Lecture Notes of the Institute for Computer Sciences, Social Informatics and Telecommunications Engineering 301

More information about this series at http://www.springer.com/series/8197

Guan Gui · Lin Yun (Eds.)

Advanced Hybrid Information Processing

Third EAI International Conference, ADHIP 2019
Nanjing, China, September 21–22, 2019
Proceedings, Part I

 Springer

Editors
Guan Gui ⓘ
Nanjing University
Nanjing, China

Lin Yun
Harbin Engineering University
Harbin, China

ISSN 1867-8211   ISSN 1867-822X (electronic)
Lecture Notes of the Institute for Computer Sciences, Social Informatics
and Telecommunications Engineering
ISBN 978-3-030-36401-4   ISBN 978-3-030-36402-1   (eBook)
https://doi.org/10.1007/978-3-030-36402-1

This Springer imprint is published by the registered company Springer Nature Switzerland AG
The registered company address is: Gewerbestrasse 11, 6330 Cham, Switzerland

Preface

We are delighted to introduce the proceedings of the Third European Alliance for Innovation (EAI) International Conference on Advanced Hybrid Information Processing (ADHIP 2019). This conference has brought together researchers, developers, and practitioners from around the world who are leveraging and developing information processing technology for a deeper and wider use of hybrid information.

The technical program of ADHIP 2019 consisted of 104 full papers in oral presentation sessions at the main conference tracks. The conference topics were: Topic 1 – Big Data Processing; Topic 2 – Real Applications of Aspects with Big Data; and Topic 3 – Huge Signal Data Processing.

Coordination with the Steering Committee members, Imrich Chlamtac, Yun Lin, Shuai Liu, and Guanglu Sun, was essential for the success of the conference. We sincerely appreciate their constant support and guidance. It was also a great pleasure to work with such an excellent Organizing Committee team, and we thank them for their hard work in organizing and supporting the conference. In particular we thank the Technical Program Committee (TPC), led by our TPC co-chairs, Prof. Shuai Liu, Prof. Zhen Yang, Prof. Liang Zhou, Prof. Fumiyuki Adachi, Prof. Hikmet Sari, and Prof. Xiaodong Xiong, who completed the peer-review process of technical papers and made a high-quality technical program. We are also grateful to conference managers and all the authors who submitted their papers to the ADHIP 2019 conference and workshop.

We strongly believe that the ADHIP 2019 conference provides a good forum for all researcher, developers, and practitioners to discuss all science and technology aspects that are relevant to hybrid information processing. We also expect that the future ADHIP conferences will be as successful and stimulating, as indicated by the contributions presented in this volume.

September 2019

Miao Liu
Jinlong Sun
Wei Zhao

Organization

Steering Committee

Imrich Chlamtac	Bruno Kessler Professor, University of Trento, Italy
Yun Lin	Harbin Engineering University, China
Shuai Liu	Inner Mongolia University, China
Guanglu Sun	Harbin Engineering University, China

Organizing Committee

General Chairs

Shuai Liu	Inner Mongolia University, China
Zhen Yang	Nanjing University of Posts and Telecommunications, China

General Co-chairs

Liang Zhou	Nanjing University of Posts and Telecommunications, China
Fumiyuki Adachi	Tohoku University, Japan
Hikmet Sari	Nanjing University of Posts and Telecommunications, China
Xiaodong Xiong	Yangtze University, China

TPC Chair and Co-chairs

Zhiping Lin	Nanyang Technological University, Singapore
Tomohiko Taniguchi	Fujitsu Laboratories Limited, Japan
Qun Wan	University of Electronic Science and Technology of China, China
Mingwu Zhang	Hubei University of Technology, China
Yun Lin	Harbin Engineering University, China
Li Xu	Akita Prefectural University, Japan
Guangjie Han	Hohai University, China
Bo Gu	Kogakuin University, Japan
Guan Gui	Nanjing University of Posts and Telecommunications, China

Sponsorship and Exhibit on Chairs

Local Chairs

Ying Lu	Nanjing Sari Intelligent Technology Co., Ltd, China
Shujie Lu	NARI Group Corporations/State Grid Electric Power Research Institute, China

Workshops Chairs

Xin Liu	Dalian University of Technology, China
Xi Shao	Nanjing University of Posts and Telecommunications, China
Xingguo Zhang	Tokyo University of Agriculture and Technology, Japan
Wenmei Li	Nanjing University of Posts and Telecommunications, China
Zhiyi Lu	Nanjing Sari Intelligent Technology Co., Ltd, China

Publicity and Social Media Chairs

Lei Chen	Georgia Southern University, USA
Sheng Zhou	Tsinghua University, China
Yue Cao	Northumbria University, UK
Lin Bai	Beihang University, China
Haibo Zhou	Nanjing University, China
Xianpeng Wang	Hainan University, China
Shuai Han	Harbin Institute of Technology, China
Ying Cui	Shanghai Jiaotong University, China
Wei Peng	Huazhong University of Science and Technology, China
Zheng Wang	Nanjing University of Aeronautics and Astronautics, China
Yimu Ji	Nanjing University of Posts and Telecommunications, China
Yongjun Xu	Chongqing University of Posts and Telecommunications, China
Yingsong Li	Harbin Engineering University, China
Tingting Yang	Dalian Maritime University, China
Yu Gu	Hefei University of Technology, China
Xiao Zheng	Anhui University of Technology, China
Yuan Wu	Zhejiang University of Technology, China
Jumin Zhao	Taiyuan University of Technology, China

Publications Chairs

Miao Liu   Nanjing University of Posts and Telecommunications,
                                     China
Jinlong Sun   Nanjing University of Posts and Telecommunications,
                                     China
Wei Zhao   Anhui University of Technology, China

Web Chairs

Jian Xiong   Nanjing University of Posts and Telecommunications,
                                     China
Hao Jiang   Southeast University, China
Jie Yang   Nanjing University of Posts and Telecommunications,
                                     China

Posters and PhD Track Chairs

Panels Chairs

Guohua Zhang   BOCO Intel-Telecom Co., Ltd, China
Yunjian Jia   Chongqing University, China
Lin Shan   National Institute of Information and Communications
                                     Technology, Japan
Wang Luo   NARI Group Corporations/State Grid Electric Power
                                     Research Institute, China
Zhaoyue Zhang   Civil Aviation University of China, China

Demos Chairs

Tutorials Chairs

Nan Zhao   Dalian University of Technology, China
Guoyue Chen   Akita Prefectural University, Japan
Wei Xu   South University, China
Xuangou Wu   Anhui University of Technology, China

Technical Program Committee

Fang-Qing Wen   Yangtze University, China
Zheng Wang   Nanjing University of Aeronautics and Astronautics,
                                     China
Jinlong Sun   Nanjing University of Posts and Telecommunications,
                                     China
Wenmei Li   Nanjing University of Posts and Telecommunications,
                                     China
Miao Liu   Nanjing University of Posts and Telecommunications,
                                     China
Yue Cao   Northumbria University, UK
Yun Lin   Harbin Engineering University, China

Contents – Part I

Contents – Part II

Modeling Analysis of Network Spatial Sensitive Information Detection Driven by Big Data

Ruijuan Liu[1(✉)], Bin Yang[1], and Shuai Liu[2]

[1] College of Arts and Sciences, Yunnan Normal University,
Kunming 650000, China
liuruijuan552@163.com
[2] College of Computer Science, Inner Mongolia University,
Hohhot 010012, China

Abstract. The dissemination of sensitive information has become a serious social content. In order to effectively improve the detection accuracy of sensitive information in cyberspace, a sensitive information detection model in cyberspace is established under the drive of big data. By using word segmentation and feature clustering, the text features and image features of current spatial data information are extracted, the dimension of the data is reduced, the document classifier is built, and the obtained feature documents are input into the classifier. Using the open source database of support vector machine (SVM) and LIBSVM, the probability ratio of current information belongs to two categories is judged, and the probability ratio of classification is obtained to realize information detection. The experimental data show that, after the detection model is applied, the accuracy of the text-sensitive information detection in the network space is improved by 35%, the accuracy of the image information detection is improved by 29%, and the detection model has the advantages of obvious advantages and strong feasibility.

Keywords: Big data · Sensitive information · Spatial data · Information detection

1 Introduction

The rapid development of Internet has brought people unprecedented convenience of information. It is more convenient for people to get all kinds of information from Internet. However, the network also has a serious negative impact, in the good buckwheat coexistence of the network information is full of a large number of sensitive information. The harm of sensitive information, especially to teenagers, is enormous. At present, Chinese netizens under 24 years old account for about half of the total number of netizens, and the majority of them are college students and primary and secondary school students. Young people's self-control is not strong, and they are easily induced by bad network information in cyberspace. They are addicted to the network not to make progress, to throw away their time, and even to cause a lot of social problems. The network harm has caused the national relevant department to attach great importance to, and has adopted a series of measures. On March 26, 2012,

G. Gui and L. Yun (Eds.): ADHIP 2019, LNICST 301, pp. 1–11, 2019.
https://doi.org/10.1007/978-3-030-36402-1_1

the China Internet Association issued the <China Internet Industry Self-Discipline Convention>, which prohibits the dissemination of sensitive information in cyberspace. On May 10, 2013, the Ministry of Culture issued the <Interim Provisions on the Administration of Internet Culture>, which states that Internet operators providing sensitive information and other illegal information products should be strictly dealt with [1, 2].

The 21st century is a highly information-based era, with the rapid progress of science and technology, especially with the continuous acceleration of the construction of big data's network. The increasing bandwidth and transmission rate of the mobile operating network provide a large number of channels for the transmission of network data, and the content services and data services for intelligent terminals will also be continuously enriched. All these make the mobile network soon to follow newspapers and periodicals, broadcast, and so on. Television, like the Internet, has become an important carrier of cultural communication and information exchange. With the rapid development of communication technology and the remarkable improvement of network bandwidth technology, with the help of the Internet and mobile network, information exchange and dissemination account for more and more proportion, people can not only through the traditional text information, and also through the picture, video and other multimedia information dissemination and communication. Under this background, the detection and filtering of sensitive information in cyberspace has become an important task in network construction. Therefore, based on the current big data domain driver, a network spatial sensitive information detection model is established to analyze and detect the spatial sensitive information and improve the network security [3, 4].

2 Design of Network Spatial Sensitive Information Detection Model

In order to construct a practical sensitive information detection model, the correlation principle of information must be considered. The information in the same domain usually has some common properties, and the information in different fields has its own characteristics. Under the influence of big data, this paper firstly analyzes the characteristics of sensitive information, including bad text and bad image, in the context of related applications, and then extracts representative independent feature vectors from these information. An information filtering classifier based on these feature vectors is designed, and a pattern recognition method is adopted to achieve the purpose of classification and detection of sensitive information according to the probability ratio [5, 6].

After the above analysis, it is clear that after obtaining the information by big data driver, it is necessary to judge whether it contains text or image information first, and then pre-process the information. If the text content is included, the text is immediately segmented, and the word frequency is counted to extract the feature of the entry, and the text classifier is used to identify and judge the probability of the text belonging to the category. This probability is used as a parameter to describe the whole information. An upper and lower threshold is defined for the output of the text analysis module, which specifies that if the parameter is within a predefined range, it is not sufficient to determine the category of information, and further image analysis is required. The image part is input into the image classification module for processing. If the parameter value is higher than the predefined upper limit, it indicates that the content has been judged to be sensitive information, and no longer needs to be processed by the image classification module, so it is directly masked. If the parameter value obtained by text analysis is lower than the predefined threshold, it indicates that the content can be judged as normal information and can be released directly without blocking. After the contents of the image to be detected are put into the image processing module, the extracted features and the parameters obtained from the text analysis are combined into a high-dimensional vector, and the classification results are obtained by the classifier decision-making. The flow diagram of the model is as shown in Fig. 1.

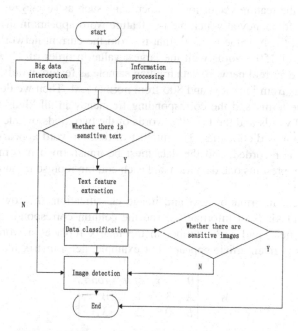

Fig. 1. Flow chart of sensitive information detection

2.1 Information Feature Extraction Driven by Big Data

Big data-driven text and images may extract a large number of different features, some of which are of great significance to information classification and sensitive detection, and some of them are not. If all the features are included in the sensitive feature vector, it not only increases the time-consuming of feature extraction and the computation of the classifier, but also may introduce noise to the classification. Therefore, first of all, we need to find an independent method for extracting and reducing the dimension of the sensitive information feature vector, that is, feature clustering algorithm [7, 8].

The clustering algorithm allocates every row of data in the current data set driven by big data to a group or a point in the hierarchical structure, and each data exactly corresponds to a group, which represents the average level of the members in the group. Sensitive data feature extraction is to try to find new data rows from the data set and combine these newly found data rows to construct the data set. Unlike the original data set, each row of data in the new data set does not belong to a cluster, but is constructed by a combination of several features [9].

The essence of word segmentation technology in document feature extraction is to calculate the first few words with the highest TF x IDF value for all words appearing in the document as document features. According to the frequency of feature words appearing in two kinds of documents, the probability of each word belonging to two categories is calculated, and the calculated probability is stored in the database according to the fixed vocabulary order.

For a document to be classified, a vector representing the frequency of each feature word appears as the feature vector for the document, such as $(w_1.w_2.w_3....w_n)$, where w_i represents the frequency at which the i-th feature word appears in the document. In the actual design, the N value is 1500, that is, from the current network data training sample, the total of 1500 words with the largest value in order of TF x IDF size are extracted from the current network data training sample as feature words. This includes 700 feature words from junk text and 800 from normal text. Then we do the TF x IDF calculation of the terms and the corresponding frequency in all kinds of documents, take the first 700 words and the first 800 words of the two kinds of calculation results, and generate two new dictionaries. The number of times a word appears in all articles and each article is recorded, and the data must be transformed into matrix form, in which each row represents one data item and each column represents an attribute of the data item [10, 11].

For the current information text and image classification, the row of the matrix corresponds to all kinds of information, and the column corresponds to the word or pattern in the article, and each number in the matrix replaces a word in one. The number of times a given article appears. For example, get a matrix like Eq. 1.

$$W = \begin{vmatrix} 0 & sex & star & road \\ A & 3 & 1 & 0 \\ B & 0 & 2 & 3 \end{vmatrix} \tag{1}$$

This matrix represents the eigenvector sex three times in class A, and start appears twice in class B, and so on. There are two information to focus on from this matrix:

The first is allwords, which records the number of times a word is used in all articles, and it can be used to determine which words should be seen as part of a feature and the other is articlewords, which is the number of times a word appears in each article [7].

According to the definition of feature dimension information, the common words in all kinds of articles carry small amount of information, poor classification performance, and few words have little meaning to classification, so reduce the size of matrix. Words that appear in only a few documents should be removed, and words that appear in too many articles should be removed. Only words that meet the requirement of less than 60% of all articles that have appeared in more than three documents are considered here. After the above pretreatment, a document matrix with word counting information can be obtained. The next step is to extract important features from the matrix to achieve the purpose of dimensionality reduction [12].

The non-negative matrix factorization method is used to factorize the document matrix and two smaller matrices are found so that the document matrix can be obtained by multiplying the two matrices. These two matrices are characteristic matrix and weight matrix respectively. In the feature matrix, each row corresponds to a document category and each column corresponds to a feature word. The numbers in the matrix represent the importance of a word to a document category. The function of the weight matrix is to map the document category to the document matrix, in which each row corresponds to a training sample, that is, a document, and each column corresponds to a document category. The numbers in the weight matrix represent the extent to which each document category is applied to each sample. This allows you to list the top 450 word features of the two document categories, which are the most important words in the document category, and you can select these 900 words as a text feature. That is to say, the text feature vector is reduced from 1500 to 900D, and the data document can be used as feature extraction document at this time.

2.2 Classifier Construction

In order to recognize sensitive information, the feature document extracted in the previous section should be regarded as a high-level semantic feature, and this mapping is accomplished by a system classifier [13].

Automatic classification is a new pattern classification and recognition technology introduced in statistical learning theory. It is defined as a set of training samples that have already been assigned class tags (these class tags need to be meaningful). To assign class labels to the new sample. In the network filtering technology, the classifier needs to accurately identify an infinite number of unknown samples, but in the learning stage of the classifier, it is impractical to collect a complete database of samples with rich representativeness and diversity. Therefore, classifiers need to start from a small number of learning samples, constantly learn and improve their classification performance. More and more learning methods are used in automatic classification, in which support vector machine (Support Vector Machines, SVM) method has advantages in solving problems such as small sample, nonlinear high-dimensional pattern recognition and so on, and has better generalization ability. Considering the influence of the small sample training set on the classifier, the computational complexity of the classifier and the processing time of the system, the SVM classification algorithm is introduced. The idea is to try to find a line as far away from all categories as possible, which is called the maximum interval hyperplane, as shown in Fig. 2 (For the sake of simplicity, only the example of linear separability is given. SVM can be extended to high dimensional space).

The basis for selecting this dividing line is: Two parallel lines passing through the corresponding coordinate points of each classification are searched, and the distance between them and the dividing line is made as far as possible. For new data points, the classification can be determined by observing which side of the boundary line it belongs to. It is to be noted that only the coordinate points located at the edge of the spacer are necessary to determine the position of the boundary, and if all the remaining data is removed, the dividing line will still be in the same position. Coordinate points near this demarcation line are referred to as support vectors [14, 15]. Support vector machine (SVM) is an algorithm for finding support vectors and finding boundary lines by using support vectors.

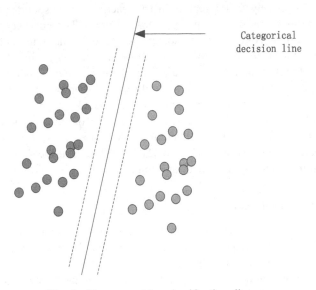

Categorical
decision line

Fig. 2. Vector machine classification diagram

The solid lines in Fig. 2 show two possible decision planes, each of which correctly classifies the data into two categories. Similarly, for new data points, the classification of the new data points can be determined by observing which side of the boundary line it belongs to. The two dashed lines parallel to the solid line are the maximum offset positions of the decision face without causing misclassification. The distance between the two dashed lines is the classification interval of the decision face. The purpose of SVM is to find the decision surface with the maximum classification interval in all sample points. In fact, only the sample points at the edge of the spacer are necessary for classification, and in the case of linear separability, the function of the decision plane is $\bar{w} \cdot x - b = 0$. In which, x is any sample point to be detected, W and constant b are obtained by training the sample point. Let the input of SVM algorithm be a linear separable sample set $D = \{(y_i, x_i)\}$ be the classification of x. "+1" indicates that it is a positive example and "−1" is a counterexample.

The SVM problem is to find w and b that satisfy the conditions shown in Eq. 2, and the module of vector w is minimal (The classification interval is equal to 2 divided by the module of w).

$$\begin{cases} \bar{w} \cdot x - b > 1 & y_i = +1 \\ \bar{w} \cdot x - b < 1 & y_i = -1 \end{cases} \tag{2}$$

The classification function is required to classify all samples correctly, that is, satisfying Eq. 3.

$$y_i[(w \cdot x_i)] + b - 1 \geq 0 \tag{3}$$

Because the programming workload of the support vector machine algorithm is very large, an open source library called LIBSVM is introduced, which can train an SVM model, give the prediction, and test the prediction result with the data set. LIBSVM also provides support for radial basis functions and many other core methods, which is written in C++ and has a version of ava. We need to select the appropriate LIBSVM compiled version based on the platform you are using, and because the design model is developed in the windows environment, you need to include a DLL file named svmc.dll. The LIBSVM documentation details how to use classifier functions.

A minimum threshold is defined for each classification. For the data information to be assigned to a certain category, the probability must be greater than a pre-specified threshold compared to the probability for all other classifications. The default threshold is 3, which means that the probability of document classification for sensitive classes is at least three times higher than that for ordinary documents. This threshold can be adjusted according to the actual application of the individual.

2.3   Realization of Sensitive Detection

Because the design adopts a dictionary-based word segmentation method, firstly, a complete dictionary is needed, the documents in the training sample library are pre-processed and segmented according to the dictionary and the stop word list, two new dictionaries are generated after the word segmentation, the number of times the words appear in all articles and in each article are recorded, which are the preliminary text features. However, if the text is classified directly by these features, it will result in a high dimension of the feature vector and a poor classification effect. Therefore, according to the two dictionaries, each feature generated above is subjected to a dimension reduction process to obtain an independent feature, that is, the feature of the text classification.

Independent features are used to treat the detected text for feature extraction. The extracted feature entries are combined into a high-dimensional vector to represent the text to be detected. Then the classifier is inputted into the classifier and the probability of the class of the information to be detected and the class of the document are obtained by decision-making. The probability ratio of documents belonging to two categories is judged, and if it is greater than 3, the information is directly judged to be sensitive; If it is less than 3, it continues to extract the image features, and combines the document probability and the image features into the feature vector of the whole web page information to the system classifier for further judgment to see whether it is sensitive information or not. The histogram feature extracted from each image is 192, the color aggregation vector is 48, the skin region feature is 4, the face feature is 2, plus the probability that the document obtained from the text recognition module belongs to junk text and normal text, respectively. A total of 248 features. Combining these features into a high-dimensional vector, a feature vector $(t_1, t_2, \ldots, t_{248})$ can be used to describe the information to be detected. Then the high-dimensional vector is input to the system classifier for training or classification decision-making, so that the sensitive data can be monitored.

3 Experiment

The C# language is used to realize the sensitive information filtering system in Windows XP, and the classification performance of the system is tested with a large number of experimental data. The hardware environment of the development platform is CPU of Intel (R) Pentium (R) dual-core T2390d. 80 GHZ, 2.79 GHZ 1G memory, 256 m graphics card. Software configuration: windows XP professional version of the operating system, Microsoft Visual Studio C# integrated development environment.

The experimental data includes text and image, and the information filtering system is tested respectively. Among them, the text class sample uses the Chinese natural language open processing platform (http://www.nlp.org.cn), collected a total of 2270 texts, divided into three groups, each group of two categories, each class selected 450 features, the total selected feature vector dimension of 900. The images in the image library are mainly collected from the network, because compared to landscape images, character images are more difficult to classify because they contain human body and skin regions and sensitive images. So the two kinds of images are divided into two groups to train and test the system. Due to limited sources of information, the graphics library consists of only 570 images divided into five groups, the first of which consists of 60 sensitive images and 40 normal landscape images, the first for training and the other four for testing. After each set of images is tested, it is used to train the system to analyze the influence of the number of training samples on the classification results of the system, in which the linear SVM. is used for the SVM classifier. It is important to note that when training the image feature base of SVM classifier, because there is no input of the text classifier, the probability parameter of the document belonging to the classification of the 248 feature components is set to 0. 5.

3.1 Text Sensitivity Detection

The text sensitivity detection is carried out in the above experimental environment, and the contrast detection method is the traditional ULL detection model. Its monitoring effect is shown in the chart below. The results are shown in Fig. 3.

As can be seen from Fig. 3, the detection accuracy of traditional detection model is poor, while the detection accuracy of designed model is higher than that of traditional detection model.

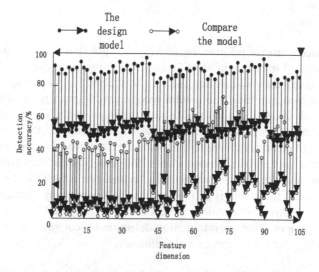

Fig. 3. Comparison of detection effects between the two models

3.2 Image Detection

According to the experimental method mentioned above, the network space image detection is carried out, and the detection results are as follows:

Table 1. Image detection results table

Data set	Design model	Traditional model
1	82	57
2	79	45
3	85	50
4	95	69
5	92	70
6	89	52
7	91	49
8	86	70
9	93	42

According to the Table 1 data, it can be seen that in all 10 sets of image data, the monitoring accuracy of the designed detection model is also higher than that of the traditional model. According to the comparison of the data, the accuracy rate increases by more than 29%.

4   Conclusion

The content-based sensitive information filtering is a hot spot research direction. It is actually a problem of information identification and information classification. It is an application of many-door disciplines such as text classification, image processing, computer vision, programming and pattern recognition. Human physiology and psychology are closely related, and have wide application prospect. The popularization of high-speed information high-speed highway has further promoted the development of this technology. At present, the sensitive information filtering technology has been paid attention at home and abroad, among which, the text classification technology has become mature, and the image classification technology is still in the research, is gradually refined and the mouth is perfect, and has produced many application and test examples. The sensitive information detection model proposed by the design can achieve the purpose of effective information detection by comprehensively using the relevant technology of the information classification.

Acknowledgment. The authors would like to thank State Key Laboratory of Complex Electromagnetic Environment Effects on Electronics and Information System Director Fund (CEMEE2019K0104B).

References

1. Bi, J., Li, H., Xing, M.: Analysis on talent training mechanism and mode of cyberspace security under the background of big data. Mod. Vocat. Educ. **7**, 159 (2018)
2. Liu, S., Bai, W., Liu, G., et al.: Parallel fractal compression method for big video data. Complexity 2016976 (2018)
3. Wang, W.: Research on the current situation and countermeasures of cyberspace security under the background of big data. China Strateg. Emerg. Ind. **156**(24), 100+102 (2018)
4. Miao, L., Shuai, L., Weina, F., et al.: Distributional escape time algorithm based on generalized fractal sets in cloud environment. Chin. J. Electron. **24**(1), 124–127 (2015)
5. Tang, W., Wang, Y., Wang, J., et al.: Research on alienation control model of network public opinion information in the context of big data. China New Commun. **20**(10), 140 (2018)
6. Bing, J., Shuai, L., Yongjian, Y.: Fractal cross-layer service with integration and interaction in internet of things. Int. J. Distrib. Sensor Networks **10**(3), 760248 (2018)
7. Wu, J.: Research on college students' virtual cyberspace behavior management from the perspective of big data. Inf. Comput. (Theory Ed.) **7**, 223–224 (2018)
8. Lu, M., Liu, S., Sangaiah, A.K., et al.: Nucleosome positioning with fractal entropy increment of diversity in telemedicine. IEEE Access **6**, 33451–33459 (2018)
9. Xia, Y., Lan, Y., Zhao, Y.: Research on alienation control model of online public opinion information in the context of big data. Mod. Intell. **38**(2), 3–11 (2018)
10. Shu, X., Yao, D., Bertino, E.: Privacy-preserving detection of sensitive data exposure. IEEE Trans. Inf. Forensics Secur. **10**(5), 1092–1103 (2017)
11. Liu, S., Bai, W., Zeng, N., et al.: A fast fractal based compression for MRI images. IEEE Access **7**, 62412–62420 (2019)
12. Fan, P.: Analysis on network information security protection strategy in the era of big data. China New Commun. **20**(09), 134 (2018)

13. Zheng, X.: Promoting the construction of network trust system under the condition of big data intelligence. China Nat. People's Congr. **455**(11), 51 (2018)
14. Zhang, Y.: Development trend of information technology and network space security. Farm-staff **580**(08), 240 (2018)
15. Wei, W., Shuai, L., Wenjia, L., et al.: Fractal intelligent privacy protection in online social network using attribute-based encryption schemes. IEEE Trans. Comput. Soc. Syst. **5**(3), 736–747 (2018)

Research on Communication Individual Identification Method Based on PCA-NCA and CV-SVM

Xinghao Guo[1($\boxtimes$)] and Shuai Liu[2]

[1] Harbin Engineering University, Harbin, China
s317080023@hrbeu.edu.cn
[2] Inner Mongolia University, Hohhot, China

Abstract. In recent years, high-dimensional data has often appeared in the fields of science and industry, such as computer vision, pattern recognition, biological information, and aerospace. Feature dimension reduction and selection are the process of reducing data from high dimensionality to low dimensionality to reveal the nature of the data. In the field of wireless communication, in view of the feature redundancy caused by the high-dimensional features of wireless device startup transient signals, this paper converts the high-dimensional features of signals into low-dimensional features that are conducive to classification through the feature dimensionality reduction and selection method based on PCA-NCA. In addition, this paper also carried out parameter optimization for SVM classifier, and the established CV-SVM classifier improved the classification performance. This paper also carries out simulation devices on the measured start-up signals of ten identical walkie-talkies. When the SNR is greater than 0 dB, the recognition accuracy of the PCA-NCA algorithm is 10% higher than recognition accuracy of the PCA algorithm alone; when the SNR is greater than 10 dB.

Keywords: PCA · Individual identification · Feature selection

1 Introduction

Feature selection refers to selecting a subset of features from the original feature set that optimizes certain evaluation criteria. With feature selection, some task-independent or redundant features are removed, and simplified data sets are often more accurately modeled and easier to understand [1]. Feature selection is a hot issue in related fields such as machine learning and pattern recognition. Many scholars at home and abroad have studied this and proposed a series of algorithms [1–3].

The feature selection methods are mainly divided into 2 types according to whether the classification accuracy is used as an evaluation function: a filtering method and a wrapper method [4]. Since the filtering method does not use the classification accuracy as evaluation index. However, since the method evaluates the classification effect during each cycle, it leads to a long time. Jain [5] experiments show that genetic algorithms are prone to premature convergence, and when the structure of genetic algorithms is applied to large-scale data, the operating efficiency will decline [6].

© ICST Institute for Computer Sciences, Social Informatics and Telecommunications Engineering 2019
Published by Springer Nature Switzerland AG 2019. All Rights Reserved
G. Gui and L. Yun (Eds.): ADHIP 2019, LNICST 301, pp. 12–19, 2019.
https://doi.org/10.1007/978-3-030-36402-1_2

Neighborhood components analysis (NCA) is a supervised learning method proposed by Goldberger et al. [7]. It measures the sample data according to a given distance measurement algorithm, and then classifies the multivariate data. In terms of function, it has the same purpose as k-nearest neighbor algorithm, and directly USES the concept of random nearest neighbor to determine the labeled training samples adjacent to the test samples. It has been widely used in speech recognition [8], image recognition [9, 10] and text recognition [11, 12]. Based on the research of PCA and NCA methods, this paper combines the two algorithms and improves the traditional SVM algorithm. The remaining papers are arranged as follows: in the second chapter, this paper will introduce the basic theory of PCA, NCA and CV-SVM algorithm; In chapter 3, this paper takes the measured startup transient signals of ten interphones of the same model as the data set to verify the effect of the method proposed in this paper. In the fourth chapter, the thesis will put forward the conclusion.

2 Algorithm Theory

2.1 PCA Feature Dimensionality Reduction

PCA is widely used in various fields because it can concentrate information, simplify the structure of indexes and make the process of analyzing problems simple, intuitive and effective. Suppose, a training set is $X = \{x_1, x_2, \cdots, x_m\}$, x_i is a n-dimensional vector. Meantime, a lower dimensional data set is $Y = \{y_1 y_2, \cdots, y_m\}$, y_l is a one-dimensional vector.

(1) Data preprocessing

Make $X = \{x_1, x_2, \cdots, x_m\}$ have a mean of 0.

$$\mu_x = \frac{1}{m} \sum_{i=1}^{m} x_i \tag{1}$$

$$x_i' = x_i - \mu_x \tag{2}$$

The processed matrix is $X' = \{x_1', x_2', \dots x_m'\}$

(2) Obtain the covariance matrix

$$C_x = X' X'^T \tag{3}$$

(3) Calculate feature values and feature vectors

$$C_x a = \lambda a \tag{4}$$

The eigenvalues are arranged in descending order according to the value, the eigenvector related to the first eigenvalue is selected, and then used to form the transformation matrix A.

$$\Lambda = \begin{bmatrix} \lambda_1 & & \\ & \ddots & 0 \\ 0 & & \ddots \\ & & \lambda_n \end{bmatrix}, \lambda_1 \geq \lambda_2 \geq \cdots \geq \lambda_n \tag{5}$$

$$\frac{\sum\limits_{i=1}^{l} \lambda_i}{\sum\limits_{i=1}^{n} \lambda_i} \geq k \tag{6}$$

$$A = \{a_1, a_2 \cdots, a_l\} \tag{7}$$

k represents the proportion of energy in the reduced data to the original data. We usually set k to $85\% \sim 90\%$.

(4) Calculate the dimensionality reduction matrix Y

The sample $\mathbf{Y} = \{y_1 y_2, \cdots, y_m\}$ is multiplied by the transpose matrix of the feature vector. The sample $\mathbf{Y} = \{y_1 y_2, \cdots, y_m\}$ is subtracted from the mean of the training samples to ensure that the training sample and the test sample are converted to the same sample space.

$$Y = A^T \times X' \tag{8}$$

2.2   NCA Feature Selection

Neighborhood component analysis is a distance measurement learning method. Its purpose is to obtain a linear space transfer matrix by learning on the training set, and to maximize the classification effect of LOO in the new transformation space. The key of this algorithm is to find A positive definite matrix A related to the spatial transformation matrix, which can be obtained by defining A differentiable objective function of A and using iterative methods (such as conjugate gradient method, conjugate gradient descent method, etc.). One of the benefits of this algorithm is that the number of categories K can be defined by a function f (determining scalar constants). Therefore, the algorithm can be used to solve the problem of model selection.

To define the transformation matrix A, we first define an objective function that represents the classification accuracy in the new transformation matrix, and try to determine that A* maximizes this objective function.

$$A^* = \operatorname{argmax}_A f(A) \tag{9}$$

When classifying a single data point, we need to consider the k nearest neighbors determined by a given distance metric, and get the class of the sample according to the category label of the k neighbors.

In the new conversion space, we do not use the left-sort method to find k nearest neighbors for each sample point, but consider the entire data set as a random nearest neighbor in the new space. We use a squared Euclidean distance function to define the distance between a data point and other data in the new conversion space. The function is defined as follows:

$$
p_{ij} = \begin{cases} \dfrac{e^{-\left\|Ax_i - Ax_j\right\|^2}}{\sum_k e^{-\left\|Ax_i - Ax_j\right\|^2}}, & \text{if } j \neq i \\ 0, & \text{if } j = i \end{cases}
\tag{10}
$$

The classification accuracy of the input point i is the classification accuracy of the nearest neighbor set C_i adjacent to it: $p_i = \sum_j^n p_{ij}$, Where p_{ij} denotes the probability that j is the nearest neighbor of i. The objective function defined by the global data set as the nearest neighbor classification method of random nearest neighbors is defined as follows:

$$
f(A) = \sum_i \sum_{j \in C_i} p_{ij} = \sum_i p_i
\tag{11}
$$

The objective function can be better chosen as:

$$
\frac{\partial f}{\partial A} = -2A \sum_i \sum_{C_i} p_{ij} \left(x_{ij} x_{ij}^T - \sum_k p_{ik} x_{ik} x_{ik}^T \right)
\tag{12}
$$

A continuous gradient descent algorithm is used here.

2.3 CV-SVM Classifier

The SVM classifier uses the nonlinear mapping function to optimally classify the sample signals in high-dimensional space to separate the training sample points and maximize the distance from the optimal separation surface [13, 14]. The SVM classifier is used to construct the optimal classification hyperplane in high dimensional space.

$$
f(x) = a\rho(x) + b = \sum_{k=1}^m a_k \rho(x_k) + b = 0
\tag{13}
$$

Where a is a weight vector, b is a threshold, and a and b determine the location of the classification plane. Introduce a relaxation factor to measure the distance between the SVM output value and the practice indicator value, thereby transforming the problem of optimizing the sample signal separation surface into

$$\begin{cases} \min \frac{1}{2} \|a\|^2 + C \sum_{i=1}^{m} \mu_i; i = 1, \cdots, m \\ s.t. \begin{cases} y_i(ax_i + b) \geq 1 - \mu_i \\ \mu_i \geq 0 \end{cases} \end{cases} \tag{14}$$

Among them, the penalty parameter C is used to control the degree of penalty of the wrong sample. Secondly, the Lagrangian multiplier is introduced to make the above problem a secondary plan. Then introduce the RBF kernel function to get RBF-SVM.

$$f(x) = sign\left(\sum_{i,j=1}^{m} \alpha_i y_i \exp\left\{ -g\|x - x_i\|^2 \right\} + b \right) \tag{15}$$

C and g that take values within a certain range are used as the original data set. Then, step by step, gradually increase the values of C and g, and calculate the classification accuracy under this group C and g. The final parameters are obtained by C and g with the highest classification accuracy. Since the search process for this optimal parameter is a cross-validation, grid search process, the final SVM is called CV-SVM.

3   Simulation Analysis

In order to verify the effect of Hilbert transform, NCA-PCA feature selection method and CV-SVM classifier, this paper collects the startup transient signals for the same model of the same manufacturer, and uses MATLAB to simulate noise interference.

This simulation verifies the method proposed in this paper from two aspects: the classification results between different methods and the classification results of different individuals. In this paper, the antenna of the walkie-talkie is directly connected to the input of the oscilloscope cable to reduce the fading of the signal, ignoring the multipath phenomenon, the delay phenomenon, and the temperature during the transmission. A high-performance Agilent oscilloscope is used to connect the communication station with a cable, and the startup transient signal is directly collected at a sampling rate of 40 MHz, and the number of sampling points is 159901. For 10 devices, each device collects 50 noise-free signals, and divides the 500 signals into training samples and test samples in a ratio of 2:3. It is necessary to artificially add Gaussian white noise after acquiring the signal. Because the time domain length of the captured transient signal is long, the computer memory will be required in the subsequent processing. So, we did a simple sampling at every 50 points, and the length of the signal Hilbert envelope dropped to 3187.

Firstly, this paper uses five methods of 'PCA+SVM', 'PCA+NCA+SVM', 'PCA +NCA+CVSVM', 'PCA+KNN' and 'PCA+NCA+KNN' to identify the startup transient signals of 10 walkie-talkies. The results are shown in Fig. 1. After the Hilbert transformation and sampling of the experimental data used in this paper, PCA dimension reduction is carried out. In this paper, the dimension when the contribution rate is 90% is taken as the dimension after dimension reduction. In the three methods of 'PCA+NCA+SVM', 'PCA+NCA+CVSVM' and 'PCA+NCA+KNN', we also use the NCA feature selection method on the basis of PCA to select features with feature weights greater than 1 for classification. We can see that: (1) when 'PCA+SVM' and 'PCA+NCA+SVM' are less than 10 dB, the recognition rate is always greater than 10%, which proves that the feature selection method proposed in this paper can effectively improve the performance of the classifier. Not only that, from the 'PCA+ KNN' and 'PCA+NCA+KNN' these two methods of the results of comparison, can also explain the superiority of the method proposed in this paper; (2) from a general view of the recognition rate curve of 'PCA+NCA+CVSVM' method, it can be seen that when the traditional gaussian kernel function SVM is modified to CV-SVM, the recognition accuracy is improved a little. Thus, the PCA-NCA and CV-SVM methods proposed in this paper can both effectively improve the accuracy of individual communication recognition.

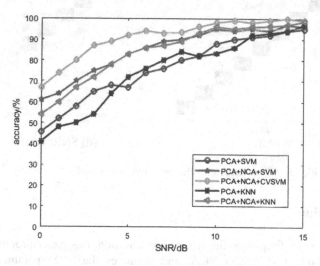

Fig. 1. Accuracy of five methods

Next is the confusion matrix of the recognition results of 'PCA+NCA+CVSVM' method under the SNR of 0, 5, 10 and 15 dB, respectively. It can be seen that when SNR = 0 dB, the recognition rate of devices NO.1, NO.4, NO.6, NO.7 and NO.8 does not exceed 70%, which is caused by the overlapping feature distribution between them, which makes it difficult to correctly classify the classifier. When SNR is greater than 5 dB, the feature distribution is gradually clear, and the location of different types of feature distribution is also gradually far away. Therefore, when the SNR increases, the classification accuracy of each device also increases gradually (Fig. 2).

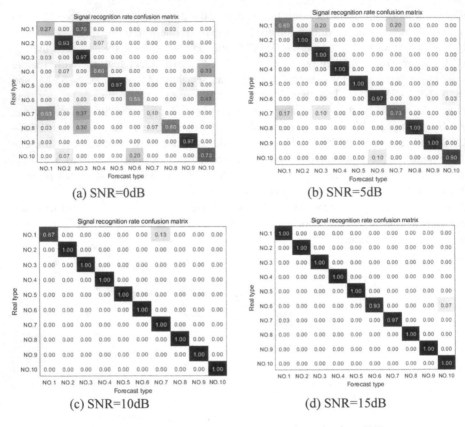

Fig. 2. Classification result confusion matrix under four SNRs

4   Conclusion

In the field of radio frequency fingerprint identification, this paper proposes a feature selection method of PCA and NCA, and improves the SVM parameter selection method to select the optimal parameters of SVM by cross validation method [15]. In this paper, PCA is used to remove the correlation between features, and then NCA feature selection method is used to select the features that are most conducive to classification, so as to solve the problem of high feature dimension of power-on transient signal. Experimental results show that this algorithm can effectively reduce feature redundancy and improve recognition accuracy while reducing data dimensions.

Acknowledgment. The authors would like to thank State Key Laboratory of Complex Electromagnetic Environment Effects on Electronics and Information System Director Fund (CEMEE2019K0104B).

References

1. Yu, L., Liu, H.: Efficient feature selection via analysis of relevance and redundancy. J. Mach. Learn. Res. **5**(12), 1205–1224 (2004)
2. Mao, K.Z.: Fast orthogonal forward selection algorithm for feature subset selection. IEEE Trans. Neural Netw. **13**(5), 1218–1224 (2002)
3. Hua-Liang, W., Billings, S.A.: Feature subset selection and ranking for data dimensionality reduction. IEEE Trans. Pattern Anal. Mach. Intell. **29**(1), 162–166 (2007)
4. Liu, Y., Zheng, Y.F.: FS_SFS: a novel feature selection method for support vector machines. Pattern Recogn. **39**, 1333–1345 (2006)
5. Jain, A.K., Duin, R., Mao, J.C.: Statistical pattern recognition a review. IEEE Trans. Pattern Anal. Mach. Intell. **22**(1), 4–37 (2000)
6. Martin-Bautista, M.J., Vila, M.A.: A survey of genetic feature selection in mining issues. In: Proceeding of the 1999 Congress on Evolutionary Computation, pp. 13–23. IEEE Press (1999)
7. Goldberger, J., Roweis, S., Hinton, G., et al.: Neighbourhood components analysis. In: Proceedings of 2005 Conference on Neural Information Processing Systems. MIT Press (2005)
8. Singh-Miller, N., Collins, M., Hazen, T.J.: Dimensionality reduction for speech recognition using neighborhood components analysis. In: Proceedings of Interspeech 2007, Antwerp, Belgium (2007)
9. Butman, M., Goldberger, J.: Face recognition using classification based linear projections. EURASIP J. Adv. Signal Process. **2008**, 1–7 (2008)
10. Xing, E.P., Ng, A.Y., Jordan, M.I., et al.: Distance metric learning, with application to clustering with side-information. In: Proceedings of 2002 Conference on Neural Information Processing Systems. MIT Press, Cambridge (2002)
11. Globerson, A., Roweis, S.T.: Metric learning by collapsing classes. In: Proceedings of 2006 Conference on Neural Information Processing Systems. MIT Press, Cambridge (2006)
12. Liu, S., Bai, W., Liu, G., et al.: Parallel fractal compression method for big video data. Complexity **2018**, 2016976 (2018)
13. Zhang, X., Lu, X., Shi, Q., Xu, X.Q., Leung, H.C.E., Harris, L.N., et al.: Recursive SVM feature selection and sample classification for mass-spectrometry and microarray data. BMC Bioinform. **7**(1), 1–13 (2006)
14. Miao, L., Shuai, L., Weina, F., et al.: Distributional escape time algorithm based on generalized fractal sets in cloud environment. Chin. J. Electron. **24**(1), 124–127 (2015)
15. Lu, M., Liu, S., Sangaiah, A.K., et al.: Nucleosome positioning with fractal entropy increment of diversity in telemedicine. IEEE Access **6**, 33451–33459 (2018)

Termination for Belief Propagation Decoding of Polar Codes in Fading Channels

Chen Zhang, Yangzhi Luo, and Liping Li[⊠]

Key Laboratory of Intelligent Computing and Signal Processing of the Ministry of Education of China, Anhui University, Hefei, China
liping_li@ahu.edu.cn

Abstract. In additive white Gaussian channel (AWGN), the performance of polar codes under the successive cancellation (SC) decoding is not as good as that of the belief propagation (BP) decoding. However, in a fading channel, the performance of BP decoding is found in our study to be worse than the SC decoding. In this work, we propose a termination criterion for the BP decoding of polar codes to improve the performance and the average number of iterations at the same time. Simulation results show that BP decoding can still achieve a better performance than the SC decoding in fading channels with the proposed termination.

Keywords: Polar code · Belief propagation · Successive cancellation decoding · Fading channels

1 Introduction

Polar codes proposed by Arıkan [3] is the first constructive and provable coding scheme which achieves the capacity of binary-input discrete memoryless symmetric channels (B-DMCs) with a low complexity successive cancellation (SC) decoding. The SC decoding is a particular instance of the belief propagation (BP) decoding shown in [6]. Overall, the performance of the SC decoding of polar codes is not as good as that of the BP decoding [2,6].

The existing decoding techniques of polar codes, including the SC decoding, the BP decoding [5,6], the successive cancellation list (SCL) decoding [12], and the CRC aided SCL decoding [9] are all studied under additive white Gaussian noise (AWGN) channels. With the adoption of polar codes as the coding scheme for the control channel of the enhanced mobile broadband (eMBB) scenario of 5G [1], it is of importance to study the performance of polar codes in fading channels. In [11], a new coding technique considering the fading characteristics is proposed to improve the performance of polar codes. In [10], the construction of polar codes is proposed for polar codes in fading channels. Until now, there is no work reported to study the performance of the BP decoding of polar codes in fading channels.

© ICST Institute for Computer Sciences, Social Informatics and Telecommunications Engineering 2019
Published by Springer Nature Switzerland AG 2019. All Rights Reserved
G. Gui and L. Yun (Eds.): ADHIP 2019, LNICST 301, pp. 20–30, 2019.
https://doi.org/10.1007/978-3-030-36402-1_3

In this paper, polar codes with the BP decoding are studied under fading channels. The first observation of our study shows that the BP decoding performance even deteriorates compared to the SC decoding in fading channels. For example, with the code block length $N = 256$ and the code rate $R = 0.36$, the BP performance is worse than that of the SC performance when the number of iterations is fixed to be 30 in fading channels. This is shown in Fig. 1. From Fig. 1, it can be observed that the BP decoding outperforms the SC decoding in AWGN channels. With the same fixed number of iterations, BP decoding does not hold this advantage any more over the SC decoding in fading channels.

To improve the BP decoding performance of polar codes in fading channels, this paper proposes the following procedures: (1) increase the maximum number of iterations of the BP decoding; (2) set an early termination criterion. The early termination of the BP decoding of polar codes is studied in [5,13]. Both criterions in [5,13] are studied in AWGN channels. This paper investigates the characteristics of the early termination criterions of BP decoding and proposes a new termination criterion. The results show that the BP decoding of polar codes with the proposed termination achieves the best error performance among the existing termination criterions in fading channel.

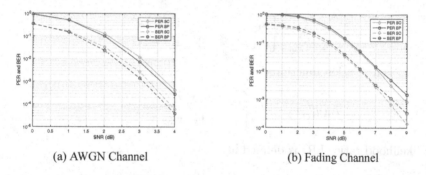

(a) AWGN Channel   (b) Fading Channel

Fig. 1. Performance comparisons of polar codes with the code length $N = 256$, the code rate $R = 0.36$. For BP decoding, the number of iterations is fixed to be 30 in both AWGN and fading channels.

The rest of this paper is organized as follows. Section 2 provides the preliminaries of polar codes. In Sect. 3, the early termination of BP decoding is introduced. Based on our study, a new early terminations is proposed for fading channels. Section 4 provides the simulation results of the BP decoding with the proposed procedures. Finally, Sect. 5 concludes the paper.

2   Preliminaries

For any B-DMC $W: \mathcal{X} \rightarrow \mathcal{Y}$, where $\mathcal{X} = \{0,1\}$ denotes the input alphabet and $\mathcal{Y}$ denotes the output alphabet, the channel transition probability is defined as

$W(y|x)$, $x \in \mathcal{X}$, $y \in \mathcal{Y}$. According to the channel combining and the splitting process, N binary input channels $W_N^{(i)}$ can be obtained with $i = 1, 2, ..., N$. For the symmetric channels [3], the K most reliable bit channels with indices in the information set $\mathcal{A}$ are used to transmit information bits. The remaining bit channels with indices in the complementary set $\mathcal{A}^C$ transmit known bits which are called frozen bits.

Polar code encoding is performed as $x_1^N = u_1^N G_N$, where G_N denotes the generator matrix of the polar code, $u_1^N \in \{0,1\}^N$ denotes the source vector $(u_1, u_2, ..., u_N)$ and $x_1^N \in \{0,1\}^N$ denotes the codeword. The source vector u_1^N consists of information bits $u_{\mathcal{A}}$ and frozen bits $u_{\mathcal{A}^c}$. Here $u_{\mathcal{A}}$ means the sub-vector of u_1^N taking elements specified by the set $\mathcal{A}$. The generator matrix is defined as $G_N = B_N F_2^{\otimes n}$. Here B_N is the bit-reversal permutation matrix, $F_2 = \begin{bmatrix} 1 & 0 \\ 1 & 1 \end{bmatrix}$, and $\otimes$ denotes the Kronecker product [3].

2.1 Successive Cancellation Decoding (SC)

For any given polar code (N, K, A, u_{A^c}) [3], the SC decoding estimates bit u_i (denoted as $\hat{u}_i$) based on the following:

$$\hat{u}_i \triangleq \begin{cases} u_i, & \text{if } i \in \mathcal{A}^c \\ h_i(y_1^N, \hat{u}_1^{i-1}), & \text{if } i \in \mathcal{A}, \end{cases} \tag{1}$$

where h_i is a decision function defined as:

$$h_i(y_1^N, \hat{u}_1^{i-1}) \triangleq \begin{cases} 0, & \text{if } L_N^{(i)}(y_1^N, \hat{u}_1^{i-1}) \geq 1 \\ 1, & \text{otherwise}, \end{cases} \tag{2}$$

The likelihood ratio (LR) is defined as:

$$L_N^{(i)}(y_1^N, \hat{u}_1^{i-1}) = \frac{W_N^{(i)}(y_1^N, \hat{u}_1^{i-1}|0)}{W_N^{(i)}(y_1^N, \hat{u}_1^{i-1}|1)}, \tag{3}$$

which can be recursively calculated [3]:

$$L_N^{(2i-1)}(y_1^N, \hat{u}_1^{2i-2})$$
$$= \frac{L_{N/2}^{(i)}(y_1^{N/2}, \hat{u}_{1,o}^{2i-2} \oplus \hat{u}_{1,e}^{2i-2}) L_{N/2}^{(i)}(y_{N/2+1}^N, \hat{u}_{1,e}^{2i-2}) + 1}{L_{N/2}^{(i)}(y_1^{N/2}, \hat{u}_{1,o}^{2i-2} \oplus \hat{u}_{1,e}^{2i-2}) + L_{N/2}^{(i)}(y_{N/2+1}^N, \hat{u}_{1,e}^{2i-2})}, \tag{4}$$

$$L_N^{(2i)}(y_1^N, \hat{u}_1^{2i-1})$$
$$= [L_{N/2}^{(i)}(y_1^{N/2}, \hat{u}_{1,o}^{2i-2} \oplus \hat{u}_{1,e}^{2i-2})]^{1-2\hat{u}_{2i-1}} \cdot L_{N/2}^{(i)}(y_{N/2+1}^N, \hat{u}_{1,e}^{2i-2}). \tag{5}$$

The initial LR is:

$$L_1^{(1)}(y_i) = \frac{W(y_i|0)}{W(y_i|1)}. \tag{6}$$

2.2 Belief Propagation (BP) Decoding

The BP decoding for polar codes [2,5] is based on the factor graph. Figure 2 shows an example when $N = 8$, where circles represent variable nodes (VNs) and squares are check nodes (CNs). Given a polar code of length $N = 2^n$, messages are passed from layer 0 to layer n, then from layer n to layer 0 iteratively. Here layer 0 is the layer with inputs from the underlying channels. The messages passed in the graph are log likelihood ratio (LLR) values.

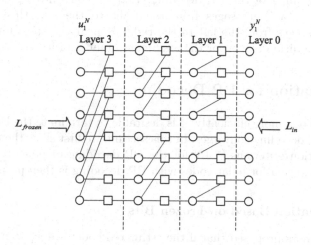

Fig. 2. BP decoding graph with the code length $N = 8$.

The initialization of the LLR is done:

$$L_{in}(i) = \ln \frac{P(y_i|x_i = 0)}{P(y_i|x_i = 1)}, \tag{7}$$

$$L_{frozen} = \begin{cases} \infty, & j \in A^c \\ 0, & j \in A, \end{cases} \tag{8}$$

where L_{in} are the LLR calculated from the channel. The initial LLRs are fed to the factor graph from the right to the left. The initial LLR L_{frozen} are the input to the factor graph from the left to the right, as shown in Fig. 2. Let $L_{v \to c}(\lambda, i)$ denote the message from the VN on the i-th row of the λ-th VN layer to the CN on the i-th row of the $(\lambda + 1)$-th CN layer ($1 \leq i \leq N$, $0 \leq \lambda \leq n - 1$). Similarly, let $L_{c \to v}(\lambda, i)$ denote the message from the CN on the i-th row of the $(\lambda + 1)$-th CN layer to the VN on the i-th row of the λ-th VN layer. Finally, let $L_{v \to c}(n, i)$ be the messages flooded to the n-th VN layer, which is used for estimation of the information bits. For bit u_i, $L_{v \to c}(n, i) + L_{frozen}(i)$ is taken as the decision metric for $\hat{u}_i$ (the estimation of u_i), and $L_{c \to v}(0, i) + L_{in}(i)$ is taken as the decision metric for the estimated coded symbol $\hat{x}_i$:

$$\hat{u}_i = \begin{cases} 0, & L_{v \to c}(n, i) + L_{frozen}(i) > 0 \\ 1, & \text{otherwise.} \end{cases} \tag{9}$$

$$\hat{x}_i = \begin{cases} 0, & L_{c \to v}(0, i) + L_{in}(i) > 0 \\ 1, & \text{otherwise.} \end{cases} \tag{10}$$

At the beginning of the BP decoding, $L_{in}(i)$ is put into $L_{v \to c}(0, i)$. Then update all $L_{v \to c}(\lambda, i)$ messages from the right to the left, then update all $L_{c \to v}(\lambda, i)$ messages from the left to the right. Repeat the steps until an early termination condition is met, or the maximum number of iterations is reached.

3   Termination for BP Decoding

In order to decode more efficiently, it is desirable to terminate the BP iterations early when the decoding converges. In this section, we first show the two existing early termination criterions [5,13] for the BP decoding of polar codes. A new termination criterion for polar codes with BP decoding is then proposed.

3.1   Termination Based on Frozen Bits

In [5], the authors proposed that if the estimated codeword $\hat{x}_1^N$ can produce all zero frozen bits, then the BP iteration can be terminated. Note that in [5], the frozen bits are set to be all zeros in the encoding process. Here we formally state this termination criterion as Termination I.

Termination I: Let G_N^{-1} be the inverse matrix of the generator matrix G_N. Let $\tilde{u}_1^N$ be the vector calculated from the estimated codeword $\hat{x}_1^N$: $\tilde{u}_1^N = \hat{x}_1^N G_N^{-1}$. Then the estimated codeword $\hat{x}_1^N \in \{0, 1\}^N$ is a real codeword, if and only if: $\tilde{u}_i = 0, \forall i \in \mathcal{A}^c$.

Note that Termination I requires a matrix inversion, which can be avoided by employing the special features of the generator matrix G_N. In [7], it is proven that the inverse of $F^{\otimes n}$ is itself. In [3], it is also shown that $B_N^{-1} = B_N$. Therefore

$$G_N^{-1} = (B_N F^{\otimes n})^{-1} = (F^{\otimes n})^{-1} B_N^{-1} = F^{\otimes n} B \tag{11}$$

Figure 3 shows the number of iterations of a polar system employing Termination I. Here the maximum number of iterations is set to be 70. The plot shows the number of iterations for each polar block. The red cross shows that a block is in error. It can be seen that there are quite a large number of blocks in error with a small iteration number when employing Termination I. There are also blocks that are in error while the maximum number of iterations is reached. These are the cases where BP decoding does not converge, and therefore can not be corrected by the BP decoding.

3.2   Termination Based on Estimated Codewords

Before introducing Termination II, recall that the encoding process is $x_1^N = u_1^N G_N$ for a given source vector u_1^N. Hence if $\hat{u}_1^N$ and $\hat{x}_1^N$ are the valid estimates, $\hat{x}_1^N = \hat{u}_1^N G_N$ must also hold. Therefore, $\hat{x}_1^N = \hat{u}_1^N \cdot G_N$ can be used to detect valid $\hat{u}_1^N$ and $\hat{x}_1^N$ [13].

Termination II: Let the calculated codeword be $\tilde{x}_1^N = \hat{u}_1^N G_N$. Then the condition for the termination of the BP iterations is when $\hat{x}_1^N = \tilde{x}_1^N$.

Note that from [4], it is observed that systematic polar codes achieve better BER performance than the counterpart of the normal non-systematic polar codes. Observe that in Termination II, the operation $\tilde{x}_1^N = \hat{u}_1^N G_N$ is exactly what systematic polar codes perform after obtaining estimates of $\hat{u}_1^N$. This operation produces less errors in $\tilde{x}_1^N$ than those in $\hat{u}_1^N$. Therefore, it can be predicted that Termination II results in less errors than Termination I.

With Termination II, the iteration number is shown in Fig. 4. It can see observed that the error cases with small numbers of iterations are far less than that employing Termination I. However there are still a few blocks in error with small numbers of iterations. These are the cases where the early termination criterion fails.

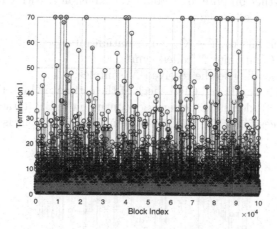

Fig. 3. The number of iterations of the BP decoding of the polar code with the code length $N = 256$ and the code rate $R = 0.36$. The maximum number of iterations is 70 in the fading channel. Termination I is employed to determine whether BP should stop.

3.3   Proposed Termination Criterion

The termination criterion is to detect a valid codeword. It is equivalent to determine whether the estimated information bits are correct. In this sense, the cyclic redundancy check (CRC) [8] can perform the same role: determine whether the estimated codeword is correct.

In this paper, the CRC based early termination is proposed to be used in the BP decoding of polar codes. This requires that before the polar code encoding, CRC check bits are added to the information bits. Let K_{crc} be the number of CRC check bits. If the original information set $\mathcal{A}$ has a size of K, then $K - K_{crc}$ information bits plus the K_{crc} check bits go to the polar encoder. In the decoding side, when the estimates of the K bits are obtained in every BP decoding iteration, CRC check can be done: if the estimated information bits pass the CRC check, then the BP decoding can stop. Otherwise, the BP decoding continues until the CRC check succeeds or the maximum number of iterations is reached. In this paper, we call this termination the CRC-based Termination (written as Termination-CRC).

Figure 5 shows the number of iterations and the error cases. It can be seen that except the uncorrectable blocks, the number of blocks in error with small iteration numbers are greatly reduced compared with Termination I and Termination II, showing the effectiveness of Termination-CRC.

When the errors in the CRC check bits and the errors in the information bits align, it can happen that the CRC check succeeds while the estimated information bits are incorrect. This can be confirmed from Fig. 5: there are six blocks in error (among 10^5 polar blocks) with small numbers of iterations. To remove these error cases, we further propose to combine Termination II with CRC checks. The scheme works as the following:

- Add K_{crc} check bits to $K - K_{crc}$ information bits;
- Encoding the K bits into N coded symbols;
- Perform BP decoding to the received N samples;
- Employ Termination II and CRC check of the estimated bits. If both succeed, terminate the BP decoding. Otherwise, continue the BP iterations until both checks are successful or the maximum number of iterations is reached.

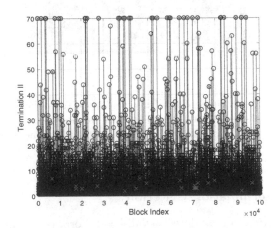

Fig. 4. The number of iterations of the BP decoding of the polar code with the code length $N = 256$ and the code rate $R = 0.36$. The maximum number of iterations is 70 in the fading channel. Termination II is employed to determine whether BP should stop.

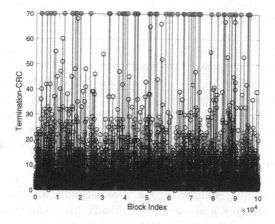

Fig. 5. The number of iterations of the BP decoding of the polar code with the code length $N = 256$ and the code rate $R = 0.36$. The maximum number of iterations is 70 in the fading channel. Termination-CRC is employed to determine whether BP should stop.

This combination of Termination II with CRC checks are termed Termination II-CRC in the paper. The iteration numbers and the error cases are reported in Fig. 6. It can be observed that except for the uncorrectable blocks, the error due to the incorrect early termination does not occur with the proposed Termination II-CRC. In the next section, the error performance of different termination criterions is presented to show the effectiveness of every termination criterion.

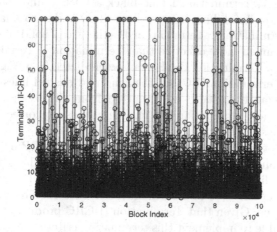

Fig. 6. The number of iterations of the BP decoding of the polar code with the code length $N = 256$ and the code rate $R = 0.36$. The maximum number of iterations is 70 in the fading channel. Termination II-CRC is employed to determine whether BP should stop.

4   Simulation Results

Binary phase shift keying (BPSK) modulation is employed to the coded symbols of polar codes. The polar code simulated has the block length $N = 256$ and the code rate R is 0.36. The maximum number of iterations for the BP decoding is 70. The modulated coded symbol x is transmitted through a fading channel: $y = hx + n$, where h follows a standard normal distribution, and n is the additive white Gaussian noise (AWGN) with mean zero and variance σ^2. With Termination-CRC and Termination II-CRC, 16 CRC check bits (with the polynomial 0×8810) are added to the information bits.

Figure 7 shows the bit error rate (BER) and packet error rate (PER) of the polar code in the fading channel. In the receiver side, assume the sign of the fading channel parameter h is estimated already from the channel estimation function, denoted as s_h. The receiver then performs the operation $\tilde{y} = s_h y = |h|x + s_h h$. After this operation, the SC or the BP decoding can start.

In Fig. 7, the line with the legend "BP I = 70" refers to the BP decoding with a fixed number of iterations of 70. It can be observed that with this fixed number of runs, the performance of the BP decoding is slightly better than the SC decoding, unlike the results in Fig. 1-b where the BP decoding performance (a fixed iteration number of 30) is worse than that of the SC decoding. This shows that in the fading channel, the BP decoding requires a larger number of iterations to converge than in the AWGN channels.

However, as shown in Figs. 3, 4, 5 and 6, the majority of blocks converge earlier than the maximum number. Given that the maximum number is already larger than that of the AWGN channels, it is desirable to stop the BP decoding when it converges.

Seen from Fig. 7, Termination I (the black solid line and the black dashed line) is not effective: it exhibits an error floor. This is due to a large number of incorrect early terminations. Termination II (the green solid and dashed lines with triangles) is much more effective than Termination I. Termination-CRC is slightly better than Termination II, also can be predicted from Figs. 4 and 5. The best criterion is Termination II-CRC (the solid and dashed lines with squares). This best performance can also be predicted from Fig. 6: there are no early termination errors for Termination II-CRC. Only those uncorrectable blocks are left with the proposed Termination II-CRC.

Figure 8 shows the average number of iterations of the BP decoding employing different termination criterions. The flat line with the legend "BP I = 70" refers to BP decoding with a fixed number of runs of 70. It can be seen that, on average Termination-CRC and Termination II-CRC requires almost the same number of iterations. Given that Termination II-CRC produces the best performance, it is desirable to implement this termination criterion in the BP decoding of polar codes in fading channels.

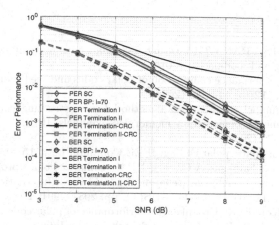

Fig. 7. BER and PER performance comparison of polar codes with the code length $N = 256$, code rate $R = 0.36$. The maximum number of iterations is 70 in the fading channel.

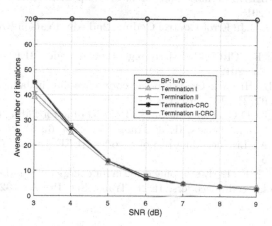

Fig. 8. Average number of iterations for BP decodings with different termination criterions. The label with "BP I = 70" is the BP decoding with a fixed number of iterations of 70.

5   Conclusion

This paper studies the performance of BP decoding in fading channels. Different termination criterions are investigated and a new termination criterion is proposed. The proposed termination can achieve the best BP decoding performance in fading channels among the existing termination criterions.

References

1. 3GPP: 3GPP TSG RAN WG1 meeting #87, chairmans notes of agenda item 7.1.5 channel coding and modulation (2016)
2. Arikan, E.: A performance comparison of polar codes and reed-muller codes. IEEE Commun. Lett. **12**(6), 447–449 (2008)
3. Arikan, E.: Channel polarization: a method for constructing capacity-achieving codes for symmetric binary-input memoryless channels. IEEE Trans. Inf. Theory **55**(7), 3051–3073 (2009)
4. Arikan, E.: Systematic polar coding. IEEE Commun. Lett. **15**(8), 860–862 (2011)
5. Guo, J., Qin, M., i Fabregas, A.G., Siegel, P.H.: Enhanced belief propagation decoding of polar codes through concatenation. In: 2014 IEEE International Symposium on Information Theory Proceedings (ISIT), pp. 2987–2991 (2014)
6. Hussami, N., Korada, S., Urbanke, R.: Performance of polar codes for channel and source coding. In: IEEE International Symposium on Information Theory (ISIT), pp. 1488–1492, June 2009
7. Li, L., Zhang, W.: On the encoding complexity of systematic polar codes. In: Proceedings of IEEE International System-on-Chip Conference (SOCC), pp. 508–513, September 2015
8. Lin, S., Costello, D.J.: Error Control Coding, 2nd edn. Pearson Prentice Hall, New Jersey (2004)
9. Niu, K., Chen, K.: CRC-aided decoding of polar codes. IEEE Commun. Lett. **16**(10), 1668–1671 (2012)
10. Deng, R., Li, L., Hu, Y..: On the polar code encoding in fading channels. Veh. Technol. Conf. **62**(24), 1–5 (2017)
11. Si, H., Koyluoglu, O.O., Vishwanath, S.: Polar coding for fading channels: binary and exponential channel cases. IEEE Trans. Commun. **62**(8), 2638–2649 (2014)
12. Tal, I., Vardy, A.: List decoding of polar codes. IEEE Trans. Inf. Theory **61**(5), 2213–2226 (2015)
13. Yuan, B., Parhi, K.K.: Early stopping criteria for energy-efficient low-latency belief-propagation polar code decoders. IEEE Trans. Sig. Process. **62**(24), 6496–6506 (2014)

Secrecy Capacity Analysis for Indoor Visible Light Communications with Input-Dependent Gaussian Noise

Bo Huang[1] and Jianxin Dai[2,3]($\boxtimes$)

[1] College of Telecommunications and Information Engineering,
Nanjing University of Posts and Telecommunications, Nanjing 210003, China
[2] School of Science, Nanjing University of Posts and Telecommunications,
Nanjing 210023, China
daijx@njupt.edu.cn
[3] National Mobile Communications Research Laboratory, Southeast University,
Nanjing 210096, China

Abstract. This paper mainly focus on the performance of secrecy capacity in the physical layer security (PLS) for the eavesdropping channel in visible light communication (VLC) system. In this system, due to the effects of thermal and shoot noises, the main interference of the channel is not only from additive white Gaussian noise (AWGN), but also dependent on the input signal. Considering a practical scenery, based on the input-dependent Gaussian noise, the closed-form expression of the upper and lower bounds of secrecy capacity are derived under the constraints of non-negative and average optical intensity. Specifically, since the entropy of the output signal is always greater than the input signal, on this basis, the derivation of lower bound is using the variational method to obtain a better input distribution. The upper bound is derived by the dual expression of channel capacity. We verified the performance of secrecy capacity through numerical results. The results show that the upper and lower bounds are relatively tight when optical intensity is high, which proves validity of the expression. In the low signal-to-noise ratio (SNR) scheme, the result of bounds with more input-dependent noise is better than less noise. And in the high SNR scheme, the result of bounds with less input-dependent noise outperforms that noise is more.

Keywords: Input-dependent Gaussian noise · Secrecy capacity · Visible light communication

1 Introduction

With the rapid progress of mobile communication technology, people have higher requirements for terminal transmission rate and security. For traditional wireless communication, there exists a series of problems, such as limited spectrum resources and easy signal fading [1]. And with the extensive use of light-emitting

© ICST Institute for Computer Sciences, Social Informatics and Telecommunications Engineering 2019
Published by Springer Nature Switzerland AG 2019. All Rights Reserved
G. Gui and L. Yun (Eds.): ADHIP 2019, LNICST 301, pp. 31–46, 2019.
https://doi.org/10.1007/978-3-030-36402-1_4

diodes (LEDs) in life, visible light communication (VLC) has received more attention. In VLC system, LEDs can be used for data signal transmission while they are used for illumination [2]. LEDs have many advantageous features such as high brightness, high reliability, low power consumption and long lifespan. The VLC system consisting of LEDs has the advantages of energy saving, environmental protection, safety and reliability, and is considered as the development direction of indoor communication in the future [3].

Despite the fact that VLC has many advantages and research work on it has also been done a lot, there are still many problems to be solved for data signal transmission security. Typically, it is a challenging problem for system designers to secure the safe data signal transmission over a VLC channel in the presence of unauthorized eavesdroppers. This problem is usually solved by encryption without being considered the defects caused by the channel [4]. In this model, the primary method of secure communication is to use a secret key. Subsequently, Wyner proposed the concept of physical layer security (PLS) in his paper [5] in 1975. In [6], the secrecy capacity based on duality and multi-antenna technology in the amplitude-limited eavesdropping channel is studied. The same authors analyzed the secrecy capacity of another scenery of the free-space optical channel in [7]. On this basis, the authors in [8] studied the performance of secrecy capacity in the typical indoor eavesdropping channel under the amplitude constraints. By introducing a randomly degraded wiretap channel model, the possibility of secure communication without relying on encryption is demonstrated. The authors in [9] studied the PLS in MIMO scenery and derived the secrecy capacity and optimal deployment of the receiver. Then, the same author studied another indoor eavesdropping channel in [10] and analyzed the performance of secrecy capacity under the different optical intensity constraints, respectively. But, the noise in the channel of system model assumed by the above research work is independent additive white Gaussian noise (AWGN). In the actual VLC scenarios, since the thermal and shot noise are related to the LED illumination intensity, the noise of channel is dependent on the input signal. On this basis, Moser studied the secrecy capacity of VLC system under the input-dependent Gaussian noise in [11]. However, Moser only analyzes the situation where only legitimate receiver exists, it may also include eavesdroppers in real scenery. So the research work of secrecy capacity for eavesdropping channel is not the same.

Inspired by the previous work, this paper mainly studied the secrecy capacity of the eavesdropping channel under input-dependent Gaussian noise. Firstly, we suppose that the output signals of both legitimate receiver and eavesdropper channels are affected by input-dependent Gaussian and input-independent Gaussian noise. Under this premise, we want to secure data signal transmission for legitimate receiver and hidden information to eavesdropper. We studied the eavesdropping channel under non-negative and average optical intensity constraint and derived the upper and lower bounds of secrecy capacity on this basis.

The reminder of this paper is arranged as the follows. In Sect. 2, we describe the system and channel model. In Sect. 3, we derive the upper and lower bounds of secrecy capacity based on the information theory. We put numerical results to compare performance of the secrecy capacity in Sect. 4. Finally, we provide concluding observations in Sect. 5.

Notations: In this paper, we use $\mathbf{R}$ to represent the real set, and $\mathbf{R}^+$ is positive real set. The natural logarithm is denoted by $\ln(\cdot)$. We use $I(\cdot\ ;\ \cdot)$ and $\mathcal{H}(\cdot)$ for mutual information and entropy, respectively.

2   System Model

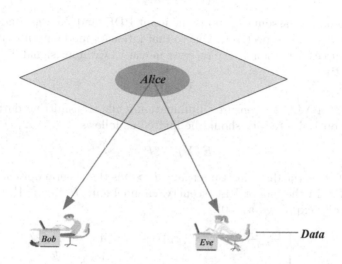

Fig. 1. An VLC network with one transmitter, one legitimate receiver and one eavesdropper.

In this paper, we consider an indoor VLC system consisting of one transmitter (Alice), one legitimate receiver (Bob), and one eavesdropper (Eve), as shown in Fig. 1. Alice acts as the transmitter to transmit data signal with one light fixture. Two receivers fixed on the desk receive the transmitted optical signal by one photodiode (PD) individually. Alice transmits data signal to Bob via VLC channel with the presence of Eve who can also receive the data signal from Alice to Bob. The received optical signals at two receivers can be mathematically expressed as [11]

$$\begin{cases} Y_{\mathrm{B}} = rH_{\mathrm{B}}X + \sqrt{rH_{\mathrm{B}}X}Z_1 + Z_{\mathrm{B}} \\ Y_{\mathrm{E}} = rH_{\mathrm{E}}X + \sqrt{rH_{\mathrm{E}}X}Z_2 + Z_{\mathrm{E}} \end{cases} \tag{1}$$

where the X is the input optical signal and is non-negative, H_{B} and H_{E} are the channel gains representing Bob and Eve, respectively. r indicates the photoelectric conversion coefficient whose value is generally set to one. Y_{B} and Y_{E} are the received signals of Bob and Eve, respectively. $Z_{\mathrm{B}} \in N\left(0, \sigma_{\mathrm{B}}^2\right)$ and $Z_{\mathrm{E}} \in N\left(0, \sigma_{\mathrm{E}}^2\right)$ are independent AWGN, $Z_1 \in N\left(0, \varsigma_1^2\sigma_{\mathrm{B}}^2\right)$ and $Z_2 \in N\left(0, \varsigma_1^2\sigma_{\mathrm{E}}^2\right)$ are input-dependent AWGN. We assume that Z_{B}, Z_{E}, Z_1 and Z_2 are irrelevant. ς_1^2 and

ς_2^2 represent the ratio of Bob and Eve's input-dependent Gaussian noise and input-independent noise variance, respectively.

The conditional probability density function (PDF) of eavesdropping channel can be expressed as [11]

$$
\begin{cases}
f_{Y_\mathrm{B}|X}\left(y_\mathrm{B}\,|x\,\right) = \dfrac{1}{\sqrt{2\pi\left(1+H_\mathrm{B}x\varsigma_1^2\right)\sigma_\mathrm{B}^2}}\,e^{-\frac{\left(y_\mathrm{B}-H_\mathrm{B}x\right)^2}{2\left(1+H_\mathrm{B}x\varsigma_1^2\right)\sigma_\mathrm{B}^2}} \\[4mm]
f_{Y_\mathrm{E}|X}\left(y_\mathrm{E}\,|x\,\right) = \dfrac{1}{\sqrt{2\pi\left(1+H_\mathrm{E}x\varsigma_2^2\right)\sigma_\mathrm{E}^2}}\,e^{-\frac{\left(y_\mathrm{E}-H_\mathrm{E}x\right)^2}{2\left(1+H_\mathrm{E}x\varsigma_2^2\right)\sigma_\mathrm{E}^2}}
\end{cases}
\tag{2}
$$

Furthermore, we assume $f_X\left(x\right)$ is the input PDF, and $f_{Y_\mathrm{B}}\left(y_\mathrm{B}\right)$ and $f_{Y_\mathrm{E}}\left(y_\mathrm{E}\right)$ are the output PDFs respectively. Due to that intensity modulation at the transmitter and direct detection at the receiver in the VLC, input signal X is limited to non-negative

$$X \geq 0 \tag{3}$$

Since indoor VLC also ensures illumination while transmitting data signals, the average optical intensity should be limited as follows

$$E\left(X\right) = \xi P \tag{4}$$

where $\xi \in (0,1]$ is the dimming target, and $P > 0$ is the general optical intensity level of LEDs. In the indoor VLC scenery, channel gain H_k (k = B, E) can be mathematically expressed as [10]

$$
H_k = \begin{cases}
\dfrac{(m+1)A_r}{2\pi D_k^2}T_s g\cos^m(\varphi_k)\cos(\psi_k), & \text{if } 0 \leq \psi_k \leq \Psi \\[3mm]
0, & \text{if } \psi_k \geq \Psi
\end{cases}
\tag{5}
$$

where m is the order of the Lambertian emission, A_r is the physical area of the PD, T_s and g are the optical filter gain and the concentrator gain of the PD, respectively. Ψ is the field of view (FOV) of the PD. D_k, φ_k and ψ_k are the distance, the angle of irradiance and the angle of incidence between LED and PD.

3   Secrecy Capacity Analysis

In this section, we mainly analyze the secrecy capacity in VLC system of an input-dependent Gaussian noise under average optical intensity constraint. When the channel of Bob is worse than the Eve, i.e., $H_\mathrm{B}/\sigma_\mathrm{B} < H_\mathrm{E}/\sigma_\mathrm{E}$, the channel Bob is stochastically faded with regarding to the channel of Alice-Eve, and the value of the secrecy capacity is near zero. Conversely, when the channel of Bob is better than the channel of Eve, i.e., $H_\mathrm{B}/\sigma_\mathrm{B} \geq H_\mathrm{E}/\sigma_\mathrm{E}$, the secrecy capacity can be expressed as [8]

$$
\begin{aligned}
C_s &= \max_{f_X(x)}\left[I\left(X\,;Y_\mathrm{B}\right) - I\left(X\,;Y_\mathrm{E}\right)\right] \\
\text{s.t.} \quad &\int_0^\infty f_X\left(x\right)\mathrm{d}x = 1 \\
&E\left(X\right) = \int_0^\infty x f_X\left(x\right)\mathrm{d}x = \xi P
\end{aligned}
\tag{6}
$$

where C_s indicates the secrecy capacity and $f_X(x)$ represents the PDF of input data signal. The upper and lower bounds of secrecy capacity will be derived in this part. Based on this analysis, the security performance is analyzed.

3.1 Lower Bound Analysis

For any two arbitrary functions $f_1(x)$ and $f_2(x)$, there exists the inequality $\max_x (f_1(x) - f_2(x)) \geq \max_x f_1(x) - \max_x f_2(x)$ [11]. Therefore, the secrecy capacity in (6) can be lower-bounded as following

$$C_s \geq \max_{f_X(x)} I(X;Y_B) - \max_{f_X(x)} I(X;Y_E)$$
$$\geq I(X;Y_B) - I(X;Y_E)|_{any\ f_X(x)} \tag{7}$$
$$= \mathcal{H}(Y_B) - \mathcal{H}(Y_B|X) - \mathcal{H}(Y_E) + \mathcal{H}(Y_E|X)$$

where $\mathcal{H}(\cdot)$ denotes entropy. By using the entropy power inequality (EPI) and variational method, we derived the expression of lower bound of secrecy capacity according to the theorem as follows.

Theorem 1. *The secrecy capacity of input-dependent Gaussian noise channel with the input signal satisfies the constraints (3) and (4) is lower-bounded by*

$$C_s \geq \sqrt{\frac{6}{\pi \xi P}} - \ln\left[\frac{3\sqrt{3}}{\sqrt{2\pi}(\xi P)^{\frac{3}{2}}}\right] + \frac{1}{2}\ln\left(H_B + \frac{2\varsigma_1^2 \sigma_B^2}{\xi P}\right) - 1 - \frac{\xi P}{\varsigma_1^2 \sigma_B^2}$$
$$- \frac{1}{2}\ln\left\{2\pi e\left[\frac{2}{3}H_E^2\xi^2 P^2 + \frac{16}{\sqrt{2\pi}}H_E\xi P\varsigma_2^5\sigma_E^5 + \sigma_E^2\right]\right\} \tag{8}$$
$$+ \frac{\sqrt{\xi P(H_B\xi P + 2\varsigma_1^2\sigma_B^2)}}{\varsigma_1^2\sigma_B^2} + \frac{1}{2}\ln\left(\frac{\sigma_E^2}{\sigma_B^2}\right) + \frac{\varsigma_2^2}{2\varsigma_1^2}$$

Proof. See Appendix A.

3.2 Upper Bound Analysis

The dual expression based on mutual information in [6] gave an analysis of the upper bound of the secrecy capacity. The method is effective for solving the upper bound of secrecy capacity on the general eavesdropping channel, and the method will also be cited in this paper.

Proposition 1. Consider a VLC channel $f(\cdot|\cdot)$ with input as $X \in \mathbf{R}^+$, and output as $Y \in \mathbf{R}$. For any one of the output distributions $Y(\cdot)$, we have

$$C \leq E_{f_X^*}\left(D\left(f_{\cdot|X}(\cdot|x)\|Y(\cdot)\right)\right) \tag{9}$$

where the $D(\cdot\|\cdot)$ denotes relative entropy [12], $f_X^*(x)$ denotes the capacity-achieving distribution of input signal.

Based on the above ideas, the upper bound of the secrecy capacity can be derived. It is known from Proposition 1, an upper bound of secrecy capacity can be obtained for any distribution of output signal. Our goal is to choose a better distribution that makes the upper bound more closer to the lower bound. As for any PDF $g_{Y_B|Y_E}(y_B|y_E)$, we have [13]

$$I(X;Y_B|Y_E) + E_{XY_E}\left\{D\left(f_{Y_B|Y_E}(y_B|Y_E)\middle\| g_{Y_B|Y_E}(y_B|Y_E)\right)\right\} \\ = E_{XY_E}\left\{D\left(f_{Y_B|XY_E}(y_B|X,Y_E)\middle\| g_{Y_B|Y_E}(y_B|Y_E)\right)\right\} \tag{10}$$

According to non-negative properties based relative entropy, we have

$$I(X;Y_B|Y_E) \leq E_{XY_E}\left\{D\left(f_{Y_B|XY_E}(y_B|X,Y_E)\middle\| g_{Y_B|Y_E}(y_B|Y_E)\right)\right\} \tag{11}$$

Noted that, the upper bound of $I(X;Y_B|Y_E)$ can be derived for any PDF $g_{Y_B|Y_E}(y_B|y_E)$.

$$I(X;Y_B|Y_E) = \min_{g_{Y_B|Y_E}(y_B|Y_E)} E_{XY_E}\left\{D\left(f_{Y_B|XY_E}(y_B|X,Y_E)\middle\| g_{Y_B|Y_E}(y_B|Y_E)\right)\right\} \tag{12}$$

It's clear that, in order to obtain secrecy capacity, there exists an input distribution to maximize the $I(X;Y_B|Y_E)$ satisfying the constraint in (6). Therefore, we have

$$\begin{aligned} C_s &= \max_{f_X(x)} I(X;Y_B|Y_E) \\ &= I(X^*;Y_B|Y_E) \end{aligned} \tag{13}$$

where X^* denotes the optimal distribution of input signal, the corresponding PDF is $f_{X^*}(x)$. According to (3.2) and (13), we have

$$C_s \leq E_{X^*Y_E}\left\{D\left(f_{Y_B|XY_E}(y_B|X,Y_E)\middle\| g_{Y_B|Y_E}(y_B|Y_E)\right)\right\} \tag{14}$$

It can be seen from (14) that the choice of any $g_{Y_B|Y_E}(y_B|y_E)$ will cause the upper bound. In order to get a better result, we should find a better choice of $g_{Y_D|Y_E}(y_B|y_E)$. By using dual expression, the upper bound in (6) can be given by the theorem as follows.

Theorem 2. *The secrecy capacity of input-dependent Gaussian noise channel in (1) under the constraints (3) and (4) is upper bounded by*

$$C_s \leq \begin{cases} I_1 + \ln\left[4e\left(\sqrt{\dfrac{3}{\pi^2 H_B \varsigma_1^2 \sigma_B^2 \varepsilon P}} + \dfrac{H_B \varepsilon P}{2}\right)\right], & if \sqrt{\dfrac{3}{\pi^2 \varepsilon P\left(\frac{H_E^2}{H_B^2}\varsigma_1^2\sigma_B^2 + H_E\varsigma_2^2\sigma_E^2\right)}} \geq \dfrac{H_E}{H_B}\left(\sqrt{\dfrac{3}{\pi^2 H_B\varsigma_1^2\sigma_B^2\varepsilon P}} + \dfrac{H_B\varepsilon P}{2}\right) \\ I_1 + \ln\left[4e\dfrac{H_B}{H_E}\sqrt{\dfrac{3}{\pi^2\varepsilon P\left(\frac{H_E^2}{H_B^2}\varsigma_1^2\sigma_B^2 + H_E\varsigma_2^2\sigma_E^2\right)}}\right], & if \sqrt{\dfrac{3}{\pi^2\varepsilon P\left(\frac{H_E^2}{H_B^2}\varsigma_1^2\sigma_B^2 + H_E\varsigma_2^2\sigma_E^2\right)}} < \dfrac{H_E}{H_B}\left(\sqrt{\dfrac{3}{\pi^2 H_B\varsigma_1^2\sigma_B^2\varepsilon P}} + \dfrac{H_B\varepsilon P}{2}\right) \end{cases} \tag{15}$$

where I_1 can be written as

$$
\begin{aligned}
I_1 = & \frac{1}{2} + \frac{1}{\sqrt{\pi}} - \frac{\sqrt{2}}{2} + \ln\left(\frac{\sigma_E}{\sigma_B}\right) \\
& - \frac{\varsigma_2^2}{2\varsigma_1^2} - \frac{\ln(2\pi)}{\sqrt{\pi}} - \left(\frac{1}{\sqrt{\pi}} + \frac{\sqrt{2}}{2}\right)\left(\frac{H_E^2}{H_B^2}\sigma_B^2 + \sigma_E^2\right) \\
& - \xi P\left(\frac{1}{2} + \frac{\sqrt{2\pi}}{4}\right)\left(\frac{H_E^2}{H_B^2}H_B\varsigma_1^2\sigma_B^2 + H_E\varsigma_2^2\sigma_E^2\right)
\end{aligned}
\tag{16}
$$

Proof. See Appendix B.

4 Numerical Results

In this section, we consider a typical indoor VLC network scenery in a $10 \times 10 \times 5\,\mathrm{m}^3$ conference room. Room lighting is provided by one LED that emits the optical power signal. Alice is placed in the center of the ceiling and modulated to transmit data signals. Bob and Eve are placed at the height of 0.9 meters above the ground. Other parameters for simulation are shown in Table 1.

Table 1. Main simulation parameters

Parameter	Value
Order of the Lambertian emission m	6
Physical area of the PD A_r	$1\,\mathrm{cm}^2$
Optical filter gain T_s	1
Concentrator gain g	3
Noise variance $\sigma^2 = \sigma_B^2 = \sigma_E^2$	-120 dBm
FOV of PD	70^0
Position of Bob	$(0\,\mathrm{m},\, 0\,\mathrm{m},\, 0.9\,\mathrm{m})$
Position of Eve	$(2.57\,\mathrm{m},\, -3.86\,\mathrm{m},\, 0.9\,\mathrm{m})$

In Fig. 2, we assume that the dimming target is $\xi = 0.3$, giving the gap between the upper and lower bounds under different ς_1/ς_2. It can be seen from the figure that when P is small (i.e., the low SNR scheme), the upper and lower bounds increase with the increase of P; when P is larger (i.e., the high SNR scheme), the upper and lower bounds tend to be constant as the P grows. With the decrease of ς_1/ς_2, the upper and lower bounds are more tighter. The gap between the upper and lower bounds of the secrecy capacity is smaller when P is larger. At a low SNR scheme, the performance of bound with high value ς_1/ς_2 outperforms that with low value ς_1/ς_2. At a high SNR scheme, the bounds of secrecy capacity performance become better as the ς_1/ς_2 is big.

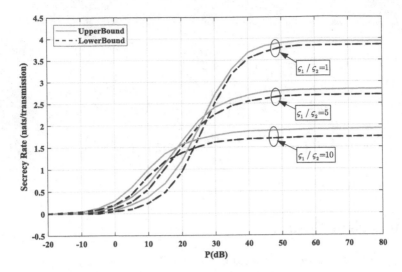

Fig. 2. Secrecy capacity under the different ς_1/ς_2 while the dimming target is $\xi = 0.3$.

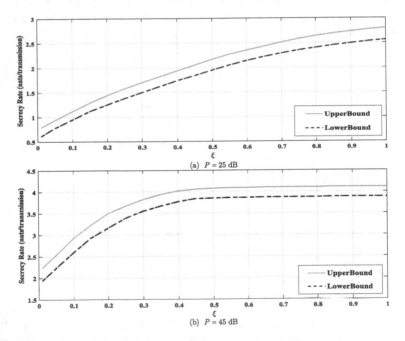

Fig. 3. Secrecy capacity under the different diming target ξ while the $\varsigma_1/\varsigma_2 = 1$.

It can be seen from Fig. 3 that, the upper and lower bounds of the secrecy capacity increase with increase of ξ when P is small. When P grows to a certain value, the bounds of secrecy capacity tends to be constant while ξ is larger. And when P is larger, the upper and lower bounds stays unchanged with the increase of ξ.

5   Conclusion

In this paper, we analyzed the secrecy capacity of VLC system with input-dependent Gaussian noise channel in typical indoor scenery. Under the constraint of average optical intensity, the closed-form expression of the upper and lower bounds of the secrecy capacity are derived. The numerical results show that the gap between the upper and lower bounds is smaller when SNR is high. The input-dependent Gaussian noise work done in this paper is a supplement to the previous research of VLC system. The channel model considered in previous works can be regarded as a special case of this paper (i.e., $\varsigma_1 = \varsigma_2 = 0$).

6   Appendix

6.1   Appendix A

For expression (7), according to [10], we have

$$\mathcal{H}(Y_B) \geq \mathcal{H}(H_B X) + f_{low}(\xi P) \tag{17}$$
$$= \mathcal{H}(X) + \ln(H_B) + f_{low}(\xi P)$$

According to Theorem 17.2.3 in [12], an upper bound of $\mathcal{H}(Y_E)$ is given by

$$\mathcal{H}(Y_E) \leq \frac{1}{2} \ln\left[2\pi e \mathrm{var}(Y_E)\right] \tag{18}$$

Substituting (17) and (18) into (7), C_s can be written as

$$C_s \geq \mathcal{H}(X) + \ln(H_B) + f_{low}(\xi P) - \mathcal{H}(Y_B | X) - \frac{1}{2} \ln\left[2\pi e \mathrm{var}(Y_E)\right] + \mathcal{H}(Y_E | X) \tag{19}$$

where $f_{low}(\xi P)$, $\mathcal{H}(Y_B | X)$ and $\mathcal{H}(Y_E | X)$ are given by

$$f_{low}(\xi P) = \frac{1}{2} \ln\left(H_B + \frac{2\varsigma_1^2 \sigma_B^2}{\xi P}\right) - \frac{\xi P + \varsigma_1^2 \sigma_B^2}{\varsigma_1^2 \sigma_B^2} + \frac{\sqrt{\xi P(H_B \xi P + 2\varsigma_1^2 \sigma_B^2)}}{\varsigma_1^2 \sigma_B^2} \tag{20}$$

$$\mathcal{H}(Y_B | X) = \frac{1}{2} E_{fx} \left\{\ln\left[2\pi e \sigma_B^2 \left(1 + \varsigma_1^2 X\right)\right]\right\}$$
$$= \frac{1}{2} \ln\left(2\pi e \sigma_B^2\right) + \frac{1}{2} E_{fx} \left[\ln\left(1 + \varsigma_1^2 X\right)\right] \tag{21}$$

$$\mathcal{H}(Y_E | X) = \frac{1}{2} \ln\left(2\pi e \sigma_E^2\right) + \frac{1}{2} E_{fx} \left[\ln\left(1 + \varsigma_2^2 X\right)\right] \tag{22}$$

Then C_s in (19) can be written as

$$C_s \geq \mathcal{H}(X) + \frac{1}{2} \ln\left(H_B + \frac{2\varsigma_1^2 \sigma_B^2}{\xi P}\right) - \frac{\xi P + \varsigma_1^2 \sigma_B^2}{\varsigma_1^2 \sigma_B^2}$$
$$+ \frac{\sqrt{\xi P(H_B \xi P + 2\varsigma_1^2 \sigma_B^2)}}{\varsigma_1^2 \sigma_B^2} - \frac{1}{2} \ln\left[2\pi e \mathrm{var}(Y_E)\right] + \frac{1}{2} \ln\left(\frac{\sigma_E^2}{\sigma_B^2}\right) \tag{23}$$
$$+ \frac{1}{2} E_{fx} \left\{\ln(X)\right\} + \frac{1}{2} E_{fx} \left\{\ln\left(\frac{1 + \varsigma_2^2 X}{X + \varsigma_1^2 X^2}\right)\right\}$$

where the $E_{fx} \left\{\ln\left[(1 + \varsigma_2^2 X)/(X + \varsigma_1^2 X^2)\right]\right\}$ is tends to zero when X is infinite.

We select an input distribution $f_X(x)$ to maximizes the $\mathcal{H}(X)+1/2$ $\{E_{f_X}[\ln(X)]\}$ under the input constrains (3) and (4). Such an optimization problem as following can be solved to find the better input PDF.

$$\max_{f_X(x)} \left\{ \mathcal{H}(X) + \tfrac{1}{2} E_{f_X}[\ln(X)] \right\}$$

$$\text{s.t.} \quad \int_0^\infty f_X(x)\,dx = 1 \tag{24}$$

$$E(X) = \int_0^\infty x f_X(x)\,dx = \xi P$$

Then an optimal distribution problem can be transformed as

$$\max_{f_X(x)} F[f_X(x)] \overset{\triangle}{=} \int_0^\infty \left\{ \tfrac{1}{2}\ln(x) - \ln[f_X(x)] \right\} f_X(x)\,dx$$

$$\text{s.t.} \quad \int_0^\infty f_X(x)\,dx = 1 \tag{25}$$

$$E(X) = \int_0^\infty x f_X(x)\,dx = \xi P$$

This problem can be solved by variational method. Assuming that optimal result in (24) is $f_X(x)$, then define a perturbation function as

$$\tilde{f}_X(x) = f_X(x) + \varepsilon\eta(x) \tag{26}$$

where ε is a variable, and $\eta(x)$ is a function, where x is the independent variable of the function. And the perturbation function in (26) should also satisfy the constraints in (24). So we have

$$\begin{cases} \int_0^\infty \eta(x)\,dx = 0 \\ \int_0^\infty x\eta(x)\,dx = 0 \end{cases} \tag{27}$$

Then define a function $\rho(\varepsilon)$, where ε is the independent variable of the function.

$$\rho(\varepsilon) = F\left[\tilde{f}_X(x)\right] = F[f_X(x) + \varepsilon\eta(x)] \tag{28}$$

The extremum value is obtained when $\varepsilon = 0$, the first variation can be expressed as

$$\left.\frac{d\rho(\varepsilon)}{d\varepsilon}\right|_{\varepsilon=0} = \int_0^\infty \left\{ \frac{1}{2}\ln(x) - \ln[f_X(x)] - 1 \right\} \eta(x)\,dx = 0 \tag{29}$$

So we have

$$f_X(x) = \sqrt{x}e^{-cx-b} \tag{30}$$

where b and c are the free parameters. Submitting (30) into the constrains in (25), we have

$$\begin{cases} b = \ln\left[\dfrac{\sqrt{2\pi}(\xi P)^{\frac{3}{2}}}{3\sqrt{3}} \right] \\[2mm] c = \dfrac{3}{2\xi P} \end{cases} \tag{31}$$

And $f_X(x)$ in (30) can be written as

$$f_X(x) = \frac{3}{\xi P}\sqrt{\frac{3}{2\pi\xi P}}\sqrt{x}e^{-\frac{3}{2\xi P}x} \tag{32}$$

The unknowns $\mathcal{H}(X)$, $\frac{1}{2}E_{fx}\{\ln(X)\}$ and $\frac{1}{2}E_{fx}\{\ln[(1+\varsigma_2^2 X)/(X+\varsigma_1^2 X^2)]\}$ in (23) can be solved as following

$$\begin{aligned}
\mathcal{H}(X) &= -\int_0^\infty f_X(x)\ln[f_X(x)]\mathrm{d}x \\
&= -\frac{3\sqrt{3}}{\sqrt{2\pi}(\xi P)^{\frac{3}{2}}}\left\{\ln\left[\frac{3\sqrt{3}}{\sqrt{2\pi}(\xi P)^{\frac{3}{2}}}\right]\int_0^\infty \sqrt{x}e^{-\frac{3}{2\xi P}x}\mathrm{d}x \right.\\
&\quad \left. +\frac{1}{2}\int_0^\infty \sqrt{x}e^{-\frac{3}{2\xi P}x}\ln(x)\mathrm{d}x - \frac{3}{2\xi P}\int_0^\infty \sqrt{x}e^{-\frac{3}{2\xi P}x}x\mathrm{d}x\right\} \\
&\leq \frac{1}{2}+\sqrt{\frac{6}{\pi\xi P}}-\ln\left[\frac{3\sqrt{3}}{\sqrt{2\pi}(\xi P)^{\frac{3}{2}}}\right]
\end{aligned} \tag{33}$$

$$\begin{aligned}
\frac{1}{2}&E_{fx}\{\ln(X)\}+\frac{1}{2}E_{fx}\left\{\ln\left(\frac{1+\varsigma_2^2 X}{X+\varsigma_1^2 X^2}\right)\right\} \\
&= \frac{1}{2}E_{fx}\left\{\ln\left(\frac{1+\varsigma_2^2 X}{1+\varsigma_1^2 X}\right)\right\} \\
&\leq \frac{1}{2}\int_0^\infty \frac{3\sqrt{3}}{\sqrt{2\pi}(\xi P)^{\frac{3}{2}}}\sqrt{x}e^{-\frac{3}{2\xi P}x}\left(\frac{1+\varsigma_2^2 x}{1+\varsigma_1^2 x}-1\right)\mathrm{d}x \\
&= \frac{1}{2}\left(\frac{\varsigma_2^2}{\varsigma_1^2}-1\right)erfc(0) = \frac{\varsigma_2^2}{2\varsigma_1^2}-\frac{1}{2}
\end{aligned} \tag{34}$$

As for $\mathrm{var}(Y_E)$, we have

$$\begin{aligned}
\mathrm{var}(Y_E) &= \mathrm{var}(H_E X) + \mathrm{var}\left(\sqrt{H_E X}Z_2\right)+\mathrm{var}(Z_E) \\
&= H_E^2\mathrm{var}(X) + H_E\mathrm{var}\left(\sqrt{X}Z_2\right)+\mathrm{var}(Z_E)
\end{aligned} \tag{35}$$

The $\mathrm{var}(X)$ and $\mathrm{var}\left(\sqrt{X}Z_2\right)$ can be written as

$$\mathrm{var}(X) = E(X^2) - [E(X)]^2 = \frac{2}{3}\xi^2 P^2 \tag{36}$$

$$\mathrm{var}\left(\sqrt{X}Z_2\right) = E\left[\left(\sqrt{X}\right)^2 Z_2^2\right] - \left[E\left(\sqrt{X}Z_2\right)\right]^2 = \frac{16}{\sqrt{2\pi}}\xi P\varsigma_2^5\sigma_E^5 \tag{37}$$

Submitting (36) and (37) into (35), we have

$$\mathrm{var}(Y_E) = \frac{2}{3}H_E^2\xi^2 P^2+\frac{16}{\sqrt{2\pi}}H_E\xi P\varsigma_2^5\sigma_E^5+\sigma_E^2 \tag{38}$$

Then substituting (33), (34) and (38) into (23), (8) can be derived.

6.2   Appendix B

Expression (14) can be written as

$$C_s \leq \underbrace{E_{X^*}\left\{\int_{-\infty}^{\infty}\int_{-\infty}^{\infty} f_{Y_{\mathrm{B}}Y_{\mathrm{E}}|X}\left(y_{\mathrm{B}},y_{\mathrm{E}}|\,X\right)\ln\left[f_{Y_{\mathrm{B}}|XY_{\mathrm{E}}}\left(y_{\mathrm{B}}|\,X,y_{\mathrm{E}}\right)\right]\mathrm{d}y_{\mathrm{B}}\mathrm{d}y_{\mathrm{E}}\right\}}_{I_1}$$

$$\underbrace{-E_{X^*}\left\{\int_{-\infty}^{\infty}\int_{-\infty}^{\infty} f_{Y_{\mathrm{B}}Y_{\mathrm{E}}|X}\left(y_{\mathrm{B}},y_{\mathrm{E}}|\,X\right)\ln\left[g_{Y_{\mathrm{B}}|Y_{\mathrm{E}}}\left(y_{\mathrm{B}}|\,y_{\mathrm{E}}\right)\right]\mathrm{d}y_{\mathrm{B}}\mathrm{d}y_{\mathrm{E}}\right\}}_{I_2} \quad (39)$$

I_1 can be written as

$$\begin{aligned}
I_1 &= E_{X^*}\left\{\int_{-\infty}^{\infty}\int_{-\infty}^{\infty} f_{Y_{\mathrm{B}}|XY_{\mathrm{E}}}\left(y_{\mathrm{B}}|\,X,y_{\mathrm{E}}\right)\ln\left[f_{Y_{\mathrm{B}}|XY_{\mathrm{E}}}\left(y_{\mathrm{B}}|\,X,y_{\mathrm{E}}\right)\right]\mathrm{d}y_{\mathrm{B}}\mathrm{d}y_{\mathrm{E}}\right\} \\
&= -\mathcal{H}\left(Y_{\mathrm{B}}|\,X^*,Y_{\mathrm{E}}\right) \\
&= -\left[\mathcal{H}\left(Y_{\mathrm{B}}|\,X^*\right) + \mathcal{H}\left(Y_{\mathrm{E}}|\,X^*,Y_{\mathrm{B}}\right) - \mathcal{H}\left(Y_{\mathrm{E}}|\,X^*\right)\right]
\end{aligned} \quad (40)$$

Obtained by (21) and (22), $\mathcal{H}\left(Y_{\mathrm{B}}|\,X^*\right)$ and $\mathcal{H}\left(Y_{\mathrm{E}}|\,X^*\right)$ can be written as

$$\begin{cases} \mathcal{H}\left(Y_{\mathrm{B}}|\,X^*\right) = H\left(Y_{\mathrm{B}}|\,X\right) = \frac{1}{2}\ln\left(2\pi e\sigma_{\mathrm{B}}^2\right) + \frac{1}{2}E_{fx}\left[\ln\left(1+\varsigma_1^2 X\right)\right] \\ \mathcal{H}\left(Y_{\mathrm{E}}|\,X^*\right) = H\left(Y_{\mathrm{E}}|\,X\right) = \frac{1}{2}\ln\left(2\pi e\sigma_{\mathrm{E}}^2\right) + \frac{1}{2}E_{fx}\left[\ln\left(1+\varsigma_2^2 X\right)\right] \end{cases} \quad (41)$$

As for $H\left(Y_{\mathrm{E}}|\,X^*,Y_{\mathrm{B}}\right)$, the conditional PDF $f_{Y_{\mathrm{E}}|Y_{\mathrm{B}}}\left(y_{\mathrm{E}}|\,y_{\mathrm{B}}\right)$ can be expressed as

$$f_{Y_{\mathrm{E}}|Y_{\mathrm{B}}}\left(y_{\mathrm{E}}|\,y_{\mathrm{B}}\right) = \frac{1}{\sqrt{2\pi\left[\left(\frac{H_{\mathrm{E}}^2}{H_{\mathrm{B}}^2}+\frac{H_{\mathrm{E}}^2}{H_{\mathrm{B}}^2}x\varsigma_1^2\right)\sigma_{\mathrm{B}}^2 + \left(1+H_{\mathrm{E}}x\varsigma_2^2\right)\sigma_{\mathrm{E}}^2\right]}}e^{-\frac{\left(y_{\mathrm{E}}-\frac{H_{\mathrm{E}}}{H_{\mathrm{B}}}y_{\mathrm{B}}\right)^2}{2\left[\left(\frac{H_{\mathrm{E}}^2}{H_{\mathrm{B}}^2}+\frac{H_{\mathrm{E}}^2}{H_{\mathrm{B}}^2}x\varsigma_1^2\right)\sigma_{\mathrm{B}}^2 + \left(1+H_{\mathrm{E}}x\varsigma_2^2\right)\sigma_{\mathrm{E}}^2\right]}} \quad (42)$$

$\mathcal{H}\left(Y_{\mathrm{E}}|\,X^*,Y_{\mathrm{B}}\right)$ can be expressed as

$$\begin{aligned}
\mathcal{H}\left(Y_{\mathrm{E}}|\,X^*,Y_{\mathrm{B}}\right) &= -\int_0^{\infty} f_{X^*}\left(x\right)\int_{-\infty}^{\infty} f_{Y_{\mathrm{B}}|X^*}\left(y_{\mathrm{B}}|\,x\right)\int_{-\infty}^{\infty} f_{Y_{\mathrm{E}}|Y_{\mathrm{B}}}\left(y_{\mathrm{E}}|\,y_{\mathrm{B}}\right)\ln f_{Y_{\mathrm{E}}|Y_{\mathrm{B}}}\left(y_{\mathrm{E}}|\,y_{\mathrm{B}}\right)\mathrm{d}y_{\mathrm{B}}\mathrm{d}y_{\mathrm{E}}\mathrm{d}x \\
&= \frac{3\sqrt{3}}{2\sqrt{2\pi}(\xi P)^{\frac{3}{2}}}\left\{\ln\left(2\pi\right)\int_0^{\infty}\sqrt{x}e^{-\frac{3}{2\xi P}x}\mathrm{d}x \right.\\
&\quad + \int_0^{\infty}\sqrt{x}e^{-\frac{3}{2\xi P}x}\ln\left[\left(\frac{H_{\mathrm{E}}^2}{H_{\mathrm{B}}^2}+\frac{H_{\mathrm{E}}^2}{H_{\mathrm{B}}^2}x\varsigma_1^2\right)\sigma_{\mathrm{B}}^2 + \left(1+H_{\mathrm{E}}x\varsigma_2^2\right)\sigma_{\mathrm{E}}^2\right]\mathrm{d}x \\
&\quad \left. + \sqrt{2\pi}\int_0^{\infty}\sqrt{x}e^{-\frac{3}{2\xi P}x}\sqrt{\left(\frac{H_{\mathrm{E}}^2}{H_{\mathrm{B}}^2}+\frac{H_{\mathrm{E}}^2}{H_{\mathrm{B}}^2}x\varsigma_1^2\right)\sigma_{\mathrm{B}}^2 + \left(1+H_{\mathrm{E}}x\varsigma_2^2\right)\sigma_{\mathrm{E}}^2}\mathrm{d}x\right\} \\
&\geq \frac{1}{\sqrt{\pi}}\left[\ln\left(2\pi\right)-2\right] + \left(\frac{1}{\sqrt{\pi}}+\frac{\sqrt{2}}{2}\right)\left(\frac{H_{\mathrm{E}}^2}{H_{\mathrm{B}}^2}\sigma_{\mathrm{B}}^2 + \sigma_{\mathrm{E}}^2 + 1\right) \\
&\quad + \left(\frac{\xi P}{2}+\frac{\sqrt{2\pi}\xi P}{4}\right)\left(\frac{H_{\mathrm{E}}^2}{H_{\mathrm{B}}^2}\varsigma_1^2\sigma_{\mathrm{B}}^2 + H_{\mathrm{E}}\varsigma_2^2\sigma_{\mathrm{E}}^2\right)
\end{aligned} \quad (43)$$

Substituting (43) and (41) into (40), we have

$$
\begin{aligned}
I_1 \leq \frac{1}{2} + \frac{1}{\sqrt{\pi}} - \frac{\sqrt{2}}{2} + \ln\left(\frac{\sigma_E}{\sigma_B}\right) - \frac{\varsigma_2^2}{2\varsigma_1^2} \\
- \frac{\ln(2\pi)}{\sqrt{\pi}} - \left(\frac{1}{\sqrt{\pi}} + \frac{\sqrt{2}}{2}\right)\left(\frac{H_E^2}{H_B^2}\sigma_B^2 + \sigma_E^2\right) \\
- \xi P\left(\frac{1}{2} + \frac{\sqrt{2\pi}}{4}\right)\left(\frac{H_E^2}{H_B^2}H_B\varsigma_1^2\sigma_B^2 + H_E\varsigma_2^2\sigma_E^2\right)
\end{aligned}
\tag{44}
$$

One of the difficulties in solving I_2 is that the input signal X has no peak intensity constraints so it is difficult to find the bounds of upper bound because the signal range can be arbitrarily large. In order to get I_2, $g_{Y_B|Y_E}(y_B|y_E)$ can be chosen as [10]

$$
g_{Y_B|Y_E}(y_B|y_E) = \frac{1}{2s^2}e^{-\frac{|y_B - \mu y_E|}{s^2}}
\tag{45}
$$

where s and μ are free parameters.

Let $p = \left[H_E^2/H_B^2 + (H_E^2/H_B)x\varsigma_1^2\right]\sigma_B^2 + (1 + H_E x\varsigma_2^2)\sigma_E^2$ and $q = (1 + H_B x\varsigma_1^2)$ σ_B^2. Therefore, $f_{Y_B Y_E|X}(y_B, y_E|X)$ can be written as

$$
f_{Y_B Y_E|X}(y_B, y_E|X) = \frac{1}{\sqrt{2\pi q}}e^{-\frac{(y_B - H_B x)^2}{2q}} \times \frac{1}{\sqrt{2\pi p}}e^{-\frac{\left(y_E - \frac{H_E}{H_B}y_B\right)^2}{2p}}
\tag{46}
$$

Substituting (46) into (39), I_2 can be written as

$$
I_2 = \ln\left(2s^2\right) + \frac{1}{s^2}E_{X*}\left\{\frac{1}{\sqrt{2\pi q}}\frac{1}{\sqrt{2\pi p}}\int_{-\infty}^{\infty}e^{-\frac{(y_B - H_B x)^2}{2q}}\int_{-\infty}^{\infty}e^{-\frac{t^2}{2p}}\left|\left(1 - \mu\frac{H_E}{H_B}\right)y_B - \mu t\right|dt dy_B\right\}
\tag{47}
$$

Then I_2 can be upper-bounded by

$$
\begin{aligned}
I_2 \leq \ln\left(2s^2\right) + \frac{\left|1 - \mu\frac{H_E}{H_B}\right|}{s^2}E_{X*}\left\{\frac{2}{\sqrt{2\pi q}} + H_B x\right\} + \frac{2|\mu|}{s^2}E_{X*}\left\{\frac{1}{\sqrt{2\pi p}}\right\} \\
\leq \ln\left(2s^2\right) + \frac{\left|1 - \mu\frac{H_E}{H_B}\right|}{s^2}H_B\xi P + \frac{2\left|1 - \mu\frac{H_E}{H_B}\right|}{s^2}E_{X*}\left\{\frac{1}{\sqrt{2\pi q}}\right\} + \frac{2|\mu|}{s^2}E_{X*}\left\{\frac{1}{\sqrt{2\pi p}}\right\} \\
= \ln\left(2s^2\right) + \frac{2}{s^2}\underbrace{\left[\left|1 - \mu\frac{H_E}{H_B}\right|\left(\sqrt{\frac{3}{\pi^2 H_B\varsigma_1^2\sigma_B^2\xi P}} + \frac{H_B\xi P}{2}\right) + |\mu|\sqrt{\frac{3}{\pi^2\xi P\left(\frac{H_E^2}{H_B}\varsigma_1^2\sigma_B^2 + H_E\varsigma_2^2\sigma_E^2\right)}}\right]}_{I_3}
\end{aligned}
\tag{48}
$$

Case1: when $\mu < 0$, I_3 is given by

$$
I_3 = -\mu \left[\frac{H_E}{H_B} \left(\sqrt{\frac{3}{\pi^2 H_B \varsigma_1^2 \sigma_B^2 \xi P}} + \frac{H_B \xi P}{2} \right) + \sqrt{\frac{3}{\pi^2 \xi P \left(\frac{H_E^2}{H_B} \varsigma_1^2 \sigma_B^2 + H_E \varsigma_2^2 \sigma_E^2 \right)}} \right]
$$
$$
+ \left(\sqrt{\frac{3}{\pi^2 H_B \varsigma_1^2 \sigma_B^2 \xi P}} + \frac{H_B \xi P}{2} \right)
$$
$$
\geq \sqrt{\frac{3}{\pi^2 H_B \varsigma_1^2 \sigma_B^2 \xi P}} + \frac{H_B \xi P}{2}
\tag{49}
$$

Case2: when $0 \leq \mu \leq H_B/H_E$, I_3 is given by

$$
I_3 = \mu \left[\sqrt{\frac{3}{\pi^2 \xi P \left(\frac{H_E^2}{H_B} \varsigma_1^2 \sigma_B^2 + H_E \varsigma_2^2 \sigma_E^2 \right)}} - \frac{H_E}{H_B} \left(\sqrt{\frac{3}{\pi^2 H_B \varsigma_1^2 \sigma_B^2 \xi P}} + \frac{H_B \xi P}{2} \right) \right]
$$
$$
+ \left(\sqrt{\frac{3}{\pi^2 H_B \varsigma_1^2 \sigma_B^2 \xi P}} + \frac{H_B \xi P}{2} \right)
\tag{50}
$$

So I_3 can be lower-bounded by

$$
I_3 \geq \begin{cases} \sqrt{\frac{3}{\pi^2 H_B \varsigma_1^2 \sigma_B^2 \xi P}} + \frac{H_B \xi P}{2}, \quad if \sqrt{\frac{3}{\pi^2 \xi P \left(\frac{H_E^2}{H_B} \varsigma_1^2 \sigma_B^2 + H_E \varsigma_2^2 \sigma_E^2 \right)}} \\ \quad \geq \frac{H_E}{H_B} \left(\sqrt{\frac{3}{\pi^2 H_B \varsigma_1^2 \sigma_B^2 \xi P}} + \frac{H_B \xi P}{2} \right) \\ \frac{H_B}{H_E} \sqrt{\frac{3}{\pi^2 \xi P \left(\frac{H_E^2}{H_B} \varsigma_1^2 \sigma_B^2 + H_E \varsigma_2^2 \sigma_E^2 \right)}}, if \sqrt{\frac{3}{\pi^2 \xi P \left(\frac{H_E^2}{H_B} \varsigma_1^2 \sigma_B^2 + H_E \varsigma_2^2 \sigma_E^2 \right)}} \\ \quad < \frac{H_E}{H_B} \left(\sqrt{\frac{3}{\pi^2 H_B \varsigma_1^2 \sigma_B^2 \xi P}} + \frac{H_B \xi P}{2} \right) \end{cases}
\tag{51}
$$

Case3: when $\mu > H_B/H_E$, I_3 is given by

$$
I_3 = \mu \left[\frac{H_E}{H_B} \left(\sqrt{\frac{3}{\pi^2 H_B \varsigma_1^2 \sigma_B^2 \xi P}} + \frac{H_B \xi P}{2} \right) + \sqrt{\frac{3}{\pi^2 \xi P \left(\frac{H_E^2}{H_B} \varsigma_1^2 \sigma_B^2 + H_E \varsigma_2^2 \sigma_E^2 \right)}} \right]
$$
$$
- \left(\sqrt{\frac{3}{\pi^2 H_B \varsigma_2^2 \sigma_B^2 \xi P}} + \frac{H_B \xi P}{2} \right) \geq \frac{H_B}{H_E} \sqrt{\frac{3}{\pi^2 \xi P \left(\frac{H_E^2}{H_B} \varsigma_1^2 \sigma_B^2 + H_E \varsigma_2^2 \sigma_E^2 \right)}}
\tag{52}
$$

From three cases, I_3 can be expressed as

$$
I_3 \geq
\begin{cases}
\sqrt{\dfrac{3}{\pi^2 H_{\mathrm{B}} \varsigma_1^2 \sigma_{\mathrm{B}}^2 \xi P}} + \dfrac{H_{\mathrm{B}} \xi P}{2}, & if \ \sqrt{\dfrac{3}{\pi^2 \xi P \left(\frac{H_{\mathrm{E}}^2}{H_{\mathrm{B}}} \varsigma_1^2 \sigma_{\mathrm{B}}^2 + H_{\mathrm{E}} \varsigma_2^2 \sigma_{\mathrm{E}}^2\right)}} \\[4mm]
\quad \geq \dfrac{H_{\mathrm{E}}}{H_{\mathrm{B}}} \left(\sqrt{\dfrac{3}{\pi^2 H_{\mathrm{B}} \varsigma_1^2 \sigma_{\mathrm{B}}^2 \xi P}} + \dfrac{H_{\mathrm{B}} \xi P}{2} \right) \\[4mm]
\dfrac{H_{\mathrm{B}}}{H_{\mathrm{E}}} \sqrt{\dfrac{3}{\pi^2 \xi P \left(\frac{H_{\mathrm{E}}^2}{H_{\mathrm{B}}} \varsigma_1^2 \sigma_{\mathrm{B}}^2 + H_{\mathrm{E}} \varsigma_2^2 \sigma_{\mathrm{E}}^2\right)}}, if \ \sqrt{\dfrac{3}{\pi^2 \xi P \left(\frac{H_{\mathrm{E}}^2}{H_{\mathrm{B}}} \varsigma_1^2 \sigma_{\mathrm{B}}^2 + H_{\mathrm{E}} \varsigma_2^2 \sigma_{\mathrm{E}}^2\right)}} \\[4mm]
\quad < \dfrac{H_{\mathrm{E}}}{H_{\mathrm{B}}} \left(\sqrt{\dfrac{3}{\pi^2 H_{\mathrm{B}} \varsigma_1^2 \sigma_{\mathrm{B}}^2 \xi P}} + \dfrac{H_{\mathrm{B}} \xi P}{2} \right)
\end{cases}
\tag{53}
$$

Substituting (53) into (48) I_2 can be written as

$$
I_2 \leq
\begin{cases}
\ln \left[4e \left(\sqrt{\dfrac{3}{\pi^2 H_{\mathrm{B}} \varsigma_1^2 \sigma_{\mathrm{B}}^2 \xi P}} + \dfrac{H_{\mathrm{B}} \xi P}{2} \right) \right], & if \ \sqrt{\dfrac{3}{\pi^2 \xi P \left(\frac{H_{\mathrm{E}}^2}{H_{\mathrm{B}}} \varsigma_1^2 \sigma_{\mathrm{B}}^2 + H_{\mathrm{E}} \varsigma_2^2 \sigma_{\mathrm{E}}^2\right)}} \\[4mm]
\quad \geq \dfrac{H_{\mathrm{E}}}{H_{\mathrm{B}}} \left(\sqrt{\dfrac{3}{\pi^2 H_{\mathrm{B}} \varsigma_1^2 \sigma_{\mathrm{B}}^2 \xi P}} + \dfrac{H_{\mathrm{B}} \xi P}{2} \right) \\[4mm]
\ln \left[4e \dfrac{H_{\mathrm{B}}}{H_{\mathrm{E}}} \sqrt{\dfrac{3}{\pi^2 \xi P \left(\frac{H_{\mathrm{E}}^2}{H_{\mathrm{B}}} \varsigma_1^2 \sigma_{\mathrm{B}}^2 + H_{\mathrm{E}} \varsigma_2^2 \sigma_{\mathrm{E}}^2\right)}} \right], if \ \sqrt{\dfrac{3}{\pi^2 \xi P \left(\frac{H_{\mathrm{E}}^2}{H_{\mathrm{B}}} \varsigma_1^2 \sigma_{\mathrm{B}}^2 + H_{\mathrm{E}} \varsigma_2^2 \sigma_{\mathrm{E}}^2\right)}} \\[4mm]
\quad < \dfrac{H_{\mathrm{E}}}{H_{\mathrm{B}}} \left(\sqrt{\dfrac{3}{\pi^2 H_{\mathrm{B}} \varsigma_1^2 \sigma_{\mathrm{B}}^2 \xi P}} + \dfrac{H_{\mathrm{B}} \xi P}{2} \right)
\end{cases}
\tag{54}
$$

Then substituting (44) and (54) into (39), the secrecy capacity (15) can be derived.

References

1. Andrews, J.G., Buzzi, S., Choi, W., Hanly, S.V.: What will 5G be. IEEE J. Sel. Areas Commun. **32**(3), 1065–1082 (2014)
2. Komine, T., Nakagawa, M.: Fundamental analysis for visible-light communication system using LED lights. IEEE Trans. Consum. Electron. **50**(1), 100–107 (2004)
3. Karunatilaka, D., Zafar, F., Kalavally, V., Parthiban, R.: LED based indoor visible light communications: state of the art. IEEE Commun. Surv. Tut. **17**(3), 1649–1678 (2015)
4. Shannon, C.E.: Communication theory of secrecy systems. Bell Syst. Tech. J. **28**(4), 656–715 (1949)
5. Wyner, D.: The wire-tap channel. Bell Syst. Tech. J. **54**, 1355–1387 (1975)
6. Lapidoth, A., Moser, S.M.: Capacity bounds via duality with applications to multiple-antenna systems on flat fading channels. IEEE Trans. Inf. Theory **49**(10), 2426–2467 (2003)
7. Lapidoth, A., Moser, S.M., Wigger, M.A.: On the capacity of free-space optical intensity channels. IEEE Trans. Inf. Theory **55**(10), 4449–4461 (2009)

8. Mostafa, A., Lampe, L.: Physical-layer security for MISO visible light communication channels. IEEE J. Sel. Areas Commun. **33**(9), 1806–1818 (2015)
9. Wang, J.-Y., Dai, J., Guan, R., Jia, L., Wang, Y., Chen, M.: On the channel capacity and receiver deployment optimization for multi-input multi-output visible light communications. Opt. Exp. **24**(12), 13060–13074 (2016)
10. Wang, J.-Y., Liu, C., Wang, J., Wu, Y., Lin, M., Cheng, J.: Physical layer security for indoor visible light communications: secrecy capacity analysis. IEEE Trans. Commun. **66**(12), 6423–6436 (2018)
11. Moser, S.M.: Capacity results of an optical intensity channel with input dependent Gaussian noise. IEEE Trans. Inf. Theory **58**(1), 207–223 (2012)
12. Cover, T., Thomas, J.: Elements of Information Theory, 2nd edn. Wiley, Hoboken (2006)
13. Csiszar, I., Korner, J.: Information Theory: Coding Theorems for Discrete Memoryless Systems. Academic, New York (1981)

The Recursive Spectral Bisection Probability Hypothesis Density Filter

Ding Wang, Xu Tang, and Qun Wan[✉]

University of Electronic Science and Technology of China,
No. 2006, Xiyuan Ave, West Hi-Tech Zone,
Chengdu 611731, Sichuan, People's Republic of China
{wangding, tangxu, wanqun}@uestc.edu.cn

Abstract. Particle filter (PF) is used for multi-target detection and tracking, especially in the context of variable tracking target numbers, high target mobility, and other complex environments, it is difficult to detect, estimate and track targets in these situations. This paper discusses the probability hypothesis density (PHD) filtering which is widely used in the field of multi-target tracking in recent years. The PHD filter algorithm can estimate the number of targets effectively, however, existing algorithms does not make full use of particle information. This paper proposes a target state extraction method based on the recursive spectral bisection (RSB) node clustering algorithm, which focus on eigenvector centrality, algebraic connectivity, and the Fiedler vector from the established field of spectral graph theory (SGT). The method makes full use of the geometric distance relationship and the weight of particles to construct the particle neighborhood graph, then use the algebraic connectivity and Fiedler vector obtained by the eigenvalue decomposition of the Laplace matrix, finally extracts the target state from each class of particle group. Simulation results demonstrate that the new algorithm provides more accurate state estimations for multi-target detection and tracking.

Keywords: Multitarget tracking · Probability hypothesis density · Recursive spectral bisection · Fiedler vector · Algebraic connectivity

1 Introduction

In multi-target tracking problem, due to the need of considering the disappearance of targets, the emergence of new targets, the derivation and combination of existing targets, observation has problems such as miss detection, false alarm and so on, which leads to the uncertainty of target number and target trajectory. The traditional multi-target tracking technology needs to use data association and filtering. When the multi-target distance is very close, traditional methods such as MHT, JPDA and PF are difficult to determine the number of targets. For this tracking problem, it is generally processed based on the random finite set theory, which use the random finite set represents target. Then, the number of targets is the number of elements in the set, state of each target is represented by the set element, observation data are characterized by random finite sets. For a random finite set, estimation can also be performed as for a

G. Gui and L. Yun (Eds.): ADHIP 2019, LNICST 301, pp. 47–56, 2019.
https://doi.org/10.1007/978-3-030-36402-1_5

single variable, which can avoid the data association problem encountered in traditional methods. However, for the multi-target environment, it is very difficult to implement the integral of set function in the Bayes recursive formula. R. Mahler proposed an approximate estimation method using the first moment of multi-target posterior probability density function, namely PHD filtering algorithm based on random finite set [3–7, 18–21].

In this article, we review key concepts and basic techniques from the field of SGT theory. Then considering the particles themselves, can learn important information about the particle network topology and its topology-related properties, without relying on an external observer. The two important matrices in this theory are the adjacency matrix and the Laplace matrix. Constructing these two matrices by particles is the key to solve the problem in this paper. There are some important concepts in SGT theory, one of these concepts is eigenvector centrality, which forms the basis of the celebrated Google Pagerank algorithm [8]. Eigenvector centrality allows the identification of central particles but also allows the assignment of a measure of the network-wide influence of each node. Another important concept from SGT is the algebraic connectivity and the associated Fiedler vector [9–11]. The latter is able to identify densely connected particle clusters that only have a few cross links to other clusters, which also reveals the invalid particles in the particle network. As the number of particles increases, the classification of particles will be a big data processing problem [18]. It is also highlight the potential applicability of these techniques in several distributed signal processing tasks such as big signal processing data, distributed estimation, base station or cluster head selection, topology selection, resource allocation, and node subset selection [12, 13].

2 Background

2.1 Multi-target Tracking Model

This section provides a formulation of the PHD filter and its implementation based on particle filter for multi-target tracking. In multi-target tracking problem [16], the number of targets in surveillance region is usually time-varying and unknown; meantime, their states and observations evolve in time, too. Therefore, the states of N_k tracked targets at time k can be naturally represented as a random set $\Gamma_k = \{x_{k,1}, x_{k,2}, \ldots, x_{k,N_k}\}$, where $x_{k,i}$ is the state of an individual target. Similarly, m_k measurements can be given by a random set $Z_k = \{z_{k,1}, z_{k,2}, \ldots, z_{k,M_k}\}$, where $z_{k,j}$ is an observation from a target or due to clutter. Then the goal of multi-target filtering is to estimate the target states and the number N_k at time step k based on the observation collection $Z_{1:k} = \{Z_1, Z_2, \ldots, Z_k\}$.

2.2 PHD Particle Filter

The first-order moment of the multi-target posterior probability density is expressed by PHD [4, 7, 20], expressed as $D_{k|k}$, and the PHD filter also includes prediction and update steps. The prediction is expressed as follows:

$$D_{k|k-1} = \int \phi_{k|k-1}(x, x_{k-1}) D_{k-1|k-1} dx_{k-1} + \gamma_k(x) \tag{1}$$

$$\phi_{k|k-1}(x, x_{k-1}) = P_S(x_{k-1}) f_{k|k-1}(x, x_{k-1}) + b_{k|k-1}(x, x_{k-1}) \tag{2}$$

Where $\gamma_k(x)$ is the intensity function of the new target random set at time k, b_k stands for derived target PHD, P_S represents the target survival probability, $f_{k|k-1}(x|x_{k-1})$ is the state transition equation. The update process is shown as follows:

$$D_{k|k} = \left[v(x) + \sum_{z \in Z_k} \frac{\psi_{k,z}(x)}{\kappa_k(z) + \langle D_{k|k-1}, \psi_{k,z} \rangle} \right] D_{k|k-1} \tag{3}$$

$$\psi_{k,z(x)} = P_D(x) g(z|x) \tag{4}$$

$$\langle D_{k|k-1}, \psi_{k,z} \rangle = \int D_{k|k}(x_t|z_{1:t}) \varphi(x_k) d(x_k) \tag{5}$$

Where $v(x) = 1 - P_D(x)$, $P_D(x)$ represents target detection probability, $g(z|x)$ represents a single-target likelihood function, $\kappa_k(z)$ Is the intensity function of the random set of clutter at time k.

From what has been discussed above, PHD filtering algorithm is a bayesian approximation algorithm, which is realized by the first-order moment of multi-target joint posterior probability density. However, the calculation is difficult to achieve due to the integral operation, particle filter is exploited for the implementation of the PHD [14]. The target detection probability [19] is calculated from the unnormalized weight:

$$\overline{M}_b = P_b[1 - \hat{P}_{k-1}] \sum_{p=1}^{L_{k-1}} \bar{w}_k^{*p}$$

$$\overline{M}_c = [1 - P_d] \hat{P}_{k-1} \sum_{p=L_{k-1}+1}^{J_k} \bar{w}_k^{*p} \tag{6}$$

$$M_c = \frac{\overline{M}_c}{\overline{M}_b + \overline{M}_c} \quad M_b = \frac{\overline{M}_b}{\overline{M}_b + \overline{M}_c} \tag{7}$$

$$\hat{P}_k = \frac{\overline{M}_b + \overline{M}_c}{\overline{M}_b + \overline{M}_c + P_d \hat{P}_{k-1} + [1 - P_b][1 - \hat{P}_{k-1}]} \tag{8}$$

Where P_b represents the target birth probability, $\hat{P}_{k-1}$ represents the target detection probability of time k-1, L_{k-1} represents the number of surviving and derived target particles, $\bar{w}_k^{*p}$ represents the unnormalized particle weight, P_d represents the target death probability, $L_{k-1} + 1, \ldots, J_k$ represents the new born target particles.

2.3 RSB Clustering Algorithm

In accordance with WSN literature, the vertices of a network graph are referred to as "nodes" and the edges of the graph are referred to as "links" [8–12, 17]. We consider the network graph where the set of nodes is denoted by Q, containing $|Q|$ elements, and the set of links is denoted by E. We denote B_k as the set of neighbors of node k, and $|B_k|$ is referred to as the degree of node k. Two commonly used matrices in SGT are the adjacency matrix and the Laplace matrix. The entries of the adjacency matrix $A = [a_{mn}]_{J \times J}$ are defined as

$$a_{mn} = a_{nm} = \begin{cases} 1 & \text{if } n \in B_m \\ 0 & \text{otherwise} \end{cases} \tag{9}$$

The entries of the laplacian matrix $L = [l_{mn}]_{J \times J}$ of an undirected graph are defined as

$$l_{mn} = l_{nm} = \begin{cases} \sum_{j \in K} w_{mj}, & \text{if } m = n \\ -w_{mn}, & \text{if } n \in B_m \\ 0, & \textit{otherwise} \end{cases} \tag{10}$$

The algebraic connectivity λ_2 and the fiedler vector f contain important information about the connectivity and clustering properties of the network graph. The RSB-based algorithm is a top-down clustering algorithm, starting from the complete network graph and subsequently dividing it into smaller clusters. In this paper, the network graph Q composed of all nodes (particles) in the observation area at a certain time.

3 Multi-target Detection and Tracking Based on RSB-PHD

In this section, We First introduce the traditional PHD particle filter, and propose a method which construct the adjacency matrix and Laplace matrix using the particle neighborhood information. Then estimate the number of target N_k according to the unnormalized particle weight using PHD particle filter, and use the RSB clustering algorithm to divide the particles into N_k classes. Finally, extract the target state from each class of particles.

3.1 Multi-target State Estimation

A single target PHD can be used for multi-target state estimation on the problem of multi-target detection and tracking, among which the number of targets estimated by the unnormalized PHD particle weights. The number of single target PHD will be bigger than the number of estimated target if the observation were drowned by noise at time k. This problem can be solved by calculating the weight sum of each observation, finding the single target PHD of the Nth target from the largest to the smallest according to the weight sum, and then extracting the target state.

Suppose there are N_{k-1} targets exist in the observation area at time k-1, the PHD $D_{k-1|k-1}(x|z_{1:k-1})$ represents by a set of particles and their weights $\{\tilde{x}_{k-1}^i, \bar{w}_{k-1}^i\}_{i=1}^{L_{k-1}+J_k}$.

If there are M_k observations and N_k targets in the observation area at time k, according to the PHD particle filter algorithm, the PHD at time k can be represented by particle set $\{\tilde{x}_k^i, \bar{w}_k^i\}_{i=1}^{L_{k-1}+J_k}$, where

$$\bar{w}_k^{(i)} = \left[v(\tilde{x}_k^{(i)}) + \sum_{z \in Z_k} \frac{\psi_{k,z}(\tilde{x}_k^{(i)})}{\kappa_k(z) + C_k(z)} \right] \bar{w}_{k|k-1}^{(i)} \tag{11}$$

However, the reality is that we can only get the observation based on all the targets at the same time, and cannot get the observation based on each target at that time alone. Therefore, it is difficult to implement the above algorithm when solving practical problems. To solve this problem, an RSB-PHD algorithm is proposed in this paper.

3.2   Construct the Particle Neighborhood Graph

A particle is a neighbor of any other particle if it lies within a fixed radius γ or is one of the K closest points to it, see Fig. 1. The neighborhood graph is constructed with edges equal to the distance between the particles, the edges of the graph are referred to as "links". The entries of the adjacency matrix $A = [a_{mn}]_{J \times J}$ are defined as

$$a_{mn} = a_{nm} = \begin{cases} 1 & \text{if } d_{mn} < \gamma \\ 0 & \text{otherwise} \end{cases} \tag{12}$$

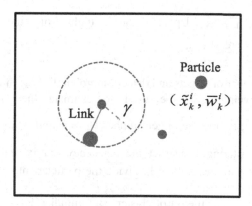

Fig. 1. Construct the particle neighborhood graph within a fixed radius

Where d_{mn} represents the distance between particle m and particle n.

The entries of the Laplacian matrix $L = [l_{mn}]_{J \times J}$ of an undirected graph $(w_{mn} = w_{nm})$ are defined as

$$l_{mn} = l_{nm} = \begin{cases} \sum_{j \in K} w_{mj}, & \text{if } m = n \\ -w_{mn}, & \text{if } d_{mn} < \gamma \\ 0, & \text{otherwise} \end{cases} \tag{13}$$

Where K here represents all particles in the graph, for an unweighted network graph, L has the same definition where the weight for link (m, n) is set to $w_{mn} = 1$ such that $L = D - A$ where $D = diag(|B_1|, \ldots, |B_k|)$. We denote B_k as the set of neighbors of particle k, and $|B_k|$ is referred to as the degree of particle k.

3.3   RSB-PHD Algorithm

The adjacency matrix and Laplacian matrix are constructed based on the particles at time k, from which we can compute the Fiedler vector and algebraic connectivity. According to the estimated number of targets N_k computed by the PHD filter, we use RSB clustering algorithm to divide particles into N_k classes and extract the target state. The complete RSB-PHD algorithm described as follow:

(1) Initialization: For $i = 1, \ldots, L_0$, particles $x_0^{(i)}$ obtained by sampling from the prior distribution $q_0(X_0)$, and $w_0^{(i)} = 1/L_0$

(2) Prediction: To survival and derivative targets, For $i = 1, \ldots, L_{k-1}$, sampling $\tilde{x}_k^{(i)} \sim q_k(\cdot | x_{k-1}^{(i)}, Z_k)$, Calculate the weights of the predicted particles: $\bar{w}_{k|k-1}^{(i)} = \frac{\phi_k(\tilde{x}_k^{(i)}, x_{k-1}^{(i)})}{q_k(\tilde{x}_k^{(i)} | x_{k-1}^{(i)}, Z_k)} w_{k-1}^{(i)}$. To new born targets, For $i = L_{k+1} + 1, \ldots, L_{k-1} + J_k$, sampling $\tilde{x}_k^{(i)} \sim p_k(\cdot | Z_k)$, Calculate the weight of the new particle: $\bar{w}_{k|k-1}^{(i)} = \frac{1}{J_k} \frac{\gamma_k(\tilde{x}_k^{(i)})}{p_k(\tilde{x}_k^{(i)} | Z_k)}$

(3) Update: For each observation $z \in Z_k$, compute $C_k(z) = \sum_{j=1}^{L_{k+1}+J_k} \psi_{k,z}(\tilde{x}_k^{(j)}) \bar{w}_{k|k-1}^{(j)}$, For $i = 1, \ldots, L_{k-1} + J_k$, Update the weight of the particle $\bar{w}_k^{(i)} = \left[v(\tilde{x}_k^{(i)}) + \sum_{z \in Z_k} \frac{\psi_{k,z}(\tilde{x}_k^{(i)})}{\kappa_k(z) + C_k(z)} \right] \bar{w}_{k|k-1}^{(i)}$.

(4) Estimate the number of targets and detection probability $\hat{P}_k$: in PHD particle filter, the sum of weights can be used to estimate the number of targets $\tilde{N}_k = \sum_{j=1}^{l_{k-1}+J_k} \bar{w}_k^{(i)}$, Round the target number $\hat{N}_k = round(\tilde{N}_k)$.

(5) RSB particle clustering: construct the adjacency matrix and Laplacian matrix according to the particles at time k, divide the particles into $\hat{N}_k$ classes by using RSB node cluster algorithm.
  ① Let V denote the set of clusters and initialize $V \leftarrow \{g_1\}$ where $g_1 = Q$
  ② $\forall g_i \in V, i = 1 \ldots |V|$, compute the cluster-level Fiedler vector $f(g_i)$ and algebraic connectivity $\lambda_2(g_i)$, where bridge links between clusters are ignored.
  ③ Find $g^* \leftarrow \arg\min_{g \in C}[(\lambda_2(g))/|g|]$
  ④ Partition $g_+^* g_-^*$ into two clusters g_-^* and g_+^*, where g_-^* contains the nodes which have negative entries in $f(g^*)$, and where g_+^* contains the nodes which have positive entries in $f(g^*)$.
  ⑤ Set $V \leftarrow \{g_-^*, g_+^*\} \cup V \setminus \{g^*\}$
  ⑥ If $|V| < N_k$, return to step 2.

(6) Target state extraction: we can compute the eigenvector centrality to identify the central particle of each class particle group; or compute the target state using $\left(\tilde{x}_k^{(i)}, \bar{w}_k^{(i)}/\tilde{N}_k\right)_{i=1}^{L_{k-1}+J_K}$

(7) Resampling particles: resampling the particle set $\left(\tilde{x}_k^{(i)}, \bar{w}_k^{(i)}/\tilde{N}_k\right)_{i=1}^{L_{k-1}+J_K}$ to new particle set $\left(x_k^{(i)}, w_k^{(i)}/\tilde{N}_k\right)_{i=1}^{L_k}$, the weight of particles times $\tilde{N}_k$ to get the particles $\left(x_k^{(i)}, w_k^{(i)}\right)_{i=1}^{L_k}$ which will be used at the next prediction step.

4 Simulation

In this paper, we use optimal subpattern assignment (OSPA) [15] metric to evaluate the performance of multi-target tracking. OSPA is still based on a Wasserstein construction, but completely eliminates most of the problems of the OMAT metric. Denote by $d^{(c)}(x,y) = \min(c, d(x,y))$ the distance between $x, y \in W$ cut off at $c > 0$, and by $\prod_k$ the set of permutations on $\{1, 2, \ldots, k\}$ for any $k \in \mathbb{N} = \{1, 2, \ldots\}$. For $1 \le p < \infty$, $c > 0$, and arbitrary finite subsets $X = \{x_1, \ldots, x_m\}$ and $Y = \{y_1, \ldots, y_n\}$ of W, where $m, n \in \mathbb{N}_0 = \{0, 1, 2, \ldots\}$, define

$$\bar{d}_p^{(c)}(X, Y) = \left(\frac{1}{n}\left(\min_{\pi \in \prod_n} \sum_{i=1}^{m} d^{(c)}(x_i, y_{\pi(i)})^p + c^p(n-m)\right)\right)^{1/p} \tag{14}$$

If $m \le n$, and $\bar{d}_p^{(c)}(X, Y) = \bar{d}_p^{(c)}(Y, X)$, if $m > n$, moreover

$$\bar{d}_\infty^{(c)}(X, Y) = \begin{cases} \min_{\pi \in \Pi_n} \max_{1 \le i \le n} d^{(c)}(x_i, y_{\pi(i)}), & \text{if } m = n \\ c, & \text{if } m \ne n \end{cases} \tag{15}$$

in either case set the distance to zero if m = n = 0. We call the function $\bar{d}_p^{(c)}$ the OSPA metric of order p with cut-off c.

Consider multi-target tracking, the target motion model described as:

$$s_k = Fs_{k-1} + v_k \tag{16}$$

Where, $F = \begin{bmatrix} 1 & T & 0 & 0 \\ 0 & 1 & 0 & 0 \\ 0 & 0 & 1 & T \\ 0 & 0 & 0 & 1 \end{bmatrix}$, $s = [x, \dot{x}, y, \dot{y}]$, represents the position and speed of the x direction, and the position and speed of the y direction, v_k is gaussian noise, and $v_k \sim N(0, 0.1)$. The target observation model described as:

$$z_k = Hs_k + w_k \tag{17}$$

Where, $H = \begin{bmatrix} 1 & 0 & 0 & 0 \\ 0 & 0 & 1 & 0 \end{bmatrix}$, $z = [x \quad y]$ represents the location of the target, w_k is gaussian noise, and $w_k \sim N(0, 2.5)$.

Suppose there are three targets in total, and the initial state of each target is X1 = [0, −0.5, 0, −0.5], X2 = [−5, 0.5, 5, 0.5], X3 = [5, 0.4, 0, −0.3], assume that both distance and velocity units are normalized. Observation data in each frame includes 3 targets and 2 clutter points. The simulation duration is 100 s, assuming the existence time of target 1 and 2 is 1–100 s, and the existence time of target 3 is 21–100 s. Considering the OSPA distances for $p = 2$ and $c = 20$.

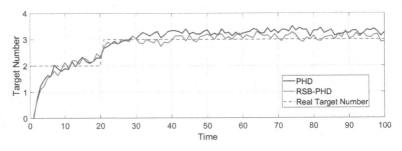

Fig. 2. 100 MC run average target number versus time, contrast of RSB-PHD and PHD algorithm

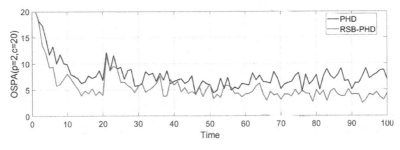

Fig. 3. 100 MC run average OSPA versus time, contrast of RSB-PHD and PHD algorithm

To capture the average performance, we run 100 Monte Carlo (MC) trials for each filter with the same target tracks but independently generated measurements. Figure 2 shows the estimate number of targets by RSB-PHD and PHD filter, these results confirm that the RSB-PHD filter provide more accurate result. Figure 3 shows the average OSPA distance for p = 2 and c = 20, it is obviously that RSB-PHD filter perform better for multi-target tracking. Figure 4 shows the detection probability of each target, since RSB-PHD filter still using unnormalized weight of particles to compute this probability, there is not much difference in performance between the two algorithms.

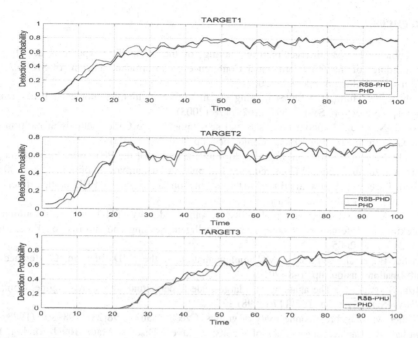

Fig. 4. 100 MC run average detection probability versus time for target 3, contrast of RSB-PHD and PHD algorithm

5 Conclusions

This paper has identified the limitations of PHD particle filter in full use of particle information in multi-target systems. And proposes a target state extraction method based on the recursive spectral bisection (RSB) node clustering algorithm. By setting the distance radius and particle position information, the particle adjacency matrix and Laplace matrix are constructed. Through the RSB algorithm based on the Laplace matrix eigen-decomposition, the Fiedler vector is calculated to cluster the particles effectively and eliminate the redundant invalid particles, so that the estimation is more accurate. Simulation results show that the RSB-PHD filtering algorithm requires more computation, and does not affect the target detection probability, but it is more accurate in the estimation of target number. Moreover, smaller OSPA distance error is of great significance in multi-target environment. As the number of particles increases, the classification of particles will be a big data processing problem. In the next part, research on the application of RSB-PHD in TBD will be carried out, and analyze the influence of particle distance radius which can be used to construct the adjacency matrix and the Laplace matrix.

Acknowledgment. The authors would like to thank the anonymous reviewers for their careful review and constructive comments. This work was supported in part by the National Natural Science Foundation of China (NSFC) under Grant 61771108, National Science and technology major project under Grant 2016ZX03001022, and the Foundation of Sichuan Science and Technology Project under Grant 18ZDYF0990.

References

1. Sidenbladh, H.: Multi-target particle filtering for the probability hypothesis density. In: Proceedings of the 6th International Conference on Information Fusion, FUSION 2003, Cairns, Australia, pp. 800–806 (2003)
2. Mahler, R.: Multitarget Bayes filtering via first-order multitarget moments. IEEE Trans. Aerospace Electron. Syst. **4**(39), 1152–1178 (2003)
3. Vo, B.-N., et al.: Random finite sets and sequential Monte Carlo methods in multi-target tracking. In: International Radar Conference, pp. 486–491 (2003)
4. Vo, B.-N., et al.: Sequential monte carlo implementation of the PHD filter for multi-target tracking. In: International Conference on Information Fusion, vol. 2, pp. 792–799 (2003)
5. Zhao, L., et al.: A new multi-target state estimation algorithm for PHD particle filter. In: Conference on Information Fusion, pp. 1–8 (2010)
6. Panta, K., et al.: Improved probability hypothesis density (PHD) filter for multitarget tracking. In: International Conference on Intelligent Sensing and Information Processing, pp. 213–218 (2005)
7. Ristic, B., et al.: Improved SMC implementation of the PHD filter. In: Conference on Information Fusion, pp. 1–8 (2010)
8. Brin, S., Page, L.: The anatomy of a large-scale hypertextual web search engine. Comput. Netw. ISDN Syst. **30**, 107–117 (1998)
9. Fiedler, M.: Algebraic connectivity of graphs. Czech. Math. J. **98**(23), 298–305 (1973)
10. Mohar, B.: Laplace eigenvalues of graphs: a survey. Discrete Math. **109**(1–3), 171–183 (1992)
11. Mohar, B.: The Laplacian spectrum of graphs. In: Alavi, Y., Chartrand, G., Oellermann, O., Schwenk, A. (eds.) Graph Theory, Combinatorics, and Applications, pp. 871–898. Wiley, New York (1991)
12. Tu, S.-Y., Sayed, A.H.: Mobile adaptive networks. IEEE J. Sel. Top. Signal Process. **4**(5), 649–664 (2011)
13. Cattivelli, F., Sayed, A.H.: Diffusion LMS strategies for distributed estimation. IEEE Trans. Signal Process. **3**(58), 1035–1048 (2010)
14. Vo, B., Singh, S., Doucet, A.: Sequential Monte Carlo implementation of the PHD filter for multi-target tracking. In: Proceedings of the 6th International Conference on Information Fusion, FUSION 2003, Cairns, Australia, pp. 792–799 (2003)
15. Schuhmacher, D., Vo, B.-T., Vo, B.-N.: A consistent metric for performance evaluation of multi-object filters. IEEE Trans. Signal Process. **8**(56), 3447–3457 (2008)
16. Tang, X., Chen, X.: A multiple-detection probability hypothesis density filter. IEEE Trans. Signal Process. **8**(63), 2007–2019 (2015)
17. Sun, Y., Zhang, F., Wan, Q.: Wireless sensor network-based localization method using TDOA measurements in MPR. IEEE Sens. J. **10**(19), 3741–3750 (2019)
18. Wang, Y.-D.: Data-driven probability hypothesis density filter for visual tracking. IEEE Trans. Circ. Syst. Video Technol. **8**(18), 1085–1095 (2008)
19. Li, C.: PHD and CPHD filtering with unknown detection probability. IEEE Trans. Signal Process. **14**(66), 3784–3798 (2018)
20. Schlangen, I.: A second-order PHD filter with mean and variance in target number. IEEE Trans. Signal Process. **1**(66), 48–63 (2018)
21. Sithiravel, R.: The spline probability hypothesis density filter. IEEE Trans. Signal Process. **24**(61), 6188–6203 (2013)

Research on LAN Network Malicious Code Intrusion Active Defense Technology

Lei Ma[✉], Ying-jian Kang, and Hua Han

Telecommunication Engineering Institute, Beijing Polytechnic, Beijing, China
malei235@tom.com

Abstract. Traditional LAN networks had low defense efficiency and poor stability. In order to solve this problem, a new malicious code intrusion active defense technology was studied, and the defense technology structure was designed and the work-flow was studied. The system structure was divided into hardware layer, kernel layer and executive layer. The work-flow was divided into four steps: file judgment, file compression, file processing and file display. The working effect of the technology was verified by comparison with the traditional method. It was known from the experimental results that the studied technology had high defense efficiency and strong stability.

Keywords: Local area network · Malicious code · Code intrusion · Active defense

1 Introduction

Malicious code refers to a set of instructions that run on a computer and the system performs tasks according to the attacker's wishes. The term "malware" is used in the Microsoft Computer Virus Protection Guide as a collective noun to refer to viruses, worms, and Trojan horses that intentionally perform malicious tasks on computer systems. According to the running characteristics of malicious code, it can be divided into two categories: the program that needs to be hosted and the program that runs independently [1]. The former is actually a fragment of the program, they cannot exist independently of certain specific applications or system environments. Independent programs are complete programs that the operating system can schedule and run; According to the spread characteristics of malicious code, malicious programs can also be divided into two categories that cannot be self-replicating and self-replicating [2]. The specific malicious code types are shown in Table 1.

At present, malicious code targeted attacks are getting stronger and stronger, and personal online banking accounts, game accounts, and Internet accounts have become new targets [3]. It can be seen that if the security of the internal network terminal is not fully protected, the malicious code is bound to enter the internal terminal at will, blocking the operation of the anti-virus software, installing and setting the backdoor program, and stealing the password. Moreover, ARP spoofing infects the entire intranet to occupy network bandwidth, which seriously affects work efficiency and increases support costs, causing the company's intellectual property and personal property to be stolen and lost. The means of malicious code dissemination has become diversified.

G. Gui and L. Yun (Eds.): ADHIP 2019, LNICST 301, pp. 57–64, 2019.
https://doi.org/10.1007/978-3-030-36402-1_6

Table 1. Malicious code type.

Malicious code name	Failure mode
Computer virus	It needs a host and can be replicated automatically
Worm	An independent program; automatic replication; less human intervention
Malicious mobile code	Composed of lightweight programs; independent programs
Back door	Separate program segments, providing intrusion channels
Trojan Horse	The general need for a host; a strong concealment
Rootkit	Generally need a host; replace or modify the system state
Combined malicious code	A combination of the above technologies to enhance failure capacity

In the early days, malicious code was mainly spread through emails, system vulnerabilities, network shares, files, and so on. And the mode of communication is mainly by attracting users to click. With the development of the network, the channels and methods of information exchange and sharing are more diverse and convenient, but it also brings about the diversification of malicious code transmission [4]. There have been transmission methods such as attacks, online horses, exploits, mobile storage devices, network sharing, and network downloads. Among them, mobile storage devices such as infected disks, and the use of infected LANs and web pages have become the most popular three routes. And these three complement each other, can effectively improve the spread range and ability of the virus, as long as there is a computer poisoning in the LAN, the virus will soon spread to the entire network. It can cause network congestion such as network congestion and theft of confidential information, which poses a great threat to the normal operation of enterprise LANs and campus networks [5].

The main shortcomings of the traditional defense against malicious code intrusion technology are as follows: (1) According to CERT statistics, nearly 90% of malicious code infections are exploited by system vulnerabilities, and traditional viruses are used to kill and cure the symptoms. (2) The virus database update is lagging behind, and it is impossible to guarantee the killing of the latest virus, worm, Trojan and other malicious code. (3) The anti-virus software uses the feature matching method to detect and kill the virus, and cannot detect and kill the new malicious code. (4) After the malicious code infects the terminal, the anti-virus software is first stopped, and the anti-virus software is difficult to isolate. Since traditional eigenvalue-based scanning-based anti-virus software is very passive, the industry's defense method that can actively detect and intercept unknown threats is called "active defense" [6]. Active defense refers to the anti-virus technology based on behavior detection, that is, the virus behavior blocking technology that determines whether it is a virus and processes it through the behavioral characteristics of the virus. The technology combines the characteristics of these viruses to determine whether they are viruses by extracting the common characteristics of computer viruses, such as modifying the registry, self-replication, and constantly connecting to the network. That is to say, the behavior of the whole process is monitored, and once the "violation" behavior is found, the user is notified or the process is directly terminated.

The protection of malicious code can not be solved by one or several technologies alone. It is a system engineering, relying on the common prevention of technology, management and user security awareness. Only the combination of technology, management, and security awareness can prevent malicious code from destroying system and user information to the greatest extent. This paper designs a malicious code defense system based on Windows platform - AV-System. The system is based on active defense. From the perspective of defense, the malicious object's destruction object is protected, and the destructive power of malicious code is greatly reduced.

2 Lan Network Malicious Code Intrusion Active Defense Technology Structure Design

The structure of the malicious code defense system AV-System based on the Windows platform is as shown in Fig. 1:

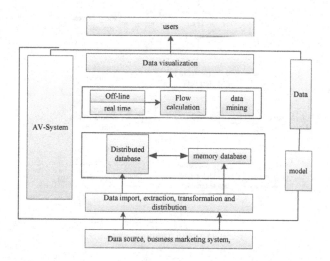

Fig. 1. Malicious code defense system AV-System structure

Looking at Fig. 1, this layer of direct dealing with hardware is called the hardware abstraction layer. The purpose of this layer is to isolate all hardware-associated code logic into a specialized module. So that the above hierarchy is as independent as possible from the hardware platform. Above the hardware abstraction layer is the kernel layer, sometimes called the microkernel, which contains basic primitives and functions such as threads and processes, thread scheduling, interrupt and exception handling, synchronization objects, and various synchronization mechanisms [7]. Above the kernel layer is the execution layer, the purpose of this layer is to provide some functions and semantics that can be directly called by the upper application or kernel driver. The kernel's executable contains an object manager for consistently managing objects in the executable. The execution body layer and the kernel layer are located in the same binary module, that is, the kernel base module. The kernel layer and the execution layer are divided. The kernel layer implements the basic mechanism of the operating system, and all the policies are decided to be left to the executable. Most of the objects in the executable encapsulate one or more kernel objects and are exposed to the application in some way, such as object handles.

3   Lan Network Malicious Code Intrusion Active Defense Technology Work-Flow Analysis

The malicious code prevention technology based on Windows platform is a more complicated work, and the working process is as shown in Fig. 2:

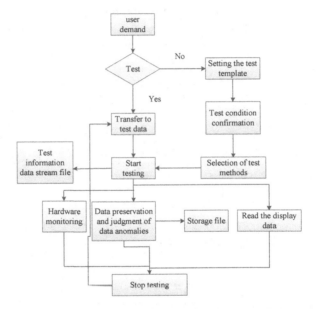

Fig. 2. Based on the Windows platform for malicious code prevention technology flow

The work-flow of Fig. 2 is described in detail as follows: The file type is judged by the type detection module. This is the premise for classifying the malicious code. For the compressed file, the file is decompressed first, and then the extracted file is returned to the type detection module for processing [8]. Consider a recursive decompression module that handles problems such as multiple and mixed compression. For non-compressed types of objects, there are different ways of handling them depending on the type. For the executable file, first of all, through a shell detection module, to determine whether it has passed, and the current popular executable file packer processing. This shelling module is also recursive until it is not required to be unpacked, and finally handed to the binary detection engine for processing [9]. For text type files, the main purpose is to perform script virus detection, which is first handed to the parser for processing, and the result of the parser is then passed to the detection engine for matching processing. The macro virus detection of some anti-virus software is done by the script processing engine. The source code of the macro is extracted by the pre-processor, and then passed to the parser [10].

The host of the propagation model maintains three states that are susceptible to infection, infection, and immunity. The differential equation expression for the model is:

$$\frac{dJ(t)}{d(t)} = \beta J(t)[N - J(t)] \tag{1}$$

$$\frac{dR(t)}{d(t)} = \gamma I(t) \tag{2}$$

$$J(t) = I(t) + R(t) = N - S(t) \tag{3}$$

In the formula, I(t) represents the number of hosts that are still infectious at time t; R(t) represents the number of hosts that have been immunized from the infected machine at time t; J(t) represents the number of all infected hosts at time t, including those that are still infectious and have been immunized from the infected machine. β is the infection rate; γ is the recovery rate of the host removed from the infected machine; S(t) represents the number of hosts that are still vulnerable at time t; N represents all node hosts in the network. When the infected node is immune, it is equivalent to remove this node from the entire network node host, and the total number of network nodes changes from N to N-1.

4 Experimental Study

In order to detect the management effect of the malicious code intrusion active defense technology of the LAN network studied in this paper, compared with the traditional technology, a comparative experiment was designed.

4.1 Experimental Parameters

The experimental parameters are as follows (Table 2):

Table 2. Experimental parameters.

Project	Parameter
Operating system	Windows XP SP3
Cpu	Intel Core 2 T5750
Virtual machine	Vmware workstation
Debugger	WinDbg X76
Memory	2 GB
Compiler	IFS DDK 2005
Development tool	VC++ 6.0 SP6

4.2   Experiment Procedure

Experiments were carried out according to the parameters set above, and the working results of the two methods were analyzed and compared.

4.3   Experimental Results and Analysis

The experimental results obtained are shown below.

Looking at Fig. 3, we can see that the defense efficiency is increasing with time, but the efficiency of the defense system in this paper is always higher than the traditional method. This article's defense system is able to detect malicious code attacks in a timely manner and prevent further spread of malicious code. It is a new way to effectively defend against malicious code attacks.

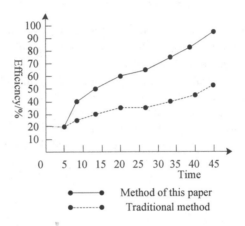

Fig. 3. Defense efficiency experiment results

4.4   Experimental Results

According to the above experimental results, the following experimental conclusions are obtained: Although both the traditional method and the method can prevent malicious code intrusion, the active defense system of this method can indeed intercept the unknown virus or Trojan. The process monitoring module, the registry monitoring module, and the file access monitoring module all run well. The process detection tool and the file detection tool can detect hidden processes and files well. In the process of using, the protection of files, registry, and processes is realized under the condition that the resources are scarce. The efficiency and stability of the operating system are both good, and will not cause any bad feedback to the user, and achieve the expected results.

5 Conclusions

In the communication network engineering, risk assessment and safety protection work protection have been carried out for many years, and certain experience and achievements have been obtained. With the development of communication technology, the deepening of network interconnection applications, the security of computer systems and the security of network security of communication networks are increasing. Traditional passive defense technologies have been unable to cope with the current automated, complex and large-scale network attacks. The active defense technology system can be effectively applied to the construction of network security assurance projects, which can ensure the safe and reliable operation of the network and meet the communication security requirements. Accurately analyze the causes of communication failures and security incidents, and develop and adopt effective solutions and countermeasures to provide a basis for scientific decision-making. The research results will help to analyze the security posture of the network operation, enhance the network operation, maintenance and management level, and improve the reliability of the system.

This paper first studies the development of malicious code prevention technology at home and abroad, analyzes the current status of automatic detection of malicious code at home and abroad, and points out their problems. Then research on the technology related to malicious code prevention: Windows kernel mechanism, Windows file system filter driver, Windows service, Windows device driver preparation, Windows PE file principle, registry principle. Based on the research of the above related technologies, a malicious code prevention system AV-System based on Windows platform is designed and implemented. Based on the research of the above related technologies, a malicious code prevention system AV-System based on Windows platform is designed and implemented.

References

1. Wang, Z., Yu, A., et al.: Construction of network security immune system. Eng. Sci. Technol. Power Monit. Control Syst. Trusted Comput. Technol. **49**(2), 28–35 (2017)
2. Tong, Q., Zhang, Z., Wu, J.X.: Inf. Secur. J. Divers. Hardware Softw. **2**(1), 1–12 (2017)
3. Intrusion detection research and implementation based on pattern recognition method. Hubei Mechanization **12**(6), 61 (2017)
4. Network security active defense technology and application. Netw. Secur. Technol. Appl. **56**(5), 28 (2017)
5. Wang, Z., Yu, A., et al.: Based on trusted computing technology, the network security immune system of power monitoring and control system. Eng. Sci. Technol. **49**(2), 28–35 (2017)
6. Li, X.: Analysis of the design and implementation of network active defense system. Electron. Des. Eng. **25**(1), 27–30 (2017)
7. Wang, Z., Hu, H., Cheng, G., et al.: The architecture of mimic defense under the software definition network architecture. Netw. Inf. Secur. J. **3**(10), 52–61 (2017)
8. Su, S.X., Zhu, Z.: Design and implementation of embedded active defense system based on honeypot. Internet Things Technol. **7**(7), 86–88 (2017)

9. Yu, A., Wang, Z.H., Zhao, B.: Research and application of trusted computing technology in power systems. Inf. Secur. Res. **3**(4), 353–358 (2017)
10. Chen, J.: Mobile network optimization design for effective intrusion prevention design of intrusion signals. Comput. Simul. **34**(7), 277–280 (2017)

Network Information Security Privacy Protection System in Big Data Era

Lei Ma[✉], Ying-jian Kang, and Jian-ping Liu

Telecommunication Engineering Institute, Beijing Polytechnic, Beijing, China
malei235@tom.com

Abstract. Traditional information security protection is based on an information data set, at least one information can not be distinguished from its own location information. Therefore, this paper studies the network information security privacy protection system in the era of big data. The hardware of network information security privacy protection system is composed of independent monitoring layer, host layer and mixed layer. It disturbs the original data by adding random numbers and exchanging, shields the original data to unauthorized users, and achieves the purpose of privacy protection and recommendation accurate and non-destructive. The system software encrypts information according to the degree of privacy protection set by users, adopts the key management mode, solves the problem of communication security and node key update, and realizes the network information security privacy protection system.

Keywords: Privacy protection · Information security · Information encryption · Key management

1 Introduction

In the era of big data, the privacy protection of network information security needs to be constantly updated and developed. There are still many problems that can be further studied and discussed. Below is a brief introduction to some classical location privacy protection systems. Literature [1] puts forward that in an information data set, at least one information cannot be distinguished from its own location information, so it can be said that this location information and other location information meet technical requirements. The system can obtain the real location of the attacker, so as to protect information security and privacy. However, this method cannot achieve the privacy protection accuracy in this field. Literature [2] proposed a protection method and corresponding safe data exchange model for protection and control of information transmission risk, and established a simulation platform for this purpose. Simulation results show that the transmission risk of protection control information can optimize the message processing mechanism under normal circumstances and ensure the reliable transmission of key messages under abnormal circumstances. However, the implementation process of this model is complex and cannot be widely applied.

In this paper, a privacy protection system for network information security in the era of big data is proposed. The method of generalized concealment of coordinate

G. Gui and L. Yun (Eds.): ADHIP 2019, LNICST 301, pp. 65–73, 2019.
https://doi.org/10.1007/978-3-030-36402-1_7

positions hides the user's position into a region, where there are many location nodes. After this generalized concealment process, the whole region is regarded as the user's position. In this way, privacy attackers can not query the location information of specific users. Continuous mobile users initiate location queries at different times to form a trajectory. By attacking the trajectory information, we can infer the user's daily life trajectory and habits, so that the privacy information is broken. In order to protect the security of information network, it is necessary to establish corresponding information security protection system. The means of information security protection mainly include identity authentication, information encryption, intrusion detection, boundary integrity detection, etc. Traditional information security protection systems usually take protective measures from a certain aspect, which can not constitute a defense system in depth, leaving an opportunity for attackers to take advantage of. The present information security protection system pays more attention to multi-level comprehensive defense, establishes the defense system in depth, and improves the reliability of information security protection.

2 Hardware Design

Because virtualization technology has changed the computer architecture, it provides a new solution to traditional security problems. As mentioned above, some studies have introduced virtualization technology into the field of security, using the characteristics of virtual machine manager to achieve security functions. However, there are some obvious problems when the Universal Virtual Machine Manager provides security services for clients. There are two main aspects: First, the Trusted Computing Base of Universal Virtual Machine Manager is huge. Trusted Computing Base (TCB) refers to the collection of all security protection mechanisms for the realization of computer system security protection, which can appear in the form of hardware, firmware or software. Once a vulnerability occurs in one part of the trusted computing base, it will seriously endanger the security of the whole system. On the contrary, if there are vulnerabilities in other parts of the trusted computing base, the harm to the whole system is relatively small. Thus, the trusted computing base is very important to the overall security of the system. Virtual Machine Manager (VM) is a layer of software between computer hardware and operating system. It is responsible for managing system resources and providing isolated running environment for multiple VMs in the upper layer.

2.1 Independent Monitoring Layer

The VMM of the independent monitoring layer runs directly on the bare machine and has the highest privilege level. It is responsible for the management of the underlying hardware resources. All access to the real hardware of the client operating system must be completed through VMM. When users get personalized recommendation, they can use the system anonymously without requiring their real identity, and they can also get personalized information. The implementation of independent monitoring layer needs to ensure that each tuple can not be distinguished from other tuples, and attackers can not judge the owner of privacy information, so as to ensure the security of users' personal privacy [3]. Usually the system allows a user to enter with multiple identities, which can protect the user's identity in different activities. It can be divided into two categories: concealment and generalization. Hiding is to protect users' privacy attributes by cutting off the relationship between privacy attributes and non-privacy attributes. Require ordered values in their own data tables not less than the prescribed occurrence rate. Some scholars have proposed an anonymity scheme based on adding, deleting and increasing noise nodes. By adjusting the degree of nodes, the anonymity of node degrees can be realized. By assigning different sensitive attribute values to noise nodes, the number of occurrences of sensitive attributes can be adjusted to achieve attribute anonymity. Generalization refers to dividing local user attributes into several equivalent classes and publishing their generalization attributes for different equivalent classes [4].

2.2 Host Layer

All access to the hardware of the host layer client operating system needs to go through VMM and then through the host operating system, and the association rules must be obeyed. As one of the most important methods in data mining, association rule mining has also achieved some research results in privacy protection, which can be used in personalized services based on Association rules. The basic strategies of privacy protection in association rules are data interference and query restriction. Data jamming strategy is to pre-transform the original data according to certain rules. It disturbs the original data by adding random numbers and exchanging, shields the original data for unauthorized users, and then runs data mining algorithm on the jammed data to get the required patterns and rules. However, the technology needs to ensure that the disturbed data can meet the needs of relevant applications, and ensure that the data is not distorted. Query restriction strategy is to change the support and confidence of specific rules through data hiding, and then use probability and statistics or distributed computing methods to get the desired mining results [5].

2.3 Mixing Layer

Hybrid layer is based on the interest of similar user groups to generate recommendations to target users. It only relies on the user's score matrix for the project. Therefore, it has good adaptability to various specific applications and can improve the scalability and recommendation quality of personalized systems. Mixed layer is mainly divided into two categories: data encryption and data transformation [6]. Among them, data encryption is a common security measure. Based on the cryptography principle, it realizes the invisibility and lossless of the original data, and achieves the purpose of privacy protection and accurate recommendation. The main idea of data transformation is to disguise or slightly change users' real privacy data without affecting the use of the original data. Common data transformation includes random perturbation method and data geometry transformation method. Mixed layer can protect privacy information in data very well, but because of the role of social relations, users with unmarked attributes may also be inferred to have some privacy attributes, which can not be directly used to protect the privacy security of users in personalized recommendation. In attribute social networks, we must take into account the influence of social structure information on attribute distribution and the characteristics of attribute distribution itself, in order to better achieve the goal of attribute privacy protection [7].

3 Software Design

3.1 Information Encryption

Information encryption can protect network information security. Data can be disrupted by encryption. Only authorized managers can access the data. This is to make the data more confidential. The encryption process is to put the original data together with the key and process it by mathematical formula to get a data that no one can understand. Encrypted data is usually called ciphertext. In order to make the encrypted data readable, when the receiver receives the data, it decrypts the data with the key in the opposite way. However, the above encryption and decryption process will increase the processing time and memory occupancy cost of the computer CPU. Complicated encryption keys are more conducive to improving data security than simple keys. However, a longer key will be more complex to encrypt and decrypt, and it will take a shorter CPU time to encrypt and decrypt, and it will also increase the size of the target data. Generally, there are two types of encryption. One is symmetric encryption. The other is asymmetric encryption. Symmetric encryption is called symmetric encryption when the encryption key used is the same as the key. Symmetric encryption and decryption algorithm is simpler than asymmetric encryption and decryption algorithm. Because symmetric encryption and decryption have the same key and simple algorithm, symmetric encryption is faster than asymmetric encryption in operation speed. Therefore, symmetric encryption is suitable for encrypting and decrypting massive data, while asymmetric encryption is more suitable for small data [8]. The symmetric encryption algorithm is shown below. If the random variable x is the value of the finite set X, then the definition formula of the entropy of the random variable x is as follows:

$$h(x) -- \sum x \in Xp(x) \tag{1}$$

In formula (1), h is the probability of variable value x, and p represents an event set. When an attacker attacks the privacy information, successfully breaking the privacy information into an event set p, and the attacker successfully recognizes that the privacy information of a user is an event in the event set p, the degree of privacy protection can be measured by the attacker successfully attacking the information of the user.

The definition formula of asymmetric encryption is as follows:

$$p = \frac{1}{n+1}, n \geq m \tag{2}$$

In formula (2), p is the hidden area of event set, n is the number of neighbor nodes, and m is the location point of neighbor. According to the privacy protection degree set by users, the hidden area can be obtained. According to the number n of neighbor nodes in the hidden area, it can be judged whether to insert the location points randomly. If $n > m$, it needs to insert $m - n$ points, and if $n < m$, m neighbor location points will be selected randomly. Because the number of coordinates of the nearest neighbor is m and the real coordinate points are added, the hidden area is composed of $m + 1$ points. When there is no background knowledge, the attacker can successfully obtain the probability of user location information [9].

3.2   Key Management

According to different application environments, the content of key management scheme is designed to ensure the security of data communication and sharing and the validity of key [10]. First, reduce the consumption of key update. In the application of key management to ensure the security of broadcast content and subscription of radio and television programs, most of them adopt group key management mode. In order to alleviate the burden of updating the key on the server side, group members coordinate and generate the group key. The burden of key generation is borne by the group members, and the burden of distributing the group key to users is also saved. By using this method of generating group key, the server is released to a great extent and the resources of group members are utilized more fully. From the point of view of software, a new software structure is proposed. This structure is used to encrypt the generated key and the distributed key, which not only reduces the cost of key update in terms of the number of encryption operations [11]. Considering the execution time of encryption operation, hardware accelerator is used to make digital signature more time-saving. In addition, key generation, management and storage are all in hardware, which improves the security of key usage. The acceleration of encryption operation reduces the time complexity, and the key management by hardware greatly improves the security of the key. However, the limitation of hardware resources should be included in the practical feasibility study.

In view of the frequent changes of node topology in mobile wireless networks, a density function is proposed to dynamically create communication packets for multi-level network nodes based on this function. To a certain extent, it solves the problem of communication security and node key updating, but the time complexity of constructing and selecting responsible nodes is also high. The linear regression formula is used to improve the security of the key. The linear regression formula is as follows:

$$z = \begin{bmatrix} \delta_1 \\ \delta_2 \\ \cdots \\ \delta_n \end{bmatrix}, X = \begin{bmatrix} X_1 \\ X_2 \\ \cdots \\ X_n \end{bmatrix} \tag{3}$$

In formula (3), z represents independent variables, $\delta_1, \delta_2, \ldots, \delta_n$ represents merchant features, X represents the requirement of each feature vector, and $[X_1, X_2, \ldots, X_n]$ represents system recommendation features. The linear regression formula is used to calculate the weight of the feature in the recommendation system. The size of the weight value represents the influence of the corresponding feature on the result. Z is the sum of all the eigenvalues of z, Z is $(-\infty, \infty)$, so the value can be compressed to the range of 0 to 1 by linear function formula, and the sample can be further divided into 0 or 1 by discrete method, that is, to buy or not to buy. First, the prediction function is constructed. The formula is as follows:

$$F(X) = \frac{1}{1 + e^{-\theta}} \tag{4}$$

In formula (4), F represents the probability of result 1. When the input value is X, the probability of output results 1 and 0 is higher. Because the input of constructing prediction function must be 0 or 1 that can be recognized by computer, it is required to convert all feature attributes into Boolean values. The concrete method is divided into the following steps: Step 1 is to count all the features and label all the feature attributes so that the feature values can be distinguished. For example, the shop area characteristic value is 3 and the shop score value is 3. They can not be distinguished according to the value, and tags can distinguish the feature attributes. Step 2: Statistics all features, list all features, establish a feature dictionary table, and then sort all features. Step 3: The string is mapped to Boolean variables. According to the dictionary table, the existence of this feature is observed in all dimensions. If there are corresponding features, the value is 1. If there are no corresponding features, the value is 0. All character features are mapped to form Boolean variables. "1" represents that the sample has this attribute, and "0" represents that the sample does not have this feature. After the above steps, the feature can be transformed into model training to achieve key management. So far, complete the network information security privacy protection [12].

4   Experimental Analysis

Through the processing of user privacy by the network information security privacy protection system proposed in this paper, the experiment will measure the feasibility of the system from function test and performance test. Functional test verifies the function of the system. Firstly, test the function of the lightweight virtual machine manager, then test the password protection function of the system by keyboard recording attack, and then test the function of the system by common web Trojan Horse attack test system. In order to analyze the advantages and disadvantages of the system, the performance loss of the system is evaluated by performance testing, and the micro-performance loss and macro-performance loss of the system are tested respectively.

4.1   System Password Protection Function Test

According to the introduction above, there are many types of keyboard record attack methods and password protection products. In order to verify the password protection function of the system, the system and the existing password protection products are tested and compared. Anti-KeyLogger Tester is one of the keylogger attack tools, because Anti-KeyLogger Tester basically contains a variety of common Keylogger attack methods. The experimental results are as follows:

From Table 1, we can see that the network information security privacy protection system can provide general password protection similar to 360 safe box and Jinshan secret guard, and the strength of password protection is similar to that of Internet banking plug-in and QQ password box special password protection.

Table 1. Comparing test results of system password protection function

SPEC CPU2006	Native OS		Network information security privacy protection system		Running time ratio
400.perlbench	6.32 s	5.32 s	7.32 s	6.32 s	102.3%
401.bizp2	11.23 s	5.36 s	7.36 s	6.36 s	103.2%
403.gcc	16.23 s	5.31 s	7.36 s	6.31 s	100.6%
429.mcf	6.32 s	3.21 s	16.36 s	6.54 s	1006%
445. gobmk	8.36 s	11.23 s	19.36 s	16.32 s	100.5%
456.hmmer	3.61 s	13.32 s	24.00 s	25.00 s	100. 6%
464.h264ref	3.63 s	0.25 s	26.32 s	23.11 s	100.6%

Based on the above experimental results, the efficiency of information security and privacy protection (%) of different methods is mainly compared. Literature [1] method and literature [2] method are selected as comparison methods for simulation experiment. The specific comparison results are shown in Fig. 1:

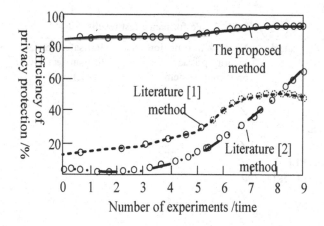

Fig. 1. Comparison results of information security and privacy protection efficiency of different methods

It can be seen from the above analysis that the efficiency of information security privacy protection of different information security privacy protection methods varies with the number of experiments. At the early stage of the experiment, the efficiency of privacy protection of each method presents a straight upward trend. When the number of experiments is 5, the efficiency of information security and privacy protection of literature [1] begins to decline, but the efficiency of information security and privacy protection of the other two methods presents a stable trend. Through the analysis of specific experimental data, it can be seen that the efficiency of information security and privacy protection of the proposed method has been significantly improved compared with the traditional method, which fully verifies the superiority of the proposed method.

4.2 System Performance Test

Hardware virtualization technology is used in network information security privacy protection system. In this paper, the performance of hardware virtualization of network information security privacy protection system is tested using standard test set SPEC CPU 2006. The performance of hardware virtualization of network information security privacy protection system is still considered by using native operating system as a reference standard. The running time of SPEC CPU 2006 in native operating system is normalized to 100%. The ratio of running time between network information security privacy protection system and native operating system is obtained as follows:

As can be seen from Table 2, the hardware virtualization cost of network information security privacy protection system is very small, and the average additional performance loss of each test is only about 1.3%. It can be inferred that, compared with the original operating system, the performance loss caused by each test of network information security privacy protection system is smaller, the average performance loss is only about 0.52%. The test results show that the overall performance of network information security privacy protection system is very good.

Table 2. Performance test results.

Keyboard recording attack method	Network information security privacy protection system	360 safety box, Jinshan secret protection	Internet banking plug-in
GetKey State	✓	×	✓
GetAsyncKeyState	✓	×	✓
GetKeyboardstate	✓	×	✓
GetRawInputData	✓	×	✓
WH KEYBOARD LL	✓	×	✓
WH JOURNALRECORO	✓	×	✓
Screenshots	✓	×	×

5 Conclusion

The exposure of personal data security issues has aroused unprecedented concern. Data security protection systems are generally designed and developed for enterprises, units, government organs and other large organizations. Personal data security systems are still implemented by encryption software alone. This method not only affects the convenience of users to operate data, but also proves that encrypted documents are not safe. This system adopts a low-cost, high-security solution to control the process of file operation and monitor the process of file operation. Considering the external storage of files and the key renewal and protection of files, it is a relatively perfect solution.

References

1. Deng, W.: Research on information security and privacy protection in the big data era. China New Commun. **19**(3), 1226–1227 (2017)
2. Wang, S., Du, W.: Progress of New Zealand's privacy protection in the big data era and its enlightenment to China. E-government **23**(11), 2165–2171 (2017)
3. Maliwei, Meng, W., Zhang, Y.: Research on personal information security in big data era. Netw. Secur. Technol. Appl. **22**(4), 1364–1365 (2018)
4. Gao, Y., Dai, G., Yan, S.: Research on information security in network environment in big data era. Inf. Syst. Eng. **22**(2), 2189 (2017)
5. Liu, Y.: Banking information security protection strategy in the age of big data network. Electron. Technol. Softw. Eng. **32**(7), 1211 (2017)
6. Liu, W.: Opportunities and challenges of network information security in the era of big data. Netw. Secur. Technol. Appl. **32**(11), 2176–2177 (2017)
7. Chen, H.: Computer information security and privacy protection strategy in the background of big data. Netw. Secur. Technol. Appl. **32**(11), 1168 (2017)
8. Zhang, Y., Wang, X.: Research on information security and privacy protection in big data environment. Digit. Technol. Appl. **32**(7), 3190–3191 (2017)
9. Zhu, X., Zhang, H., Ma, J.: Android platform privacy protection system based on hook technology. J. Netw. Inf. Secur. **32**(4), 1621–1693 (2018)
10. Yan, W., Yao, Y., Zhang, W., et al.: Logistics system privacy protection scheme based on two-dimensional code and information hiding. J. Netw. Inf. Secur. **3**(11), 2222–2228 (2017)
11. Li, C., Shi, Z., Gao, H., et al.: Development and design of personal privacy protection system for mobile intelligent terminal. Comput. Appl. Softw. **34**(6), 217–220 (2017)
12. Li, C., Zhang, Z., Zhang, C., et al.: Data fusion algorithm for privacy protection in wireless sensor networks. Inf. Secur. Res. **3**(6), 523–527 (2017)

Multi-path Channel Modeling and Analysis of Embedded LTE Wireless Communication Network Under Cloud Computing

Yanhua Qiao[1,2(✉)], Lin Zhao[1,2], and Jianna Li[1]

[1] Department of Information and Automation,
Tianjin Tianshi College, Tianjin, China
qiaoyanhua12985@163.com
[2] State Key Laboratory of Reliability and Intelligence of Electrical Equipment,
Hebei University of Technology, Tianjin, China

Abstract. The multi-path channel modeling analysis of conventional communication network can analyze the modeling of multi-path channel in communication network. However, for the multi-path channel modeling analysis of embedded LTE wireless communication network under cloud computing, there is a shortage of high analysis error rate. To this end, the multi-path channel modeling analysis of embedded LTE wireless communication network under cloud computing is proposed. The LTE multipath channel modeling and analysis program structure is built, and the single-frequency signal is subjected to time-varying channel technology, and the digital signal is designed by multipath time-varying channel technology to complete the key technology design of multipath channel modeling and analysis. The multipath channel modeling and analysis program is used to determine the multi-path channel modeling Rayleigh distribution and Rice distribution, and the related characteristics analysis to realize multi-path channel modeling analysis of embedded LTE wireless communication network under cloud computing. The experimental data show that the proposed multipath channel modeling analysis is more than the conventional multipath channel modeling analysis, and the analysis error rate is reduced by 14.35%, which is suitable for multi-path channel modeling analysis of embedded LTE wireless communication networks under cloud computing.

Keywords: Embedded LTE · Wireless communication · Network multipath channel · Modeling and analysis

1 Introduction

The multipath channel modeling analysis of conventional communication network can analyze the multipath channel modeling of communication network. However, when modeling and analyzing multipath channel in embedded LTE wireless communication network, the key technology of multipath channel modeling and analysis is limited. Literature [1] proposes a multipath channel modeling and analysis method for wireless communication networks based on improved subgradient algorithm. To transfer process of communication signals, on the basis of the instantaneous signal to noise ratio

G. Gui and L. Yun (Eds.): ADHIP 2019, LNICST 301, pp. 74–83, 2019.
https://doi.org/10.1007/978-3-030-36402-1_8

will repair network port priority selection problem is transformed into the constraint optimization problems, according to the network port repair choice optimization criterion, combined with the gradient algorithm, at the same time to determine the network port repair priority selection of the optimal solution, wireless communication network modeling analysis of multipath channel. Simulation results show that the method takes longer time and has lower precision. Literature [2] proposes a multipath channel modeling and analysis method for wireless communication networks based on multipath fading channel. By using the energy differential function of the received signal and the primary synchronization signal, the precise symbol timing synchronization and fractional carrier frequency deviation are obtained respectively in the time domain, and the multipath channel analysis of wireless communication network is completed. Experimental results show that the accuracy of this method is low and the practical application effect is poor. Therefore, the multipath channel modeling analysis of embedded LTE wireless communication network is proposed. Based on the LTE physical layer protocol and OFDM modulation, the LTE multipath channel modeling and analysis program structure is built, the single frequency signal passing through the time-varying channel technology is constructed, and the digital signal passing through the multipath time-varying channel technology is designed. The key technologies of multipath channel modeling and analysis are designed; The multipath channel modeling and analysis program is used to analyze the Rayleigh distribution and Rice distribution, and the proposed multipath channel modeling analysis for embedded LTE wireless communication network is completed. In order to ensure the effectiveness of the multipath channel modeling and analysis of the designed communication network, the simulation of the embedded LTE wireless communication network environment is carried out, and two different communication network multipath channel modeling and analysis are used to simulate the error rate analysis. The experimental results show that the proposed multipath channel modeling analysis is highly effective.

2 System Objectives and Analysis

Cloud computing is an Internet-based computing model that distributes computing tasks across resource pools of large numbers of computers. Consumers can acquire computing power, storage space, and various software services as needed, and pay for usage. Cloud computing has caused another innovation in the computer field, and has brought many new security problems. To this end, the multi-path channel model of embedded LTE wireless communication network under cloud computing is designed.

Multi-path channel modeling and analysis of embedded LTE wireless communication networks under cloud computing mainly includes:

(1) Analysing the signal processing flow of LTE physical layer protocol and FDM modulation, builds the LTE multipath channel modeling and analysis program structure, and designs the single frequency signal and digital signal through time-varying channel technology.

(2) Using the discrete multipath analysis and scattering multipath analysis, analyze the finite number of multipath components and multipath components, and determine the multipath channel modeling and analysis program.

(3) The characteristics of multipath time-varying channel, Rayleigh distribution and Rice distribution are analyzed by using multipath channel modeling and analysis program, and the shortcomings of modeling and analysis of multipath channel in conventional communication network are solved.

3   Key Technology Design of Multipath Channel Modeling and Analysis for Embedded LTE Wireless Communication Network Under Cloud Computing

3.1   Building a LTE Multipath Channel Modeling and Analysis Program Structure Under Cloud Computing

The emerging "cloud computing" technology is the most noteworthy technological revolution in the world in the next few years. It is designed with the concept of dynamic resource allocation and on-demand service, and is valued and promoted by the scientific and technological community and more and more commercial giants. However, while cloud computing is rapidly developing, it also brings many new security threats. Among them, multipath channel transmission is affected. Wireless channel is the most complex channel. The wireless propagation environment is the basic factor that affects the wireless communication system. During the process of signal propagation, the signal will be reflected, diffracted and scattered under the influence of various environments, so that the signal arriving at the receiver is the superposition of many path signals [3]. Therefore, the superposition of these multipath signals in the case of no line-of-sight propagation obeys the Rayleigh distribution. When the multipath signal contains a line-of-sight propagation path, the multipath signal is distributed from Rice. In the channel with multipath transmission, due to the different transmission time of each path, the transmission characteristic is not ideal, and the influence of the channel noise, received signal is widened in time, which extends to adjacent symbol. Such channels can cause inter-symbol interference.

LTE uses OFDMA (Orthogonal Frequency Division Multiple Access) as the downlink multiple access mode. OFDM is a transmission technology of multi-carrier modulation. The signal processing flow of OFDM modulation is as follows: the data stream is transformed into a multi-channel sub-data stream (N-channel) after series-parallel transformation, and then they are used to modulate the N-channel subcarriers respectively, and finally to transmit in parallel. OFDM signals have a strong ability to resist multipath fading and pulse interference, because the rate of sub-data stream becomes 1/N, the symbol period becomes NT times as long as the symbol period after serial-parallel transformation. The designer can divide a wideband frequency selective channel into N narrow band flat fading channels by designing the symbol period much longer than the delay spread of the channel [4]. This process is a simplification of channel equalization operation, because of its simple implementation, it is especially suitable for high-speed wireless data transmission. The signal processing flow of LTE downlink OFDM modulation is shown in Fig. 1.

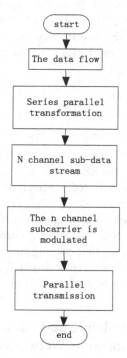

Fig. 1. Signal processing flow of LTE downlink OFDM modulation

3.2 Design of Single Frequency Signal Passing Through Time-Varying Channel

The effect of multipath propagation on signal is called multipath effect, which has great influence on the quality of signal transmission. When a single frequency signal is input and transmitted through a multipath time-varying channel, the waveform envelope of the received signal fluctuates randomly with time, and the output is not a single frequency signal, it is a narrow band signal, and the bandwidth is determined by speed of upper variable factor. After multipath time-varying channel transmission, delay and attenuation of multipath channel are different, which leads to different amplitude and frequency of received signal. A single frequency signal with a amplitude of 1 and a frequency of 10 Hz is transmitted by 20 paths to obtain the waveform and spectrum. The attenuation of the 20 paths is the same, but the time delay varies with time. Time delay variation of each path is sinusoidal. The frequency of the change is extracted from 0–2 Hz randomly. After multipath propagation, the different path delays are different at the same time. The superposition of delay signal causes the time domain graphics to no longer be single sinusoidal, and other frequencies appear. (because of the sampling frequency, it looks like a smooth curve) burrs appear in frequency domain, that is diffusion in frequency domain [5].

3.3   Design of Digital Signal Over Multipath Time-Varying Channel

Multipath time-varying channels generate time domain dispersion for digital signals. Intersymbol interference occurs when the digital signal passes through a multipath time-varying channel. Due to the different delay of each path, the attenuation of each path is different, and the signal reaches the receiving end through multiple paths to form inter-symbol interference. A three-path transmission channel:

$$s(t) = \sum_{i=1}^{3} u_i b(t - \tau_i) \tag{1}$$

In the formula, $u_1 = 0.5, u_2 = 0.707, u_3 = 0.5; \tau_1 = 0, \tau_2 = 1, \tau_3 = 2$, the waveform of the output signal in the transmission channel is closer to that of the input signal. Because the channel amplitude characteristic is not very ideal, will cause the input signal distortion. Analog signal is reflected in waveform distortion and digital signal is reflected in inter-symbol interference.

Relying on the LTE multipath channel modeling and analysis program structure, the single-frequency signal undergoes time-varying channel technology, and the digital signal is designed through multi-path time-varying channel technology to realize multi-path channel modeling and analysis of embedded LTE wireless communication network under cloud computing. Key technology design.

4   Multi-path Channel Modeling and Analysis of Embedded LTE Wireless Communication Network Under Cloud Computing

4.1   Determination of Multipath Channel Modeling and Analysis Program

There are two main programs for analyzing multipath channel models, discrete multipath analysis (finite number of multipath components)and scattering multipath analysis (continuum of multipath components). In mobile wireless channels, the first model is usually used to simulate the waveform level of mobile wireless channels, while the second model is usually used in narrowband modulated tropospheric channels. In the two case, the channel is modeled as a linear time-varying system with complex low pass equivalent response $c(\tau, t)$. If there are N discrete multipath components, the channel output is the sum of five delayed and fading input signals. So $y(t) = \sum_{k=1}^{N(t)} a_k(t)x(t - \tau_k(t))$ impulse response $c(\tau, t)$ is:

$$c(\tau, t) = \sum_{k=1}^{N(t)} a_k(t)\delta(\tau - \tau_k(t)) \tag{2}$$

In the formula, $N(t)$ is the number of multipath components, $a_k(t)$ and $\tau_k(t)$ are the complex fading and delay of the K path at the moment.

4.2   Analysis of Rayleigh Distribution and Rice Distribution

In practice, for digital communication systems, the period of modulation symbols is larger than the delay spread caused by multipath propagation, so all frequency components in a symbol period will undergo the same attenuation and phase shift [6]. The channel is flat for all frequency components, so this kind of channel is defined as flat fading channel. The theoretical analysis and experimental results show that the amplitude of flat fading is consistent with Rayleigh distribution or Rice distribution in most cases. Because of the complexity of the mobile communication channel, the simulation is usually based on the flat fading channel modeling, and then on this basis, the frequency selective channel is modeled and simulated. The characteristics of Rayleigh distribution and Rice distribution are deduced and simulated [7, 8].

When there is a line-of-sight propagation signal, the line-of-sight component of the received signal is described by a generic time-varying component as:

$$m(t) = m_1(t) + jm_2(t) = \rho e^{j(2\pi f_\rho + \theta_\rho)} \tag{3}$$

In the formula, ρ, f_ρ, and θ_ρ are the amplitude of the stadia signal component, the Doppler frequency of the stadia signal component and the phase respectively of the stadia signal component.

The envelope of the received signal is expressed as:

$$\xi(t) = \sqrt{(\mu_1 + \rho)^2 + \mu_2^2} \tag{4}$$

It is distributed from Rice distribution, where μ_1 and μ_2 are two independent and dependent real Gao Si processes with normal distribution, it is satisfy $\mu_1, \mu_2 \in N(0, \sigma_0^2)$.

The probability density function of the envelope of the received signal is:

$$P_\xi(x) = \frac{x}{\sigma_0^2} \exp\left[-\frac{x^2 + \rho^2}{2\sigma_0^2}\right] \cdot I_0\left[\frac{x\rho}{\sigma_0^2}\right], (x > 0) \tag{5}$$

In the formula, $I_0(x)$ is a modified Bessel function of the first kind [9]. The ratio K between the reflected signal power and the dispersive signal power is called the Rice factor, it is can be expressed as:

$$K = \frac{\rho^2}{2\sigma^2} \tag{6}$$

When there is no line-of-sight propagation signal, $\rho = 0$ (K = 0, $I_0 = 1$), the envelope of the received signal is represented as:

$$\zeta(t) = |u(t)| = \sqrt{u_1^2(t) + u_2^2(t)} \qquad (7)$$

It takes the Rayleigh distribution, and its probability density function is:

$$P_\zeta(x) = \frac{x}{\sigma_0^2} \cdot \exp\left[-\frac{x^2}{2\sigma_0^2}\right], (x > 0) \qquad (8)$$

So Rayleigh channel can be regarded as a special case of Rice channel with K factor 0 and no line-of-sight propagation path [10].

4.3   Characteristic Analysis of Multipath Time-Varying Channel

Time-varying channel refers to the channel in which the channel parameters change with time. Its characteristic is that the transmission attenuation of the signal changes with time, and the transmission delay of the signal also changes with the time, and the signal passes through multiple paths to the receiving end. And the length and decay of each path vary over time. The influence of time-varying channel on signal transmission diffuses the frequency of input signal.

In multipath channel, the input signal is transmitted by more than one path, and the receiver receives the signal from multiple transmission paths at the same time. These signals may be Co direction addition, or reverse phase subtraction. The effect of multipath propagation on the signal is called multipath effect, which can greatly affect the signal transmission quality.

For the multipath signal of mobile station at different positions, the initial distance from the mobile station to the base station is set to r0 = 1000, r0 = 9000, r0 = 14000. When other conditions remain unchanged, the condition of receiving the signal is such as to make the mobile station static. Because of the reflection path, the received signal is weaker than the signal without the reflection path, and the fading occurs. Signals of different frequencies pass through the multipath channel f = 3e8, f = 9e8, f = 27e8, if f increases gradually and some frequencies are weakened and f is sufficiently large, the synthesis signal is weakened. Those frequency ranges that are affected are basically consistent, called coherent bandwidth. At the same location, because of the presence of the mirror signal, the frequency at which different signals are transmitted, the signals received at the receiver are either strengthened or weakened. This is called frequency selective fading.

The multipath signal of different speed signal of mobile station is changed, and the signal of different speed of mobile station passes through the multipath channel v = 0, v = 300. When other conditions are invariant, the mobile station has velocity, even at the same frequency, the same position, at different time points, the intensity of the composite signal is different, some local signal attenuation, some local signal enhancement. When the velocity increases from 0 to 300, the direct path signal weakens, the reflection path signal increases, and the composite signal weakens.

Based on the key technology design of multi-path channel modeling and analysis of embedded LTE wireless communication network under cloud computing, and the multipath channel modeling analysis program, the characteristics analysis, Rayleigh distribution and Rice distribution of multipath time-varying channel are completed. Analysis and analysis of multi-path channel modeling of embedded LTE wireless communication network under cloud computing.

5 Experiment and Result Analysis

In order to ensure the effectiveness of multi-path channel modeling and analysis of embedded LTE wireless communication network under cloud computing proposed in this paper, simulation simulation analysis is carried out. In the course of experiment, different embedded LTE wireless communication networks are used as experimental objects to simulate the error rate. Simulation and simulation of different structure, data volume and so on of embedded LTE wireless communication network are simulated. In order to ensure the effectiveness of the experiment, the multipath channel modeling and analysis of conventional communication network is used as the comparison object, the results of the two simulation experiments are compared, and the experimental data are presented in the chart.

5.1 Parameter Setting

In order to ensure the accuracy of the simulation experiment, the parameters of the test are set. In this paper, different embedded LTE wireless communication networks are used as experimental objects, and two kinds of multipath channels are used to model and analyze the simulation results. Because the analytical results and the analytical methods obtained by different methods are different, it is necessary to ensure the consistency of the experimental environment parameters in the experiment process. The results of the experimental data set in this paper are shown in Table 1.

Table 1. Parameter setting

Parameter	Scope of implementation	Remarks
Communication network load	1–10^4 GHz	Analysis under variable load using two different analytical methods
Embedded LTE wireless communication network environment	good	Within the rated range, two different design methods are used to analyze the design in an ideal environment
Simulation system	DJX-2016-3.5	Windows terrace

5.2 Analysis of Experimental Results

In the process of experiment, two different modeling and analysis methods of multipath channel in communication network are used to analyze the change of error rate in simulation environment. At the same time, because two different communication network multipath channel modeling and analysis, its analysis results can not be compared directly, so the third party analysis recording software is used to record and analyze the experimental process and results. The results are shown in the curve of the experiment. In the simulation experiment result curve, the function of the third-party analysis recording software is used to eliminate the uncertainty caused by the operation of the personnel in the simulation laboratory and the factors of the simulation computer equipment, and only for different embedded LTE wireless communication networks. Modeling and analysis of multipath channels in different communication networks. The contrast curve of the experimental results is shown in Fig. 2. According to the results of the test curve, the third-party analysis and recording software is used to analyze the multi-path channel of the proposed communication network, and the arithmetic error rate of the analysis error rate of the multi-path channel modeling analysis of the conventional communication network is processed.

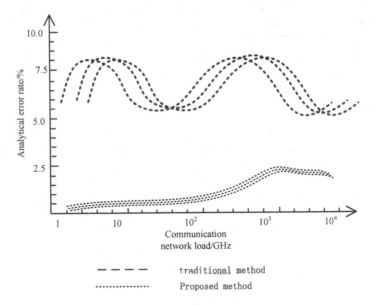

Fig. 2. Experimental result contrast curve

According to the test curve in Fig. 2, the arithmetic error rate of the bit-error rate analysis of the multipath channel modeling analysis method of traditional communication network is between 5.5 and 8.5, while the arithmetic error rate of the method in this paper is only between 0.1 and 2.5. The lower the error rate, the better the accuracy of the method and the better the application effect. It can be proved that the method in this paper is more suitable for multi-path channel modeling and analysis of embedded LTE wireless communication network under cloud computing. This is because the method in this paper establishes the LTE multipath channel modeling and analysis program structure, and combines time-varying channel technology or multi-path time-varying channel technology to realize the key technology design of multipath channel modeling and analysis, so as to effectively improve the accuracy of analysis.

6 Conclusion

This paper proposes multi-path channel modeling and analysis of embedded LTE wireless communication network under cloud computing. The key technology design of multi-path channel modeling and analysis based on cloud computing embedded LTE wireless communication network, and the determination of multipath channel modeling and analysis program. The characteristics analysis, Rayleigh distribution and Rice distribution of multipath time-varying channels are analyzed to realize the research of this paper. The experimental data shows that the method designed in this paper is extremely effective. It is hoped that the research in this paper can provide a theoretical basis for multi-path channel modeling and analysis of communication networks.

References

1. Liu, W., Han, L., Yang, X.: The optimal network port selection model of the simulation analysis of communication. Comput. Simul. **33**(8), 248–251 (2016)
2. Sun, Y., Chen, Y.: Research on time and frequency synchronization estimation of railway communication with LTE-R under multipath fading channel. Railway Standard Des. **60**(11), 148–152 (2016)
3. Liao, X., Li, Z., Xi, Y.: Modeling and analysis of users' knowledge network in innovative community based on clustering. Comput. Simul. **33**(4), 316–319 (2016)
4. Zhang, H.: On the security system and key schemes of metro CBTC based on TD-LTE technology. Urban Mass Transit **3**(4), 36–39 (2016)
5. Dan, Z., Matthe, M., Mendes, L.L., et al.: A study on the link level performance of advanced multicarrier waveforms under MIMO wireless communication channels. IEEE Trans. Wirel. Commun. **16**(4), 2350–2365 (2017)
6. Huang, J., Wang, C.X., Feng, R., et al.: Multi-frequency mmWave massive MIMO channel measurements and characterization for 5G wireless communication systems. IEEE J. Sel. Areas Commun. **35**(7), 1591–1605 (2017)
7. Sangeetha, M., Bhaskar, V.: NR-DCSK based chaotic communications in MIMO multipath channels. Wirel. Personal Commun. **103**(5), 1–16 (2018)
8. Nawaz, S.J., Wyne, S., Baltzis, K.B., et al.: A tunable 3-D statistical channel model for spatio-temporal characteristics of wireless communication networks. Trans. Emerg. Telecommun. Technol. **28**(12), e3213 (2017)
9. Sen Gupta, A.: Estimation and equalization for shallow water communication channel using geometric encoding of channel multipath. J. Acoust. Soc. Am. **142**(4), 2645–2645 (2017)
10. Oh, H.S., Kang, D.W.: Performance analysis on channel estimation with antenna diversity of OFDM reception in multi-path fast fading channel. Wirel. Pers. Commun. **103**(3), 2423–2431 (2018)

Layered Encryption Method for Monitoring Network User Data for Big Data Analysis

Yanhua Qiao[1,2(✉)], Lin Zhao[1,2], and Jianna Li[1]

[1] Department of Information and Automation,
Tianjin Tianshi College, Tianjin, China
qiaoyanhua12985@163.com
[2] State Key Laboratory of Reliability and Intelligence of Electrical Equipment,
Hebei University of Technology, Tianjin, China

Abstract. The conventional monitoring network user data layered encryption method had a low security when layered encryption of modern network data. Therefore, a layered encryption method for monitoring network user data for big data analysis was proposed. Big data technology was introduced, and a layered framework of network user data was built to monitor and encrypt network user data. Relying on the determination and layering of different levels of user data, the data layered encryption model was embedded to realize the layering and encryption of monitoring network user data. The test data showed that the proposed layered encryption method for monitoring network user data for big data analysis would improve the security of the data by 46.82%, which was suitable for users of different levels to encrypt their own network data.

Keywords: Big data analysis · Network users · Data layering · Network data

1 Introduction

Network layering is the process of sending or forwarding, packing or unpacking data to be completed by network nodes, loading or unloading control information, and different hardware and software modules. This can make the complicated problem of communication and network interconnection easier. The OSI model is divided into seven layers. From top to bottom, the application layer refers to the network operating system and specific applications. Corresponding server, FTP server and other application software represent layer data syntax conversion, data transmission and other session layers establish a conversation relationship between the two ends, and responsible for the data transmission layer is responsible for the error check and repair to ensure the quality of the transmission, is where TCP works. The network layer provides an addressing scheme, where the IP protocol works (data packet). The data link layer wraps the unprocessed bit data transmitted by the physical layer into physical devices such as network cables, network cards, and interfaces of the physical layer of the data frame.

Literature [1] proposed an efficient hierarchical data encryption method based on cognitive radio network, constructed the framework of markov decision process, based on remote sensing results and residual energy, and combined with private key

G. Gui and L. Yun (Eds.): ADHIP 2019, LNICST 301, pp. 84–93, 2019.
https://doi.org/10.1007/978-3-030-36402-1_9

encryption method, realized the hierarchical encryption method of big data analysis. However, the accuracy of the method is poor and the application effect is not ideal. Literature [2] proposes a joint data stratification and encryption method based on wireless energy audit network, which completes the stratification and encryption of big data analysis by taking advantage of the compression and encryption characteristics of compressed sensing and combining with the reconstruction mechanism based on machine learning. However, this method is too simple and has limited application.

In order to solve the problems of traditional methods, a hierarchical encryption method is proposed to monitor network user data for big data analysis. Better implementation of network data encryption, and improve the security of data.

2 Construction of Hierarchical Data Encryption Method for Monitoring Network User Data in Big Data Analysis

Symmetric encryption is the same key used for encryption and decryption, representing the algorithm AES, DES. This encryption mode has a big disadvantage: it is assumed that the information is transmitted by Party A to Party B. If Party A uses the key for encryption, then it must find a way to tell the party to the key. How to save and transfer keys has become a very troublesome thing.

2.1 Introduction of Big Data Technology

After establishing a TCP connection, the server transmits the response HTML to the client through a TCP packet through the TCP protocol. The network layer of the client reorders the received TCP packets, adjusts them, and hands them over to the application layer. At this point, the HTTP request is completed. With the popularity of scalable video coding, security issues for scalable video have also received increasing attention. Most of the current encryption schemes are for H. Designed by the 264/AVC coding standard. The new technology adopted by SVC is analyzed, and a new layered encryption scheme based on its characteristics is proposed. The scheme selects different key information of the previous video, such as inter-layer prediction motion vector, quality scalable key frame, etc. as the encryption object, and performs algorithm design according to the type of selected information and the security level required by the user. The experimental results show that the scheme has the advantages of good encryption effect, low key quantity and high real-time performance, and can adapt to the application of different security requirements [3] (Fig. 1).

The physical layer is the lowest layer of the reference model. This layer is a data transmission medium for network communication, consisting of a cable and devices connected to different nodes. The main function is to use the transmission medium to provide physical connection for the data link layer, which is responsible for processing data transmission and monitoring data error rate, and achieving transparent transmission of data streams [4].

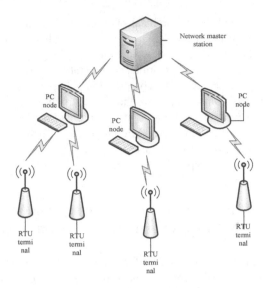

Fig. 1. Network data layering system

2.2   Building a Network User Database Framework

The hierarchical encryption method for network user data seems to be very simple. However, certain aspects of this layer sometimes require special attention. The physical layer is actually wiring, fiber, network cards, and other things that connect two network communication devices together. The elimination of network failures often involves a layer of problems. We can't forget the legendary story of connecting five levels of lines across the entire floor. Since the office chairs are often pressed from the cable, the network connection is intermittent. Unfortunately, this type of failure is very common, and it takes a long time to eliminate such a failure [5]. Currently, it is only necessary to know that the second layer converts the data frame into a binary bit for one layer of processing [6] (Fig. 2).

The application of layered encryption method for monitoring network user data for big data analysis realizes the construction of networked data layered encryption system under the background of big data.

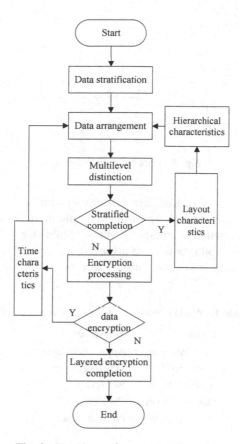

Fig. 2. Data layered encryption flow chart

3 Analysis of Hierarchical Encryption Method for Monitoring Network User Data Under Big Data Analysis

Hubs belong to the first tier because they are just electronic devices and have no knowledge of the second tier. The second level of related issues has its own part in this webinar. Therefore, the details of this issue will not be discussed in detail at present. Cognitive wireless network technology with characteristics of cognition, autonomy and variability, as an important technology to improve the capacity of wireless networks, has attracted the attention of academic circles, standards organizations and industry [7]. Aiming at the fact that existing power control technology can not describe the hierarchical decision-making of multiple cognitive nodes, a multi-user dynamic layered power control algorithm in cognitive wireless networks is proposed [8] (Fig. 3).

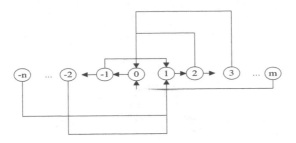

Fig. 3. Data layering diagram

Based on the proposed Stall Kohlberg capacity maximization game model, a distributed power control method is designed for multiple users with cognitive information asymmetry in cognitive wireless networks. Multi-stage dynamic interaction between leader users and follower users ia achieved, and overall network performance is achieved while ensuring individual utility (Table 1).

Table 1. Working mode of network layered model.

Client	The server
Application layer	Application layer
Transport layer	Transport layer
Network layer	Network layer
Data link layer	Data link layer
Physical layer	Physical layer

The bridge works on the second layer and only focuses on the MAC address on the Ethernet. If you are talking about MAC addresses, switches or network cards and drivers, it is in the second layer. The specific situation is shown in Fig. 4.

Big data is a research hotspot in the current academic and industrial circles, and it is affecting people's daily life patterns, work habits and thinking patterns. However, at present, big data is faced with many security risks in the process of collection, storage and use. Privacy leakage caused by big data causes serious trouble to users, and false data will lead to wrong or invalid big data analysis results. The data analysis has the following formula:

$$z = (x - \bar{x})/s \tag{1}$$

Among them, s is the standard deviation. For the technical challenges of massive computational analysis and complex cognitive reasoning in big data computing, traditional computer-based algorithms can not meet the increasingly demanding data processing requirements. The group computing based on human-machine collaboration is an effective solution. The size of Internet users is shown in Table 2:

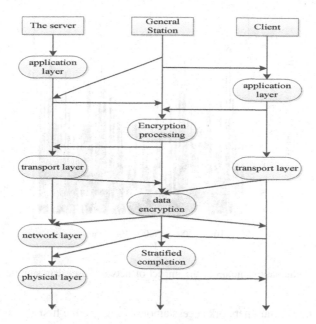

Fig. 4. Network user data layered framework

Table 2. Comparison of internet user size.

Project	2010	2011
Micro-blog	63110000	249880000
Space	294500000	319850000
Instant messaging	352580000	415800000
E-mail	249690000	245770000

The inherent complexity of large data problems, high-speed growth, form diversity, and low value density pose serious challenges for traditional computing methods. On the one hand, the large-scale and high-speed growth of big data brings the demand for massive computational analysis. On the other hand, the characteristics of form diversity and low value density make big data computing tasks highly dependent on complex cognitive reasoning techniques (Fig. 5).

The rapidly evolving Internet has become an indispensable part of people's lives, and people have left many data footprints on the web. These data footprints are cumulative and relevant, and when multiple data footprints are brought together, individual privacy information can be discovered. It brings a lot of trouble or economic loss to the individual's life. The network traffic ratio is expressed as the following formula:

$$M = \sum ap \tag{2}$$

$$p \le \frac{(t+a)(t+a+1)}{2} \tag{3}$$

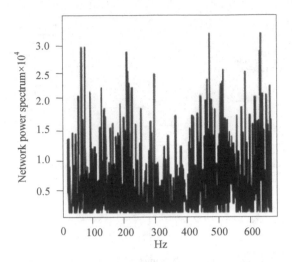

Fig. 5. Schematic diagram of the impact of network user data stratification

Among them, a certain network access amount is a, and the first access amount is p. With the development of smart grid, communication network technology and sensor technology, data on the power user side has increased exponentially and complexity, and gradually formed user-side big data. The traditional data analysis mode can no longer meet the demand, and it is urgent to solve the problem of analysis and processing of big data on the power user side. Analyze the source of user big data, and focus on the large amount of data, large variety and fast speed of user-side big data, pointing out the challenges faced by network users in big data in terms of data storage, availability, and processing. The embedding process is shown in Fig. 6.

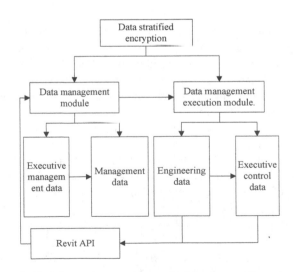

Fig. 6. Data layered encryption method implementation process

With the development of information technology, emerging services such as blogs, Weibo, and social networks based on new technologies and the Internet of Things have produced unprecedented types of data at an unprecedented rate. Cloud computing provides a basic platform for data storage, which has brought about the official arrival of the era of big data. Big data contains great value and is a valuable asset of the company. But big data also brings huge challenges.

4 Simulation Experiment

In order to ensure the effectiveness of the modeling and analysis of the hierarchical network encryption method for monitoring network user data proposed in this paper, simulation analysis is carried out. Different methods are used to conduct data layered encryption for network users as test objects, and the analysis accuracy simulation test is carried out. The network user data layered encryption method is simulated. In order to ensure the validity of the test, the previous method was used as the test comparison object to carry out the simulation test.

4.1 Test Data Preparation

Layered encryption of network user data is based on the direction of the general direction. You want users to work toward what core goals, and users grouping them is to split them into finer granularity. The two are complementary. According to the 28th rule, 80% of the product's revenue is contributed by 20% of users. In this way, our core users are actually not many. How do we find them, how to use the value of other traffic, how to train more users to become core users, to achieve these goals, and to achieve a cultured operation.

4.2 Analysis of Test Results

During the test, two different methods were used to layer the network user data at the same time, and the accuracy rate was analyzed. In order to ensure the accuracy of data processing, the hierarchical data encryption of network users is monitored by means of big data analysis. The statistical results of the results are obtained and the test results are obtained. The simulation accuracy curve is shown in Fig. 7.

According to the results of the test curve, it is possible to realize network data layering by LSI. Experimental data show that the data stratification encryption time of the proposed method is always lower than that of the traditional method under different experiment times, with the maximum difference of 50 min. The shorter the time, the higher the efficiency of the method, which proves that the method in this paper is more suitable for data stratification in all walks of life. This is because the method in this paper constructs a layered network user data framework, and at the same time, combined with embedded data layered encryption model, can effectively improve the efficiency of monitoring and encrypting network user data, and better realize the hierarchical encryption of monitoring network user data.

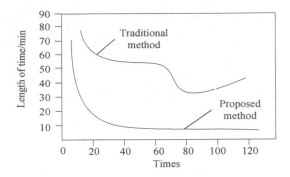

Fig. 7. Layered encryption method effectiveness simulation curve

5 Conclusions

Under this structure, the core users of the network, both in the direction of content production and in the direction of consumption, represent two types of operational strategies. User layering of the dual pyramid structure is not uncommon. User layering, generally four or five layers of structure can be, too much layering will become complex, not suitable for the implementation of operational strategies. User tiering is a top-down structure, but the user community cannot be fully summarized by structure. If you continue to increase the number of layers, the conditions will become complicated and the business needs will not be solved. So we use a horizontal structure of user grouping. Groups within the same tier continue to be segmented to meet higher refinement needs.

References

1. Do-Vinh, Q., Hoan, T.-N.-K., Koo, I.: Energy-efficient data encryption scheme for cognitive radio networks. IEEE Sensors J. **PP**(99), 1 (2018)
2. Tan, R., Chiu, S.Y., Nguyen, H.H., et al.: A joint data compression and encryption approach for wireless energy auditing networks. ACM Trans. Sensor Networks **13**(2), 1–32 (2017)
3. Shenashen, M.A., Hassen, D., El-Safty, S.A., et al.: Axially oriented tubercle vein and X-crossed sheet of N-Co 3 O 4 @C hierarchical mesoarchitectures as potential heterogeneous catalysts for methanol oxidation reaction. Chem. Eng. J. **313**, 83–98 (2017)
4. Hu, E., Feng, Y., Nai, J., et al.: Construction of hierarchical Ni–Co–P hollow nanobricks with oriented nanosheets for efficient overall water splitting. Energy Environ. Sci. **33**(S1), 542–546 (2018)
5. Yoshioka, T., Tashiro, K., Ohta, N.: Observation of water-stimulated supercontraction of uniaxially oriented Poly(vinyl alcohol) and the related hierarchical structure change revealed by the time-resolved WAXD/SAXS measurements. Macromolecules **136**, 352–361 (2017)
6. Dong, P., Zheng, T., Du, X., et al.: SVCC-HSR: providing secure vehicular cloud computing for intelligent high-speed rail. IEEE Network **32**(3), 64–71 (2018)

7. Liu, Y., Zheng, F.B.: Object-oriented and multi-scale target classification and recognition based on hierarchical ensemble learning. Comput. Electr. Eng. **62**, 515–521 (2017)
8. Li, C.K., Ye, Y., Liu, Y.S., et al.: A facile step for heterogeneous crystal structure in hierarchical architecture with vacancy-driven defects by oriented attachment growth mechanism. J. Mater. Chem. A **38**, 534–541 (2018)

Research on Emergency Communication Command and Scheduling Algorithm Based on Pattern Recognition

Jun Li[✉] and Jun Xing

Shenzhen Academy of Inspection and Quarantine, Shenzhen, China
zwm20171028@sina.com

Abstract. In the process of regular pattern recognition, due to the limitation of the algorithm, the emergency communication command and dispatch has a delay and a certain deviation. In order to solve the above problems, an emergency communication command and scheduling algorithm based on pattern recognition is proposed. The delay time constraint is determined by the time interval calculation, and the channel line selection is performed on the basis of the established condition, and the control transmission amount is below the maximum amount supported by the selected channel line, according to the information length, the priority level is divided and the ratio of the command scheduling algorithm is studied. The proposed algorithm is compared with the traditional command and dispatch algorithm, and the balance is more than 10% higher than the traditional algorithm; the scheduling time is also saved by about 30 s, which fully proves the feasibility of the scheduling algorithm.

Keywords: Pattern recognition · Emergency communication · Scheduling algorithm

1 Introduction

Command and dispatch generally refers to a behavior that is taken when an emergency situation occurs, and can command evacuation and solve problems in an emergency. This method is referred to the pattern recognition, and the data is transmitted and monitored in real time during the recognition operation of the computer [1]. When an emergency situation occurs, the command and dispatch will be started immediately to avoid network communication and ensure the smooth communication. The general communication command and dispatch system will be established according to the scope and characteristics of communication, and the dispatching systems at all levels will be closely connected to each other, thus establishing a more complete command and dispatch system. The dispatching command system is the future intelligent information digital conference system will replace the traditional analog system, and enter digital, network and intelligent. Therefore, the communication usage rate of communication data information will become more and more frequent, and with the development of society, the communication data exchange volume will continue to increase, and the construction of dispatching command system is the inevitable development

G. Gui and L. Yun (Eds.): ADHIP 2019, LNICST 301, pp. 94–103, 2019.
https://doi.org/10.1007/978-3-030-36402-1_10

trend of search and rescue dispatching command. With the acceleration of social information, the dispatching command system has brought communication and communication environment and convenient command and dispatch operation environment to all relevant units. The construction of dispatching command system is an indispensable information infrastructure for information systems.

2 Design of Communication Command and Scheduling Algorithm

The communication command and dispatch algorithm mainly achieves four basic objectives: to ensure that the system throughput of the communication system achieves the best performance, and to ensure that the packet loss rate of the communication system is controlled within a reasonable range, to ensure that the quality of communication meets the normative standards and that the speed of communication can meet the standards for emergency handling. The pursuit of maximizing system throughput is an important aspect of wireless communication system design. In the communication scheduling [2], it is necessary to ensure that the communication system has sufficient throughput under the premise of comprehensive consideration of various factors. Packet loss rate is an important indicator to measure the reliability of communication transmission. If the communication system cannot be guaranteed to have sufficient reliability, the communication quality of the system will be greatly reduced. Reducing the packet loss rate can also effectively reduce the number of retransmissions, thereby reducing the load on the transmitter. The emergency communication command and dispatcher issues dispatching instructions during operation, and then each line and equipment implements scheduling processing. Therefore, the communication command and dispatch needs to coordinate the quota allocation of each line, select the optimal scheduling path, and avoid the conflict in the execution of the scheduling process. In the process of efficient scheduling of emergency information resources for pattern recognition, the emergency task set in the communication line is first expressed, and the value density of the emergency task is calculated. The priority of all emergency task scheduling sequences in the line is obtained, the resource priority is calculated, the emergency information resource scheduling criterion is given, and the emergency information resource is efficiently scheduled. Data communication mainly includes three parts: communication source system, communication transmission system and communication destination system. The main function of the source system is to encode the data of the input end data. The main function of the transmission system is to transmit and receive the signal. The main function of the destination system is to decode the analog signal at the output end. The access network scheduling algorithm ensures the reasonable state distribution of the data stream, mainly for the source system of the pattern recognition data communication and the destination system for scheduling. Through the data transmission mechanism, the modem capability is improved to ensure stable data communication in the whole frequency band. Its pattern recognition scheduling communication data structure is shown in Fig. 1.

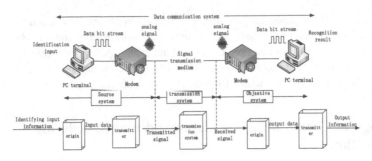

Fig. 1. Pattern recognition data communication structure

It can be seen from the figure that the structure of pattern recognition data communication is divided into three layers, which is more perfect than the previous communication structure, and this structure provides the basic security for pattern recognition emergency communication scheduling.

2.1 Determining the Delay Time Constraint

The main factor of delay generation is limited by the line resources, and is related to the transmission protocol, topology, line load, node driving method, information frame loss and other factors used in the communication control system. Its delay characteristics may be random, fixed, bounded or unbounded [3]. The stability and real-time performance of the system are constrained by the induced delay. Especially in systems with high real-time requirements, it is necessary to improve the real-time performance of the network, which is sufficient to ensure the practicability and security of the communication system. In pattern recognition, delays can generally be summarized into two categories, one is due to hardware delays caused by processor resources due to operations such as computing data. The other type is the transmission waiting delay due to the mutual constraint between the lines. Expressed as:

$$D = \sum_k D_k^c + \sum_l D_l^p \tag{1}$$

The D_k^c in the above formula represents the delay overhead spent on the k-th processor resource for the data that needs to be calculated. It is not only related to the type of specific processor resources, but also to the size of the amount of data that needs to be processed. And D_l^p represents the delay overhead incurred when the transmitted data is transmitted over the l link. In another case, when the two are on different processor resources, the delay generated is not only related to the amount of delayed data generated $c_{i,j}$, but also related to the positional relationship between the two. In any time interval t, the minimum time sent by the message i can be calculated by using Eq. 1:

$$X_i(t) = \left[\frac{t}{T_{RL}}\right] w_i \tag{2}$$

In Eq. 1, TRL represents the channel rotation period, and w_i represents the assigned weight, and each message in the message set has sufficient time to be transmitted within its allowed minimum delay time.

2.2 Channel Line Selection

In the emergency command and dispatch of pattern recognition, in the case of an emergency, the line that is normally operated and not occupied by other signals should be selected for grooming. Each line should be reasonably evenly distributed to avoid congestion, local conflicts, etc. The pattern recognition channel line is shown in Fig. 2.

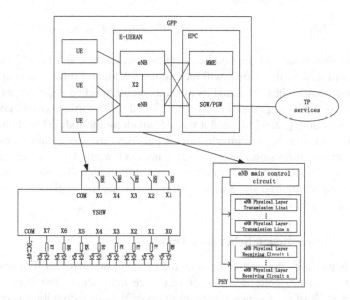

Fig. 2. Channel wiring diagram

It can be seen from the figure that there are multiple lines running in parallel in the entire communication system, and physical equipment is used to detect the line quality in the process of command and dispatch. Determining the allocation of the line to be used for scheduling after the line channel does not have a hardware failure, in the distributed scheduling algorithm, each node can only generate conflict-free scheduling plans and aggregation trees based on local information, such as its own information and surrounding one-hop neighbor information. This undoubtedly brings greater challenges to the MLASDC problem [4]. In order for nodes to avoid conflicts locally, this chapter first investigates the causes of conflicts. Under the protocol interference model, when scheduling node u, the following two conflicts may occur: The parent node $p(u)$ of node u is located within the transmission radius of a certain sending node, and this conflict is called a negative conflict; A node that is receiving a packet is located within the transmission radius of node u. This conflict is called a positive conflict. Assume that node x: has generated its own transmission schedule, ready to send the packet to node has generated its own transmission schedule, ready to send the packet to node y2 at time slot 3. To handle negative conflicts, this chapter defines a special set, $F2R(u)$ (forbidding the collection of time slots). For each node $u \in V$, $F2R(u)$ stores a set of time slots in which node u cannot be selected as a parent node by other nodes, such as a time slot in which u's neighbor node v is transmitting. This collection can be updated by the following formula:

y2 at time slot 3. To handle negative conflicts, this chapter defines a special set, F2R(u) (forbidding the collection of time slots). For each node $u \in V$, $F2R(u)$ stores a set of time slots in which node u cannot be selected as a parent node by other nodes, such as a time slot in which u's neighbor node v is transmitting. This collection can be updated by the following formula:

$$F2R(u) = \{t | t = sch(v) \cdot t(v), \forall v \in NB(u) \ \& \ sch(v) \in S\} \tag{3}$$

After the neighbor node v of the node u completes scheduling and broadcasts its own scheduling information, the node u will receive the scheduling information and update $F2R(u)$. When node x2 has generated its own transmission schedule, it is ready to send the packet to node YZ at time slot 3, and the "Schedule" information will contain the transmission schedule [x2, y2, 3], and it will be broadcast by node x2 to its neighbors. When the node y1 receives the information, it puts the time slot 3 into its own set of forbidden reception time slots. In this case, if node x1 wants to select y1 as its own parent node in time slot 3, y1 will directly return a "Forbidden" message, prohibiting x1 from selecting y1 in time slot 3 as its own parent node. In this way, congestion and negative conflicts are avoided.

2.3   Control Transmission Scheduling Quota

If the quota is too large during the transmission process, problems such as overheating of components and unstable processor performance may occur. Therefore, the command and dispatch of emergency communication of pattern recognition needs to calculate and control the maximum amount of scheduling that the line can bear, ensuring that the communication information can smoothly pass through the channel line and maintain the normal operation of the entire schedule. In each priority packet queue, when the queue is not empty, counting starts, and for each data, the queue length is incremented by 1, until the operation of the queue transmission is performed. The maximum number of frames sent by the transmitted data in one time slot is N. In the process of transmitting data, the number of transmitted messages is subtracted [5]. The determining rule of the maximum number of transmitted information N is to determine the maximum number of bytes that can be sent in one time slot according to the network transmission rate. The number of bytes sent by N messages should be no more than the maximum number of bytes, and the maximum amount can be obtained. The calculation of the maximum amount will not only affect the rate of transmission, so the transmission rate factor needs to be considered in the calculation.

2.4 Priority Ratio

To control the amount of scheduling, the order of scheduling is arranged, and the arrangement is calculated and assigned according to the priority level. The specific priority comparison process is shown in Fig. 3.

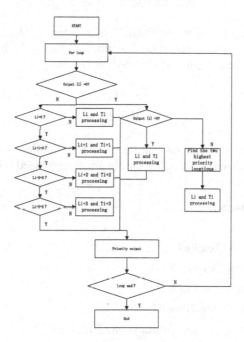

Fig. 3. Output priority flow chart

Priority allocation: set the information period to x, the information arrival time to y, the information deadline to z, and the comprehensive evaluation period to T. The comprehensive evaluation time is a combination of information cycle time, information arrival time, and information deadline by weight distribution, in order to assign priorities. Let the pre-overrun length flag of each queue be lengthflag(i), if a queue length exceeds the preset value, then lengthflag$(i) = 0$; Otherwise, lengthflag$(i) = 1$. Similarly, the pre-timeout flag lengthflag(i) can be set, timeout lengthflag$(i) = 0$; no timeout is lengthflag$(i) = 1$; The information priority is determined based on the obtained comprehensive evaluation time T, and the information frame priority is allocated in comparison with the clock cycle division section.

2.5 Command and Dispatch

The shortest path selection process divides the communication node into five parts: source node, untagged node, temporary marker node, permanent marker node, and multiple target nodes. Let S be the set of the end points of the shortest path that has been found from S_0, initialize it to an empty set, and let i be the number of shortest paths that have been searched, and set its initial value to 0. Use d to indicate the shortest possible distance from S_O, to the end point v_i, take the initialization value and select v_j to:

$$d_i = L_{(s_o,v_i)} \cdot W_{(s_o,v_i)}, v_i \in V \tag{4}$$

$$d_j = \min\{d_i | v_i \in V - S\} \tag{5}$$

It satisfies $Dis(S_O, v_j) < R$, where $Dis(i, j)$ is a distance calculation function, representing the linear distance from node i to node j, then v_i is the end point of the shortest path starting from S_O, if $v_j \in D$ is let $i = i+1$, let

$$\begin{aligned} S &= S \cup \{v_j\} \\ V &= V - \{v_j\} \end{aligned} \tag{6}$$

The emergency communication command and scheduling algorithm for pattern recognition can be realized by selecting the final path combined with the transmission quota:

```
public Insert()
{
Input1=new TextField(15);
input2=new TextField(15);
input3=new TextField(15);
Panel panel=new JPanelU;
panel.setLayout(new GridLayout(5,2));
paneLadd(new Label(', circuit'),BorderLayout.CENTER);
panel.add(input1);
paneLadd(new Label(', limit'),BorderLayout.CENTER);
panel. add(input2);
panel.add(new Label(', priority"),BorderLayout. CENTER;
panel.add(input3) ;
panel.add(new Label(', live location"));
Connection con=DriverManager.getConnection
(dbURL,user,password);//get connected
Statement st=con. createStatement();//obtain Statement object
ResultSet rs=st. executeQuery(sqlStr);//operation dispatching
con.close(); //close junction
}
```

3   Simulation Experiment

The simulation experiments were carried out using all the communication information of the same pattern recognition system. In the context of Grid Sim, a simulation platform for emergency communication command and dispatch of pattern recognition is built. Grid Sim is a simulation tool for analog communication systems. The parameter settings of the simulation platform are shown in Table 1.

Table 1. Simulation platform parameter configuration

Configuration item	Configuration parameter
Integrated environment	Eelipse6. 5, jdk1.5
Communication Systems	LTE, FDD, 5 M bandwidth
Operating system	Windows xp32bit
Processor	Intel (r) Core (tm)2 Duo CP, 2.53 Ehz
Channel environment	Ethernet connection, ideal channel
Database	Oracle9i

Use Grid Sim to set up 6 resources with different processing rates and prices, and set the local resource scheduling policy to SPACE_SHARED. And six task sets are formed to conduct experiments, and the task set includes the number of tasks in the order of 300, 600, 900, 1600, 2400, 2600. In the experiment, a value is randomly taken in the interval [5, 20] as the length of the information, and the unit is MIP (mega instruction).

3.1   Scheduling Equilibrium Experiment

In order to ensure the rigor of the experiment, the traditional command and dispatch method is adopted. As a comparison of experimental argumentation, the equilibrium of the algorithm scheduling is compared and analyzed. The experimental result curve is shown in Fig. 4.

From the experimental results in the figure, it can be concluded that with the increase of the number of tasks, the balance of emergency communication command and dispatch using pattern recognition algorithm is gradually increased. After smoothing, it is about 10% higher than the traditional scheduling method, thus greatly ensuring the stability of scheduling.

3.2   Scheduling Time Experiment

The same hardware equipment and data information are used in the experiment, which is compared with the traditional command and dispatch method. The experimental comparison results are shown in Fig. 5.

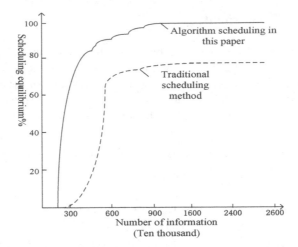

Fig. 4. Schematic diagram of scheduling equilibrium experiment results

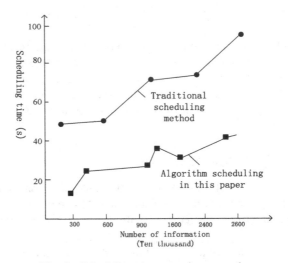

Fig. 5. Scheduling time experiment results

It can be seen from the figure that as the scheduling data increases, the time required for the scheduling process increases gradually. However, compared with the traditional scheduling method, the command scheduling algorithm proposed in this paper always saves about 30 s of scheduling time and solves the problem of scheduling delay in the past.

4 Conclusion

In response to the increasing use of pattern recognition in various industries, the requirements for emergency communication systems in pattern recognition have gradually increased. Through design and research, the algorithm which is more in line with the emergency standard is proposed, which greatly increases the scheduling efficiency. It is a good reference for the research of scheduling algorithms in the emergency communication system of pattern recognition in China.

Acknowledgments. National Key R&D Program (2018YFC0809105)

References

1. Zhao, J., Yu, Z., Xu, F., et al.: Time-efficient scheduling for multi-path routing in WSNs. J. China Acad. Electron. Inf. Technol. **13**(3), 35–39 (2018)
2. Hu, Z., Xu, J., Xia, J.: Design and implementation of communication platform based on ARINC659 bus node. J. Xi'an Polytech. Univ. **30**(03), 316–321 (2016)
3. Wang, X.: Efficient scheduling algorithm simulation grid space emergency information resources. Comput. Simul. **34**(9), 292–295 (2017)
4. Li, Z.: Research on ship scheduling algorithm for emergency. Ship Sci. Technol. **41**(2), 49–51 (2018)
5. Wang, J., Wu, C., Song, W., et al.: Research on emergency communication system for earthquake rescue site. China Earthq. Eng. J. **39**(5), 214–219 (2017)

Multi-source Heterogeneous Data Acquisition Algorithm Design Different Time Periods

Jun Li[✉] and Jun Xing

Shenzhen Academy of Inspection and Quarantine, Shenzhen, China
zwm20171028@sina.com

Abstract. The traditional algorithm was affected by dynamic error and data loss, resulting in low efficiency of collection. In order to solve this problem, a time division collection algorithm based on data format transformation was proposed. According to the data format conversion process multi-source heterogeneous configuration files, and access to the content of the whole configuration file and the GDAL, according to the results of the configuration process design algorithm, under the constraints of the input data for approximate operation, minimize the objective function, through the fixed matrix other factors influence on partial derivatives root, period of time the multi-source heterogeneous data acquisition algorithm design. The experimental results showed that the maximum collection efficiency of the algorithm can reach 90%, which provided an effective solution for scientific researchers to solve the problems caused by differences in data format.

Keywords: Multiple source · Heterogeneous data · Period of time · Acquisition · Dynamic error · Packet loss

1 Introduction

Information physics fusion system has a wide range of applications, and the complexity of object orientation determines that the information it obtains in the physical world is heterogeneous. In recent years, information acquisition means have been increasing, such as ocean monitoring instruments, ocean satellite remote sensing, global buoy program, numerical model calculation, etc. On the one hand, the data obtained by these means enriches the data information and provides a very favorable foundation for research in various fields. On the other hand, it also brings about a variety of problems in data formats in various fields. Therefore, how to read these data is one of the primary problems that researchers need to solve [1].

In view of this problem, a multi-source heterogeneous data integration system is constructed by using traditional algorithm. However, users can only access the data in the system, but still cannot process their own data formats.

For the above problems and the deficiencies of existing integrated systems, a time-division acquisition algorithm of multi-source heterogeneous data is proposed [2]. For project developers, this can reduce the workload of development and shorten the development cycle, and for users or data researchers, it is convenient for them to conduct follow-up processing of data.

G. Gui and L. Yun (Eds.): ADHIP 2019, LNICST 301, pp. 104–111, 2019.
https://doi.org/10.1007/978-3-030-36402-1_11

2 Based on Data Format Conversion Algorithm Design

Since the storage mechanism of multi-source heterogeneous data format is different, some data formats can be read through the same third-party library function, so they can be processed together [3]. The entire data format transformation process is shown in Fig. 1.

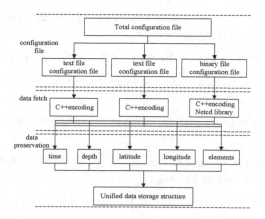

Fig. 1. Data format conversion process

It can be seen from Fig. 1 that when using the data conversion system to process data, the multi-source heterogeneous data format is divided into 4 categories for interpretation, which are text file classes, mainly including text format files. Binary file classes, mainly including binary format files; GDAL files, mainly including NetCDF format files, rattle format files, HDF format files (including HDF4 and HDF5 formats), remote sensing image files; MATLAB file, mainly including Mat format file [4].

2.1 File Configuration

The configuration files in the system are divided into two parts: one is the general configuration file, whose purpose is to convey what type of data the system will analyze next; The other part is the sub-configuration file corresponding to the 4 class files. The sub-configuration file mainly completes the description of each file class [5]. Take the GDAL file class as an example to detail the specific contents of the config-uration file:

(1) the general configuration file is as follows:

File type: 2 (default in this system: the number "0" stands for text file class, the number "1" stands for binary file class, the number "2" stands for GDAL file class, and the number "3" stands for MATLAB file class);

(2) the sub(GDAL file class) configuration file is as follows:

File path: that is, the path of the file to be read (you can choose to read individual files or all files under a folder);

Depth file: that is, the depth file corresponding to the file to be read. If it exists, write the depth file name; otherwise, write "0";

① Name of the time variable: the name of the time set in the file to be read;

Time range: that is, the data reader can freely choose the time range of reading within the time range of the file to be read;

② Name of the depth variable: the name of the depth set in the file to be read;

Depth range: that is, the data reader can freely choose the depth range to read within the depth range of the file to be read;

③ Name of the latitude variable: the name of the middle latitude set of the file to be read;

Latitude range: that is, the data reader can freely choose the latitude range to read in the latitude range of the file to be read;

④ Name of the depth variable: that is, the name of the depth set in the file to be read;

Depth range: that is, the data reader can freely choose the depth range to read within the depth range of the file to be read;

⑤ Name of the slave latitude variable: that is, the name of the middle latitude set of the file to be read;

Latitude range: that is, the data reader can freely choose the latitude range to read in the latitude range of the file to be read;

⑥ Longitude variable name: the name of longitude set in the file to be read;

Longitude range: that is, the data reader can freely choose the longitude range read within the longitude range of the file to be read;

⑦ The name of a scheduled element: the name of the set of variables to be read in the file to be read.

⑧ Proportion factor: the scale factor of the set of variables to be read;

⑨ Null value: that is, invalid value data in the set of variables to be read;

⑩ Bonus units: units of the set of variables to be read [6].

2.2   Algorithm Design

In the case of data format transformation, the multi-source heterogeneous file is configured and the time-division acquisition algorithm of multi-source heterogeneous data is designed according to the configuration results [7]. The parameters and operation symbols used in the algorithm are as follows:

λ is the set of all relational matrices Rxy, where $x, y \in \{1, \ldots, r\}$ is; Z^t constraint matrix, where $t \in \{1, 2, \ldots, \max_x t_x\}$; The rank of p_q matrix, where $q \in \{1, \ldots, r\}$; A, B factor matrix.

The specific design of algorithm flow is as follows:

Start with x from 1 to r to initialize BX.

Repeat the following process until convergence:

Construct matrix C and D according to the above definition.

Obtain the value of E according to the calculation result of formula $E = (B^T B)^{-1} B^T C B (B^T B)^{-1}$.

Start x from 1 to r, and set B_x^e to the 0 matrix.

Start x from 1 to r, and set B_x^d to the 0 matrix.

For each relation matrix ruler C_{xy} belonging to λ, perform the following operations:

$$B_x^e + = \left(C_{xy} B_y E_{xy}^T \right)^+ + B_x \left(E_{xy} B_y^T B_y E_{xy}^T \right)^- \tag{1}$$

$$B_x^d + = \left(C_{xy} B_y E_{xy}^T \right)^- + B_x \left(E_{xy} B_y^T B_y E_{xy}^T \right)^+ \tag{2}$$

$$B_x^e + = \left(C_{xy}^T B_y E_{xy}^T \right)^+ + B_x \left(E_{xy}^T B_y^T B_y E_{xy} \right)^- \tag{3}$$

$$B_x^d + = \left(C_{xy}^T B_y E_{xy}^T \right)^- + B_x \left(E_{xy}^T B_y^T B_y E_{xy} \right)^+ \tag{4}$$

T to 1 to $\max_x t_x$, do the following:

X from 1 to r, do the following:

$$B_x^e + = [\theta_x^t]^- B_x \tag{5}$$

$$B_x^d + = [\theta_x^t]^+ B_x \tag{6}$$

constructing matrix structure:

$$B = B \circ Diag \left(\sqrt{\frac{B_1^e}{B_1^d}}, \sqrt{\frac{B_2^e}{B_2^d}}, \ldots, \sqrt{\frac{B_r^e}{B_r^d}} \right) \tag{7}$$

For the initialization of each B_x, the random hcol algorithm is adopted in this algorithm: the value of each column of B_x is calculated by averaging the elements of the random subset of the column in ruler C_{xy}. And for the matrix A, you don't have to initialize it, because it can be calculated from the value of the matrix B.

The time-division acquisition algorithm based on data format transformation performs approximate operation on the input data according to the constraint conditions to minimize the objective function, where the objective function is:

$$\min_{B \geq 0} J(B : E) = \sum C_{xy} \in \lambda \left\| C_{xy} - B_x E_{xy} B_y^T \right\|^2 \tag{8}$$

The functions II*ll and tr(*) respectively represent the f-normal form and the trace function, and λ is the set of all relationships between objects. The missing relational matrix is replaced by the 0 matrix. Although it can achieve the purpose of the objective function optimization, it will also bring an unexpected relational matrix in the factorization and distort the relationships between objects.

To solve the minimization problem, the factor matrix needs to be initialized first, and then keep E unchanged, change B or keep B unchanged, change the value of E and iterate over them until the expression converges. Changing the values of B_x and E_{xy} is the local optimum of their convergence to the optimization problem. By fixing the value of one of B and E and the influence of Lagrangian other matrix factors on partial derivative roots, the multiplication and updating rules of relational matrix were changed, thus completing the design of time-division acquisition algorithm for multi-source heterogeneous data.

3   Experiment

To test the validity of the algorithm based on the data format conversion, the following experiment has been conducted.

3.1   Experiment Platform Design

NS2 and MATLAB r2000b are used as experimental platforms. NS2 is a powerful network simulation platform, while MATLAB has a powerful matrix processing function. NS2 is an object-oriented network simulator, which is essentially a discrete event simulator. NS2 itself has a virtual clock, and all events are driven by discrete events. At present, NS2 can be used for simulation of different IP networks, and some simulations have been implemented: (1) network transmission protocols such as TCP/UDP; (2) generate business source traffic; (3) routing queue management mechanism, etc. Since NS2 is open source, some research groups continue to enrich the component library, making it more advantageous. As shown in Fig. 2, NS2 structure diagram introduces each component.

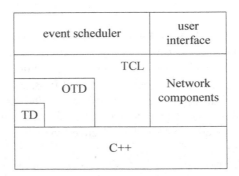

Fig. 2. NS2 structure diagram

The development language of NS2 is C++ and Otcl. Objects and variables in both C++ and Otcl are related by Tcl. C++ classes and objects are compiled classes and objects, whereas OTcl classes and objects are called explanatory classes and explanatory objects.

3.2 Experimental Results and Analysis

The traditional algorithm is compared with the time-division acquisition algorithm based on data format conversion in the case of dynamic error and packet loss, and the results are as follows.

3.2.1 Dynamic Error

The comparison and analysis results of the two algorithms under dynamic error are shown in Fig. 3.

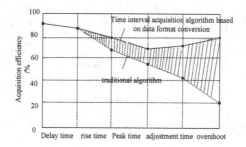

Fig. 3. Comparison and analysis results of acquisition efficiency of the two algorithms under dynamic error

As can be seen from the trend of broken lines in Fig. 3, the accuracy of the initial analysis results of the two algorithms can reach 90%. When the dynamic response is within the delay period, the efficiency of the traditional algorithm is the same as that of the time-division acquisition algorithm based on data format transformation, both of which are 85%. When the dynamic response is within the rising period, the collection efficiency of the traditional algorithm is affected by the regional environment, resulting in a low collection efficiency of 65%. Although the time-division acquisition algorithm based on data format transformation will not be affected by the regional environment, the collection efficiency will be reduced to 80% as the experiment is controlled under the dynamic environment. When the dynamic response is within the peak period, the collection efficiency of the traditional algorithm reaches 55%, while the collection efficiency of the time-division acquisition algorithm based on data format transformation can reach 70%. When the dynamic response is within the adjustment period, the adjustment effect of the traditional algorithm is poor, resulting in the acquisition efficiency falling to 41%. The efficiency of time - segment acquisition algorithm based on data format conversion increased to 75%. When the dynamic response is in the overshoot process, the acquisition efficiency of the traditional algorithm has reached the minimum, at 20%. And the efficiency of the time - segment acquisition algorithm based on data format conversion continues to increase, reaching 80%. According to the analysis results, the traditional algorithm is affected by the regional environment and cannot effectively analyze errors in the dynamic response process, resulting in a low collection efficiency. The time - segment acquisition algorithm can avoid the influence of regional environment and maintain high efficiency.

3.2.2   Packet Loss

The comparison and analysis results of the acquisition efficiency of the two algorithms in the case of packet loss are shown in Fig. 4.

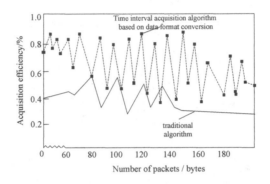

Fig. 4. Comparison and analysis results of acquisition efficiency of the two algorithms in the case of packet loss

According to the comparison diagram in Fig. 4, when the number of lost packets is less than or equal to 60 bytes, the maximum collection efficiency of the time-division acquisition algorithm based on data format conversion is 0.87, while the maximum value of the traditional algorithm is 0.43. When the number of packets is greater than 60 and less than or equal to 143 bytes, the maximum collection efficiency of the time-division acquisition algorithm based on data format conversion is 0.9, while the maximum value of the traditional algorithm is 0.6. When the number of lost packets is greater than 143 and less than 160 bytes, the maximum collection efficiency of the time-division acquisition algorithm based on data format conversion is 0.89, while the maximum value of the traditional algorithm is 0.4. When the number of lost packets is greater than or equal to 143 and less than 200 bytes, the maximum collection efficiency of the time-division acquisition algorithm based on data format conversion is 0.82, while the maximum value of the traditional algorithm is 0.39. According to the analysis results, when packet loss occurs in the network, the time-division acquisition algorithm based on data format conversion is more efficient.

3.3   Experimental Conclusions

According to the packet loss situation, the two algorithms can obtain the following comparison results: when the number of packet loss is less than or equal to 60 bytes, the maximum collection efficiency difference between the two algorithms is 0.44. When the number of lost packets is greater than 60 and less than or equal to 143 bytes, the maximum collection efficiency of the two algorithms differs by 0.3. At that time, when the number of packet loss was greater than 143 and less than 160 bytes, the maximum value difference of acquisition efficiency of the two algorithms was 0.49. When the number of lost packets is greater than or equal to 143 and less than 200 bytes, the maximum collection efficiency of the two algorithms differs by 0.43. Therefore, the design of time - segment acquisition algorithm based on data format transformation is reasonable.

4 Conclusions

The design method of time-division acquisition algorithm based on data format transformation can still maintain a good collection efficiency under the problems of dynamic error and data loss. By summarizing the typical cases in the daily combined test, it can be seen that the maximum difference between the collection efficiency of the algorithm and that of the traditional algorithm is 0.71, which has significant application effect.

Acknowlegements. National Key R&D Program of China (2017YFF0211100). Shenzhen Science and Technology Project (KJYY20160229141621130).

References

1. Liu, S., Li, N., Fu, J.: A peak-valley time division model based on high-dimensional norming and SGHSA algorithm. China Electr. Power **51**(1), 179–184 (2018)
2. Li, B., Huang, J., Wu, Y., et al.: Short-term load forecasting of typhoon based on meteorological information particle reduction. J. Electr. Technol. **33**(9), 2068–2076 (2018)
3. Wang, S., Shi, C., Qian, G., et al.: Chaotic time series prediction based on fractional order maximum correlation entropy algorithm. J. Phys. **20**(1), 248–255 (2018)
4. Liu, C., Hu, N., Guo, Z., et al.: Numerical simulation of wave field in viscous fluid biphasic VTI medium based on fractional time derivative constant Q viscoelastic constitutive relation. Geophysics **19**(6), 24–25 (2018)
5. Shi, J., Zhang, J.: Vehicle routing problem model and algorithm for batch distribution with stochastic travel time. Comput. Appl. **38**(2), 573–581 (2018)
6. Wang, Z., Yi, Lin, Lin, Y.: Similarity measurement of time series based on coefficient matrix arc differential. Comput. Eng. **20**(2), 9–16 (2018)
7. Wang, Y., Lian, C.H., Jin, Q.: Single quantum bit storage time refreshes the world record - single ion qubit. Physics with more than 10 minutes of coherent time, **47**(5), 320–322 (2018)

Research on Data Security Acquisition System Based on Artificial Intelligence

Yingjian Kang[✉], Lei Ma, and Leiguang Liu

Telecommunication Engineering Institute, Beijing Polytechnic, Beijing, China
kangyingjian343@163.com

Abstract. The traditional acquisition system had low collection efficiency and poor acquisition accuracy. In order to solve the above problems, a new data security acquisition system was studied. Artificial intelligence technology was introduced to design the hardware and software parts of the system. The hardware part mainly designed the system A/D acquisition module, serial data acquisition module and parallel port communication module. The software part was divided into three steps: data screening, data analysis and data acquisition. By comparing with the traditional system, the actual working effect of the system was verified. The experimental results showed that the data security acquisition system based on artificial intelligence had higher collection efficiency and better precision. The system was worthy of recommendation.

Keywords: Artificial intelligence · Secure acquisition · Acquisition system · Data acquisition

1 Introduction

There are usually two explanations for data collection: one refers to terminal computer equipment such as inventory machines and handheld computers; the other refers to software for network data collection. The equipment of the data acquisition system refers to the process of automatically collecting information from analog and digital units to be tested such as sensors and other devices to be tested. The data acquisition system is a flexible [1], user-defined measurement system that combines computer-based measurement software and hardware products to collect content such as web pages and forums in batches. The system can directly save the collected data to a database or publish to the network. The original webpage can be automatically collected according to the rules set by the user, the content required in the format webpage can be obtained, and the data can be processed [2].

It mainly has the following characteristics: ① System with strong software and hardware support. All the hardware and software resources of the general-purpose microcomputer system can be used to support the system to work. ② With independent development capabilities [3]. ③ The application configuration of the software and hardware of the system is relatively small, and the cost of the system is relatively high. However, when the secondary development is performed, the software and hardware expansion capabilities are better. ④ The reliability of the operation in the industrial environment is poor, and the environment for placing is high [4]. ⑤ The system does

G. Gui and L. Yun (Eds.): ADHIP 2019, LNICST 301, pp. 112–119, 2019.
https://doi.org/10.1007/978-3-030-36402-1_12

not have the ability to develop independently. Therefore, the software and hardware development of the system must rely on development tools. ⑥ The software and hardware design and configuration scale of the system are all based on the principle of meeting the functional requirements of the data acquisition system. Therefore, the software and hardware applications of the system have a configuration ratio close to 1, and have the best cost performance. ⑦ The system is reliable and easy to use. The application runs in ROM without being destroyed by external interference, and the system immediately enters the user state after power-on [5].

2 Research on Hardware of Data Security Acquisition System Based on Artificial Intelligence

In the campus network performance data acquisition system, the acquisition system needs to transmit the analog parameters such as motor speed and current loop to the monitoring host on the one hand, and collect various parameters and image data of the lower computer on the other hand. At the same time, the monitoring host also sends various control signals to the lower computer. In order to balance various needs, the design combines analog and digital acquisition methods, which can realize 8-channel A/D sampling, 2-channel serial data acquisition and 2-channel parallel data acquisition. The block diagram of the system is shown in Fig. 1:

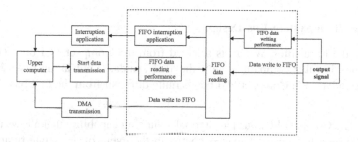

Fig. 1. Data security acquisition system hardware based on artificial intelligence

2.1 Acquisition Module Design

The acquisition system uses the digital signal processing chip TMS320F2812 as the control core, and the F2812 has a maximum operating frequency of 150 MHz. In addition to a wealth of internal memory resources, it also has a variety of peripheral resources such as ADC, SCI, SPI, etc. The design utilizes its ADC and SCI modules for analog signal and serial digital signal acquisition [6]. Data collection for parallel data is directly exchanged with the host without going through the DSP. Because the host and peripheral speed do not match, the dual-port RAM chip IDT70V24 is selected as the data cache. It is a high-speed, low-power dual-port RAM with a storage capacity of 8 k bytes. The logic control of the system is completed by CPLD chip XC95108. Its main functions are PCI local bus arbitration and address decoding. The implementation of the three acquisition modules is as follows:

(1) A/D acquisition module. The analog signal is sampled using the F2812's own digital-to-analog converter module ADC. The ADC has 16 analog input channels with two built-in S/H (sampler keeper), conversion accuracy of 12 bit, maximum conversion rate of 12.5 MSPS, and support for data input ranging from 0 to 3 V [7].

(2) Serial data acquisition module. F2812's SCI module has two serial communication interfaces, which can be configured to 65,536 different baud rates, with parity check mark, can work in half-duplex or full-duplex mode, can be set to interrupt or query mode [8]. In addition, SCI has two enhanced features: ① Both transmit and receive have separate FIFOs with a FIFO depth of 16 words and the trigger stage can be configured to any number within 16. This flexible setting is very convenient for practical use, because the data length collected by the lower computer is often not an integer multiple of 16, and the FIFO trigger level is set according to the data length, so that one frame of data can be transmitted and processed in time; ② The baud rate can be automatically detected, which is very suitable in the case of the unknown communication terminal baud rate or the need to replace the communication terminal.

(3) Parallel communication module. For signals with a large amount of data transmission such as image signals, it is necessary to use parallel port communication. The acquisition system provides two parallel ports, the data width is 8 bits, and the address width is 8 bits. They exchange data with the host through the dual port RAM.

2.2 Acquisition System Bus Design

The bus of the acquisition system is selected from the Compact PCI bus. The Compact PCI bus is fully compatible with the PCI standard, but as an open industrial computer standard, the Compact PCI bus is quite different from the PCI bus. It mainly reflects in:

① The Compact PCI bus has thermal switching capability that allows the entire system to replace damaged boards in the event of an uninterrupted power supply, which is critical for systems with high reliability requirements.

② The Compact PCI bus uses a European card (Eurocard) for better mechanical properties. The assembly technology of the European plug-in card is very mature. The plug-in card is inserted vertically into the chassis to facilitate ventilation and heat dissipation.

③ High-density pinhole bus connectors are completely airtight and offer higher shock resistance and reliability than desktop PCI slots.

④ The Compact PCI backplane accommodates up to eight cards and doubles the original PCI specification to better meet the needs of industrial systems.

2.3 Compact PCI Interface Design

At present, many PCI protocol chips also support hot swap, so that the original PCI bus-based hardware system can be easily ported to the CPCI framework without major modifications in hardware and software. This design uses the PCI9054 from PLX, which complies with the PCI 2.2 specification and the CPCI 2.1 hot swap specification. For the hot swap specification of CPCI, PCI9054 provides the pin ENUM# and LEDon/LEDin. The activation of ENUM# indicates that the plug-in status of the card is about to change. The LEDon/LEDin pin is used to drive an external LED to indicate the current system software layer connection and disconnection. The PCI9054 also provides a hot swap control register HS_CSR to record board status and control status. The definition of HS_CSR is shown in Table 1:

Table 1. Hot swap control status register hs_csr.

Position	Explain
0	Retain
1	EMUM
2	Retain
3	EMUM
4	Retain
5	Retain
6	EMUM
7	Retain

When the board is inserted, HS_CSR [3] is set to 1, the blue light is lit, PCI9054 sets HS–_CSR [7] to 1, and the ENUM# signal is activated to cause an interrupt. The interrupt is cleared until the device driver is installed, HS_CSR [3] is set to 0, and the blue light is extinguished. When the board is unplugged, HS_CSR [6] is set to 1. The activation of the ENUM# signal causes an interrupt. After the host unloads the driver, HS_CSR [3] is set to 1. Lights up in blue, indicating that the board can be safely removed.

2.4   Hot Swap Power Management

The signals used for hot plug control in the CPCI specification are: BD_SEL#, HEALTHY, and PCI_RST#. The pins of the connector J1 of the CPCI bus are divided into a long pin, a medium long pin, and a short pin. The long pin is the power and ground signal, the long pin is the PCI bus signal, and the short pin is BD_SEL# and IDSEL. When the board is inserted, the power signal is first contacted, and the PCI bus signal is precharged to 1 V. This is to reduce the impact on the PCI bus signal during hot plugging. Then there is the PCI bus signal connection, and finally the BD_SEL# signal connection. BD_SEL# is effective to indicate that the board has been plugged in and can be powered on. The card removal process is just the opposite. HEALTHY# is a signal that reflects whether the board's power supply status is good.

The LTC1646 is a hot-swap power management IC from Linear for CPCI interfaces. The LTC1646 requires two external N-channel transistors as switches to control the supply of 3.3 V and 5 V power to the board. The OFF/ON# pin of the LTC1646 is connected to BD_SEL#. When BD_SEL# is low, the transistor is turned on, and the 3.3 V and 5 V power supplies are powered up at a certain rate. PWRGD# is connected to HEALTHY#, which is low when the board power supply is within tolerance. PCI_RST# is connected to the RESETIN# pin of LTC1646. It is ORed with the HEALTHY signal to obtain the output signal RESETOUT#. This signal is connected to the RST# pin of PCI9054 as the reset signal of the CPCI board. The LTC1646 provides an output pin, PRECHARGE, which is connected to the bus signal of the PCI9054 to pre-charge the bus signal during board insertion and removal.

3   Research on Data Security Acquisition System Software Based on Artificial Intelligence

Modifications to hardware operating parameters are achieved by means of interrupts. Customize a 16-bit control register User_CSR with the upper 4 bits used as the command word and the lower 12 bits used as the control word. When the application writes data to User_CSR through the PCI bus, the CPLD sends an interrupt signal to the external interrupt pin XINT2 of F2812 through the decoding logic. The software workflow is shown in Fig. 2 below:

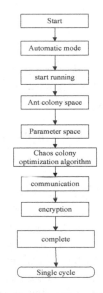

Fig. 2. Software workflow

After the F2812 responds to the interrupt, it reads the value of User_CSR, determines which parameter needs to be modified according to its command word, and then obtains a new parameter value according to its control word, and writes it to the corresponding register to complete the modification. Due to space limitations, the specific implementation method is explained by taking the modification of the SCIA setting as an example. User_CSR defines SCIA as follows (Table 2):

Table 2. Partial definition of User_CSR.

Bit15 ~ 12	11 ~ 0
Command word	Control word
0000	SCI
0001	SCIA
0010	SCIB

The hardware configuration that can be modified through this interface has the baud rate of the SCI, the trigger level of the transceiver FIFO, and the size of the dual-port RAM space occupied by each acquisition channel.

The software work-flow can be represented by the following calculation process:

$$X = \left(r^2 k_1 + r^4 k_2\right) + \left(r^2 + 2x^2\right)P \tag{1}$$

$$Y = \left(r^2 k_1 + r^4 k_2\right) + \left(r^2 + 2x^2\right)P \tag{2}$$

$$Z = \left(r^2 k_1 + r^4 k_2\right) + \left(r^2 + 2x^2\right)P \tag{3}$$

In the above formula, X, Y, and Z respectively represent the three-dimensional coordinates of the acquired data, r represents the acquisition coefficient, k_1 represents the parent band constant, k_2 represents the child constant, and P represents the detection constant.

4 Experimental Results

In order to test the actual working effect of the acquisition system designed in this paper, a comparative experiment was designed.

4.1 Experimental Parameters

The experimental parameters are shown in Table 3 below:

Table 3. Experimental parameters.

Project	Data
Working voltage	220 V
Working current	50 A
Work environment	UMA
Standard of execution	RE
Execute a command	TVA
Working frequency	30 MHz
Working hours	20 min

4.2   Experiment Procedure

Experiment according to the parameters set above, select the traditional acquisition system and the acquisition system of this paper to collect the data of the same computer, record the collection efficiency, and analyze the experimental results.

4.3   Experimental Results and Analysis

Collection efficiency experiment results (Fig. 3)

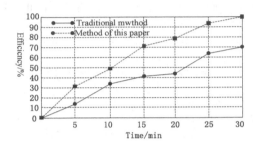

Fig. 3. Collection efficiency experiment results

Observing the above figure, when the working time is 5 min, the collection efficiency of the traditional system is 13%, and the collection efficiency of the system is 31%; When the working time is 10 min, the collection efficiency of the traditional system is 34%, and the collection efficiency of the system is 49%; When the working time is 15 min, the collection efficiency of the traditional system is 40%, and the collection efficiency of the system is 70%; When the working time is 20 min, the collection efficiency of the traditional system is 42%, and the collection efficiency of the system is 80%; When the working time is 25 min, the collection efficiency of the traditional system is 65%, and the collection efficiency of the system is 90%; When the working time is 30 min, the collection efficiency of the traditional system is 70%, and the collection efficiency of the system is 100%.

4.4   Experimental Results

According to the above experimental results, the following experimental conclusions are obtained: the artificial intelligence-based data acquisition system designer has the good ability, and process the data streams were obtained by sampling the analog signals, such as multiplication and accumulation summation operations. For example, there are two types of commonly used digital signal processing chips, one is a dedicated DSP chip, and the other is a general purpose DSP chip. The characteristics of the data acquisition system based on DSP digital signal microprocessor are as follows: high precision, good flexibility, high reliability, easy integration, time-division multiplexing, etc., but at the same time its price is high. (4) Based on hybrid computer acquisition system. This is a system structure that has developed rapidly in the field of computer applications with the emergence of 8-bit single-chip microcomputers in recent years. It is connected by a general-purpose computer (PC) and a single-chip microcomputer through a standard bus (for example, RS-485 standard). The part of the MCU and its peripheral circuits is specially configured for the functions of data acquisition and other functions. The host computer undertakes the tasks of man-machine dialogue, large-capacity calculation, recording, printing and graphic display of the data acquisition system. The computer data acquisition system based on artificial intelligence technology has the following characteristics: ① It usually has self-development capability. ② The system configuration is flexible, and it is easy to form various large and medium-sized measurement and control systems. ③ The host can be separated from the site to form various local area network systems. ④ Make full use of the host resources, but it will not occupy the full CPU time of the host.

5 Conclusions

This design uses TMS320F2812 as the control core of the data acquisition system, which satisfies the real-time requirements of the system, saves peripheral resources and improves the cost performance of the system. Applying the Compact PCI bus to the acquisition system gives the system the ability to plug in and out, improving the reliability of the entire system and adapting to the needs of the industrial work environment. The innovation of this paper is to combine the advantages of Compact PCI bus and DSP chip, which greatly improves the reliability and real-time of the system. At the same time, it provides a good interface for application developers, which facilitates the modification of hardware working parameters and improves the flexibility of the system.

References

1. Hu, D., Dong, S.: Research and simulation of information data acquisition in remote experiment, simulation of computer simulation 34(4), 186–189 (2017)
2. Li, M.: Research on rapid diagnosis of agricultural tractor engine fault based on artificial intelligence. Agric. Mechanization Res. 39(11), 229–233 (2017)
3. Gao, J.: Artificial intelligence and artificial self healing drive chemical base quality safety. Jiangsu Saf. Prod. 15(11), 13 (2017)
4. Zhang, H.: Design and implementation of artificial intelligent image detection system based on the Internet of Things. Comput. Meas. Contr. 25(2), 15–18 (2017)
5. Zhou, R., Zhang, W.: Financial technology innovation risk and control analysis based on large data, artificial intelligence, block chain research. China Manage. Inf. 12(19), 33–36 (2017)
6. He, X., Shi, W., Li, W., et al.: Based on large data large capacity power electronic system reliability research. China J. Electr. Eng. 37(1), 209–220 (2017)
7. Yan, A.Q., Tian, J.: Non coal mine mountain intelligent control system design. Metal Mine 3(2), 113–116 (2017)
8. Wang, X.: The practice of information security in the construction of mobile financial control system based on artificial intelligence 3(11), 1000–1005 (2017)

Weak Coverage Area Detection Algorithms for Intelligent Networks Based on Large Data

Ying-jian Kang[✉], Lei Ma, and Ge-cui Gong

Telecommunication Engineering Institute, Beijing Polytechnic, Beijing, China
kangyingjian343@163.com

Abstract. Aiming at the problem of abnormal location often occurring in traditional weak coverage area detection algorithm of intelligent network, a detection algorithm of weak coverage area in intelligent network based on large data is proposed. Firstly, the detection data is collected by data acquisition method based on local characteristics, and then the gray level conversion of these detection data is used to realize the pre-processing of the detection data and the detection after pre-processing. The feature vectors are used to describe the feature points so as to realize the accelerated feature matching of the detected data. Then the region feature detection of the detected data is carried out, and finally the weak coverage area detection algorithm of the intelligent network based on large data is realized. Experiments verify the detection performance of the weak coverage area detection algorithm based on large data in intelligent networks, and draw a conclusion that the detection algorithm based on large data has a much smaller probability of abnormal location than the traditional weak coverage area detection algorithm in intelligent networks.

Keywords: Bigdata · Intelligent network · Weak coverage area · Detection algorithm

1 Introduction

Due to the huge information contained in image and video, it is impossible to accurately express the information of image and video with simple words. The weak coverage area detection of intelligent network under large data needs complex calculation to analyze the semantic information and then get the regional feature information and detect it correctly [1]. In the actual use of large data, it may face various transformations [2, 3]. Therefore, how to reduce the impact of noise, how to detect the weak coverage area of intelligent network based on large data and extract the feature information needs of the weak coverage area of intelligent network have become one of the hotspots in the current computer field [4, 5].

G. Gui and L. Yun (Eds.): ADHIP 2019, LNICST 301, pp. 120–128, 2019.
https://doi.org/10.1007/978-3-030-36402-1_13

2   Weak Coverage Area Detection Algorithms for Intelligent Networks Based on Large Data

2.1   Data Acquisition

According to the type of feature information, the current data acquisition methods of weak coverage area detection algorithms in intelligent networks are mainly divided into data acquisition methods based on global features and data acquisition methods based on local features [6, 7]. Data acquisition based on global features is to describe the whole image with one feature through mathematical operations according to global features such as color and texture. Data acquisition based on local features is to find the more important region or location (called feature points) in the image by analyzing the image, and then describe each feature point with the image information around it, and get the feature value of the feature. With the application of large data more and more widely, data acquisition based on global characteristics has been unable to meet the data needs of large data detection. Therefore, as the basis of weak coverage area detection in intelligent networks, data acquisition method based on local features can effectively extract image feature information for image or video retrieval, which is widely used in image retrieval engine, network filtering and other systems.

2.2   Data Preprocessing

Intelligent network weak coverage area detection algorithm based on large data needs to convert the original image of image data into gray image after data acquisition [8]. Every point of gray image is represented by gray value. Then the integral image is calculated according to the gray image. The values of each point in the integral image are expressed by the gray sum of points in the rectangle formed by the coordinates of the origin and the current point in the gray image. For example, point D is expressed by its gray level in gray level image, while point D is expressed by the gray sum of all points in gray level area in integral image, it is shown as Fig. 1. In this way, the gray level and sigma of rectangular ABCD can be calculated conveniently by formula (1).

$$\sum = A - B - C + D \tag{1}$$

A, B, C and D are the values of points in the corresponding integral image. In the later feature detection and description, it is often necessary to calculate the gray sum of points in a rectangular region, so the integral image can reduce a lot of repeated memory access and computation. And no matter how large the area of rectangular ABCD is, after image abstraction, only four memory accesses and three addition and subtraction operations are needed to calculate the gray sum of interior points.

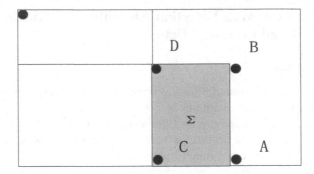

Fig. 1. Calculating the sum of the gray levels of a rectangle using an integral image

2.3   Feature Description

Characteristic vectors are used to describe feature points: centering on the feature points, sampling the area around the current feature points, and identifying some features in the area as the feature vectors of the feature points [9]. In order to ensure the stability of the feature vectors for rotation transformation, the algorithm needs to calculate the main direction of each feature point. When matching, the principal directions of the two feature points are aligned to ensure the stability of the feature for rotation transformation. The calculation method of characteristic direction is shown in Fig. 2.

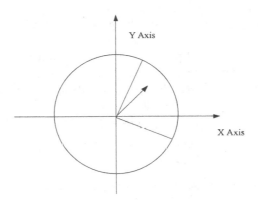

Fig. 2. Characteristic direction calculating method

(1)   With the feature as the center and the radius of 6S (s representing the scale of the feature point) as the circle, the Haar wavelet transform of the feature point is calculated and its gradient information (dx, dy) is obtained.

(2)   After obtaining the gradient information of the points around the feature points, the sum of the gradient values of all X-axis and Y-axis directions in the 60-degree sector area is calculated every 0.15 rad, and the Σdx, Σdy and the weight $\left(\sum dx\right)^2 + \left(\sum dy\right)^2$ are obtained at the end point.

(3) The main direction of the feature points is expressed by the angle between the Y axis and the X axis.

After obtaining the main direction of feature points, the weak coverage area detection algorithm based on large data in intelligent networks needs to describe these feature points and generate a vector. The calculation feature window is used to show how to calculate the description of the feature points. The arrow represents the offset direction of the point relative to the direction of the feature points, the length of the arrow represents the gradient of the point, and the circular range represents the sampling range. Its radius is determined by the size of the S parameter of the image where the feature points are located in Gaussian filtering. It is 20s (s represents the scale of the feature points). The feature window is evenly divided into 16 sub-regions. In each sub-region, 25 points are sampled for Haar wavelet transform, and each sub-region is represented by vector $(\sum dx, \sum dy, \sum |dx|, \sum |dy|)$. In this way, the calculated feature window forms a 64-dimensional vector. Finally, the vector is standardized to get the description of the current feature points. In addition, the feature description can also be achieved through data image analysis [10]. Firstly, the characteristics of data image in weak coverage area of intelligent network are analyzed, and the characteristics of the number and distribution of feature points are analyzed. It is found that the number of image and the number of feature points are basically similar to the normal distribution. The ordinates in the coordinates are used to indicate the number of feature points in the image, and the abscissa is used to indicate the number of images with the current number of feature points. It can be seen that the number of feature points in most images is between 300 and 800; some images have no feature points; the largest number contains more than 2200 feature points; an average image contains 620 feature points; the largest number of images contains 500 feature points. On the other hand, we analyze whether the distribution of feature points has obvious regularity, divide the image into blocks, and then count the probability of the occurrence of feature points in each block, that is, the number of feature points in the current block divided by the total number of feature points. For convenience, we divide the result by the maximum value in all the blocks, and we can find that the feature points are concentrated in the central region and the bottom. The probability of feature points appearing in the upper left and upper right corner is less.

2.4   Accelerated Feature Matching

Accelerated feature matching can be accelerated from two aspects, one is to reduce the scale of computation at the algorithm level, and the other is to use parallel hardware, such as multi-core processor, GPGPU or reconfigurable processor, to achieve acceleration. The main idea of software algorithm level optimization is to reduce the number of feature points extracted from each image under the condition of ensuring accuracy. Because if two images are matched in people's cognitive range, most of these images have far more matching points than reducing the number of feature points. Reducing the number of feature points per image will not affect the matching of most images. Therefore, reducing the number of feature points does not have much effect on the accuracy on the premise of maintaining the size of feature points. The commonly used process is to detect the salient region of the image by using the image salient region detection algorithm, and then to extract the features from the salient region of the image. Combining these two methods to calculate the salient map of the original image and then to extract the feature from the region of the salient map not only reduces the number of feature points and speeds up the time of feature matching but also accelerates the time of feature extraction.

2.5   Area Feature Detection

An intelligent network weak coverage detection algorithm based on big data is based on the eigenvalue of Hessian matrix. For each point, the Hessian matrix is calculated. According to the Hessian matrix, a eigenvalue can be obtained, and the point with the largest eigenvalue in a certain region is selected as the feature point. We consider that the region with the most concentrated distribution of image feature points is the salient region of the image. The Hessian matrix can quickly calculate the matrix and the largest subregion, so the distribution matrix of the feature points can be transformed and then the suitable region can be calculated by using the Hessian matrix. An Intelligent Network weak coverage region Detection algorithm based on big data the box filter method is used to approximate the eigenvalues of the Hessian matrix. The formulas are as follows:

$$Det = Dxx * Dyy - 0.81 * Dxy * Dxy \qquad (2)$$

Dxx, Dyy, Dxy is the sum of the corresponding weights of each point in the corresponding box filter. When calculating Dxy, all white points have a weight of 1, a black weight of -1 and a gray weight of 0. When calculating Dyy, the weight of white area is 1, the weight of black is -2, and the box filter corresponding to gray weight is $90°$ of box filter rotation of Dyy, the weight of white area is -1, black weight is 2, gray weight is 0. The sum of gray levels in each area can be calculated using the previously abstracted integral image. In this way, the eigenvalue Q can be easily calculated:

$$Q = (1 - A)x \qquad (3)$$

Where A is a matrix and x is a set of all eigenvalues. In order to ensure that the extracted feature points are not affected by image size transformation, big data's intelligent network weak coverage region detection algorithm adopts pyramid method to solve this problem. For an image, it is first calculated for its views with different zoom sizes, each not small and of the same size, as a layer, called a scale, and several scale put together to form a octave, Several octave groups form a pyramid. In the pyramid of each image, each octave represents an image of different sizes, while several scale in each octave are called interval, and each interval calculates the eigenvalues with different box filter sizes.

In the pyramids, for each scale, the local largest point is found as the candidate feature point, that is, the point with the largest eigenvalue of the eight sampling adjacent points. After finding the candidate feature points, for each candidate feature point, in its corresponding octave, the points adjacent to the 26 points around it, that is, the points on the cube centered on the candidate feature points, are compared, if the eigenvalues of the points are the largest. Then the candidate feature point is considered to be the feature point, otherwise it is not.

Finally, the corresponding position of the feature points in the original image is calculated from the feature points of the integral image.

2.6 Implementation of Weak Coverage Area Detection Algorithms in Intelligent Networks

The traditional weak coverage area detection algorithm in intelligent network firstly obtains three salient maps according to the brightness, color and direction characteristics of each pixel in the image, and then synthesizes three salient maps to generate salient areas of the image. After obtaining the salient region of the image, the local feature extraction algorithm is used to detect the feature points in the salient region, that is, the feature points with high contrast. Finally, the feature vectors of each feature point are calculated in the description stage. The weak coverage area detection algorithm based on large data in intelligent network assumes that the area with the most concentrated distribution of feature points in the image is the salient area of the image. In the processing of the algorithm, an adaptive matrix is generated according to the distribution of feature points in the image obtained during the feature detection stage, and then the maximum sub-matrix of the adaptive matrix, i.e. the region with the most concentrated distribution of feature points, is obtained by using the dynamic programming algorithm. The whole algorithm can quickly detect the salient area of the image with less loss to determine whether the area is the weak coverage area of the intelligent network. It reduces the computation of salient region detection algorithm while effectively reducing the feature information. The feature points detected by the weak coverage area detection algorithm of intelligent network based on large data are usually the dark spots in the bright spots or the bright spots in the dark spots in the image, and the salient areas of the image are the areas where the feature points are most distributed. Therefore, the problem of finding salient regions can be transformed into the problem of finding regions with the most concentrated distribution of feature points in images. In order to achieve the selection of salient feature regions, first of all, images need to be partitioned, and the information of feature points contained in each image sub-block is recorded in a matrix.

In order to find the region with the most concentrated distribution of feature points, we consider that we can use the algorithm of finding elements and the largest continuous region in the matrix. However, since the elements of the distribution matrix are natural numbers, the matrix needs to be processed to contain negative numbers.

For each image algorithm, we first need to get a feature point distribution matrix B of $m*n$ according to its feature point distribution. The calculation process is divided into the following steps:

(1) The coordinate position of the feature points can be obtained by detecting the feature points in the feature detection stage.

(2) The image is segmented into m*n blocks (m denotes the number of row blocks and n denotes the number of column blocks, m and N can be determined according to the actual situation);

(3) According to the coordinate position information of feature points, the number of feature points in each block area is recorded as distribution matrix B.

After obtaining the distribution matrix B of the image, it is necessary to study whether the image has the characteristics of feature point set, that is, whether a region with an area ratio of X can be found in general images, and the percentage of feature points is y (x > y). Among the 10,000 image samples, an average of 15.62% of the regions accounted for 27.22% of the features, and 36.75% of the regions accounted for 61.91 features. It shows that there are key areas in the image.

In order to obtain the region R with the most concentrated distribution of feature points in matrix B, the region R is defined as the largest sub-region in which the number of feature points per unit area is larger than the number of feature points per unit area in the whole image, generally P > 1. That is to say:

$$\max\{R|\frac{\sum_{i,j\in R}b[j][j]}{\sum_{i,j\in all}b[i][j]} \geq Q\} \tag{4}$$

Where $b[i][j]$ represents the number of feature points in column j of row i. $\sum_{i,j\in R}b[i][j]$ is the number of feature points contained in region R. $\sum_{i,j\in all}b[i][j]$ is the number of feature points of the whole image. R is the area of region R and all is the area of the whole image.

Through the above process, we can find the largest sub-region with the most dense feature points, so as to realize the detection algorithm of weak coverage area in intelligent network based on large data, which provides a feasible experimental premise and basis for this method.

3   Experimental Results and Analysis

In order to ensure the effectiveness of weak coverage area detection algorithm in intelligent networks based on large data, simulation experiments are designed. In the process of experiment, the weak coverage area of an intelligent network is taken as the experimental object to detect the weak coverage area of the intelligent network. In order to ensure the effectiveness of the experiment, the traditional algorithm is compared with the algorithm in this paper, and the experimental results are observed. All possible sub-matrices of the matrix are traversed by using the weak coverage area detection algorithm of intelligent network. First, the starting and ending positions of rows are determined, then the starting and ending positions of columns are determined, and then the sum of the sub-rectangular regions is traversed. The complexity of the algorithm is $O(m^3 * n^3)$, m for rows and n for columns.

In order to better compare the advantages and disadvantages of the algorithm, the simulation experiment uses the data set containing exception set A and B. Figure 3 is a comparison of abnormal location performance between traditional weak coverage area detection algorithm and large data-based weak coverage area detection algorithm in intelligent networks.

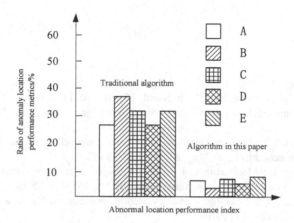

Fig. 3. Comparison of performance measures for anomaly localization

By comparing the performance of anomaly location between the traditional weak coverage area detection algorithm and the large-data-based weak coverage area detection algorithm, it can be seen that the probability of anomaly location of the large-data-based weak coverage area detection algorithm in intelligent network is much smaller than that of the traditional weak coverage area detection algorithm in intelligent network.

4   Concluding Remarks

Aiming at the problem of anomaly location which often occurs in traditional weak coverage area detection algorithm of intelligent network, a detection algorithm of weak coverage area of intelligent network based on large data is proposed. Firstly, the detection data are collected by the data acquisition method based on local features, and then the gray conversion of these detection data is used to realize the pre-processing and pre-processing detection of the detection data. The feature vectors are used to describe the feature points, and the accelerated feature matching of the detected data is realized. Then, the detected data are detected by region feature detection. Finally, an intelligent network weak coverage area detection algorithm based on large data is implemented. Weak coverage area detection algorithm based on large data in intelligent network achieves weak coverage area detection in intelligent network. It has smaller abnormal location probability and less computing overhead, and improves the detection rate of weak coverage area in intelligent network. By comparing the abnormal location performance of traditional weak coverage area detection algorithm with that of the weak coverage area detection algorithm based on large data, experiments verify the detection performance of the weak coverage area detection algorithm based on large data in intelligent network. It can be seen that the abnormal location of the weak coverage area detection algorithm based on large data in intelligent network is abnormal. Bit probability is much less than the traditional weak coverage area detection algorithm.

References

1. Liu, W., Dong, J., Ren, Y., et al.: Large data analysis and network weak coverage optimization. Telecommun. Eng. Tech. Stand. **15**(16), 110–113 (2018)
2. Wang, Z.: Cuban streets wireless network weak coverage solution. Sci. Technol. Vis. **29**, 94–95 (2017)
3. Qian, D., Fan, C.: Research on intelligent acceleration algorithms for large data mining in communication network. Laser Mag. **37**(33), 132–135 (2016)
4. Niu, Q., Cheng, L.: Monitoring and intelligent diagnosis research based on big data of environmental protection. Environ. Sci. Manag. **20**(21), 167–170 (2018)
5. Lin, Z., Yin, L., Li, X.: Intelligent laundry algorithms based on big data platform. Fujian Comput. **32**(12), 112–113 (2016)
6. Li, C., Hua, Z., Liu, M.: LTE network structure evaluation method based on MR big data. Telecommun. Eng. Technol. Stand. **10**(11), 117–121 (2015)
7. Wang, H., Zhao, D., Yang, H., et al.: Research methods of swarm intelligence in the era of big data. Comput. Modernization **15**(12), 111–116 (2015)
8. Wang, H.: Research on information security situational awareness system based on big data and artificial intelligence technology. Netw. Secur. Technol. Appl. **14**(13), 138–139 (2018)
9. Zhang, F.: Solution to weak coverage of WCDMA network particular area. Electron. Design Eng. **24**(3), 141–143 (2016)
10. Li, X.: Establishing a customer experience-based association analysis system by introducing network-aware big data. Inf. Commun. **21**(22), 2234 (2018)

Research on RF Fingerprinting Extraction of Power Amplifier Based on Multi-domain RF-DNA Fingerprint

Yihan Xiao[✉] and Xinyu Li

College of Information and Communication Engineering,
Harbin Engineering University, Harbin, Heilongjiang 150000, China
{xiaoyihan,lixinyu_2019}@hrbeu.edu.cn

Abstract. The uniqueness of the RF signal is caused by the difference in the hardware structure of the transmitter and the differences between the different devices. Among them, RF power amplifier is one of the key components of RF fingerprinting of wireless transmitter. It is an important breakthrough for RF fingerprint generation mechanism and individual identification. This paper proposes a new identification method of power amplifier based on new intelligent feature set, firstly, processing the received signal. The time domain, frequency domain, time-frequency domain, fractal domain transformation and feature extraction are performed. Secondly, the new intelligent feature set of each power amplifier individual can be characterized, and the RF-DNA fingerprint is visualized. Finally, the support vector machine is used to realize the individual recognition by selecting the optimal RBF kernel function. By simulating and verifying the eight power amplifier signals, a new intelligent feature set can be used to uniquely characterize the power amplifier. Under low SNR, the power amplifier individual can be quickly and effectively identified. The recognition rate of more than 80% can be achieved above the −5 dB signal-to-noise ratio.

Keywords: Individual identification · RF-DNA · SVM

1 Introduction

When a wireless device transmits a signal, the subtle features of each device are attached to the radio frequency signal due to hardware differences, and the individual identification of the device can be realized by using these subtle differences, and the power amplifier is a key component of the wireless device transmitter, and has a significant non- Linear characteristics are an important source of RF fingerprint generation and the key to studying the mechanism of RF fingerprint generation. The concept of "radio frequency fingerprint" was first put forward in 2003 [1]. In 2016, Yu Jiabao et al. conducted a comprehensive review of RF fingerprinting technology, pointing out that RF fingerprinting is a method for extracting RF fingerprints of devices by analyzing the communication signals of wireless devices for device identification. It should be universal, unique and short. Time invariance, independence and robustness [2]. In fact, as early as 1995, Choe [3] and Toonstra [4] and others have begun to use

© ICST Institute for Computer Sciences, Social Informatics and Telecommunications Engineering 2019
Published by Springer Nature Switzerland AG 2019. All Rights Reserved
G. Gui and L. Yun (Eds.): ADHIP 2019, LNICST 301, pp. 129–142, 2019.
https://doi.org/10.1007/978-3-030-36402-1_14

communication signals for individual identification of devices. RF fingerprint technology can be applied to wireless network security authentication, indoor wireless positioning, fault diagnosis, communication countermeasures and radar countermeasures. This technology has been listed by the US military as one of the key technologies for current development, and has high application value in civil and military applications.

In fact, the early technology of radio frequency fingerprint was based on transient signals. Radio frequency fingerprint technology based on steady-state signal was first proposed in 2008 [5]. Because of its good classification performance and higher feasibility of the method, more and more attention has been paid to the technology of RF fingerprint extraction and recognition based on steady-state signals. Radio frequency different native attributes (RF-DNA) is a method to extract features from radio frequency (RF) signals. The signals emitted by each device have unique characteristics and can be used to distinguish the device from other similar devices. This is called fingerprint recognition. Randall W. Klein et al. proposed an RF-DNA fingerprint recognition algorithm based on time domain (TD) features [6]. McKay D et al. proposed RF-DNA fingerprint feature extraction technology based on spectral domain (SD) features [7]. Donald R et al. proposed that the normalized amplitude of the preamble of IEEE802.16e WiMAX signal be transformed into discrete Gabor transform, and the RF-DNA fingerprint signal is generated by Gabor coefficient [8, 9]. Kang used bispectrum theory to extract SURF features [10]. Gok uses variational mode decomposition (VMD) to compute fingerprint features [11]. D'Agostino S uses time domain amplitude characteristics [12]. Ru X uses frequency domain features to accomplish individual recognition of radiation sources [13, 14].

The fingerprint recognition technology based on RF-DNA is one of the hotspots in the field of RF fingerprint identification in recent years. It constructs radio frequency fingerprint of transmitter by extracting statistical features from radio frequency signal, so as to realize the identity authentication of equipment [15]. Based on this research, this paper proposes a method for identifying the power amplifiers by constructing RF-DNA gene profiles: By intercepting the information of the power amplifiers, this paper transforms them into the time domain, the frequency domain, the time-frequency domain and the fractal domain. Genes that can characterize power amplifiers are extracted from various domains to construct RF-DNA gene profiles, which can uniquely characterize power amplifiers and realize the individual identification of power amplifiers (Fig. 1).

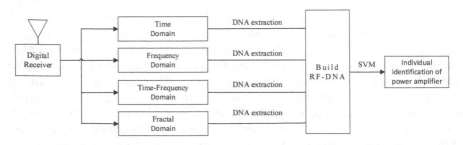

Fig. 1. RF-DNA construction and identification technology block diagram

2   Construction of Power Amplifier RF-DNA

The gene extracted by transforming the intercepted signal in the time domain, the frequency domain, the time-frequency domain, and the fractal domain can reflect the uniqueness of the Power Amplifier, which can be defined as RF-DNA.

2.1   Time Domain RF-DNA RF Fingerprint Extraction Process

For time domain RF-DNA radio frequency fingerprints (F), the basic signal characteristic is instantaneous amplitude. I/Q quadrature sampling is a commonly used method of signal acquisition equipment. The complex time domain signal can be expressed as follows:

$$s_{TD}(n) = I_{TD}(n) + jQ_{TD}(n) \tag{1}$$

Where, $I_{TD}(n)$ and $Q_{TD}(n)$ are the Instantaneous in-phase component and quadrature phase component of $S_{TD}(n)$.

According to the Hilbert transform, the instantaneous amplitude a(n) of the signal can be conveniently calculated according to the Eq. (2).

$$a(n) = \sqrt{I_{TD}^2(n) + Q_{TD}^2(n)} \tag{2}$$

In order to eliminate the influence of the deviation of the acquisition equipment on the subsequent processing, it is necessary to centralize the basic feature. The instantaneous amplitude is centered according to the Eq. (3).

$$a_c(n) = a(n) - \mu_a \tag{3}$$

Where $n = 1, 2, ..., N_M$, N_M is the total number of samples of the sampled signal, and μ_a is the mean of the instantaneous amplitude of the signal samples.

For the above basic signal characteristic, if directly used as the classification recognition process of the signal, the signal may be limited in data processing due to the high complexity. Applying the inherent statistical characteristics of the basic signal feature as classification features can reduce the feature space dimension used for device classification and reduce the computational burden. Common statistical features commonly used in feature extraction include standard deviation (σ), variance (σ^2), skewness (γ), and kurtosis (κ).

2.2   Frequency Domain RF-DNA RF Fingerprint Extraction Process

In the field of signal processing, most signal processing methods are only for the amplitude information of the signal, and the phase information is also very important for characterizing a signal. Higher-order spectra and higher-order cumulants can describe both the amplitude information of the signal and the phase information of the signal. Therefore, the process of introducing high-order spectra and high-order cumulants is the simplest, the most in-depth, and the most widely used bispectrum. Some research has been done on the role of bispectrum in the recognition of power amplifier based on RF-DNA.

In this paper, the nonparametric indirect bispectrum estimation results of the power amplifier output signal are analyzed, and the bispectral distribution entropy, bispectral singular spectral entropy, bispectral energy entropy and waveform entropy are extracted, and the four characteristic entropies are combined into four-dimensional features. The vector acts as a fingerprint feature that distinguishes the signals of different power amplifiers. The research will be carried out in the following aspects.

(a) Receive signals from different power amplifiers;
(b) Calculate the bispectrum estimate of the signal using the indirect estimation method in the nonparametric method;
(c) Divide a certain quadrant of the bispectrum into a frequency region of 8 * 8, and calculate a distribution entropy of the bispectrum estimation. The formula is as follows

$$\|A\| = \sum_{i=1}^{N} |a_i| \ , \quad P_i = \frac{|a_i|}{\|A\|} \tag{4}$$

Where $a_i(i = 1, 2, \ldots, N)$ represents bispectrum mean of N frequency planes. The bispectral distribution entropy can be defined as

$$E_a = -\sum_{i=1}^{N} p_i \cdot \lg p_i \tag{5}$$

(d) Performs the singular value decomposition on the bispectrum estimation result, and gets a series of singular values $\lambda_i(i = 1, 2, \ldots, L)$. Then calculates the bispectral singular spectral entropy according to formula (6,7).

$$p_i = \lambda_i / \sum_{i=1}^{L} \lambda_i \tag{6}$$

$$E_{svd} = -\sum_{i=1}^{L} p_i \cdot \lg p_i \tag{7}$$

(e) Energy entropy and waveform entropy are calculated by the surrounding-line integral bispectrum.

$$p_i = b_i / \sum_{i=1}^{M} |b_i| \tag{8}$$

$$E_b = -\sum_{i=1}^{L} p_i \cdot \lg p_i \tag{9}$$

$$N_{i,j} = \sum_{i,j} |n(i,j)| \tag{10}$$

$$p_{ij} = |n(i,j)|/N_{i,j} \tag{11}$$

$$E_n = -\sum_{i,j} p_{ij} \cdot \lg p_{ij} \tag{12}$$

In the above formula, E_b and E_n represent waveform entropy and energy entropy. In formula (8), M is the number of lines in the perimeter integral and b_i represents the integral of each circle. In formula (10), n(i, j) represents the result of the third-order cumulant bispectrum estimation.

(f) Form the four-dimensional eigenvector $F = [E_a, E_{svd}, E_b, E_n]$.

2.3   Time-Frequency Domain RF-DNA RF Fingerprint Extraction Process

In a majority of previous related work, RF-DNA fingerprints were predominantly extracted from TD and SD responses, with Wavelet Transform (WT) coefficients being AFIT's first application of joint 2D features. The use of WT coefficients is consistent with conclusions in [9] indicating that the use of momentary and/or time localized energy as a function of frequency can be effective for describing signals. This motivated the use of Wave Translate (WT) which is calculated as follows:

Step 1. Perform a n-layer wavelet decomposition on the signal to obtain a series of wavelet coefficients.

Step 2. The obtained wavelet coefficients include n detail coefficients (corresponding to high frequency components of wavelets) and an approximation coefficient (corresponding to low frequency components of wavelets).

Step 3. According to the wavelet coefficients, reconstructing the signal at a specified level by using high frequency or low frequency components of the original signal.

Step 4. Calculate the energy of each reconstructed signal to form a feature vector $F=[e_1, e_2, \ldots, e_n]$.

2.4   Fractal Domain RF-DNA RF Fingerprint Extraction Process

Fractal is a general term for a self-similar graphic structure that has no meaning length. This graphic structure's essence cannot be described by Euclidean measures. Therefore, using dimensions to portray such graphics has been employed widely.

Fractal dimensions can quantitatively describe the complexity of a collection of parts. The definition of fractal dimension is different from the definition of European geometric dimension. It is application-dependent, and its fractal dimension is defined differently depending on the application. In the field of modulation mode identification, the box dimension and information dimension are commonly used. Among them, the box dimension reflects the collection scale of the classification set, and the information dimension reflects the information of the distribution of the classification set. In this paper, we choose box dimension and information dimension as the basic features in fractal domain.

Box Dimension. The steps of feature extraction based on box dimension are as follows:

(a) The signal sequence after the pre-processing can be expressed as

$$\{g(i), i = 1, 2, \cdots\cdots, N\} \tag{13}$$

Where N is the length of the signal sequence

(b) According to the definition of the box dimension, the signal sequence $\{g(i)\}$ is placed in the unit square, and the minimum interval of the abscissa is q = 1/N. N (q) can be expressed as

$$N(q) = N + \frac{\left\{\sum_{i=1}^{N-1} max\{g(i), g(i+1)\}q - \sum_{i=1}^{N-1} min\{g(i), g(i+1)\}q\right\}}{q^2} \tag{14}$$

(c) The box dimension can be calculated by the following formula

$$D_b = -\frac{\ln N(q)}{\ln q} \tag{15}$$

Information Dimension. The following are the steps for feature extraction using information dimensions.

(a) Same as box dimension, the preprocessed signal can be expressed as

$$\{f(i), i = 1, 2, \cdots, N\} \tag{16}$$

(b) Signal reconstruction. In the frequency domain, the signal is reconstructed as follows.

$$s(i) = fs(i+1) - fs(i), i = 1, 2 \cdots, N - 1 \tag{17}$$

The purpose of this is to reduce the impact of some of the in-band noise, and to facilitate the calculation of information dimensions using the following method.

(c) Calculate information dimension using reconstructed signals.

$$L = \sum_{i=1}^{N-1} s_i, P_i = \frac{s_i}{L} \tag{18}$$

$$D_I = \sum_{i=1}^{N-1} P_i \lg(1/P_i) \tag{19}$$

Fractal features are expressed in vector form as $V_F = [D_b, D_I]$

2.5 Conclusion

This chapter introduces the characteristics of the multi-domain which will be used in this paper to identify the amplifiers. The extraction methods of each feature are also be introduced. Table 1 shows the summary of the used features.

Table 1. Feature extraction in different transform domains.

Domain	Feature
Time domain	Standard deviation (σ)
	Variance (σ^2)
	Skewness (γ)
	Kurtosis (κ)
Frequency domain	Waveform entropy
	Energy entropy
	Distribution entropy
	Singular value entropy
Time-frequency domain	The energy of the Reconstructed signal used the 1–4th order high frequency coefficient of wavelet.
Fractal domain	Box dimension
	Information dimension

3   Power Amplifier Individual Recognition Based on SVM

3.1   Individual Recognition Based on Support Vector Machine

The basic learning principle of Support Vector Machine (SVM) is the principle of SRM (Structure Risk Minimization). The main advantages are fast learning speed, global optimality, fast convergence speed and small mean square error. The support vector machine method is based on the concept of decision plane, which is solved by transforming the classification problem into the quadratic programming problem of the data. Decision planes can distinguish a set of elements belonging to different categories, Assume the following samples exist.

$$(x_1, y_1), \cdots, (x_l, y_l), x \in R, y \in \{+1, -1\} \tag{20}$$

l is the number of samples. After the training samples are given, a decision plane is constructed by SVM, also called the optimal classification hyperplane, so that the distance between the different types of training samples to the optimal classification hyperplane is maximized, and then achieves more accurate classification in the training of test samples.

By introducing the concept of kernel function, support vector machine (SVM) can deal with the problems of non-linearity and high-dimensional space. It plays an important role in the theory of SVM. The kernel function is a technique generated as a spatial map. The kernel function is mapped to a higher dimensional space, and the complex inner product operation between two points in the high-dimensional feature space is replaced by a kernel function of the original input space. Thereby avoiding the increase of the SVM algorithm in the case of nonlinear separability. The kernel function selected in this paper is RBF kernel function.

$$K(x, y) = \exp(-\gamma \|x - y\|^2) \tag{21}$$

In formula, $\gamma = 1/2\sigma^2$, γ is the distance between the optimal classification hyperplane and the nearest point. By changing the value of width σ, a larger γ can be selected to reduce the error.

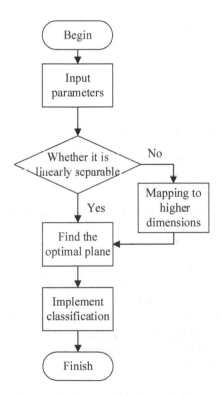

Fig. 2. Flow chart of support vector machine recognition

Classification process: For linear separable categories, support vector machine directly achieves classification by seeking the optimal classification hyperplane; for linear inseparable samples in low-dimensional space, an important idea of support vector machine is to map them to higher-dimensional data space through kernels, so that samples can be classified linearly in high-dimensional space. The flowchart of the support vector machine implementation classification is shown in Fig. 2.

4 Simulation and Verification of Individual Recognition of Power Amplifier

4.1 Experimental Configuration

Eight 433 MHz RF power amplifiers of the same model and the same batch were selected as the research object. The experimental configuration is shown in Fig. 3. The vector signal generator is used to repeatedly transmit an edited 16QAM modulated signal. The carrier frequency of the signal is set to 433 MHz. The sampling rate is 1 MHz and the output power is 0 dB. The 16QAM signal is connected to the power amplifier through a coaxial line. The power amplifier is powered by a 5 V DC voltage. After the amplified signal passes through the 30 dB attenuator, it is directly connected to the RF recorder by a coaxial line. The RF recorder uses quadrature sampling technology with a center frequency set to 433 MHz and a sampling rate set to 4 MHz.

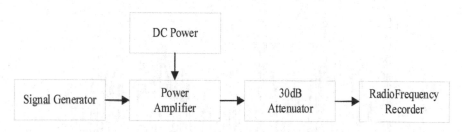

Fig. 3. Experimental configuration

4.2 Data Preprocessing

Since the signal source continuously transmits a QAM signal repeatedly, after using a radio frequency recorder records a piece of data for about 5 s, it is necessary to perform segmentation interception processing on the signal, and intercept each segment of the QAM signal. Specific steps are as follows:

(a) Instantaneous amplitude calculation. Calculate the instantaneous amplitude characteristic a(n) of the recorded signal.
(b) Detection of mutation points. The abrupt point detection is performed on a(n), and the index value of the first 40 mutation points of the recorded signal file, that is, the index value of the start time and the end time of each QAM signal is obtained. (According to a complete QAM signal playback time of 90 ms, there are about 55 repeated cycles of QAM signal in 5 s record data.)

(c) QAM signal interception. For each of the power amplifier's recorded signals, 20 waveforms were intercepted as experimental data, and 8 amplifiers totaled 160 waveforms.

4.3   Analysis of Results

This paper used features of the multi-domain which are introduced in Sect. 2 to construct RF-DNA of the power amplifier. After extracting the multi-domain RF-DNA fingerprint of the signal, a set of high-dimensional eigenvectors is obtained. The main feature extracted from RF-DNA is used as the input of support vector machine, which is divided into test set and training set according to a certain proportion (4:1) for individual classification and recognition. The results are analyzed as follows.

Before the feature extraction, the normalization operation is first performed. The purpose of this step is to avoid the data dominate that SVM model parameters are dominated by data with a larger or smaller distribution range. The comparison chart before and after normalization is as follows:

Figures 4 and 5 represent the signal waveforms before and after normalization. This operation can effectively prevent the subsequent processing from being affected by the wild value.

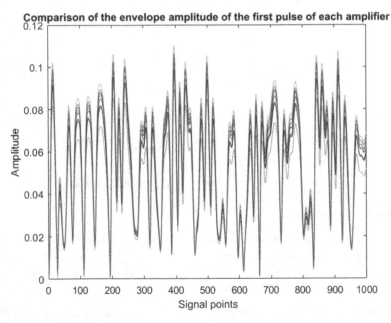

Fig. 4. Comparison of RF signals of eight power amplifiers before normalization

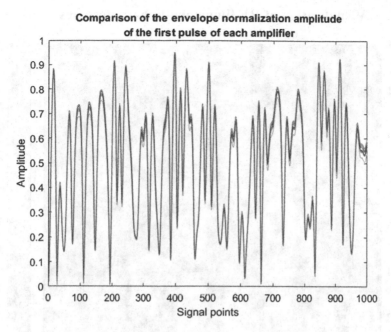

Fig. 5. Normalized comparison of RF signals of eight power amplifiers

Feature Visualization. After feature extraction in different domains, this paper carried out feature fusion to construct multi-domain RF-DNA.

Figure 6 is a graphical representation of the statistical average of the multi-domain fusion features of the eight power amplifiers. The color represents the statistical average of the features extracted from the 20 samples. From this picture, we can see that the characteristics extracted between different power amplifiers are quite different.

This figure can be analyzed from the following aspects:

(a) From the perspective of a single domain, amplitude features of time domain are more effective than wavelet features of time-frequency domain. This is reflected in the higher recognition rate of time domain features. The main reason for this result is that the 16QAM signal is an amplitude modulation signal, and the amplitude has a greater influence on the signal itself.

(b) As can be seen from Fig. 7, using multi-domain RF-DNA for individual recognition is better than single domain. The recognition accuracy of eight power amplifiers has reached 95% when the SNR is −3 dB.

c) From the rising trend of the three curves, the multi-domain RF-DNA and time-domain amplitude characteristics have great similarities in the rising trend, which indicates to some extent that the time-domain amplitude characteristics play a major role in the fusion characteristics.

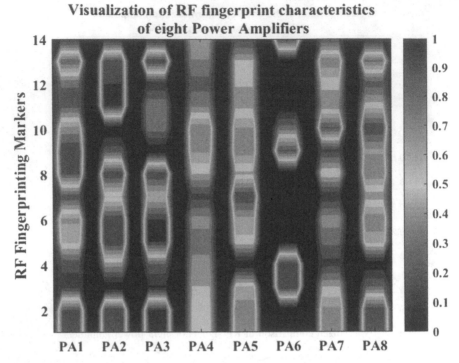

Fig. 6. Visualization of RF fingerprint characteristics

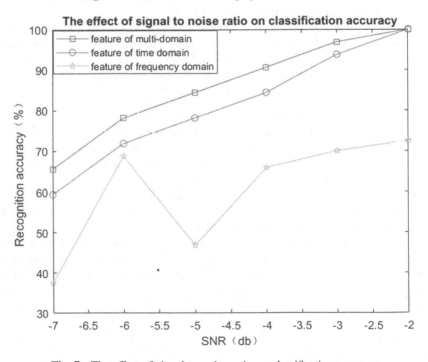

Fig. 7. The effect of signal to noise ratio on classification accuracy

5   Conclusion

In this paper, firstly, the signal is transformed into time-domain, frequency-domain, time-frequency domain and fractal domain to extract 14 features to form RF-DNA. Then we put them together and as the input of the support vector machine, which is determined by selecting the optimal RBF kernel function. Eventually, the recognition rate of the eight power amplifiers is over 95%. This proves that multi-domain RF-DNA is very effective in the identification of individual amplifiers. And even in the case of very low signal-to-noise ratio, the recognition accuracy can meet the required requirements.

Acknowledgment. The authors would like to thank State Key Laboratory of Complex Electromagnetic Environment Effects on Electronics and Information System Director Fund (CEMEE2019K0101A).

References

1. Hall, J., Barbeau, M., Kranakis, E.: Detection of transient in radio frequency fingerprinting using signal phase. In: IASTED International Multi-conference on Wireless and Optical Communications (2003)
2. Yu, J.-B., Hu, A.-Q., Zhu, C.-M., Peng, L.-N., Jiang, Y.: RF fingerprinting extraction and identification of wireless communication devices. J. Cryptologic Res. 3(5), 433–446 (2016)
3. Toonstra, J., Nsner, W.: Transient analysis and genetic algorithms for classification. In: Communications, Power, and Computing, pp. 432–437 (1995)
4. Choe, H.C., Poole, C.E., Andrea, M.Y., et al.: Novel identification of intercepted signals from unknown radio transmitters. In: SPIE's 1995 Symposium on OE/Aerospace Sensing and Dual Use Photonics. International Society for Optics and Photonics, pp. 504–517 (1995)
5. Kennedy, I.O., et al.: Radio transmitter fingerprinting: a steady state frequency domain approach. In: Vehicular Technology Conference, VTC 2008-Fall, pp. 1–5. IEEE (2008)
6. Klein, R.W., Temple, M.A., Mendenhall, M.J.: Application of wavelet-based RF fingerprinting to enhance wireless network security. J. Commun. Netw. 11(6), 544–555 (2012)
7. Williams, M.K.D., et al.: RF-DNA fingerprinting for airport WiMax communications security. In: International Conference on Network and System Security, pp. 32–39. IEEE (2010)
8. Reising, D.R, Temple, M.A., Oxley, M.E.: Gabor-based RF-DNA fingerprinting for classifying 802.16e WiMAX mobile subscribers. In: International Conference on Computing, Networking and Communications, pp. 7–13. IEEE (2012)
9. Reising, D.R., Temple, M.A., Jackson, J.A.: Authorized and rogue device discrimination using dimensionally reduced RF-DNA fingerprints. IEEE Trans. Inf. Forensics Secur. 10(6), 1180–1192 (2015)
10. Ru, X., Huang, Z., Liu, Z., et al.: Frequency-domain distribution and band-width of unintentional modulation on pulse. Electron. Lett. 52(22), 1853–1855 (2016)
11. Ru, X.H., Liu, Z., Huang, Z.T., et al.: Evaluation of unintentional modulation for pulse compression signals based on spectrum asymmetry. IET Radar Sonar Navig. 11(4), 656–663 (2017)

12. Dubendorfer, C.K., Ramsey, B.W., Temple, M.A.: An RF-DNA verification process for ZigBee networks. In: Military Communications Conference, Milcom – 2012, pp. 1–6. IEEE (2013)
13. Chen, Y., et al.: Detecting and localizing wireless spoofing attacks. In: Securing Emerging Wireless Systems, pp. 1–18. Springer, Boston (2009). https://doi.org/10.1007/978-0-387-88491-2_8
14. Yuan, H.L.: Research on physical-layer authentication of wireless network based on RF fingerprinting. Southeast University (2011)
15. Bihl, T.J., Bauer, K.W., Temple, M.A.: Feature selection for RF fingerprinting with multiple discriminant analysis and using ZigBee device emissions. IEEE Trans. Inf. Forensics Secur. **11**(8), 1862–1874 (2016)

Fault Feature Analysis of Power Network Based on Big Data

Cai-yun Di[✉]

State Grid Jibei Electric Power Company Limited Skills Training Center,
Baoding Technical College of Electric Power, Baoding, China
cjj998799@163.com

Abstract. During the operation of the power network, there was a sharp change in current and voltage at the time of failure, which made it difficult for the grid operators to quickly and accurately determine the fault. This paper proposed a big data-based power network fault feature analysis method design. Taking the symmetrical fault component method as the main analysis method, a two-phase short-circuit equivalent model was constructed by accurately analyzing the fault characteristics of the power network, and the fault features were detected and located by the big data network preprocessor. The experimental results shown that the big data power network fault feature analysis method could effectively feedback and locate the fault location and complete the maintenance of the power network in time.

Keywords: Big data environment · Power network · Fault characteristics · Analytical method

1 Introduction

With the increase of the scale of power networks, the safe operation of power grids is becoming more and more important to society [1]. However, due to the frequent occurrence of natural disasters in China and the aging of power equipment, power grid failures are inevitable and bring losses to the economy and residents' lives. Therefore, it is necessary to study the characteristics of power network faults before, during and after the fault to effectively avoid faults and quickly eliminate faults. By means of the symmetrical component method, the principle of current and voltage characteristics of typical faults of 220 kV and above power grids is analyzed and summarized, and the fault feature quantities of the multiple center electrical network are transformed into a single comprehensive feature quantity to monitor the operating state of the distribution network [2]. The fault area can be determined and located according to the association situation of each node and the size of the local anomaly factor. A two-phase short-circuit equivalent model is established, and the big data network preprocessing is used to improve the accuracy and reliability of the fault analysis of the power network. Through the method of experimental argumentation analysis, the effectiveness of the big data power network fault feature analysis method designed in this paper is determined. During the failure analysis, the fault location can be effectively feed backed and located, and the maintenance of the power network can be completed in time.

G. Gui and L. Yun (Eds.): ADHIP 2019, LNICST 301, pp. 143–151, 2019.
https://doi.org/10.1007/978-3-030-36402-1_15

2   Analytical Method Design

The analysis method designed in this paper shows the fault processing process of power network as shown in Fig. 1. It is divided into four parts: symmetric fault component [3], two short-circuit equivalent models and big data preprocessing.

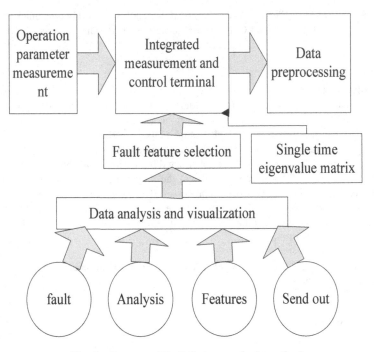

Fig. 1. Process of fault feature analysis method

2.1   Symmetric Fault Component Design

Most of the faults in the power grid are asymmetric faults (single-phase, two-phase grounding, etc.). When this type of fault occurs in the power grid [4], the current and voltage at the fault point are no longer symmetrical, and a symmetrical component method is needed to perform the short circuit calculation.

The symmetrical component method is a basic method for analyzing the asymmetric operating state of a symmetric system. Any asymmetric three-phase phasor F_a, F_b, F_c can be decomposed into three sets of symmetric components with different phase sequences: positive sequence component $F_{a(1)}$, $F_{b(1)}$, $F_{c(1)}$; negative sequence component $F_{a(2)}$, $F_{b(2)}$, $F_{c(2)}$; zero sequence component $F_{a(0)}$, $F_{b(0)}$, $F_{c(0)}$. That is, the following relationship exists:

$$\left.\begin{array}{l} \boldsymbol{F}_a = \boldsymbol{F}_{a(1)} + \boldsymbol{F}_{a(2)} + \boldsymbol{F}_{a(0)} \\ \boldsymbol{F}_b = \boldsymbol{F}_{b(1)} + \boldsymbol{F}_{b(2)} + \boldsymbol{F}_{b(0)} \\ \boldsymbol{F}_c = \boldsymbol{F}_{c(1)} + \boldsymbol{F}_{c(2)} + \boldsymbol{F}_{c(0)} \end{array}\right\} \qquad (1)$$

The symmetrical component method is cited in the calculation of the imbalance of the power network system [5], that is, any three-phase unbalanced current, voltage or impedance is decomposed into three balanced phasor components, i.e., positive phase sequence ($\boldsymbol{U}_{U1}$, $\boldsymbol{U}_{V1}$, $\boldsymbol{U}_{W1}$); negative phase sequence ($\boldsymbol{U}_{U2}$, $\boldsymbol{U}_{V2}$, $\boldsymbol{U}_{W2}$) and zero phase sequence ($\boldsymbol{U}_{U0}$, $\boldsymbol{U}_{V0}$, $\boldsymbol{U}_{W0}$).

$$\left.\begin{array}{l} \boldsymbol{U}_U = \boldsymbol{U}_{U1} + \boldsymbol{U}_{U2} + \boldsymbol{U}_{U0} \\ \boldsymbol{U}_V = \boldsymbol{U}_{V1} + \boldsymbol{U}_{V2} + \boldsymbol{U}_{V0} \\ \boldsymbol{U}_W = \boldsymbol{U}_{W1} + \boldsymbol{U}_{W2} + \boldsymbol{U}_{W0} \end{array}\right\} \qquad (2)$$

The phase sequence of the positive phase sequence (clockwise direction) is equal to $\boldsymbol{U}_{U1}$, $\boldsymbol{U}_{V1}$, $\boldsymbol{U}_{W1}$ and equal in size, 120° apart; The phase sequence of the negative phase sequence (counterclockwise direction) is $\boldsymbol{U}_{U2}$, $\boldsymbol{U}_{V2}$, $\boldsymbol{U}_{W2}$ in order, equal in size, 120° apart; The zero phase sequence is equal in magnitude and in phase [6]. The operator a is quoted in the symmetrical component method, which is defined by the fact that the unit phasor is rotated 120° counter clockwise, then:

$$\left.\begin{array}{l} \boldsymbol{U}_{U0} = \dfrac{1}{3}\boldsymbol{U}_U + \boldsymbol{U}_V + \boldsymbol{U}_W \\[2mm] \boldsymbol{U}_{U1} = \dfrac{1}{3}\boldsymbol{U}_U + a\boldsymbol{U}_V + a^2\boldsymbol{U}_W \\[2mm] \boldsymbol{U}_{U2} = \dfrac{1}{3}\boldsymbol{U}_U + a^2\boldsymbol{U}_V + a\boldsymbol{U}_W \end{array}\right\} \qquad (3)$$

In the above calculations, all are based on the U phase, and are vector calculations.

2.2 Construction of Two-Phase Short-Circuit Equivalent Model

The double instantaneous fault in the face of current and voltage is the same as the fault current and voltage characteristics in a single phase for a short time [7]. The difference is that there is still a fault current after the fault phase switch is overlapped, and the coincidence is unsuccessful, and the switch three-phase trips, as shown in Fig. 2.

According to the analysis of Fig. 2, the current and voltage characteristics of the phase-to-phase unground fault are as follows: the fault current of the two fault phases is large, and the fault current of the non-fault phase is zero; The non-fault phase voltage is equal to the pre-fault voltage [8], the fault voltage amplitude is reduced by half; the zero sequence current is zero.

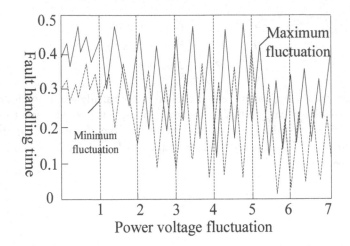

Fig. 2. Instantaneous ground fault recording

The two-phase short-circuit equivalent model construction steps are as follows:

Assuming that the V, W phase is short-circuited by two phases, the voltage at the fault point three relative to ground and the phase current flowing out of the point (short-circuit current) have the following boundary conditions:

$$\left.\begin{array}{l} U_{fu} = 0 \\ I_{fu} = 0 \\ I_{fv} = -I_{fw} \end{array}\right\} \tag{4}$$

According to formula (3), the conversion is as follows:

$$\begin{bmatrix} I_{f(1)} \\ I_{f(2)} \\ I_{f(0)} \end{bmatrix} = \frac{1}{3} \begin{pmatrix} 1 & a & a^2 \\ 1 & a^2 & a \\ 1 & 1 & 1 \end{pmatrix} \begin{bmatrix} 0 \\ I_{fv} \\ -I_{fv} \end{bmatrix} = \frac{jI_{fv}}{\sqrt{3}} \begin{bmatrix} 1 \\ -1 \\ 0 \end{bmatrix} \tag{5}$$

The above process shows that there is no zero sequence current at the two-phase short-circuit fault point.

Combine the composite network diagram and the formulas (1) and (5) to obtain:

$$I_{fv} = -j\sqrt{3}\frac{U_{f|0|}}{Z\sum(1) + Z\sum(2)} \tag{6}$$

$$I_{fw} = j\sqrt{3}\frac{U_{f|0|}}{Z\sum(1) + Z\sum(2)} \tag{7}$$

It can be seen that when the positive sequence impedance is equal to the negative sequence impedance, the non-fault phase voltage is equal to the pre-fault voltage, and the fault phase voltage amplitude is reduced by half.

The technical support system for power network fault analysis is based on two-phase short circuit, supplemented by energy management system [9]. At the same time, it provides fault characteristics for the control center of power equipment, and completes the construction of the two-phase short-circuit equivalent model. Figure 3 shows the two-phase short-circuit equivalent model structure.

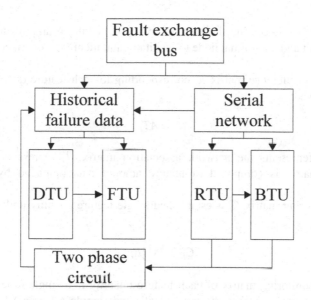

Fig. 3. Two-phase short-circuit equivalent model structure

2.3 Big Data Network Preprocessing

The big data network pre-processing is used to perform preliminary screening and pre-processing on the raw data uploaded by each sensing device, reducing the amount of irrelevant data and generating the required initial feature quantity matrix. This part mainly includes selecting the fault feature quantity, constructing the correlation matrix, and processing the area difference [10]. In the process of selecting the fault feature quantity, the electrical characteristic quantity selected in this paper is current and power. Among them, three-phase current, negative sequence current, and zero-sequence current and corresponding power or no power are covered.

The association matrix is constructed, the process is: First, each terminal node E_j in the distribution network is numbered, and the area Z_j between the nodes is also numbered, and finally the matrix is constructed according to the rules shown in Table 1.

Table 1. Building a big data network matrix rule.

Correlation value	Association relationship
−1	The node is located in the area, but the current power of the node is directed outside the region
0	Nodes are not in the region
1	The node is located in the area, and the current power of the node points to the region

The purpose of processing the area difference is mainly to amplify the difference between the fault and the normal node to facilitate fault identification. Specific steps are as follows:

The regional difference matrix R_i corresponding to each feature quantity is calculated and obtained:

$$R_i = AT_i \tag{8}$$

Where: A represents the network association matrix; T_i represents the column matrix. The matrix is composed of feature amount data uploaded by each node terminal.

Fault monitoring matrix C_i is established(single feature quantity under single time period):

$$C_i = |A^T|R_i \tag{9}$$

The state monitoring matrix of each feature quantity in a single time period (take one power frequency cycle as the time length and sample 64 times) [11], spatially expands into a related state monitoring matrix $W_i = (i = 0\text{–}19)$ of multiple electrical feature quantities, and further merge into a multiple time and multiple electrical feature quantity high-dimensional spatiotemporal state monitoring matrix W:

$$\begin{aligned} W_i &= [C_1 C_2 \cdots C_w] \\ W &= [W_1 W_2 \cdots W_W] \end{aligned} \tag{10}$$

3 Experimental Argumentation Analysis

In order to verify the feasibility of the fault analysis method designed in this paper, a 10 kV smart distribution network with dual DG is taken as the research object, as shown in Fig. 4.

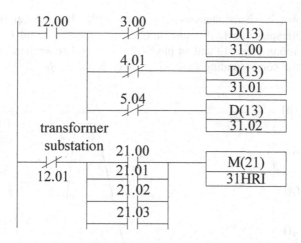

Fig. 4. Power network topology diagram

Figure 5 shows a visual analysis of multidimensional scaling and corresponding LOF values for normal operation of the distribution network. It can be seen that under normal operating conditions, there are no outliers, and each node (1–17, 17 is a generalized node) is similar. The dimensionality reduction result in Fig. 5 is expressed as a point-like area at the origin of the coordinates, and the LOF values are all in the vicinity. According to the decision rule, there is no fault in the distribution network at this time.

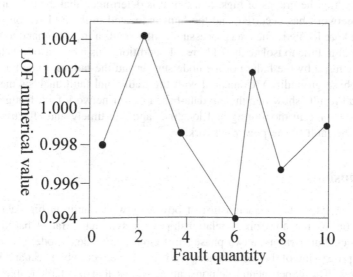

Fig. 5. Grid fault monitoring data in the operating state

Figure 6 shows a visual analysis of the multiple dimensional dimensionality reduction and corresponding LOF values for a single-phase ground fault in the Z11 feeder section. Among them, 13 and 14 physical nodes and generalized nodes (17) are all outliers, and the corresponding LOF value reaches about 96.

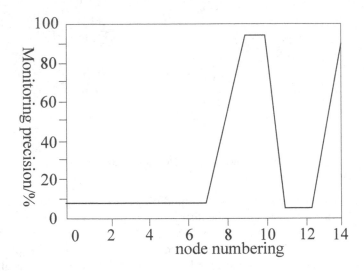

Fig. 6. Z11 feeder section fault monitoring data

By analyzing the graphs of Figs. 5 and 6, it is determined that the relevant fault of the power network has occurred, and the fault is located in the Z11 region where the nodes 13, 14 are located. The data processing center sends a trip command to the faulty node terminal in time to isolate the Z11 area. In addition, this paper also tests the power failure test caused by the failure of the node sensor and the failure of the bus node Z2 area (two-phase grounding). Compared with the traditional fault analysis method, the experimental results show that the big data-based power network fault feature analysis method is effective in monitoring and locating, and can timely and effectively report and locate the fault of the power network.

4   Conclusions

This paper analyzes the characteristics of power network faults in big data environment, and builds the component relationship with symmetric faults based on fault characteristics. Furthermore, a two-phase short-circuit equivalent model is constructed, and the preprocessing of the big data network is used to effectively detect and locate the fault features. The experimental demonstration shows that the fault feature analysis method designed in this paper has extremely high effectiveness. While completing the monitoring and positioning of the fault characteristics of the power network, it effectively reports and locates the fault location and completes the maintenance of the power network in time. It is hoped that the research in this paper can provide theoretical basis and reference for the analysis method of fault characteristics of power network in China.

References

1. Zhu, Y., Li, L., Song, Y., et al.: Large data storage and parallel processing methods for power equipment monitoring based on ODPS platform. J. Electr. Technol. **32**(9), 199–210 (2017)
2. Chai, Q., Zheng, W., Pan, J., et al.: Research on state monitoring and fault processing of intelligent distribution network based on large data analysis. Mod. Electr. Technol. **16**(4), 105–108 (2018)
3. Lei, W., Qing, C., Gao, H., et al.: Intelligent substation fault tracking architecture based on large data mining. Power Syst. Autom. **56**(3), 84–91 (2018)
4. Wang, S., Zhao, D.: Review and prospect of power grid fault diagnosis. Autom. Electr. Power Syst. **41**(19), 164–175 (2017)
5. Wei, H., Le, Z., Yong, M., et al.: Study on post-fault transient stability assessment of power system based on in-depth learning. Power Grid Technol. **26**(10), 40–46 (2017)
6. Yu, Y., Zhu, Z., Huang, C., et al.: Distribution network fault trend judgment based on large data analysis. Power Supply Technol. **23**(1), 132–134 (2018)
7. Ge, X., Ai, M., Li, Z., et al.: Large data ETL method of distribution network operation monitoring signal based on CEP engine. New Technol. Electr. Energy **36**(9), 36–42 (2017)
8. Li, G., Yu, C., Liu, Y., et al.: Power transformer fault prediction and health management: challenges and prospects. Power Syst. Autom. **41**(23), 156–167 (2017)
9. Wang, D., Li, J.: Query optimization method for large data of condition monitoring of substation equipment. Power Syst. Autom. **41**(2), 165–172 (2017)
10. Wang, Y., Jia, Y.: Improved matrix algorithm for fault location of distribution network containing distributed generation. Comput. Simul. **35**(04), 58–64 (2018)
11. Hao, S., Ming, L., Ma, H., et al.: Research on large data application planning method in power supply chain. China Electr. Power **50**(6), 69–74 (2017)

Design of All-Pass Filter System for Power Communication with High Anti-harmonic Interference

Caiyun Di[(✉)] and Zhi Zhao

State Grid Jibei Electric Power Company Limited Skills Training Center,
Baoding Technical College of Electric Power, Baoding, China
cjj998799@163.com

Abstract. In the traditional system, the prediction sensing unit was lacking, which caused the output voltage and current harmonic content to deviate greatly from the actual value. In order to solve this problem, the design of the all-pass filtering system for power communication with high anti-harmonic interference was proposed. According to the hardware structure block diagram of the system, the predictive sensing module was designed to obtain readable and unreadable information. In order to make the system only transmit readable information, the closed switch was designed, and the client module at the end of the hardware was set to display the prediction results and improve the harmonic interference problem; For the above system hardware control module, the software part was designed, and the filter system function was determined according to the software design flow, thereby completing the design of the all-pass filter system for power communication with high anti-harmonic interference. The experimental results showed that the output voltage and current harmonic content of the system were consistent with the actual value, which provided a certain reference for the filter anti-interference.

Keywords: High anti-harmonic interference · Power communication · All-pass filter · Perception · Prediction

1 Introduction

Data communication through power lines is undoubtedly an economical and convenient way, but in the transmission of signals in the power grid, the background must contain a large number of power grids and their harmonic components to drown the communication signals, bringing great difficulty to the detection. Generally, an all-pass filter is used to eliminate one or more harmonic interferences in the signal without affecting the frequency components of the communication signal, thereby improving the detection signal-to-noise ratio [1]. A filter is a frequency selective network that transforms an input signal into a desired output signal in a prescribed manner, allowing signals of certain frequencies to pass through to block or attenuate signals of other frequencies. The theory and technology of filters have been steadily developing rapidly.

© ICST Institute for Computer Sciences, Social Informatics and Telecommunications Engineering 2019
Published by Springer Nature Switzerland AG 2019. All Rights Reserved
G. Gui and L. Yun (Eds.): ADHIP 2019, LNICST 301, pp. 152–160, 2019.
https://doi.org/10.1007/978-3-030-36402-1_16

It has been widely used in various electronic devices. Without the penetration of filters into electronic technology, there is no modern electronic world [2].

At present, it is common practice to suppress a certain harmonic interference component by a second-order notch with an all-zero point and an all-pole cascade, or to design a single-frequency point trap by a second-order all-pass filter, and then The suppression of multiple harmonic interferences is achieved by cascading [3]. Literature [4] proposed All-Pass-Filter-based Active Damping for VSCs with LCL Filters Connected to Weak Grids. Based on making the open loop phase at the resonant frequency zero. This strategy will be shown to provide sufficient oscillation damping and can be implemented in two different ways: at the design stage (if design constraints make it possible) or an all-pass filter in series with the current controller.

Literature [5] proposed Design and Simulation of the Integrated Navigation System based on Extended Kalman Filter. The structure of the INS/GPS integrated navigation system consists of four parts, namely GPS receiver, inertial navigation system, extended Kalman filter and integrated navigation scheme. We then illustrate how to use the extended Kalman filter to simulate an integrated navigation system by measuring position, velocity and attitude. In particular, an extended Kalman filter can estimate the state of a nonlinear system in a noisy environment. In the extended Kalman filter, the estimation of the state vector and the error covariance matrix is calculated by the following steps: (1) time update and (2) measurement update. Finally, the simulation process is implemented by Matlab.

However, due to the influence of the coefficient quantization effect, these filters have higher sensitivity, especially in the low frequency band, making the notch frequency point easily offset. In the background noise of the power line communication signal, the largest components such as the 3rd and 5th harmonics of the fundamental wave are in the low frequency band relative to the acquisition frequency. Whether the interference components can be accurately filtered out will directly affect the communication quality. In the medium voltage large-capacity variable frequency drive device, in order to solve this problem, a high-pass filter system design for power communication with high anti-harmonic interference is studied, because the numerator and denominator polynomial of the all-pass filter transfer function are mirrored. The symmetry relationship makes the filter have the lowest coefficient sensitivity in the low frequency band and can obtain an efficient lattice operation structure.

2   Hardware Design of All-Pass Filter System

According to the characteristics of harmonic interference, the overall structure block diagram of the all-pass filter system under this condition is designed, as shown in Fig. 1.

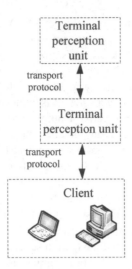

Fig. 1. System overall structure

It can be seen from Fig. 1 that the overall structure of the system is mainly composed of the terminal sensing unit, the control unit and the client. The terminal sensing unit is mainly responsible for monitoring the information parameters and intelligently controlling the monitoring switch. The control unit is mainly responsible for transmitting the network terminal parameters collected by all nodes to the filtering server, and issuing a command signal to the relevant node server; The client is mainly responsible for real-time monitoring of network terminal information monitoring results and remote monitoring, and automatically controls the filters in the intelligent control priority control unit.

2.1   Predictive Perception

The predictive sensing module is mainly responsible for predicting and sensing the data information transmitted during the power communication process. The module uses the Kalman filter prediction method to realize the two-way intelligent communication of the predicted information in the power communication process. When the collected data information is transmitted to the control unit through the prediction sensing module, it needs to pass five nodes, which are the system total power switch node, the sensing node, the collecting node, the processing node and the receiving node, between the five nodes. The relationship is shown in Fig. 2.

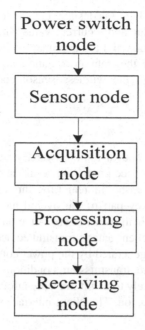

Fig. 2. Predictive perception framework

It can be seen from Fig. 2 that in addition to the harmonic interference prediction sensing information, the above five nodes also include readable information and unreadable information. The sensing node monitors readable and unreadable information to ensure that each data information has a specific attribute; The collection node collects the system operation data in real time; the receiving node acquires the data information from the collection node; the processing node processes the received information [6].

2.2 Control Unit

The control unit is composed of a wireless sensor coordinator and a network server. When predicting harmonic interference, it is necessary to accurately transmit the data transmitted by the device, and the generation of the sensor data needs to be controlled by a switch [7]. In order to make the control effect better, a closed switch with readable and unreadable information is designed, as shown in Fig. 3.

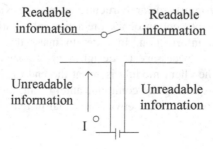

Fig. 3. Readable and unreadable information closure switch

The closed switch shown in Fig. 3 is designed in a reverse connection manner, with one node as a voltage input value and a current value with a positive characteristic in the loop. The readable information and the unreadable information are simultaneously transmitted to the circuit, and the data information collected by all the nodes is transmitted to the host through the wireless sensor coordinator, and the readable information is transmitted [8].

2.3 Client Module

The client module is set at the end of the hardware, which is mainly responsible for displaying the harmonic interference prediction result, and the staff can view the network terminal data prediction result in real time through the client interface. The system prediction switch is a key part of the overall hardware structure design. The server at the front end of the client uses the error-free and non-repetitive information prediction of the data, and the client data is transmitted according to the TCP protocol [9]. Since the data information generated by the power communication is different, it is necessary to fully consider the transmission condition of the signal, and use the wireless sensing device to securely transmit the node information to ensure the security of the data information transmission. The client interface settings are shown in Fig. 4.

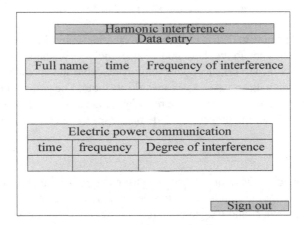

Fig. 4. Client interface settings

The design of the system hardware structure adopts the Kalman filter prediction method to realize the fast perception of the prediction information, thereby obtaining readable and unreadable information. In order to make the system only transmit readable information, it is necessary to design a closed switch to make the data communication better. The client module is set at the end of the hardware, which is mainly responsible for displaying the communication result, and the athlete can view the data communication result of the network terminal in real time through the client interface.

3 System Software Part Design

For the above system hardware control module, the software part is designed, as shown in Fig. 5.

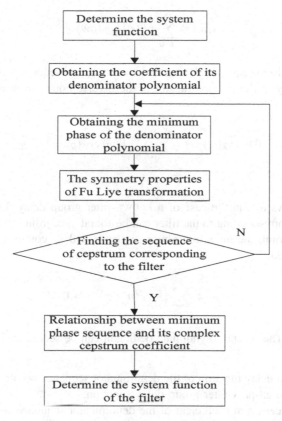

Fig. 5. System software design process

The system function of the digital all-pass filter can be obtained from Fig. 5:

$$F(x) = \frac{A(x)}{B(x)} = \frac{\sum_{m=0}^{M} q_{M-m}^{x-m}}{\sum_{m=0}^{M} q_{m}^{x-m}} \tag{1}$$

Where $q_0 = 1$, it can be seen from Eq. (1) that the system function $F(x)$ can be completely determined by its denominator polynomial coefficient. Since $F(x)$ is a stationary filter, its denominator polynomial must have a minimum phase. The relationship between a minimum phase filter group delay function and its complex cepstrum coefficients is as follows:

$$\alpha(w) = \sum_{i=0}^{\infty} p\beta(p)\cos(pw) \tag{2}$$

The complex cepstrum sequence $\beta(p)$ must be a real causal sequence. According to the symmetry property of the Fourier transform, the inverse Fourier transform is obtained for Eq. (2):

$$\begin{aligned} \mathrm{IDFT}(\alpha(w)) &= \frac{1}{N}\sum_{j=0}^{N-1}\sum_{i=0}^{\infty} p\beta(p)\cos(pw)Q_N^{-jn} \\ &= \frac{n\beta(n)}{2} \end{aligned} \tag{3}$$

Equation (3) shows that in the case of a known filter group delay function, the cepstrum sequence corresponding to the filter can be found. According to the basic theory of complex cepstrum, the minimum phase sequence and its complex cepstrum coefficients are satisfied:

$$s(p) = \sum_{i=0}^{p} \left(\frac{p}{n}\right)\beta(n-p), n > 0 \tag{4}$$

Where $s(0) = 1$. The parent polynomial coefficient can be scored by Eq. (4). Its main steps are:

First, the group delay function of the denominator sequence is calculated according to the specified all-pass filter group delay function;
Secondly, the cepstrum coefficient of the denominator sequence is obtained by the denominator group delay function;
Finally, the coefficients of the scoring parent polynomial are obtained from the cepstral coefficients, and the system function of the filter is determined.

4 Simulation

In order to verify whether the above design method is reasonable, the filter design experiment was completed in the 380 V/2.2 kW cage asynchronous motor speed control system driven by the three-level inverter developed in the laboratory. The result is shown in Fig. 6.

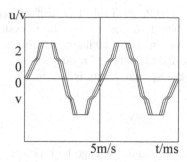

（a）Inverter output voltage waveform without filter rated load

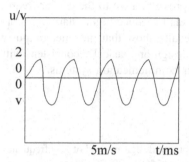

（b）Inverter output voltage waveform after filtered rated load

Fig. 6. Experimental waveform

Figure 6(a) shows the output voltage and current waveform of the inverter when the rated load of the all-pass filter for power communication with high anti-harmonic interference is high; Fig. 6(b) shows the output voltage and current waveform of the inverter when the rated load is filtered.

According to the above content, the output voltage and current harmonic content of the all-pass filter system of the conventional system and the high-anti-harmonic interference power communication are compared and analyzed. The results are shown in Table 1.

Table 1. Two system output voltage and current harmonic content

	Traditional system	All pass filter system	Actual value
Near maximum voltage harmonic content/%	10.1	2.2	2.1
The maximum current harmonic content in the vicinity/%	0.32	6.65	6.60
Total harmonic distortion/%	23.5	5.4	5.5

According to the comparison results of Table 1, it can be seen that the output voltage and current harmonic content of the all-pass filter system is a high-anti-harmonic power communication system. The total harmonic distortion is much smaller than that of the traditional system, and the obtained results are basically consistent with the actual values, indicating that the system design is reasonable.

5   Conclusions

The higher harmonic problem is the medium-voltage high-power multi-level variable frequency drive device inherent in the all-pass filter system for power communication of harmonic interference. The reasonable design of the filter can reduce the insulation requirement of the motor and improve relative to the carrier frequency and increasing the number of output voltage levels to reduce higher harmonics are simpler and more economical. The experimental results show that the filter output voltage and current harmonic content of the system design are basically consistent with the actual values, and can be widely used in power communication systems.

References

1. Biao, W., Lei, Z., Jin, M.: An optimal design method of low frequency resonant filter based on NSGA-II. Electr. Meas. Instrum. **55**(10), 20–26 (2018)
2. De, W.W., Jie, S., Tai, B., et al.: Test and research on anti-jamming performance of power line carrier communication. Electr. Meas. Instrum. **54**(14), 53–56 (2017)
3. Li, X., Sun, Z.: Design and implementation of 10 kV low voltage distribution system for building electricity under harmonic interference. Mod. Electron. Technol. **40**(10), 164–167 (2017)
4. Roldán-Pérez, J., Bueno, E.J., Peña-Alzola, R., et al.: All-pass-filter-based active damping for VSCs with LCL filters connected to weak grids. IEEE Trans. Power Electron. **PP**(99), 1 (2018)
5. Zhou, W., Hou, J., Liu, L., et al.: Design and simulation of the integrated navigation system based on extended Kalman filter. Open Phys. **15**(1), 182–187 (2017)
6. Liu, X., Liu, Z., Shan, J.: Design of composite hierarchical anti-jamming autopilot for missile system. Control Eng. **24**(3), 500–504 (2017)
7. Li, F.: Design and implementation of anti-jamming detection system for abnormal signals in network intrusion. Mod. Electron. Technol. **40**(6), 10–13 (2017)
8. Zhou, T., Xu, Y., Wang, J.: Passive filter design considering harmonic characteristics of electrified railway. Power Capacit. React. Power Compens. **38**(3), 12–18 (2017)
9. Ma, X.: Design and experimental analysis of interference suppressor for communication signal in tilt initiation of high power microwave projectile. Bull. Sci. Technol. **33**(1), 110–113 (2017)
10. Wei, Z.: Simulation study on information recognition of communication transmission interference in big data network. Comput. Simul. **35**(04), 422–426 (2018)

Improved Design of Classification Algorithm in Cloud Computing and Big Data Environment

Yihuo Jiang[✉]

Fuzhou University of International Studies and Trade, Fuzhou, China
Wz26677@163.com

Abstract. With the rapid improvement of China's economic level, science and technology are also progresses, and the scope of the application of science and technology in daily life is becoming more and more extensive, and the large data of cloud computing is also applied to all aspects of our daily life. The classification algorithm is the key to reflect the large data computing ability of the cloud computing. It can further improve the analysis ability of the related data, make the operation of the related data more convenient, more close to the needs of the searcher for information, and avoid a large number of invalid information, because this is very demanding for the classification algorithm. On this basis, we analyzed the operation of the classification algorithm in the cloud computing environment, and used the clustering algorithm to improve the design, improve the efficiency of the related data and improve the accuracy of the data collection.

Keywords: Cloud computing · Big data · Sorting algorithms · Improved design

1 Introduction

With the continuous development of China's economy and the continuous advancement of science and technology, China has entered the era of cloud computing big data. The classification research of related information and related searches are all carried out by using cloud computing big data [1]. The wide application of this technology helps to improve the search speed of information. The collection of information is more comprehensive, and the processing speed of data is more satisfied with the needs of modern information processing [2]. Cloud computing large data is mainly designed and calculated algorithms to improve the speed and accuracy of data calculation, to ensure the accuracy and speed of information search [3]. Therefore, the requirements of the algorithm are very high, and the related algorithms need to be improved continuously. Relevant personnel have also made some improvements to the classification algorithm.

Reference [4] proposes a stream data concept drift detection algorithm and a parallel decision tree classification algorithm in large data environment, which are mainly used to detect and process the implicit concept drift of unstable stream data. Based on the proposed P-HT parallel decision tree classification algorithm, a parallel modeling algorithm and a real-time classification evaluation framework for stream data based on

G. Gui and L. Yun (Eds.): ADHIP 2019, LNICST 301, pp. 161–170, 2019.
https://doi.org/10.1007/978-3-030-36402-1_17

distributed flow processing platform are designed. The traditional classification algorithm will be improved by incremental quantization to meet the needs of stream data processing. This method has high efficiency and anti-concept drift performance, but its operation process is complex. Reference [5] proposes a deep neural network classification algorithm based on particle swarm optimization (PSO). The weights are optimized by combining the automatic coder in deep learning with PSO algorithm. The weighted sum of the error function of the coder itself and the cost function of the Softmax classifier is used as the evaluation function of the PSO algorithm to make the coded data more accurate. Adaptive classifier. This method has high classification accuracy on mail classification, but it has great limitations. Reference [6] proposes a data stream classification algorithm based on clustering assumption. The clustering assumption that the samples classified by clustering algorithm may be of the same category is used to fit the distribution of samples by clustering results on training data sets. In the classification stage, samples that are difficult to classify or have potential concept drift are purposefully selected. The new model and so on, the algorithm can reduce the number of samples needed to update the model under the premise of adapting to concept drift, and achieve better classification effect, but the improvement of the algorithm does not consider the processing of invalid information.

Based on the above problems, this paper proposes to improve the design of classification algorithm in cloud computing and big data environment. In the context of cloud computing large data, classification algorithm has been fully improved and improved. The improvement of the algorithm requires a series of preparatory analysis of related operations. In order to improve the operation accuracy, it is necessary to improve the operation efficiency and save the corresponding calculation time. This makes the classification algorithm has been effectively improved, and the related design is more convenient, easy to use, and more practical.

2 Algorithm Research in Cloud Computing Big Data Environment

At the current stage of information technology development, the scope of use of cloud computing has also been greatly enhanced, and the technical level has also been greatly improved. Many large companies such as Alibaba use cloud computing to collect and organize information when conducting statistical analysis of data. And this technology has been widely promoted and popularized in recent years, and has been valued by many large companies and large enterprises [7]. In the context of the Internet environment formed at this stage, cloud computing is very conducive to the further development of Internet technology at this stage. Cloud computing technology can not only analyze and calculate data, but also use cloud computing technology to predict and analyze related data. It plays a certain degree of reference for high-level decision-making, making the decision-making more accurate, more conducive to making better decisions, and improving the company's own economic benefits.

Cloud computing technology is currently a platform for data storage, management and computing, and has been widely used by users. Compared with the previous information exchange and processing technology, cloud computing technology has been greatly improved. It has greatly improved the information processing speed and processing range compared with the previous information processing system. Therefore, in the context of the current Internet, cloud computing technology has been widely applied and popularized. Based on the use of data center technology and Internet information technology, cloud computing technology has been developed to support the theory and practice. It provides powerful support for the rapid development of cloud computing technology and promotes the rapid development of cloud computing technology [8]. Cloud computing technology realizes the visualization of communication between information and improves the speed of calculation between data. It provides a corresponding basis for effective interaction and contact between information, so that users who want to perform information operations can make full use of Internet resources to realize the transmission of information and collect the required information. The cloud computing technology sends information through the cloud, achieves effective interaction between human and machine, creates a better environment for computing information for users, expands the calculation ideas between information, and achieves effective calculation between information. Cloud computing can achieve the sharing of information, so that the information between multiple users forms a diversified interaction mode, so that there is a certain relationship between information and information, and the communication between data usage is realized. The data is delivered to the usage mode, which satisfies the needs of various users for data usage, realizes the sharing of information, improves the ability to filter and process information, and embodies the applicability and convenience of data. The communication between the information and the processing capacity of the information itself is improved, and it is adapted to the current high-tempo information needs, and its use has been further enhanced. On this basis, through the cloud computing, a large amount of required information can be searched, and the searched information can refer to the big data, so that the data itself has scalability. And for the new information that just appeared, the information can be obtained in time on the basis of cloud computing. Unlike the low speed of information circulation in the past, it is not conducive to the communication and sharing of information under modern information technology, enhance the load capacity of information itself, and strengthen the ability of information itself to identify and distinguish information. Moreover, it has a certain fault tolerance for the processing of information. In the case of processing the information itself, the data can be kept running smoothly, and the information is not processed erroneously, so that the ability to process information is improved. Behind the cloud computing, there is a high-speed server supporting its calculations, so that the efficiency of computing is continuously improved, and the accuracy of calculations is improved. Therefore, we must continue to improve the performance of the server to meet the growing demand for data processing. As shown in Fig. 1:

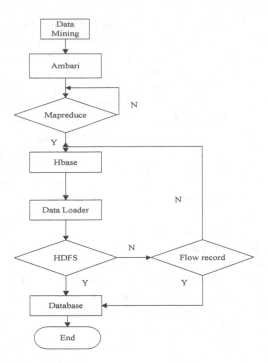

Fig. 1. Cloud computing website classification system architecture

In the context of cloud computing big data, the calculation and processing of related data has been greatly improved, fully embodying the arrival of the modern information age. It allows more people to reach the convenience of the information age, improve the convenience requirements that people need to meet the information needs, and enable people to enjoy the convenience brought by the information age. In the process of utilizing cloud computing big data, it can be fully applied to all aspects of Internet companies. For example, Taobao, according to the user's search needs, combined with the user's browsing page, can be recommended to the user related products again, to improve the convenience of the user to browse again [9]. It allows everyone to quickly and easily purchase products, reduce the time of purchase, improve the convenience of purchase, so that everyone can choose their favorite products without leaving home. For example, the Gaode map can also use big data to perform related calculations in the map software, calculate relevant walking routes and related walking time, and improve the convenience of people's travel. It allows everyone to go out without worrying about other problems. With a mobile phone, you can go to any place you want to go. The map can be automatically positioned according to people's travel needs. And according to the calculation of big data, the processing of related information can be improved, and the burden of travel can be reduced [10].

3   Research on Improved Design of Classification Algorithm

To improve the classification algorithm in the cloud computing big data environment, it is necessary to carry out research on related algorithms. The clustering algorithm should be used to improve the related design, improve the efficiency of the relevant data, and improve the accuracy of data collection.

The constraint is set to:

$$u_{ij} \in \{0, 1\}, j = 1, 2 \ldots m \tag{1}$$

$$\sum_{j=1}^{m} u_{ij} = 1, i = 1, 2, \ldots \ldots . n \tag{2}$$

Design the algorithm as:

$$J(I, U) = \sum_{i=1}^{n} \sum_{j=1}^{m} u_{ij} d(x_i, \theta_j) \tag{3}$$

Where i represents the relevant parameter of the operational data, and j represents the operational coefficient of the correlation operation, u represents the analysis of the relevant algorithm to be performed during the operation, and n represents the degree of infinity of the data, m represents the required analysis required to perform correlation analysis using data, x represents the possibility of adding data for the future which makes the data operation more convenient, and the data processing and operation efficiency are effectively improved. To randomly divide the collected data into multiple test clusters, in the process, the values will be calculated and compared with the subset. Also, the mean value is used as the value of the operation, and finally the out-of-cluster data that produces any other data points is selected. In the operation of the data, the related data can be integrated, so that the final expression of the data can present a complete process for related operations. It makes the analysis of the results of the operation relevant and universal, and completes the corresponding operations on the relevant information. Also, it enables the final calculation results to fully meet the conditions for the relevant collection and display, to make the specific information systematized, and to carry out systematic calculations to achieve the ultimate goal. As shown in Table 1:

Table 1. Data classification results

Alfalfa	Sample	Scores
Corn	6	96.25
Oats	144	99.01
Grass	48	91.89
Pasture	24	96.23
Windrowed	32	94.65

In the related data calculation, fully consider the steps that the data should perform in the correlation operation. In the process of data processing in each step, the relevant feasibility analysis and processing should be fully carried out, so that the final generated data has corresponding correctness, and the accuracy degree is effectively improved. Fully improving the correlation operation for it, so that the speed of calculation and the degree of correlation can be effectively improved, and the processing of related data can be fully optimized. The center of the optimal result at the initial center of the data is far from the sampling of the data point. The level of the sampled data is to be searched for random sampling by hierarchical clustering, and the center of the clustered cluster is used as the initial center point. Finally, using the global optimal technique, it is calculated by the relevant genetic algorithm to ensure that the optimal solution is finally obtained. As shown in Table 2:

Table 2. Data traffic statistics

Groups of the median	In the group values	Frequency
27.73–28.67	28.2	1
28.67–29.98	29.14	18
29.98–30.55	30.08	30
30.55–31.49	31.02	32
31.49–32.43	31.96	23
32.43–33.37	32.9	11

When performing optimization and upgrade of related algorithms, the algorithm can be designed as:

$$J(\theta, U) = \sum_{i=1}^{n}\sum_{j=1}^{m} u_{ij}^q d(x_i, \theta_j) - \sum_{i=1}^{n} \partial_1 \left(\sum_{j=1}^{m} u_{ij} - 1 \right) \tag{4}$$

In the above formula, u_{ij}^q denotes the value of the i object in property q, d represents the distance of the sample classification data.

$$\frac{\partial J(\theta, U)}{\partial \theta} = \sum_{I=1}^{N} u_{ij}^q \frac{\partial d(x_i, \theta_j)}{\partial \theta_i} = 0, j = 1, 2, \ldots, m \tag{5}$$

In the formula, ∂d represents the value of the sample classification data in the case of a specific distance. θ_i represents the value of i under θ data.

After the optimization of the algorithm, the computational efficiency of the algorithm can be greatly optimized and improved. As an improved algorithm design in the cloud computing big data environment, it can fully improve the accuracy of the operation and enhance the efficiency of the operation. In the process of algorithm-related optimization, we must fully consider the feasibility of the operation, can not blindly pursue the innovation of the algorithm and forget the essence of the break-through, and can not achieve the effect of the operation. In the process of performing the operation, it is necessary to improve the control ability of the algorithm for the data, and perform the calculation of the data step by step. It is not only possible to perform the related disordered operation, and the effect of the operation is not achieved, and the feasibility of the operation cannot be improved. As shown in Fig. 2:

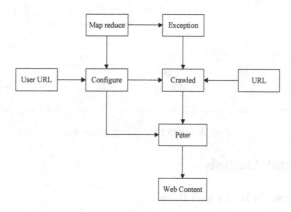

Fig. 2. Data import flow chart

When designing the algorithm, first of all, we must consider the accuracy of the algorithm operation to ensure accurate data collection. The final result of the operation is reasonable, and the phenomenon of operational errors cannot occur, so as to avoid unnecessary misunderstanding and inaccurate calculation information; Secondly, the corresponding feasibility analysis should be carried out to avoid making the design of the algorithm unsuitable for the corresponding calculation. It is also necessary to make the algorithm's operation process too complicated or too simple to accurately process related information; Thirdly, it is necessary to improve the computational efficiency of the algorithm, make the related operations more convenient, and make the operation more cumbersome, which is not conducive to the programmer's editing and operation of the algorithm; Finally, while taking into account the correctness, the design of the algorithm should allow more people to perform related operations and operations. It is necessary to improve the popularity of related algorithms, so as not to produce poor application effects for related algorithms, resulting in related computational difficulties, and their general practicability is poor. As shown in Fig. 3:

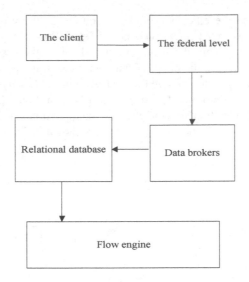

Fig. 3. Data processing process

4   Experimental Analysis

4.1   Experimental Platform and Data

The experimental platform cluster consists of four computers and four nodes. The software environment is: operating system: CentOS 6, JDK version: 1.7, Hadoop version: 2.5.2, Mahout version: 0.10.1. After Hadoop platform is built, Mahout is used to implement the proposed algorithm. To run Mahout, Hadoop needs to be installed in advance. Hadoop has been installed. Now we will use Mahout to run the classification algorithm proposed in this paper. The experimental data came from 20-News groups in UCI.

4.2   Analysis of Experimental Results

The document set selected in this experiment is part of the data in 20-Newsgroups, the experiment was carried out 20 times. Choosing the Value of the Experimental Data and Choosing the Mean Value. By comparing the methods of this paper, reference [4], reference [5], and reference [6], the classification results of the experiments are shown in Table 3.

Table 3. Accuracy comparison of different classification methods

Experimental methods	Test document number/number	Number of correct classifications/number	Correctness/%
The method in this paper	300	288	96%
Reference [4] method	300	189	63%
Reference [5] method	300	201	67%
Reference [6] method	300	196	65.3%

From the data in Table 3, it can be seen that the classification accuracy of this method is as high as 96%, while the classification accuracy of reference [4], reference [5] and reference [6] are all more than 60%. The accuracy of this method is about 30% higher than that of the other three methods, which shows that this method is accurate in data classification. It is more accurate and reliable.

The experimental results show that the proposed method, the reference [4], the reference [5], and the reference [6] are effective in terms of the classification time and the number of classifications. The experimental results are shown in Fig. 4.

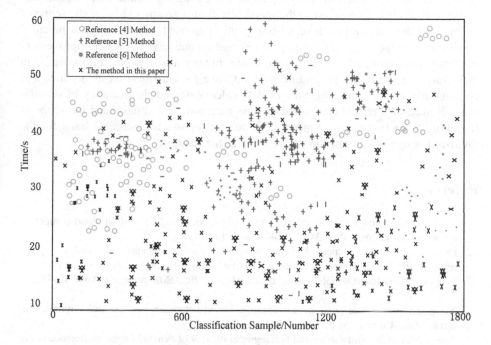

Fig. 4. Comparison of sample data classification under different methods

From Fig. 4, we can see that the improved classification algorithm in this paper can classify the sample data in a shorter time and a larger number of classifications. But when using reference [4], the number of classifications is relatively small and the classification time is relatively long. When using this method to classify the sample data, only a part of the data can be classified. This method can not classify large quantities of data when it is increased; when the reference [5] method and reference [6] method are used, the classification takes a long time and can only classify local data; therefore, experiments show that the improved method in this paper has more advantages in data classification.

5   Conclusions

In the cloud computing big data environment, the improved research of classification algorithm fully realizes the optimization and upgrade of the algorithm, and the data processing and computing ability has been effectively improved. It further enhances the analysis ability of related data, makes the calculation process of related data more convenient, is closer to the searcher's demand for information, and avoids a large amount of invalid information. Moreover, it realizes the improvement of the classification algorithm and can also apply the cloud computing big data to more aspects and realize the effective calculation of the algorithm. It also greatly enhances the scope of its use, and the technology has also been greatly improved, which has great practical significance for future research and operation, and is conducive to further improvement and improvement of the algorithm in the future. In the era of data-based information in the future, it is necessary to continuously improve the classification algorithms, and continuously improve the efficiency of data calculation and the accuracy of calculations. It makes the related computing process more simple and easy, and the scope of feasibility is continuously expanded. This paper proposes a theoretical basis for the improved design of classification algorithms in the future.

References

1. Yi, L.: Research on a remote sensing processing service model based on cloud computing model. Comput. Appl. Res. **36**(9), 124–125 (2017)
2. Fang, S.: Commercial spectral remote sensing image classification m based on sparse representation and spectral information. Electron. J. Inf. Sci. **26**(2), 155–158 (2017)
3. Feng, C.: Spark based remote sensing data analysis method. Microcomput. Appl. **12**(3), 21–29 (2017)
4. Yong, T.: Map reduce performance optimization in heterogeneous resource environment. Small Micro-Comput. Syst. **7**(6), 125–129 (2017)
5. Xiong, X., Lin, Z.: Simulation study on regional filtering of demand target interference in big data networks. Comput. Simul. **33**(10), 376–380 (2017)
6. Kreijns, K., Kirschner, P.A., Jochems, W.: The sociability of computer-supported collaborative learning environments. Educ. Technol. **12**(6), 266–271 (2017)
7. Gunawardena, N., Lowe, C., Anderson, T.: Analysis of a global online debate and the development of an interaction analysis model for examining social construction of knowledge in computer conferencing. J. Educ. **52**(12), 521–536 (2017)
8. Barbierato, E., Gribaudo, M., Iacono, M.: Performance evaluation of NoSQL big-data applications using multi-formalism models. Futur. Gener. Comput. Syst. **18**(3), 115–124 (2017)
9. Plantenga, T.D., Choe, Y.R., Yoshimura, A.: Using performance measurements to improve MapReduce algorithms. Proc. Comput. Sci. **15**(7), 304–310 (2017)
10. Plantenga, Y.R., Choe, A.Y.: Using performance measurements to improve MapReduce algorithms. Proc. Comput. Sci. **52**(6), 152–163 (2017)

Research on Dynamic Access Control Model of Distributed Network Under Big Data Technology

Yi-huo Jiang[✉]

Fuzhou University of International Studies and Trade, Fuzhou, China
Wz26677@163.com

Abstract. The traditional distributed network dynamic access control management model has the defects of poor control management efficiency and poor expansibility. In order to solve the above problems, the dynamic access control management model of the distributed network is constructed by the large-data technology. According to the requirement of distributed network dynamic access control management model, the mining model is constructed. Based on this model, the direct trust value and indirect trust value are calculated by big data technology, and the final trust value is obtained by combining them. Based on the final trust value obtained, the dynamic access control management process is formulated and executed to realize the control and management of distributed network dynamic access. The simulation results show that compared with the traditional distributed network dynamic access control management model, the distributed network dynamic access control management model greatly improves the efficiency and expansibility of the model. It fully shows that the distributed network dynamic access control management model has better control and management performance.

Keywords: Big data technology · Distributed network · Dynamic access · Control · Management

1 Introduction

The security of distributed network has been paid more and more attention. As an important security technology, dynamic access control has penetrated into all aspects of operating system, database and network. Therefore, in recent years, the research on distributed network dynamic access control management model has been regarded as one of the most important research topics by scholars all over the world [1].

The traditional distributed network dynamic access control management model can be divided into two kinds: one is autonomous access control, the other is autonomous access control. The basic idea is that the subject (user or user process) in the distributed network can freely grant the access to the object (all or part) to other subjects. In fact, this method generally establishes the distributed network access control matrix, the row of the matrix corresponds to the main body of the distributed network, the column corresponds to the object of the distributed network, and the element represents the

G. Gui and L. Yun (Eds.): ADHIP 2019, LNICST 301, pp. 171–180, 2019.
https://doi.org/10.1007/978-3-030-36402-1_18

access authority of the subject to the object. However, the cost of the model is difficult to pay, and the efficiency is quite low, so it is difficult to meet the needs of large-scale applications, especially network applications. The other is mandatory access control, which is a model to restrict the object access according to the sensitive mark of the information in the object and the access level of the subject who accesses the sensitive information. The model used in forced access control is mainly the BLP model [2]. Reference [3] proposes a new access control model based on hierarchical system and a new hierarchical system with inclusive relationship, which is more compatible with the open distributed network environment and has universality. Access control model based on hierarchical system. In this model, four kinds of attributes are formally defined and the POL module is designed based on the obligation mechanism. The module divides the authority management into two parts, taking into account the fine-grained and coarse-grained authorization access control, and the fine-grained authorization has the highest priority. This method not only reduces the possibility of policy conflict, but also solves the problem of policy library expansion. But the efficiency of this method is not high. Reference [4] focuses on the analysis of security requirements in multi-domain environment, draws lessons from existing key technologies, proposes a trust evaluation mechanism based on time attenuation and role level, and improves the cross-domain authorization mechanism on the basis of inter-domain role mapping, based on the combination of trust evaluation model and role-based access control model. A cross-domain authorization model based on user domain set is proposed. This method can effectively improve efficiency, but its scalability is not high.

Based on the human existence of the above problems, this paper proposes a distributed network dynamic access control model under the big data technology.

2   Construction of Distributed Network Dynamic Access Control Management Model

In the distributed network environment, the information resources that need to be managed and controlled are huge and complex, and the terminal needs frequent interaction in order to cooperate to complete the specific service. The traditional dynamic access control management model can not meet its dynamic and open requirements, which can easily lead to privacy disclosure and other security risks. In order to solve this problem, a dynamic access control management model based on trust constraints is proposed. In that model, the role-based dynamic access control management model is expanded through an integrated trust and a context, and the dynamic trust value calculation is carried out on the user history and the external recommendation through a lightweight trust level mechanism, Fine-grained and dynamic security access authorization performance can be provided. The model evaluation results show that the model has excellent environmental adaptability and dynamic performance [5]. The model is easy to implement and can effectively enhance the security of dynamic access control management in distributed network environment.

2.1   Construction of the Whole Frame of the Model

Under the distributed network environment, the user's scale changes dynamically, the user's identity can not be determined in advance, and it has the open characteristic. The traditional model is static because the role assignment mode is static, and the user identity is based on proof and the role assignment authority does not satisfy the minimum permission principle, so it is no longer applicable. In order to solve this problem, according to the dynamic and open characteristics of distributed network environment, the dynamic access control management model is improved as follows:

The first is to increase the level of trust. Before the user role is granted, the trust level of the user needs to be measured in a specific context. Only those who are considered to be able to trust can take the next step, and the authentication process is only used as an alternate option. The user is not directly related to the role and overcomes the security threat when the user's identity is unknown in advance.

The second is to restrict authorization. In order to meet the dynamic and fine-grained requirements of authorization, users need to use role activation constraint, object operation activation constraint and authorization time constraint to obtain the operation authority of the object finally.

Where the character activates the constraint. Under specific session conditions, the user trust value of the requesting access system is evaluated, and when the specified threshold is greater than the specified threshold, a certain role can be activated. Role assignment is dynamic and prevents access requests from malicious users; object actions activate constraints. After the user acquires a specific permission, it needs to be confirmed by the authorization checking mechanism before the operation. In order to prevent malicious users from trying to take illegal actions after obtaining permissions by accumulating trust, it not only satisfies the minimum permission principle of access control, but also satisfies the need of fine-grained authorization; authorization time constraint. As an important context constraint, the validity of authorization time is a kind of Important security mechanisms can effectively overcome the traditional access control once granted permanent defects.

Thirdly, a trust measurement algorithm is constructed. In the dynamic access control management model, in order to meet the characteristics of dynamic authorization and fine-grained authorization, integrated rewards and punishments, security classification and trend prediction strategies, a trust measurement method considering experience, knowledge and recommendation is presented.

The diagram of dynamic access control management model based on trust constraint is shown in Fig. 1.

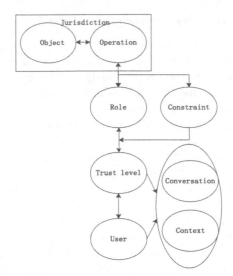

Fig. 1. A schematic diagram of dynamic access control management model based on trust constraints

As shown in Fig. 1, the model defines the relationship between an element set and an element set that includes the following types: user, trust level, role, session, context, operation, object, permissions, and constraints. Among them, the concept of user refers to autonomous entities, including other networks, autonomous programs and natural persons. The user set is used to obtain the user set of the distributed network service. Each trust level in the trust level is a subset between [0, 1] and can be discrete or continuous [6]. A user has a trust level according to the session and context at a given time, and the role is assigned to the role according to the user's trust level, and the role set refers to the work function associated with the same semantic responsibilities. A session corresponds to a user and a set of trust levels, representing the process in which a user acquires a trust level. A user can perform multiple sessions to obtain a different level of trust in each session. Having different levels of trust means having different access permissions; context refers to the specific environment information at the time of the visit, such as access time state and access location and other environment variables; The object is an operable set of data and a part of the resources available in a distributed network, operation refers to a mirror image of the operation. Constraints are defined as assertions applied to model element relationships or assignment relationships that return a quantity of acceptance or not. it can be seen as a condition for the application of an element relationship or element assignment; the right is a binary group that is authorized to perform a specific task in the system [7]. Permissions are always associated with roles, that is, permissions give role-specific rights. The type of permissions depends on the distributed network, and the model itself makes no assumptions.

2.2 Measurement of Trust Level

Trust is defined as the ability of entities to safely and reliably execute beliefs in a specific context environment. The basis of the level of trust is the determination of the nature of the event. Set up P is a positive event set, Q is a negative event set, satisfying $A = P \cup Q$. Whether the nature of an event is a positive event or a negative event depends on the nature of the event itself, that is, the event is empirically classified as whether the influence of the event on trust is positive or negative. Let a_i denote the i th event in a specific time interval, and if $a_i \in Q$ mark it. If $a_i \in P$, then mark $P_i = 1$. That is,

$$P = \begin{cases} 0, & if \quad a_i \in Q \\ 1, & if \quad a_i \in P \end{cases} \tag{1}$$

Direct trust is an entity based on experience And direct knowledge Measurement, experience and direct knowledge are historical experiences that entities themselves can acquire directly. Experience is a record of the success of interaction. The smaller the interval between the measurement of trust relationship and the time interval, the greater the influence on the value of trust relationship measure [8].

Entity A To entity B The direct trust value is

$$DT_{(A \to B)} = \alpha \cdot E + (1 - \alpha) \cdot DK, (0 \le \alpha \le 1) \tag{2}$$

Of which, α represents the entity's coefficient based on experience.

Indirect trusted section includes recommendation RC and indirect knowledge IK Two parts, the recommendation comes from the directly related entity (referrer), indirect knowledge mainly refers to the trend. Set the number of directly associated nod Each associated node gives a recommendation value as a referrer (Direct creditable value of the relevant referrer), Then the metric recommendation RC It's all m. The average of the recommended values, then entity A To entity B Indirect trust value of

$$IT_{(A \to B)} = \beta \cdot RC + (1 - \beta) \cdot IK, (0 \le \beta \le 1) \tag{3}$$

Of which, β represents the coefficient that measures the recommended value.

After the direct and indirect trust values are obtained, the final trust value is

$$TL^{[t_1, t_n]} = \frac{\sum_{i=1}^{n} w_{t_i} T^{(t_i)}}{\sum_{i=1}^{n} w_{t_i}}, (w_{t_i} = \lambda^{t_n - t_1}, 0 < \lambda < 1) \tag{4}$$

Of which, $T^{(t_i)}$ represents the current trust value, $T^{(t_i)} = \gamma DT + (1 - \gamma)IT$, $(0 \le \gamma \le 1)$, γ is the calculation parameter of the current trust value; λ represents the model extensibility parameters.

2.3   Dynamic Access Control Management Process

In the previous section, the trust-level measure considered the security of access, but did not examine the security of the resource itself during the visit. Therefore, it is necessary to introduce authorization checking mechanism into this model. The core part of the mechanism is role activation constraint, object operation activation constraint and authorization time constraint. Authorization checking mechanism is designed to guarantee the security of resource province during dynamic access [8–10].

Execute according to the authorization check function, its purpose is to check the validity of authorization. However, only checking the validity of authorization checking function can not complete the access process, and it is also necessary to make decision on access. Therefore, the current authorization needs to meet certain conditions in order to finally determine whether the access is successful or not [11].

In distributed network environment, because the terminal is mostly embedded system and its resource, power and processing speed are relatively limited, the consistency maintenance method of dynamic constraint conflict is less complicated because it does not need to detect all potential constraint conflicts. More applicable. In order to effectively detect and resolve the internal constraint conflicts in the dynamic access control management model, the graph theory method is used to study the relationship among users, roles and permissions [12].

A constraint conflict graph is a multi-graph that describes multiple conflicts, Expressed as $G(C) = (V, E)$. Of which, V Vertex set, which means the user, role and authority associated with the constraint; E means two vertices The constraint between v_1, v_2 is *lable*, *id* is the label of the constraint edge.

Constraint collision graph can detect all constraint conflicts in distributed networks, and there are two possible constraint conflicts. The first one is that the source node v_1, the target node v_2 are a set of conflict elements, and *id* is the SoD constraint between the set of conflict elements. The second case is v_1 As a pre-emptive constraint, v_2 is a member of a set of elements that are pre-constrained, *id* Prior constraint identification.

A typical constraint conflict graph, as shown in Fig. 2. It contains five constraints, Expressed as $cr_1 : (r_1, r_2, r_3)$, $prc_1 : (r_1, r_2)$, $ppc_1 : (p_1, p_2)$, $ppc_2 : (p_2, p_3)$, $ppc_3 : (p_3, p_1)$. Of which, cr_1 represents a conflicting role set; prc_1 represents a pre-requisite constraint, r_2 is the precondition of r_1. ppc_1 ppc_3 and ppc_2 are pre-emptive constraints. p_2 p_3 and p_1 are prerequisites for p_1 p_2 and p_3, respectively.

Based on the constraint conflict diagram shown in Fig. 2, a consistency maintenance algorithm is proposed. The steps of the algorithm are: to detect constraint conflicts; to use priority resolution strategy to resolve the detected constraint conflicts until the constraint conflicts are resolved; to delete the tasks that can not be accomplished by priority resolution strategies; Output constraint consistency maintenance results.

Through the above-mentioned process, the dynamic access control and management of distributed network is realized, and the security of distributed network is guaranteed more effectively.

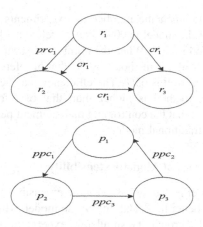

Fig. 2. Constraint conflict diagram

3 Experimental Results and Analysis

In order to validate the performance of the model, a simulation experiment is designed to analyze the model based on 879 MHz CPU PC with 256 MB main memory and Windows XP sp2. The experiment mainly compares the efficiency of model management and control, the extensibility of model and the stability of model, and obtains the experimental data.

3.1 Comparative Analysis of Model Control Management Efficiency

Through the simulation experiment, the comparison of the model control management efficiency is shown in Table 1.

Table 1. Comparison of model control management efficiency.

Number of experiments	Build model	Reference [3] method	Reference [4] method
10	90%	50%	65%
20	88%	49%	54%
30	95%	66%	59%
40	79%	70%	64%
50	86%	63%	62%
60	83%	44%	58%
70	96%	52%	49%
80	89%	50%	48%
90	90%	49%	65%
100	88%	40%	62%

As shown in Table 1, when the number of experiments is 10, the control and management efficiency of the model is 90%, that of reference [3] method is 50%, and that of reference [4] method is 65%. When the number of experiments is 50, the control and management efficiency of this method is 86%, that of reference [3] method is 63%, and that of reference [4] method is 65%. The efficiency was 62%. By comparison, the control efficiency of this method is higher than that of reference [3] method and reference [4], which proves that the control and management performance of the model is better than that of the traditional model.

3.2   Comparative Analysis of Model Extensibility

The scalability of the model is mainly based on the extensibility parameter 1 Denote, 1 The higher the value, the better the scalability of the model, which means the better the performance of the model. Through the simulation experiment, the model expansibility is compared as shown in Fig. 3.

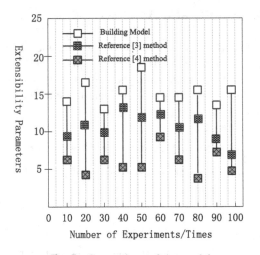

Fig. 3. Comparison of the model

As shown in Fig. 3, when the number of experiments is 10, the scalability of this method is 14, that of reference [3] method is 9, and that of reference [4] method is 6. When the number of experiments is 50, the scalability of this method is 18, that of reference [3] method and reference [4] method is 13 and 5, respectively. Reference [3] method > Reference [4] method, which proves that the expandability of this method is better.

3.3   Contrast Experiment of Model Signal Stability Performance

In order to further verify the operability of the model, the stability performance of the signal is experimented, and the stability of the signal of this method, reference [3] method and reference [4] method is compared to verify the stability of the method.

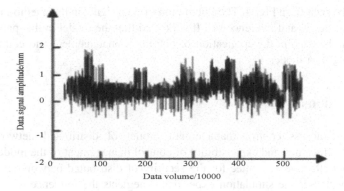

(A) Data signal fluctuation under reference [3]

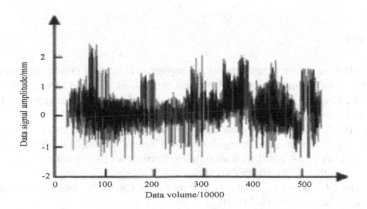

(B) Data signal fluctuation under reference [4]

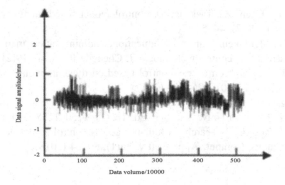

(C) The fluctuation of data signal in this method

Fig. 4. Data signal fluctuation comparison under different methods

As can be seen from Fig. 4, The fluctuation of data signal in this method is less than that in reference [3] and reference [4]. It is proved that the model in this paper is more stable. It can be used in the application of automatic management and control system under the big data mode.

4 Conclusions

The dynamic access control management model of distributed network greatly improves the efficiency and expansibility of control management of the model, and can provide more effective guarantee for the security of distributed network. But because the experiment uses the simulation experiment, neglects the influence of the interference factor in the actual control and management process, it will cause the experiment result to have the certain deviation, therefore, the distributed network dynamic access control management model needs to be further studied and optimized.

References

1. Huang, H.: Research on security model and algorithm of learning flow access control under large data of the Yellow River Qing. J. Minnan Norm. Univ. (Nat. Ed.) **100**(2), 30–39 (2018)
2. Zhang, R., Tang, T., Wanke: Fine-grained access control and audit management in large data environment. Inf. Secur. Res. **3**(6), 509–515 (2017)
3. Yu, H., Hong, R., Shi, W.: Research on the model of enterprise theme network public opinion analysis system based on big data. Mod. Comput. (Prof. Ed.) **613**(13), 73–77 (2018)
4. Xing, X., Tian, X.: A novel reputation-based dynamic access control model. J. Shanghai Electr. Power Inst. **12**(6), 80–85 (2017)
5. Li, L., Shao, L., Wang, C., et al.: Access control of CA-RBAC for ubiquitous networks. Netw. Space Secur. **8**(2), 48–54 (2017)
6. Hu, X.: Research and simulation of dynamic access control method for cloud computing storage data. Comput. Simul. **34**(3), 365–368 (2017)
7. Liu, F., Ding, H.: Role-based secure access control method. Electron. World **45**(1), 166–167 (2017)
8. Liu, H., Zhang, L., Chen, Z.: Task access control model based on fuzzy theory in P2P network. J. Commun. **38**(2), 44–52 (2017)
9. Li, Q.: Research and implementation of educational administration management system based on role-based access control technology. J. Chengde Pet. Coll. **19**(2), 40–44 (2017)
10. Chen, Y., Hao, T.: Research on access control based on dynamic monitoring of role trust. Comput. Technol. Dev. **27**(10), 106–110 (2017)
11. Wang, Y., Yang, J.: A role-based and attribute-based access control model for cloud computing data. J. Tsinghua Univ. Nat. Sci. Ed. **16**(11), 1150–1158 (2017)
12. Li, H., Song, F., Wang, L.: Research on four-tier access control model based on time and environment constraints. Comput. Appl. Softw. **35**(1), 59–64 (2018)

Intelligent Data Acquisition Method for Cross-border E-commerce Guidance and Purchase Considering User Demand

Jiahua Li[✉]

Guangzhou Vocational and Technical University of Science and Technology,
Guangzhou, China
lijiahua010122@163.com

Abstract. At present, due to the unknown online procurement, and remote distance for the cross-border e-commerce shopping guide, business considerations for users were not so full. Based on this, a cross-border e-commerce shopping guide big data intelligent collection method considering user needs was proposed. Through the mobile port of big data to collect and explore the online social retail collection method of big data, it focused on promoting the way of big data onto intelligent collection, and promoted cross-border e-commerce shopping guide big data to better carry out commodity circulation of user needs. Experiments showed that the big data collection method studied in this paper better combined user needs and merchant profit, and helped to improve user experience.

Keywords: User needs · Cross-border E-commerce shopping guide · Big data · Intelligent acquisition · Optimization

1 Introduction

In the past ten years, with the Internet economy growing exponentially, e-commerce has achieved rapid and vigorous development in China, and people's shopping experience has gradually shifted from offline to online, that is, from physical operation to network operation; With the popularity of mobile devices such as mobile phones and tablets, online shopping penetration is still increasing [1]. As of the end of December 2013, the number of e-commerce platform users in China reached 302 million, and the proportion of online users using e-commerce platforms increased to 48.9%. According to the statistics of China Internet Network Information Center CNNIC, the total transaction volume of China's e-commerce platform online in 2013 was 1.85 trillion yuan, a year-on-year increase in 40.09% compared with previous years. It is expected that the growth rate will gradually slow down in the next few years in 2014 to 2017. The annual online shopping market will reach 21.6 trillion yuan to 2017 [2] (Fig. 1).

In this context, shopping websites represented by Tmall, Amazon, JD, etc. have gradually developed into a comprehensive shopping platform. The information architecture and user experience of the website are also becoming mature, and the initiative of consumers is stimulated by good humanized design [3]. At the same time, a large

G. Gui and L. Yun (Eds.): ADHIP 2019, LNICST 301, pp. 181–188, 2019.
https://doi.org/10.1007/978-3-030-36402-1_19

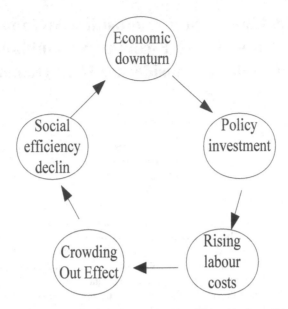

Fig. 1. Cross-border e-commerce shopping guide flow chart

number of goods and discount information outside the website occupy our vision, and the effectiveness of the information is greatly reduced. This is actually the lack of user experience and path design when the information reaches the online shopping user. Information access as the entrance to the e-commerce website plays a vital role in the distribution of traffic. However, the design research of the current design system is in a relatively blank stage [4]. How to better use the user experience design method to improve the efficiency of information access, and form a good user reputation, has long been a problem that has to be considered in front of the designer. Therefore, the establishment of a more complete information architecture, interactive interface, and access system has become a key step for the e-commerce platform to provide users with an excellent shopping experience [5].

2   Design of Intelligent Data Collection Method for Cross-border E-commerce Shopping Guide Big Data

2.1   Big Data Mobile Port Collection

Differentiating the two ports of the mobile PC, consumers can't do without the support of the terminal Internet access device. The terminal Internet access devices of China's network users are mainly composed of the start end represented by smart phones and tablets, and the PC side represented by W desktops and laptops. Compared with the PC, the convenience of the replacement side enables the consumer to purchase goods at any time, complete the payment online [6], track the inquiry order and other service functions. Of course, the value of the mobile end is not only to expand the source of traffic, but also to better combine the various services of offline physical retail stores with local relevance and irreplaceability, so that online and offline channels are all connected and connected. The objectives are shown in Table 1.

Table 1. Indexes

	Min	Max	Average value	Standard deviation	Kurtosis
Hl–1	2	5	5.61	0.948	759
Hl–2	2	5	5.12	0.912	759
Hl–3	2	5	6.26	0.881	759
H2–1	2	5	3.86	0.982	759
H2–2	2	5	4.98	0.901	759
H2–3	2	5	3.98	0.791	759
H2–4	2	5	3.09	0.819	759
H2–5	2	5	2.98	0.298	759
H2–6	2	5	2.00	1.920	759
H3–1	2	5	8.73	1.911	759
H3–2	2	5	4.98	1.910	759
H3–3	2	5	6.21	1.009	759
H3–4	2	5	7.02	1.091	759
H4–1	1	5	9.22	1.681	759
H4–2	2	5	3.92	0.879	759
H4–3	2	5	2.98	0.712	759
H4–4	1	5	4.01	0.971	759
H4–5	2	5	5.01	0.491	759

Therefore, the mobile terminal is neither a general extension of the PC side nor a simple complement of the PC side, but a more stage of the evolution of the network retail format. From the history of online retail format development [7], in the past ten years, the PC side is the main port for the development of online retail formats. However, with the gradual saturation of the desktop and notebook markets, the development speed of the PC-side shopping market tends to slow down, and the PC-side portal is gradually maturing. At the same time, with the development of mobile networks and the popularity of smart handwriting, the mobile shopping market has experienced explosive growth in recent years, and the mobile terminal has almost infiltrated into every aspect of online retail [6].

According to the statistics of iResearch, in 2011–2014, the transaction volume of the mobile shopping market was spurred from 11.68 billion yuan to 940.66 billion yuan, and the compounding rate was as high as 331%. The growth rate is far better than the PC-side shopping market. It is expected that the main move in the future development of online retail formats lies in the development of the mobile shopping market. However [8], because the screen of the mobile terminal is usually smaller, it can only describe products by limited words and photos, which makes consumers' product experience value low. Therefore, network zero enterprises should constantly improve the design of mobile shopping scenes, actively promote mobile payment applications and other measures to enhance the development of mobile terminals. Secondly, at the same time, we will deepen the two domestic and international markets. On the one hand, we must promote the zero net Qiao road to sink, and actively develop the rural market [9].

2.2 Large Data Network Social Retail Collection

The essence of network social retail is the coincidence of social platform and network retailing, which refers to the process of retailing by network retail enterprises or individuals through social platform. Network social retailing combines the user resources of social platform sea children with the convenience of network retail. The reasons for the rise are mainly H aspects under W. First, the Internet business era, who can more quickly and more directly to mass users will represent unlimited business opportunities, and the rise of the mobile Internet has made the W Internet as a medium of social activities more and more common, with the help of this advantage, network social retail began to rise. Second, the traditional B2C or C2C network retail model has not been able to solve the trust problem between merchants and consumers, and social networking is a kind of social retail based on W strong relationship, sellers are selling goods. At the same time, it is also the feeling of selling friends, through this acquaintance relationship, the problem of trust between merchants and consumers is well solved. Third, online social retailing is a good way to help consumers solve the problem of "what to buy? Where to buy?". On the one hand, from the point of view of the hacker, social network retailing runs through the whole process of product purchase, such as store selection before purchase, product price comparison, communication with sellers during purchase, interaction, etc. evaluation, experience sharing, usage guidance, etc. On the other hand, from the perspective of network companies or individuals, accurate product marketing and promotion can be better achieved by actively cooperating with social media, network or social tools, as shown in Fig. 2.

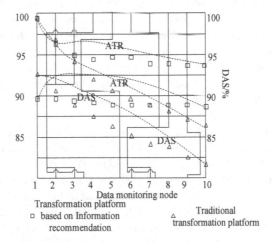

Fig. 2. Traditional B2C network sales trend

In addition, in the traditional B2C or C2C network retail period, the popularity of the online retail platform, the advertisements and information provided by the merchants, the ratings of the consumers to the merchants, or the evaluation of the products constitute the most important purchase basis for the consumers. However, today, when social platforms are prevalent, consumers are more inclined to consult their friends and friends in various social circles. It can be said that the process of online social retailing focusing on, sharing, communicating, discussing, interacting and other social elements in online retail transactions greatly caters to the trend of the times, and it will become an important direction for the evolution of online retail formats in the future. For any target highlighting, five different eigenvalues X{X1, X2, X3, X4, X5} can be extracted, then the membership functions are:

$$\mu(X) = e^{-D(X)} \tag{1}$$

Where

$$D_i(X) = |X_1 - M_1| + |X_2 - M_2| + |X_3 - M_3| + |X_4 - M_4| + |X_5 - M_5| \tag{2}$$

Based on this formula, the membership functions are:

$$\mu_{A1}(X), \mu_{A2}(X), \mu_{A3}(X), \mu_{A4}(X) \tag{3}$$

So the maximum is:

$$\alpha = \max[\mu_{A1}(X), \mu_{A2}(X), \mu_{A3}(X), \mu_{A4}(X)] \tag{4}$$

When $\mu_A(X) = \alpha$, then X belongs to the third category, namely, the sphere.
When $\mu_A(X) = \beta$, then X belongs to the second category, namely, the triangular prism.
When $\mu_A(X) = \delta$, then X belongs to the first category, namely, the cube.

3 Experimental Results and Analysis

In order to ensure the effectiveness of the research on the intelligent data collection method of cross-border e-commerce shopping guide big data considering the needs of users, this experiment was carried out. The experiment of cross-border e-commerce shopping guide big data intelligent collection method considering user needs selected two types of programs. In the experiment, the two types of experimental targets are placed in the same debugging environment, in order to observe the data intelligent integration goals in different time, and record the data at any time. The schematic diagrams of the experimental demonstration results are shown in Figs. 3 and 4, respectively.

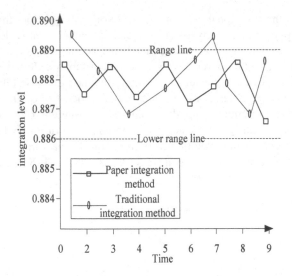

Fig. 3. Experimental target result structure chart

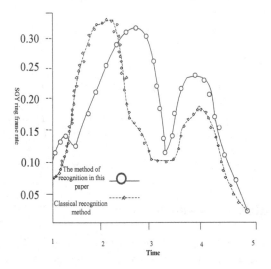

Fig. 4. Experimental intention trend structure

At present, first- and second-tier cities are the user concentration areas of online retail enterprises, and also the core area of competition in the network sales market. However, the development of online retail enterprises in first- and second-tier cities is gradually deepening. The more successful the online retail enterprises in the first- and second-tier cities The smaller, at the same time, with the speed of urbanization construction and the improvement of rural residents' ability to eliminate. The potential of the rural online retail market is huge. According to the statistical report in the Internet information of China, as of June 2015, the number of netizens in China reached 6.68, of which the proportion of netizens in rural areas was 27.9%, compared with the end of 2014 there are 8 million people increased. However, the Internet penetration rate in rural areas of China is only 30.1%. Compared with the penetration rate of 64.2% in urban areas, there is still much room for growth in rural areas. Moreover, in the population aged 10–40, the Internet penetration rate in rural areas is 15–27% points lower than that in urban areas. This part of the population happens to be a relatively low-difficult Internet population, and there is much room for conversion in the future. Therefore, online retail enterprises should focus on promoting the sinking of online retail channels and actively develop rural markets. On the other hand, we must promote the development of cross-border network retailing and fully expand overseas markets.

4 Conclusions

This paper mainly studies the intelligent data collection method for cross-border e-commerce shopping guide big data considering user needs. It fully considers the specific needs of online users to collect intelligent collection methods from cross-border e-commerce shopping guide big data, and optimize cross-border e-commerce shopping guides. In order to help us get more reference value cross-border e-commerce shopping guide big data, for us to better use and use cross-border e-commerce shopping guide big data to improve the use of online users.

Through the analysis of this paper, we can know that the research on cross-border e-commerce shopping guide big data intelligent collection method considering user needs has important and far-reaching significance. Although, in recent years, the cross-border e-commerce shopping guide big data intelligent collection method considering user needs has achieved great gains. There are still many problems waiting for us to solve. To this end, we must not be afraid of difficulties, overcome difficulties, and constantly improve the cross-border e-commerce shopping guide big data intelligent collection method to consider user needs, to obtain effective image information, in turn, it is better to improve the user demand for cross-border e-commerce shopping guide big data intelligent collection method business services.

Acknowledgements. "Innovation Research on Cross-border E-commerce Shopping Guide Platform Based on Big Data and AI Technology", Funded by Ministry of Education Humanities and Social Sciences Research and Planning Fund (No.: 18YJAZH042); Key Research Platform Project of Guangdong Education Department (No.: 2017GWTSCX064); The 13th Five-Year Plan Project of Philosophy and Social Science Development in Guangzhou (No.: 2018GZGJ208).

References

1. Maridn, R.J., Duncan, C.P.: The transformation of retailing institutions: beyond the wheel of retailing and life cycle theories. J. Macromark. **16**(4), 58–66 (2017)
2. Rousseau, D.M., Sitkin, S.B., Burt, R.S., Camerer, C.: Not so different after all: a cross-discipline view of trust. Acad. Manag. Rev. **23**(3), 438–458 (2018)

3. Sillence, E., Briggs, P., Harris, P., et al.: A framework for understanding trust factors in web-based health advice. Int. J. Hum. Comput. Stud. **64**(8), 697–713 (2016)
4. Chellappa, R.K., Pavlou, P.A.: Perceived information security, financial liability and consumer trust in electronic commerce transactions. Logistics Inf. Manag. **15**(5/6), 358–368 (2018)
5. Yang, H., Yin, D., Hong, R.: Research on bridge automatic identification methods in high-resolution remote sensing images. Comput. Simul. **23**(9), 119–122 (2016)
6. Shankar, V., Urban, G.L., Sultan, F.: Online trust: a stakeholder perspective, concepts, implications, and future directions. J. Strateg. Inf. Syst. **11**(3), 325–344 (2012)
7. Willemyns, M., Gallois, C., Callan, V.: Trust me, I'm your boss: trust and power in supervisor —supervisee communication. Int. J. Hum. Resour. Manag. **14**(1), 117–127 (2018)
8. Zhang, P., Dran, G.V., Blake, P., Pipithsuksunt, V.: A comparison of the most important website feature in different domains: an empirical study of user perceptions. In: Proceedings of the Sixth AMCIS Conference on Information System, vol. 6, pp. 1367–1372 (2018)
9. Choo, C.W., Detlor, B., Turnbull, D.: Information seeking on the web: an integrated model of browsing and searching. First Monday **9**, 2 (2018)

Optimization Design of Cross-Border E-commerce Shopping Guide System Combining Big Data and AI Technology

Jiahua Li[✉]

Guangzhou Vocational and Technical University of Science and Technology,
Guangzhou, China
lijiahua010122@163.com

Abstract. In the era of Internet economy, cross-border e-commerce shopping guides were conducted under the conditions of virtual network environment. Therefore, the traditional cross-border e-commerce shopping guide system had long been unable to meet the diversified needs of cross-border e-commerce shopping guides. A cross-border e-commerce shopping guide system combining big data and AI technology was proposed and designed. Using big data and AI technology, the hardware and software of the cross-border e-commerce shopping guide system were analyzed respectively, and the optimized design of the cross-border e-commerce shopping guide system was completed. The experimental data showed that the cross-border e-commerce shopping guide system combining big data and AI technology had better performance than the traditional system, and could better meet the technical requirements of cross-border e-commerce shopping guide.

Keywords: Big data · AI technology · Cross-border · E-commerce shopping guide system · Optimized design

1 Introduction

In order to promote the development of the national economy, the import trade industry is developing rapidly. Free trade zones have been established in China, the first time in the Shanghai region. Practice shows that the establishment and development of free trade zones are the important way to promote economic development at home and abroad [1]. Simply, it is to explore and establish a new market economy suitable for China's national conditions. The main core contents of the free trade pilot zone include further clarifying the role of the government in market economic activities, comprehensive reform of the existing financial system, and promotion of the development model of new trade models. China's free trade pilot zone does not copy foreign trade zones, but combines the new situation of international trade with China's economic development requirements, and establishes an economic model with Chinese characteristics that can sustainably guarantee the rapid growth of China's economy [2]. As consumers have huge consumer demand for overseas goods, the advantages of the free trade zone in bonded import will undoubtedly greatly change the consumption habits of

G. Gui and L. Yun (Eds.): ADHIP 2019, LNICST 301, pp. 189–196, 2019.
https://doi.org/10.1007/978-3-030-36402-1_20

existing users. The establishment of a large-scale cross-border e-commerce integrated service platform on the business model of the Pilot Free Trade Zone can also solve the problem of foreign brand retail goods entering China through online platforms [3]. With the help of the policy opportunities of the free trade pilot zone to promote the construction of cross-border e-commerce platforms, we can first change the current chaos of the cross-border e-commerce shopping guide "cross-border online shopping" model, and regulate the behavior of the entire cross-border e-commerce shopping guide industry. Secondly, it can also solve the problems of after-sales service, goods return, temporary commodity taxation and payment risk that have long plagued cross-border e-commerce industry in the past, paving the way for the rapid development of cross-border e-commerce shopping guide [4].

2   Optimization Design of Cross-Border E-commerce Shopping Guide Hardware System Combining Big Data and AI Technology

At present, in the cross-border e-commerce shopping guide operators, the two most important problems in cross-border supply chain management are the operation mode and logistics operation system of overseas suppliers [5]. For overseas suppliers, cross-border B2C e-commerce platform are relatively smooth development in most areas, but in the investment and business introduction this link is relatively weak: some regional well-known brands have no willingness to enter the Chinese market due to their limited production capacity; For some internationally renowned brands, expanding the cross-border e-commerce shopping guide retail channel is likely to create a conflict of interest with the costly establishment of international agents and channels. If high-quality investment is not possible, the cross-border e-commerce shopping guide platform will not be able to effectively control the quality of overseas goods. The phenomenon of shoddy, counterfeit and shoddy caused by secondary times will cause a fatal credibility crisis for the e-commerce platform and the entire cross-border e-commerce shopping guide industry (Fig. 1).

In terms of cross-border logistics implementation, there are currently two main problems: the first is the cross-border circulation speed of goods, and the second is the customs clearance optimization ability of goods [1]. At present, small parcels for cross-border e-commerce shopping guides mainly rely on transshipment companies to complete cross-border logistics through transshipment companies. It will inevitably lead to the break of the supply chain "three streams in one" ("flow of funds", "information flow" and "material flow" in e-commerce), which will cause significant obstacles to the speed of cargo flow [6]. However, the ability to optimize customs clearance is mainly determined by the number of customs duties and the clearance time. Once the customs clearance time is longer or the tariff changes greatly, it will greatly affect the customer experience of e-commerce consumers, and affect the reputation and promotion of cross-border e-commerce brands.

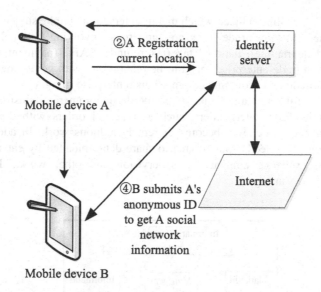

Fig. 1. Cross-border supply chain

3 Optimization Design of Cross-Border E-commerce Shopping Guide Software System Combining Big Data and AI Technology

In the framework of constructing a unified customs service platform, the General Administration of Customs takes the lead in taking the lead. Therefore, the internal system of the Customs Administration can directly communicate with the data of the platform, and the customs clearance of goods is regulated by means of "three-in-one comparison". "Three orders" refers to the customs declaration form provided by the e-commerce enterprise, the payment list provided by the payment enterprise, and the logistics operation note provided by the logistics enterprise [7]. After the "three singles" data is confirmed, it can be released, thus saving customs clearance time and improving customs clearance efficiency.

Through a unified customs clearance service platform, it is possible to provide a simpler and more effective supervision method for the General Administration of Customs and local customs, and assist the supervision department to effectively cope with the current fragmentation trend of foreign trade orders [8]. By comparing enterprise data and customs data, it can effectively cope with the small number of small parcels and small orders, and improve the efficiency of customs clearance while reducing the burden of customs supervision.

3.1 Public Service Construction Management with Big Data Technology

The construction of cross-border e-commerce public services in the free trade zone, the meaning of this "public service" has two-way. Firstly, it builds a public information platform between the functional departments of local governments, and then, Its main service object is the public subject, which mainly refers to the public subject in the field of foreign trade. Sunshine trade links are numerous, involving national inspection (inspection and quarantine), national tax (tax refund), SAFE (payment settlement), traditional foreign trade enterprises need to be one-on-one with government commissions or foreign trade and economic commissions (enterprise filing, data statistics) and other government functions and banks. Cross-border e-commerce industry due to the particularity of its fragmented orders, such as repeated orders with the functional departments for each order will become extremely arduous work. In addition, government functions also need a public area to share data uploaded by enterprises, and data collection, exchange comparison, supervision and other work.. The system framework is shown in Fig. 2:

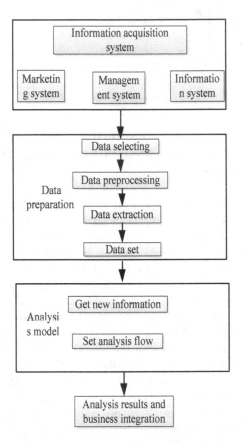

Fig. 2. Official service platform framework

Therefore, the public service platform invested by the government has become the fundamental means to solve these problems. As with the customs clearance service platform, the local public service platform also generally adopts the "three-single comparison" approach for supervision. The "three-single" formalities are complete and supervised and approved, so that they can enjoy the normal foreign exchange tax rebate. The cross-border e-commerce public service platform serves as a platform for government-level construction. In addition to communicating with government functions, some local platforms can directly interface with customs clearance service platforms. The public service platform not only forms a circle of intersections between various government departments(National Inspection Bureau, State Administration of Taxation, SAFE, Foreign Trade and Economic Cooperation Commission, Commercial Committee, Economic and Information Commission, etc.), but also builds a bridge of communication between relevant government functions and foreign trade. It is a service window opened by the functional department for foreign trade enterprises, which can effectively promote the sharing of resources, efficient operation, unified collaboration and innovative services.

3.2   Artificial Intelligence Algorithm

A cross-border e-commerce integrated service platform built by large-scale cross-border e-commerce enterprises provides agency services for these small and medium-sized enterprises and individual sellers. As the country's cross-border e-commerce regulatory policies become clearer, customs and governments around the country are gradually tightening the regulatory gap. Some traditional small and medium-sized foreign trade enterprises and cross-border e-commerce platform individual sellers have gradually developed an uncomfortable and urgency in the face of emerging regulatory policies. This part of the foreign trade unit has a common feature. It has long been used for postal transportation, and it is not taxable. It is not familiar enough with the sunny cross-border chain, and it seems to be at a loss in the face of the era of e-commerce supervision. The competent government department shall promote the internationalization of the mature e-commerce integrated service platform in China, as shown in Fig. 3.

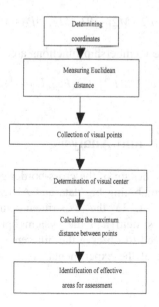

Fig. 3. Integrated service flow chart

Some large cross-border e-commerce companies have extensive experience in dealing with problems arising from cross-border e-commerce chain links in government and customs departments. These large-scale cross-border e-commerce companies can establish a bridge between foreign trade enterprises and consumers, providing agency services for sellers, including finance, customs clearance, logistics, tax rebates, foreign exchange and other aspects. The cross-border e-commerce integrated service platform provides convenient solutions for related enterprises in reducing foreign trade thresholds, dealing with foreign trade issues, and reducing foreign trade risks. At present, such platforms are suitable for a variety of formats such as small parcels and small orders, and will also develop deeper and more professional services with the development of cross-border e-commerce, as shown in Table 1.

Table 1. Characteristics of electronic target procurement service.

	P1	P2	P3	P4	P5
Cube	3.21	0.23	5.61	6.72	7.45
Triangular prism	3.42	0.41	5.12	6.21	7.82
Globe	3.64	0.72	6.26	5.27	7.31

For any of the target highlights, five different eigenvalues $P\{P1, P2, P3, P4, P5\}$ can be extracted, then the membership functions are:

$$P(X) \sum = \xi e \sum_{C}^{W} L \tag{1}$$

Where

$$P = |P1-M1| \cdot |P2-M2| \cdot |P3-M3| \cdot |P4-M4| \cdot |P5-M6| \tag{2}$$

Based on this formula, the membership functions are:

$$U = \{U1(P1), U2(P2), U3(P3), U4(P4), U5(P5)\} \tag{3}$$

4   Experimental Results and Analysis

In order to ensure the absolute design of the cross-border e-commerce shopping guide system optimization design combining big data and AI technology, the experimental demonstration was carried out. In the experiment, the traditional cross-border e-commerce shopping guide system and the system optimization designed in this paper were compared and tested to observe the difference and record the data at any time. The schematic diagram of the experimental demonstration results is shown in Table 2 and Fig. 4.

Table 2. Test parameters.

Name	parameter values
Network size	300 × 300
Number of nodes	200 and 300
Communication radius (m)	32
Base station position	(0,0)
Eelec(nJ/b)	50
Eda(nJ/b)	5
Packet size (bits)	1000
Initial energy (J)	2
α	2
β	1
γ	0.5

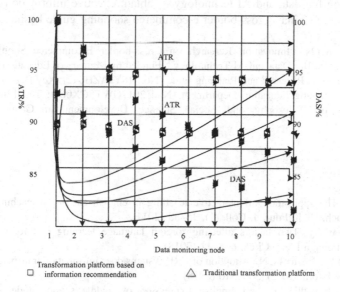

Transformation platform based on
□ information recommendation   △ Traditional transformation platform

Fig. 4. Experimental comparison chart

Through experimental comparison, we can find that in the case of the same data node, the system optimization under the support of big data and artificial intelligence is outstanding in ATR (Customer Terminal Performance) compared to the original system method. It also performs well in DAS (the desire to purchase goods), which is much higher than the original system design. Thereby changing the order picking mode of the e-commerce logistics distribution center, and improving the accuracy and efficiency of order picking.

5   Conclusions

This paper mainly studies the optimization design of cross-border e-commerce shopping guide system combining big data and AI technology. It can use big data and AI technology to effectively obtain information from it and identify the target to help us obtain more valuable cross-border e-commerce shopping guide information. It develops and utilizes cross-border e-commerce shopping guides to enhance valuable information resources.

Through the discussion and analysis of this paper, we can understand that the research on the optimization design of cross-border e-commerce shopping guide system combining big data and AI technology has important and far-reaching significance. Although the design of cross-border e-commerce shopping guide system has achieved great gains in recent years, there are still many problems waiting for us to solve. To this end, we must not be afraid of difficulties, overcome difficulties, and constantly optimize the design technology of cross-border e-commerce shopping guide system combining low-resolution big data and AI technology to obtain effective information. In turn, it will better serve China's cross-border e-commerce shopping guide business.

Acknowledgements. "Innovation Research on Cross-border E-commerce Shopping Guide Platform Based on Big Data and AI Technology", Funded by Ministry of Education Humanities and Social Sciences Research and Planning Fund (No.: 18YJAZH042); Key Research Platform Project of Guangdong Education Department (No.: 2017GWTSCX064); The 13th Five-Year Plan Project of Philosophy and Social Science Development in Guangzhou (No.: 2018GZGJ208).

References

1. Shawina: The application of interactive teaching in english classroom teaching. Chengdu Electr. Mach. High. Educ. J. Coll. (1), 35–38 (2017)
2. Junming, Wang: Two factors affecting foreign language learning and foreign language teaching. Foreign Lang. Circle **6**, 8–11 (2018)
3. Al-Jabri, I.M., Roztocki, N.: Adoption of ERP systems does information transparency matter. Telematics Inform. **32**(2), 300–310 (2018)
4. Yan, S.: Difficulties in oral English expression of middle school students and their countermeasures. Eng. Teach. Res. Prim. Middle Sch. (1), 2 (2018)
5. Luo, Y.: On the role of teachers and students in english role-playing teaching. New Curriculum Res. Teach. Educ. **8**(1), 8–11 (2018)
6. Zheng, Y.: Role playing teaching in primary english teaching. Educ. Forum, (3), 44 (2012)
7. Canale, M., Swain, M.: Theoretical basis of communicative approaches to second language teaching and testing. **8**, 1–47 (2017). Oxford University Press, London
8. Laudon, K.C., Traver, C.G.: E-Commerce 2016 Business Technology and Society, vol. 9, pp. 143–159. Addison Wesley, Boston (2018)

Research on Balanced Scheduling Algorithm of Big Data in Network Under Cloud Computing

Lunqiang Ye[⊠]

Southwest Minzu University, Chengdu, China
feiyun001b@163.com

Abstract. In order to find the optimal big data balanced scheduling scheme under cloud computing and reduce the completion time of the task, an improved ant colony algorithm based algorithm for large data equalization scheduling under cloud computing was proposed. Firstly, a balanced scheduling algorithm structure was established, then the equilibrium problem to be explored was described, finally, the ant colony algorithm was used to simulate the ant search food process to solve the objective function. And the local and global information deep update methods was introduced to improve, speed up the search speed, and finally the performance test experiments on CloudSim simulation platform was performed. The results show that compared with the discrete particle swarm optimization (DPSO), the algorithm not only greatly reduces the execution time of cloud computing tasks (2.5 s), but also solves the problem of unbalanced data load, and achieves the balanced scheduling of large network data under cloud computing.

Keywords: Cloud computing · Big data · Balanced scheduling · Ant colony algorithm

1 Introduction

The development of a series of new network applications, such as online social networking, search websites and business representatives, a large amount of Internet data integration and data aggregation, has caused a burst of data processing applications and demand, and the amount of business that the Internet has to analyze or process is becoming increasingly heavy [1]. For example, the central processing system of foreign social software Face hook receives an average of more than 3 billion messages and nearly 1000T network data per day; And China's Alibaba's Taobao. The emergence and application of a large amount of data has accelerated the arrival of the "big data era." For mass data services, how to effectively balance these data to provide convenient and fast network search services for network users has become an important issue facing the Internet. In this case, a new type of computing technology was born, which is the cloud computing technology [2]. The cloud computing platform such as Hadoop is the practical application result of cloud computing technology. In a cloud computing platform, the resource and job scheduling strategy is its core, which plays a vital role in

G. Gui and L. Yun (Eds.): ADHIP 2019, LNICST 301, pp. 197–206, 2019.
https://doi.org/10.1007/978-3-030-36402-1_21

the allocation of computing resources and the execution of the entire system. Therefore, the research of scheduling algorithms in cloud computing environment is of great significance. This study proposes an ant colony algorithm based algorithm for large data equalization scheduling in cloud computing. Ant colony algorithm is an intelligent algorithm, which is applied to cloud computing, which can shorten task execution time, improve load balance, better solve big data management and scheduling in cloud computing, and load balancing of virtual machines.

2 Balanced Scheduling Algorithm Based on Ant Colony Algorithm

Load balancing is applied in many professional fields. The load balancing of computers is accompanied by the demand for computing power and the emergence of clustering technology. It is the performance index of cluster systems and develops with the development of cluster technology [3]. The scheduling mechanism of the load balancing algorithm can solve the problem of unbalanced data load in the cluster environment, promote the reasonable distribution of data resources and improve the quality of service.

The early balanced scheduling algorithm only distributes the tasks evenly to the data nodes, so that the data is not idle and improves system efficiency. Excessive node load can lead to a large number of tasks queuing, directly affecting the task completion time and system throughput. The first phase is the application data phase when the task comes. In this phase, the task needs to be assigned to the data node with lower load. The second phase is to balance the load for the node, and transfer some tasks of the node to the node with low load when the data node load is too high during task execution.

Ant colony algorithm is similar to genetic algorithm, and it is a natural heuristic algorithm. The ant population is divided into foragers, followers and harvesters. In the process of foraging, workers are responsible for finding food sources. The rate of return from food sources depends on the quantity or quality of food and the distance from the nest. By observing the wagging dance of the follower, the follower decides which follower to harvest according to the rate of return, so the rate of return on the food source is proportional to the follower's probability of choosing the food source. When his followers arrived at the source of food, he became a harvester and began to harvest [4]. The flow chart of ant colony algorithm is shown in Fig. 1. The breeder is responsible for collecting the status information of the system resources and displaying it in the "ant nest". The followers of "ant nest" can understand the rate of return of different resources and take corresponding actions according to the rate of return of resources. When followers acquire resources, they become reapers and begin harvesting, and evaluate the solutions they have obtained.

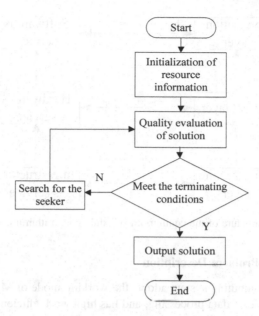

Fig. 1. Ant colony algorithm

Using ant colony algorithm to balance data scheduling is based on information collection of system load data and information broadcasting in honeycomb. This is a typical centralized control method. The follower can obtain detailed system load data information in the cell, and track the operation according to the profit margin of different nodes. Because of the high output, low-load nodes are easy to be chosen by followers [5].

2.1 Balanced Scheduling Algorithm Structure

In cloud computing, the system is usually divided into three layers as shown in Fig. 2, which are the application layer, the virtual layer, and the infrastructure layer. There are many hierarchical models of cloud computing, but all hierarchical models are based on these three layers, and the balanced scheduling algorithm model is also based on these three layers. The application layer is an interface for cloud computing to display services to users and users to apply for services to cloud computing. It is mainly responsible for submitting tasks to the virtual layer and collecting applications from users [6]. The virtual layer is all the resources that the application layer user can see. It is responsible for assigning the virtual machine resources to the specific application of the user, and handing over the tasks satisfying the operating conditions to the infrastructure layer for execution. The infrastructure layer is the actual server cluster.

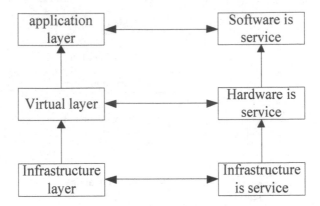

Fig. 2. Three-layer structure of the equilibrium scheduling algorithm under cloud computing

2.2 Equilibrium Problem Description

The current cloud computing system adopts the working mode of Map/Reduce, which is suitable for large-scale data processing, and has high work efficiency. The execution process is as shown in Fig. 3.

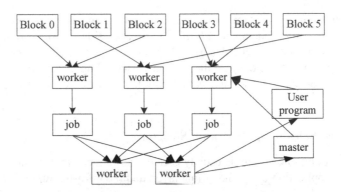

Fig. 3. Map/Reduce execution process

Map/Reduce mainly has two key stages, Map and Reduce, as shown below.

(1) The Map stage subdivides the task into multiple sub-tasks. The sub-tasks are generally in the range of $16 \sim 64$ MB. Then the sub-tasks are assigned to the cloud computing data (worker) execution, and the results are fed back to the main node after execution [7].

(2) The Reduce phase aggregates the results of each worker in the Map phase and outputs the final result to R output data.

Big data equalization scheduling is a complex problem. Each task is divided into M, N subtasks of Map, Reduce stage, and the number of M and N is much larger than the number of workers. Each worker has to complete many subtasks, so it is reasonable to schedule tasks to ensure data load balancing becomes a key problem for task scheduling algorithms in cloud computing environments.

Equilibrium scheduling of big data in the network under cloud computing can be described by 3-tuple: {T, R, ETC}, T is a collection of tasks: t1, t2, ..., tm, m is the number of tasks; R is a collection of resources, r1, r2, ..., rn, n is the number of resources. The objective function of the equilibrium scheduling of big data of the network under cloud computing is to make the number of data on the node relatively balanced and ensure the task completion time is as short as possible under the condition that the task completion time meets the user requirements [8].

2.3 Standard Ant Colony Algorithm

Set the number of ants in the ant colony m. Starting from the starting node, the probability formula for the ant to select the next node according to the transition probability is

$$p_{ij}^k(t) = \frac{\vartheta_{ij}^a \cdot \theta_j^b}{\sum\limits_{j=1}^{i} \vartheta_{ij}^a \cdot \theta_j^b} \tag{1}$$

Where, θ_j is a heuristic information function associated with the edge (i, j); a and b are pheromones and heuristics; and ϑ_{ij} is a pheromone on the edge (i, j).

In order to prevent unrestricted accumulation of pheromones, a pheromone volatilization mechanism is introduced. When the ants complete a search from the start point to the end point, the pheromone on each side is updated, specifically

$$\vartheta_{ij}(t+1) = c\vartheta_{ij}(t) + \Delta\vartheta_{ij}(t) \tag{2}$$

$$\Delta\vartheta_{ij}(t) = \sum_{k=1}^{m} \Delta\vartheta_{ij}^k(t) \tag{3}$$

Where, $\Delta\vartheta_{ij}(t)$ and $\Delta\vartheta_{ij}^k(t)$ are the increments of pheromone on the side (i, j) of ant k and all ants; c is the pheromone volatilization coefficient.

$\Delta\vartheta_{ij}^k(t)$ uses the ant week system calculation method, specifically

$$\Delta\vartheta_{ij}^k(t) = D/E_k \tag{4}$$

Where D is a constant; E_k is the path length of ant k.

The process of balancing the network big data using the standard ant colony algorithm is shown in Fig. 4.

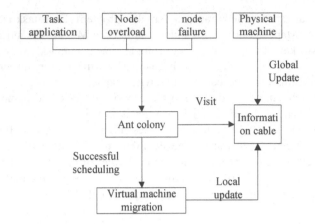

Fig. 4. Ant colony algorithm equilibrium scheduling structure

2.4 Improved Ant Colony Algorithm

In the ant colony algorithm, the value of the pheromone volatilization coefficient c has a great influence on the performance of the algorithm. In order to improve the adaptability of the algorithm, the pheromone volatilization coefficient of the basic ant colony algorithm is dynamically adjusted:

$$c(t) = \begin{cases} c_{min} & \vartheta_{ij} \leq \vartheta_{min} \\ \vartheta(t)\vartheta_{min} < \vartheta_{ij}(t) < \vartheta_{max} \\ c_{max} & \vartheta_{ij}(t) \geq \vartheta_{max} \end{cases} \tag{5}$$

Where c_{min} and c_{max} are the maximum and minimum values of the volatilization coefficient; ϑ_{min} and ϑ_{max} are the minimum or maximum limit values for preventing pheromone.

Since the equilibrium scheduling of big data of the network under cloud computing is complex, in order to establish the mapping of tasks and data, the improved ant colony algorithm pheromone function will reward the global optimal path solved. That is, the pheromone concentration on the path it contains is strengthened, and at the same time, the solved local iterative worst path is punished. That is, the pheromone concentration on the path included is weakened, so that the difference between the optimal path and the worst path information concentration is further expanded, so as to achieve the purpose of searching the ant colony as close as possible to the optimal path [9]. The global pheromone concentration update method of the improved ant colony algorithm is

$$\vartheta_{ij}new = \begin{cases} (1 - c) \cdot \vartheta_{ij}old + \sigma(L1 - L2) \\ \text{If the road segment } (i,j) \text{ belongs to the global optimal path} \\ \text{If the road segment } (i,j) \text{ belongs to the global worst path} \\ 0, \text{ otherwise} \end{cases} \tag{6}$$

Where $L1$ is the global optimal path, $L2$ is the iterative worst path, and σ is a parameter introduced in the algorithm.

After each ant completes the search for the path, it must perform a partial update on the path it has taken. The local update method refers to the basic ant colony algorithm model. The formula for partial update is:

$$\vartheta_{ij}new = (1 - c) \cdot \vartheta_{ij}old + \Delta\vartheta_{ij}, c \in (0, 1) \tag{7}$$

In the formula, c is the information evaporation coefficient.

$$\Delta\vartheta_{ij} = \begin{cases} D/E_k, \\ 0, \text{ otherwise} \end{cases} \text{ If the ant passes the path } (i, j) \tag{8}$$

In the formula, E_k, is the path distance obtained by the k-th ant, and D is a parameter introduced in the algorithm. The process of equalizing the scheduling of network big data by using the improved ant colony algorithm is shown in Fig. 5.

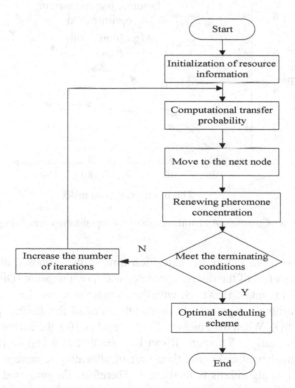

Fig. 5. Improved ant colony algorithm for the equilibrium scheduling solution process

3   Comparative Experiment

The scheduling algorithm is run on the cloud simulation software CloudSim. The experiment is in the case where multiple users of different SLAs compete for the same resources. Comparing the nonSLA-MPS and SLA-MPS algorithms from the average response time of the task, the SLA default rate of the cloud service provider and the total revenue of the cloud service provider, the effects of the two algorithms on the interests of the cloud service providers are tested. The maximum number of virtual machines that are enabled in each data center is 30, and the total number of tasks specified in the experiment is 400, 600, 800, and 1000.

The ant colony algorithm based on cloud computing network completes the comparison of balanced scheduling time between large data balanced scheduling algorithm and discrete particle swarm optimization balanced scheduling algorithm, as shown in Fig. 6.

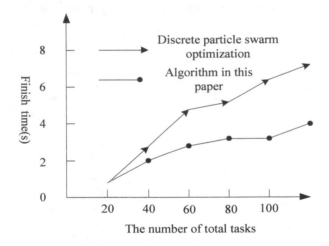

Fig. 6. Comparison of time required for equalization scheduling

As can be seen from Fig. 6, the execution time of the proposed algorithm is not much different from that of the discrete particle swarm optimization (DPSO) algorithm when the task load is small. However, with the increase of tasks, the execution time of the proposed algorithm is significantly shorter than that of the discrete particle swarm optimization (DPSO). When the number of tasks reaches 100, the execution time of the two algorithms is nearly 2.5 s apart. It can be seen that in a certain range, with the increase of the number of tasks, the time cost of allocating resources and executing resources of the two algorithms is increasing. Therefore, the proposed algorithm can balance the scheduling of large network data more effectively in cloud computing.

Ant colony algorithm based on cloud computing network completes the comparison of balanced scheduling errors between large data balanced scheduling algorithm and chaotic particle swarm optimization scheduling algorithm, as shown in Fig. 7.

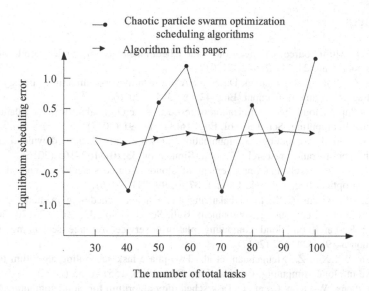

Fig. 7. Comparison of equilibrium scheduling errors

Analysis of Fig. 7 shows that with the increasing number of tasks, the equilibrium scheduling error of the chaotic particle swarm equilibrium scheduling algorithm is larger, and the error fluctuations constantly. The maximum scheduling error of this method can reach 2.0, which shows that the method has a high error in large data scheduling. The error of this algorithm is basically 0, which shows that this algorithm can schedule with zero error, and fully proves the overall effectiveness of this algorithm.

4 Conclusions

In summary, in the cloud computing environment, the balanced scheduling of data resources is the key to ensuring the quality of cloud computing services. In order to perform reasonable task assignment in the cloud computing environment, shorten the time to complete the total task, Each node achieves load balancing as much as possible, and applies the improved ant colony algorithm to the cloud computing data balanced scheduling. The simulation test shows that with the increase of the task amount, compared with the traditional data balance scheduling algorithm, the data scheduling time is significantly reduced, and the load balancing degree of the node is significantly improved.

Acknowledgements. Supported by Educational and Teaching Research and Reform Funds for Southwest Minzu University, "A Study on the Construction and Application of Teaching Resources in the SPOC Blended Teaching Mode" Project No.: 2018YB25.

References

1. Ying, T.J.: Multi source heterogeneous data scheduling algorithm under cloud computing. Sci. Technol. Eng. **21**(34), 268–272 (2017)
2. Jinfang, Z., Qingxin, W., Jiaman, D., et al.: A big data dynamic migration strategy in cloud computing environment. Comput. Eng. **42**(5), 13–17 (2016)
3. Luo Nan Super Cloud: The optimization of resource scheduling algorithm for balancing load under cloud computing. Sci. Technol. Eng. **16**(34), 86–91 (2017)
4. Xin, L.: Cloud computing communication network information download balanced scheduling optimization research. Comput. Simulation **33**(10), 162–165 (2016)
5. Xiaofeng, L.: Research and improvement of cloud resource scheduling method in cloud computing optical fiber network. Laser J. **37**(5), 99–103 (2016)
6. Junying, W., Xinrui, C.X.: Load balancing and efficient scheduling method for diversity resources in cloud computing environment. Bull. Sci. Technol. **33**(12), 167–170 (2017)
7. Kai, Z.: Research on cloud computing platform service resource scheduling. Comput. Simulation **34**(9), 424–427 (2017)
8. Xiaonian, W., Xin, Z., Mengchuan, et al.: Two-phase task scheduling algorithm for multi-objective in cloud computing. Comput. Eng. Des. **38**(6), 1551–1555 (2017)
9. Han, H., Peng, W., Kun, C., et al.: Task scheduling algorithm for cloud computing based on multi-scale quantum harmonic oscillator algorithm. J. Comput. Appl. **37**(7), 1888–1892 (2017)

Optimization of Rational Scheduling Method for Cloud Computing Resources Under Abnormal Network

Lunqiang Ye[✉]

Southwest Minzu University, Chengdu, China
feiyun001b@163.com

Abstract. When the traditional heuristic algorithm was used to schedule the cloud computing resources under the abnormal network, there was a problem that the scheduling speed was slow and the effect was poor. Aiming at the above problems, combined with the characteristics of cloud computing and the actual needs of cloud computing resource allocation, based on the advantages of genetic algorithm and ant colony algorithm, a hybrid optimal cloud computing resource scheduling algorithm was designed. The improved algorithm combines the advantages of genetic algorithm and ant colony algorithm, and the genetic algorithm can effectively improve the search efficiency; The ant colony algorithm was used in the later stage of the algorithm to improve the accuracy of the optimal solution and to complete the reasonable scheduling of cloud computing resources under the abnormal network. The results show that the hybrid algorithm was faster than the single genetic algorithm and ant colony algorithm. It only took 10 s, the resource load was more balanced, and the scheduling effect was better.

Keywords: Abnormal network · Cloud computing · Resource scheduling · Genetic algorithm · Ant colony algorithm

1 Introduction

In the cloud computing environment, particle swarm optimization, genetic algorithm and ant colony algorithm are applied to the current resource scheduling [1]. They have adaptive search capabilities, they first establish a mathematical model for specific application problems, and then solve it [2]. Resource scheduling in the cloud computing environment is an NP-Hard problem. When solving a single algorithm, there are some limitations. For example, the population diversity of the late stage of genetic algorithm is seriously degraded, and the search ability of the bureau is poor. The ant colony algorithm has no initial hormone mechanism, and the search efficiency is low at the beginning stage.

In order to overcome the limitations of a single algorithm, it is better to balance the tasks between resources. The genetic algorithm and the ant colony algorithm are combined, and the genetic algorithm can be used to obtain the feasible solution of resource scheduling in the cloud computing environment. Then, using the characteristics of late search ability of ant colony algorithm, the resource scheduling scheme is

G. Gui and L. Yun (Eds.): ADHIP 2019, LNICST 301, pp. 207–215, 2019.
https://doi.org/10.1007/978-3-030-36402-1_22

searched twice to find the best scheduling scheme. Finally, the simulation experiment is carried out on Cloud Sin platform to test its performance. The results show that the improved hybrid algorithm is more efficient. It only takes 10 s, the resource load is more balanced, and the scheduling effect is better.

2 Hybrid Optimization Algorithm

In view of the advantages and disadvantages of traditional allocation algorithms, this paper designs a hybrid optimization algorithm. It is a new heuristic grid task scheduling algorithm with both time and efficiency [3]. The overall framework of its algorithm design is shown in Fig. 1.

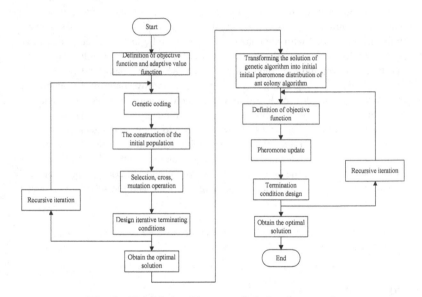

Fig. 1. Hybrid algorithm overall design framework

2.1 Dynamic Fusion Critical Point Determination of Two Algorithms

The key step of the new algorithm is the best combination of the two algorithms. The dynamic fusion strategy can determine the optimal fusion time between the genetic algorithm and the ant colony algorithm.

(1) Set the minimum number of genetic iterations and set the maximum number of iterations.
(2) In the iteration process, we need to calculate the evolutionary rate of descendants and set the minimum evolution rate.

(3) Within the set number of iterations, if the continuous N generation, the evolution rate of the offspring population is less than the minimum evolution rate, indicating that the genetic algorithm optimization speed is low, so the genetic algorithm process can be terminated and enter the ant colony algorithm [4].

2.2 Objective Function

According to the characteristics of cloud computing resource scheduling, the following constraints are added, so that the algorithm can be better applied to practical problems. The specific constraints are: The processing time of the task is about ProcessTime(e), network bandwidth constraint Band math(e), and network delay constraint NetDelay(e) [5]. The objective function is defined as follows, depending on the situation after the resource is subject to the above constraints:

$$Res(e) = \frac{\left(A_{\text{ProcessTime}(e)} + B_{\text{NetDelay}(e)}\right)}{C_{\text{Bandmath}(e)}} \tag{1}$$

$$s.t. \begin{cases} \text{ProcessTime}(e) < \text{MaxT} \\ \text{NetDelay}(e) < \text{MaxN} \\ \text{Band math}(e) < \text{MinB} \end{cases} \tag{2}$$

The maxT, minB, and maxN in the formula (2) represent the upper limit of the task processing time, the minimum limit of the bandwidth, and the upper limit of the network delay, respectively, and the weight values of the three constraints are represented by A, B, and C, respectively.

2.3 Fitness Function

The fitness index is used to evaluate the goodness of the individual in the population. The greater the fitness value, the better the individual's performance. By defining the fitness function as follows, the principles of the genetic algorithm can be well followed.

2.4 Genetic Coding

To perform a global search for resource scheduling problems based on genetic algorithms, it is first necessary to encode the scheduling scheme of the problem into chromosomes. The binary method is generally used for chromosome coding, that is, one chromosome corresponds to one binary string, and corresponds to a resource scheduling scheme [6].

2.5 Initial Population

Let the population size be M, the number of sub-tasks be n, the number of processing units be m, and the maximum depth of the task be h. The algorithm flow for generating the initial population is shown in Fig. 2.

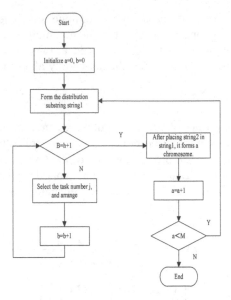

Fig. 2. Algorithm flow for generating an initial population

Assuming there are two resources, the two solutions that can be generated using this algorithm are:

Solution 1 : (**212212   212221**)

Solution 2 : (**111212   122121**)

Their corresponding resource rational scheduling schemes are:

Distribution plan 1 : Y1 : X2→X4→X5

Y2 : X1→X3→X6

Distribution plan 2 : Y1 : X3→X1→X6

Y2 : X5→X4→X2

2.6   Select Copy

After calculating the appropriate values of all chromosomes, it is necessary to select the chromosomes that satisfy the conditions with specific constraints, and set the appropriate values by roulette, to randomly select chromosomes with better performance from all chromosomes, follow the steps below:

Step1: The chromosomes are selected from the initial population according to the probability Pe, and then the appropriate values of the selected chromosomes are calculated, and the sum Mi of the moderate values of all the chromosomes is calculated.

Step2: A random number M0 is selected from [0, Mi] using a random number algorithm.

Step3: The appropriate value of the chromosome is added according to the numbering order of the chromosomes, and when the accumulated value is $\geq$ Mo, the last accumulated chromosome is copied.

Step4: Step 2, Step 3 are repeated, and when the number of new chromosomes reaches the original number of chromosomes, the selection and copying operations are terminated.

2.7   Crossover Operator

First, two chromosomes are randomly selected, and then the position of the intersection is randomly determined, and the second half (including the intersection) is exchanged from the intersection to generate two new sub-individuals [7].

If the new individual does not satisfy the constraint, re-select the intersection. If the newly generated individuals satisfy the constraint relationship, calculate their fitness values separately. The number of individuals in the offspring is twice the number of individuals in the father. The elite retention strategy is used to rank the individuals in descending order according to the fitness value, and the first half of the individuals are retained to generate new populations.

2.8   Mutation Operator

The mutation operator here essentially transfers a resource to another task for execution. In order to prevent a certain resource from being migrated and the execution time increases and the population is degraded, it is stipulated that the resources occupied by the post-migration task are not randomly generated. Instead, in the collection of resources other than the resources currently occupied by the task, the resource that minimizes the execution time of the subtask is selected and migrated to the task for execution [8].

2.9   Iterative Termination Condition

The specific values of the parameters can be determined by combining empirical parameters related to the genetic algorithm.

2.10   Ant Colony Algorithm for Obtaining Optimal Solution

The chromosome population is evaluated according to the objective function, and when the evolution rate of the chromosome population is small, the final genetic algorithm is terminated; Since the grid scheduling has the shortest task scheduling length as the solution target, when used for the grid task scheduling problem, the basic ant colony algorithm needs to be modified appropriately. The specific changes are: in the traveling salesman problem, the basic ant colony algorithm uses pheromones to describe the path distance between the various attractions; In the problem of rational resource scheduling, pheromone is used to describe the real-time computing power of each computing node. The ant colony algorithm obtains the optimal solution process as follows:

Initial pheromone conversion:
In order to ensure the high efficiency of the algorithm, the optimal solution obtained by the genetic algorithm needs to be transformed and used as the initial pheromone of the ant colony algorithm. The calculation formula is as follows:

$$A_i(t) = A_0 + A_i^{GA}(t) \tag{3}$$

In the formula (3), A_0 represents a pheromone constant, and A_i^{GA} represents a pheromone value converted according to the calculation result of the genetic algorithm.

Objective function design:
The ant colony algorithm optimization solution is mainly a quadratic solution to the better solution obtained by the genetic algorithm. Here, the node domain of the ant colony algorithm is regarded as an undirected graph Gaco (V, E), and V and E represent nodes of all resources and a network set, respectively. The ultimate goal of the ant colony algorithm is to find an optimal path from the network geometry of all resources of the undirected graph.

Pheromone update:
In the actual solution, in order to avoid trapping the local optimal solution, the local pheromone of the ant selected line should be updated first. After the ant is transferred from node i to j, the pheromone of Aij can be updated by formula (4).

$$A_{ij}(t+1) = (1 - \psi)A_{ij}(t) + \sum_{k=1}^{m} \Delta A_{ij}^k(t) \tag{4}$$

$$\Delta A_{ij}^k(t) = \begin{cases} \dfrac{B}{\text{Re}source(e_{ij})}, \text{The k-th ant chooses } e_{ij} \text{ between t and t} + 1 \\ 0, \end{cases} \tag{5}$$

In the formula, $\psi \in (0,1)$ and $1 - \psi$ respectively represent the update coefficient and residual coefficient of the pheromone; $\Delta A_{ij}^k(t)$ represents the pheromone left by the k-th ant on the path at time t; B represents the strength of the pheromone.

Equations (4) and (5) are mainly for global update of pheromone after an iterative update for all ants.

Termination condition design:
The ant colony algorithm can be terminated as long as any of the following conditions are met:

(1) The maximum number of design iterations is reached;
(2) The evolution rate of the offspring of the new population is lower than the design value.

3 Comparative Experiment

In order to verify the effectiveness of the hybrid algorithm, experiments are needed. CloudSim, a cloud computing simulation tool, is used to build an experimental simulation platform for resource rationality in cloud computing environment. The experimental environment is as follows: Select the cluster data that the network exposes, including 100 physical nodes, each node is configured as 24 Core, 64 G memory, 10 Gbps network. Using genetic algorithm, ant colony algorithm and hybrid algorithm, the reasonable scheduling of cloud computing resources under abnormal network is simulated.

The genetic algorithm, ant colony algorithm and hybrid algorithm were used to conduct reasonable scheduling experiments on 100 resources. The time required for the three algorithms to complete the rational scheduling of resources is shown in Fig. 3.

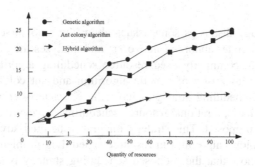

Fig. 3. The time required for the three algorithms to complete the rational scheduling of resources

It can be seen from Fig. 3 that compared with the other two algorithms, the hybrid algorithm requires the least time for reasonable resource scheduling, and it takes only 10 s to complete the scheduling. And from the time span, although the number of resources is constantly increasing, the average value has good stability.

In order to further verify the advantages of the hybrid algorithm in the scheduling effect, the resource load situation after three algorithms is analyzed. The result is shown in Fig. 4.

Figure 4 shows the load data of each resource point when the number of resources is 100. From the ant colony algorithm, the ant colony calculation and the resource load degree of the hybrid optimization algorithm, it can be seen that some resource points have a higher load level and some resource points have a lower load level. The ant colony algorithm and the genetic algorithm load on the resource points 5, 7, and 8 respectively, and the load on the resource points 3, 4, and 8 is small. The load of the hybrid optimization algorithm is more balanced, indicating that the overall load balancing performance of the hybrid algorithm is optimized.

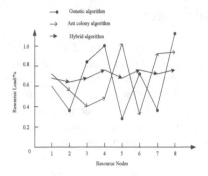

Fig. 4. Resource load situation after scheduling by three algorithms

4 Conclusions

In summary, this study discusses some issues about the rational scheduling of cloud computing resources under abnormal networks, and analyzes the advantages and disadvantages of current commonly used resource scheduling algorithms. Through in-depth research and comparison of genetic algorithm and ant colony algorithm, it is found that the two scheduling strategies have the characteristics of complementary advantages; On this basis, a rational resource scheduling strategy based on genetic-ant colony algorithm is proposed. This strategy integrates the dual advantages of genetic algorithm and ant colony algorithm in resource scheduling problems. The simulation experiment results show that the proposed scheduling strategy is superior to genetic algorithm and ant colony algorithm in large-scale task environment, and is superior to ant colony genetic algorithm in general. How to use the genetic ant colony algorithm based resource scheduling strategy for practical work will be the next research goal.

Acknowledgements. Supported by the Fundamental Research Funds for the Central Universities, Southwest Minzu University, "A Study on the Cloud Load Balancing of Data Stream Storage in Desktop Cloud Environment" Project No. 2019NQN54.

References

1. Qiu, X., Dai, Y., Xiang, Y., et al.: Correlation modeling and resource optimization for cloud service with fault recovery. IEEE Trans. Cloud Comput. **7**(3), 693–704 (2017)
2. Mao, L., Qi, D.Y., Lin, W.W., et al.: An energy-efficient resource scheduling algorithm for cloud computing based on resource equivalence optimization. Int. J. Grid High Perform. Comput. **8**(2), 43–57 (2016)
3. Zuo, L., Shu, L., Dong, S., et al.: A Multi-objective optimization scheduling method based on the ant colony algorithm in cloud computing. IEEE Access **3**, 2687–2699 (2017)
4. Jin, A., Song, W., Wang, P., et al.: Auction mechanisms toward efficient resource sharing for cloudlets in mobile cloud computing. IEEE Trans. Serv. Comput. **9**(6), 895–909 (2016)
5. Zhang, R., Wu, K., Li, M., et al.: Online resource scheduling under concave pricing for cloud computing. IEEE Trans. Parallel Distrib. Syst. **27**(4), 1131–1145 (2016)

6. Cui, X., Zeng, C., Xu, Z., et al.: Resource scheduling strategy in cloud computing based on greedy algorithm. Microelectron. Comput. **33**(6), 41–43 (2016)
7. Kumar, D., Baranwal, G., Raza, Z., et al.: A systematic study of double auction mechanisms in cloud computing. J. Syst. Softw. **125**, 234–255 (2017)
8. Meng, L.X., Meng, L.W.: Simulation of resource load balancing scheduling under cloud computing. Comput. Simul. **35**(4), 386–389 (2018)

Design of Agricultural Product Quality and Safety Big Data Fusion Model Based on Blockchain Technology

Kun Wang[1,2]([envelope])

[1] Institute of Agricultural Information,
Jiangsu Agri-Animal Husbandry Vocational College, Taizhou, China
wangkun332@tom.com
[2] Taizhou Agricultural Internet of Things Engineering Technology
Research Center, Taizhou, China

Abstract. In the process of processing agricultural product quality and safety data, the traditional model will have problems such as long delay and redundant storage. Therefore, based on blockchain technology, combined with historical data, real-time data features, external shared data features and previous research results, the data is deeply integrated, the agricultural product quality and safety big data fusion model is designed. Create a big data fusion framework based on blockchain technology to collect and process agricultural product quality and safety data reasonably and efficiently, realizing the quality and Safety of the Integration of Agricultural products big data. The data architecture is proposed in the big data fusion model, and the collection and data storage methods of the quality and safety supervision system are designed to achieve efficient collection and storage of data. The experiment proves that the agricultural product quality and safety big data fusion model has certain advantages over the traditional model.

Keywords: Blockchain · Agricultural product quality · Big data fusion model · Data source · Acquisition · Storage

1 Introduction

Based on the block chain technology, according to the construction of China's agricultural product traceability system, combined with the actual situation of the traceability system construction in a certain region, the evaluation and analysis are carried out to clarify the main problems in the quality and safety of agricultural products. The block chain technology does not depend on the consumption data and product prices in the actual market operation. By designing the agricultural product quality and safety big data fusion model, it solves the problems of poor correction of traditional models, low system security, long delay, redundant storage, etc. The model was created by comparing the quality and safety satisfaction of the agricultural product market with the willingness to pay and the upper limit of the traceable agricultural products. The quality and safety of agricultural products are closely related to the stability of agricultural development, the happiness of people's lives, and the orderliness of social stability. Based on the perspective of agricultural product supply chain, considering the problems

G. Gui and L. Yun (Eds.): ADHIP 2019, LNICST 301, pp. 216–225, 2019.
https://doi.org/10.1007/978-3-030-36402-1_23

existing in the model, the blockchain technology is applied to the quality and safety supervision of agricultural products. Through the design of agricultural product quality and safety big data fusion model, analyze the game mechanism between government, supermarket, farmer professional cooperatives, agricultural product cold chain enterprises, agricultural products production and processing enterprises, consumers, third-party testing institutions and other multi-stakeholders. Establish an effective incentive mechanism to coordinate the interests of various entities, weaken conflicts and enrich the content of agricultural product quality and safety supervision [1].

2 Design of Big Data Fusion Model for Agricultural Products Quality and Safety

The big data fusion model can solve a wide range of business analysis decisions for users. The importance of big data is not how much data it has, but how it is handled. Relying on big data means you can get data from any source and analyze the data to find the answer. When the data is combined with high-performance analysis, you can complete complex tasks related to the business. Currently, the mainstream big data framework is based on blockchain technology. Blockchain technology is a distributed system infrastructure developed by the Apache Foundation. Users can make full use of the power of the cluster for high-speed computing and storage without developing the underlying details of the distributed, and develop distributed programs. Blockchain technology enables a distributed file system with high fault tolerance and is designed to be deployed on low-cost hardware; And it provides high throughput to access application data, suitable for applications with very large data sets [2]. Blockchain technology relaxes the requirements of hardware systems and can access data in file systems in streaming form. The core design of the blockchain technology framework is to provide storage for massive amounts of data and to provide calculations for massive amounts of data. Taking agricultural products as an example, the big data fusion model is as follows.

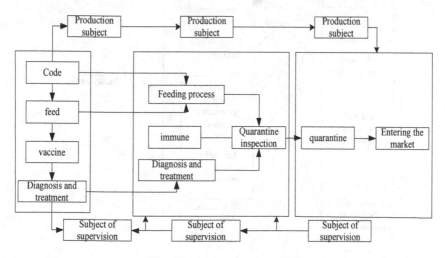

Fig. 1. Big data fusion model

Figure 1 is a big data fusion model consisting of many elements, the bottom of which is the file on all storage nodes in the fuzzy cluster. The upper layer of the system is the engine, which consists of servers and hardware. Through the process of processing the distributed file system at the core of the distributed computing system. In order to achieve effective supervision of corporate behavior and government regulatory actions in the production, processing, circulation, and consumption of agricultural products. The system relies on the unified coding of agricultural product information to realize the data of automatic associated enterprise product information and consumption feedback, and finally establishes a big data fusion model [3].

2.1   Identify the Data Source

In order to ensure the reasonable and efficient collection and processing of agricultural product quality and safety data, it is necessary to scientifically divide existing data sources and data items. At present, agricultural product quality and safety data mainly comes from agricultural research units, colleges and universities, agriculture-related government agencies, agriculture-related enterprises, and agricultural product wholesale markets [4]. Therefore, through the full investigation of historical data and real-time data characteristics, external shared data features, and previous research results, the data is deeply integrated. The quality and safety data of agricultural products are divided into four categories according to agricultural basic data, production process data, market information data and macro management data [5]. The data source processing is as follows:

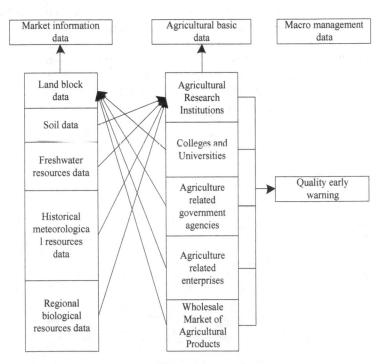

Fig. 2. Data source processing

Figure 2 shows the data source processing process. The specific structure is as follows: Agricultural basic data: mainly includes soil data, soil block data, freshwater resources data, historical meteorological resource data, regional biological resource data, and historical disaster data. Production process data: Mainly divided into planting production data and aquaculture production data according to different types of production [6]. Among them, planting production data includes seed information, plot farming history information, seedling information, seeding information, pesticide and fertilizer information, mulch information, water-saving irrigation information, agricultural machinery use information and agricultural tracking information. The production data of the aquaculture industry mainly includes the spectrum information of the breeding system, the characteristics of the individual's own characteristics, the information of the feed formula, the environmental information of the housing, and the situation of the epidemic. Market information data: including market supply information, product sales information, agricultural product circulation information, price quotes, and production materials market information. The macro management data mainly includes basic information of the national economy, domestic agricultural production information, agricultural product trade information and emergency information.

In the core database of agricultural product quality and safety big data, data can help information resource library administrators and information resource library developers to easily find the data they care about. Data is data describing the structure and establishment method of data in the information resource library, which can be divided into two categories according to their uses: technical data and business data. The data center in the data resource library is constructed by using various technologies such as centralized storage technology, computer technology, and database technology. It stores, interacts, accesses, and changes the integrated data to provide data support for Binzhou City Agricultural Products Quality and Safety Traceability Management Platform. In addition, the data center can also implement data association within the platform, providing data extraction, data mapping and other services. The repository data structure is as follows:

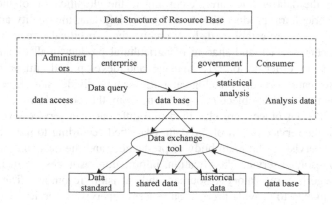

Fig. 3. Resource library data structure

Figure 3 is a data structure diagram of the resource library. The data standard adopts the public warehouse metamodel standard. The construction content includes architecture, technical metadata, business metadata, metadata management tools, etc. [7]. The information service layer is at the top of the platform construction structure, and is a service platform for users to interact with each application management. The information service mainly integrates all the resources of the platform information through a unified web page, and displays the information of the platform to system operation roles such as enterprise administrators, government administrators and consumers. All the operation pages constitute the function of the platform design, so the information service layer directly connects the target users through HTNH. Based on the public warehouse metamodel standard, combined with agricultural product quality and safety related business information and technical processes, establish a data system, the data architecture is as follows:

Table 1. Data architecture

	Business	Technology	Operation
Display structure	Report format, index meaning, user privileges	Technical standard	Data release and display process
Application structure	Exchange rules and standards	Data validation process	Processing processes and rules
Storage structure	Index system, Catalog, data model	Original data standard	Data storage management
Collection structure	Definition of data acquisition indicators	Interface communication standard	Data auditing algorithm
Basics structure	Index coding	Index database data model	Audit and verification relationships among indicators

Table 1 is the data architecture. According to the classification of the core data resources of agricultural product quality and safety big data, the quality and safety of agricultural products are established. Data architecture, specifically realize the collection, management, service and sharing of agricultural product quality and safety big data resources, in order to orderly manage and develop and utilize information resources. Information resource catalog categories can be divided into three categories. According to the service object classification, from the perspective of the use of information, different objects are classified into different data service levels from the perspective of the service object of the data. Classified according to the main body of government supervision, the main body of production, and the decision-making level. According to resource service classification, information resources are mainly divided into two categories: regulatory resources and decision resources. The regulatory resources are mainly to provide production process supervision services for regulatory entities and enterprises, and the decision resources are mainly to provide services for decision makers [8].

2.2 Realizing the Quality and Safety of Agricultural Products Big Data Fusion

When collecting and processing data for the agricultural product quality and safety supervision system, it needs to be regarded as a very important link. It mainly includes spatial data such as administrative division maps, main roads, water system maps, distribution maps of polluting enterprises, catalogues of safe edible agricultural products certification enterprises, and lists of agricultural standardized production demonstration bases over the years. At the same time, it is necessary to comprehensively evaluate the environmental assessment standards for the production of pollution-free food, green food and organic agricultural products. Therefore, in this system, the big data fusion model is adopted to evaluate the quality safety factor of agricultural products, and it provides auxiliary and decision support for the leadership to do product evaluation and planning certification [9].

The agricultural product quality and safety supervision system based on blockchain technology collects and processes data, and the dynamic equation of replication due to the proportion of government supervision departments selecting "strict supervision" is as follows:

$$f(x) = \frac{ai}{an} = i(m_k - m_{k^v}) \tag{1}$$

In formula (1), f represents the income of the farmer group, a represents the income of the enterprise group, $i(m_k - m_{k^v})a$ represents the demand for the product, n represents the sales volume of the product, and m_{k^v} represents the actual sales volume of the agricultural product. The big data fusion model is a model for the evaluation of origin from both the product and the enterprise entity, but it needs to be specific to each plot evaluation. Because the data volume and indicator system are too complex, other methods are needed for model construction [10]. This project evaluates each plot using a distributed high-speed algorithm. The specific index calculation method is as follows:

$$l = \sqrt{\frac{max_n + ave_i}{2}} \tag{2}$$

Formula (2), max_n represents the food index, ave_i is the impact index, and l represents the average of the key index. When $l < 1$, indicating that the quality of agricultural products is not up to standard, early warning and deletion of the list are required. When $l = 1$, indicating that it is in a critical state, it is necessary to pay attention to the quality of agricultural products; $I < 1$, indicating that the quality of agricultural products is up to standard, suitable for the production of quality agricultural products [11].

The distributed high-speed algorithm can query the user's data in the filing management system. When a certain data collected by the user is the calculated result of several other data, the system defaults to the user calculating the result according to the calculation formula. And it displays to the text input box where the data item is located, improves the user's data filling speed, and reduces data errors caused by manual calculation, ensuring the accuracy of the data. However, the algorithm is easily interfered by the surrounding environment in the process of calculation, and then the data verification function is designed in the agricultural product quality and safety big data fusion model. This function can test the results of the distributed algorithm calculation, and use the hash function to test the calculation results. The hash function formula is as follows:

$$b = \{m_j - h\} = \frac{1}{m} \tag{3}$$

In the formula (3), b represents a data group element sum, m represents a data output value, and h represents a random variable. The data inspection function enables efficient management of agricultural product quality inspection data, and achieves matching with production data to meet the needs of government regulatory authorities for comprehensive control of inspection data. Specifically, it conducts unified management of basic information such as test samples, test sites, test methods, production subjects, and test results in the data of agricultural input products, quality inspection of planting products, and production of animal products, and it implements the basic data query function [12, 13]. At this point, the integration of agricultural product quality and safety big data is realized.

3 Experimental Results

In order to verify the effectiveness of the agricultural product quality and safety big data fusion model based on blockchain technology, the function, performance test of the model. In the experiment, by comparing the response speeds of the two models and analyzing the development efficiency and system performance, the stability of the traditional big data fusion model and the agricultural product quality and safety big data fusion model based on blockchain technology is proved. The test environment is as follows:

Divided into three test environments. The first hardware environment is Intel(R) Core(TM) i7-4790CPU@3.60 GHz Quad core eight Memory threads: 8 GB 1600 MHz DDR3, the operating system is ubuntu 14.04.1 LTS, the server is NodeJS 7.9.0, the application server is Tomcat 8.5.16, the database is MysSql 5.6.17 MongoDB, the performance testing tool is ApacheBench 2.3, the browser is 64 Chrome;

The second hardware environment is Intel(R) Core(TM) i7-4790CPU@3.50 GHz Quad core eight Memory threads: 12 GB 1600 MHz DDR3, the operating system is ubuntu 13.03.1 LTS, the server is NodeJS 6.0.0, the application server is Tomcat 2.6.10, the database is MysSql 4.6.16 MongoDB, the performance testing tool is ApacheBench 1.3, the browser is 56 Chrome;

The third hardware environment is Intel(R) Core(TM) i7-4790CPU@3.50 GHz Quad core eight Memory threads: 12 GB 1600 MHz DDR3, the operating system is ubuntu 10.3.1 LTS, the server is NodeJS 5.0.0, the application server is Tomcat 4.6.10, the database is MysSql 4.6.16 MongoDB, the performance testing tool is ApacheBench 1.3, the browser is 16 Chrome (Fig. 4).

Testing the functionality of the agricultural product quality and safety big data fusion model, mainly testing the business logic and system function realization degree realized by the system. Testable use cases are written according to system functions and tested according to test cases. The problems found have been solved in time, and the test results are as follows:

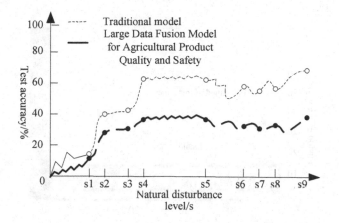

Fig. 4. Compares the experimental results

From the above test data, it can be seen that compared with the traditional model, the agricultural product quality and safety big data fusion model based on blockchain technology is more stable in performance testing and model function. The response speed of blockchain technology in processing agricultural product quality and safety data is significantly improved, and the higher the concurrent request volume, the more obvious the performance advantage after separation (Fig. 5).

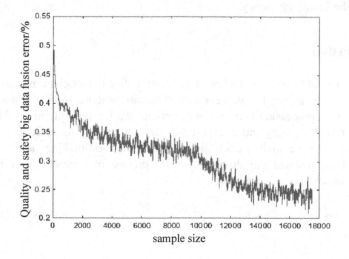

Fig. 5. Quality and safety of agricultural products big data fusion error

It can be seen from the above figure that with the increase of the number of samples, the safety big data fusion error shows a decreasing trend, which proves that the research method of this paper has a better effect on the quality and safety of agricultural products. The reason is that this method combines historical data, real-time data features, external shared data features and previous research results, and deeply integrates the data, greatly improving the quality and safety of agricultural products.

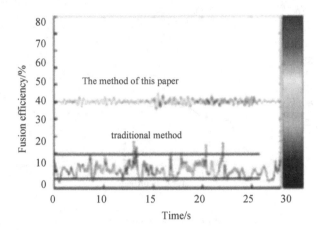

Fig. 6. Analysis of fusion efficiency of different methods

It can be seen from Fig. 6 that with the change of fusion time, the fusion efficiency of the method is always about 40%, which is nearly 30% higher than the traditional method. The main reason is that this method adopts BlockChain technology to create a big data fusion framework, which can collect and process agricultural product quality and safety data reasonably and effectively, and reduce the data fusion error, thus improving the fusion efficiency.

4   Conclusion

Through the use of blockchain technology, it can realize the efficient management and application of full-caliber, full-process and all-factors in terms of data collection, data supervision, data processing and data decision-making for agricultural production and agricultural product quality and safety. It provides a great help for agricultural industry managers to improve their work efficiency and decision-making ability, and can comprehensively manage and clearly define the process of agricultural products from production, processing to circulation.

References

1. Zhao, K., Xing, Y.: Overview of Internet of Things security driven by block chain technology. Inf. Netw. Secur. **12**(5), 1111–1116 (2017)
2. Yang, X., Li, X., Wu, H., et al.: Application model and realistic challenges of block chain technology in education. Mod. Distance Educ. Res. **12**(2), 2134–2145 (2017)
3. Yang, X., Li, X., Wu, H., et al.: Application model and realistic challenges of block chain technology in education. Mod. Distance Educ. Res. **23**(2), 2134–2145 (2017)
4. An, R., He, D., Zhang, Y., et al.: Design and implementation of anti-counterfeiting system based on block chain technology. J. Crypt. **4**(2), 1299–1308 (2017)
5. Zhang, C., Zhang, X., Wang, Z., et al.: Traceable research progress on quality and safety of agricultural products. China Agric. Sci. Technol. Rep. **19**(1), 3218–3228 (2017)
6. Li, T., Zhu, W.: Study on supervision of fresh agricultural products quality and safety—taking pesticide residues in vegetables as an example. Jiangsu Soc. Sci. **23**(2), 2184–2191 (2017)
7. Jinfen, Zheng, B., Qian, Y.: Scientific and technological innovation and breakthrough direction of agricultural product quality and safety in China. Agric. Prod. Qual. Saf. **23**(3), 2113–2118 (2017)
8. Guo, Z., Xu, B.: Building a three-dimensional model of a city based on social media data. Geospatial Inf. **15**(10), 1246–1248 (2017)
9. Wei, X., Yu, Z., Tian, C., et al.: Click-through rate prediction model of internet advertising based on big data platform. Comput. Eng. Design **38**(9), 2504–2508 (2017)
10. Li, W., Yang, W., Zhao, Y., et al.: Prediction model for mechanical properties of hot rolled strip based on large data and metallurgical mechanism. J. Iron Steel Res. **12**(4), 1653–2363 (2018)
11. Wang, X., Hong, W.N.: Dynamic forecasting model of export product sales based on large data of controllable correlation of cross-border e-commerce. Comput. Appl. **37**(4), 1038–1043 (2017)
12. Zhou, L., Fan, H., Pan, J.: Research on knowledge service framework of big data based on knowledge fusion process. Libr. Sci. Res. **23**(21), 2353–2359 (2017)
13. Yang, Y.: Improvement of massive multimedia information filtering technology in big data environment. J. of Xi'an Polytech. Univ. **04**, 569–575 (2017)

Artificial Intelligence Integration Method for Agricultural Product Supply Chain Quality Data Based on Block Chain

Kun Wang[1,2(✉)]

[1] Institute of Agricultural Information, Jiangsu Agri-Animal Husbandry
Vocational College, Taizhou, China
wangkun332@tom.com
[2] Taizhou Agricultural Internet of Things Engineering Technology
Research Center, Taizhou, China

Abstract. Traditional supply chain quality data integration methods costed a lot in integrating product quality, but the integration accuracy was very low and the effect is poor. In order to solved this problem, a supply chain of agricultural products was set up based on the artificial intelligence integration method of block chain using quality data. The framework of agricultural product supply chain was designed. The supply chain included four steps of production, processing, trade and consumption. Based on the frame, the workflow of the supply chain of agricultural products was expounded. The feasibility of the construction of agricultural product supply chain was verified by the experiment. The experimental results showed that the design of intelligent integration method can effectively reduce cost and improve the accuracy of integration.

Keywords: Block chain · Agricultural product supply chain · Supply chain quality · Intelligent integration method · Artificial intelligence

1 Introduction

With the development of the international trend of food economy and trade, agricultural products have become the focus of research in the global food safety field. The quality and safety inspection system of agricultural products is extremely complex and is the key to establishing a reasonable, stable and sustainable global agricultural product supply chain, which can promote the sustainable and stable development of agriculture [1]. With the popularization and application of data encryption currency such as Bitcoin, the blockchain has gradually emerged. Blockchain technology has become the first new technology. In recent years, the application research of blockchain technology has experienced an explosive growth. It is widely regarded as another subversive innovation in the computing paradigm following personal computers and mobile social networks, and is expected to reshape the activities of human society [2].

Reference [3] proposes an improved oversampling unbalanced data integration classification algorithm, using the AdaBoost algorithm to deal with the advantages of unbalanced data, using the decision tree as the basic classifier, using the oversampling

G. Gui and L. Yun (Eds.): ADHIP 2019, LNICST 301, pp. 226–234, 2019.
https://doi.org/10.1007/978-3-030-36402-1_24

method to synthesize samples at each iteration, balancing The training information, the final classification model, and the improved oversampling unbalanced data integration classification algorithm can significantly improve the classification accuracy, and thus improve the performance of the classifier. Reference [4] explores the way in which production fragmentation affects the unsalable sales of agricultural products through the mediation of supply chain integration and the regulation of information network capabilities under the theoretical framework of "resources-capacity-circulation". The higher the information network capability, the stronger the intermediary role of supply chain integration, and the role of regulated mediation.

The time dimension of the above integrated method data is limited. This paper proposes an artificial intelligence integration method based on blockchain for agricultural product supply chain quality data. The design quality system integration framework uses blockchain technology to asymmetrically encrypt data to ensure data security and increase the time dimension of the data to make it traceable.

2 Design of Agricultural Product Supply Chain Quality System Integration Framework

The process of obtaining the quality data integration of agricultural product supply chain is more complicated, and the calculation formula is as follows:

$$m = \frac{xy + 3y}{2x} \tag{1}$$

In formula (1), x, y and m represent the supply material, labor cost and product quality respectively. After obtaining the product quality, formula (1) is substituted into formula (2) to calculate the product quality level.

$$T = \frac{xy - 2y}{m} \tag{2}$$

After obtaining the product quality level, the product integration of the supply chain is calculated:

$$\kappa = \frac{T}{m} \tag{3}$$

Through the above calculation process, the integration of agricultural product supply chain quality data is completed.

Figure 1 shows the agricultural product supply chain basic structure. As it shows, the agricultural product supply chain includes the production, processing, trading and consumption of products. Since the agricultural product supply chain is a complete chain, the management of agricultural product safety should be started from the source [5].

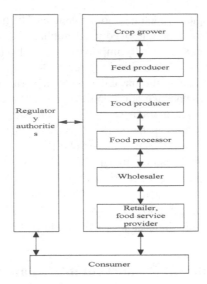

Fig. 1. Agricultural product supply chain basic structure

The quality chain of the agricultural product supply chain must ensure that all agricultural-related industry groups can participate, and the quality safety should be the first in the process of participation [6]. The agricultural product supply chain includes a number of elements, such as: crop growers, food manufacturers at all levels, and food distributors at all levels, ensuring supply chain quality by integrating resources such as logistics, information flow and capital [7].

Within the various quality chain organizations, product design, production, marketing, services and other elements work together to ensure product quality, the interlaced internal structure of the organization is constructed with internal mass structure. When perfecting the internal structure of the product, it is necessary to always consider the product quality, taking quality as the core goal, and ensuring that the quality data meets the production requirements [8].

3 Artificial Intelligence Integration Process Design of Agricultural Product Supply Chain Quality Data

The artificial intelligence integration method is highly flexible, and the fault tolerance and computing power are also unmatched by traditional methods, so it has been widely concerned by the research community. The integration approach mimics human nature and seeks some advice before making a decision. This method evaluation can be divided into multiple independent pattern classifiers, and the data is integrated after they are integrated. The performance of this method is better than the performance of any single classifier [9, 10].

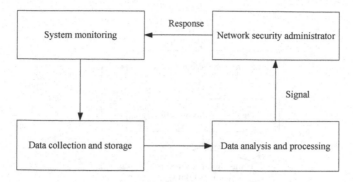

Fig. 2. Artificial intelligence integrated system module

As shown in Fig. 2, the artificial intelligence integrated system process involves data collection, data processing, selection, analysis, and result classification. The system can be divided into four modules: data acquisition and storage, data analysis and processing, network security administrator and system monitoring. Based on these modules, the system can be divided into different types. The system can measure the system performance according to the threshold, order and probability [11]. The artificial intelligence-based integrated classifier can improve the performance of the classifier.

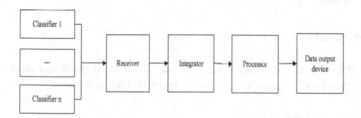

Fig. 3. Hardware design of artificial intelligence integrated system for agricultural product supply chain quality data

As shown in Fig. 3, the data is collected by a plurality of classifiers, and the data collected by each classifier is received and preprocessed by the receiver. Then the data is integrated through the integrator, the integrated data information is processed by the processor, the information we need is obtained, and finally the data information is output and fed back to the user [12].

As shown in Fig. 4, firstly, the data collected by the classifier is standardized, the data is input, and then the data is detected and classified, the data is converted into a signal, and the standard data is judged according to the signal, and the matched data is subjected to secondary detection and classification, obtaining test results.

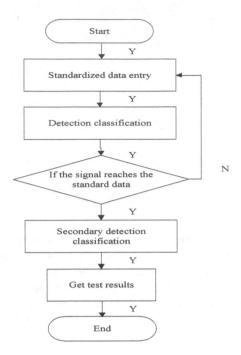

Fig. 4. Software design of artificial intelligence integrated system for agricultural product supply chain quality data

4   Experiments

In order to test the actual working effect of the artificial intelligence integration method designed in this paper, a comparative experiment is designed.

4.1   Experimental Parameters

The experimental parameters are described below in Table 1:

Table 1. Experimental parameters

Project	Data
Power type	High efficiency and energy saving power supply
Processing instruction	Cache instruction
Hard disk	160 GB
Video card	ATI Mobility Radeon discrete graphics
Detection signal form	TUV radio frequency signal
Caching method	Three level caching
Data display form	DSP processing signal
Memory capacity	4 GB
Radiation level	B
Operation and maintenance voltage	220 V
Power	≥ 200 W

4.2   Experiment Process

The experiment is performed according to the parameters set above, comparing the traditional agricultural product supply chain system with the agricultural product supply chain system studied in this paper, respectively recording the cost, system work efficiency and system accuracy experiment of the agricultural product supply chain system, the working results of two agricultural product supply chain systems are analyzed according to the three experimental results.

4.3   Experimental Results and Analysis

The experimental results obtained are shown below:

(1)   Operation cost

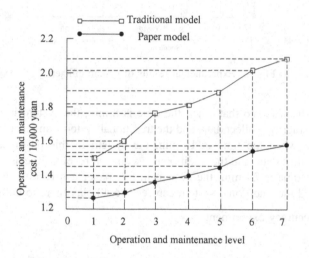

Fig. 5. Experimental results of operation cost

From Fig. 5, when the operation and maintenance level is 1, the operation and maintenance cost of the traditional system is 14,900 yuan, and the operation and maintenance cost of the system in this paper is 12,700 yuan; when the operation and maintenance level is 3, the operation and maintenance cost of the traditional system is 17,600 yuan, and the operation and maintenance cost of the system in this paper is 13,500 yuan; when the operation and maintenance level is 5, the operation and maintenance cost of the traditional system is 18,700 yuan, and the operation and maintenance cost of the system in this paper is 14,300 yuan; when the operation and maintenance level is 7, the operation and maintenance cost of the traditional system is 120,900 yuan, and the operation and maintenance cost of the system in this paper is 15,600 yuan;

(2) System efficiency

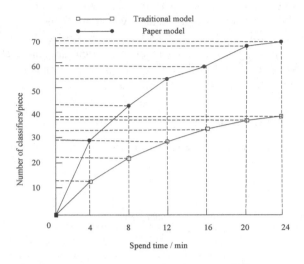

Fig. 6. Experimental results of system efficiency

It can be seen from Fig. 6 that when the time is 8 min, the system in this paper can receive 40 classifiers to collect data, and the traditional system can receive 20 classifiers to collect data; when the time is 16 min, the system in this paper can receive 60 classifiers to collect data, and the traditional system can receive 30 classifiers to collect data; when the time is 24 min, the system in this paper can receive 70 classifiers to collect data, and the traditional system can receive 40 classifiers to collect data.

(3) System accuracy experiment

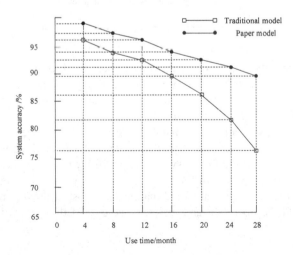

Fig. 7. System accuracy experiment

As can be seen from Fig. 7, when the system usage time is 4 months, the traditional system accuracy is 96%, and the system accuracy of this paper is 99%; when the system usage time is 12 months, the traditional system accuracy is 93%, and the system accuracy of this paper is 96%; when the system usage time is 20 months, the traditional system accuracy is 86%, and the system accuracy of this paper is 93%; when the system usage time is 28 months, the traditional system accuracy is 76%, and the system accuracy of this paper is 89.5%;

According to the above experimental results, the following experimental conclusions are obtained: The traditional agricultural product supply chain and the agricultural product supply chain based on the blockchain can improve the working efficiency of the whole system by adopting the artificial intelligence integration method, but the work cost of the agricultural product supply chain operation in this paper is much smaller than the traditional agricultural product supply chain with higher precision.

In summary, the agricultural product supply chain constructed in this paper has low cost, short time-consuming and high efficiency, which can effectively reduce the labor intensity and has a good development potential.

5 Conclusions

The core advantage of the blockchain is decentralization, which enables peer-to-peer transactions, collaboration, and coordination among different distributed systems by using timestamps, data encryption, economic incentives, distributed consensus, etc., thereby reducing costs and improving efficiency. This system adds time dimensions to the data, making it traceable, and the blockchain technology encrypts the data with asymmetric cryptography to ensure data security.

Although the agricultural product supply chain studied in this paper has a series of advantages and lacks a certain practical operation foundation, there may be some potential problems in the future use, which needs further research and discussion.

References

1. Ruimin, Z., Zhang, W.: Risk and control of financial science and Technology Innovation – based on large data, artificial intelligence, block chain research. China Manag. Inf. **13**(19), 33–36 (2017)
2. Fang, H., Tong, S., Du, J., et al.: Design and research of intelligent learning robot based on block chain technology - intelligent learning robot. Distance Educ. Mag. Large-Scale Learn. Serv. Syst. **35**(4), 42–48 (2017)
3. Zhang, F., Wang, L., Chai, Y.: An improved unbalanced data integration classification algorithm for oversampling. Minicomput. Syst. **39**(10), 36–42 (2018)
4. Qin, L., Tian, Y., Jiao, H.: The influence of production fragmentation on supply chain integration and unsalable agricultural products-an adjusted intermediary model. Jiangsu Agric. Sci. **46**(09), 335–340 (2018)
5. Chaoyang, Xu, P., Lou, J., et al.: Chemical recommendation model. J. Northeast. Norm. Univ. (Natural Science), **49**(2), 84–88(2017)

6. Xie, W.: GMIC global financial innovation summit: when big data, artificial intelligence, block chain technologies encounter finance. China Econ. Wkly. **12**(18), 50–51 (2016)

7. Zhao, B., Xu, S., Huang, Z.: Simulation of robot path intelligent search method under intensive obstacle environment simulation. Comput. Simul. **34**(2), 393–396 (2017)

8. Fresh, J.: The important direction of the future transformation and development of China's financial industry: "block chain +". Southern finance **12**(12), 87–91 (2016)

9. Xing, G.: Artificial intelligence, financial digital new side. China Financ. Comput. **12**(5), 15–18 (2017)

10. Yuxiang, H.: FiMAX "endorsement" block chain new standard. Chin. Financ. **21**(2), 75–76 (2018)

11. Li, F.: Electrocardiogram point diagram - new vision for large data analysis. Pract. Electrocardiol. J. **27**(1), 7–8 (2018)

12. Xia, D., Wang, Y., Zhao, X., et al.: Incremental interactive data integration method for intelligent people's livelihood. Comput. Res. Dev. **54**(3), 586–596 (2017)

Research on Adaptive Scheduling Method of Communication Resource Information in Internet of Things Environment

Chao Wang[✉]

School of Software, Nanyang Institute of Technology, Nanyang, China
wangchao7887@163.com

Abstract. The continuous expansion of information resources of communication resources under the Internet of things environment had led to information management problems becoming one of the core issues of communication information integration. This paper proposed an adaptive scheduling method for communication resource information in the Internet of things environment. Based on GIS technology, communication resource management was used for database communication resource information sharing. Next the three-level distributed database was used to establish the upload and storage of Internet of things communication resource information with obvious hierarchical relationship. The database synchronization mechanism was used to ensure that each database communication resource configuration was synchronized, and a network channel was established to increase the network load. Finally, based on the browser information, the communication resources were adaptively scheduled. The experimental data showed that compared with the traditional resource information scheduling method, the resource transmission speed of the designed communication resource information resource adaptive scheduling method was increased by 65%, and the information resource transmission matching rate was increased by 27%.

Keywords: Internet of things · Communication resource · Self-adaption · Scheduling method

1 Introduction

The Internet of things is the carrier of the modern Internet traditional telecommunication network, which enables a large number of ordinary object entities with independent functions to have an interconnection network. It can be said that the Internet of things is the most important component of modern electronic information technology and the most important development of modern information. As the modern Internet of things environment continues to evolve, the amount of relevant information continues to increase. The resource scheduling problem of a large amount of Internet of things communication resource information has become a key point of resource information utilization and configuration. Adaptive scheduling of communication resources can be seen as a high-precision resource supply and resource allocation in a massive information environment. The key is the collection and matching of information resource

G. Gui and L. Yun (Eds.): ADHIP 2019, LNICST 301, pp. 235–244, 2019.
https://doi.org/10.1007/978-3-030-36402-1_25

information. In addition, in the later research, it was found that in all Internet of things environment communication information, more than 80% of the information has spatial location. Adding geographic data based on the general information database and using GIS positioning can realize Internet of things data collection. To establish an information subsystem for database communication resource information sharing. Specifically, the third-level distributed database is used to establish and upload and store the information of the Internet of things communication resources with obvious hierarchical relationship through data positioning. The database synchronization mechanism is used to ensure the synchronization of each database communication resource configuration. Finally, the communication resources are adaptively scheduled based on the browser information [1].

2 Design of Adaptive Resource Information Scheduling Method in Internet of Things Environment

2.1 Communication Resource Management Based on GIS Core

Communication resource information management mainly includes five aspects of content as shown in Fig. 1.

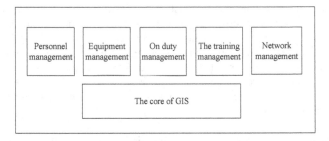

Fig. 1. Schematic diagram of communication resource management content

The five aspects shown in Fig. 1 need to be built on the GIS core data program, and the five aspects of work share the specific Internet of things data service. The communication related thematic data can be directly superimposed on the GIS data as the thematic data layer, and the low price position is the geographic coordinates of each communication data. Personnel management is to uniformly record the information of personnel related to the communication information business into the database, and centrally manage the information resources. On the basis of exerting its own information and communication management, it realizes the allocation of human resources information. Equipment management is to centrally allocate, adjust, store and scrape the equipment needed for IoT communication information transmission, and realize centralized management guarantee of data transmission hardware. Previous management refers to the unified storage management and application of all parts of the communication duty. While exerting the communication duty management function, the daily IoT information is statistically analyzed to provide an auxiliary basis for the later information management transmission [2].

Network management is a direct reflection of communication information institutions through maps or charts and other information, comprehensive analysis of data quality and performance, and provides a network basis for subsequent data communication [3].

2.2 Data Classification Based on Three-Level Distributed Database

In order to improve the adaptive scheduling rate of data communication resource data, it is necessary to establish a three-level distributed database to classify the communication data. Each Internet of things data transmission unit needs to arrange a primary database to ensure that the database can run on the data local area network. The upper-level database data must completely cover the sub-database data, and the three-level database data table is completely consistent [4]. For example, each database needs to contain all the data of all data collection points of its subordinate branches. Each database needs long-term maintenance to ensure normal data storage and transmission. After the database data is updated, the maintenance program will send the modified data to the upper database to synchronize the data of the upper and lower levels. Although the upper-level database can receive the communication resource data played by the lower-level database, it cannot be subjectively changed. The data management structure is shown in Fig. 2.

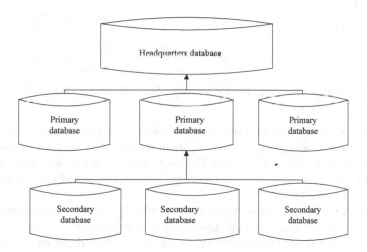

Fig. 2. Database layering diagram

The establishment of the database does not need to be limited to a special database product. Data stratification is performed by not using the data triggering device and snapshot replication feature of the Oracle database, but by modifying the communication data in the primary database record. Each time you quit, you only need to consult your own modification mark, and directly submit the modified data and added data, and then insert it into the upper-level database [5]. The spatial thematic attribute data in the primary database can be centrally managed through the Oracle91 program. Units at all levels are added to the data management as a professional GIS layer for real-time management.

2.3   Database Data Synchronization

Because the key of the upper and lower level database lies in the database synchronization problem, the lower level database needs to send the information data in real time to the upper level database through the data wide area network. The specific way is to transfer the working database and the temporary database. The upper level database is divided into two users: system users and temporary library users [6]. The ability is given to system users to modify database data and temporary library permissions. The user of the temporary library can only modify the permissions of the temporary database, and cannot modify the working rate data for the login system. It is only used when the temporary library unit sends real-time data to the upper database unit. The relationship between the working library, the temporary library, and the system user database is shown in Fig. 3 [7].

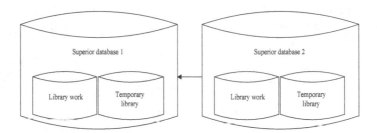

Fig. 3. Working library temporary library relationship diagram

In order to ensure the database transmission rate, a data transmission network channel of the Internet of things communication resource data needs to be established between the databases at various levels. The load channel is mainly used to improve the high load information data between databases. Establishing a load channel requires a balanced load based on TIRS.

The TIRS load channel design is mainly to directly apply the adjustment code of the database network channel to the database wide area network, and directly connect the network with the adjustment code IPS user transmission port and the channel using the user IP address. The main functions are as follows: The first is to ensure that the database information at all levels can be correctly transmitted. The other is to balance the load information that needs to be transmitted to ensure the stability of data transmission. When the data transmission is performed through the network channel, the TIPS information load protocol can directly improve the load stability of the entire network load path and the transmission result. The detailed resume process is shown in

Fig. 4. By establishing a communication channel, the data transmission path can be effectively increased, thereby increasing the network load [8].

By using multiple load protocols used by the channel, the data transmission scale can be directly increased, the data synchronization rate can be ensured, and multiple lines of database data can be evenly distributed. This ensures that the overall load capacity of the network transport channel is within a relatively safe and controllable area. In addition, when the network channel uses the network channel to perform data equalization processing on the load information used for database transmission, in order to ensure the data transmission frame number and the adaptability of the file package, it is necessary to perform the load reduction processing on the transmitted network information and the divided channels in advance according to the type of communication data. In order to avoid the information channel being stalled due to excessive channel congestion due to excessive channel information. In the process of equalization and data synchronization in the data database, the upper and lower limits of the equilibrium load are determined by the actual definition of the TIRS load balancing protocol. In general, the lower limit is 0. Table 1 shows the contents of the designed TIRS load balancing protocol [9].

Table 1. TIRS equalization protocol content

The TIRS wire transfer character		
Load balancing transmission time		
Link load identification code		
The load sequence		
Check code		
P	Regional correlation	Overload

The load balancing protocol can effectively widen the file transmission path of the load channel, thus ensuring the database synchronization rate [10].

In the actual design, the data samples and transmission extremes faced by different database network channel establishments are also different. In order to realize the simultaneous operation of multiple data channels of different levels of databases, load balancing needs to be implemented through network offloading.

R and W respectively represent the highest bandwidth of the data transmission channel of the database communication resource and the success rate of the load transmission. The formula for calculating the maximum unit load of the channel bandwidth is:

$$f = \frac{R}{W} \tag{1}$$

Since the database network channel capacity can be centrally organized and transmitted by the channel load construction protocol table proposed above, under the premise that the network bandwidth of each database has the same identity, the maximum network data channel transmission power can be utilized for network

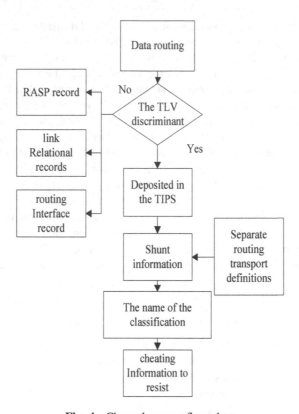

Fig. 4. Channel resume flow chart

transmission, thereby effectively reducing the average load pressure of each data channel.

If the maximum load rate of the database network data channel is k, then the maximum value of the data transmission station is N, then the formula for expressing the maximum traffic of the database network channel is:

$$C = \frac{1}{2}\log 2(1 + \frac{p}{N})$$ (2)

Equation (2) is an expression for determining the maximum split flow of a normal network channel.

In the normal local routing network channel state, the network channel load definition domain in each level database will perform vertical shunting and protocol amplification according to the protocol process. Through the amplified load process, the limit value of the load shunt can be obtained. The formula expression is:

$$C_j = \frac{1}{2}\log 2(1 + \frac{pm}{N})$$ (3)

In the formula, m is the limit value after the amplification of the protocol process. The smoothness of the channel data protocol can be guaranteed by Eqs. (1), (2) and (3).

2.4 Adaptive Scheduling Based on Browser Information Communication Resources

Information resource management and scheduling needs to be based on an information browser. In order to distinguish between different databases, the CLIENT/DATE-based client browser is upgraded to the BROWER/SERVER/DATAbase three-tier structure. The three-tier organization can share the database and GIS positioning kernel. The server side of the three-tier structure system is implemented by JAVA, which directly completes the client logic task. The browser adds the JAVA runtime environment plugin to display the server query results. The database is the core of the client browser upgrade, and the data codes are different in different storage locations of the database. In order to improve the scheduling efficiency of the browser information resources, some data codes in the database are given, as shown in Table 2.

Table 2. Part of the resource code

Section head	In the middle	The tail domain
Group{	MFVec2f	set crossSection
Group{	MFRotation	set orientation
eventIn	MFVec2f	set scalc
eventIn	MFVec3f	spine
children[	appearance Appearance{I	beginCapTRUE
children[	SFBool	TRUE
DEF desktop Shape{	SFBool	appearance Appearance{
DEF desktop Shape{	appearance Appearance{	crossSection
field	SFBool	endCapTRUE
field	MFRotation	orientation 0
field	MFVec2f	scale 1
field	MFVec2f	TRUE
field	SFBool	scale
field	MFVec3f	spine

3 Simulation Experiment

In order to verify the design of the Internet of things environment, the communication resource information adaptive scheduling method application effect, experimental comparison. The comparison group selects the traditional communication resource information configuration scheduling mode, so that the experimental group selects the adaptive scheduling method of communication resource information in the designed Internet of things environment. The scheduling resource transmission speed and the information resource transmission matching rate are compared. For the accuracy of the results, third-party software is used for parameter result recording. The verification process is as follows (Fig. 5):

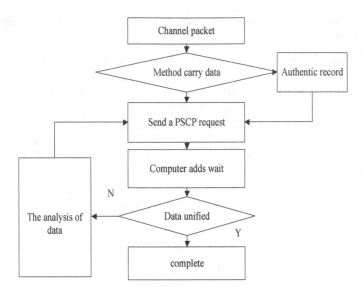

Fig. 5. Experimental flow chart

First, the resource transmission speed is compared and verified. The result is shown in Fig. 6.

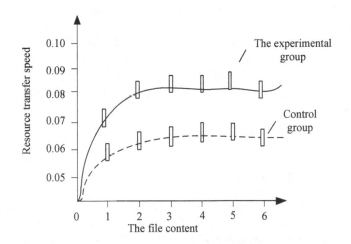

Fig. 6. Resource transmission speed comparison

It can be seen from Fig. 6 that the transmission speed of the experimental group is significantly higher than that of the comparison group. After actual quantification, it can be determined that the transmission speed of the experimental group has increased by nearly 65%. The comparison of information resource adaptive matching is shown in Fig. 7.

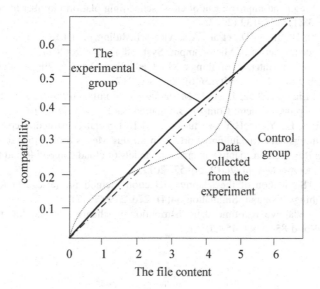

Fig. 7. Matching degree comparison chart

Figure 7 is a comparison of adaptive matching degrees. After actual quantization, it can be determined that the information resource transmission matching rate is increased by 27%. It has a certain advantage.

4   Conclusions

An adaptive scheduling method for communication resource information in the Internet of things environment is designed. First, GIS positioning is used to achieve Internet of things data collection. An information subsystem is established for sharing information of database communication resources, and a network channel is established to increase the transmission rate. Through the three-level distributed database and data location, the information uploading and storage of Internet of things communication resources with obvious hierarchical relationship is established. The database synchronization mechanism is used to ensure the synchronization of each database communication resource configuration. Finally, the communication resources are adaptively scheduled based on the browser information.

References

1. Zhang, H.B., Kuang, Y.H.: Simulation study on load balancing optimal scheduling of Internet of things communications resources. Comput. Simul. **34**(6), 310–313 (2017)
2. Wang, Q.W., Wu, L.M., He, R.J., et al.: Smart city information system in cloud computing and Internet of things. Eng. Technol. Primer **8**(2), 00278–00279 (2017)
3. Pan, H.P.: Design and improvement of cloud scheduling platform in fiber Internet of things. Laser Mag. **38**(1), 135–139 (2017)
4. Xu, J.Y., Chi, H., Jiang, D., et al.: A service scheduling model for IoT device processing based on feedback network. Microcomput. Syst. **38**(1), 24–28 (2017)
5. Qin: Based on the internet of things RFID adaptive Octree collision algorithm study. J. Changchun Normal University **36**(6), 23–27 (2017)
6. Wang, H.Z., Liu, K., Zhou, J., et al.: Modeling and simulation research on short-term load forecasting of power system. Comput. Simulation **33**(2), 175–179 (2016)
7. Liang, L., Liu, L., Yang, H.Y.: Diffusion model of metal construction cost efficiency of Internet of things data scheduling. World Non-ferrous Metals **8**(6), 115–116 (2016)
8. Wang, L.L.: Research on adaptive interaction models of cloud computing and the Internet of things. Microcomput. Appl. **7**(10), 56–57 (2017)
9. Yang, C.Y.: Simulation of the adaptive detection method for false data features in the Internet of things. Comput. Simulation **34**(4), 276–279 (2017)
10. Lu, W.: An adaptive real-time data distribution mechanism of the Internet of things. Commun. World **85**(3), 44–45 (2017)

Research on Dynamic Network Load Evaluation Algorithm Based on Throughput Monitoring

Chao Wang[✉]

School of Software, Nanyang Institute of Technology, Nanyang, China
wangchao7887@163.com

Abstract. In order to solve the problem of too low total load of individual nodes, a dynamic network load evaluation algorithm based on throughput monitoring was proposed. The node monitoring quantity analysis and evaluation parameter determination were used to complete the monitoring description of the dynamic network throughput rate. On this basis, through the improvement of load effect, evaluation mechanism establishment and correction factor calculation, the new evaluation algorithm was completed. The experimental results showed that after applying the dynamic network load evaluation algorithm based on throughput monitoring, the problem of too low total load of individual nodes was effectively solved.

Keywords: Throughput monitoring · Load evaluation · Network algorithm · Node monitoring · Equilibrium mechanism · Correction factor

1 Introduction

The throughput rate originally refers to the total amount of service data that the business system can provide in a unit of time. However, with the advancement of scientific and technological means, this concept has gradually been applied to many fields such as computer and data application communication. It refers to the average rate of network data passing through the communication channel in a unit time, and can also be described as the average rate at which the node successfully completes the data delivery processing per unit time. Usually, bit/s is used as the description unit [1]. Under the premise of accurately measuring the network throughput rate, by testing the performance of dynamic data under the condition of overloaded resources, the processing method of obtaining the overall workload level is the load evaluation method of the dynamic network. In the past, for a long time, relevant research departments in China used virtual machine delivery means to divide the load of dynamic networks. Then, through the method of fixed-point throughput calculation, the trend of network load in each operating area is counted, and a detailed load evaluation algorithm is developed according to the development of monitoring nodes in the functional area. Although this algorithm construction method can fully reflect the importance of network throughput monitoring parameters, with the gradual increase of application time, the total load of individual nodes can not be effectively averaged, resulting in large

G. Gui and L. Yun (Eds.): ADHIP 2019, LNICST 301, pp. 245–253, 2019.
https://doi.org/10.1007/978-3-030-36402-1_26

deviations in the evaluation results. In order to avoid the above situation, a new dynamic network load evaluation algorithm based on throughput monitoring is proposed by means of equalization evaluation mechanism and correction factor. And through the way of comparing experiments, the practical application value of the new algorithm is proved.

2 Dynamic Network Throughput Monitoring Description

2.1 Dynamic Monitoring of Web Nodes

Web network dynamic node monitoring is a non-functional description attribute. It can realize real-time analysis of node monitoring by determining load condition response time, service throughput, information access frequency, and node available service rate. Applying this analysis result can fully represent the basic access status of dynamic throughput in the Web dynamic network environment. The quality of service in the Web monitoring environment can further influence the distribution of dynamic nodes on the network. It evaluates the monitoring of dynamic nodes of the Web network from the perspectives of node accuracy, distribution security, and average response time, and can obtain multiple conditional indicators with description functions [2]. Assume that the average response delay in the web network environment is q, and the access frequency of each node monitoring is p. Under the condition that the basic evaluation index remains unchanged, the dynamic monitoring amount of the Web network can be expressed as:

$$R = \frac{qe + pw + u(i - 1)}{yt^2} \tag{1}$$

Where R represents the dynamic network monitoring amount of the web network, e represents the load condition response time, and w represents the service throughput parameter, i represents the information access frequency limit, u represents the node available service rate, y represents the analysis condition index coefficient, and t represents the basic access adjustment frequency. The flow chart of the web network is as follows (Fig. 1):

2.2 Throughput Load Evaluation Parameter Determination

When the user issues an access service to the Web dynamic network node, the evaluation parameter value of the throughput load situation and the Web service load parameter may cause a certain discrepancy. When the access value is small, the user's access request will not be affected, and the expected value of the load evaluation algorithm will not cause a large deviation. However, when the access value is large, the execution time of the user access request will gradually increase as the frequency of access increases, until the average response delay reaches the full operating cycle of the server [3, 4]. The positive attribute has a decisive influence on the throughput load evaluation parameter. The non-affirmative attribute needs to be combined with the Web

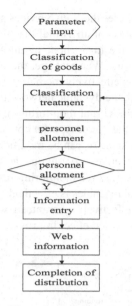

Fig. 1. Flow chart of the web network

service evaluation to reflect the impact on the throughput load evaluation parameters. The specific parameter determination criteria are as shown in formula (2).

$$D = 1 + \frac{1}{n}\left(\sum_{a=1}^{s}\frac{fG - H_1}{R} + \frac{H_2 - lG'}{R'}\right) \tag{2}$$

Where D represents the throughput load evaluation parameter, n represents the Web service load parameter, and a represents the execution lower limit value of the complete operation cycle. s represents the execution upper limit value of the complete running cycle, f represents the discriminating threshold of the function execution condition, and G represents the affirmative attribute operator. H_1 represents the original variable of orientation, R' represents the opposite of the monitoring amount of the dynamic node of the network, and H_2 represents the quantitative operator related to the non-positive attribute. l represents the average deviation degree parameter, and G' represents the opposite of the affirmative attribute operator.

3 Load Assessment Algorithm Based on Monitoring Description Results

3.1 Dynamic Network Service Load Effect Is Perfect

The dynamic network service load improvement is the key to the establishment of new evaluation algorithms. With the support of the Xen paravirtualized operating platform, all virtual machines are created and debugged by the simultaneous operation of multiple physical servers. It then uses the Web Services service of the dynamic network configuration to deploy the location of all virtual machines [5]. When all the dynamic network load factors that meet the throughput monitoring requirements exist in the Tomcat container in the state of the War package, the migration scheduling operation of the network virtual machine is effectively mediated. In order to achieve a high level of dynamic network service load, the dynamic network load resources are balanced and monitored with the support of the virtual monitoring module and the cluster selection module. Under the premise that the server Apache hot start function is not affected, the throughput of all network dynamic loads can be modified and configured to ensure that the algorithm automatically generates continuous access path backups during the evaluation process. And by collecting the monitoring result scheduling scope, the load information of all running virtual machines is effectively summarized, and the dynamic network service load effect is effectively guaranteed when the total amount of data remains unchanged [6, 7]. The detailed effect improvement process is shown in Fig. 2.

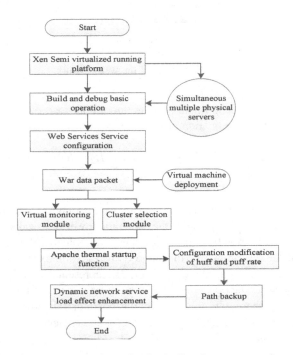

Fig. 2. Dynamic network service load effect improvement flow chart

3.2 Equilibrium Evaluation Mechanism

The equilibrium evaluation mechanism is the key to ensuring the efficiency of the new algorithm. When the dynamic network service accesses the starting load request to the virtual machine, the load on the server side will be transiently over-excited, resulting in a large deviation between the load service instance selection and the standard result. In order to avoid the above situation, the server selects the algorithm service type, selects the overload limit value of the current network running state on the core virtual machine, and maintains the overall service load value at a stable level through subsequent equalization adjustment. Using the above adjustment results, the load service information of the dynamic network is organized and improved. After all the destination migration nodes meet the service maintenance requirements, select the most suitable virtual machine running position as the transition node of the load information, and then create a new connection path, so that the true value of the equilibrium evaluation result gradually approaches the target value. After all dynamic network load service items are migrated to the virtual machine node, the establishment of a new algorithm equalization evaluation mechanism is completed. Detailed mechanism analysis is shown in Fig. 3.

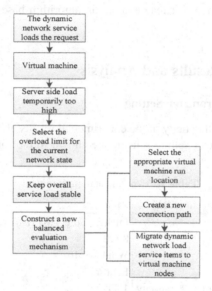

Fig. 3. Analytical diagram of establishing principle of equilibrium evaluation mechanism

3.3   Load Evaluation Correction Factor Calculation

The load evaluation correction factor can guarantee the authenticity of the dynamic network throughput monitoring results and make the evaluation results of the algorithm more convincing. The web network server has two kinds of load transmission modes: CPU occupation and background occupation. The CPU usage can cause the throughput of the to-be-detected to be gathered by triggering the network load, and the total amount of the core CPU can be effectively controlled by executing the load connection request. When the throughput of the network dynamic load reaches a certain level, all background processing rights are released, and the CPU usage no longer fluctuates with the change of the load evaluation correction factor. The background occupancy mode can directly obtain the throughput rate monitoring result of the dynamic network load situation, and trigger a series of evaluations to take up the occupation. At this time, the evaluation accuracy reaches the boundary state, and as the application time of the algorithm increases, the accuracy of the load evaluation correction factor will gradually increase. The specific factor is calculated as follows:

$$\phi = \frac{\int (\frac{\eta k}{D} + |c \cdot \lambda|)}{M + xv} \tag{3}$$

Where ϕ represents the load evaluation correction factor, η represents the total amount of CPU carried, and k represents the occupied load stator. c represents the throughput aggregation period, λ represents the dynamic network load monitoring coefficient, M represents the call extreme value of the load evaluation process, x represents the authority liberation parameter, and v represents the absolute value of the background occupancy operator. Integrating the above operating principles, the construction of a dynamic network load evaluation algorithm based on throughput monitoring is completed.

4   Experimental Results and Analysis

4.1   Experimental Parameter Setting

In order to ensure the authenticity of the experimental results, the experimental running environment and parameter setting scheme are shown in the following Table 1.

Table 1. Experimental environment

Experimental environment index	Parameter
Computer CPU	Intel(R) Core(TM) i7-6700 CPU@3.40 GHZ
RAM	8 GB
Operating system	Windows 10
The development tools	Eclipse
Computer built-in hard disk capacity	1 TB
External hard disk capacity	5 TB

The relevant experimental parameters can be set according to the following table.

Table 2. Experimental parameter setting table.

Parameter name	Experience group	Control group
EPT/(min)	50	50
NLP	0.66 (high speed) 0.82 (low speed)	0.66 (high speed) 0.82 (low speed)
TNL/(/T)	9.82×1011 (high speed) 9.94×1011 (low speed)	9.82×1011 (high speed) 9.94×1011 (low speed)
DNS/(%)	92.75	92.75
AEP	0.43	0.43

In the above table, the EPT parameter represents the experimental time, the NLP parameter represents the node load parameter, the TNL parameter represents the total node load, the DNS parameter represents the dynamic network stability, and the AEP parameter represents the algorithm evaluation parameter. In order to ensure the authenticity of the experimental results, the experimental parameters of the experimental group and the control group were always consistent.

4.2   Individual Node Load Total Comparison

In order to avoid the impact of sudden events on the authenticity of the experimental results, this experiment is divided into two parts. As an experimental execution condition, the values of dynamic network stability, algorithm evaluation parameters, etc. remain unchanged. Under the condition that the running experiment computer keeps running at high speed and the node load parameter is 0.66, 50 min is used as the experiment time, and the changes of the total load of individual nodes after the application of the experimental group and the control group algorithm are respectively recorded; Under the condition of running the experimental computer to keep the low speed operation and the node load parameter of 0.82, the experiment time was recorded with 50 min as the experiment time, and the change of the total load of the individual nodes after the application experiment group and the control group algorithm were respectively recorded. The specific experimental comparisons are shown in Tables 3 and 4.

Table 3. Comparison of individual node load totals (high speed).

The change of the total load of the individual node in the experimental group/($\times$ 1011 T)	Experimental time/(min)	The change of the total load of the individual node in the control group/($\times$ 1011 T)
6.78	5	6.57
6.78	10	6.34
6.78	15	6.20
7.89	20	6.12
7.89	25	5.99
7.89	30	5.83
9.31	35	5.71
9.31	40	6.02
9.31	45	6.15
10.42	50	6.73

Comparing Tables 2 and 3, it can be seen that under the condition that the running experiment computer maintains high speed operation and the node load parameter is 0.66, with the increase of experimental time, after applying the experimental group load evaluation algorithm, the total load of individual nodes shows a step-wise increasing trend. When the experiment time is 50 min, the total load of each node reaches the maximum value of 10.42 $\times$ 1011 T, which exceeds the target upper limit value of 9.82 $\times$ 1011 T.

Table 4. Comparison of individual node load totals (low speed).

The change of the total load of the individual node in the experimental group/($\times$ 1011 T)	Experimental time/(min)	The change of the total load of the individual node in the control group/($\times$ 1011 T)
7.21	5	8.35
7.35	10	8.35
7.66	15	8.35
7.84	20	8.35
7.91	25	8.35
8.26	30	8.35
7.93	35	8.35
9.98	40	8.35
10.23	45	8.35
9.79	50	8.35

Comparing Tables 2 and 4, it can be seen that under the condition that the running experiment computer keeps running at a low speed and the node load parameter is 0.82, with the increase of experimental time, after applying the experimental group load evaluation algorithm, the total load of individual nodes shows a trend of rising and falling alternately. When the experimental time is 45 min, the total load of individual nodes reaches the maximum value of 10.23 $\times$ 1011 T, exceeding the target upper limit value of 9.94 $\times$ 1011 T; After applying the load evaluation algorithm of the control group, the total load of individual nodes is always stable, which is 8.35 $\times$ 1011 T from the beginning to the end, which is much lower than the experimental group. In summary, under the condition that the experimental computer keeps running at low speed and the node load parameter is 0.82, the dynamic network load evaluation algorithm based on throughput monitoring can increase the total load of individual nodes by 1.88 $\times$ 1011 T.

5 Conclusions

The dynamic network load evaluation algorithm based on throughput monitoring uses the Web platform as the background. By continuously improving the node monitoring and basic load conditions, the evaluation accuracy of the algorithm reaches the expected level. Compared with the prior art, the influence of a large number of operation processes on the execution efficiency of the algorithm is avoided, and a complicated carrying manner is not required to ensure the execution of the algorithm. From the perspective of practicality, this new algorithm does have certain application feasibility.

References

1. Liu, C., Wang, J., Zhang, R.: Simulation research on load balancing selection in heterogeneous network communication. Comput. Simul. **35**(01), 269–274 (2018)
2. Lai, X.C., Liu, Q.L., Ren, Z.L., et al.: Channel occupancy rate-based adaptive fairness algorithm for Ad Hoc network. J. Dalian Univ. Technol. **56**(1), 41–49 (2016)
3. Tang, L., Liang, R., Zhang, Y., et al.: Load balance algorithm based on POMDP Load-aware in heterogeneous dense cellular networks. J. Electron. Inf. Technol. **39**(9), 2134–2140 (2017)
4. Li, G., Qu, W.L., Tian, F., et al.: A dynamic load balancing algorithm for multi-type services. Modern Electron. Tech. **33**(7), 1991–1993 (2016)
5. Wang, J., Guo, Y.J., Sun, L.J., et al.: Multi service load balancing algorithm for two tier satellite networks. Syst. Eng. Electron. Technol. **38**(9), 2156–2161 (2016)
6. Liu, W.J., Cheng, C., Chai, X.Q., et al.: Low power lossy network routing protocol based on minimum link cost ranking optimization. Comput. Eng. Des. **38**(2), 313–317 (2017)
7. Wang, S.Q., Sun, D.J., Zhang, Y.W.: Performance analysis for ALOHA protocol of underwater acoustic networks with a serial route. J. Harbin Eng. Univ. **37**(3), 360–367 (2016)

Research on the Classification Method of Network Abnormal Data

Bozhong Liu[(⊠)]

School of Electronic and Information Engineering, Guang'an Vocational
Technical College, Guang'an, China
`liubozhong77@163.com`

Abstract. As people use the network more and more and release more and
more personal information to the Internet, it also caused the leakage of personal
information. According to the above background, the optimization research on
the classification detection method of network anomaly data was proposed.
Correlation analysis was carried out for the conventional algorithm, and the
related model was constructed. A new algorithm was proposed to detect the
network anomaly data to improve the processing ability of the network anomaly
data. The experimental data showed that the proposed network anomaly data
classification detection optimization algorithm improved the processing range
by 31% when processing abnormal data, and the efficiency of processing data
was increased by 36%. It proved the effectiveness of the new method and
provided a theoretical basis for the processing of future abnormal data.

Keywords: Network anomaly · Data classification · Detection method ·
Improved design

1 Introduction

Under the development of modern science and technology, people's information
security is also reduced. Many information is badly bought and sold online, and
people's privacy cannot be effectively guaranteed. This is not conducive to the
improvement of network security, causing great damage to personal information,
affecting the security of personal information. In this context, the network technology
department has also improved the network data anomaly detection, and fully enhanced
the algorithm to improve the security of information. By making relevant predictions
about the data that may cause attacks in advance, the security of information is
improved, and relevant prevention of virus attacks is carried out in advance. In the
construction of firewall, its performance should be fully improved. On the basis of
traditional prevention, protection of personal privacy information should be strengthened to improve personal security performance. In the process of technical improvement, the research on the classification detection method of network abnormal data
should be strengthened. There are different methods of classification detection for
different network intrusion methods to maintain the data, so as to protect the data well
[1]. At present, China's research on the classification detection method of network
abnormal data is still in its infancy, and the technology is not very mature. It is not well

G. Gui and L. Yun (Eds.): ADHIP 2019, LNICST 301, pp. 254–262, 2019.
https://doi.org/10.1007/978-3-030-36402-1_27

protected against malicious online information attacks, resulting in the loss of personal information, which has a great negative impact on individuals. Therefore, the protection of personal information should be constantly strengthened, the relevant technology of network abnormal data classification detection method should be improved continuously, the operation of its algorithm should be improved, and its safety performance should be increased. It provides effective technical support for the protection of personal information and future security performance, and guarantees the privacy of individuals. As shown in Table 1:

Table 1. Attribute representation of abnormal traffic data

Abnormal	The source IP address	Destination IP address
DDOS	Scattered	Concentrated
Attack	Concentrated	Concentrated
The worm	Concentrated	Scattered
IP scanning	Scattered	Concentrated
Port scanning	Scattered	Scattered

2 Classification and Detection of Network Abnormal Data

2.1 The Method of Artificial Intelligence Is Used for Relevant Detection

Using artificial intelligence to classify network abnormal data is the trend of network abnormal data detection in the future. The relevant procedures are edited manually and the machine is used for the related detection operations. The relevant detection can be improved through the related automatic calculation, saving manpower, improving the efficiency of detection and reducing the working pressure of people [2]. At present, with the improvement of science and technology, the attack technology of network information is further improved. A series of simple methods used in the past to monitor data have been unable to meet the needs of network abnormal data detection. The traditional method is relatively simple. Now, the detection method for complex data should be updated so that it can carry out stronger detection for the update method of complex network abnormal data. Improve related processing, use artificial intelligence to perform related detection, and edit complex programs in advance so that they can cope with complex problems and solve them accordingly. The artificial intelligence can continuously update and learn according to the relevant complexity, can automatically deal with related problems, improve the processing technology for information, and improve the efficiency of processing problems. It makes the processing of information more difficult, and the scope of processing related problems is expanded accordingly, and various complex data can be solved in a related manner. Artificial intelligence can link related abnormal data, so that the processing of network abnormal data can be solved in a series of ways. It has changed the traditional solution to only a single abnormal data, and improved the processing efficiency of abnormal data [3]. As shown in Fig. 1:

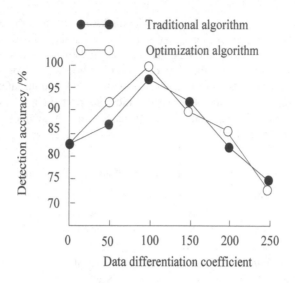

Fig. 1. Algorithm detection results

2.2   Data Mining for Correlation Detection

When using the data mining method for related detection, it is necessary to conduct a large amount of mining of the originality of the abnormal data to find out the root cause of the problem. Correlate the root cause of the abnormal data and solve the problem of abnormal data processing. Using this method to detect and analyze related data, the source of the relevant abnormal data can be solved and analyzed, and the source of the virus is processed from the root cause. On this basis, the information processing process can be fully simplified, and it is no longer necessary to search for abnormal data one by one, which wastes a lot of time. When performing related detection through data mining [4], not only can the problem be processed, but also relevant differential detection can be performed by analyzing the data. Analyze the degree of abnormality of the data, compare it with the previous data, compare the source and difference of different abnormal data, in order to make more reasonable editing of the development and update of the algorithm, and simplify the processing of the abnormal data afterwards. In the response to the processing of various complex information, the way of data mining is particularly important, which can highlight the handling of related complex problems and solve the problems from the root. As shown in Fig. 2:

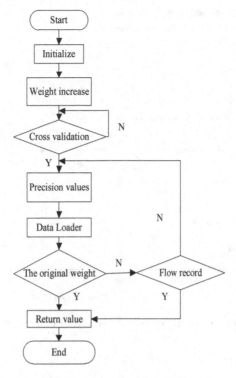

Fig. 2. Algorithm general flow

2.3 Using Information Entropy Method to Detect Abnormal Data

The method of information entropy is to detect the details of the anomaly information, and use the relevant algorithm to further detect and analyze the abnormal data in detail. The detection of network problems is not limited to the processing of the surface, but the details are analyzed. On this basis, the editing of the relevant algorithms is performed according to the details. On this basis, the relevant calculations are carried out, and the details of the problem are analyzed in detail, so that the details are handled very delicately, not only the surface is processed, but the abnormal data is repeated and cannot be cured [5]. In the process of using the information entropy method to detect abnormal data, it is necessary to continuously update the abnormal data, and continue to perform detailed operations on the algorithm to improve the processing of details and improve personal information security. Under the premise of safe handling of information, it is guaranteed that individuals can effectively protect the security of individuals and strengthen the processing of information. The relevant abnormal data is detected in advance, and the detailed problems are processed firstly on the basis of the detection, and the security of the personal information is improved on the basis of the processing [6]. As shown in Fig. 3:

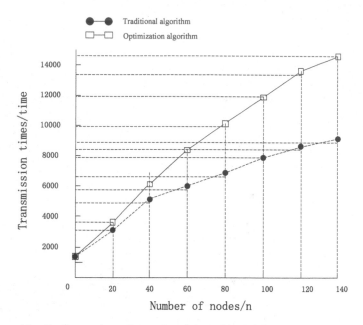

Fig. 3. Comparison of experimental results of different algorithms

3 Case Analysis

In order to ensure the effectiveness of the network anomaly data classification detection method proposed in this paper, it is necessary to analyze its effectiveness. In the test process, different classification detection methods are used as the test object, and the optimization ability of the detection method is analyzed in detail, and the test objects of different specifications are used for simulation analysis. In order to ensure the accuracy of the experimental process, the parameters of the experiment should be set [7]. In this paper, the test data is used as the test object, and two different design methods are used to conduct the classification test. The simulation results are analyzed. Since the analysis results obtained in different methods are different from the analysis methods, it is necessary to ensure the consistency of the test environment parameters during the test. The test data setting results in this paper are shown in Table 2:

Table 2. Different methods for detecting network result data tables

Abnormal characteristic number	K mean accuracy	Accuracy of neural network detection
12	81	77
21	83	80
31	79	78
41	74	77
51	78	81
15	74	78
37	76	79
42	77	91

3.1   Analysis of Results

Algorithm:

$$\sum_{j=1}^{n} z_j b_j = 1, b_j > 0 \tag{1}$$

In the form, $\sum_{j=1}^{n} z_j b_j$ represents the label information of network abnormal data subblock b_j; z_j represents Acquired j an effective network abnormal data block; n represents the total number of data blocks. Perform related update operations according to the above algorithm to optimize the related algorithms:

$$(z)y = sign\left(\sum_{j=1}^{n} b_j z_j + c\right) \tag{2}$$

In the form, $(z)y$ represents the optimized network abnormal data feature fusion error domain; c represents the center of mass of the sample. Using this algorithm, effective monitoring of abnormal data can be realized, and analysis and processing of abnormal data can be optimized [8]:

$$\max \sum_{j=1}^{n} \theta_k = \frac{1}{2} \sum_{j=1}^{n} \sum_{k=1}^{n} z_j b_j (z)y \tag{3}$$

In the form, $\max \sum_{k=1}^{m} \theta_k$ represents the network anomaly data detection model.
As shown in Table 3:

Table 3. Sample data statistics

Number of experiment	Sample quantity	Identifiable abnormal data characteristics
1	324	67
2	342	45
3	532	55
4	123	37
5	432	27
6	124	34
7	864	43

According to the method described above, the updated algorithm is used to analyze and process the abnormal data, reduce the existence of abnormal data, improve the security of information, and strengthen the protection of information [9]. J represents the correlation coefficient of the processed information, k represents the analysis of the coefficient, and m represents the security of the data, b represents the range of data processing, z represents the range of calculations used by the running data, and the detection of abnormal data [10]. As shown in Fig. 4:

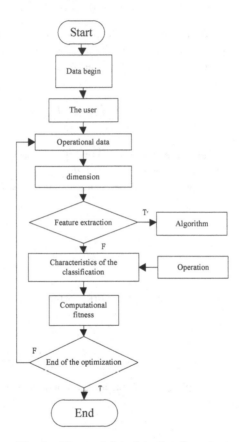

Fig. 4. Abnormal data detection flow chart

In the process of performing related operations, as shown in Fig. 5:

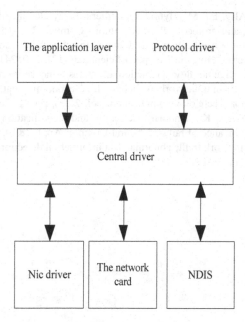

Fig. 5. Driver structure

4 Conclusions

In this paper, the network anomaly data is analyzed and processed in the context of informationization. Based on the analysis of the traditional algorithms, the related algorithms are optimized. Based on the classification and detection of network anomaly data, the optimization algorithm is processed. A large number of algorithms are used to process related data, which ensures the security of user information, improves the protection of user information, and enhances the information security for users.

References

1. Nemanja, B., Duan, K.Z.: Improved real-time data anomaly detection using context classification. Expert Syst. Appl. **23**(14), 23–36 (2017)
2. Sun, Y., Wong, A.C., Kamel, M.S.: Classification of imbalanced data: a review. Int. J. Pattern Recognit. Artif. Intell. **12**(3), 501–520 (2017)
3. Wang, B., Zhao, Y., Hu, F., et al.: Anomaly detection with subgraph search and vertex classification preprocessing in Chung-Lu random networks. IEEE Trans. Signal Process. **66**(20), 5255–5268 (2018)
4. Hussain, J., Lalmuanawma, S., Chhakchhuak, L.: A two-stage hybrid classification technique for network intrusion detection system. Int. J. Comput. Intell. Syst. **9**(5), 863–875 (2016)
5. Xin, D.U., Huang, X., Hongga, L.I., et al.: Research on classification of plant community using projection pursuit learning network algorithm on high resolution remote sensing images. J. Geo-Inf. Sci. **18**(1), 124–132 (2016)

6. Al-Obeidat, F., El-Alfy, E.S.M.: Hybrid multicriteria fuzzy classification of network traffic patterns, anomalies, and protocols. Pers. Ubiquitous Comput. **2**, 1–15 (2017)
7. Nguyen, H.A., Choi, D.: Application of data mining to network intrusion detection: classifier selection model. Lecture Notes in Computer Science **36**(12), 230–241 (2017)
8. Pang, M., Hao, X.: Traffic flow prediction of chaos time series by using subtractive clustering for fuzzy neural network modeling. In: Second International Symposium on Intelligent Information Technology Application, vol. 2(13), pp. 12–26 (2017)
9. Jerome, R.B., Hätönen, K.: Anomaly detection and classification using a metric for determining the significance of failures. Neural Comput. Appl. **28**(6), 1–11 (2016)
10. Ying, W.: Wireless network traffic abnormal data information detection simulation. Comput. Simul. **34**(9), 408–411 (2017)

Research on Key Information Retrieval Method of Complex Network Based on Artificial Intelligence

Bozhong Liu[✉]

School of Electronic and Information Engineering, Guang'an Vocational
Technical College, Guang'an, China
liubozhong77@163.com

Abstract. Aiming at the problem of poor retrieval accuracy and slow retrieval speed of information retrieval method based on hyperlink, a key information retrieval method based on artificial intelligence was proposed. The method was mainly divided into three steps, and each step was completed with the help of artificial intelligence. First, file information was preprocessed (information processing and information filtering), then keywords were extracted from information content, and finally semantic similarity calculation and semantic information matching were conducted to complete key information retrieval in complex networks. The results showed that the accuracy of key information retrieval method of complex network based on artificial intelligence was improved by 2.27% and the speed of retrieval was improved by 3.06 s.

Keywords: Artificial intelligence · Complex networks · Information retrieval · Keywords extraction · Semantic similarity · Semantic information matching

1 Introduction

With the passage of time, China's enterprises and institutions, the party and government departments of the number of files is increasing. In order to facilitate the preservation and access, the paper version of file information is converted into electronic version, and then stored in the department or organization's computer network system. However, these personal network systems are mostly self-organization, self-similarity, attractor, small world, scale-free, namely complex network [1]. The structure of complex network is complex, the connection mode is disordered and the nodes are various. Therefore, when people need to retrieve the information or data they need in a complex network, they will not only be slow, but also may be wrong. Therefore, many key information retrieval methods come into being in order to improve the efficiency of information retrieval. Hyperlink based information retrieval method is the most widely used, but with the emergence of more and more disordered archival data, the retrieval method is also unable to meet the actual needs of enterprises, institutions, party and government organs and other departments, and the problem of poor accuracy and slow speed of retrieval starts to appear [2]. The key information retrieval method based on artificial intelligence is proposed. The application of artificial intelligence in the key

G. Gui and L. Yun (Eds.): ADHIP 2019, LNICST 301, pp. 263–270, 2019.
https://doi.org/10.1007/978-3-030-36402-1_28

information retrieval of complex networks is one of the main research directions in the field of information retrieval. In this study, the file information was preprocessed by artificial intelligence first, then the key words were extracted by artificial intelligence, and finally the semantic similarity calculation and semantic information matching were conducted by artificial intelligence to complete the key information retrieval in the complex network. To verify the effectiveness of the method, a comparative experiment was carried out. The results show that compared with hyperlink based information retrieval method, the retrieval accuracy is improved by 4% and the retrieval speed is improved by 2.3 s

2　Information Retrieval Under Artificial Intelligence

Artificial intelligence, or AI for short, is a branch of computer science, mainly used in robot manufacturing, language recognition, image recognition, natural language processing and so on. Artificial intelligence can replace human brain to complete heavy scientific and engineering calculation, and can do it faster and more accurately than human brain [3]. The artificial intelligence technology is applied to the key information retrieval, that is, intelligent retrieval. It is based on the needs of users, and searches out the parts required by users in the large and complex network [4]. The process of intelligent information retrieval method is shown in Fig. 1.

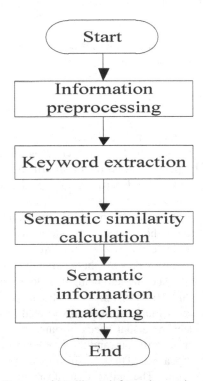

Fig. 1. Process of intelligent information retrieval method

2.1   Information Preprocessing

Information is stored at random. The information stored in the complex network will become confused over time and flow of system data, and there is a risk of being mixed in by other information. The format is mixed and cannot be read. Therefore, it is necessary to use artificial intelligence to preprocess information. Information preprocessing is a complex work, which needs two steps (information processing and information filtering) [5]. Only when the information is sorted out well, can the efficiency of subsequent key information retrieval be accelerated to achieve the goal of this research.

2.1.1   Information Processing

Information processing is mainly aimed at the problem of information format and content. The information processing process is shown in Fig. 2.

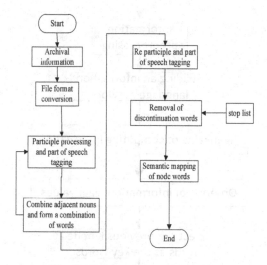

Fig. 2. Information preprocessing

2.1.2   Information Filtering

After the completion of the information processing, the information obtained is still confused, only the internal or format of the simple correction and processing. Further treatment is therefore required. This process is actually a complex set of language rules. These language rules are incorporated into information filtering software, and in the ai information retrieval system [6]. The artificial intelligence will collect all the above preliminarily processed file information, then label the existing garbage information and send it to the isolation area. The information in the isolation area will be tested and processed again. If there is a problem, it will be isolated, and if there is no problem, it will be allowed to pass. Then, with the above unannotated information, it is sorted out according to the language rules in the artificial intelligence input in advance, and finally stored in the database in an orderly way [7].

2.2   Keywords Extraction

When users search for archival information, the key words of the content to be searched must be entered in the human-computer interaction interface. Therefore, in order to improve the efficiency of information retrieval, keyword extraction of information content stored in complex networks is needed to speed up subsequent information matching and complete information retrieval [8]. The powerful computing power of artificial intelligence is used to calculate the importance of each node (words in the information), and then the nodes are sorted by importance, and a certain number of keywords are extracted according to the set requirements. The specific process is shown in Fig. 3.

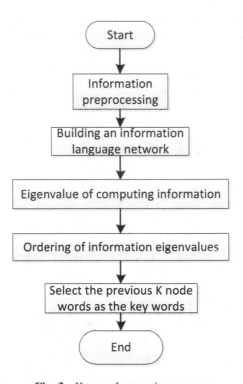

Fig. 3. Keyword extraction process

The formula in step 3 is as follows:

$$\xi = \frac{a \cdot B_i}{\sum\limits_{i=1} B_i} + \frac{(1+a) \cdot C_i}{2} \tag{1}$$

In the formula, ξ is the eigenvalue; B_i is the importance of the node; C_i is the aggregation coefficient of nodes i; a is an adjustable parameter.

2.3 Semantic Similarity Calculation and Matching

After the user enters the search keywords, the ai will search similar keywords according to the keyword semantics. This keyword is extracted according to the information content in the above chapters, and then the user will present the file information content listed according to the importance in the human-computer interaction interface. In this link, there are mainly two steps: semantic similarity calculation and semantic information matching [9].

2.3.1 Semantic Similarity Calculation

Suppose the semantic similarity of the keywords E1 and E2 is, and the calculation formula is:

$$sim(E1, E2) = \alpha \cdot simA(E1, E2) + \beta \cdot simB(E1, E2) + \gamma \cdot simC(E1, E2) \qquad (2)$$

$$\alpha + \beta + \gamma = 1 \qquad (3)$$

The formula, $simA(E1, E2)$ is the semantic similarity of distance; $simB(E1, E2)$ is the semantic similarity based on content; $simC(E1, E2)$ is the semantic similarity based on attributes.

2.3.2 Semantic Information Matching

After the similarity calculation of keywords is completed, semantic information matching should be conducted according to the similarity. In the hyperlink based information retrieval method, the polysemy of a word cannot be distinguished, and the artificial intelligence can easily make up for this shortcoming [10]. It will, like the human brain, automatically identify and match the semantic information. For example, users use hyperlinked information retrieval methods to retrieve information about financial aspects. After entering the key word "finance" through the search interface, this method, because it completely ignores the semantic information of the search term, only USES the word "finance" to search mechanically, and finally retrieves only the meaning of the word "finance", or the related information with the word "finance". And after the use of artificial intelligence for retrieval, to "financial" a more precise definition for the term, "financial" contains "tax", "debt", "spending" and other subsystems, so the use of artificial intelligence can not only provide users with the word "finance" keywords information, also can retrieve the relevant information, to satisfy the user may need to know about the "financial" related subclass information [11–13].

3 Contrast Experiment

In order to verify the effectiveness of the key information retrieval method of complex network based on artificial intelligence, a comparative experiment was conducted. The accuracy and speed of retrieval are taken as indicators to judge the effectiveness of the method. It is assumed that there are 1,500 files in a company's file information storage system, which are divided into five types: employee personal information files (800), business files (200), financial files (250), personnel flow files (200), and company development history records (50).

Now, the key information retrieval method of complex network based on artificial intelligence and information retrieval method based on hyperlink are used to retrieve the information of 15,000 files. The results are shown in Table 1.

Table 1. Search results of 15,000 documents by two methods

Category	The number of all file letters that belong to this type	Key information retrieval method for complex networks based on artificial intelligence			Information retrieval method based on hyperlink		
		The number of correctly retrieved/share	Accuracy rate/%	Average accuracy/%	The number of correctly retrieved/share	Accuracy rate/%	Average accuracy/%
1	800	790	98.75	98.95	795	99.38	96.68
2	200	200	100		198	99	
3	250	250	100		250	100	
4	200	200	100		190	95	
5	50	48	96		45	90	

As can be seen from Table 1, the average accuracy rate is 98.95% when 1,500 files are retrieved intelligently using the key information retrieval method of complex network based on artificial intelligence. The average accuracy rate was only 96.68% when 1500 files were retrieved by hyperlink based information retrieval method. The former was 2.27% higher than the latter.

Now to verify the difference in retrieval speed between the two methods. The two methods were used to search 250 financial files. The retrieval results are shown in Table 2.

Table 2. Compare the speed of information retrieval between the two methods

Retrieval times	Key information retrieval method for complex networks based on artificial intelligence/s	Information retrieval method based on hyperlink/s
1	2.3	5.4
2	2.5	5.6
3	2.4	5.4
4	2.3	5.8
5	2.6	5.2
Average time consuming/s	2.42	5.48

As can be seen from Table 2, the average time spent in retrieving 250 financial files is 2.42 s when using the key information retrieval method of complex network based on artificial intelligence. The average time spent in retrieving 250 financial files was 5.48 s using hyperlink based information retrieval method. Compared with the latter, the former is 3.06 s shorter than the latter.

All in all, the key information retrieval method based on artificial intelligence is superior to the information retrieval method based on hyperlink in terms of both retrieval accuracy and retrieval speed.

4 Conclusions

To sum up, archival information, as an important basis for the development of enterprises, institutions, party and government departments, and its storage mode has gradually begun to develop toward informatization, networking and intellectualization. However, due to the fact that the archival information is mostly stored in the complex network with personal nature, it will be difficult to find information when users want to look up certain information, and it will be difficult to retrieve it for a while. Even if it is retrieved, the retrieved content is not accurate. A key information retrieval method based on artificial intelligence is proposed. The experimental results show that the retrieval time of this method is shorter than that of the traditional method, and the accuracy of information retrieval is higher, and the average accuracy is 98.95%. This method not only improves the accuracy of information retrieval, but also improves the efficiency of information retrieval, which provides great convenience for file information retrieval.

References

1. Zanganeh, M.Y., Hariri, N.: The role of emotional aspects in the information retrieval from the web. Online Inf. Rev. **42**(4), 520–534 (2018)
2. Ou, S., Tang, Z., Su, J.: Construction and usage of terminology services for information retrieval. J. Libr. Sci. China **42**(2), 32–51 (2016)
3. Wang, L.: Text information retrieval algorithm simulation analysis under massive data. Comput. Simul. **33**(4), 429–432 (2016)
4. Liu, J., Cao, S.: Analysis on the information retrieval experience: a perspective of flow theory. Libr. Inf. Serv. (8), 67–73 (2017)
5. Cai, J., Tang, Y.: A new randomized Kaczmarz based kernel canonical correlation analysis algorithm with applications to information retrieval. Neural Netw. Official J. Int. Neural Netw. Soc. **98**, 178 (2017)
6. Huang, Y.Y., Li, Y.: Research on cognitive information retrieval model based on the "scarcity theory". J. Intell. **35**(11), 136–140 (2016)
7. Ashwin, K.T.K., Thomas, J.P., Parepally, S.: An efficient and secure information retrieval framework for content centric networks. J. Parallel Distrib. Comput. **104**, 223–233 (2017)
8. Kralj, J., Robnik-Šikonja, M., Lavrač, N.: HINMINE: heterogeneous information network mining with information retrieval heuristics. J. Intell. Inf. Syst. **50**, 29–61 (2017)
9. Cheng, Y., Lai, M.: Research on the information retrieval model based on D-S theory. Libr. Inf. Serv. **61**(21), 5–12 (2017)
10. Liu, P., Feng, M., Ming, L.: Practical k-agents search algorithm towards information retrieval in complex networks. World Wide Web **1**, 1–21 (2018)

11. Craswell, N., Croft, W.B., Rijke, M.D., et al.: Neural information retrieval: introduction to the special issue. Inf. Retrieval J. **21**(2–3), 1–4 (2017)
12. Kishore, C.B.D.J., Reddy, T.B.: An efficient approach for land record classification and information retrieval in data warehouse. Int. J. Comput. Appl. 1–10 (2018)
13. Min, Y., Duan, J., Huang, M.: Research on information retrieval and intelligent fusion based on cloud computing environment. Modern Electron. Tech. (6), 162–164 (2018)

Optimized PointNet for 3D Object Classification

Zhuangzhuang Li[1], Wenmei Li[1,2(✉)], Haiyan Liu[1], Yu Wang[1], and Guan Gui[1]

[1] College of Telecommunications and Information Engineering,
Nanjing University of Posts and Telecommunications, Nanjing 210003, China
liwm@njupt.edu.cn
[2] School of Geographic and Biologic Information, Nanjing University
of Posts and Telecommunications, Nanjing 210023, China

Abstract. Three-dimensional (3D) laser scanning technology is widely used to get the 3D geometric information of the surrounding environment, which leads to a huge increase interest of point cloud. The PointNet based on neural network can directly process point clouds, and it provides a unified frame to handle the task of object classification, part segmentation and semantic segmentation. It is indicated that the PointNet is efficient for target segmentation. However, the number of neural network layers and loss function are not good enough for target classification. In this paper, we optimize the original neural network by deepen the layers of neural network. Simulation result shows that the overall accuracy increases from 89.20% to 89.35%. Meanwhile, the combination of softmax loss with center loss function is adopt to enhance the robustness of classification, and the overall accuracy is up to 89.95%.

Keywords: Point cloud · PointNet · Object classification · Center loss

1 Introduction

The three-dimensional (3D) images contain special information that allows the object to be naturally separated from the background. In recent years, the 3D coordinates of object surface can be acquired accurately and quickly with the development of 3D imaging technology [1]. Point clouds are better than images to describe the objects because they contain the largest amount of raw information. However, it is difficult to process point clouds directly. Since point clouds are not irregular and uneven distribution [2].

Deep learning has been applied in many fields, such as computer vision, natural language processing and wireless communications. Deep learning can automatically learn how to extract features from inputted raw data using deep neural networks [3–6]. Convolutional neural networks (CNN) have made great achievements in image classification and segmentation. Most researchers have changed their strategies and started to convolve with raw point clouds after transforming raw data to regular 3D voxel grids. They feed raw data to 3D CNN for feature extractions to segment point clouds [7]. Some scholars have tried to use a multi-view method to take two-dimensional

G. Gui and L. Yun (Eds.): ADHIP 2019, LNICST 301, pp. 271–278, 2019.
https://doi.org/10.1007/978-3-030-36402-1_29

images of the same object from different angles and then convolve with images to extract features [8, 9].

Charels et al. proposed a new novel type of neural network named PointNet. The main idea of PointNet is to process raw point clouds by a mini-network, feed them to the network, and finally extract global features with max pooling [7]. Ge et al. proposed the Hand PointNet network, which can directly consume 3D point clouds for hand regression. The gesture regression network can capture complex hand structures and accurately return to a low dimensional representation of the 3D hand [10].

The loss function is a way to measure the difference between the predicted output of neural network and labels. Wen et al. put forward a new loss function, namely center loss, to address the face recognition task. It is able to find a center for deep features of every class. With the center updating every time, the differences between deep features become smaller. If the distances are too far, they will be paid the penalty [11]. With the combination of the center loss and softmax loss, the highly discriminative deep features are obtained. Meanwhile, center loss is easy to realize in the CNN.

In this paper, we would optimize the network from two aspects to improve the performance of classifier model. First, the number of layers is increased in the hidden layer to get more abstract features. Second, the joint supervision of the center loss and softmax loss are applied to judge the score. The performance of model is improved with a proper parameter. The contributions of this paper can be summarized as below:

(a) Optimize the PointNet by increasing the numbers of hidden layers to get more abstract features.
(b) The joint supervision of softmax loss function and center loss have been put forward to extract deep features on the PointNet, which improves the performance of the model.

2 Related Work

In recent years, most researchers dedicated to work on driverless car technology and augmented reality. It is especially important to understand the applications of 3D scenes. 3D data has many popular representations such as point clouds, mesh, volumetric, and multi-view images. Point clouds are used more and more widely because it is close to raw sensor data and representationally simple. Volumetric CNNs are the pioneers to apply 3D CNN to process point clouds. The main idea of volumetric CNNs is to transform unordered point cloud into regular voxel grids, and apply 3D CNN to learn the features automatically. It shows good performance in classification tasks. However, it is challenging to spend more time to compute due to high space and time complexity [7]. In addition, this method results in the loss of local information, which is difficult to apply to object detection and location determination. Multi-view CNNs are different with volumetric CNNs, which apply 2D CNN to classify them. Multi-view CNNs can get more and more abstract features than a single image. However, multi-view CNNs are too constrained by 2D images due to the loss of space information to understand scene information [12]. The k-means algorithms are applied into unsupervised classification works with point clouds, but these methods are constrained on the accuracy.

The above methods transform point clouds into 3D voxels and image grids, which result in the loss of geometric information. Charels et al. put forward a new novel type of neural network that can directly process raw point clouds [13]. The PointNet provides a unified structure for object classification, part segment, and semantic scene segment. It uses max pooling to aggregate the information from each point regardless of the input order. Although it is very simple, the PointNet shows strong performance on the test set [13]. Ge et al. improved the PointNet to capture complex hand structures and accurately regress a low dimensional representation of the 3D hand [10].

The loss function is used to estimate the differences between the predicted and labels of the model. The smaller the loss function is, the stronger the robustness of the model is. Generally, we choose cross entropy loss function, but the disadvantage of softmax is not enough focused on the classification results of boundary points. So contrastive loss was put forward in the siamese network. It can reduce dimensionality reflected in the process of feature extraction [14]. Triplet loss sets the threshold between intra-class differences and intra-class distances based on contrastive loss. The neural networks extract features automatically, which can enlarge intra-class feature distances and inter-class feature variations [15].

3   Methodology

In this section, we would introduce two approaches to optimize the PointNet. The first method is based on increasing the number of hidden layers to extract abstract features. Furthermore, inspired by the improvement of the loss function in the face recognition, the second approach is to combine softmax loss function with center loss to enhance discriminative ability.

A. Increase the number of convolution layer

A convolution layer is added into the original network. The optimized PointNet architecture is shown in Fig. 1. The input represents inputting 3D raw point clouds (n × 3) and the raw point clouds are transformed by affine transformation matrix (3 × 3) to implement the data alignment. The aligned data is used to extract deep features by three-layer perception (64, 64, 64) with shared parameters. Each point extracts 64-dimensional features. The affine transformation matrix is predicted by the extracted features. In addition, the three-layer perception (64, 128, 1024) is continued used for feature extractions and aggregate point global features by max pooling. Finally, the fully connected layers are used to classify the features vectors. And the output represents classification scores for 40 classes.

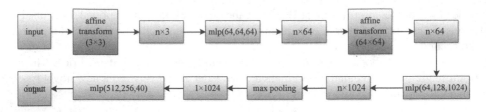

Fig. 1. Optimized PointNet.

B. The joint supervision of softmax loss and center loss

Cross entropy is an important branch of shannon's information theory. It is mainly used to measure the differences between two probability distributions. The cross entropy has two characteristics: one is non-negative, and the other is close to zero when the predicted output is close to label. The softmax converts the output of the neural network into a probability and the distances between the logits and labels are generated. The softmax loss function is formulated in Eq. 1.

$$L = -\sum_{i=1}^{M} \log \frac{e^{W_{yi}^T x_i + b_{yi}}}{\sum_{j=1}^{n} e^{W_{yj}^T x_i + b_j}} \tag{1}$$

The x_i denotes the ith feature in the y_ith class. W_j is the jth column of the weights and b is the bias term. The deep features extracted by CNN are not only separable but also higher distinguishability. If the deep features are more discriminative, the generalization performance of model will be better. The center loss function could be applied to minimize the intra-class distances and the formula of center loss is shown in Eq. 2.

$$L_c = \frac{1}{2} \sum_{i=1}^{m} \|x_i - c_{yi}\|_2^2 \tag{2}$$

Where c_{yi} is the y_ith class center of deep features. The equation effectively demonstrates the intra-class variations. It is challenging for the whole training set to update the center when the deep features change. So two necessary modifications are made to solve this problem. First, the center is updated based on mini-batch rather than the whole training. Second, a parameter α is used to control the learning rate of the centers. The formulas for the gradients of L_c and the update of c_{yi} are as follows:

$$\frac{\partial L_c}{\partial x_i} = x_i - c_{yi} \tag{3}$$

$$\Delta c_j = \frac{\sum_{i=1}^{m} \delta(y_i = j) \cdot (c_j - x_i)}{1 + \sum_{i=1}^{m} \delta(y_i = j)} \tag{4}$$

Many experimental studies have shown that the central loss function individually does not perform well in classification tasks. The combination of softmax loss function and center loss is used to train the neural network for discriminative feature extraction. Softmax loss function can enlarge the inter-class distances, and center loss reduce the intra-class differences. The joint supervision of softmax loss function and center loss is formulated as:

$$
\begin{aligned}
L &= LS + \lambda LC \\
&= -\sum_{i=1}^{M} \log \frac{e^{Wyi^T xi + byi}}{\sum_{j=1}^{n} e^{Wyj^T xi + bj}} + \frac{\lambda}{2} \sum_{i=1}^{m} \|xi - cyi\|_2^2
\end{aligned}
\tag{5}
$$

The parameter λ can control the weight of softmax function and center loss. Different λ can make great differences in the deep feature distribution. A proper λ can make feature extraction yield twice the result with half the effort. The detailed information is shown in Table 1.

Table 1. Center loss.

Algorithm: Center loss
Input: Training data $\{xi\}$. Initialized parameters θc in convolution layers. Parameters W and $\{cj|j=1,2\dots,n\}$ in loss layers, respectively. Hyperparameter λ, α and learning rate μt. The number of iteration $t\leftarrow 0$.
Output: The parameters θc.
1: while not converge do
2:   $t\leftarrow t+1$
3:   Compute the joint loss by $L^t = L_S^t + L_S^T$
4:   Compute the backpropagation error $\dfrac{\partial L^t}{\partial x_i^t}$ for each i by $\dfrac{\partial L^t}{\partial x_i^t} = \dfrac{\partial L_s^t}{\partial x_i^t} + \lambda \cdot \dfrac{\partial l_c^t}{\partial x_i^t}$
5:   Update the parameters W by $W^{t+1} = W^t - \mu^t \cdot \dfrac{\partial L^t}{\partial W^t} = W^t - \mu^t \cdot \dfrac{\partial L_s^t}{\partial W^t}$
6:   Update the parameters cj for each j by $c_j^{t+1} = c_j^t - \alpha \cdot \Delta c_j^t$
7:   Update the parameters θc by $\theta_C^{t+1} = \theta_C^t - \mu^t \sum_i^m \dfrac{\partial L^t}{\partial x_i^t} \cdot \dfrac{\partial x_i^t}{\partial \theta_C^t}$
8: end while

4 Experiment

Experiments can be divided into two parts: (1) the performances of optimized PointNet and joint supervision of softmax loss function and center loss, and (2) the sensitivity of parameter λ.

4.1   The Performances of Improved Model

The neural network learns global feature by max pooling that can be used to classify the objects. ModelNet40 shape classification dataset is used to evaluate the performances of our optimized model, which has 40 man-made object categories such as airplanes, tables, pianos. There are 12,311 models in the dataset represented by a triangular mesh, which can be split into 9843 for training and 2468 for testing. the raw input point cloud is normalized in the data preprocessing. All layers include 1×1 convolution, RELU and batch normalization. Adam optimizer with initial learning rate 0.001, momentum 0.9 and batch size 32 are used in this paper. Dropout is the most commonly used regularization in the convolution neural network to reduce the complexity of the network, which is used on the last fully connected layer. Dropout with keep radio 0.7 is set in the experiment. It takes 6–7 h to train with TensorFlow and a GTX 1080 GPU. In Table 2, the performances of optimized neural network are compared with previous work. Especially, we use center loss based on PointNet rather than optimized neural network. The performance of our optimized model is shown better than other methods.

Table 2. The results of methods.

	Input	Views	Accuracy avg. class	Accuracy overall
SPH	Mesh	–	68.2%	–
3DShapeNets	Volume	1	77.3%	84.7%
Voxnet	Volume	12	83.0%	85.9%
Subvolume	Volume	20	86.0%	89.2%
LFD	Image	10	75.5%	–
PointNet baseline	Point cloud	–	72.6%	77.4%
PointNet	Point cloud	1	86.2%	89.2%
Ours (increasing layers)	Point cloud	1	85.7%	**89.3%**
Ours (center loss)	Point cloud	1	**86.67%**	**89.95%**

4.2   The Sensitivity of Parameter λ

If the softmax loss function or center loss is used individually, the extracted features would contain large intra-class differences or inter-class distances. The parameters of λ and α are restricted in [0, 1]. A scalar λ is used for balancing the weights for the two loss functions. A proper λ can help to extract more discriminative features, which is crucial for object classification. In the experiment, we fix α to 0.3 and vary λ from 0.0001 to 0.0007. We evaluate the average accuracy and accuracy overall of using center loss on the test set, which are up to 86.67% (accuracy average class) and 89.95% (accuracy overall) respectively. When $\lambda = 0.0005$, the verification accuracies of these parameter variations on the ModelNet40 shape dataset are shown in Fig. 2.

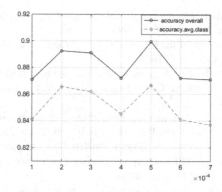

Fig. 2. The performances are influenced by different λ.

5 Concluding Remarks

In this paper, we have proposed two approaches to improve the accuracy of PointNet based 3D classification model. The first method increases the number of hidden layers to extract more abstract features. The second approach is to combine softmax loss function with center loss to obtain the discriminative features. Both of the two methods obtained better performance compared to the original PointNet. The overall accuracy is up to 89.35% and 89.95%, respectively. There are still some problems to be studied further, such as network optimization with lightweight network or deep volume layer network (ResNet, VGG). And a wide range of λ, α may enhance the discrimination of target.

References

1. Yanaka, K., Yamanouchi, T.: 3D image display courses for information media students. IEEE Comput. Graph. Appl. **36**(2), 68–73 (2016)
2. Grubisic, I., Gjenero, L., Lipic, T., Sovic, I., Skala, T.: Active 3D scanning based 3D thermography system and medical applications. In: Proceedings of the 34th International Convention MIPRO, pp. 269–273 (2011)
3. Ravi, D., et al.: Deep learning for health informatics. IEEE J. Biomed. Heal. Inform. **21**(1), 4–21 (2016)
4. Huang, H., Yang, J., Song, Y., Huang, H., Gui, G.: Deep learning for super-resolution channel estimation and DOA estimation based massive MIMO system. IEEE Trans. Veh. Technol. **67**(9), 8549–8560 (2018)
5. Zhang, L., Jia, J., Gui, G., Hao, X., Gao, W., Wang, M.: Deep learning based improved classification system for designing tomato harvesting robot. IEEE Access **6**, 67940–67950 (2018)
6. Li, W., Liu, H., Wang, Y., Li, Z., Jia, Y., Gui, G.: Deep learning-based classification methods for remote sensing images in urban built-up areas. IEEE Access **7**, 36274–36284 (2019)

7. Garcia-Garcia, A., Gomez-Donoso, F., Garcia-Rodriguez, J., Orts-Escolano, S., Cazorla, M., Azorin-Lopez, J.: PointNet: a 3D convolutional neural network for real-time object class recognition. In: Proceedings of the International Joint Conference on Neural Networks, vol. 2016, pp. 1578–1584, October 2016

8. Wang, X., Liu, M.: Multi-view deep metric learning for volumetric image recognition. In: Proceedings - IEEE International Conference on Multimedia and Expo, Mvdml, 2018, vol. 2018, pp. 1–6, July 2018

9. Gao, Y., Radha, H.: Multi-view image coding using 3-D voxel models. In: Proceedings - International Conference on Image Processing, ICIP, vol. 2, pp. 257–260 (2005)

10. Ge, L., Cai, Y., Weng, J., Yuan, J.: Hand PointNet: 3D hand pose estimation using point sets. In: Proceedings of the IEEE Computer Society Conference on Computer Vision and Pattern Recognition, pp. 8417–8426 (2018)

11. Li, Z.: A discriminative learning convolutional neural network for facial expression recognition. In: 2017 3rd IEEE International Conference on Computer and Communications, pp. 1641–1646 (2017)

12. Ge, L., Liang, H., Yuan, J., Thalmann, D.: Robust 3D hand pose estimation in single depth images: from single-view cnn to multi-view CNNs. IEEE Conference on Computer Vision and Pattern Recognition (CVPR) 2016, pp. 3593–3601 (2016)

13. Qi, C.R., Su, H., Mo, K., Guibas, L.J.: PointNet: deep learning on point sets for 3D classification and segmentation. In: Proceedings - 30th IEEE Conference on Computer Vision and Pattern Recognition, CVPR 2017, vol. 2017, pp. 77–85, January 2017

14. Chen, Y., Chen, Y., Wang, X., Tang, X.: Deep learning face representation by joint identification-verification. In: International Conference on Neural Information Processing Systems, pp. 1988–1996 (2014)

15. Schroff, F., Kalenichenko, D., Philbin, J.: FaceNet: a unified embedding for face recognition and clustering. In: Proceedings of the IEEE Computer Society Conference on Computer Vision and Pattern Recognition, 07–12 June, pp. 815–823 (2015)

Deep Learning Based Adversarial Images Detection

Haiyan Liu[1], Wenmei Li[1,2(✉)], Zhuangzhuang Li[1], Yu Wang[1],
and Guan Gui[1]

[1] College of Telecommunications and Information Engineering,
Nanjing University of Posts and Telecommunications, Nanjing 210003, China
liwm@njupt.edu.cn
[2] School of Geographic and Biologic Information,
Nanjing University of Posts and Telecommunications, Nanjing 210023, China

Abstract. The threat of attack against deep learning based network is gradually strengthened in computer vision. The adversarial examples or images are produced by applying intentional a slight perturbation, which is not recognized by human, but can confuse the deep learning based classifier. To enhance the robustness of image classifier, we proposed several deep learning based algorithms (i.e., CNN-SVM, CNN-KNN, CNN-RF) to detect adversarial images. To improve the utilization rate of multi-layer features, an ensemble model based on two layer features generated by CNN is applied to detect adversarial examples. The accuracy, detection probability, fake alarm probability and miss probability are applied to evaluate our proposed algorithms. The results show that the ensemble model based on SVM can achieve the best performance (i.e., 94.5%) than other methods for testing remote sensing image dataset.

Keywords: Adversarial detection · Deep learning · Ensemble model · Support vector machine (SVM) · K-nearest neighbors (KNN) · Random forest (RF)

1 Introduction

In the field of deep learning applications, it has been great progress in image classification, speech recognition and computer vision [1]. As a classical network model of deep learning, convolutional neural network (CNN) is indispensable and profoundly meaningful to the development of computer vision, especially in the field of massive image processing [2].

In the subsequent study of the adversary, adversarial training is found to be useful in improving the robustness of classifier based on neural network [3]. It is good news for the acquisition and storage of many precious datasets (e.g. HSRRS images, remote sensing images with high spatial resolution, abundant color, complex texture and similar shape). There are two types of adversarial training, one is the Black-box attack, and the other is White-box attack [4]. White-box attack is undoubtedly catastrophic for neural networks, as it masters almost overall structures and parameters of a particular neural network. Therefore, the performance of neural networks can be better improved by adversarial training [5, 6]. The Fast Gradient Sign Method (FGSM) is the most

© ICST Institute for Computer Sciences, Social Informatics and Telecommunications Engineering 2019
Published by Springer Nature Switzerland AG 2019. All Rights Reserved
G. Gui and L. Yun (Eds.): ADHIP 2019, LNICST 301, pp. 279–286, 2019.
https://doi.org/10.1007/978-3-030-36402-1_30

representative of White-box attack. It has the characteristics of specific adversarial perturbation and one-step target classification in computer vision. Kurakin et al. [6] noted that for ImageNet, the top-1 error rate for the adversarial examples generated by FGSM is approximately 63–69%. Therefore, the input image generated by FGSM makes sense to checkout and improve the performance of neural networks.

The detection is found to be as a technique for defensing against adversarial attacks [7, 8]. Literally, the 'detection only' approach refers to merely monitoring tar-get classification result of deep neural network on adversarial examples with no further processing (e.g. SafetyNet, Additional Class Augmentation). Li et al. [8] applied CNN-based neural networks into the convolution filters statistics to classify the test images. A cascaded classifier is designed to detect adversarial examples generated by the FGSM methods with the accuracy more than 85%. And Meng et al. proposed a framework that utilizes single or multiply external classifier to detect an adversarial image effectively. For the specified remote sensed dataset, Zhang et al. [9] proposed a method based on CNN to achieve classification by obtaining promising features in hyperspectral image. In brief, CNN and external classifier both have good performance in attack detection, but the detection performance is needed to be further improved.

Generally speaking, a single learner is more susceptible to erroneous predictions against adversary. To achieve complicated learning goals, ensemble model is de-signed to construct and combine multiple weak learners into strong learners [10, 11]. It greatly improves the robustness for integral neural network. To solve the limitation of single-dimensional feature representation, this paper is planned to integrate high level and low dimensional features through SVM to detect adversarial attack. The two dimensional features are extracted by CNN first or second full-connection layer. At the same time, CNN's output will be compared to verify the effectiveness of the integrated network (CNN-classifier). The objective of this paper is briefly summarized as the following two points:

(a) Multi-layer features fusion: It combines the features of different scales of the full connected layer, reduce the influence of feature positions and improve the robustness of the classification.
(b) Adversarial samples detection based on machine learning: Cooperation with three typical classification algorithms, convolutional neural network can obtain better performance in detecting adversarial attack.

The paper is organized as follows. Section 2 several classification algorithms and hybrid model cascaded based on CNN are presented. Section 3 the main experimental method is stated. Section 4 the experimental results are analyzed and in Sect. 5, conclusions and prospect are drawn.

2   Methodology

2.1   CNN

A CNN is a representative method for image classification in computer vision. The classical CNN mainly consists of the convolutional layer, pooling layer and fully connected layer. Among them, the convolutional layer is to extract key features in images and to migrate learning of different features. The multi-use of the max pooling layer facilitates feature extraction, reduces feature dimension and prevents over fitting effectively. In addition, the fully connected layer integrates the feature representations, greatly reducing the impact of feature locations on the classification results. The classical structure of CNN is shown in Fig. 1.

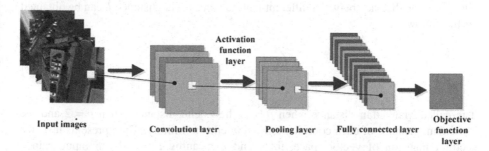

Fig. 1. The classical structure of CNN.

In our experiment, the input image is provided with the width and height of 128 and the color channel is 3. For feature extraction, the convolution layer is set as two 3 × 3 kernels with dimension 128 and 64, respectively. The ReLU is applied as the activation function of the convolutional layer. And the pooling layer is described as max pooling with 2 × 2 kernel. In addition, the Dropout is set to 0.25. For classification part, the 1024, 512 and 10 respectively indicate the number of neural units of the first (Dense1), second full connected layer (Dense2) and the number of final classification labels. The activation function is still ReLU, except for Softmax in the output.

2.2 Several Classification Algorithms

2.2.1 SVM

The SVM is a kind of supervised learning with stable effects and fast prediction capacity, which is applied widely in its application in two or multiple and linear or nonlinear classification. It is designed to find a hyperplane to segment the positive and negative examples and ensure the largest interval between the two classes. Given a linearly separable training dataset, the classification hyperplane is obtained by maximizing or equivalently solving the corresponding convex quadratic programming problem,

$$f(x) = sign(w \cdot x + b) \qquad (1)$$

$$w \cdot x + b = 0 \qquad (2)$$

where the Eqs. (1) and (2) is decision function and hyperplane representation, respectively. The value of function $sign(x)$ takes -1 when the variable is less than 0; otherwise, $+1$. The hyperplane divides the feature space into two parts: a positive class and a negative class. The points in side with positive normal vector belong to positive class, and the other side is negative class.

2.2.2 KNN

The KNN is a fundamental classification and regression method. For classification, its model is designed to divide the eigenvector space by training dataset. The KNN input is a vector and the output is category, a scalar. As shown in Eq. (3), the criteria for the division is the distance between different feature values. The distance L can be obtained by the following:

$$L = \left(\sum_{l=1}^{n} \left| x_i^{(l)} - x_j^{(l)} \right|^p \right)^{\frac{1}{p}} \tag{3}$$

It is called Manhattan distance when $p = 1$, the Euclid distance when $p = 2$ and the Maximum distance of each coordinate when p tends to infinity. The l presents instance vector dimension of vector space, the i and j, meaning i-th and j-th input trained instance vector. The values i, j, l are smaller than the dimension n of the vector space R^n. Known the relationship between the dataset and the category, and the label of the test dataset is compared with its corresponding feature. To predict the label, the KNN uses the majority voting rule to select the data of the similar feature.

$$f : R^n \rightarrow \{c_1, c_2, \cdots, c_k\} \tag{4}$$

$$P(Y \neq f(X)) = 1 - P(Y = f(X)) \tag{5}$$

$$\frac{1}{k} \sum_{x_i \in N_k(x)} I(y_i \neq c_j) = 1 - \frac{1}{k} \sum_{x_i \in N_k(x)} I(y_i = c_j) \tag{6}$$

where Eqs. (4, 5, 6) present classification function, misclassification probability and local misclassification probability, respectively. The function f exists in the n dimension vector space, which contains k categories. In the formula (5), the total probability that the instance X corresponds to any label Y equals to 1. In the formula (6), I presents indication function related label y_i and category c_j. The set $N_k(x)$ is constituted by k neighbor trained points x.

2.2.3 RF

As a representative model of ensemble learning, RF implements relatively simple. It is not sensitive to partial feature deletions on massive and highly parallel sample training. Due to the random sampling, the trained model has a small variance and a strong generalization ability. Since the decision tree node partitioning feature has been randomly selected, the model can be trained effectively when the dimension of sample feature is high.

RF uses the CART decision tree as a weak learner, and it uses the majority voting method of weak learners to determine the final classification result. For classification issues, RF utilizes the information gain to measure the amount of information, and determine the direction of feature split. The Eq. 7 describes that D presents training data set, A_i is the i th feature of D, $H(D)$ denotes the information entropy, $H(D/A_i)$ means the mutual information.

$$g(D, A_i) = H(D) - H(D/A_i) \tag{7}$$

2.2.4   Ensemble Method

Considering the disadvantage of CNN in adversary, the hybrid model is developed to strengthen the robustness of classifier and detect adversarial images. The specific flow-chart of the integrated model is shown in Fig. 2. The above classifier integrates different features for predictive classification. These features are extracted from the first and second full connected layer, respectively. Then the classifier gains a prediction result.

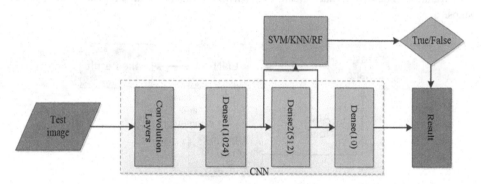

Fig. 2. Flow chart of ensemble model.

2.3   Metric Evaluation

A confusion matrix, where the positive class is set to the adversarial image, is the basic evaluation criteria of experimental performance for adversarial detection. The accuracy (Acc), detection probability (P_D), fake alarm probability (P_{FA}) and miss probability (P_M) are all applied to evaluate the performance of classifier. The TP, TN, FP, FN in confusion matrix are all key parameters for calculating the above metrics. The calculation process is carried out by following,

$$
\begin{aligned}
P_D &= \frac{TP}{TP + FN} \\
Acc &= \frac{TP + TN}{TP + TN + FP + FN} \\
P_{FA} &= \frac{FP}{TP + FP} \\
P_M &= \frac{FN}{TP + FN}
\end{aligned}
\tag{8}
$$

3   Experiment

This experiment adopts a high spatial resolution remote sensing (HSRRS) image as the test data, with 10 labels, each containing 100 samples. The clean test images and the fake images generated by FGSM are feed into the classifier.

3.1   Adversarial Attack and Detection

The Fig. 3 shows the flowchart of adversarial attack and detection. The adversarial image is generated by adding perturbation or noise on clean image (original HSRRS image). The perturbation originated from FGSM. Then, we train CNN to achieve target prediction. The same feature extraction process by consecutive four convolutional layers from clean image. The fully connected layer integrates gradually features for classification. Then we replace clean image with adversarial image repeating the above steps.

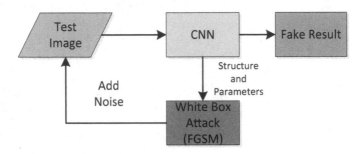

Fig. 3.   The flowchart of adversarial attack and detection.

3.2   Adversarial Detection on Ensemble Model

The full connected layer is regarded as a classifier in above step. We design a framework that combines the fully connected layer with the real classifier to select promising features, then integrate these features and predict results. These promising features are extracted from the first and second full connected layer, respectively. They work together on the SVM classifier, then SVM makes the final prediction. Same process is repeated, just replacing the classifier SVM with KNN or RF. Finally, the experimental results are presented using the confusion matrix, also the relevant metric results are calculated at the same time.

4   Results and Analysis

Due to the FGSM perturbation, the classification accuracy of CNN has declined from 96.4% to 33.3%. The experimental results are carried out in the following two aspects: (1) for each ensemble model, the feasibility of each full connected layer, and (2) for each metric, the performance comparison of classifier. Table 1 illustrates the metrics of several ensemble methods.

With respect to first aspect, CNN-SVM gains a best performance of accuracy, the detection probability and the miss probability, especially in the first full connected layer (Dense1), followed by CNN-KNN and CNN-RF. Yet the CNN-KNN gets a terrible performance in detection probability and miss probability, 0.880 and 0.120, respectively. CNN-RF has a moderate advantage at each metric. In addition, the feature integration by classifier significantly improves the classification performance of each fully connected layer. As it gains a better performance than the best between Dense1 and Dense2. Above all, the robustness of ensemble model based on other classifier is improved to the greatest extent.

In terms of second aspect, the metric of ensemble model is described as following. For the accuracy, CNN-SVM is at a dominant position in the above three models, followed by CNN-KNN and CNN-RF. For the detection probability and the miss probability, CNN-SVM is best, CNN-RF is moderate and CNN-KNN is worst. For the fake alarm probability, CNN-KNN is best, followed by CNN-SVM and CNN-RF.

From the perspective of fake alarm probability, we can choose CNN-KNN for classification prediction. In addition, CNN-RF is the most suitable choice for the moderate performance requirements. It also can be summarized that CNN-SVM possesses a good advantage for its highest accuracy and highest detection probability, lowest miss probability in feature analysis and classification. What's more, CNN-KNN tends to identify clean image as adversarial one, especially for the features collected in Dense1.

Table 1. Four metrics of the three ensemble methods

Method		Accuracy	Detection Probability (P_D)	Fake Alarm Probability (P_{FA})	Miss Probability (P_M)
CNN-SVM	Dense1	94.0%	0.933	0.054	0.067
	Dense2	93.3%	0.923	0.058	0.077
	Dense1&2	94.5%	0.933	0.044	0.067
CNN-KNN	Dense1	92.1%	0.880	0.040	0.120
	Dense2	93.7%	0.917	0.045	0.083
	Dense1&2	93.8%	0.907	0.032	0.093
CNN-RF	Dense1	92.8%	0.923	0.067	0.077
	Dense2	92.5%	0.927	0.064	0.073
	Dense1&2	94.3%	0.927	0.058	0.073

5 Conclusion

The adversarial detection approaches based on machine learning are proposed, and the original classifier model is based on CNN. These methods have improved the precision of target prediction and classification. What's more, we verified the validity of the ensemble model and found its better performance for adversarial images detection.

The results show that CNN-SVM obtains the best performance in classification with the detection probability 0.933 and the accuracy 94.5% in Dense1&2. Considering the overall performance, CNN-SVM is the most appropriate choice for adversarial images detection.

There are still some promotions need to be done in the future work. For example, robust light network or other neural networks for HSRRS images classification. A better feature representation acquired by preprocessing data. And the defense or detection of adversarial examples in DNN based classifiers.

References

1. Gui, G., Huang, H., Song, Y., Sari, H.: Deep learning for an effective nonorthogonal multiple access scheme. IEEE Trans. Veh. Technol. **67**(9), 8440–8450 (2018)
2. Huang, H., Yang, J., Huang, H., Song, Y., Gui, G.: Deep learning for super-resolution channel estimation and DOA estimation based massive MIMO system. IEEE Trans. Veh. Technol. **67**(9), 8549–8560 (2018)
3. Goodfellow, I.J., Shlens, J., Szegedy, C.: Explaining and harnessing adversarial examples. In: International Conference on Learning Representations (ICLR), pp. 1–11 (2015)
4. Tabacof, P., Valle, E.: Exploring the space of adversarial images. In: Proceedings of International Joint Conference on Neural Networks (IJCNN), pp. 426–433 (2016)
5. Liang, B., Li, H., Su, M., Li, X., Shi, W., Wang, X.: Detecting adversarial image examples in deep neural networks with adaptive noise reduction. IEEE Trans. Dependable Secur. Comput. (2018). https://doi.org/10.1109/TDSC.2018.2874243
6. Kurakin, A., Goodfellow, I., Bengio, S.: Adversarial machine learning at scale. In: International Conference on Learning Representations (ICLR), pp. 1–17 (2017)
7. He, W., Wei, J., Chen, X., Carlini, N., Song, D.: Adversarial example defenses: ensembles of weak defenses are not strong (2017). http://arxiv.org/abs/1706.04701
8. Li, X., Li, F.: Adversarial examples detection in deep networks with convolutional filter statistics. In: IEEE International Conference on Computer Vision (ICCV), pp. 5775–5783 (2017)
9. Zhang, M., Li, W., Du, Q.: Diverse region-based CNN for hyperspectral image classification. IEEE Trans. Image Process. **27**(6), 2623–2634 (2018)
10. Fawzi, A., Moosavi-Dezfooli, S.-M., Frossard, P.: Robustness of classifiers: from adversarial to random noise. In: 30th Conference on Neural Information Processing Systems (NIPS), pp. 1632–1640 (2016)
11. Carlini, N., Wagner, D.: Towards evaluating the robustness of neural networks. In: IEEE Symposium on Security and Privacy (SSP), pp. 39–57 (2017)

Detection for Uplink Massive MIMO System: A Survey

Lin Li and Weixiao Meng[✉]

Communications Research Center, Harbin Institute of Technology, Harbin, China
wxmeng@hit.edu.cn

Abstract. In this paper, we make a compressive survey for the research on detection in uplink Massive multiple input and multiple output (MIMO) system. As one key technology in Massive MIMO system, which is also one primary subject for the fifth generation wireless communications, this research is significant to be developed. As a result of large scaled antennas, the channel gain matrix in Massive MIMO system is asymptotic diagonal orthogonal, and it is an non-deterministic polynomial hard problem to obtain the optimum bits error rate (BER) performance during finite polynomial complexity time. The traditional detection algorithms for MIMO system are not efficient any more due to poor BER performance or high computational complexity. The exiting detection algorithms for Massive MIMO system are able to solve this issue. However, there are still crucial problems for them, including employing the deep learning technology for detection in Massive MIMO system, and not work for the millimeter wave Massive MIMO system in the strong spatial correlation environment even exiting keyhole effect, which is not rich scattering, as well as application in Hetnets wireless communications, and etc. Therefore, the research on detection for uplink Massive MIMO system is still in its early stage, there are lots of significant and urgent issues to overcome in the future.

Keywords: Massive MIMO · Low complexity detection · Optimum performance

1 Introduction

The technology of Massive multiple input and multiple output (MIMO) system was firstly proposed by Marzetta in 2010 [1–3]. As a hot research spot for 5G communications, the study on Massive MIMO system is getting increasing attention. In general, Massive MIMO system is defined as following: large scaled MIMO system whose base station is equipped with thousands and hundreds of antennas, which serve tens of user terminals simultaneously at the same frequency, as shown in Fig. 1. In order to provide ever-increasing throughput for

This work was sponsored by National Natural Science Foundation of China: No. 61871155.

© ICST Institute for Computer Sciences, Social Informatics and Telecommunications Engineering 2019
Published by Springer Nature Switzerland AG 2019. All Rights Reserved
G. Gui and L. Yun (Eds.): ADHIP 2019, LNICST 301, pp. 287–299, 2019.
https://doi.org/10.1007/978-3-030-36402-1_31

assigned cell consecutively and steadily, from the initial point to point MIMO system, to the following multi-user (MU) MIMO system, the technology of multiple antennas equipped at both the base station and user terminals, has been widely applied. In order to satisfy the higher demand of big throughput and etc. for the coming 5G area, the technology of Massive MIMO system has great potential, and its corresponding research is urgent to be developed.

The outstanding advantages of Massive MIMO system are summarized as the following aspects. Firstly, though Massive MIMO technology, the system capacity is increased by even more than 10 times. Secondly, the energy efficiency achieves to be more than 100 times. Thirdly, Massive MIMO system is able to be built up with low power devices, and its required cost is much lower. Fourthly, considering anti-unintentional jamming and anti-deception jamming, Massive MIMO system has much higher robustness. Fifthly, Massive MIMO system is able to cut down the air interface delay obviously. At last, Massive MIMO technology is able to simplify the multiple access.

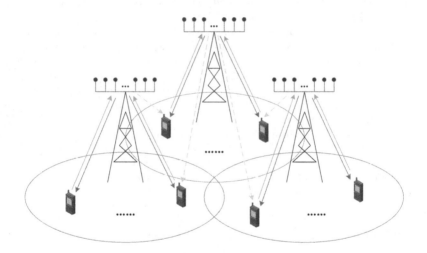

Fig. 1. Massive MIMO system

However, Massive MIMO system faces many challenges, which are generally introduced as following. Firstly, the uplink channel and the downlink channel of Massive MIMO system do not satisfy the reciprocity, which resulted that the time division duplexing (TDD) technology and etc. are not able to be realized or applied directly. Due to the large scaled antennas in Massive MIMO system, a large amount of pilot sequences are not orthogonal with each other any more. This generates the serious pilot pollution, which is one of the important and hard issue to overcome in Massive MIMO system. As a result of serving hundreds and thousands of users terminals simultaneously at the same frequency, the channel distribution in the propagation model is random and different from each other, which lead the channel estimation and capacity analysis method for

Massive MIMO system to be rather complex and hard to be solved. Due to the large scaled antennas, the traditional signal detection and estimation algorithms for MIMO system are not able to obtain the optimum bit error ratio (BER) performance of maximum likelihood (ML) algorithm during finite polynomial complex time, the research and develop on the low computational complexity detection algorithms in Massive MIMO system, is the premise of the communication in Massive MIMO system to be practice and realized, and is also one of the important and urgent problem to be solved [4]. Further more, the other emphasis research topics in Massive MIMO system include the trade-off problem between energy efficiency and spectral efficiency, beam forming problem, precoding technology, combination with millimeter wave (MMW) communication technology, application in Hetnets wireless communications and etc. We focus on and carry out the research on the low complexity detection algorithms in Massive MIMO system in this paper.

The reminder of this paper is organized as follows: The introduction to the research on detection algorithms for Massive MIMO system is discussed in Sect. 2. The crucial questions for the future research are presented in Sect. 3. Finally, the conclusion is introduced in Sect. 4.

2   Detection Algorithms for Massive MIMO System

The optimum detection algorithms including the ML detection algorithm by hard decision and Maximum a posteriori (MAP) detection algorithm by soft decision have the optimum BER performance. Essentially, ML detection algorithm is by means of ergodic method to obtain the optimum BER performance. The BER performance of ML detection algorithm is taken as the evaluation criterion of the optimum BER performance and the optimization objective for the detection algorithms both in MIMO system and in Massive MIMO system. However, the computational complexity of ML detection algorithm exponentially increased with the number of the transmitting antennas, and further pointed that it was an NP-hard problem for the detection algorithms in MIMO system to obtain the optimum BER performance during finite polynomial complexity time. Therefore, due to the large scaled antennas equipped in Massive MIMO system, the exponential computational complexity is too high, and it is impossible for ML detection algorithm to achieve the optimum BER performance over finite low complexity time. Neither ML detection algorithm nor the MAP detection algorithm is appropriate or able to employed in the practical detection for Massive MIMO system.

Then, considering the high computational complexity of the optimum detection algorithms in MIMO system, lots of researchers developed the study on the sub-optimum detection algorithms which have low computational complexity. The sub-optimum detection algorithms for MIMO system is divided into the linear detection algorithms and nonlinear detection algorithms.

Firstly, the linear detection algorithms include matched filtering (MF) detection algorithm, zero forcing (ZF) detection algorithm and minimum mean square error (MMSE) detection algorithm and etc. The computational complexity of linear detection algorithms polynomially increased with the number of transmitting antennas, compared with the exponential computational complexity of the optimum detection algorithms including ML detection algorithm and etc., the linear detection algorithms have much low computational complexity. However, the BER performance of linear detection algorithms is rather bad, and there was a big gap compared to the optimum BER performance. Under the demand of high quality detection performance in Massive MIMO system, the linear detection algorithms are required to be improved and optimized. Therefore, due to the bad BER performance, linear detection algorithms are not appropriate for directly applying in practical detection in Massive MIMO system.

Secondly, the nonlinear detection algorithms, which are divided into the following several categories. The fist category is represented as the interference cancellation based detection algorithms, including successive interference cancellation (SIC) detection algorithm and parallel interference cancellation (PIC) detection algorithm and etc., have the comparative polynomial computational complexity as that of linear detection algorithms, but obtain the bad BER performance which has a quite big gap compared to the optimum BER performance of ML detection algorithm. The second category is introduced as the sphere decoding (SD) detection algorithm, which is also included into the tree searching based detection algorithms, is able to obtain the approximate optimum BER performance of ML detection algorithm, so it usually substitute the ML detection algorithm and has been widely employed in practical system detection. However, under the condition of a medium fixed signal to noise ratio (SNR), the computational complexity of the SD detection algorithm still exponentially increases with the number of transmitting antennas, and not appropriate for Massive MIMO system equipped with large scaled antennas. The last category is denoted as the lattice reduction aided (LRA) detection algorithm, which has got much attention for the research on MIMO system recently. LRA detection algorithm is able to approach the optimum BER performance of ML detection algorithm under the condition of high SNR in small scaled MIMO system, the computational complexity of LRA polynomially increases with the number of transmitting antennas. The principle of the LRA detection algorithm is by means of orthogonalization the channel gain matrix. However, the channel gain matrix of Massive MIMO system is asymptotic orthogonal itself, which has been introduced and proved in the next section. Thus, the LRA detection algorithm does not work any more for the orthogonal channel gain matrix. The traditional LRA detection algorithm is based on and to improve the linear detection algorithms. For Massive MIMO system, the BER performance of the traditional LRA detection algorithm is not able to be better, and still has a big gap compared to the optimum BER performance of ML detection algorithm. With the worse BER performance, the traditional LRA detection algorithm is not appropriate for the practical detection in Massive MIMO system.

Further more, we make an essential analysis for the reason why the traditional detection algorithms for MIMO system is not efficient for Massive MIMO system any more.

The density of channel gain matrix $\mathbf{H}^H\mathbf{H}$ versus the scale of antennas number $N_t = N_r$ in MIMO system is shown in Fig. 2, where $\mathbf{H} \in \mathbb{R}^{N_r \times N_t}$ is channel gain matrix, whose entry obeys to the complex Gaussian distribution with zero mean and unit variance, N_t and N_r denote the number of the transmitting antennas and that of the receiving antennas, respectively. From Fig. 2, the channel gain matrix of the MIMO system is becoming more and more diagonal gradually versus the increasing of the antennas numbers' scale in MIMO system. Considering the large scaled antennas, it is easy to conclude that the channel gain matrix in Massive MIMO system is asymptotic diagonal.

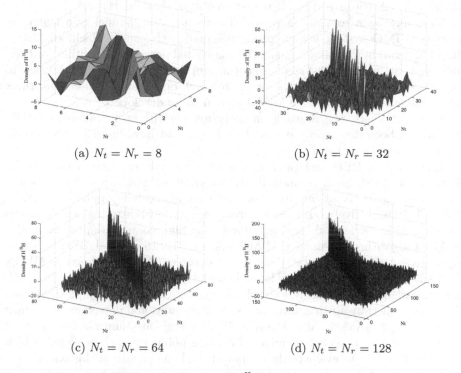

(a) $N_t = N_r = 8$

(b) $N_t = N_r = 32$

(c) $N_t = N_r = 64$

(d) $N_t = N_r = 128$

Fig. 2. The density of channel gain matrix $\mathbf{H}^H\mathbf{H}$ versus the scale of antennas number $N_t = N_r$ in MIMO system

For arbitrary matrix, whether it is orthogonal or not, is decided by the criterion of orthogonality deficiency (od), as shown in the following,

$$\mathrm{od}(\mathbf{H}) = 1 - \frac{\det(\mathbf{H}^H\mathbf{H})}{\prod_{n=1}^{N_t} \|\mathbf{h}_n\|^2} \tag{1}$$

where the channel gain matrix $\mathbf{H} = [\mathbf{h}_1, \cdots, \mathbf{h}_n, \cdots, \mathbf{h}_{N_t}]$, $\mathbf{h}_n$ is its nth column vector entry, and $n = \{1, 2, \cdots, N_t\}$. For arbitrary channel gain matrix $\mathbf{H}$, it is always satisfied that $0 \leq \text{od}(\mathbf{H}) \leq 1$. When $\text{od}(\mathbf{H}) = 1$, the channel gain matrix $\mathbf{H}$ is singular; When $\text{od}(\mathbf{H}) = 0$, the channel gain matrix $\mathbf{H}$ is orthogonal. Take the LRA detection algorithm as example, its objective in principle is to minimize the orthogonality deficiency of the channel gain matrix $\text{od}(\mathbf{H})$ until to be 0, thereby the orthogonal basis are obtained, and the original detection results are optimized and improved to be better. However, according to the theorem of Marčenko Pastur (M-P) law in large scaled random matrix theory, the matrix is asymptoticly diagonal little by little versus the growth of the matrix's dimension. As shown in Fig. 2, when the scale of the antennas number $N_t = N_r$ in MIMO system is increasing, the density of the diagonal entries is bigger and bigger than those of the off-diagonal entires in the channel gain matrix $\mathbf{H}^H\mathbf{H}$, till to be totally diagonal. Furthermore, when $N_t = N_r \to \infty$, $\mathbf{H}^H\mathbf{H} \approx N_r\mathbf{I}_{N_r}$, and $\|h_n\|^2 \approx N_r$. According to (1), it is easy to obtain that, $\text{od}(\mathbf{H}) \approx 0$.

Therefore, as a result of large scaled antennas, the channel gain matrix of Massive MIMO system is asymptotic diagonal orthogonal, which was introduced in detail in the following, and the traditional detection algorithms or their improvements for MIMO system are not appropriate for Massive MIMO system any longer. It is very imperative for the research on novel detection algorithms which are efficient for Massive MIMO system to be developed.

In recent years, the research on detection algorithms for Massive MIMO system has been developed, and is classed into and introduced by the several aspects, as shown in Fig. 3.

Examples for BER performance of the traditional detection algorithms for detecting 4-QAM signal in Massvie MIMO system are shown in Fig. 4, where the number of transmitting antennas and that of receiving antennas is $N_t = N_r = 128$ respectively, and the environment is rich scattering which means the channel is Rayleigh flat fading. Due to the high computational complexity of MLD algorithm in Massive MIMO system, the theoretical BER of single input and single output (SISO) system for detecting M-QAM signal in AWGN channel, is always taken as the lower bound for the BER performance of ML detection algorithm. Similarly, examples for the computational complexity versus the number of transmitting antennas N_t of the traditional detection algorithms for detecting 4-QAM signal in Massvie MIMO system are shown in Fig. 5, where we use the magnitude of the number of floating points operations (flops), which is denoted as $O(\cdot)$ to evaluate the computational complexity in this paper.

Firstly, the local search based detection algorithms have been employed in Massive MIMO system. As one of the research hot spot in combination optimization technology, the local search method has been widely generalized and employed in many fields. In wireless communications feild, the local search algorithms are initially applied to detect multiuser in CDMA system, and then are gradually extended to be employed for detecting and estimating signal in MIMO system up to Massive MIMO system [5]. The local search detection algorithms for Massive MIMO system include the likelihood ascent search (LAS) detection algorithm [6], the randomized search (RS) detection algorithm and the reactive tabu search (RTS) detection algorithm [7] and etc. In Massive MIMO system equipped with large scaled antennas, the local search based detection algorithms are able to obtain the optimum BER performance of the ML detection algorithm during finite polynomial complexity time. However, both of the BER performance and computational complexity are decisively influenced by those of the initial solution vector. The traditional LAS based detection algorithm usually takes the detection result of linear detection algorithm as initial solution vector, such as that of MMSE detection algorithm, which is denoted as MMSELAS detection algorithm. Its BER performance and computational complexity is shown in Figs. 4 and 5, respectively. The computational complexity of MMSELAS detection algorithm is in the same magnitude order with that of MMSE detection algorithm. Furthermore, the MMSELAS detection algorithm is just efficient to detect low order modulation signal in Massive MIMO system, such as Binary Phase Shift Keying (BPSK) modulation signal or 4-Quadrature Amplitude Modulation (QAM) signal. Otherwise, for the high order modulation signal including 16-QAM signal or 64-QAM signal and etc., the BER performance of the MMSELAS detection algorithm is very poor and similar to that of the MMSE detection algorithm, which means that neither the MMSE detection algorithm nor the MMSELAS detection algorithm is appropriate to detect high order modulation signal in Massive MIMO system. When the RTS detection algorithm is employed for high order modulation signal in Massive MIMO system, its BER performance is getting worse and worse versus the increasing of either the antennas' number scale or the modulation order.

Secondly, the Markov Chain Monte Carlo (MCMC) [8] detection algorithm is also applied for Massive MIMO system. On account of the strong efficiency and flexible easy to operate, the MCMC method has been widely used in many research fields including financial industry and etc. In wireless communication field, the MCMC algorithm was extended to be employed for the receiver design in CDMA system and in MIMO system, until now to be applied to detect and estimate signal in Massive MIMO system. In Massive MIMO system, by means of the MCMC detection algorithm, as shown in Figs. 4 and 5, respectively, it is able to obtain the approximate optimum BER performance of ML detection algorithm, along with the low computational complexity which polynomially increases with the number of transmitting antennas. However, just like the LAS based detection algorithm, either the BER performance or the computational complexity of the MCMC detection algorithm is substantially effected by those of the initial solution vector. The exiting MCMC detection algorithm usually chooses the detection results of linear detection algorithms such as ZF detection algorithm or MMSE detection algorithm as initial solution vector, whose computational complexity is in the same order with that of linear detection algorithm, and BER performance approximates to the optimum one of ML detection algorithm for low modulation order signal, but is quite bad as that of linear detection algorithm for detecting high oder modulation signal. The traditional MCMC detection algorithm is not appropriate to detect high order modulation signal in Massive MIMO system. Although the multiple starts mixed Gibbs sampling improved MCMC detection algorithm provided the solution for high order modulation signal in medium small scaled MIMO system, its BER performance got rather worse versus the growth of the number of antennas or the modulation order, and is still not appropriate for detecting high order modulation signal in Massive MIMO system equipped with large scaled antennas.

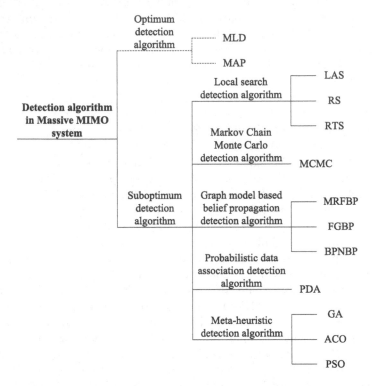

Fig. 3. The detection algorithms for Massive MIMO system

Thirdly, as one of the most important soft decision detection algorithm, the probabilistic data association (PDA) detection algorithm [9] has been also employed for the low complex detection in Massive MIMO system. At the beginning, the PDA detection algorithm was applied for multiple target tracking technology in remote sensing and radar fields. Along with the development of subjects fusion, the PDA algorithm has been gradually applied in communications filed, from the multiuser detection technology in CDMA wireless communication system, to be extended for the signal detection and estimation in MIMO system, until now for the signal detection and estimation in Massive MIMO system. In Massive MIMO system, as shown in Figs. 4 and 5, respectively, the PDA detection algorithm is able to obtain the approximate optimum BER performance over polynomial computational complexity. However, compared to other detection algorithms in Massive MIMO system, due to the PDA detection algorithm is one of the soft decision detection algorithms based on the bits domain, its computational complexity is more than one order higher than other low complexity detection algorithms. Further more, the BER performance of the PDA detection algorithm is poor for high order modulation signal. The PDA detection algorithm is still not appropriate to detect high order modulation signal in Massive MIMO system.

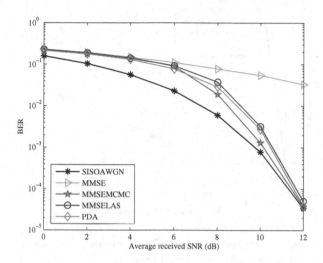

Fig. 4. Examples for BER performance of the traditional detection algorithms for detecting 4QAM signal in Massive MIMO system, where the number of transmitting antennas and that of receiving antennas is $N_t = N_r = 128$

Fourthly, the graph model based belief propagation (BP) detection algorithm is also one of the most important soft decision detection algorithms, and has been applied in the signal detection and decoding in Massive MIMO system. As the analysis method for the problem of probability distribution in complex system, the graph model based algorithm has been widely employed in lots of fields including engineering design and etc. The frequently-used major graph models include the Bayesian belief networks graph model, the Markov random fields (MRF) graph model and the factor graph (FG) model and etc. As one simple efficiency technology, the graph model based BP algorithm has been widely applied in many science domains such as the image processing, the computational biology and etc. In the communications field, various graph models based BP algorithm was initially employed in the multiuser detection in CDMA system, and then extended to be applied in signal detection and estimation in MIMO system, until now employed to solve the issue of signal detection and estimation in Massive MIMO system [10]. Along with polynomial computational complexity, the graph model based BP detection algorithm is able to achieve the approximate optimum BER performance of the ML detection algorithm. Whereby, the computational complexity of the FG model based BP detection algorithm linearly increases with the number of transmitting antennas as shown in Fig. 5, but due to its poor BER performance for high order modulation signal, the FG model based BP detection algorithm is not appropriate to detect high order modulation signal in Massive MIMO system.

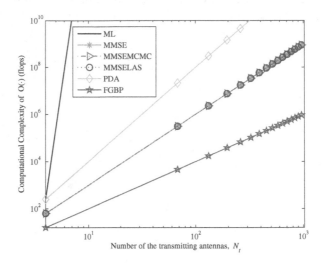

Fig. 5. Examples for computational complexity of the traditional detection algorithms for detecting 4QAM signal in Massive MIMO system

Finally, the meta-heuristic algorithm among the swarm intelligent technology based detection algorithm is another primary detection algorithm in Massive MIMO system, including the Genetic detection algorithm, ant colony optimization (ACO) detection algorithm [11] and particle swarm optimization (PSO) detection algorithm and etc. The BER performance of the meta-heuristic detection algorithm approaches the optimum one of ML detection algorithm during finite polynomial complexity time. However, the exiting research just presented the meta-heuristic based detection algorithm for media small scaled MIMO system. Along with the coming big data era, the artificial intelligent (AI) technology including the swarm intelligent technology is developing and improving in rapid speed. Therefore, the research on meta-heuristic based detection algorithms in Massive MIMO system has great and extensive application prospect and development potential.

Consequently, although the exiting research on the detection algorithms in Massive MIMO system has obtained essential developed, there are still lots of future work to be solved.

3   Crucial Questions for the Future Research

Through synthesizing the above discussion and analysis, the research on the detection algorithms for Massive MIMO system is still in a fledging period, there are lots of problems required to be solved and further improved in the future. Briefly, the crucial questions for the future research work are summarized and presented as follows.

3.1 Deep Learning Technology for Detection Algorithm in Massive MIMO System

Recently, the research on artificial intelligent (AI) is the leading edge science. As a research hot-spot in AI, the deep learning technology has got more and more attention, which has got many advantage achievements in the relevant fields. In 5G wireless communications, the deep learning technology has been employed for many aspects, including the channel estimation, the channel state information (CSI) feedback and reconstruction, the precoding [12,13], and etc. Further more, the inherent problem of the low complexity detection in Massive MIMO system is similar as that of big data processing, especially the one with high dimension. In consideration of the powerful processing ability of the deep learning technology for the high dimensional data, it has promising prospects to employ the deep learning technology for detection algorithm in Massive MIMO system, in order to obtain the optimum BER performance, and achieve the theoretical spectral efficiency with lower average receiving SNR, along with lower finite polynomial computational complexity, which is also a crucial and difficult question to be solved for the future research.

3.2 MMW Massive MIMO System: Strong Spatial Correlation Environment Even Existing the Keyhole Effect

Further more, the exiting detection algorithms for Massive MIMO system always take the transmission environment as rich scattering. However, in the more and more complex practical communications environment, this assumption is hard to be satisfied. For instance, the devices for Massive MIMO system are tending to be miniaturization by employing MMW technology, in order to be applicable for indoor communications. However, the channel space of Massive MIMO system in the indoor environment is usually strong spatial correlation at both between the transmitting and receiving antennas, and even generates the keyhole effect, which stops the signal transmission [14]. The exiting detection algorithms for Massive MIMO system are not able to detect signal in the strong space fading coherent environment and have no ability to eliminate the keyhole effect. Therefore, the research on detection algorithms for the strong space fading coherent environment even exiting the keyhole effect in MMW Massive MIMO system is difficult but important to carry out in the future.

3.3 Massive MIMO System in Hetnets Wireless Communications

When Massive MIMO system applied in outdoor mobile communications, many researches in 5G intend to combine the Massive MIMO technology with Hetnets wireless communications [15]. As a result of the wide coverage area, the channel propagation environment is random and diversity, which is different from the rich scattering environment where the traditional detection algorithms for Massive MIMO system usually assumed to state. Fortunately, the method of employing random matrix theory (RMT) both in the channel estimation and signal detection for Massive MIMO system in Hetnets makes it realizable. Thus, the research on low complexity detection algorithms for Massive MIMO system in Hetnets wireless networks, which is not limited by the channel conditions, is significant and challenge.

4   Conclusion

In this paper, a survey for the detection in Massive MIMO system is presented. From the introduction of Massive MIMO system, the research on low complexity detection algorithms is the hot spot among the key technologies. Through the comprehensive survey for the development of research on the low complexity detection algorithms in Massive MIMO system, as a result of the large scaled antennas, the channel gain matrix is asymptotic diagonal orthogonal, along with poor BER performance and high computational complexity, the traditional detection algorithms or their improvements for MIMO system are not appropriate for Massive MIMO system. The exiting detection algorithms for Massive MIMO system obtained the approximate optimum BER performance of ML detection algorithm over finite polynomial complex time. However, there are crucial problems to be solved, including the deep learning technology for the low complexity detection in Massive MIMO system, the detection research for the MMW Massive MIMO system which has strong spatial correlation environment even existing the keyhole effect, and the research on detection algorithms for Massive MIMO system in Hetnets wireless networks which is not limited by the channel conditions, and etc. In conclusion, the research on low complexity detection algorithms for Massive MIMO system is still in the initial beginning stage, lots of difficult but important issues are urgent to be solved, and the corresponding research work are significant to develop in the future.

References

1. Shafi, M., et al.: 5G: a tutorial overview of standards, trials, challenges, deployment, and practice. IEEE J. Sel. Areas Commun. **35**(6), 1201–1221 (2017)
2. Björnson, E., Hoydis, J., Sanguinetti, L.: Massive MIMO has unlimited capacity. IEEE Trans. Wireless Commun. **17**(1), 574–590 (2018)
3. Matthaiou, M., Smith, J.P., Ngo, Q.H., Tataria, H.: Does massive MIMO fail in ricean channels? IEEE Commun. Lett. **8**(1), 61–64 (2019)
4. Yang, S., Hanzo, L.: Fifty years of MIMO detection: the road to large-scale MIMOs. IEEE Commun. Surv. Tutorials **17**(4), 1941–1988 (2015)
5. Mann, P., Sah, K.A., Budhiraja, R., Chaturvedi, K.A.: Bit-level reduced neighborhood search for low-complexity detection in large MIMO systems. IEEE Wireless Commun. Lett. **7**(2), 146–149 (2018)

6. Sah, K.A., Chaturvedi, K.A.: An unconstrained likelihood ascent based detection algorithm for large MIMO systems. IEEE Trans. Wireless Commun. **16**(4), 2262–2273 (2017)
7. Elghariani, A., Zoltowski, M.: Low complexity detection algorithms in large-scale MIMO systems. IEEE Trans. Wireless Commun. **15**(3), 1689–1702 (2016)
8. Hedstrom, C.J., Yuen, H.C., Chen, R., Farhang-Boroujeny, B.: Achieving near MAP performance with an excited markov chain Monte Carlo MIMO detector. IEEE Trans. Wireless Commun. **16**(12), 7718–7732 (2017)
9. Yang, S., Xu, X., Alanis, D., Ng, X.S., Hanzo, L.: Is the low-complexity mobile-relay-aided FFR-DAS capable of outperforming the high-complexity CoMP? IEEE Trans. Veh. Technol. **65**(4), 2154–2169 (2016)
10. Sen, P., Yılmaz, ö. A.: A low-complexity graph-based LMMSE receiver for MIMO ISI channels with M-QAM modulation. IEEE Trans. Wireless Commun. **16**(2), 1185–1195 (2017)
11. Mandloi, M., Bhatia, V.: Multiple stage ant colony optimization algorithm for near-OPTD large-MIMO detection. In: 2015 23rd European Signal Processing Conference (EUSIPCO), pp. 914–918. Nice (2015)
12. Huang, H., Song, Y., Yang, J., Gui, G., Adachi, F.: Deep-learning-based millimeter-wave massive MIMO for hybrid precoding. IEEE Trans. Veh. Technol. **68**(3), 3027–3032 (2019)
13. Wang, T., Wen, C., Jin, S., Li, Y.G.: Deep learning-based CSI feedback approach for time-varying massive MIMO channels. IEEE Wireless Commun. Lett. **8**(2), 416–419 (2019)
14. Chen, R., Xu, H., Wang, X., Li, J.: On the performance of OAM in keyhole channels. IEEE Wireless Commun. Lett. **8**(1), 313–316 (2019)
15. Chen, C., Zhao, X., Yuan, J.: Coverage analysis of inter-tier interference cancellation for massive MIMO HetNet with repulsion. IEEE Commun. Lett. **23**(2), 350–353 (2019)

Big Data-Based User Data Intelligent Encryption Method in Electronic Case System

Xin Liu[✉]

School of Railway Operation and Management,
Hunan Railway Professional Technology College, Zhuzhou, China
liuxin001100@163.com

Abstract. When the user data of the conventional electronic case system was encrypted, there was a shortage of low analysis accuracy. To this end, an intelligent encryption method for user data of the electronic case system based on big data was proposed. Introducing the big data technology, building a framework for intelligent encryption of user data of electronic case system, and realizing the construction of intelligent encryption of user data of electronic case system; Relying on the determination of the data intelligent encryption algorithm, the electronic case system model was embedded to realize the intelligent encryption of the user data of the electronic case system. The experimental data showed that the proposed big data modeling and analysis method was 61.64% more accurate than the conventional method, which was suitable for intelligent encryption of user data in electronic case system.

Keywords: Big data · Electronic case system · Data encryption

1 Introduction

Electronic Medical Record (EMR) is also called a computerized medical record system or Computer-Based Patient Record (CPR). It replaces handwritten paper cases with digitized patient medical records that are stored, managed, transmitted, and reproduced using electronic devices. It is digitally stored, managed, transmitted, and reproduced using electronic devices. Its content includes all information about paper cases [1] Electronic cases are also generated by the network management of hospital computer, the application of information storage media–discs and IC cards, and the globalization of the Internet. Electronic cases are also the inevitable outcome of information technology and network technology in the medical field, are an inevitable trend of modernization of hospital cases, and its preliminary application in the clinic has greatly improved the hospital's work efficiency and medical quality [2], but this is only the beginning of electronic case application. The electronic case system is a set of software and hardware systems that support electronic cases, including data collection and transmission, data storage and extraction, and data processing and display. It can realize the collection, processing, storage, transmission and service of patient information. With the advancement of medicine, medical technology and information technology, the traditional medical model has been challenged as never before. "Digital Hospital" is becoming an inevitable trend in the development of hospital information in the world,

G. Gui and L. Yun (Eds.): ADHIP 2019, LNICST 301, pp. 300–309, 2019.
https://doi.org/10.1007/978-3-030-36402-1_32

and the research and promotion of electronic case systems is one of the important aspects of the development of "digital" hospitals. Especially in hospitals [3], patients have more information during admission, including diagnostic data of clinicians, hospitalization data, family information of patients, and various medical expenses for patients. The amount of information is quite large. If you manage the storage with old paper files in the past, it will take time and effort to lose some information [4].

Electronic cases are the inevitable outcome of the widespread application of information technology and network technology in the medical field, and are also the inevitable trend of modern management of hospital medical records. Its intelligent encryption method can not be underestimated [5].

2 Electronic Case Encryption Technology Design

The electronic case system is medical-specific software. The hospital electronically records the patient's visit information through electronic cases, including: home page, disease record, inspection test results, medical orders, surgical records, nursing records, etc. There are both structured information, unstructured free text, and graphic image information. It involves the collection, storage, transmission, quality control, statistics and utilization of patient information [6].

"Structuralization" is accompanied by electronic cases, that is, "structuring" has been invented in order for computers to be able to handle cases. The core of the case is that the medical staff records the condition, symptoms, medication, and disposal contents of the patient during the diagnosis and treatment. However, due to the complexity of medical services and the differences among individual patients, this record naturally has the dual attributes of "normative" and "differential". Unfortunately, the nature of computers is good at dealing with "normative (structured)" data. For the analysis and utilization of unstructured data, it is limited to late-stage fields such as "full-text search" and "smart segmentation". For example, the library field, or the use of medical big data. However, as a business system application "unstructured" data processing, the computer is powerless. Therefore, the pursuit of "structured" cases is a balance between "human readable" and "computer readable" [7].

The so-called structured, semi-structured, and superior and inferior disputes are basically a pseudo-proposition. The structural maturity evaluation of the electronic case system needs to be carried out in a more sophisticated and multi-dimensional indicator system. Thats is: the background support capability of "node, structured, and coded", and the extent to which the relevant template data in the system achieves the above three capabilities.

2.1 Electronic Case Encryption Components

(1) Clinical documentation: Located at the top of the electronic case data structure, it is a collection of data on the clinical diagnosis and guidance intervention information of patients (or health care subjects) generated and recorded by specific medical service activities (health events). Such as: outpatient cases (emergency), inpatient medical records, consultation records, etc. [8].

(2) Document segment: Structured clinical documents are generally split into logical segments, i.e. document segments. The document segment provides a clinical context for the data that makes up the document segment, i.e. adding specific constraints to the generic definition of the data elements therein. Structured document segments typically consist of data sets and are specifically defined by data sets. Document segments are not explicitly defined in this standard, but the concept of document segments is implicit.

(3) Data group: It consists of several data elements, which constitutes a basic unit of clinical documents as a collection of data elements, and has the characteristics of clinical semantic integrity and reusability. Data groups can have nested structures, and larger data groups can contain smaller sub-data sets. Such as: document identification, complaints, medication, etc.

(4) Data element: Located at the bottom of the electronic case data structure, it is the smallest, non-subdividable data unit that is assigned by a series of attributes such as definition, identification, representation, and allowable values. The allowed values for data elements are defined by the value range. The structure of electronic case data is shown in Fig. 1.

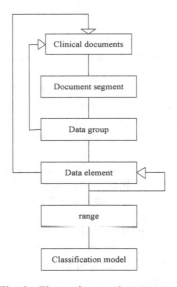

Fig. 1. Electronic case data structure

2.2 Framework for Electronic Case Encryption Technology

In the case editor, the user can see that the segment of the case is split into individual nodes. From the technical backend, each node is saved as a "value pair" so that the database can process the data further. Since 2002, the industry has developed a dedicated electronic case editor to handle nodes in case templates, so this technology threshold has been surpassed by most manufacturers today.

2.2.1 Nodeization of Electronic Case Encryption

A hierarchical relationship between time nodes is required. For example, the previous step "node", after implementation, we can quickly query in the background, for example, query the patient's case "blood pressure diastolic pressure: 90 mm Hg" such a value as reference. But in reality, the questions we need to answer are often: diastolic pressure before medication, diastolic blood pressure after medication, or the range of hypertension in a family history. Therefore, it is meaningless to just save "nodeization" and "value pairing" without knowing the context. The hierarchical relationship definition of case nodes can solve the problem of logical relationship between nodes. At this stage, adding and deleting nodes requires defining the application scenario (document template type, node chapter, etc.) of the node, and giving a unique ID number according to certain rules, so as to facilitate the reuse and query of the node project.

2.2.2 Encoding of Electronic Case Encryption

The definition of the definition of the data content within the node. From the technical background, it is the range of values and data types of node values; from the clinical business point of view, it is the standard dictionary code maintenance for diagnosis, inspection, operation, and medication. Engineers with experience in ICD-10 know that this is not only a question of data coding dictionary compilation, but also the unification of the description dimensions of the same objective subject under different clinical professions and different disease conditions. In real life, it is often necessary to compile and correspond to different coding rules according to the specific purpose of use. The terminology registration service in the hospital information platform can help solve the problem of partial coding and correspondence of coded data. However, in practical applications, it is impossible to achieve 100% data coding. It is often necessary to find an balance of the ratio of input and output between flexibility and normativeness.

2.2.3 Measurement of Electronic User Data

Since the intelligence level of the electronic medical record system is mainly described according to the number of disclosures of the user data by the attacker, the current measurement of the electronic user data is basically measured by the disclosure risk. Disclosure risk is defined as the probability that an attacker may disclose data and other related content provided by an electronic medical record system. Let S be the electronic user encrypted data, SK is defined as the electronic user encrypted data S that the attacker can disclose according to the related content K, then the electronic medical record system user data encryption intelligence degree can be described by the following formula:

$$r(s, k) = P_r(S_k) \tag{1}$$

3 Construction of Intelligent Encryption of Electronic Case System

3.1 Symmetric Encryption Process

Symmetric key encryption is also called Secret Key Encryption, that is, both sides transmitting and receiving data must use the same/symmetric key to encrypt and decrypt plaintext. The most famous symmetric key encryption standard is the Data Encryption Standard (DES). DES is a block encryption algorithm that uses a 56-bit key to operate a 64-bit block of data. The basic flow of symmetric encryption is shown in Fig. 2.

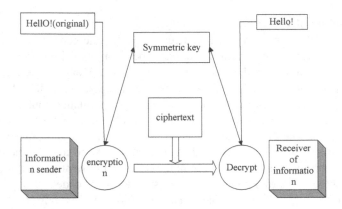

Fig. 2. Basic process of symmetric encryption

Commonly used algorithms in symmetric encryption algorithms are: DES, 3DES, TDEA, Blowfish, RC2, RC4, RC5, IDEA, SKIPJACK, AES, etc. RC5 is a relatively new algorithm, and Rivets designed a special implementation of RC5, so the RC5 algorithm has a word-oriented structure:

$$RC5 - w/r/b, \tag{2}$$

where w is the word length and its value can be 16, 32 or 64. For different word length plaintext and ciphertext blocks, the packet length is 2w bits, r is the number of encryption rounds, and b is the key byte length. Since the RC5 packet length variable cipher algorithm is mainly processed for 64-bit packet w = 32 in this paper, the processing of RC5 encryption and decryption is described in detail below:

3.1.1 Create a Key Group

The RC5 algorithm uses 2r + 2 key-related 32-bit words for encryption: where r is the number of rounds encrypted. The process of creating this key group is very complicated but straightforward. First copy the key bytes into the array L of 32-bit words (at this time, pay attention to whether the processor is little-endian or big-endian). The last word can be padded with zeros if needed. Then initialize the array S with the linear congruential generator modulo 2:

From I=1 to 2(r+1)-1:

Where RC5 is a 32-bit group of 16-bit words,

P=0xb7e1; Q=0x9e37

For

32-bit words and 64-bit grouped RC5,

P=0xb7e15163; Q=0x9e3779b9

For 64-bit words and 128-bit packets, P=0xb7151628aed2a6b Q=0x9e3779b97f4a7c15

Finally, mix L with S, the mixing process is as follows:

I=j=0;

A=B=0;

Processed 3n times

3.1.2   Encryption Processing

After the key group is created, the plaintext is encrypted. When encrypting, the plaintext packet is first divided into two 32-bit words: A and B (in the case that the processor byte order is little-endian, w = 32, the first plaintext byte enters the lowest byte of A, and the fourth plaintext byte enters the highest byte of A, the first The five plaintext bytes enter the lowest byte of B, and so on, where the operator <<< indicates the left shift of the loop, and the add operation is the modulus (which should be modulo, w = 32 in this article). The output ciphertext is the contents of registers A and B (Table 1).

Table 1. Symmetric encryption application mode.

Encryption mode (English name and shorthand)	Chinese name
Electronic Code Book (ECB)	Electronic cryptographic model
Cipher Block Chaining (CBC)	Cipher block link mode
Cipher Feedback Mode (CFB)	Encrypted feedback mode
Output Feedback Mode (OFB)	Output feedback mode

3.2 Asymmetric Key Encryption Process

Asymmetric key encryption, also known as Public Key Encryption (Public Key Encryption), was proposed by Professor Herman of Stanford University in 1977. Unlike symmetric encryption algorithms, asymmetric encryption algorithms require two keys: a public key (pub-lackey) and a private key (private key). The public key and the private key are a pair. If the data is encrypted with the public key, only the corresponding private key can be used for decryption; if the data is encrypted with the private key, only the corresponding public key can be used to decrypt. Since encryption and decryption use two different keys, this algorithm is called an asymmetric encryption algorithm. The basic flow of asymmetric encryption is shown in Fig. 3.

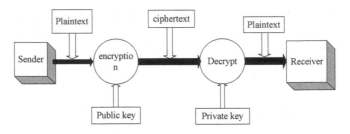

Fig. 3. Basic process of asymmetric encryption

The main algorithms used in asymmetric encryption are: RSA, Elgamal, knapsack algorithm, Rabin, D-H, ECC and so on. The RSA algorithm is the first algorithm that can be used for both encryption and digital signatures, and is also easy to understand and operate. RSA is the most widely studied key algorithm. From the time of its submission to the present, it has been tested by various attacks for more than 30 years. It is widely accepted as one of the best key scheme by 2017. The SET (Secure Electronic Transaction) protocol requires the CA to use a 2048-bit long key, and other entities use a 1024-bit key. The RSA key length increases rapidly as the level of security increases.

4 Big Data Electronic Case System User Data Intelligent Encryption Experiment

The simple process of electronic signature is as follows: when an electronic signature is required, the system will prompt the user to insert the memory card storing the individual into the card reader, and the user inserts and then returns. The system prompts the user to enter the password for reading the memory card information, and the user enters and presses Enter. The system reads the personal key and signs it, prompting the user to remove the memory card to prevent the key from being lost or leaked.

Assuming that User A wants to send a message m $[1, p - 1]$ to B and sign the message m. The first step: User A selects an x $[1, p - 1]$ as the secret key and calculates y = (mod p) as the key. The key y is stored in a public file. The second step: randomly select k $[1, p - 1]$ and calculate r = (mod p). For the general Megamall type digital signature scheme, there is a Signature Equation: $ax = b * k + c(mod(p - 1))$.

Where (a, b, c) is a permutation of the mathematical combination of (h(m), r, s). The s can be solved by the signature equation. Then (m, (r, s)) is the digital signature of A to message m.

Step 3: A sends (m, (r, s)) to B.

4.1 Preparation of Experimental Data

See Table 2.

Table 2. The length of the key corresponding to the security level

Secrecy level	Symmetric key length (bit)	RSA key length (bit)	ECC key length (bit)	Secrecy years
80	80	1024	160	2010
112	112	2048	224	2030
128	128	3072	256	2040
192	192	7680	384	2080
256	256	15360	512	2120

4.2 Analysis of Experimental Results

The results of encryption analysis are shown in Fig. 4:

According to the test curve results, it can be concluded that asymmetric encryption has obvious advantages for big data electronic case system user data. The asymmetric encryption system does not require the communication parties to transfer the key in advance or has any agreement to complete the secure communication, and the key management is convenient, and the anti-counterfeiting and the repudiation can be realized. Therefore, it is more suitable for the confidential communication requirement in the network communication.

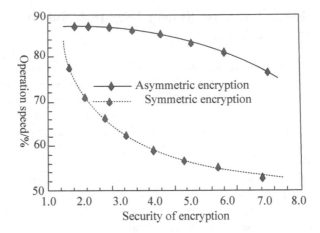

Fig. 4. Comparison of encryption results

5   Conclusions

Once the case is encrypted, the level of confidentiality will be greatly enhanced, and only authorized persons can log into the electronic case system. Moreover, all modifications and saves require identity authentication to be carried out. The details of any changes are also recorded by the computer and can be checked at any time. The purpose is to prevent tampering and prevent "deadbeat."

References

1. Han, W., Yan, H., Wang, Y.: Researchon hidden dangers and security secrets of classified electronic document. 20–23
2. Hu, J.: Analysis of the impact of big data on the development of hospital records management. Manage. Obs. (02), 108–110 (2017)
3. Yu, D.: Application of electronic medical record in hospital information management. Electron. Technol. Softw. Eng. (17), 259 2017
4. Li, A.: Problems and countermeasures of hospital information security. Network Secur. Technol. Appl. (11), 130–131 (2017)
5. Ye, J.: Application of data encryption technology in computer network communication security. Inf. Commun. (06), 173–175 (2018)
6. Wang, W., Shi, X., Liu, X., Xu, K., Yu, H.: Research on smart grid security technology based on symmetric key algorithm. Energy Environ. Prot. (12), 279–281 (2017)
7. Lei, H.Y.: Construction of hospital information resource management platform based on electronic medical record. Inf. Comput. (Theor. Version) (11), 221–224 (2018)
8. Han, T., Xie, J.: RSA encryption and decryption algorithm and related attack methods. Comput. Inf. Technol. (01), 31–32+36 (2018)
9. Liu, T.Y., Lin, K.J., Wu, H.C.: ECG data encryption then compression using singular value decomposition. IEEE J. Biomed. Health Inform. **22**(3), 707–713 (2018)

10. Bokhari, M.U., Shallal, Q.M., Tamandani, Y.K.: Reducing the required time and power for data encryption and decryption using K-NN machine learning. IETE J. Res. (15), 1–9 (2018)
11. Nasution, A.B., Efendi, S., Suwilo, S.: Image steganography in securing sound file using arithmetic coding algorithm, triple data encryption standard (3DES) and modified least significant bit (MLSB). J. Phys: Conf. Ser. **1007**(1), 012010 (2018)
12. Han, C., Yang, X., Hu, W.: Chaotic reconfigurable ZCMT precoder for OFDM data encryption and PAPR reduction. Opt. Commun. **405**, 12–16 (2017)
13. Rasmi, M., Alazzam, M.B., Alsmadi, M.K., et al.: Healthcare professionals' acceptance electronic health records system: critical literature review (Jordan case study). Int. J. Healthcare Manage. (3), 1–13 (2018)
14. Mohammed, A., Franke, K., Boakye, P.O., et al.: Feasibility of electronic health information and surveillance system (eHISS) for disease symptom monitoring: a case of rural Ghana. PLoS ONE **13**(5), e0197756 (2018)
15. Romeromuñiz, C., Nakata, A., Pou, P., et al.: High-accuracy large-scale DFT calculations using localized orbitals in complex electronic systems: the case of graphene-metal interfaces. **30**(50) (2018)

Research on Intelligent Retrieval Technology of User Information in Medical Information System Under the Background of Big Data

Xin Liu[✉]

School of Railway Operation and Management, Hunan Railway Professional Technology College, Zhuzhou, China
liuxin001100@163.com

Abstract. Intelligent information technology had made outstanding contributions to strengthening information management in hospitals and improving the level of hospital construction. It had become the key development object in the future of hospital intelligence information data management. As one of the most important data information in the hospital, the management of the user data of the medical information system had an extremely important influence and significance on the decision making of the future management of the hospital, the use of medical data, and the forensics of the judicial materials. The traditional manual operation and manual computer operation of the user data management model of medical information system had a direct impact on the development process of information intelligent management of the future hospital users. Therefore, the intelligent management of the important database of the medical information system user data was of great significance to the exchange and use of data experience within the hospital, and even the world, as well as the intelligent management of the hospital and the scientific and technological development of the medical future. Through the medical record management of the key information of medical system files, this paper effectively removes redundant data and improves data retrieval efficiency; it realizes accurate collection of medical information according to visualization technology. The effectiveness of the proposed method is verified by experiments.

Keywords: Big data · Medical information system · User information · Intelligent retrieval · Privacy protection

1 Introduction

After nearly a hundred years, the management and retrieval technology of the medical information system of user data has developed from a single information file to a high-tech medical information management discipline. As an important carrier to record patients' specific medical activities, their medical information not only provides raw materials for medical programs, teaching management, scientific research, hospital management and hospital management decisions, but also can be used to guide hospital decision management, specific business, medical statistics, education, scientific research, prevention, health care, medical results evaluation, health assessment, legal

G. Gui and L. Yun (Eds.): ADHIP 2019, LNICST 301, pp. 310–316, 2019.
https://doi.org/10.1007/978-3-030-36402-1_33

appraisal, and treatment of doctor-patient disputes, history files and assessment directly or indirectly as important data, which has far-reaching significance for strengthening the information and intelligent development of medical specialty [1]. With the rapid development of science and technology and data application, the development of intelligent means and the in-depth study of modern medical management in hospitals, in order to promote the progress of hospital management, it is necessary to speed up the management of intelligent retrieval technology of user data in medical information system under the background of large data. The intelligent management level of each unit in the hospital to some extent determines the process of the hospital in the process of intelligent management, see Table 1.

Table 1. Different data differences of the medical information system users.

	Hive	RDBMU
Query language	Hive sql	Soj
Memory	HDFS	Raw device or local file system
Carry out	Mape reduce	Executor
Delayed	High	Low
Data size	Large	Small
Expand	Fine	Poor
Fault-tolerant	Yes	No

Among them, Hive sql and Soj are two different query languages. The user data information of the medical information system embodies the aggregated information data of the various departments of the hospital, and is the main information node and source of the hospital medical information network. In all the information system user data of the hospital, the data storage has reached the maximum, the source of information is complex, the use frequency is high, the quality is high, and the use characteristic of [2] constantly growing is presented. Under the background of large data, the intelligent retrieval technology of medical information system user data is not only one of the important indicators of the hospital intelligent management, but also an important basis for assessing and comparing the hospital management level, the ability level and the frequency of medical accidents. It is one of the important means for the hospital to carry out comprehensive information and intelligence management. To this end, this paper studies the medical system user data retrieval technology in the context of big data, so as to solve the problem of low data retrieval efficiency and poor recognition accuracy.

2 User Data Intelligent Retrieval Technology

2.1 Key Information Technology of Medical Record Management

The main feature of user data management in medical information system is to store the user's medical data for future use in the hospital. At the beginning of the research and development, the intelligent retrieval technology of the medical information system user data strictly follows the standard system of medical engineering. The data content is consistent, the data storage is comprehensive, the coding sequence is consistent, the processing means are varied and the operation is convenient, so that it [3] will be easy to be updated in the future. The intelligent retrieval technology of user information in medical information system adopts the open use and operation of users. From the very beginning, attention should be paid to the user's needs, so as to improve the use of technology cycle, so as to enhance the practical and effective use of technology, and further improve the efficiency of medical records management, input speed and accuracy of statistical data and other details, as shown in Fig. 1.

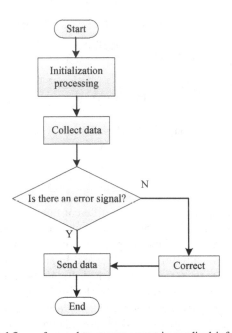

Fig. 1. The workflow of user data management in medical information system

The technology adopts the information source that is unified with the hospital network facilities, so as to complete the maximum compatibility of data collection, and contact the use of [4] hospital patient information management (Fig. 2).

The data management and retrieval work of the medical information system is a relatively standard and strict industry, which has standard requirements for the daily operation requirements, such as input, storage and classification of medical records. This requires that the process design of user information management information technology for medical information system developed in China is in line with the relevant regulations of the state. The database design meets the specific requirements issued by the Ministry of Health, and the design ideas and coding standards are consistent with the platform center of the hospital information management and retrieval system [5].

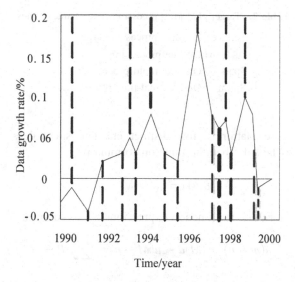

Fig. 2. Changes in data growth rate in the related year of medical system

2.2 Visualization Technology of Medical Information Retrieval

The application of visualization technology in medical diagnosis and treatment is still relatively broad, specific examples are "Visual Information Management Plan" [6]. It is a new integrated data management technology that emerged in the early twenty-first Century. It combines digital image technology, computer graphics, multimedia information technology, sensor sensing technology and other branch of computer simulation [7]. Through multi-dimensional reconstruction simulation technology, it can create a multi-dimensional body structure model, more intuitively and vividly to provide an effective learning approach for human body structure, making the teaching of anatomical application effective, scientific and natural interactive requirements. It has a very high application in medical research and education, diagnosis and treatment plan [8]. Assuming that the data class index is N, at the same time, each data category has its standard platform eigenvector, $Z_1, Z_2, Z_3, Z_4, Z_5 \ldots Z_m$, therefore, the relationship between the vector X and W_i, the platform vector Z_i of the intelligent retrieval of user data in the unknown type of medical system is:

$$M(X) = m(X - Z) = \sqrt{(X - W)}(X - Z) \tag{1}$$

Where $i = 2, 4, \ldots N$.

For example, there are three medical user information data platforms to be identified, namely, Hadoop, Spark and Storm. After many tests, the following results are obtained and analyzed. As shown in Table 2, there are three medical user, there are three types of processing characteristics of the target platform itself.

Table 2. Target platform processing type characteristics.

Terrace	Big data processing type
Hadoop	Off-line processing
Spark	Off-line, rapid processing
Storm	On-line, real-time processing

For any of these platforms, five distinct characteristic values $M\{M_1, M_2, M_3, M_4, M_5\}$. can be obtained. Then the function formula is:

$$\beta(M) = \sqrt[3]{D(M - n)} \tag{2}$$

Based on this formula, the function expressions are as follows:

$$u(m - n) = (M)d - u(M - n) = \sum {}_3 R - m \tag{3}$$

2.3 SoA Oriented Service Architecture Technology

SoA is a new technology and new idea, which is designed to solve the use of medical system in recent years. It is a kind of service architecture technology [9], which has both coarseness and comfortableness. SoA can be used in existing or newly added data applications that will not worry the patient because of the long waiting time. It will upgrade the user's data messages, as shown in Figs. 3 and 4.

In view of the particularity of the medical profession and the diversified needs of patients, more and more humanized requirements have been put forward for the collection, retrieval and analysis of medical diagnostic information. The development of medical information into visualization and intelligence provides an effective way for users to obtain the required information intuitively and conveniently [10].

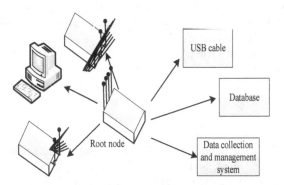

Fig. 3. Classification structure of medical system

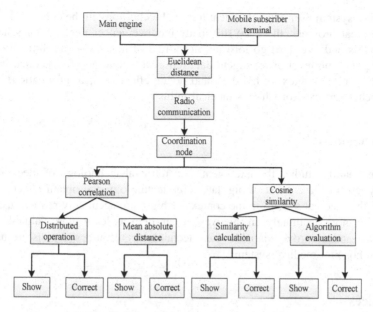

Fig. 4. SOA oriented service architecture

3 Experimental Results and Analysis

In order to ensure the effectiveness of the research on the intelligent data retrieval technology of medical information system in the context of big data, this experiment is carried out. Under the background of big data, the user information intelligent retrieval technology experiment of medical information system selected two different types of target data. In the experiment, the experimental targets are placed under the same network conditions to observe the retrieval speed and correct rate under different technical conditions, and record the data at any time. The schematic diagrams of the experimental demonstration results are shown in Fig. 5, respectively.

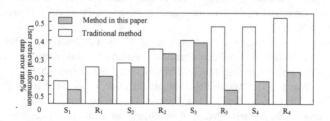

Fig. 5. Comparison of the correct rate of the target object

Through the analysis and research of this paper, we can know that the research on user information intelligent retrieval technology of medical information system under the background of big data has great significance. Although, in recent years, the medical data system user data intelligent retrieval technology in the context of big data has made great progress, there are still many inconveniences needing for scholars to study. To this end, we must go forward, not afraid of hardships and difficulties, constantly improve the level of intelligent data retrieval technology for medical information systems in the context of big data, and obtain effective data information, so as to provide better services for China's medical industry.

4   Conclusions

This paper mainly studies the intelligent data retrieval technology of medical information system in the context of big data. This technology can obtain effective information in the medical system in the context of big data, accurately retrieve user data, and identify more accurately. In this way, it can help us learn more valuable patient information and improve valuable data technology resources for us to use and strengthen hospital medical systems.

References

1. Sun, G., Yu, F., Lei, X., et al.: Research on mobile intelligent medical information system based on the internet of things technology. In: International Conference on Information Technology in Medicine and Education, IEEE, pp. 260–266 (2017)
2. Diao, L., Yan, H., Li, F., et al.: The research of query expansion based on medical terms reweighting in medical information retrieval. Eurasip J. Wireless Commun. Networking **2018**(1), 105 (2018)
3. Zhou, X., Yanyan, W.U.: Research on application of data fusion methods in medical case-based retrieval. Electron. Sci. Technol. **3**, 14 (2017)
4. Himani., S., Vaidehi, D.: A survey on medical information retrieval. In: International Conference on Information and Communication Technology for Intelligent Systems, pp. 543–550. Springer, Cham (2017)
5. Wang, J., He, Z., Yang, X.: The research on the elderly mental health and the construction of intelligent information service platform. J. Chengdu Med. Coll. (2017)
6. Yong-Wei, M.I., Rui-Chang, W.U., Yi-Yong, L.I., et al.: Research on architecture and key technologies of medical equipment management based on Internet of Things. Chin. Med. Equipment J. (2016)
7. Chen, Z., Guo, Z., Liu, X., et al.: Research on application of Internet of Things and cloud computing technology in intelligent medical system. In: International Conference on Education, Management, Information and Mechanical Engineering (2017)
8. Rong, W.U., Wang, J.H.: Acquisition and organization of medical research information based on Web 2.0. Hosp. Adm. J. Chin. Peoples Liberation Army (2016)
9. Kim, J.M., Ryu, G.S.: Implementation of intelligent medical image retrieval system HIPS. J. Korea Internet Things Soc. **2**(4), 15–20 (2016)
10. Ghoulam, A., Barigou, F., Belalem, G., et al.: Query expansion using medical information extraction for improving information retrieval in french medical domain. Int. J. Intell. Inf. Technol. **14**(3), 1–17 (2018)

Research on Embedded Innovation and Entrepreneurship Sharing Platform for College Students Under the Internet of Things

Xiao-hui Zhang[✉], Li-wei Jia, and Wei Wu

Henan Medical College, Zhengzhou, China
lr123201712@163.com

Abstract. The innovative entrepreneurship project for college students is to strengthen the training of students' innovative entrepreneurship, enhance their awareness of innovative entrepreneurship, and cultivate innovative entrepreneurship.In order to better realize information sharing, this paper proposes an embedded innovation and entrepreneurship sharing platform for college students under the Internet of Things. With embedded system as the development environment, the design of innovation and entrepreneurship sharing platform is realized through front-end UI interface module, sharing platform module and database module. The experiment shows that the embedded innovation and entrepreneurship sharing platform designed for college students is not only higher than the traditional sharing platform in the amount of information, but also about 20% higher in accuracy than the traditional platform.

Keywords: Internet of Things · Embedded · Sharing platform · Entrepreneurial innovation

1 Introduction

In the process of informationization, the rapid development of network technology and products makes the Internet of Things come into being. The Internet of Things is an important part of the new generation of information technology, and also an The core and foundation of the Internet of Things is still the Internet, which is an extension and expansion of the network on the basis of the Internet. Important stage of development in the information age. Secondly, the client extends and extends to any goods and objects, and carries out information exchange and communication, that is, things are interrelated [1]. Internet of Things (IOT) is an extension of Internet application, business and application. Therefore, application innovation is the core of the development of the Internet of Things. Innovation 2.0, with user experience as the core, is the soul of the development of the Internet of Things. Under this innovation form of the Internet of Things, it provides more choices for Chinese College students. In recent years, the contradiction between the number of college graduates and the market demand has made the employment market competition increasingly fierce, encouraging

G. Gui and L. Yun (Eds.): ADHIP 2019, LNICST 301, pp. 317–325, 2019.
https://doi.org/10.1007/978-3-030-36402-1_34

college students to start their own businesses. "Promoting employment through entrepreneurship" has gradually become an important way to alleviate employment pressure, and more college students choose to embark on the road of entrepreneurship. Through investigation and research, it is found that the level and level of College Students' entrepreneurship are rising, from the initial blind entrepreneurship to the scientific entrepreneurship and rational entrepreneurship, and the entrepreneurship theory is also developing and maturing in practice. In order to provide sufficient resources for college students' innovative entrepreneurship and help them realize their dream of entrepreneurship smoothly, we need to use some platforms to transmit and share some information. At this stage, college students' innovative entrepreneurship training plan includes innovative training projects, entrepreneurship training projects and entrepreneurship practice projects. Three types of projects gradually cultivate and exercise students' innovative ability. However, at this stage, the management of innovation and entrepreneurship information and resource acquisition are based on traditional Excel spreadsheet, which is inefficient, difficult to view project application materials, and insufficient sharing of project results. Therefore, we need to solve the problems of College Students' entrepreneurship at this stage, in order to achieve the ultimate goal of University Students' innovation and entrepreneurship information sharing.

2 Design of Embedded Innovation and Entrepreneurship Sharing Platform

This paper designs an embedded innovation and entrepreneurship sharing platform for college students. The platform chooses embedded operating system as the development environment. Embedded system is a special computer system designed for specific applications, which is completely embedded in controlled devices. The system has the advantages of small core, strong specificity, fast running speed and high reliability [2]. Providing shared information for college students can also ensure the security and reliability of shared information. On this basis, C# language is chosen as the programming language for platform development. C# is an object-oriented programming language derived from C language and C++. It has good security, stability and simplicity. It not only eliminates the complexity of C and C++, but also inherits its powerful functions [3] C# inherits the high performance of C++ and the simple visual operation of VB. Because of its powerful operation, innovative grammar style and convenient design, it is the best choice. In such a development environment for platform design and development, embedded innovation and entrepreneurship sharing platform specific development process is shown in Fig. 1.

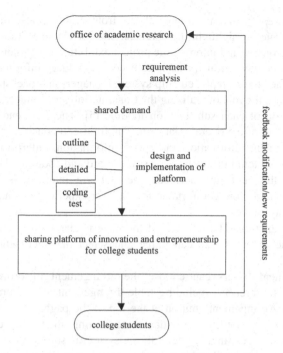

Fig. 1. Development flow chart of innovation and entrepreneurship sharing platform

From the development process in the diagram, we can see that the platform organizes, publishes and stores the innovation and entrepreneurship information of university students in the server for the visitors to share and use. It eliminates the need of users for some information, but it is difficult to find effective information accurately. The spam information mixed in the platform greatly affects the efficiency and speed of users'sharing and accessing knowledge information, and consumes it. It took precious time and energy [4]. The development of the platform is divided into two ports: the client and the server, and either end can exist as the user. At the same time, the function of the server can be realized. That is to say, when the user transmits information, the user's port is the server, and when the user inquires and gets information, it is the client. However, no matter which port type, it is necessary to realize the conversion of the relationship between the front module, the back module and the database module, as well as the transmission of information. The open information is displayed in the foreground, and the information is managed in the background. The information data operated by the user in the foreground sends requests to the background. The background extracts the data from the database and returns the data to the foreground.

2.1 Front-End UI Interface Module

The application of the front-end browsing UI module in the project management system is mainly for displaying the relevant notification, declaration workflow display, login system background and so on in the project management of College Students' innovation and entrepreneurship. In general, the front desk can also display the function of excellent projects, highlight the characteristics of College Students' innovative entrepreneurship projects, and improve the project exhibition. The main interface is not only a platform to connect ordinary users to access and query information, but also a window and interface for entrepreneurship system managers and backstage maintainers to log in. It also plays the role of realizing the transmission and connection of backstage data and information of each sub-function module [5]. The front-end UI interface is also the front-end part of the overall platform. The front-end consists of eight modules: home page, recruitment information, enterprise information, enterprise recommendation, website news, system introduction, message board and about us. The front page of the front desk is the platform interface. The platform interface is designed to be beautiful, generous and more comfortable for the user experience. It has the following several page display modes:

Classification function. The left side of the page is classified according to project level, type, instructor, etc. Users can judge and select the documents they need to download.

Page arrangement. Users can choose the arrangement of project information according to their preferences, including table arrangement and natural arrangement. Click the "Switch Arrangement" button at the top of the page.

Sort function. The platform provides three sorting methods: correlation, time descending and time ascending. By default, the system is sorted by correlation. Users can choose the sorting method independently according to their needs.

College students generally do not have the financial strength to recruit employees in the early stage of entrepreneurship, so the recruitment information released in the recruitment information section of the entrepreneurship platform is generally the kind of unpaid. The enterprise information part is to share the relevant information of every college student entrepreneurship enterprise, so that large enterprises and interested students can join in. The other modules can basically be released and invoked by college students themselves.

2.2 Function Module of Shared Platform

The function modules of the platform play a backstage role in the overall structure. Through this module, we can realize the various possibilities needed by the platform and achieve the effect of the platform's entrepreneurial information resources sharing [6]. The platform is oriented to users and servers for students, instructors, administrators and other users. It has four roles: user management, information management, information retrieval, online statistics, message management, etc. User management is mainly for teachers and students in the college, user login and registration information management. Project information management is mainly for college administrators to complete the functions of adding, deleting, modifying and checking project information. Information retrieval is mainly for platform visitors to complete the retrieval of project information and to retrieve again in the result set. Online statistics mainly completes the download statistics of visitors and project information of the platform. Message management mainly focuses on the management and reply of visitor's message. The function distribution of the embedded innovation and entrepreneurship information sharing platform for college students is shown in Fig. 2.

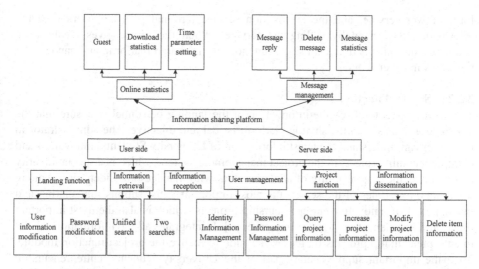

Fig. 2. Function module diagram of information sharing platform

From the platform function module in the figure, we can see that the whole platform divides the sharing function into four functions to realize, four function modules are respectively: User function module, server function module, online statistics function module and message management function module [7]. The client side mainly inquires, calls and retrieves the existing information in the platform. Users log on to the platform with their own user names to obtain the innovation and entrepreneurship information they need. The function of the server is to upload and publish the resource information that may be needed in the innovation and entrepreneurship platform, and the most important one is to share the data and information related to the entrepreneurship project. In addition, online statistics and message management function modules play an auxiliary role. While the platform can provide the required information to be shared, it maintains the normal operation of the platform, making the efficiency of resource sharing higher.

2.2.1 User Function

The client plays the main role of sharing resources acquisition in the sharing platform. The process of sharing resources acquisition is divided into four steps: retrieval, query, acquisition and invocation [8]. The retrieval can be divided into unified retrieval and secondary retrieval. Unified retrieval is to output different types of data according to storage. For example, when querying and retrieving the entrepreneurial data of a college student, the unified retrieval will retrieve the information about the entrepreneurial data, but it will not be specific to a college student. If further precise information is needed, it will be needed. The shared resources are retrieved twice. When retrieving and querying the required resource information, requests for permission are made to the server. Generally, the shared platform system defaults to passing permission immediately, but for some pertinent and patented information and data, the server needs to pass the permission request manually. The information receiving function is provided in the form of wer service, and the information service terminal provides users with the information they need by calling the service. When the server gives feedback, it completes the information acquisition function of the shared platform, and can call the resources in other work.

2.2.2   Server Function

The server needs to check the information of the landing personnel to ensure that the information released to the sharing platform is real and effective. The administrator in the server can understand the latest information of University Students' innovation and entrepreneurship projects in the project management system, which is a special identity and assumes the responsibility of administrators who manage other identities. Among the function modules of the server, the most important is the submission, sharing and management of innovative entrepreneurship projects, which is also the most important function for students to realize on the server [9]. It integrates all the information related to entrepreneurship projects on the service side to realize the project function module. Then the important supplementary part of the University Students' entrepreneurship sharing platform is the project progress record module. The module fills in project progress record information and sub-project log [10]. It prompts students to grasp the project process timely and accurately, and paves the way for the follow-up promotion. When the project is completed, the project submission and two sub-functional modules are divided into report and audit report. Because there are many modules. Attract only audit report module. In the shared platform of college students' entrepreneurship, the page management options of corresponding pages can be entered by choosing one of the two submenus of report and audit report in the left evaluation module. When making project report review, select submenu audit report and select restriction conditions, such as project specification number and query condition, to search the result through web page. If the project report needs to be reviewed, it can be obtained by clicking on the audit and submitting it. If the selection is wrong, you can cancel and return to the home page. The core function of University Students' entrepreneurship sharing platform is the release function of the project, which plays a vital role in the subsequent launch and implementation of the project.

2.2.3   Message Management Function

The message management module in the embedded innovation and entrepreneurship sharing platform for college students is connected with the message board in the UI interface of the front desk. Both the client and the server can leave messages in it. Users can ask questions about the data of innovation and entrepreneurship projects to the server. Users who share information can answer the questions in it, and the interactive function of the platform can be more realized. For some erroneous information, users can also be reminded of the release of information through message function to facilitate timely modification, to ensure the authenticity and real-time of the data in the platform. Some messages that have been resolved or do not need to be saved can also be deleted through the message management function. Through the implementation of message management function module, the sharing of the platform is more complete.

2.3 Database Module

The database mainly plays the role of data storage in the embedded innovation and entrepreneurship sharing platform for college students. Through the construction of the shared database, the huge shared data information can be effectively stored in the cloud. In the process of calling shared information, users can also save a lot of retrieval time. The working logic of the database module is shown in Fig. 3.

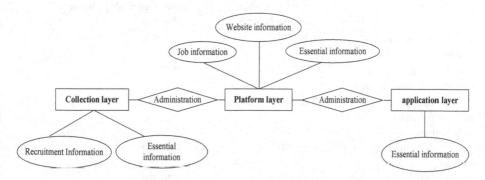

Fig. 3. The working logic diagram of the database

According to the working logic diagram of the database in the figure, the database of the embedded innovation and entrepreneurship sharing platform for college students mainly includes collection layer, platform layer and application layer. The acquisition layer collects real-time information through Internet of Things technology, which covers all data and records. The main purpose of building the Internet of Things architecture is to build reliable links between data and objects. Physical objects are used as information sources to transmit information independently and input data into the database according to the standard transformation to form data and physical correspondence. At the same time, database access rights are set to improve data security. Platform layer is the key part of database information sharing. It establishes information sharing platform to provide users with access query, information feedback and security monitoring functions. The core of platform layer is database information remote sharing method. The application layer is mostly oriented to all nodes. Users can get the required information through the corresponding devices, so as to meet the information needs of different users.

3 Experimental Analysis

The ultimate goal of the embedded innovation and entrepreneurship sharing platform for college students under the Internet of Things is to enable entrepreneurs to upload entrepreneurship data and past innovation and entrepreneurship information. In order to verify that the designed sharing platform can achieve the desired results, an experimental analysis is carried out. In order to reflect the sharing effect of the platform, the traditional sharing platform is selected as the experimental comparison. The comparison results are shown in Table 1.

Table 1. Table of experimental comparison results

	Traditional entrepreneurship sharing platform	Embedded innovation and entrepreneurship sharing platform
Upload data volume of startup projects	1.30 GB	5.80 GB
Number of uploads of entrepreneurship projects	3758	19573
Upload data volume of entrepreneurship information	3.25 GB	10.55 GB
Project download data volume	0.25 GB	3.88 GB
Number of project references	0.13 GB	3.30 GB
Accuracy of entrepreneurship information	65%	88%

From the results in the table, we can see that the data volume of entrepreneurship projects and entrepreneurship information in the embedded innovation and entrepreneurship sharing platform for college students designed in this paper is much higher than that of the traditional entrepreneurship sharing platform. The uploaded number of entrepreneurship projects in this design platform is 19573, and the downloaded data volume of projects is 3.88 GB, which shows that the entrepreneurship information in Compared with the traditional sharing platform, the designed sharing platform is 23% higher, the parameters of the designed platform are better than those of the traditional platform, which shows that there are not only a large number of entrepreneurial data information in the platform, but also a high reliability of information, which has a strong authenticity and reliability of data information.

4 Conclusion

To sum up, the design and implementation of the embedded innovation and entrepreneurship sharing platform for university students under the Internet of Things is mainly based on the actual needs of the development and management of University Students' innovation and entrepreneurship projects, with the help of the platform to achieve overall management, thus ensuring that teachers and students can participate in the various project processes, reducing the workload of management, improving the comprehensive effect of management, and providing universities with entrepreneurial needs. Students can provide more weighted data and information, provide corresponding guarantee for the effective implementation of innovative entrepreneurship projects for college students, truly play an important role in sharing platform of innovative entrepreneurship for college students, and promote the overall improvement of the quality of personnel training.

References

1. Fu, X., Liu, H., Bai, Y.S.: Research on the integration of university entrepreneurship Park and innovation and Entrepreneurship Education under the background of "Internet +". Chin. Vocat. Tech. Educ. **22**(19), 55–57 (2017)
2. Liu, H., Fu, X., Bai, Y.S.: Research on the integration mode of entrepreneurship Park and innovation and entrepreneurship education in Higher Vocational Colleges under the Internet + background. Chin. Vocat. Tech. Educ. **36**(28), 79–81 (2017)
3. Bayinchahan, Anpeng: Design and implementation of intelligent campus system based on embedded and RFID Internet of Things. Mod. Electron. Technol. **40**(16), 63–65 (2017)
4. Jiang, M., Li, F., Zhang, C.: Research and Practice on the construction of sharing service platform for scientific and technological innovation and entrepreneurship. Heilongjiang Anim. Husbandry Vet. Med. **22**(20), 280–282 (2017)
5. Li, Y., Zhang, Y., Li, J.: Research on integrated service model of regional science and technology resource sharing platform from the evolutionary perspective. China Sci. Technol. Forum **24**(2), 51–57 (2017)
6. Zhao, H., Xu, J., Yulong, C.: Beijing, Tianjin and Hebei University Innovation and Entrepreneurship Education Research under the Background of Cooperative Development. Educ. Vocat. **23**(24), 65 (2017)
7. Wu, J.: Path choice of strengthening innovation and entrepreneurship education for agricultural graduate students. Educ. Rev. **18**(2), 42–45 (2018)
8. Yang, W.: Simulation of remote sharing method of database information under the framework of Internet of Things. Comput. Simul. **29**(4), 15–19 (2018)
9. Gu, W.: Research on data scheduling method of shared resources in Internet of Things. Comput. Simul. **34**(1), 268–271 (2017)
10. Bloomberg, Yang, P., Ma, Z., et al.: Performance evaluation and analysis of ARM embedded platform based on Docker. Comput. Appl. **37**(1), 325–330 (2017)

Research on Automatic Estimation Method of College Students' Employment Rate Based on Internet Big Data Analysis

Xiao-hui Zhang[✉], Li-wei Jia, and Fa-wei Zhou

Henan Medical College, Zhengzhou 451191, Henan, China
1r123201712@163.com

Abstract. In order to solve the problem of large error and inaccuracy in employment rate estimation, an automatic employment rate estimation method based on Internet big data analysis is proposed. This method can be divided into four steps: Firstly, the data integration model based on XML middleware is used to select the sample data of employment rate estimation. Secondly, the decision tree C4.5 algorithm is used to classify the attributes of the sample data. Thirdly, the improved KPCA algorithm is used to extract the feature vectors of employment information and calculate the distance between the forecasted samples and all samples. Fourthly, non-linear mapping method is used to transform employment structure data into corner data, and grey theory is used to establish employment rate estimation model. The results show that the average employment rate estimation error of this method is 4.81% lower than that of the statistical method based on support vector machine.

Keywords: Internet big data analysis · Employment rate · Estimation method

1 Introduction

Employment has always been one of the key issues of national concern. With the increasing number of college graduates in China, the employment situation has become more and more serious. Many graduates are facing the problem of unemployment. In this case, how to effectively estimate the employment rate of students has become a major problem to be solved in the field of education. The method of estimating the employment rate of students can estimate the future employment rate of students according to the employment data of historical graduates. At present, the employment rate of colleges and universities is mainly counted by manual method, but the process of this method is complex, which requires a lot of manpower and material resources, and the cost of statistics is relatively high. With the continuous development of intelligent technology, the use of intelligent statistical methods for college employment statistics [1]. Mainstream intelligent statistical methods of employment rate include the statistical methods of employment rate in Colleges and Universities Based on particle swarm optimization algorithm; Statistical method of university employment rate based on genetic algorithm; Statistical methods of college employment rate based on support vector machine algorithm, etc. Among them, the most commonly used method is based

G. Gui and L. Yun (Eds.): ADHIP 2019, LNICST 301, pp. 326–335, 2019.
https://doi.org/10.1007/978-3-030-36402-1_35

on support vector machine (SVM). However, due to the statistical error of this method, this study proposes a new method of automatic employment rate estimation based on large data analysis of the Internet. Firstly, it integrates the employment rate data information of colleges and universities, determines the sample data needed for employment rate estimation, classifies them, extracts the characteristic vector of the employment information of students to be predicted, calculates the distance between students to be predicted and all samples, and constructs the employment rate estimation model. Finally, the experiment proves that this method has less error and higher accuracy in estimating employment rate, and achieves satisfactory results [2].

2 Automatic Estimation Method of Employment Rate Based on Big Data Analysis

"Statistical data are the reflection of objective things' quantity. Quantitative under-standing of statistics must be based on qualitative understanding of objective things. Statistical research is closely related to the quality of phenomena to study its quantity and reflect the quality of phenomena through quantity". Therefore, the concept of "employment" needs to be defined scientifically before the employment rate statistics. However, at present, the concept of "employment" has not been recognized and unified in China. According to the provisions of China's employment policy, labourers with labor capacity can combine with means of production through certain ways, and obtain certain remuneration or income from engaging in a legal social work. This is employment. Although the above definitions are different, they have common ele-ments, namely, labourers with labor capacity, workers with the same means of pro-duction, and workers with remuneration or labor. Income. Accordingly, it can be strictly said that the employment rate refers to "the total number of employed graduates * 100% of the total number of employed graduates". Essentially, the employment rate is a statistical data and an important indicator to measure the comprehensive teaching ability of colleges and universities. The employment situation of college graduates is becoming more and more serious, and many professionals are in a saturated state, which makes it difficult for college graduates to find jobs [3]. Therefore, it is necessary to make statistics on the employment rate of different majors in universities and dis-tribute educational resources rationally so as to guide students'majors effectively and ultimately promote the improvement of employment rate. The statistical method of employment rate in Colleges and universities has become a hot issue in the field of education, which has attracted the attention of many scholars.

2.1 Principle of Estimating Employment Rate

In the process of establishing the model of estimating the employment rate of students, the employment data of historical students are obtained, the employment samples of students are given and classified, and the data characteristics of students to be predicted are extracted, which are transformed into feature vectors, the distance between students to be predicted and all samples is calculated, and the model of estimating the employment rate of students is established. Detailed steps are shown in Fig. 1 below.

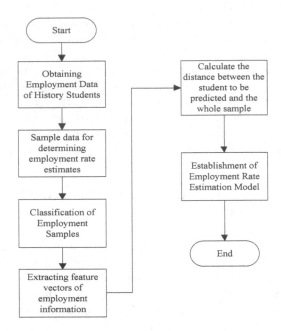

Fig. 1. Design flow of employment rate estimation method

2.2 Sample Data for Estimating Employment Rate

Due to the influence of phases, technology and other economic and human factors in the construction and implementation of data management system in Colleges and universities, a large number of employment-related data with different storage modes have been accumulated in the development process of colleges and universities. From simple file databases to complex network databases, they constitute heterogeneous data sources in Colleges and universities. Therefore, data integration is the only way to establish employment samples, and data integration needs a data integration model based on XML middleware to complete. The model is constructed through the following four steps:

(1) Establishing Data Integration Middleware

Data integration middleware is used to transfer data from data source to any target data source that needs data. External applications that want to access data can also access data from different heterogeneous data sources in a unified form through data integration middleware [4].

(2) Establishing relevant XML data model

In order to deal with all kinds of data sources in a unified way, the system must describe data from different data sources in a common mode. Generally speaking, the global data model of heterogeneous data source integration system must satisfy the following two points: First, it can describe various data formats, whether structured or semi-structured, whether it supports all query languages or simple text queries. Second, it is easy to publish and exchange data. The integrated data can be easily published and exchanged in various formats.

(3) Establishing the mapping from specific data model to common data model

Mapping between specific storage mechanisms and public data models is required, and each data source must establish a mapping from itself to the XML public model. On the basis of completing the mapping process, it is also necessary to establish a data conversion program from the specific storage format of each data source to the XML format.

(4) Solving Semantic Heterogeneity

After resolving the problem of schema heterogeneity, the problem of semantic heterogeneity is very prominent. How to clean up the data, according to certain standards, error data, duplicate data and contradictory data from different systems. It is very important to unify appropriate transformation rules, which directly affects the integrity, consistency and sharing of data after integration.

This paper presents a heterogeneous data integration model based on XML middleware, as shown in Fig. 2. Using the method of heterogeneous data integration based on middleware, the middleware system is responsible for data access, query and coordination among heterogeneous data sources, and centralizes to provide high-level retrieval services for heterogeneous data sources. According to the method of middleware heterogeneous data integration, XML Schema is used to describe the schema information and global schema information of each local data source, and XPath query is used to query data based on global schema in a unified way [5].

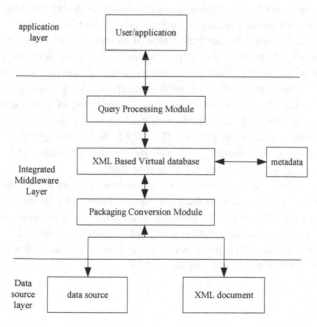

Fig. 2. Heterogeneous data integration model based on XML middleware

The whole model architecture is divided into three layers: data source layer, integration middleware layer and application layer. The integration middleware layer is the most important layer of the whole model and the key to realize heterogeneous data integration.

Data Source Layer: At the lowest level, it is a data provider, which should include various types of databases (relational database and object-oriented database), files and other information. Integration Middleware Layer: Coordinating database systems downwards, providing unified data schema and common interface for data access for applications accessing integrated data upwards, providing necessary data conversion functions or tools, transforming data into XML format, storing data into XML data space, and maintaining mapping relationship between XML data space and heterogeneous data sources [6].

Application layer: User interface layer, according to the specific application and user computing environment, adopt appropriate information access technology or application software. The application layer can access data in the application server layer of integrated data by Web browser or special client. Whether the application is in C/S mode or B/S mode, as long as the interface specification of the interface layer is followed, the underlying data sources can be operated effectively and transparently.

2.3 Data Attribute Classification

After the sample data is determined by the data integration model based on XML middleware mentioned above, it is necessary to classify different student characteristics information.

Decision Tree is a tree graph composed of a series of nodes and branches, in which branches are composed of nodes and sub-nodes. Nodes represent attributes that need to be considered in learning or decision-making, and different branches are composed of different attributes. By using the attribute value of an instance, from the root node of the decision tree to the leaf node, the case can be learned and the decision can be made. The final result of learning or decision-making is represented by leaf nodes [7].

Decision tree has the ability of multi-concept learning through analysis and induction of case sets. It is easy to use and has a wide range of applications. Decision tree algorithm is the best choice for classifying large-scale case data represented by unstructured attribute values. At present, ID3, C4.5, SLIQ and SPRINT are the most widely used decision tree learning algorithms. In this chapter, C4.5 algorithm is selected to complete the classification of sample data.

C4.5 algorithm constructs decision tree by top-down greedy algorithm for learning. The construction process starts with selecting the attributes to be tested at the root node, and then chooses the attributes to be tested at each node in the decision tree according to the criteria of maximum information gain and minimum entropy. The object set is divided by the test results. This process is repeated until the leaf nodes of a cotyledon are in the same class as the classification criteria.

2.4   Extraction of Employment Information Feature Vector

KPCA feature extraction method is a principal component analysis method based on the kernel transformation method. It maps the original data space to the high-dimensional space through the non-linear function (kernel function), and then processes the data of principal component analysis in the high-dimensional space to extract the linear and non-linear features of samples. The most important part of the method is to introduce the kernel function, which can simplify the calculation greatly by calculating the inner product in the high-bit space through the kernel function in the original space [8].

The purpose of KPCA algorithm is to preserve the feature information of samples as much as possible, and to simplify the representation of data as much as possible. The cumulative contribution rate is used to select feature vectors to reduce the dimension of feature space, which has a good effect on data dimension reduction. However, the whole process only considers the total feature information of samples without considering the category information of samples. Relevant literature also shows that the feature vectors extracted by the traditional KPCA method according to the cumulative contribution rate have no good effect on the classification of abnormal data, that is, only considering the main components of the matrix from a mathematical point of view without considering the classification of actual samples. So in this section, we improve the traditional KPCA algorithm, that is, to measure the class information by the degree of clustering within the class and the degree of dispersion between the classes of the feature vectors, which not only retains a good dimension reduction effect, but also is more conducive to the subsequent pattern classification. The improved KPCA algorithm runs as follows (Fig. 3):

According to the above process, assuming that P and O represent different types of data eigenvectors, formula (1) is used to calculate the distance d between the students to be predicted and the whole sample:

$$d = \frac{\sqrt{P+O}}{C_i \otimes X} \tag{1}$$

In the formula, C_i represents any category of student employment samples, and X represents unknown student employment samples [9].

2.5   Employment Rate Estimation Model Formation

In the process of establishing the employment rate estimation model, based on the distance between the students to be predicted and the whole sample obtained in Sect. 1.4, the employment structure data are transformed into corner data by using the non-linear mapping method, and the employment rate prediction model is established by integrating grey theory. Detailed steps are as follows:

Assuming that the original data of employment structure contains three dimensions and b represents two-dimensional corner data, it is based on the distance between the

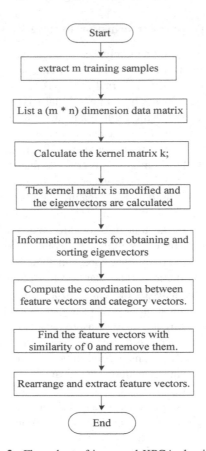

Fig. 3. Flow chart of improved KPCA algorithm

students to be predicted and the whole sample obtained in Sect. 1.4. Using the non-linear mapping method, the employment structure data are transformed into corner data by formula (2):

$$\begin{cases} \alpha_3 = b \cdot d \\ \alpha_2 = \frac{d \cdot b}{\alpha_3} \end{cases} \tag{2}$$

In formula, α_2, α_3 represents the employment structure at different stages.

Assuming that e(0) represents the original employment forecasting time series, the grey theory is used to generate the series accumulatively. Formula (3) is used to obtain the accumulative time series of one-time employment forecasting:

$$e^{(1)} = \frac{e^{(0)} \otimes \left\{ e^{(1)}(1), e^{(1)}(2), \ldots, e^{(1)}(n) \right\}}{\alpha_3 \cdot \alpha_2} \tag{3}$$

The whitening equation of GM (1,1) model is obtained by approximating the change trend of a cumulative sequence with differential equation. The whitening equation of GM (1,1) model is expressed by formula (4):

$$f_{GM(1,1)} = \frac{\{g,h\}}{W} + ge^{(1)} = h \tag{4}$$

In the formula, g represents the development coefficient of different employment stages, h represents the grey function of employment prediction. W represents a given sample of observed employment time series data.

Using Formula (5) to obtain the corresponding sequence of employment forecasting in different time periods:

$$\hat{e}^{(1)}(t+1) = \left[e^{(0)}(1) - \frac{g}{h}\right] \cdot q \tag{5}$$

In the formula, t stands for time; q stands for the certainty that the labor force has been employed.

Formula (6) is used to obtain the time response function of employment estimation in different stages:

$$\hat{e}^{(0)}(t+1) = [1-r]\left[e^{(0)}(1) - \frac{g}{h}\right] \cdot q + (\alpha_2, \alpha_3)\hat{e}^{(1)}(t+1) \tag{6}$$

In the formula, r represents the weighted coefficient of the overall employment forecast.

Assuming that j represents the mean square deviation of employment estimation and u represents the correction coefficient of prediction, the employment estimation model is established by formula (7).

$$y(t) = u(\lambda_1) \otimes \lambda_2 + \lambda_3 \ldots \frac{\delta_1(g)}{\delta_2(h)} \otimes (j, u) \tag{7}$$

In the formula, $y(t)$ represents the estimated value of t-time, δ_1, δ_2 represents the adjustment factor of constant, and λ_1, λ_2, λ_3 represents the transition process of each stage of employment estimation [10].

3   Experimental Analysis

The experimental data were collected from the statistical records of the employment situation of graduates in Liaoning Province from 2010 to 2018. In this study, the estimation method and the statistical method based on support vector machine are used to estimate the employment rate of graduates from 2010 to 2018, and the estimation errors of the two methods are detected. The results are shown in Fig. 4 below.

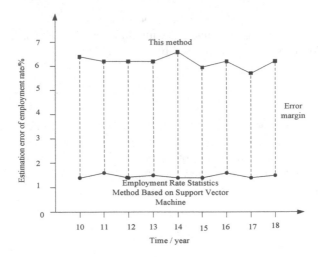

Fig. 4. Estimation error of two methods

Figure 4 shows that the average employment rate estimation error of this method is 1.34%, while that of the statistical method based on support vector machine is 6.15%. By comparing the two methods, we can see that the estimation of this method is more accurate, which makes up for the shortcomings of the statistical method of employment rate based on support vector machine.

4   Conclusion

To sum up, this study proposes an automatic employment rate estimation method based on large data analysis of the Internet, aiming at the problem of large error in employment rate estimation of statistical methods based on support vector machine. The simulation results show that the method solves the problems of the employment rate statistics method based on support vector machine, and lays a foundation for the development of employment guidance in Colleges and universities.

References

1. Wang, S.: Based on large data analysis of disadvantaged groups in colleges and universities graduates employment situation in recent years. China Univ. Students Career Guide **2**(17), 55–58 (2016)
2. Yang, H., Li, L.: Viewpoint on the employment rate of graduate students in agriculture and forestry. Heilongjiang Agric. Sci. **58**(7), 78–82 (2017)
3. Yan, Y., Deng, F.: Employment situation and characteristics for college graduates—discovery from data of 42 colleges and universities in Chengdu. J. Southwest JIAOTONG Univ. (Soc. Sci.) **17**(1), 1–8 (2016)
4. Yao, J., Chen, Y.: Employment status of graduates of food quality and safety specialty in West Anhui University. Anhui Agric. Sci. Bull. **22**(6), 177–179 (2016)

5. Liu, H.: Verification method for the maximal employment rate of university. J. Guangdong AIB Polytech. Coll. **33**(3), 48–53 (2017)
6. Zhao, X., Chen, X.: Clustering analysis based on graduates' employment quality pluralistic evaluation. J. Xinyang Agric. Coll. **26**(4), 149–151 (2016)
7. Zhang, R., Zhang, W., Wu, C.: Survey and analysis of employment status of graduates in mechanics—based on the statistic data of graduates in the Department of Engineering Mechanics at Dalian University of Technology during the past five years. China Univ. Students Career Guide **9**(11), 59–64 (2016)
8. Kong, P., Huang, C., Lu, Y.: Employment statistics and Countermeasures for aquaculture graduates—taking Guangdong Ocean University as an example. Agric. Dev. Equipments **36**(11), 38 (2016)
9. Lei, Y.: Further improve professional art school graduates' employment quality evaluation system –thinking based on MyCOS company on employment-based data analysis of music schools. Guide Sci. Educ. **12**(1), 167–169 (2016)
10. Huang, N.: On the employment situation and countermeasures of international Chinese education in application-oriented universities—a case study of Huangshan University. J. Huangshan Univ. **18**(1), 118–122 (2016)

Research on Demand Response Model of Electric Power Interruptible Load Based on Big Data Analysis

Chengliang Wang[1], Hong Sun[1], and Yong-biao Yang[2(⊠)]

[1] Jiangsu Fangtian Power Technology Co., Ltd., Nanjing, China
lxxl80112@163.com
[2] Southeast University, Nanjing, China
hy20160401@163.com

Abstract. In order to solve the problem of low precision in the analysis of power interruptible load demand using traditional power interruptible load demand response model, a power interruptible load demand response model based on big data analysis is studied in this paper. Firstly, the demand response is implemented by enabling technology, then the dynamic peak-valley price is determined by the demand response. Finally, the power interruptible load demand response model based on big data analysis is realized by using dynamic peak-valley price. The effectiveness of the demand response model based on big data analysis is verified by experiments.

Keywords: Big data analysis · Power interruptible · Load demand response model

1 Introduction

With the increasing scale of new energy access network and the construction of smart grid, the demand for demand-side response and the conditions for flexible dispatching are becoming more and more urgent and mature. As a demand-side resource, demand response has the characteristics of economy and flexibility, and it is an important means to realize flexible interaction of smart grid. At the same time, the demand response, especially interruptible load, can quickly respond to the wind power change and reduce the investment cost of the generation side. It is an ideal backup method for peak shaving in the case of large-scale wind power and other new energy sources connected to the grid. At the present stage, China is still facing the problem of power supply shortage. To ensure the safe and stable operation of the power grid, and to ensure the daily life and economic development of electricity use, is still a subject that will need to be paid attention to [1]. The practice at home and abroad shows that the demand-side management can effectively save energy and alleviate the problem of system capacity and electricity shortage by changing the user's smart electricity mode. Demand response refers to the behavior of electricity users changing their habits according to electricity price signals or other incentives. Demand response is a part of demand-side management. The participation of users in demand response can reduce the operation

© ICST Institute for Computer Sciences, Social Informatics and Telecommunications Engineering 2019
Published by Springer Nature Switzerland AG 2019. All Rights Reserved
G. Gui and L. Yun (Eds.): ADHIP 2019, LNICST 301, pp. 336–345, 2019.
https://doi.org/10.1007/978-3-030-36402-1_36

cost of power grid, save electricity and resources, have good economic and environmental benefits, and is one of the best applications of smart grid. The demand response changes the load of the power system and has a great impact on the reliability of the system. The influencing factors of power system reliability are generally system load fluctuation, component reliability column energy, electrical characteristics and network structure. Among them, the system load has the obvious dispersion characteristic, it is difficult to reflect the actual situation with the single load level index, such as peak load, average load evaluation system reliability. However, demand-side management and other means often change the smart load rate and distribution of the system, increase the uncertainty, and have a great impact on the reliability of the system. Habibian et al. [2] studied the flexibility of demanders'participation in the electricity market of power industry users and provided interruptible load reserve. The standard model of optimal strategic consumption is designed, and the reserve supply curve and consumption curve are optimized. The standard model provides an intuitive basis for this interaction. In addition, it provides tailor-made solutions to uncertainties. But the operability of the method is to be improved. Therefore, it is of great significance to study the variation of system reliability with load, to evaluate the impact of the implementation of demand response on the reliability of power system, to coordinate the demand response resources with the traditional generation resources, and to improve the system reliability. Based on big data analysis, the demand response model of power interruptible load is studied.

2 Demand Response Model of Electric Power Interruptible Load Based on Big Data Analysis

2.1 Implementing Demand Response Through Enabling Technology

Among the components of enabling infrastructure, intelligent instruments and advanced metering infrastructure are key components for implementing demand response. The new generation of electronic intelligent instruments have the ability to realize two-way information communication between end users and power supply enterprises. In the implementation of the demand response project, the intelligent instrument can receive the signals from the electric power enterprises, such as the maximum quantity of electricity that can be obtained in a certain period of time, or the signal of the electricity price determined dynamically. The application of intelligent instruments and advanced metrology infrastructure in the world is growing rapidly. AMI is a network system of millions of intelligent instruments [3]. Whether price-based or motivation-based demand response, in order to effectively participate in demand response in the implementation of automatic control, in the field of end-user such as residential, commercial or industrial buildings, The structure of energy management system is also an important part. The general EMS architecture obtains information signals from controllable or uncontrolled end-user loads, including state and power consumption of electrical equipment, etc. Moreover, the EMS can obtain information about the existing power capacity or the conventional power production situation of the renewable energy source. In addition, the signals of all the load service entities, including the instructions in the demand response activities, the price data, and the like, are transmitted to the energy management system through the advanced metering facilities. Considering all the input information, EMS makes the best operation strategy for the end user. The goal is to meet the needs of the load service entity that initiated the demand response and to meet the needs of the end user, without affecting the satisfaction degree of the power service [4]. At present, there are great regional differences in the use of EMS in the world. The United States plays a leading role in the use of EMS, especially in the home EMS market. European power companies also support a number of related pilot projects. It is widely believed that EMS is beneficial to both customers and electricity, and because many large companies, such as Siemens and Intel, have already provided commercial EMS products, EMS will further enter homes in the near future. Business and industry. The key condition for effective implementation of demand response is the ability to handle a large amount of data transmission. A low latency between the load to be controlled by the LSEs, end user EMS, etc., The appropriate bandwidth of information transmission channel is the prerequisite for the implementation of demand response action. The delay here refers to the time lag between the buyer issuing the request information and the Respondent getting the request information and therefore being able to act accordingly. Bandwidth refers to the transmission rate of each enabling device in the information transmission channel. In order to ensure better implementation of the demand response strategy, it is necessary to transmit the requirement response instructions effectively and respond quickly. Therefore, low latency and appropriate bandwidth index are the important guarantee of the demand response performance.

Based on big data's analysis, three fields of data communication should be considered in the establishment of power interruptible load demand response model: intelligent instrument field, internet field and home local area network field. Home Local area Network (HLAN) is a generic concept that can refer to residential, industrial or commercial user-end buildings. The field of intelligent instruments is a network composed of many intelligent instruments. The Internet is a platform for computing and information management in the IT industry and is used by the public through service providers. The home local area network is the gateway connecting the internet and intelligent instrument field, which is used to realize the interaction between the end user EMS and controllable load, electrical adjustment. The EMS obtains the signal through the intelligent instrument domain, and carries out the action through the home local area network [5]. The Internet is an interface where multiple systems with Internet protocols can exchange information with each other, so as to achieve a desired task, such as providing direct load control to a certain load at the end user. The communication requirements of the intelligent power grid are different due to the different application programs of the intelligent power grid, some applications of the intelligent power grid are sensitive to the time delay, the signals or other information must be transmitted in a specific time, and the other applications can adopt the low-rate communication scheme. There are many communication mechanisms suitable for delay and bandwidth standards in different data communication domains. Generally speaking, communication technology can be divided into wireless and wired technology. Wireless communication technology has lower investment cost because it avoids the cost of wiring. In addition, the wireless signal can reach the actual physical connection where difficulties, thus enhancing the location of the endpoint flexibility. However, wireless transmission has a greater signal loss in the propagation process, thus limiting the effective communication range [6]. Also, to avoid unauthorized access, wireless technology requires powerful security measures. ZigBee, Z-wave, WIFI, Wi-max, cognitive radio and recent cellular technologies can be used as major wireless communication technologies and can be used in many areas of communication in the operation of demand response smart grid. Wired communication technology can use existing lines or external wiring for signal transmission. Existing wired technologies include power line communication, optical fiber, Ethernet and so on. In order to ensure the successful implementation of demand response, the scalability, reproducibility, practicability, reliability and security of the proposed solution should be further analyzed, regardless of whether it is wireline or wireless.

2.2 Dynamic Peak-Valley Pricing Based on Demand Response

With the development and perfection of the electricity market, the main body of interest gradually presents diversification. The demand response can strengthen the interaction among the participants in the electricity market, which is an essential part of the future electricity market [7]. The demand response can be divided into DR based on electricity price and DR. based on incentive according to the different response modes of the participants in the demand response project. The classification is shown in Fig. 1.

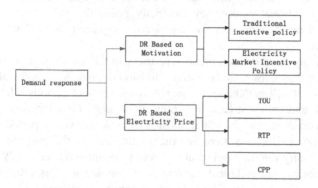

Fig. 1. Classification of requirements response

The DR based on incentive refers to the incentive contract signed in advance between the demand response implementing agency and the user. If the signing user makes the due response according to the agreement requirement, he will get a certain reward from the implementing agency. If the user fails to respond according to the contract, he will be punished accordingly. Users should fully understand the content of the agreement and choose voluntarily whether to participate in the demand response project according to their own conditions and electricity usage [8]. Incentive demand response protocols usually include the amplitude of load, the duration of load reduction and the frequency of response according to the DR signal. The incentive fee is independent of the retail price of the electric power, including both the electricity price discount and the cutting load compensation. In the establishment of the power-interruptible load demand response model based on big data analysis, the main interruptible load measures are to adopt the time-division price. The peak and valley price is especially common in time-sharing price, that is, according to the load level of power system, the whole day can be divided into three periods: peak, level and valley, and different price standards are carried out in each period. The price of electricity in normal period is close to the normal price, the price in peak period is higher than that in normal section, and the price in period of valley is lower than that in normal section [9]. Through the difference of electricity price in three periods to produce certain economic benefits, when the economic benefits are attractive to the users, the participants can be guided to adjust their own electricity consumption mode, so that the power consumption can be transferred from the peak period to the valley, and the load curve can be improved. To achieve the role of peak filling. However, the traditional peak-valley price does not fully consider the characteristics of user load, and the lack of dynamic adjustment mechanism makes it impossible to mobilize the enthusiasm of users. If the traditional fixed peak and valley price difference is too small to cause the user response, the effect of peak cutting and valley filling is very weak, and the main significance of implementing the demand response project is lost. If the price difference between peak and valley electricity is too large, it may lead to excessive response, even peak and valley inversion. The demand response model of power interruptible load based on big data's analysis needs to fully mine and extract the user characteristics, and therefore, based on the traditional peak-valley electricity price, the adjustment mechanism is introduced, and the dynamic peak-valley electricity price is formulated to avoid the above situation.

Big data analysis of the comprehensive users in the whole region shows that the daily load curve fluctuates steadily, and the division of peak, level and valley periods is more stable, and it will not change frequently in all kinds of periods. The membership degree of peak and valley at each time point is obtained by using fuzzy membership function, and based on this, the initial division of peak and valley period is carried out at each time point. Because there are fuzzy attributes in the partition results, it is necessary to classify the time points at different time intervals accurately according to the response ability and technical constraints of the actual users [10]. The common membership function includes Gao Si type, bell shape, trapezoid and triangle, and so on, which should be reasonably selected according to the characteristics of the processing target and the requirement of the processing result. The highest point corresponding to the daily load curve of electric power users must belong to the peak period, that is, the peak membership degree of this time point is 100 kum, while the valley membership degree is 0. The fluctuation of the integrated power user load curve is continuous and stable, so the higher the load value near the highest point or other points of the curve is, the higher the probability that the corresponding time point belongs to the peak period. In contrast, the lowest point of the load curve corresponds to a valley membership degree of 100, while the peak membership degree is 0. Other time points of the load curve only need to determine the corresponding load power value and the peak point and the lowest point load power comparability can get the specific peak and valley membership degree. The peak membership degree and valley membership degree of each time point of the load curve are obtained by using the linear part of the partial large-scale semi-trapezoidal membership function and the partial small semi-trapezoidal membership function. The membership function of semi-trapezoid is shown in Fig. 2.

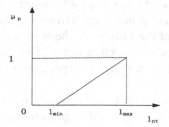

(a) Partial large-scale semi-trapezoidal membership function

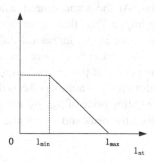

(b) Semi-trapezoidal membership function

Fig. 2. Membership function of semi-trapezoid with partial size and small size

In the semi-trapezoidal membership function of partial large and small scale, the other time points of load sequence correspond to peak and valley membership degree can be obtained from formulas (1) and (2), respectively.

$$\mu_p(l_{nt}) = \frac{l_{nt} - l_{min}}{l_{max} - l_{min}} \tag{1}$$

$$\mu_v(l_{nt}) = \frac{l_{max} - l_{nt}}{l_{max} - l_{min}} \tag{2}$$

Among that, lnt represents the time point nt corresponding load power; lmin and lmax represents the minimum and maximum values in the daily load time series, respectively; $\mu_p(l_{nt})$ and $\mu_v(l_{nt})$ represents peak membership degree and Valley membership degree of time Point nt respectively. The preliminary results of the time series of the load time series by using the fuzzy membership function can be used as an important basis for the time period division of the peak. taking into account the restriction of the user's life, the stability of production and the current limit of the electricity price technology and the facility level at present, and determining the peak, the level and the valley time duration should not be shorter than two hours so as to avoid the frequent switching of the electricity price, and the total time of each time period of each day should not be less than 4 h, in order to stabilize that production condition of the user's life and enhance the influence of the peak-to-valley electricity price [11]. The total length of the daily peak, the level and the valley time is 8 h, and the peak and valley membership of each time can be in time according to the peak of each time. Divide the constraints and adjust the peak and valley periods for determining the daily load sequence.

The determination of peak-valley price includes two aspects: dividing the peak and valley time and determining the price standard of each time period. After dividing each time period of peak and level valley, it is necessary to adjust the original peak and valley electricity price according to the load capacity in different load value difference area [12]. Because the power users are all users in a certain area, the basic shape of the clustering load curve is similar. At the same time, the load value in the numerical difference region is obviously higher than that in the non-numerical difference area. Therefore, the greater the load value in the numerical difference area, the greater the difference between peak and valley electricity prices is needed to reduce the power supply pressure during the peak period of power consumption. To improve the demand response peak filling effect. Through large numbers According to the analysis, the peak price, the average price and the valley price of p_{po}, p_{fo} and p_{vo}, are called standard peak and valley price respectively, then the peak and valley price of the predicted day can be determined by formula (3).

$$\begin{bmatrix} p_{pnd} = p_{fo} + (p_{po} - p_{fo})s_{nd} \\ p_{fnd} = p_{fo} \\ p_{vnd} = p_{fo} - (p_{fo} - p_{vo})s_{nd} \end{bmatrix} \tag{3}$$

Among this, $p_{pnd}, p_{fnd}, p_{vnd}$ respectively representing the predicted daily peak and valley electricity prices; s_{nd} represents the standard value of the day load of the nd.

2.3 Realization of Demand Response Model of Electric Power Interruptible Load

The identification of user response parameters is introduced into the demand response model of interruptible load through dynamic peak-valley pricing. In order to make dynamic peak-valley electricity price, we should fully excavate and analyze the characteristics of user load, and introduce dynamic adjustment mechanism into peak-valley electricity price, so that we can better arouse the enthusiasm of user demand response. Based on big data analysis, it is necessary to accurately identify the user response parameters and determine the response degree of the user when dealing with the different price difference of power supply to establish the demand response model of electric power interruptible load. If the price difference between peak and valley electricity is relatively small, the economic benefit is not enough to guide users to change their power consumption habits, the demand response is weak, and the load transfer rate is low, even because of the influence of non-electricity price factors or the strong randomness of users, such as negative load clipping rate, this part is called "dead zone"; If the price difference between peak and valley is too large to break through the limit of user's electricity elasticity, the potential of user's demand response will not produce any other response after being fully excavated, that is, the electricity consumption has reached. To the range threshold, this part is called "saturation zone"; Only within a reasonable range between "dead zone" and "saturation zone" is the price difference between peak and valley electricity. Through a large amount of data in the power market, the load transfer rate and the price difference of the user's response can approximate the quasi-synthetic linear function, and the load transfer rate is positive. This part is called the "linear region". Based on big data's analysis, a demand response model of power interruptible load is established. For different types of users, there are great differences in response parameters. The model is suitable not only for comprehensive users, but also for each class of specific users with significant characteristics. And because of non-price factors, Under the influence of uncertain conditions such as prime, all load transfer rates of interruptible load are constrained by reasonable range of variation and have fuzzy properties.

3 Experimental Results and Analysis

In the course of the experiment, the power-interruptible load demand in a certain area is the experimental object, and the power-interruptible load demand in the area can be analyzed by the power-interruptible load demand response model based on the big data analysis. In order to ensure the effectiveness of the experiment, the traditional power-interruptible load demand response model is compared with the power-interruptible load demand response model based on big data analysis, and the experimental results are observed. This paper first describes the peak-valley membership degree of the predicted daily load curve by using the semi-trapezoidal membership function. However, according to the peak-valley membership degree value, there is ambiguity in the partition of the peak, flat and valley periods, so it is necessary to combine the specific period partition constraints. Determine the predicted day, peak and valley time. The actual load of a power network in a certain area is selected, and the peak and valley membership degree of each time point is calculated. According to the membership degree of peak and valley at each time point, the time period of the peak and valley is preliminarily divided, and it is found that all three time points of 1 h–9 h–(23 h) are single hour for normal period. 24 h is a single hour period. Frequent switching in different time periods can easily affect the life of users and make production stable. At the same time, it brings great challenges to the technology and facility level of time-sharing electricity price. Combined with time division constraints, the prediction of peak and valley time division is finally determined. Then, according to the load standard value of the day value difference area, the electricity price of all kinds of time periods and standard peak valley electricity price of the predicted day peak level valley are obtained. And the peak and valley electricity prices on the forecast day. By using the obtained results, the experimental parameters of the power interruptible load demand response model based on big data analysis are set up. Maximum positive load rate of Random response of users without Peak-Valley Price difference $\lambda_{0max} = 0.5\%$, Maximum negative load rate $\lambda_{0min} = -0.5\%$; Demand response load transfer response critical price difference a = 0.1YUAN; Demand response load transfer saturation critical price difference b = 0.8YUAN; Maximum power transfer rate in saturated area $\lambda_{1max} = 5\%$. Under the scheme of forecasting daily peak and valley electricity price, the demand response model of interruptible load based on big data and the traditional demand response model of power interruptible load are used to analyze the demand of interruptible load in this area. The analytical accuracy of the two is shown in Fig. 3.

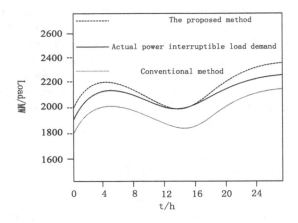

Fig. 3. Comparison of analytical accuracy

Figure 3 shows that, Using the power interruptible load demand response model based on big data analysis to analyze the power interruptible load demand in this area on the same day, compared with the traditional power interruptible load demand response model for the same day electric power demand response model in this area. The results of the analysis of interruptible load demand are closer to the actual power interruptible load demand on the same day in the region. That is, the accuracy of the analysis is higher.

4 Conduction

Using the interruptible load demand response model based on big data analysis, the analysis accuracy of the interruptible load demand can be improved, which has certain practicability and scalability. It plays an important role in improving the load curve and increasing the load rate, and can alleviate the power supply tension. Situation and improve the security of system operation.

References

1. Yang, X., Fan, Y., Yin, W.: Application of investment forecast model for power equipment replacement based on big data. East China Electr. Power **42**(10), 2002–2006 (2014)
2. Habibian, M., Zakeri, G., Downward, A., et al.: Co-optimization of demand response and interruptible load reserve offers for a price-making major consumer. Energy Syst. 1–27 (2017)
3. Yang, X., Wang, N., Yu, T., et al.: Research on real time price of electric vehicle and load demand management based on big data analysis. Hebei Electr. Power **22**(21), 324 (2018)
4. Xu, C., Zhao, H., Song, X.: Research on method of power user group identification and analysis based on large data. J. Zhengzhou Univ. (Nat. Sci. Ed.) **48**(3), 113–117 (2016)
5. Wang, F., Yanbo, Yu, J.: Design and implementation of power multidimensional analysis system based on big data. Electr. Power Inf. Commun. Technol. **15**(4), 30–35 (2017)
6. Wu, L., Chen, Q., Linghui, et al.: Application of power grid precision marketing based on large data analysis. Power Demand Side Manag. **50**(51), 437–439 (2016)
7. Li, J., Li, W., Li, H., et al.: Acquisition and application of big power data based on big data cloud platform. Electr. Meas. Instrum. **56**(12), 318–325 (2018)
8. Yang, F., Li, X., Pan, K., et al.: Operational efficiency evaluation of power supply business hall based on big data analysis. Electr. Power Inf. Commun. Technol. **15**(2), 118–123 (2017)
9. Liu, J., Luo, F., Liu, R., et al.: Study on application strategies of demand-side management under big data background. Power Demand Side Manag. **18**(22), 115–120 (2016)
10. Sousa, J., Saavedra, O.R., Lima, S.L.: Decision-making in emergency operation for power transformers with regard to risks and interruptible load contracts. IEEE Trans. Power Deliv. **2**(9), 11–17 (2017)
11. Chaudhary, R., Aujla, G.S., Kumar, N., et al.: Optimized big data management across multi-cloud data centers: software-defined-network-based analysis. IEEE Commun. Mag. **56**(2), 118–126 (2018)
12. Chen, S.-F., Gu, H., Tu, M.-Y., et al.: Robust variable selection based on bagging classification tree for support vector machine in metabonomic data analysis. J. Chemom. **32**(11), 2921–2927 (2017)

Research on Interruptible Scheduling Algorithm of Central Air Conditioning Load Under Big Data Analysis

Cheng-liang Wang[1] and Yong-biao Yang[2(✉)]

[1] Jiangsu Fangtian Power Technology Co., Ltd., Nanjing, China
[2] Southeast University, Nanjing, China
lxxl80112@163.com

Abstract. The traditional algorithm is a combination of fuzzy dynamic programming and priority-based heuristic rules. The optimization performance of interruptible load scheduling is poor. For this reason, the central air conditioning load interruptible scheduling algorithm is proposed based on big data analysis. The algorithm adopts the characteristics of central air conditioning load management and selects the time scale of central air conditioning load scheduling. By optimizing the flexibility of interruptible scheduling, based on the central air conditioning load interruptible scheduling model, the optimal individual in the last generation population is decoded by binary coding, so as to realize the central air conditioning load interruptible scheduling algorithm. The experiment proves that the central air conditioning load interruptible scheduling algorithm has strong optimization performance.

Keywords: Optimized scheduling strategy · Time dimension · Interrupt load · Internal gene

1 Introduction

Central air conditioning load management is one of the core research contents of interruptible load. Domestic and foreign scholars have conducted in-depth research on the optimal scheduling strategy for interruptible load. Some researches on scheduling strategy algorithms use traditional optimization algorithms to establish a model combining fuzzy dynamic programming with priority-based heuristic rules. The adaptive system is used to solve the problem of interruptible load optimization scheduling. By adding the model reference adaptive system, the influence of load prediction error on interruptible load scheduling can be considered. Based on the optimal power flow framework, an algorithm for interruptible scheduling of central air conditioning load under big data analysis is proposed. It aims at solving the central air-conditioning load interruptible scheduling model with the minimum total system cost as the target, and can obtain the active shadow price and the interrupted load electricity price and interruption amount of each node. It also analyzes the impact of shadow electricity prices and interruptible electricity prices on the total cost of the system, but the essence

G. Gui and L. Yun (Eds.): ADHIP 2019, LNICST 301, pp. 346–354, 2019.
https://doi.org/10.1007/978-3-030-36402-1_37

is that it can interrupt the scheduling calculation problem. An interruptible load scheduling model that considers the impact of real-time electricity prices during peak power demand, taking into account the impact of power system network losses. The scheduling target comprehensively considers the minimum of the interruptible load cost and the network loss cost purchased by the grid company, and optimizes the scheduling of the interruptible load by using the queuing method. Although the central air conditioning load interruptible scheduling model can reduce the economic benefits brought by network loss, its constraint on interruptible load is simpler [1].

2 Central Air Conditioning Load Interruptible Scheduling Algorithm

2.1 Central Air Conditioning Load Scheduling Selection

Scheduling the interruptible load depends on the results of load forecasting and the estimation of the system side output. The prediction accuracy of the two is inversely proportional to the pre-calculation time, that is, the longer the pre-calculation time, the worse the prediction accuracy is. According to the above characteristics, this paper decomposes the interruptible load scheduling into three time scales before, before and after the time dimension. The interruptible load scheduling at different time scales can be coordinated with each other. Multi-time scale interruptible load coordination optimization scheduling through the coordinated coordination of interruptible load scheduling at different time scales, the error of scheduling requirements is gradually refined. The error caused by the previous time scale is corrected by the scheduling scheme of the next time scale to improve the accuracy and adaptability of the scheduling scheme [2].

According to the concept of multi-time scale interruptible load coordination optimization scheduling mode, the interruptible load contracts are divided into the following three categories according to the difference of advance notice time and minimum interruption duration at different time scales: Type A: Type A interruptible load users are mainly involved in the pre-monthly plan, including two types: the first type is the interruptible load rotation type contract. This kind of contract scheduling is set on a weekly basis, and the user is set a reference date of seven days a week according to the user's production scheduling habits. According to the dispatching instructions of several stops per week, the user will arrange the rotation of the production plan according to the base date and stop production within the specified time period to reduce the power load. The second type is an interruptible load monthly reduction contract. This type of contract is scheduled to be reduced in part by the specified time period within the specified time period of the request interruption according to the dispatch instruction to reduce the partial power load [3]. Considering that users need to adjust their production schedules, the advance notice time is usually half a month. Type B: Type B contract users are mainly involved in the day-to-day plan. The advance notice time is 24 h, taking into account the time interval from the day before the day before the scheduled dispatch to the next day. The minimum interruption duration is specified for specific users according to different industry production characteristics. The minimum interruption duration of each user is generally not less than 2 h. Type C: Type C contract users are mainly involved in emergency planning, and the advance notice time is 2 h. This type of contract is mainly based on reliability, and its minimum interruption duration is generally short, generally not less than 0.5 h. It mainly deals with emergency power shortage caused by faults in the power grid [4].

In the interruptible load scheduling of the central air conditioning load, the excitation method with high compensation for interrupted power is used. Since the monthly, the day and the emergency advance notice time are different, the unit price of the interrupted load interruption power compensation is also increased accordingly. The monthly plan is notified in advance, and the user has sufficient time to adjust the production schedule. Therefore, the unit price of the interruption compensation is the lowest. The users participating in the monthly plan can make certain adjustments according to the nature of the industry. The planned early notice time is shorter, so the user's interrupt compensation unit price is higher than the monthly plan. In addition, the difference in user interruption characteristics will also affect the cost of the interruptible load [5]. Studies have shown that the unit time interruption load cost and power outage duration decrease exponentially, that is, users who are also involved in the planned day, the longer the minimum interruption duration, the lower the cost of participating in the interruptible load. From a power company perspective, interruptible load scheduling with smaller interrupt durations and interruption intervals is more flexible. Therefore, under the same advance notice time, the longer the general interruption duration and the longer the interruption interval, the lower the interruption compensation cost. The emergency plan has the shortest notice time in advance, and the user response is high, the interruption reliability is strong, and the compensation unit price is the highest in the three time scales. Different users can also give different interrupt compensation unit price according to the difference of the degree of interruption reliability, and give higher interrupt compensation to users with high reliability, so as to encourage other low-reliability users to improve their reliability [6].

The interruptible load dispatching mode of central air-conditioning load management relies on a more economical monthly plan to limit the long-term load peak. Sacrificing part of the economy in the event of a grid emergency, using a more reliable emergency plan to ensure the safe and stable operation of the grid. As a scheduling mode with more balanced economy and reliability, the plan to link the monthly plan with the emergency plan is an important part of the central air-conditioning load interruptible load. The interruptible load of the central air-conditioning load management is coordinated and complemented, and the coordination and unification of the economic and reliability of the interruptible load dispatching is realized. So far, the construction of the central air conditioning load interruptible scheduling model is completed [7].

2.2   Modeling of Interruptible Scheduling Algorithms

The central air-conditioning load interruptible load dispatching is based on the fact that the user has signed an interruptible load contract with the user. According to the interrupt characteristics of different users, the user's interrupt scheduling is optimized, and the best economy is achieved under the premise of meeting the load dispatching requirements. In the multi-time scale interruptible load optimization scheduling model, the monthly and pre-planning scheduling model is a single-objective optimization problem, and the multi-objective function of the emergency planning scheduling is also transformed into a single-objective optimization problem after being processed. In addition to the user's interrupt capacity and interrupt price, the interruptible load scheduling needs to consider constraints such as the interrupt duration and interruption interval of each interruptible load user. This makes the optimization problem a relatively complex discrete non-convex function optimization problem [8].

This design uses genetic algorithm to solve the interruptible load scheduling problem of central air conditioning load, and the calculation process of each algorithm is described [9].

Genetic algorithms attempt to search for the optimal solution to a problem by simulating the evolution of a population. A population represents a set of solutions to the optimization problem, which consists of a number of genetically encoded numbers. A chromosome is the main carrier of genetic material in each individual, and its internal representation is a combination of genes that determines the external manifestation of the individual. Therefore, the use of genetic algorithms to solve problems requires mapping the external representation of the problem's potential solution set to its internal genes through coding work. After genetically encoding the first generation of population, according to the principle of survival of the fittest and the survival of the fittest in nature. Individuals are selected according to the degree of fitness of each individual in the population, and the genetic operators of natural genetics are used to combine and mutate the genes among individuals in the population. This process will lead to a population of natural evolution like the Miocene population is more adaptable to the environment than the previous generation and evolved better and better approximate solutions [10]. Because the work of gene encoding is complex, and to meet the completeness, soundness and non-redundant coding specifications, we often use binary coding to simplify. The optimal individual in the last generation population is decoded, which can be used as the approximate optimal solution of the problem. The flow chart of the genetic algorithm is as follows (Fig. 1);

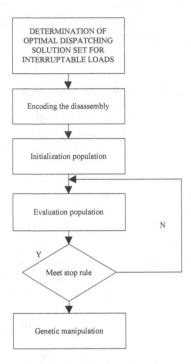

Fig. 1. Genetic algorithm flow

2.3   Implementation of Interruptible Scheduling Algorithm

With binary coding, the load interruption amount needs to be converted into a binary number for encoding. According to different ideas, two encoding methods can be used to encode it. The coding formula is as follows;

$$l_m = \frac{0102.\dots\dots b}{1111.\dots\dots b(a_i)} \times (l_{\min} - l_{i\min}) \tag{1}$$

In the formula (1), l represents the maximum value of the load amount, b represents the minimum value of the load amount, and a represents the number of codes. The advantage of this coding method is that the number of bits can be fixed, the coding is simple, and the data accuracy can be adjusted by the number of code bits [11]. The disadvantage is that if the fixed number of bits is small, there are cases where the optimization result is relatively rough.

The purpose of the interruptible load scheduling monthly plan is to minimize the scheduling compensation cost of the interruptible load on the premise of satisfying various constraints. The final fitness function formula is as follows:

$$g(t) = \frac{h}{\left(\sum_{e}^{m} [x(i,l)] \times [o(l)]\right)} \tag{2}$$

In the formula (2), g represents a constant, t represents a reduction amount, i represents a user, x represents a period number, o represents a penalty coefficient, and h represents a separation distance. The purpose of the interruptible load dispatch emergency plan is to pursue optimal economic performance on the basis of ensuring reliability. The fitness function adopted is as follows:

$$l_k = [x(i, l)] + [j(i_1 + l_2)] \tag{3}$$

In the formula (3), l represents the interrupt compensation amount, x represents the penalty coefficient, and i represents the reliability coefficient.

Regional minimum load reduction formula:

$$\sum_{m}^{n} t_{\min}(u) \Delta j_{\min} \geq o \tag{4}$$

In formula (4), t represents the demand reduction, and j represents the reduction amount. The user interruption amount constraint formula is obtained based on formula (4), and the formula is as follows;

$$y(b) \Delta v_{\min} \geq o \tag{5}$$

In formula (5), y indicates that the interrupt amount is met, and v indicates the minimum interrupt load amount. Based on the ultra-short-term load forecast, the short-time scale error correction is implemented.

The calculation result is obtained after the load scheduling task is satisfied or all interruptable load users are selected according to the sequence, and the scheduled interruptible load is statistically output. The interruptible scheduling algorithm is a bionic algorithm. The advantage is that the running process is simple, and it is easy to combine the objective function and constraints with high complexity. Moreover, the weighting of the penalty function in the constraint is set to meet different needs. For some complex optimization problems, some non-hard constraints can be ignored to achieve the purpose of solving the main problem.

Figure 2 is an interruptible scheduling algorithm that sorts the interruptible loads in order of priority. In the monthly plan and the current plan, the scheduling target is based on economy, and the system sorts the interruptible loads according to the interrupt compensation unit price of each interruptible load. In the emergency plan, the scheduling target is based on reliability and economical. The system sorts the reliability index of each interruptible load and the weighting coefficient of the interrupt compensation unit price. According to the order, the interruptible load is interrupted, and after each interruptable load is selected according to the priority order. The interruptible load is scheduled to be interrupted according to the completion of the load scheduling demand

and the interrupt limit condition for selecting the interruptible load. At this point, the central air conditioning load interruptable scheduling algorithm is implemented.

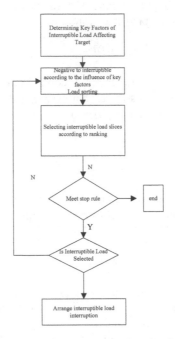

Fig. 2. Interruptible scheduling algorithm

3   Experimental Results

In order to verify the effectiveness of the central air conditioning load interruptible scheduling algorithm under big data analysis, the business solution software was used for calculation. The central air conditioning load interruptible load optimization scheduling problem is essentially a mixed integer programming problem. For such problems, the branch and bound method is generally used to solve the problem. By implicitly enumerating all possible combinations, the optimal solution of the problem can be obtained theoretically. Later, with the development of the theory of operations research, the cutting plane method was produced. Its core idea is to dynamically add the cutting plane constraint in the process of finding the optimal, and to cut off the area in the feasible domain that does not contain the integer feasible solution, and speed up the calculation process. By combining the branch and bound method with the cutting plane method, the branching plane method is formed, which greatly improves the efficiency of the mixed integer programming. The experimental data is selected as follows:

Table 1. Experimental data

Time	Hourly interrupt capacity	Actual interruption	Excess interruption
1	123	2354	3864
2	246	4579	348
3	365	479	358
4	525	5469	358
5	367	358	579
6	375	3534	382

Table 1 is the experimentally selected data, and the central air conditioning load interruptible scheduling algorithm under the big data analysis is tested. The experimental results are as follows:

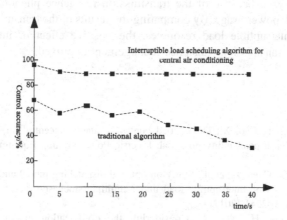

Fig. 3. Comparison of experimental results

Figure 3 is the experimental results. It can be seen that by comparing the optimization function of the central air-conditioning load interruptible scheduling algorithm under the traditional algorithm and big data analysis, the algorithm of this design has certain superiority. Traditional algorithms that minimize the number of interruptions can result in increased costs. As can be seen from Fig. 3, for some loads, the number of constraints is increased compared to the number of unconstrained interrupts. This is because the goal of the central air conditioning load interruptible scheduling algorithm is to minimize the overall system outage cost, rather than maximizing the economic compensation for individual loads. Therefore, some loads can be interrupted multiple times instead of other load interruptions to achieve the system's total number of interruptions and minimum interruption costs. The experiment proves that the central air conditioning load interruptible scheduling algorithm has a strong optimization function.

4 Conclusion

The central air-conditioning load interruptible scheduling algorithm based on big data analysis analyzes the application of the central air-conditioning load interruptible load and the continuous shortage of power system peak power consumption in the grid can reduce the power demand during the peak period of the power grid by coordinating the interrupted load dispatching on an emergency time scale one month ago, thereby ensuring the safe and stable operation of the power grid. In the power market where the interruptable load development is more mature, some high-cost peak-shaving unit output can be replaced by purchasing part of the interruptible load resources. The day-to-day economic dispatching link on the power generation side is transformed into a coordinated optimization economic dispatch of the generator set and the interruptible load, thereby reducing the marginal cost of the entire power grid purchase. Considering the network constraints, the limitations of traditional power transmission plug management are analyzed because of the transmission resistance phenomenon that may occur during peak power usage. By comparing the results of the transmission resistance plugging with interruptible load resources, the positive effect of interruptible load resources on the transmission resistance management is proved.

References

1. Zhu, Y., Wang, J., Cao, X.: Direct load control strategy of central air conditioning and evaluation of its dispatchability potential. Electric Power Autom. Equipment **22**(5), 1232–1245 (2018)
2. Ai, X., Zhou, S., Chen, Z., et al.: Study on optimal dispatching model and solution method of power system with interruptible load under multiple stochastic factors. China J. Electr. Eng. **37**(8), 2231–2241 (2017)
3. Yang, K., Wang, H., Xia, N.: Considering the optimization model of backup with interruptible load in practical engineering environment. Power Grid Clean Energy **33**(4), 248–256 (2017)
4. Gao, Z., Zhang, L., Yang, X.: Research on load aggregation of central air conditioning and suppression of wind power output fluctuation. Chin. J. Electr. Eng. **37**(11), 3184–3191 (2017)
5. Chen, H., He, X., Jiang, T., et al.: Available transmission capacity calculation of power system considering interruptible load. Power Syst. Autom. **41**(15), 2281–2287 (2017)
6. Chen, Z., Cui, W.H., et al.: Comments on the research and practice of interruptible load in market environment. DSM **19**(1), 226–230 (2017)
7. Li, J.: Application and benefit analysis of interruptible load in DSM. Ind. Technol. Innovation **23**(2), 153–155 (2017)
8. Jiang, J.T., Wang, Y., et al.: Research on navigation and scheduling algorithm for type II tasks of digital human-machine interface in nuclear power plant. Nucl. Power Eng. **33**(1), 1452–1456 (2018)
9. Yang, X., Li, W., Hu, X.: Cost calculation and benefit analysis of interruptible load for single industrial consumer. Value Eng. **36**(4), 235–237 (2017)
10. Li, Z., Yang, B., Yang, Y., et al.: Peak shaving method for large-scale central air conditioning based on day-ahead dispatch. South. Power Grid Technol. **11**(1), 2274–2279 (2017)
11. Yu, G.: Improvement of a large-scale network data caching method. J. Xi'an Polytechnic Univ. **4**, 504–509 2016

Simulation Study on Pedestrian Road Planning in Ancient Building Groups Under Cloud Computing Environment

En-mao Qiao[1(✉)] and Da-wei Shang[2]

[1] Decoration and Art Design College,
Inner Mongolia Technical College of Construction, Hohhot, China
sunyixi589@163.com
[2] Architecture and Planning College,
Inner Mongolia Technical College of Construction, Hohhot, China

Abstract. In order to guide the traffic organization in the ancient building group in an orderly manner, the simulation study on the pedestrian road planning of the ancient building group in the cloud computing environment is proposed. Based on the analysis of the characteristics of pedestrian roads, a cloud computing environment road planning simulation model is established. Using the cloud computing environment to determine the maximum number of people on the road, use the simulation software LEGION to set the structure and parameters of the model, and carry out road planning and deduction in the simulator to realize the design of the road planning simulation model. Through the method of experimental argumentation and analysis, the effectiveness of the cloud computing environment road planning simulation model is determined, which can improve the order planning of pedestrians' road planning.

Keywords: Cloud computing environment · Ancient building complex area · Road planning · Simulation model

1 Introduction

With the vigorous development of China's tourism industry, the area of ancient buildings and antique buildings has been favoured by more and more tourists, and has become a hot development area for China's tourism industry [1]. The buildings are closely connected, the roads are narrow and the steps are all over. Due to the limitations of many limitations, in the event of a dangerous accident, the traffic organization in the ancient building complex area is difficult to obtain effective control. It in turn led to traffic congestion in the ancient building complex area, and even caused casualties such as trampling.

Cloud computing is a model of the addition, use, and delivery of Internet-based related services, often involving the provision of dynamically scalable and often virtualized resources over the Internet. In the past, the cloud was used to represent the

© ICST Institute for Computer Sciences, Social Informatics and Telecommunications Engineering 2019
Published by Springer Nature Switzerland AG 2019. All Rights Reserved
G. Gui and L. Yun (Eds.): ADHIP 2019, LNICST 301, pp. 355–363, 2019.
https://doi.org/10.1007/978-3-030-36402-1_38

telecommunication network, and later used to represent the abstraction of the Internet and the underlying infrastructure. Therefore, in the cloud computing environment, you can even experience 10 trillion operations per second, and have strong computing power, which can simulate the trend of nuclear explosion, forecasting climate change and market development [2]. Literature [3] proposed the pedestrian road friendliness evaluation based on attribute measure. By constructing the index system of pedestrian environmental friendliness evaluation, the optimal planning of pedestrian road is realized by classifying the road planning samples with the principle of attribute measure. But the planning effect of this method is not ideal. Therefore, how to apply the cloud computing environment to the pedestrian road planning and simulation in the ancient building group in an optimal way has become a new direction for scholars.

This paper proposes a simulation study of pedestrian road planning in ancient buildings based on cloud computing environment. The results show that the road planning simulation model based on cloud computing environment can effectively guide the pedestrian traffic in the ancient building complex area, ensuring smooth pedestrian traffic and high efficiency.

2   Analysis of Pedestrian Traffic Characteristics

In the current pedestrian traffic environment in the ancient building complex area, the situation of pedestrians crossing the street is relatively poor, and has not yet become the focus of relevant laws and regulations and traffic management policies [3]. Assuming that the intervening gap of the pedestrian road is S_k and the speed of the incoming vehicle is X_k, the function expression of pedestrian traffic is:

$$X'_{ik} = \frac{X_{ik} - X_k}{S_k} \tag{1}$$

Where X'_{ik} represents the pedestrian pass probability; X_{ik} represents the walking gap of the pedestrian, and X_{ik} is a constant, usually $X_{ik} = \{1+i, 2+i, 3+i, \cdots, k+i\}$.

In addition, the individual differences of pedestrians are also the main factors affecting the changes of pedestrians' road characteristics, including the gender, age, personality, education level, group relationship, and cognitive level of pedestrians [4].

At the same time, the number of tourists in the scenic spot, the passage of the road, and the capacity of the ancient building complex area [5] are also the most important factors affecting the sharp increase in the characteristics of pedestrians. The factors influencing the capacity of the ancient buildings are the narrow tortuosity of the ancient buildings, the number of steps, the obstruction of the pedestrian's visual field, and the judgment of the road ahead. They all have a significant impact on the pedestrian road characteristics.

3 Establishment of Cloud Computing Environment Road Planning Simulation Model

Simulate the most complex scenic spots of pedestrian crossings in the ancient building complex area, located in the middle of the model. In addition, considering the characteristics of tourist traffic, terrain, steps, roads, etc., the optimal planning path of the model is judged [6]. The cloud computing environment road planning simulation model structure is shown in Fig. 1.

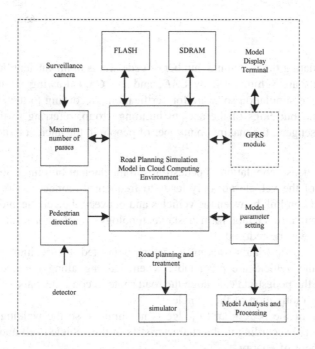

Fig. 1. Cloud computing environment road planning simulation model structure

3.1 Determine the Maximum Number of People

According to the principle of human flow density [7], the number of predicted pedestrians in the ancient building group area is determined. Combined with the functional expression [8] of the characteristics of pedestrian traffic, the maximum pedestrian density value of the pedestrian road in the ancient building group area is calculated. Among them, the pedestrian passing road feature X'_{ik} is set to a fixed value of $12\ m^2/R$, and the maximum number of pedestrians passing through the ancient building group area is shown in Table 1.

Table 1. Maximum number of passengers

Fork setting	Pedestrian area/m^2	Admissible population density/person $\cdot (m^2)^{-1}$	Maximum number of passes
Fork road 1	755	4.1	3009
Fork road 2	552	6.3	25980
Fork road 3	1135	2.5	3655
Fork road 4	281	2.7	5869
Fork road 5	281	5.9	15265
Fork road 6	569	2.1	1425
Fork road 7	785	4.5	6557

After calculating the maximum number of pedestrians in the ancient building group area, the results are summarized by *CAD*, and the *CAD* drawing is simplified and imported into the simulation software for verification. According to the characteristics of the steps and buildings of the ancient building group, referring to the maximum number of passengers, the maximum number of people in the ancient building group is obtained:

(1) Due to the dense population of pedestrians in the ancient buildings, the high-speed operation of the vehicle not only leads to frequent disconnection of the wireless communication link between the vehicles and between the vehicle and the roadside unit [9], but also cannot form a stable topology, so the maximum number of passengers will be reduced.

(2) Because the pedestrian's walking trajectory is limited, the position, direction and speed of the vehicle are predictable when walking along the pedestrian road. Therefore, the pedestrian can judge the road route to continue walking according to the driving motivation of the vehicle.

(3) The ability of the pedestrian to judge is not limited, so the walking path can be freely selected according to the characteristics of the vehicle itself and the constant replenishment of energy.

(4) Set up a global positioning system in the area of ancient buildings to accurately locate the boundaries and extension standards of roads. Under the premise of satisfying the characteristics of the maximum number of passengers, the pedestrians are provided with relevant information such as the speed and position of the vehicles, thereby ensuring the maximum number of pedestrians in the pedestrian passages in the ancient building group area.

After determining the maximum number of people in the ancient building group area, the rationality of the maximum number of people is guaranteed, and data preparation is provided for the parameter setting of the next pedestrian road planning simulation model.

3.2 Road Planning Simulation Model Parameter Setting

Pedestrian road planning modeling using traffic simulation software LEGION [10]. In this paper, the intersections in the road network are regarded as one node, each road is regarded as the connection between two nodes, and the whole road network is abstracted into a directed network diagram composed of points and connections. Therefore, this paper adopts the adjacency matrix to express the relationship between each node in the entire road network and each node and the connection. The traffic path in each pedestrian network in this paper stores two parameters, namely speed parameter and weight parameter.

The speed parameter stores the time of the average pedestrian travel speed information of the road segments existing in the entire road network [11]. Before the pedestrian enters the road network, the speed parameter needs to be initialized, and the maximum speed allowed by the given road segment is given. The unconnected road in the road network is given an initial speed of zero. After the pedestrian enters the road network, it receives the information transmitted by other pedestrians in the road network, and updates the real-time information to its own speed parameter according to the comparison time stamp. The pedestrian speed parameter matrix is as follows:

$$\tau = \begin{bmatrix} \sigma_1^2 & 5 & 4 & 3 & 2 & 1 & 0 \\ X_{1ik} & \sigma_1^2 & & & & x_1 & \\ & X_{2ik} & \cdots & & & & \\ & & X_{3ik} & \sigma_3^2 & & & \\ & & & X_{4ik} & \sigma_3^2 & & \\ & x_1 & & & X_{5ik} & \sigma_a^2 & \\ 0 & 1 & 2 & 3 & 4 & X_{6ik} & \sigma_a^2 \end{bmatrix} \tag{2}$$

Where τ represents the speed parameter of the pedestrian; $X_{1ik} \sim X_{6ik}$ represent the walking gap of the pedestrian; $\sigma_1^2 \sim \sigma_a^2$ represent the road bearing matrix during pedestrian travel; x_1 represents the average displacement of the pedestrian walking; wherein 0 to 5 are constant parameters.

The weight parameter is the weight of the road segment that exists in the entire road network. In this paper, due to the cloud computing environment [12], the weight value is affected by factors such as the length of the road segment, the congestion degree of the road segment and the maximum number of people on the road segment. Therefore, the weight parameter changes due to the change of the speed parameter. The weight parameter matrix of the road is as follows:

$$T_x = \left(A^T/Y^{-1}\right)^{-2} = \begin{Bmatrix} X_{11}, X_{1n} \in A^T \\ X_{n1}, X_{nn} \in Y \end{Bmatrix} \quad T_x = \left(A^T/Y^{-1}\right)^{-2} = \begin{Bmatrix} X_{11}, X_{1n} \in A^T \\ X_{n1}, X_{nn} \in Y \end{Bmatrix} \tag{3}$$

Where T_x represents the weight parameter of the road; A^T represents the weight change in time T; Y^{-1} represents the weight feature of the control center; X_{11} represents the pedestrian pass value; X_{1n} represents the communication weight; X_{n1} represents the road node weight; X_{nn} represents the weight of all road nodes.

The speed and weight parameters provide an intuitive way to collect road planning data and ensure that the most up-to-date data information is always stored for each location, preparing for the simulation of the road plan.

3.3   Road Planning Simulation Model Implementation

Apply the speed parameters and weight parameters of the road planning simulation model to the model realization process, and select SUMO as the traffic system simulation software SUMO C Simulation of Urban Mobility [13]. It is used as a time-discrete, spatially continuous pedestrian road planning system simulator. The implementation process is as follows:

Cloud computing environment road planning simulation model The topological relationship between roads is represented by virtual road segments within the virtual node. The virtual road segment contains the distance damping information such as distance damping information and signal time damping information when crossing the intersection, and the matrix relationship is as follows:

$$V = \sum_{W}^{B} \frac{1}{n} \tag{4}$$

Where V represents the matrix relationship between the segments; n represents the virtual segment information.

Set the road segment numbers to 30 roads, 305 roads, 408 roads, and 503 roads. By analyzing the road segments, vertices and polylines of the virtual nodes, the topological relationship between the nodes and the termination nodes is judged, and the spatial coordinates of the road planning simulation model of the cloud computing environment are established.

According to the cloud computing environment road planning simulation model, the detailed description of the actual traffic environment is different, and it is divided into microscopic simulation, mesoscopic simulation and macroscopic simulation. These three simulation techniques are applied to the model implementation process to track the planning of 30 roads, 305 roads, 408 roads, and 503 roads.

First, the static road network data information is read, including the distance between each node in the road network, the maximum traffic speed information allowed by the road segment, and the traffic congestion fee charge of the road segment, and the initial weight is calculated comprehensively. Then, based on the calculated initial weight, the weight of the road network is calculated again using a dynamic path planning algorithm based on the travel cost. Then when the vehicle continuously receives the speed information, the weight of the road network is recalculated. Repeat the above steps until the vehicle reaches the destination node, that is, the planning process for the pedestrian road is completed.

The cloud computing environment road planning simulation model is used to carry out the planning and deduction of pedestrian roads in the ancient building group area in the simulator to ensure the feasibility and effectiveness of the cloud computing environment road planning simulation model designed in this paper. So far, the road model simulation model design for the cloud computing environment is completed.

4 Simulation Experiment Demonstration and Analysis

In order to ensure the effectiveness of the road planning simulation model of the cloud computing environment designed in this paper, the simulation experiment demonstration analysis is carried out.

The experimental process is carried out in the traffic simulation software *LEGION*. The experimental object is set as a pedestrian road in an ancient building group, and the simulation and demonstration experiments are carried out. During the experiment, the arrangement of pedestrians in an ancient building group is shown in Fig. 2.

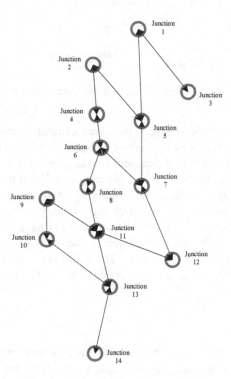

Fig. 2. Pedestrian road arrangement

In order to ensure the effectiveness of the experiment, the traditional road planning simulation model and the cloud computing environment road planning simulation model are used for comparison experiments, and the road planning quality of the two models is statistically calculated. Since the quality of road planning is not statistical, the road planning congestion rate is used as a measure of planning quality. The higher the road planning congestion rate, the lower the road planning quality; Conversely, the lower the road planning congestion rate, the higher the road planning quality. The experimental results are shown in Fig. 3.

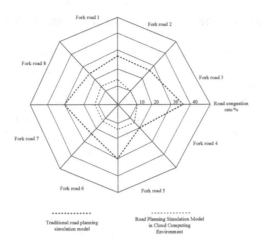

Fig. 3. Comparison of experimental argumentation results

According to the analysis of Fig. 3, the cloud computing environment road planning simulation model has a road planning congestion rate of less than 20% when planning the pedestrian roads in the ancient building group. However, the road planning crowding rate of the traditional road planning simulation model is about 40%, so we can see the advantages of the cloud computing environment road planning simulation model designed in this paper to improve the quality of road planning. When the cloud computing environment road planning simulation model is used for road planning, the planning is stable, and the location of the intersection Sect. 3 is consistent with the standard road planning model. The advantages of the cloud computing environment road planning simulation model designed in this paper can be seen more.

5   Conclusion

This paper studies and designs the pedestrian road planning simulation of the ancient buildings in the cloud computing environment, and analyzes the characteristics of the pedestrian roads in the ancient buildings based on the advantages of the cloud computing environment. On this basis, the simulation model of the pedestrian road planning for cloud computing environment is constructed. First determine the maximum number of people on the road, and then elaborate on the structure and parameter settings of the model. Finally, the cloud computing environment descendant road planning simulation model is simulated in the simulator to realize the design of this paper. The experimental results show that the cloud computing environment designed for pedestrian downlink road planning simulation model is extremely effective. When planning the pedestrian roads in the ancient buildings, it can greatly improve the planning quality of pedestrians, and can effectively reduce the simulation errors of road planning, save planning time, and improve the tourism economic benefits of ancient buildings. It is hoped that the research in this paper can provide theoretical basis and reference for the planning and design of pedestrian roads in China's ancient buildings.

Acknowledgments. 1. Research on the Classification, Conservation and Utilization of Historic buildings and blocks, supported by the Scientific Research Grant Project of institutions of higher Learning in Inner Mongolia Autonomous region (Project Plan No. NJZY18255).

2. Research on adaptation Strategy of Rural Housing in Hohhot, a scientific research grant project for colleges and universities in Inner Mongolia Autonomous region (Project Plan No. NJZY18257).

3. Study on the Conservation and Utilization in the Planning of Historic blocks in the Desert-Southern Mongolia area-taking Wulanchabu area as an example (Grant No: 18NDXT02).

This achievement is supported by the Cooperative Innovation Center for Cultural inheritance and Development of Mongolian and Northern Minority nationalities in Inner Mongolia Autonomous region.

References

1. Zhang, Y., Wang, X., Liu, X., et al.: Summary of cloud computing environmental security. J. Softw. **27**(6), 1328–1348 (2016)
2. Gazilla, H.: Data security in large data cloud computing environment. Electron. Technol. Softw. Eng. **52**(15), 173–174 (2017)
3. Sun, S.: Evaluation of pedestrian road friendliness based on attribute measure. Stat. Decis. **1**, 56–59 (2017)
4. Su, J.: Discussing the design of landscape roads in landscape planning. China Sci. Technol. Investment **52**(29), 101–103 (2016)
5. Yuan, J.: Pedestrian traffic flow model and road section performance evaluation method. Hunan Traff. Sci. Technol. **42**(3), 198–200 (2016)
6. Hong, Y., Ye, P., Zhu, C., et al.: Research on pedestrian traffic prediction in nanning garden expo. Prose Baijia (New Lang. Loop Page) **65**(4), 89–91 (2016)
7. Tian, C.: Analysis of key issues to be considered in the planning and design of municipal roads. Archit. Eng. Technol. Des. **56**(8), 203–205 (2016)
8. Su, S., He, L.: Transient dynamic congestion evacuation model for pedestrians at pedestrian traffic planning intersection. J. Jilin Univ. (Eng. Ed.) **48**(2), 440–447 (2018)
9. Li, J.: Probe into urban road traffic planning and design. Commod. Qual. **17**(6), 49–51 (2016)
10. Li, J.: Strategies on urban traffic road planning and design. Charm China **19**(31), 91–92 (2016)
11. Kong, A.: A brief talk on planning and design of urban pedestrian stereo crossing road—taking planning and design of pedestrian stereo crossing road in Shaoxing City as an example. Eng. Constr. Des. **36**(6), 52–56 (2018)
12. Luo, C.: Planning for the protection of ancient buildings in urban development—taking the planning for the protection of ancient buildings in Zhoucun street as an example. Eng. Technol.: Citation Ed. **10**(2), 103–105 (2017)
13. Li, Y.: Non-continuous hierarchical data mining method based on cloud computing. J. Xi'an Polytech. Univ. **4**, 498–503 (2017)
14. Yin, H.: Numerical simulation of pedestrian wind environment in high-rise buildings. Urban Build. **26**(2), 215–217 (2017)

Design of 3D Reconstruction Model
of Complex Surfaces of Ancient Buildings
Based on Big Data

Enmao Qiao[1](✉) and Dawei Shang[2]

[1] Inner Mongolia Technical College of Construction,
Decoration and Art Design College, Hohhot, China
sunyixi589@163.com
[2] Inner Mongolia Technical College of Construction,
Architecture and Planning College, Hohhot, China

Abstract. Over time, ancient buildings have remained in the natural environment for a long time, and damage often occurs. Therefore, in order to protect the cultural heritage of these materials, repair work is essential. Under this background, a three-dimensional construction method of complex curved surface of ancient buildings based on big data is proposed to complete the three-dimensional modeling of ancient buildings. The model construction is mainly divided into three steps: the first step uses LiDAR to obtain the LiDAR point cloud data and image data of the complex surface of the ancient building; the second step processes the data, including the processing of LiDAR point cloud data and the processing of image data; The method combines LiDAR point cloud data with image data to automatically generate a three-dimensional model of complex curved surface of ancient buildings. The results show that compared with the other two traditional methods, the accuracy of the method is higher, and the model coordinate points are closer to the real coordinates.

Keywords: Big data · Ancient architecture · Complex surface ·
Three-dimensional reconstruction model · Lidar

1 Introduction

China has a history of more than 5,000 years and its cultural heritage is profound. Therefore, the ancients have left us with many cultural heritages, which are precious treasures of mankind. Cultural heritage is divided into physical cultural heritage (tangible cultural heritage) and intangible cultural heritage (intangible cultural heritage). The material cultural heritage refers to cultural relics of historical, artistic and scientific value, including historical relics and ancient buildings. Human cultural sites have been preserved to the present, and have become invaluable treasures in China. However, with the passage of time and the influence of human natural activities and the environment, many material cultural heritages have been seriously damaged, especially ancient buildings. The ancient buildings have been exposed to the external environment

© ICST Institute for Computer Sciences, Social Informatics and Telecommunications Engineering 2019
Published by Springer Nature Switzerland AG 2019. All Rights Reserved
G. Gui and L. Yun (Eds.): ADHIP 2019, LNICST 301, pp. 364–373, 2019.
https://doi.org/10.1007/978-3-030-36402-1_39

for a long time. They are more seriously eroded by the rain, snow and wind. The outer ones are damaged, broken, and collapsed. They are gradually annihilated in the long river of history. Only the 12th and 2nd ancient buildings survived. The typical is the Forbidden City in Beijing. The Forbidden City in Beijing is the royal palace of the Ming and Qing Dynasties in China. It is located in the center of Beijing's central axis and is the essence of ancient Chinese palace architecture. But the Palace Museum we see now is not the original Forbidden City form, but has been modernized [1]. In order to preserve this great building, the country will invest a lot of money and dispatch professionals to repair the Forbidden City every year. The maintenance of ancient buildings is not a simple task, because the construction of ancient buildings is different from that of modern buildings. Therefore, maintenance must maintain the characteristics of ancient buildings and achieve the purpose of maintenance. The process is more complicated. In this context, the three-dimensional modeling of complex curved surfaces of ancient buildings, the practice of repairing the model on the model, not only can speed up the maintenance efficiency, but also minimize the secondary damage to ancient buildings. The design process of 3D reconstruction model of complex curved surface of ancient buildings is mainly divided into the following three steps: firstly, the LiDAR non-contact is used to obtain the ancient building information, then the information is processed, and finally the 3D reconstruction of the complex surface of the ancient building is completed. In order to ensure the effectiveness of the method, a set of precision simulation experiments are carried out. The results show that the method is more accurate than the other two methods [2].

2   Design of 3D Reconstruction Model of Complex Curved Surface of Ancient Buildings

Figure 1 below shows the design flow of the 3D reconstruction model of complex curved surfaces of ancient buildings.

The three-dimensional reconstruction model design of complex curved surface of ancient buildings is divided into three parts: the acquisition part, using LiDAR to obtain the complex surface LiDAR point cloud data of ancient buildings; the processing part: processing the LiDAR point cloud data and color digital image data; reconstruction Partly, the 3D reconstruction of complex curved surfaces of ancient buildings is completed [3].

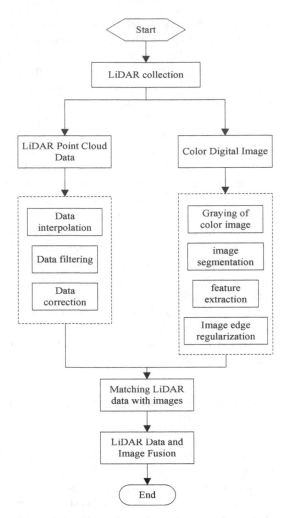

Fig. 1. Design flow of 3D reconstruction model of complex curved surface of ancient buildings

2.1 Acquisition Part

The acquisition part is the basis of the three-dimensional modeling of complex curved surfaces of ancient buildings. The main tool is Lidar, which is called LiDAR in English. The main function is to measure the three-dimensional coordinates of the ground buildings. LiDAR consists of several devices:

(1) The laser scanner is mainly used to measure the relative position and distance between the laser emitter and the ancient building, and to scan the complex surface size and shape of the ancient building;

(2) Digital camera, the main function is to obtain images of ancient buildings, and record spectral information and other related data information;

(3) Inertial Measurement System (INS): The direction in which the laser is emitted and reflected back.

(4) The central control unit, whose main function is to control and manage the operation of LiDAR;

(5) Storage unit, the main role is to save data information [4].

Here, the RB-13K255 LiDAR produced by Harbin Aosong Robot Technology Co., Ltd. is selected. The relevant parameter settings are shown in Table 1 below.

Table 1. RB-13K255 LiDAR related parameter settings

Project	Enhancement mode	Outdoor mode
Applicable scenario	Stronger performance, suitable for indoor environment	Higher reliability, suitable for outdoor environment, reliable anti-sunshine ability
Maximum measuring distance	25 km	
Sampling frequency	200 Hz	
Scanning frequency	15 Hz	
Angular resolution	0.337°	0.54°
Communication frequency	256000 bps	
Communication frequency	Supporting previous SDK/protocols	

RB-13K255 LiDAR works (see Fig. 2): Lift the aircraft above the ancient building, turn on the laser scanner and emit a laser beam (laser, semiconductor laser, etc.). When the laser beam encounters an ancient building, it will follow the launch. The route is reflected back, then received by the receiver in the laser scanner, and the time difference between each laser beam from the emission to the reflection is recorded. Finally, according to the known laser propagation speed, the laser emitter and the ancient building can be calculated. The distance between the specific calculation formula is as follows:

$$d = \frac{1}{2}v \cdot t \qquad (1)$$

In the formula, d is the distance between the laser emitter and the ancient building; v is the laser propagation speed; t is the time from the laser beam to the reflection [5].

However, it is not enough to only measure the distance data. In order to build a three-dimensional model of complex surface of ancient buildings, it is necessary to further determine its coordinates. The specific steps are as follows:

(1) The coordinates of each laser reflection point are determined according to the position and direction of laser emission.
(2) The IMU is used to measure the relevant parameters of the aircraft, including heading angle, pitch angle, yaw angle, etc.
(3) Using GPS to measure the space coordinates of aircraft;
(4) The results of step (1) are corrected by steps (2) and (3), and the accurate spatial rectangular coordinates of each laser foot point (each laser beam point on an ancient building) are obtained [6].

In addition, we need to use digital camera to record the color image of ancient buildings, which can provide a reference for the three-dimensional model of complex surface of the latter ancient buildings.

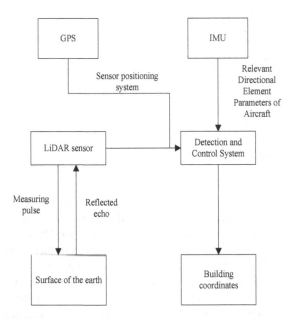

Fig. 2. The working principle of RB-13K255 LiDAR

2.2 Processing Section

In Sect. 2.2, two types of data are obtained, one is LiDAR data, the other is color digital image, so there are two tasks in the processing part.

(1) LiDAR Data Processing

(1) Data correction: Errors of LiDAR equipment and accidental errors are the main causes of data errors of LiDAR, so before registration with image data, error correction is needed to improve the accuracy of LiDAR data.

(2) Data filtering. In the process of digitalization of physical scanning, errors, redundant points and measurement noise caused by scanning environment will inevitably be introduced. These points will have a great impact on the later reconstruction of physical model. In order to extract the characteristic data of physical objects better, data filtering must be carried out to remove these errors. There are two commonly used data filtering methods: the first one is based on the abrupt elevation change; the second one is based on the echo intensity of laser foot data. In this section, the second method is used to complete the data filtering task. The principle is as follows: Because the surface of ancient buildings is not smooth, there are intensity differences in the reflected signals. Using this difference, the signals are transformed into corresponding images with different gray values, and then the filtering process is completed according to the operation flow of image filtering method. The process is as follows: the constructed smoothing filter is placed in gray. Roaming over the graded image, then collecting the gray value of each pixel in the image, sorting these gray values according to the sequence from small to large, then finding out the middle value, and finally giving the middle value to a central position pixel in the image [7].

(3) Data interpolation: After data filtering processing, there will be some empty shortcomings, such as the part below the eaves of ancient buildings which can not be illuminated by airborne LiDAR, so it is necessary to add the elevation of ground points to this position, and then build a complete ground elevation model. The above supplementary process is called data interpolation [8].

(2) Color Digital Image Processing

(1) Graying of color image. Grayscale image refers to a series of processing of color images with multiple colors to produce corresponding gray images containing only black, white and different shades of gray. There are many methods of image graying, such as component method, maximum method, average method, weighted average method and so on. In this section, the weighted average method is used to gray the image [9]. The basic idea is to assign different weights according to the importance of each component, then calculate the weighted results, and gray the weighted mean. Because the ultimate goal of color digital image processing is to get the smooth edge of the image, the optimal weights of R, G and B are 0.30, 0.59 and 0.11, respectively. This method can be described by the following mathematical formulas:

$$f(i,j) = 0.30R(i,j) + 0.59G(i,j) + 0.11B(i,j) \tag{2}$$

In the formula, R, G and B are the components of three colors. (i,j) is a coordinate pixel in gray image.

(1) Image segmentation. Image segmentation is to segment the object from the whole image. In this paper, the ancient buildings are separated from the background in the image. At present, there are four commonly used segmentation methods: threshold-based, region-based, edge-based and specific theory-based. In this paper, a threshold-based image segmentation method is adopted. Its basic principle is as follows: first, an approximate threshold is selected as the initial value of the estimated value, then the threshold is continuously improved, and finally, a new threshold is used to segment the image.

(3) Extraction of complex surface features of ancient buildings. The feature extraction of complex surface of ancient buildings is to detect the image edges of ancient buildings. Its basic principle is to use image edge enhancement operator to highlight the local edges of the image, then define the "edge intensity" in the image, and then extract the image edge points by setting threshold.

(4) Image edge regularization. The edges of building images extracted from complex surface features of ancient buildings are irregular and serrated, which can not be used for subsequent three-dimensional modeling. Therefore, image edges need to be regularized to make the edges smooth [10].

2.3 Reconstruction Part

The LiDAR data obtained above are matched with the image to synthesize a three-dimensional model of complex surface of ancient buildings. The specific process is shown in Fig. 3 below.

3 Simulation Test Experiment

In order to test the accuracy of this method, a set of simulation experiments is required. The simulation experiment object is an ancient tower building in a certain ancient city. The building has a total of six floors and has a delicate shape. It has existed for hundreds of years, and many of the outer walls have fallen off and are facing the risk of collapse. In order to reflect the superiority of the method, experiments were carried out together with two other three-dimensional model construction methods. That is to say, literature [1] method (method 1) and literature [2] method (method 2) are used to compare with this method. After the modeling is completed, 10 points are selected as the experimental precision test points, and the coordinates in the model are shown in Table 2 below.

It can be seen from Table 2 that the coordinates in the model are almost the same as the real coordinates by using this method. After modeling with the other two methods, the coordinates in the model are quite different from the real coordinates. It can be seen that the modeling accuracy of the method is higher.

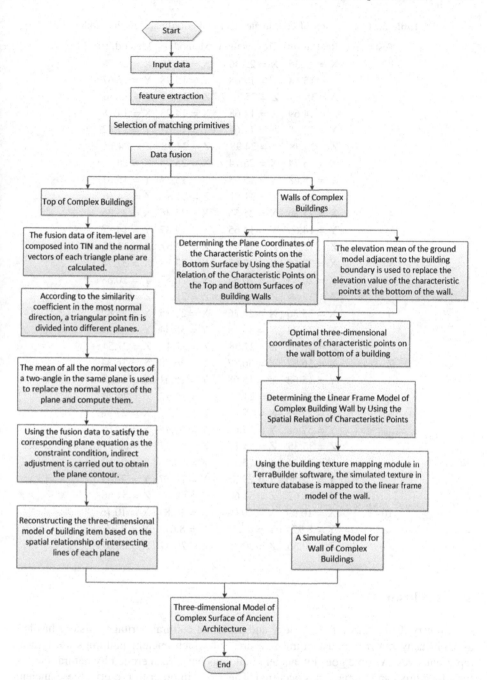

Fig. 3. Construction flow of complex surface three-dimensional model of ancient architecture

Table 2. Comparison of coordinates and real coordinates in the model

Test point	Real result	This method	Method 1	Method 2
1	X = 25.36	X = 25.36	X = 25.56	X = 25.78
	Y = 15.68	Y = 15.68	Y = 15.78	Y = 15.67
	Z = 35.35	Z = 35.35	Z = 35.37	Z = 35.36
2	X = 14.69	X = 14.68	X = 14.98	X = 14.78
	Y = 17.68	Y = 17.67	Y = 17.67	Y = 17.62
	Z = 24.98	Z = 24.98	Z = 24.78	Z = 24.78
3	X = 25.74	X = 25.74	X = 25.78	X = 25.36
	Y = 15.68	Y = 15.68	Y = 15.34	Y = 15.67
	Z = 24.87	Z = 24.87	Z = 24.87	Z = 24.36
4	X = 25.36	X = 25.36	X = 25.36	X = 25.36
	Y = 14.65	Y = 14.65	Y = 14.87	Y = 14.87
	Z = 32.53	Z = 32.53	Z = 32.67	Z = 32.75
5	X = 37.65	X = 37.65	X = 37.78	X = 37.78
	Y = 20.35	Y = 20.36	Y = 20.87	Y = 20.68
	Z = 21.68	Z = 21.67	Z = 21.36	Z = 21.36
6	X = 25.36	X = 25.36	X = 25.85	X = 25.69
	Y = 35.98	Y = 35.98	Y = 35.34	Y = 35.34
	Z = 27.98	Z = 27.98	Z = 27.44	Z = 27.54
7	X = 36.87	X = 36.87	X = 36.78	X = 36.34
	Y = 15.68	Y = 15.68	Y = 15.31	Y = 15.87
	Z = 24.71	Z = 24.71	Z = 24.67	Z = 24.24
8	X = 27.98	X = 27.99	X = 27.87	X = 27.98
	Y = 57.68	Y = 57.68	Y = 57.75	Y = 57.68
	Z = 35.35	Z = 35.37	Z = 35.87	Z = 35.67
9	X = 25.36	X = 25.36	X = 25.36	X = 25.67
	Y = 22.36	Y = 22.35	Y = 22.87	Y = 22.47
	Z = 54.62	Z = 54.60	Z = 54.62	Z = 54.66
10	X = 10.69	X = 10.68	X = 10.87	X = 10.76
	Y = 8.92	Y = 8.92	Y = 8.67	Y = 8.95
	Z = 20.36	Z = 20.36	Z = 20.87	Z = 20.67

4   Conclusion

In summary, China has a long history and profound cultural heritage. History has left us with many material and cultural treasures, of which ancient buildings are typical representatives. As time goes by, ancient buildings have been eroded by natural factors for a long time, and damage has occurred. Therefore, in order to preserve these ancient buildings and protect our history and culture, the restoration of ancient buildings is of paramount importance. Due to the complexity and fragility of the ancient building structure, direct repair is very likely to cause secondary damage to the building. In order to avoid this situation, three-dimensional modeling of complex curved surfaces of ancient buildings is generally carried out before the repair, and pre-repair is carried out on the model. In this context, this paper designs a three-dimensional reconstruction method for complex curved surfaces of ancient buildings based on big data. It is verified that the method has higher precision and can ensure the smooth progress of ancient building repair work.

Acknowledgements. (1) Research on the Classification, Conservation and Utilization of Historic buildings and blocks, supported by the Scientific Research Grant Project of institutions of higher Learning in Inner Mongolia Autonomous region (Project Plan No. NJZY18255).

(2) Research on adaptation Strategy of Rural Housing in Hohhot, a scientific research grant project for colleges and universities in Inner Mongolia Autonomous region (Project Plan No. NJZY18257).

(3) Study on the Conservation and Utilization in the Planning of Historic blocks in the Desert-Southern Mongolia area-taking Wulanchabu area as an example (Grant No: 18NDXT02).

This achievement is supported by the Cooperative Innovation Center for Cultural inheritance and Development of Mongolian and Northern Minority nationalities in Inner Mongolia Autonomous region.

References

1. Xin, J., Luo, Y., Cheng, P.: The complicated surface reconstruction of ancient buildings based on LiDAR. Geomatics Spat. Inf. Technol. **40**(7), 65–67 (2017)
2. Wang, L.: Combining point cloud data and BIM technology for 3D reconstruction and informational management of ancient buildings. Bull. Surveying Mapp. **495**(6), 121–124 + 136 (2018)
3. Bloomberg, Yang Wunian, Peng, Wang: Application of three-dimensional laser scanning technology in reconstruction of ancient building models. Geospatial Inf. **14**(3), 94–96 (2016)
4. Lin, X., Yao, T., Ma, R., et al.: Three dimensional reconstruction of the Great Wild Goose Pagoda based on massive point cloud data. Sci. Conserv. Archaeol. **29**(3), 67–72 (2017)
5. Zhang, Z., Luo, Y., Pei, N., et al.: Digital protection of ancient cultural relics Based on 3D laser scanning: a case study of Leshan confucian temple. Geomatics Spat. Inf. Technol. **7**, 42–44 (2016)
6. Zhai, C., Zhang, J., Ma, C., et al.: Research on the roof modeling techniques of ancient buildings based on SketchUp. Heilongjiang Sci. Technol. Inf. **26**, 27 (2016)
7. Zhang, J., Duan, M., Lin, X.: Comparison and analysis of models for 3D power line reconstruction using LiDAR point cloud. Geomatics Inf. Sci. Wuhan Univ. **42**(11), 1565–1572 (2017)
8. Fei, J.: Research on 3D model construction based on dual image acquisition. Digit. Technol. Appl. **7**, 137–141 (2017)
9. Yang, L., Ruan, X.: Semi-automatic model-driven 3D building reconstruction. Remote Sens. Inf. **32**(3), 115–122 (2017)
10. Song, Q., Tang, J., Xin, J.: 3-dimensional reconstruction for soybean plant of seedling stage based on growth model. Comput. Eng. **43**(5), 275–280 (2017)

3D Human Motion Information Extraction Based on Vicon Motion Capture in Internet of Things

Ze-guo Liu[(⊠)]

College of Information Engineering, Xizang Minzu University,
Xianyang, China
liuzeguo316@163.com

Abstract. In order to solve the problems of unclear contour and poor geometric precision in the process of extracting human body motion information by traditional key point detection method, a 3D human motion information extraction method based on Vicon motion capture was proposed. The motion characteristics of human body were captured by Vicon motion capture technology. According to the capture results, the change characteristics of joint force and angle in the course of human motion were collected and calculated, so that the frequency of human motion wave can be accurately grasped, the distribution of frequency change and the law of change. According to the law of change, the contour features in the process of human motion were perceived and judged, and the geometric accuracy of the moving contour was optimized by using fuzzy algorithm, thus the accurate extraction of three-dimensional human motion information was realized. The simulation results show that this method can effectively extract 3D human motion information, solve the problem of unclear contour in traditional methods, and improve the geometric accuracy of 3D human motion information extraction.

Keywords: Internet of things · Motion capture · Human motion · Information extraction

1 Introduction

With the development and maturity of the Internet of things technology, in the environment of the Internet of things, the requirement of extracting three-dimensional human motion information is gradually raised. In order to extract and analyze the human motion information more accurately, scan out the movement behavior characteristics of the object accurately, extract the motion information and the structure information of the object, the method of 3D human motion information extraction based on Vicon motion capture technology is innovated [1].

G. Gui and L. Yun (Eds.): ADHIP 2019, LNICST 301, pp. 374–382, 2019.
https://doi.org/10.1007/978-3-030-36402-1_40

2 Human Motion Information Extraction Method Based on Vicon Motion Capture

2.1 Motion Features of Human Joint Based on Vicon Motion Capture

In the process of human motion feature capture, in order to extract 3D human motion information better, combined with Vicon motion capture technology, the process of human motion feature mining is simplified, in order to carry out fast and accurate 3D human dynamic capture. The feature extraction algorithm is used to extract and calculate the change features of joint motion in the course of human motion, and the dynamic capture of the motion feature is established. The calculation process is as follows:

$$H[a] = 1.75 \frac{\partial^2 \Omega}{\partial v^2}$$

$$= -\sum_{i=1}^{n} \frac{\xi_{ij}}{\xi_i} \left\{ \sin\left[1.75\xi_i^{-1/2}\right] + \xi_i^{-1/2} \cos[1.75\xi] \right\} e^{\xi 2i/2} \tag{1}$$

In formula: $H[a]$ represents that the effective use value of capturing the joint angle in the course of human motion, and it can balance angle parameters and average sharpness to a certain extent; Ω represents a set of dense vectors representing contour operators; v^2 represents time-delay parameters of motion characteristics; $\xi_i^{-1/2}$ represents interactive vector parameters, which is a differential parameter that represents a specific capture process [2]. $e^{\xi 2i/2}$ represents annotation operator; ξ_{ij} represents visual error offset. The above formula optimizes the use condition of the key angle, and also needs to optimize the motion frame frequency. The formula is as follows:

$$\beta(s + 1, n - s + 1) = \frac{1}{(s + 1, n - s + 1)} \cdot R^S (1 - R)^{n-s}$$

$$\beta(s + a, n - s + b) = \frac{1}{(s + a, n - s + b)} \cdot R^{S+1} (1 - R)^{n-s-1} \tag{2}$$

In formula: $\beta(s + 1, n - s + 1)$, $\beta(s + a, n - s + b)$ represent the individual pixel starting coordinates and the terminal feature parameters of the visual moving image, respectively; $(1 - R)^{n-s}$ represents the frequency of the motion image; R^S represents the frequency hopping probability of the moving image. The distribution of wave frequency, frequency change and frequency hopping in human motion capture system is shown in Fig. 1.

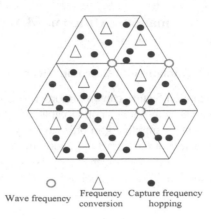

○   △   ●
Wave frequency   Frequency Capture frequency
              conversion   hopping

Fig. 1. Relationship between frequency of human motion wave and frequency change

According to the frequency of human motion wave and the relation of frequency change distribution, the calculation method of human joint motion characteristic is optimized. The formula is as follows:

$$\text{cen}_{it} = \ln\frac{I_{it}}{A} - \phi_{it}^2 \text{FDI}_{it} - \ln(H * FDI)_{it} \tag{3}$$

In formula, cen_{it} represents the tradeoff value of human motion characteristics, which is used to define the essential evaluation of parameters; H_{it} represents the texture set of moving point sub-pixel distribution; FDI represents valid values that can be qualified; ϕ_{it}^2 represents the local variance and is used for the coefficient defined by the weighting depth [3].

Through the above process, the optimization of the human motion feature operation is completed, and the optimized joint angle operation can capture the human body action.

2.2 Feature Processing of Human Motion Contour

Based on the human body motion feature mining algorithm based on Vicon, the preliminary results of motion feature estimation are obtained. In order to eliminate the errors in feature extraction process, and the human local motion capture is inaccurate, etc. Image edge features are recognized and analyzed with 3D shape algorithm in order to provide corresponding data support for Vicon action capture [4].

Set the collected 3D image as Y, image feature points are n, the set of data made up of feature points is $\{z_1, z_2, z_3, \ldots, z_n\}$, the set of image data is $\{x_1, x_2, x_3, \ldots, x_n\}$. The feature complexity coefficient is S, the perceptual time of action capture is m, the number of data samples is P, the shape of the database is described by l [5, 6].

Suppose that the initial edge of the 3D human motion image in the process of Vicon action capture is $G_t(h,l)$, the characteristic parameters of human motion contour obtained by different structures are represented by $F_a(m,n)$, and the gradient values of human motion contour can be calculated by the following formula:

$$F_a(m,n) = \sum_{a=1} UG_t(h,l) \tag{4}$$

According to the above exposition, we can more accurately extract and collect the human body motion contour features, and detect and analyze the human body motion contour region, which is conducive to more accurate recognition of three-dimensional human motion image feature data. It is beneficial to accurate extraction of 3D human motion information [7, 8].

2.3 Realization of Human Motion Information Extraction

In order to improve the timeliness and accuracy of motion feature extraction, the information extraction is greatly affected by the surrounding environment, and the resolution and edge blur of the extracted image are easy to appear in the process of motion extraction, so as to improve the timeliness and accuracy of motion feature extraction, a fuzzy algorithm is used to calculate the gradient change of salient joint motion angle in the process of human motion.

$$f_n(a,b) = \frac{a}{\delta b} n[f(a+1,b-1) - f(a-1,b+1)] \tag{6}$$

In formula: δ represents the rate of change in the angle of the joint, a, b represent the characteristic parameter of motion initiation and n is the direction of motion. According to the above algorithm, the force change of 3D human body is calculated. The algorithm is as follows:

$$P = \frac{\sum (a_n - b_n)}{n\sqrt{n^2+1}} \tag{6}$$

Because the traditional algorithm for extracting the global feature of human body motion consumes a relatively large proportion of time, it is difficult to extract the detailed features effectively [9, 10]. Combined with the previous algorithm, the accuracy of 3D human motion information processing is standardized and recorded as the standard data for feature extraction, which is used for comparison and reference. The data are as follows.

Table 1. Accuracy of 3D human motion information processing.

Resolution ratio	Standard for accuracy of edge contour feature extraction	Joint change precision standard	Kinematic trend precision standard	Force variation precision standard
−10	0.845	0.774	0.891	0.945
−20	0.945	0.798	0.885	0.912
−30	0.874	0.805	0.798	0.915
−40	0.768	0.854	0.791	0.857
−50	0.778	0.901	0.918	0.905
−60	0.748	0.872	0.926	0.984
−70	0.742	0.831	0.873	0.945
−80	0.757	0.846	0.744	0.901
−90	0.875	0.798	0.854	0.891

Combined with the high scale algorithm of Vicon motion capture technology, the feature of human body motion contour is extracted, thus avoiding the problem of extraction error and so on [11]. Combining with the mapping function, the extraction accuracy of human motion edge parameter information is optimized, and the edge feature can be accurately extracted and displayed in the process of human body motion, so as to improve the accuracy of feature information extraction. Reduce the error of motion feature extraction. Combined with fuzzy algorithm and gray mapping method, human motion information can be extracted more accurately. Combined with the data in Table 1 and the gray mapping function algorithm, the motion feature accuracy detection system is extracted and decomposed and analyzed. Suppose that the decomposition process of 3D human motion feature is shown in Fig. 2. C represents the analysis and extraction of 3D human motion feature information from S and P of the same sample.

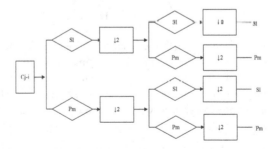

Fig. 2. 3D discrete wavelet transform

Based on the method of extracting variance of 3D human motion feature captured by Vicon, the threshold value of human motion is calculated. According to the result, the information is converted to the three-dimensional image of human motion blur, and the fuzzy membership value C of each pixel is obtained. The mean value of 3×3 neighborhood is calculated by the previous formula. Using derivative C and image convolution, the gradient of image horizontal and vertical direction is calculated accurately to determine the value of $Cj-i$, and the edge feature is judged according to the threshold value. The gradient larger than the threshold is the contour feature of human body. The second derivative of the image is calculated by the same principle, the corresponding negative points are selected, and the largest adjacent points are extracted from the negative points. If this point is positive, the difference between this point and the negative point is obtained, and the other points are set to zero. In this case, according to the statistical characteristics of the second derivative, the threshold value can be judged to obtain the joint motion angle characteristic information of the zero crossing point, and the human body motion feature can be accurately extracted according to the joint angle and motion contour feature.

3 Experimental Results and Analysis

In order to verify the validity of 3D human motion information extraction method based on Vicon motion capture in the Internet of things, a comparative simulation experiment was designed. Take a sporting event as an example. In order to ensure the effectiveness of the experiment, the movement of the same contestant at the same time cut point is selected to detect the movement. In order to ensure the validity of human body action feature extraction in the course of motion, the relevant data are set up. Data y_i after batch Operation of the balance index within the range of [68.5 to 78.6]; Set the set of indicators $K(x_i, x_j)$ within the assessment area to 15.85; In order to ensure that the human motion capture system can accurately capture and set up the H[a], $e^{\xi 2i/2}$, $N(t)$, $(2x + 1)u\pi$ are 5.28/4163.5/66.32/400; Set the test parameters as shown in the Table 2.

Table 2. Experimental parameters.

Experiment number	Range of movement/CM	Capture image frame code/PB	Correction parameter
1	20	2.5	10^{-4}
2	30	3.0	10^{-4}
3	40	3.5	10^{-4}
4	50	4.0	10^{-4}
5	60	4.5	10^{-4}
6	70	5.0	10^{-4}
7	80	5.5	10^{-4}
8	90	6.0	10^{-4}
9	100	6.5	10^{-4}

According to the parameters of the above simulation and contrast experiment, the results of the traditional method and the method in this paper are recorded in the course of the experiment, and the concrete results are shown in the Table 3.

Table 3. Comparison of experimental results.

	Moving contour	Contour feature parameter	Contour definition	Background filtering rate	Fitting degree	Identification degree
Traditional method	−2	−4	3	20	0.85	4
Paper method	7	2	7	15	1.36	9

The results of the analysis table show that the motion profile of the motion information extraction method designed in this paper is much stronger than that of the traditional method, and the definition of the contour curve is much stronger than that of the traditional method. The results show that the accuracy of the extraction of motion contour features is higher in the process of capturing motion features, and the fitting degree and identification degree are also slightly better than the traditional methods. In order to detect the geometric accuracy of the method more intuitively, the actual test results are displayed, as shown in the Fig. 3 below.

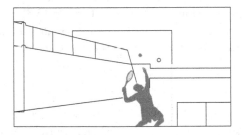

(a)Paper method

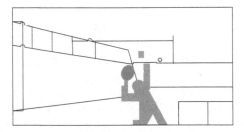

(b)Traditional method

Fig. 3. Comparison of experiment results

According to the above image, it is not difficult to find that the proposed method is obviously superior to the traditional method in extracting and displaying human motion information in the process of detection, and can perform high resolution, high definition action feature capture.

4 Conclusions

A method of extracting 3D human motion information based on Vicon motion capture in the Internet of things was proposed. The joint angle in the human motion process is calculated by using the human motion feature mining algorithm. According to the joint changing angle, the shape of the moving object is obtained, and the useful data features that accurately reflect the characteristics of the human body's motion behavior are obtained. The feature information of the original point cloud is preserved to effectively extract the human body motion information. The experimental results show that compared with the traditional method, this method has high geometric accuracy, good fit and superior performance, which fully meets the research requirements.

Acknowledgements. On the digitalized 3D model of Tibetan Xianziwu based on 3D Motion Capture.

(Innovation-Supportive Project for Young Teachers in Colleges and Universities in Tibet Autonomous Region).

QCZ2016—33.

References

1. Li, A., Cao, Y., Hou, Y., et al.: Simulation and evaluation of the influence of human movement on the ventilation and airflow distribution attached to the vertical wall. J. Xi'an Univ. Archit. Technol. (Natural Sci. Edn.) **6**, 882–889 (2017)
2. Li, X., Xiao, Q.: Human motion behavior recognition method based on automatic encoder and probabilistic neural network. Softw. Guide **1**, 11–13 (2018)
3. Li, W., Sun, J.: Human motion shape estimation based on Gaussian incremental dimension reduction and manifold Boltzmann optimization. Acta Electron. **45**(12), 3060–3069 (2017)
4. Wu, Y., Xiong, J.: Design and implementation of intelligent terminal for human motion health parameter detection system. J. Changjiang Univ. **1**, 23–26 (2018)
5. Li, M., Liu, S., Ke, P., et al.: Study on the difference of human motion amplitude in different percentiles during the course of arresting landing. Aerosp. Med. Med. Eng. **6**, 406–410 (2017)
6. Wei, L., Jia, Y., Xue, R.: Study on the characteristics of electromyography changes in the formation of human motion coordination. Fujian Sports Sci. Technol. **36**(2), 25–27 (2017)
7. Xue, R., Jia, Y., Wei, L.: Study on the change characteristics of biomechanical parameters in the process of human motion coordination. J. Hubei Sports Sci. **36**(3), 221–224 (2017)
8. Filippeschi, A., Schmitz, N., Miezal, M., et al.: Survey of motion tracking methods based on inertial sensors: a focus on upper limb human motion. Sensors **17**(6), 1257–1260 (2017)

9. Xing, C., Wu, Y., Xiang, X., et al.: Physiological characteristics of compensation strategies for human motion chains and their impact on exercise training. Chin. J. Sports Med. **36**(10), 922–926 (2017)
10. Peng, Z.: Physiological changes, body temperature regulation and exercise ability of human body in high temperature environment. Liaoning Sport Sci. Technol. **1**, 44–47 (2016)
11. Liang, W., Jing, Y., Lu, Y., et al.: Liquid crystal display design of a wearable human motion trajectory evaluation device. Chin. J. Liq. Cryst. Disp. **31**(5), 464–469 (2016)

Human Motion Attitude Tracking Method Based on Vicon Motion Capture Under Big Data

Ze-guo Liu[✉]

College of Information Engineering, Xizang Minzu University, Xianyang, China
liuzeguo316@163.com

Abstract. Aiming at the problem that the human body motion posture cannot be correctly and quickly marked in the conventional method, a human body motion attitude tracking method based on Vicon motion capture under big data is proposed and designed. Under the motion capture filtering algorithm, the human body weight measurement function is constructed by the combination of color, edge and motion features, and different images are selected according to the occlusion between limbs to establish a constrained human motion model, and the model is based on Vicon action. The tracking calculation of the capture realizes the tracking process of the human body motion posture. The effectiveness of the method is determined by the method of experimental argumentation analysis. The results show that the method can track the motion posture of the human body quickly and accurately, and the robustness is better. The tracking accuracy is 13.87% higher than the conventional method.

Keywords: Big data technology · Vicon motion capture · Human body movement posture · Tracking method

1 Introduction

At present, the tracking and recognition of human motion based on machine vision is a popular research direction in the world. It has universal applications in video surveillance, video retrieval, human-computer interaction, virtual reality and sports training. Using machine vision to track and identify human motion information in video can greatly reduce the original labor cost and complete the recognition process of human motion more quickly and accurately [1]. In order to improve the tracking rate of human body motion posture, it is extremely necessary to establish a recognition model based on attitude features. The human body motion posture features are divided into external features and internal features. External features include shape, contour, etc. Internal features include color, texture, etc. Since the human body motion posture is mainly composed of the above features, the tracking method based on human motion capture is one of the most important methods at present.

The Vicon motion capture method can capture the reflective sphere moving in the scanning space according to different cameras at the same sampling time, and obtain

G. Gui and L. Yun (Eds.): ADHIP 2019, LNICST 301, pp. 383–391, 2019.
https://doi.org/10.1007/978-3-030-36402-1_41

the three-dimensional coordinates of the reflective sphere at that moment [2]. Based on these coordinates, kinematics and dynamics analysis can be performed. The displacement, velocity, acceleration, and the variation of physical quantities such as momentum and kinetic energy are obtained. At the highest resolution, the Vicon motion capture method has a sampling frequency of 482 *spf* and a maximum sampling frequency of 10,000 *spf*. Therefore, Vicon's matching motion capture software is used to track the human body's motion posture, and its efficiency and accuracy are extremely high.

Although the conventional tracking method can capture the human body's motion posture, but the tracking time is long, and the capturing accuracy is not ideal. Based on this, this paper proposes and designs a human body motion attitude tracking method based on Vicon motion capture, and demonstrates effectiveness of our proposed method through experiments. The method of analysis verifies the effectiveness of the method. The results show that the human body motion attitude tracking method based on Vicon motion capture can improve the tracking speed of human motion posture and ensure the accuracy of tracking results, which is extremely robust.

2   Design of Human Body Motion Attitude Tracking Method

2.1   Reference Motion Capture Filter

Vicon motion capture filter provides a probabilistic verification of non-Gaussian, non-linear and multi-module observation data, while human pose tracking is a tracking problem in high-dimensional space [3], which is solved by using motion capture method. In the case of a problem, the high-dimensional state space is usually decomposed into two or more subspaces to apply dynamic processes and resampling processes in each subspace.

Consider the tracking problem in the 2-dimensional state space $s = (x, y)$ consisting of two 1-dimensional subspaces $S_A (S_A \in R)$ and $S_B (S_B \in R)$. In order to avoid searching for the correct image state in the entire 2-dimensional space, block sampling divides the search process into two steps [4]. That is, the state x is searched in the subspace S_A, and then the state y is searched in the subspace S_B. Since the survival factor of each step is a, the survival factor for 2-dimensional state tracking in the 2-dimensional space s is $2a$, and the required capture path is $2D_{min}/a$, and the 2-dimensional state is directly performed in s using the motion capture filtering method. The survival factor of the trace is a^2, and the number of particles needs to be D_{min}/a^2. Among them, represents the minimum acceptable survival diagnosis required for successful tracking [5]. Since a is much smaller than 1, the motion capture filtering method can greatly reduce the number of required capture paths and improve tracking efficiency.

Let each joint point of the human motion correspond to a filter set $\gamma_i (i = 1, 2, \cdots, n)$, and let $\gamma_i = D_{min}/a^2$ update the joint image of the human body after the filtering calculation is finished. The position of the corresponding joint point in the image at time

t is obtained by calculating the mean of each joint in the filter set. The filtering process at each joint point is as follows:

Since the number of images in each filter set is small, the sampling process is easily degraded [6]. Therefore, we perform "re-sampling" at each time step to complete the selection process of the human body motion image.

Considering that the human body pose changes between two frames of images is small, the method of this paper does not use motion models for prediction. At the time t, the tracking result of the time $t - 1$ is used as the mean value, and N filters having a Gaussian distribution are generated. Among them, the variance $\varpi = \gamma w_0$ of the Gaussian distribution, by adjusting the value of γ, changes the filter distribution area of the new image, and finally obtains the prediction result of the image Gaussian distribution.

The measurement process of the human body is realized by the combination of color, edge and motion characteristics. The measurement process of the head uses only the color features, and the measurement process of the limbs uses the fusion of the three features. The occlusion and occluded limbs are measured using different features to complete the measurement of each initial parameter [7]. By calculating the filtering state in the filter set corresponding to each joint point, the mean value is accurately estimated, and the human body weight measurement function is obtained:

$$s_k = \sum_{i=1}^{N} \pi \varpi^2 \tag{1}$$

Where s_k represents the weight measure of the human body motion; k is a constant, $k = 1, 2, \cdots, N$.

After the above definition, the estimation function of the human body motion posture is obtained, and the function is analyzed and backed up to prepare for the tracking calculation of the human body motion posture.

2.2 Establish a Constrained Human Motion Model

A rectangular model is used to establish a human body model, and the constraint relationship between the limbs is represented by a line connecting the nodes. Both frame models use nodes to describe the limbs [8], and the connections between the nodes represent the relationship between the limbs. The model structure is shown in Fig. 1.

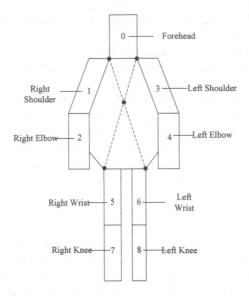

Fig. 1. Schematic diagram of the node relationship of the human body model

Analysis of Fig. 1 shows that the constrained human body appearance model designed in this paper consists of 9 "cardboards" connected by joints. Among them, there are 14 nodes, 1 virtual node and the connection between nodes. For the virtual node, Since it does not play a fixed role, it does not need to be tracked [9]. The nodes in the human body model correspond to the real joint points, the solid lines represent the real limbs, the dashed lines and arcs represent the constraints between the two adjacent joint points, and the dashed arrows indicate the one-way constraints that only affect the joint points indicated by the arrows.

It is assumed that the spatial state of the human pose is represented by X, where X is the Cartesian product $X = X^1 \times X^2 \times \cdots X^{14}$ of 14 sub-state spaces, and each sub-state space is a 2-dimensional vector space. Thus, the tracking problem in a 2-dimensional state space translates into tracking problems in two planar state spaces.

Using the Vicon motion capture method, the length of the limb, the neck and shoulders, the distance between the shoulders, the sternum, the sternum and the hips are constrained [10]. Let ε denote the distance between two nodes, then the quantized constraint can be expressed as a Gaussian function:

$$P(\varepsilon) = \frac{s_k}{\sqrt{2\pi\vartheta}} \exp\left(\frac{-(\varepsilon - \varepsilon_0)^2}{2\vartheta^2}\right) \tag{2}$$

Where $P(\varepsilon)$ represents the constrained quantification result of the human body motion posture; ε_0 represents the distance between the two joint points initialized; ϑ is the variance of the Gaussian function, since the inflection point of the Gaussian function is located at $\varepsilon = \varepsilon_0 + \vartheta$, when $\varepsilon \in \varepsilon_0 - \vartheta$, the curve of $P(\varepsilon)$ is steep; When $\varepsilon \in \varepsilon_0 + \vartheta$, the curve of $P(\varepsilon)$ becomes gentle. It can be seen that the larger the ϑ value, the looser the corresponding constraint, and the larger the allowable variation range of ε; conversely, the smaller the ϑ value, the tighter the constraint, and the smaller the allowable variation range of ε.

At this point, the constraint design of the human body posture model is completed, and the corresponding limb length constraint is determined after the initialization calibration is completed.

2.3   Design of Human Body Motion Attitude Tracking Algorithm

The human body motion attitude tracking calculation adopts an adaptive method, and combined with the Vicon motion capture method, the spatial position of the human motion posture is defined by selectively using the likelihood functions corresponding to the three characteristics according to the occlusion condition between the limbs [11]. And determine the conflict set S_0, representing a collection of limb samples that are covered. It should be pointed out that since this article only considers the situation that the human body is facing the camera, we think that the big arm is blocked when the big arm and the small arm are blocked. In the calculation, only the strong relationship between the limbs is considered, that is, only the occlusion relationship between the upper limbs and the lower limbs is considered, regardless of the occlusion relationship between the head, the upper limbs and the lower limbs. We use the motion capture filter and the constrained human body model introduced above to determine the mutual occlusion relationship of the human body's motion posture, as shown in Fig. 2.

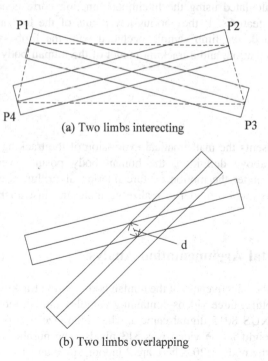

(a) Two limbs interecting

(b) Two limbs overlapping

Fig. 2. Conflict between two limbs

According to the conflict relationship between the two limbs in Fig. 2, when the intersection P_0 of the mid-line P_1, P_2, P_3 and P_4 of the two limb samples is located in the quadrilateral $P_1P_2P_3P_4$, the two limb samples intersect, and the constrained quantitative result $P(\varepsilon)$ of the human motion posture will appear. Repeat the calculation phenomenon. In order to avoid such phenomena, this calculation introduces an adaptive method to bring the constraint relationship of the human body model into the adaptive calculation process, so that only the filter that meets $P(\varepsilon)$ can pass the calculation.

According to the coverage relationship of the two limb samples in Fig. 2, it is assumed that l is the distance between the midpoints of the centerline of the two limb samples; d is the distance from the end point of the centerline of one limb sample to the centerline of the other limb sample. When both l and d are less than the threshold [12], the two limb samples are considered to be covered. The judgment is calculated as follows:

$$\kappa = \frac{P(\varepsilon)}{(l+d)^2} \qquad (3)$$

Where κ represents the extent of coverage of the limb sample. $(l+d)^2$ is the judgment coefficient, $(l+d)^2 \in W + W_1/4$.

When the spatial positional relationship of all limb samples is judged, the occluded limb samples are placed in the filter set. For all limb samples, the likelihood of each limb sample is calculated using the likelihood function corresponding to the color, edge, and motion features. If the various key points of the human body have been completely occluded, the limb sample occluded with the limb sample is used for corresponding calculation, and a tracking model of the human body motion posture is obtained:

$$c = \frac{S_m/\gamma}{N\kappa} \qquad (4)$$

Where c represents the mathematical expression of the tracking model.

Through the above definition, the human body posture weight measurement function obtained under the motion capture filtering algorithm is combined with the constrained human motion model to realize accurate and fast tracking of the human body motion posture.

3 Experimental Argumentation Analysis

In order to verify the effectiveness of the human body motion tracking method based on Vicon motion capture, three videos containing complex human motion were captured using the Cano IXUS 8015 digital camera. The video size was 640×480, and the average human height in the video was 313 pixels. The number of motion captures corresponding to the node is 20. There are 2 indoor video and 1 outdoor video. At the same time, in order to ensure the rigor of the experiment, the conventional tracking method was used to compare with the method.

The algorithm was implemented using VC++6.0, and the video clips were tested on an Intel Core2 computer with 2.0 GHz CPU. The average processing time was 5.3 *spf*, the processing time of each video and the human scale in the video and the joint points. The number of motion captures is proportional.

In this method, the number of captures of human joint movements and their distribution have an important influence on the performance of the method. Due to the interdependence of these two parameters, we simultaneously adjust the two parameter values and analyze them on a test video of 200 frames. The experimental performance, that is, the tracking accuracy and speed of the human motion posture, obtains the parameter value: the adjustment factor $\gamma = 0.6$ of the motion capture range, and the experimental results have the best performance when the number of motion captures $N = 25$, and the fixed values of the two parameters are used in the subsequent experimental tests.

3.1   Tracking Accuracy Comparison

The average tracking error of the two methods on the human body motion posture is shown in Table 1.

Table 1. Average tracking error of human joint points

Joint	Indoor 1	Indoor 2	Outdoor	Average tracking error of this method %	Average tracking error of conventional method %
Forehead	4.62	5.26	3.14	7.25	16.35
Neck	4.16	4.36	3.36	4.36	9.25
Shoulder	8.45	5.21	8.14	9.24	21.36
Elbow	6.32	3.95	5.16	1.36	7.25
Hip	6.58	5.32	3.24	5.27	15.26
Knee	4.85	6.14	4.48	7.15	14.15
Ankle	6.17	4.17	5.65	9.25	19.26

Because different sports have different technical requirements, the main parameters of the body's limb motion analysis should be determined according to the specific research of the sports project, with certain uncertainty, so there must be certain errors in the tracking results. It can be seen from the data in Table 1 that for the tracking result of the same test video, the average error of the method is smaller than the average error of the conventional method. The calculation shows that when the Vicon motion capture method is used to track the human body's motion posture, the tracking accuracy is 13.87% higher than the conventional method.

3.2   Tracking Speed Comparison

The comparison results of the average tracking speed of the two methods on the human body motion posture are shown in Fig. 3.

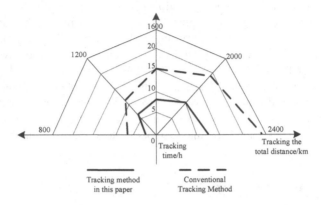

Fig. 3. Comparison of human body motion tracking speed

It can be seen from the experimental results that the proposed algorithm achieves a satisfactory tracking speed of human motion. The analysis shows that under the same tracking path, the tracking time of this method is lower than the conventional method, including complex background, human motion, clothing changes and occlusion between limbs, which can quickly capture and track the human body posture. The tracking speed of the conventional method is lower than the method of this paper. Therefore, the effectiveness of the proposed method can be determined. The results show that the human motion attitude tracking method based on Vicon motion capture can achieve satisfactory tracking results.

4   Conclusions

This paper proposes a human body motion attitude tracking method based on Vicon motion capture, which combines the color, edge and motion characteristics of human body image, combined with motion capture filter and human motion model to successfully realize the human body motion posture under big data. track. The experimental results show that the proposed method not only effectively reduces the capture path required for tracking, but also improves the operation efficiency, and greatly improves the accuracy of tracking, solves various forms of limb occlusion, and is satisfactory. Tracking Results.

Acknowledgements. On the digitalized 3D model of Tibetan Xianziwu based on 3D Motion Capture (Innovation-Supportive Project for Young Teachers in Colleges and Universities in Tibet Autonomous Region) QCZ2016—33.

References

1. Anonymous. Research on the motion characteristics of left and right ankle joints of Vicon motion capture system during human walking. Modern Inf. Technol. **2**(6), 15–17 (2018)
2. Wei, Y., Fan, X.: Tracking and recognition of human motion posture based on GMM. J. Beijing Inst. Fashion (Natural Science Edition) **100**(2), 47–55 (2018)
3. Wang, M., Hu, M., Yang, W.: Motion accuracy simulation of robot tracking gesture image. Comput. Simul. **34**(8), 346–350 (2017)
4. Gang, J., Nan, Z.: An athlete posture analysis model for tracking human joint points with multi-feature optical flow. Sci. Technol. Bull. **15**(12), 133–136 (2017)
5. He, K., Ding, X.: Human behavior tracking method based on low-dimensional manifolds. Comput. Eng. Des. **38**(5), 1361–1365 (2017)
6. Wang, Y., Li, H., Qi, H., et al.: A robust moving target tracking method inspired by three-stage memory mechanism of human brain. J. Electron. **45**(09), 12–17 (2017)
7. Man, W., Zhu, Z., Zhang, Z., et al.: Human motion posture analysis using synchronous extrusion wavelet transform. J. Xi'an Jiaotong Univ. **51**(12), 8–13 (2017)
8. Zhiping, W.: Pedestrian tracking algorithm based on human body feature recognition and Kalman filter. Electro-Optic Control **46**(11), 97–102 (2016)
9. Ying, Z., Ying, Z.: Research on motion target tracking algorithms based on computer vision. J. Chifeng Univ. (Nature Edition) **33**(4), 12–14 (2017)
10. Liu, S., Qiu, Z., Ding, Q., et al.: Research on head attitude tracking method based on adaptive filtering. Electro-optic and Control **91**(4), 33–36 (2016)
11. Wang, Q., Gong, L., Dong, C.: Passive attitude tracking control of Spacecraft Based on time-varying gain ESO. Control Decis.-Making **43**(2), 193–202 (2018)
12. Yin, C.: Multi-loop recursive attitude tracking control for capturing spacecraft. Space Control **12**(1), 54–56 (2018)

Simulation of Differential Expression in Root, Stem and Leaf of Ornamental Cunninghamia Lanceolata Under Internet of Things Environment

Hui Liu[✉]

Heze University, Heze, China
ysh201701@163.com

Abstract. With the promotion of the use of ornamental Cunninghamia lance-olata (Cunninghamia lanceolata L.), the difference of root, stem and leaf specific expression was simulated under the Internet of things environment. In the process of the research, the model was established. The selective expression of genes was carried out and the score output was calculated. Based on the output probability setting of signal states and differential gene identification, the biological function analysis of peculiar genes in roots, stems and leaves of Cunninghamia lanceolata was realized. Through the experimental analysis, the validity of the simulation is proved effectively.

Keywords: Internet of things · Cunninghamia lanceolata · Rhizome and leaf · Difference

1 Introduction

The rapid development of molecular biology in recent years shows the traditional physiology, ecological methods to reveal the resistance of Cunninghamia lanceolata (Cunninghamia lanceolata) information is very limited, and vulnerable to other factors, it is difficult to meet the needs of modern Chinese fir research. Therefore, protein two-dimensional electrophoresis technology emerged as the times require. It can not only reveal the differences in protein and exclude the phenotypic variation caused by environmental differences, but also widen the choice of research materials. Although the cost is large, the method is fast and reliable [1]. The research on proteomics of Cunninghamia lanceolata is relatively few, which is related to the late start of the research on coniferous tree species [2]. Cunninghamia lanceolata is a unique tree species in China. It is also one of the main tree species in the south of China. It is of great importance in the total amount of forest resources in China. For a long time, continuous cultivation of Cunninghamia lanceolata (Cunninghamia lanceolata) resulted in an increasingly obvious decline in the yield of Chinese fir plantation. A large number of studies have shown that phosphorus deficiency is one of the main constraints on plant growth [3]. Low phosphorus tolerance is the nature of a plant widely existing in nature. It has been widely recognized that low phosphorus tolerance of plants and its

© ICST Institute for Computer Sciences, Social Informatics and Telecommunications Engineering 2019
Published by Springer Nature Switzerland AG 2019. All Rights Reserved
G. Gui and L. Yun (Eds.): ADHIP 2019, LNICST 301, pp. 392–400, 2019.
https://doi.org/10.1007/978-3-030-36402-1_42

role in improving plant resistance and uptake of nutrients in ecosystems has been widely recognized. The results showed that phosphorus stress could lead to the decrease of plant dry matter accumulation and root parameters, the change of species and quantity of root specific exudates, and the increase of nutrient accumulation in root. However, most of the current scholars have studied in physiology and ecology, and relatively few in molecular biology. At present, there are few studies on Simulation of rhizome differences. He et al. [4] analyzed the correlations between the varietal parameters of Sirius and to determine the minimum number of parameters that need to be estimated in order to accurately simulate the effect of the genotype and environment on wheat anthesis date. So far, the mechanism of molecular effects of Chinese fir on low phosphorus stress has not been clarified. In order to study the response mechanism of Chinese fir to adversity during its growth and development, especially the mechanism of low phosphorus tolerance, it is particularly important to express differentially from stem to leaf.

2 Simulation of Differential Expression of Ornamental Cunninghamia Lanceolata Root, Stem and Leaf

2.1 Model Establishment

The xylem of Chinese fir roots, stems and leaves is composed of tubular molecules, parenchyma cells and wood fibers. It has been one of the hotspots in plant anatomy, developmental biology and cell biology because of its obvious characteristics in morphology, structure, development and physiological function. These cell types have different functions, all from the cambium meristem primordial cells. The proportion of these cell types is different among different tree species. The structure and composition of stem wood of the same tree also have great variation. This is determined by its internal genetic basis and external environmental conditions. The radial width of the ring is more or less dependent on the species of trees, while some species growing in the tropics may not have obvious rings or may form multiple rings a year, resulting in false rings. In addition to the morphological characteristics of the cell wall, the xylem cells of late wood became longer and lignin components changed (Takabe et al. 1992) [5]. Stress wood can cause secondary growth of trunks and branches in a more favorable direction of (favorable). Along with this brings about the violent development transformation, causes the wood product many aspects also to have the change.

The most important point in designing a generalized hidden Markov model (GHMM), is its topology. Choosing the topology of the model correctly can describe the data more efficiently. Usually, the topology of GHMM is fully connected, that is, every state can be reached from any other state. However, it is obvious that the ergodic topology is not suitable for the poly (A) signal structure derived from the pseudo-Chinese fir mRNA polyadenosine signal model (Fig. 1A).

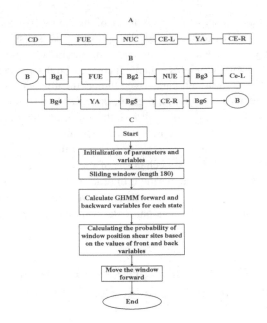

Fig. 1. A signal structure; B topology; C algorithm flow chart

The square represents the fixed-length region, while the brackets represent the variable-length region with a limited range; 3'-UTR represents the 3 'untranslated region; CD represents the coding region; FUE represents the upstream remote control element; NUE represents the upstream near-end control element; CE stands for the shear element, CE.L,CE.R for the left and right side of the poly (A) site, CS for the shear site, that is, the poly (A) site. YA represents the dimer with TA or CA at the left end of CS. It is noted that not all sites are YA, at left end of the site, so other pairs of combinations are also considered in GHMM. In order to simplify the model, it is assumed that the length of each specific signal state is fixed, while the length of the background region outside the signal is variable. At the same time, each state can only be transferred to the next state, but does not exclude the possibility of jumping directly from one signal to another, so the length of each background state in the model is set to possible zero. Finally, it is specified that all paths of the model can only begin in the first state, that is, background 1, and end in the last state IV. The GHMM topology for poly (A) site recognition is shown in figure 3.6B. Among them, B is the starting point of program scanning, Bg is the background state between cis-acting elements, and E is the end point of program scan. According to the design of GHMM model, we construct a computer program to predict the location of poly (A) sites, the core flow of which is shown in figure 3-6C. The main function of the subfunction is to calculate the probability product of the base distribution of the subsequence by the base distribution matrix, and to realize the calculation of the first-order isomeric Markov submodel [6].

2.2 Selective Expression of Genes

The selective expression of genes is very complex, and its influencing factors have both external and internal factors. Now people can make the favorable gene expression of organism by changing the external conditions, inhibit the harmful gene expression, for the benefit of human beings. Treat cancer by placing oncogenes in a state of suppression, such as through specific chemotherapy methods. RNA interference is common in animals, plants and human bodies. It is of great significance for the management of selective expression of genes, the protection of virus infection, the control of active genes and the activation of inhibitory genes. In eukaryotes, most of the genes that contain complex transcription units are genes that encode tissue and development-specific proteins, with the exception of varying numbers of introns. Its original transcription product, pre.rnRNA, can be processed into two or more mRNA, by many different ways, which can encode more than one peptide. This diversity of post-transcriptional processing is regulated by the selective expression of genes. It mainly includes the selection of transcription initiation sites, selective processing and mRNA stability control.

2.3 Score Output Calculation

At present, hidden Markov model (HMM) is a widely used statistical method in bioinformatics, mainly used in linear sequence analysis, model analysis, gene discovery and so on. HMM is developed on the basis of Markov chain [7]. Unlike Markov chain model, HMM is more complex. Its observations and states do not correspond one to one, but are related through a set of probability distributions. As shown in Fig. 1, a hidden Markov model is composed of two random variable sequences, one of which is an unobservable (both hidden) variable state sequence to describe the state transition, and the other is an observable symbol sequence generated by an unobservable state to describe the statistical correspondence between the state and the observed value. For an observer, only the observed value can be seen, but the observer who gets the observed value from which states in the model does not know, which is the so-called "hidden" of the model (Fig. 2).

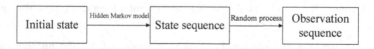

Fig. 2. HMM composition diagram

According to the description of poly (A) signal pattern, the statistical characteristics are mainly concentrated in the nucleotide sequences of upstream 130nt and down-stream 50nt of poly (A) site, indicating that this part of the sequence basically reflects the purine around poly (A) site. The pattern of the pyrimidine concentration curve, so we use a 180nt wide sliding window to calculate the output score of the sequence. For an input sequence longer than 180nt, slide along the entire sequence with the step size of Int until the end of the sequence [8]. In this way, for each base position, according to the previously designed algorithm, a score can be calculated in each window containing that base (Score, is the score of the poly (A) site in a sequence of windows). Take the maximum score as the last score of the poly (A) site at this location, described as follows:

$$Score(t) = \max\{S(t)\}$$
$$S(t) = \{\log_{10} PS_w + 120\}/2 \tag{1}$$

$$PS_w = a_t(8) \cdot \beta_t(9) \tag{2}$$

According to the definition of forward and backward variables, $a_t(8)$ represents the probability that the observed sequence $O1, O2, \cdots, Ot$ will appear when the eighth state of the model (i.e., YA on the left side of poly (A) site ends at the base position t, $\beta_t(9)$ represents the ninth state in the model (that is, Bg5 on the right side of poly (A). W refers to all window sequences containing base position t. Log values and two constants (120 and 2) are used to adjust the score so that the final output score is in a controllable range.

2.4   Output Probability Setting of Signal Status

After determining the length of the signal, we need to further calculate the output probability of the bases (A, T, C, G) in each signal state (the probability distribution of the observed symbols in the state S_i). To this end, the number of signal modes obtained by SignaSleuth from 8 K data sets is used to analyze the base distribution of FUE, CE-L and CE-R signal states (i.e. the base-to-ε output probability $D_\varepsilon = \varepsilon \in \{A, T, C, G\}$), and the calculation formula is as follows:

$$D_\varepsilon = \frac{\sum\limits_{i=1}^{N} (\varepsilon_i \times W_i)}{\sum\limits_{\varepsilon \in \{A, T, C, G\}} (\sum\limits_{i=1}^{N} (\varepsilon_i \times W_i))} \tag{3}$$

Among them, $W_i = \frac{C_i}{\sum\limits_{i=1}^{N} C_i}$ is the statistical weight of mode i, and the more the number of occurrences, the greater the weight of mode i. C_i is the number of occurrences of mode i in the signal region. ε_i is the number of occurrences of base i in mode ε, $1 \leq i \leq N$, and IV is the number of signal modes considered.

2.5   Differential Gene Identification

In order to identify the structural differences between WT and pcfs4, the gene (DPG), is based on biological significance. The top of the figure is the structure of the given gene, and the box represents the exon (exon), joining two exon lines representing the short lines below the intron (intron), exon representing the TilingArray probe [9]. The abundance of Exon 1 and Exon 2 is the same between WT and pcfs4, but Exon 3 is different. In this way, the ratio of Exon-1 between IV T and pcfs4 is the same as that of Exon-2, which is equal to 1, which is different from the ratio of Exon-3. On the contrary, if the selection utilization of poly (A) locus is not affected by PCFS4, the relative abundance of the two transcripts will be the same in WT and pcfs4, that is, the ratio of measured abundance between wT and pcfs4 will be equal in all three exon.

For a given unknown gene, it is assumed that two major transcripts (also known as transcripts) are derived from its pre.mRNA by selecting two different poly (A) sites for splicing. As described above, the selective polyadenylate of the gene FCA is the same.

Based on the above concepts, hierarchical combination statistical analysis was used to identify differentially structured genes (DPG) and differentially expressed genes (DEG) regulated by PCFS4 factors by using logarithmic converted ratio data to identify differentially structured genes (DPG) and differentially expressed genes (DEG). For each of the selected differentially structured genes, we also use the multiple mean comparison (MMC) method to analyze the differences in all pairings of the gene or transcript. And then determine which or which exorls units cause partial differences in the corresponding genes or transcripts. In order to improve the specificity of the candidate differentially expressed gene (DEG), the double-sided T-test was further applied to the entire transcript of the candidate gene, zero pseudomorphism: all probe ratios of the entire transcript. The average value equals 0. If the candidate gene is considered not to be a differentially expressed gene, the candidate gene is classified as a differentially expressed gene.

2.6   Special Allogeneic Biological Function in Root, Stem and Leaf of Cedar

The number of genes specifically expressed in leaves was the largest, with 20 genes, but mainly concentrated in auxin signal transduction pathway, including 15 genes encoding SAUR protein (9 indole-3-acetic acid inducible protein ARG7 and 6 auxin-induced protein). 2 GH3 (gretchen hagen3) and 1 gene encoding AUX/IAA protein (IAA29) In addition, jasmonic acid pathway transcriptional activator MYC2 (BbHLH28) and ethylene signal transduction activator EIN3 were also specifically expressed in leaves.

3   Methodology

3.1   Test Material

The seeds of Cunninghamia lanceolata were collected from Jiaozhou Experimental Station of Qingdao Agricultural University. After laminating, the seedlings were raised in spring 2016. After 45 days of seedling growth, individual plants with the same growth and development were selected and their roots, stems and leaves were selected for specific gene expression analysis. The leaves of 'QN-101'4' at different developmental stages, including sprouting buds (shoot tips), early leaf development (young leaves), middle developmental (mature leaves) and late developmental (senescent leaves), were used for qRT-PCR analysis.

3.2   Data Detection and Functional Annotation

The genes obtained from mapping were compared with NR (NCBI non-redundant protein library), Swiss-Prot (non-redundant protein database), Gene Ontology database and KEGG pathway database) by Blastx (E < 1e−5), and the gene annotation information was obtained. P-value < 0.05 was used as the threshold to define the metabolic pathways of significant enrichment in genes. Using iTAK software (Yi et al., 2016), using classification in database The defined transcription factor (transcription factor, TF) family was identified by hmmscan [10].

3.3   Fluorescence Quantitative PCR Verification

PrimeScriptTM reagent Kit with gDNA Eraser kit was used to reverse transcript mRNA into cDNA. The expression of differentially expressed genes was verified by Real-time Quantitive PCR. Pbactin is selected as the internal reference gene. The differential gene and the specific primer sequence of the internal reference gene are listed in Table 1:

Table 1. Real-time fluorescence quantitative PCR gene primer sequence.

Name	Gane ID	Forward primer	Reverse primer
BbHLH 28	LOC103964261	AAGACGCATCACCCAACAAC	AAAGCTTTGCCGGGAACATT
BAK 1	LOC103929041	CGGAAGGAGATGCTCTGAGT	TTCCGGAAAGGTCCAAGCT
ARG7	LOC103957880	CGTCTGCCTGCTGTΛATTCC	TGTTAGACCGCCCATTGGAT
ARG7	LOC103957860	TTGCAGTCTATGTCGGGGAG	GATCGGTTCGTGTTCACTCA
Auxin-induced protein X10A	LOC103967982	GGGTTCCGTCTTCCATCTGT	TCTTGTCTGCAGGGAATCGT
Auxin-induced protein X10A	LOC103957857	TCAGTGTCCCTTCTATGCCC	GAGATGCACTTGGACAACGG
Squalene monooxygenase	LOC104967056	ACCTCAGATATCGCCGGAAG	TTTGAAAAGCACCCATCGCA
Pbactin	GQ339778.1	ATTGGAGCTGAGAGATTCCGGT	GTCTCATGAATGCCAGCAGCTT

3.4   Analysis of Gene Expression in Different Tissues of Chinese Fir

By comparing with the reference genome, 19 443, 19 567 and 17 876 genes were obtained in roots, stems and leaves of Cunninghamia lanceolata (Cunninghamia lanceolata). There were 845894841 low-expression genes (FPKM < 10) in root, stem and leaf respectively. The number of high-expression tissue-specific genes was lower (26, 12), as shown in Fig. 3.

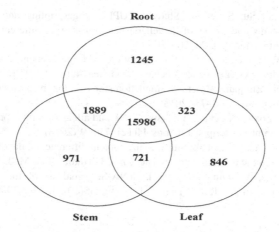

Fig. 3. Analysis of differentially expressed genes in rhizomes and leaves of Cunninghamia lanceolata

These results suggest that there are significant differences in gene expression among different tissues of Cunninghamia lanceolata, and the expression of a large number of tissue-specific genes may be related to the different biological functions of different tissues.

4 Conclusion

It was found that the expression of genes related to hormone signal transduction pathway was mainly enriched in leaves, especially auxin signal transduction pathway. Auxin regulates plant cell division and differentiation, promotes stem and leaf growth, vascular tissue differentiation and apical dominance. The genes associated with auxin signal transduction pathway are mainly expressed in leaves, which may be related to the primary site of auxin synthesis in young leaves.

References

1. Guangxin, Yu., Shuangqing, Z., Xiuhong, Z., et al.: CDNA-SRAP analysis of differential expression in stem and leaf of Aegilops alba. J. Henan Agricultural University **51**(4), 481–486 (2017)
2. Zhang, Y., Jiang, T., Ye, Y., et al.: Cloning and expression specific analysis of strawberry FaCOP1. Horticulture **44**(3), 547–556 (2017)
3. Yan, S.Y., Zhang, Y., Wang, X., et al.: Design of orderly Harvester for stems and leaves vegetables based on Pro/E. Agric. Mechanization Res. **39**(3), 139–143 (2017)
4. He, J., Gouis, J.L., Stratonovitch, P., et al.: Simulation of environmental and genotypic variations of final leaf number and anthesis date for wheat. Eur. J. Agron. **42**(1), 22–33 (2012)

5. Yan, B., Zhu, S., Su, S., et al.: Study on UPLC fingerprinting and chemical pattern recognition of stems and leaves of Scutellaria baicalensis from different areas. J. Nanjing Univ. Tradit. Chin. Med. (6), 24–26 (2017)
6. Chuang, H.S., Wang, Y., Jian, Y., et al.: Study on the finite element modeling method for sugarcane stalk-leaf system. Agric. Mechanization Res. 40(6), 19–23 (2018)
7. Le, W., Yuan, N., Zhiqiang, C., et al.: Simulation study on the dynamics of cotton leaf age. Jiangsu Agric. Sci. 46(4), 68–73 (2018)
8. Jing, D., Lu, X., Zhang, K., et al.: Analysis of SNP and allele-specific expression of Gordane hybrid and its parent transcripts. J. Crops 44(12), 71–79 (2018)
9. Hu, S., Chung, K., Yang, J., et al.: Study on the content difference of flavonoids in stems and leaves of peppermint at different harvest date. Chin. J. Tradit. Chin. Med. 3, 544–550 (2018)
10. Huan, Z., Yingjie, Y., Dingli, L., et al.: RNA-Seq analysis of the genes specifically expressed in root stem and leaf of Duli L. J. Hortic. 45(10), 18–31 (2018)

Design of Statistical Model for Difference of Leaf Color of Ornamental Begonia Based on Big Data Analysis

Hui Liu[✉]

Heze University, Heze, China
ysh201701@163.com

Abstract. Based on big data's analysis, the statistical model of the difference between different leaf colors of ornamental begonia was designed in order to solve the problem of low statistical accuracy of the difference between different leaf colors of traditional ornamental begonia. Combined with quantitative classification, the variety of ornamental begonia was investigated and analyzed, and the characters of ornamental begonia were analyzed and the coding design was carried out. On this basis, the varieties of ornamental begonia were labeled with different leaf colors. The statistical model design of the difference between different leaf colors of ornamental begonia is realized. The experimental results show that the model design has good accuracy.

Keywords: Big data analysis · Ornamental begonia · Leaf color variety

1 Introduction

The cultivation and application of ornamental begonia in China has been recorded for nearly 2000 years. During the long-term cultivation process, many varieties have been formed through natural selection and human participation. Recently, some new species with high ornamental value have been introduced in China, which greatly enriches the resources of ornamental begonia. In order to make better use of these resources, it is urgent to make a scientific and systematic statistical study on the differences between different leaf colors. At present, there are many problems in the statistical research on the difference of leaf color among ornamental begonia. The resources of ornamental begonia are unclear [1]. The investigation of ornamental begonia resources was carried out as apple rootstock and breeding resource in the early stage. The taxonomy was also rarely carried out under the species line, and some of the varieties investigated at that time had been lost, while the new variety resources had not been systematically investigated [2]. The other is regulation of genes, regulation of anthocyanin biosynthesis structure gene expression intensity and process, and pigment accumulation in space and time.

The varieties of the modern ornamental begonia are becoming more and more diverse and the ornamental characters are more abundant. The varieties are different from the original species or their parents in such characters as branch type, flower color, flower type and fruit, etc. Generally speaking, the variety of ornamental begonia,

G. Gui and L. Yun (Eds.): ADHIP 2019, LNICST 301, pp. 401–409, 2019.
https://doi.org/10.1007/978-3-030-36402-1_43

white flowers account for the majority. For example, the leaves of red jade begonia are light green, strawberry jelly begonia is dark green, the leaves of red begonia are yellow green ornamental begonia are rich in natural anthocyanin glycoside, flavonol, proanthocyanidins, etc. It can be used as ornamental tree species to beautify the urban and rural environment, as well as the construction tree species around the city forest belt, at the same time, it can be used to develop related ornamental begonia health products. It is of great significance for the development of new ornamental begonia varieties with both ornamental and medicinal value to deeply study the difference statistics among different leaf colors of ornamental begonia.

2 Design of Statistical Model for Difference of Leaf Color of Ornamental Begonia

2.1 Investigation and Analysis of Begonia Varieties

Combined with quantitative classification, a variety classification system for ornamental begonia varieties with different leaf colors was established, which laid a solid foundation for the classification of ornamental begonia varieties. In order to do a good job in classification of ornamental begonia [3], the first and urgent task is to carry out extensive investigation and research, find out the resources of ornamental begonia varieties, and analyze the leaf size, shape and color of ornamental begonia. The leaf characteristics of ornamental begonia varied in varieties, especially in leaf size, shape and color of leaves under inflorescences and new shoots during anthesis. Therefore, when the varieties were recorded, they were recorded separately. The leaves which have been fully expanded under the inflorescence at the time of anthesis are called young leaves, and the leaves on the new shoots which will be sprouted from leaf buds are called mature leaves or old leaves when they are fully expanded and reach their proper size [3]. The young leaf characters were recorded at flowering stage, with the records of flowers and inflorescences, while the records of old leaves were recorded in autumn, and the records of fruit characters were carried out at the same time. Leaf blade shape is round, ellipsoid, ovate, Obovate, in which the most oval and ellipsoid. The classification and coding of the characters of the varieties of Malus were carried out as shown in the table.

Table 1. Trait characteristics and coding.

	Character	Detailed coding
1	Flower color	Flowers red, pink, white
2	Flower pattern	Double cultivar single petal
3	Footpath among flowers	Flower diameter reaches 5 cm
		Flower diameter less than 4 cm
4	Florescence duration	Long viewing period
5	Flower quantity	Flower diameter covering leaf
6	Fruit size	Fruit diameter greater than 2 cm
7	Leaf color	Larger result
8	Tree form	Leaf purple red

Table 1 is the classification and coding of the characters of the begonia cultivars. The maximum width axis of a rectangular leaf and two nearly parallel leaf edges cover the middle of the long axis of the leaf, and the maximum width axis of the elliptic leaf is perpendicular to the midpoint of the leaf axis in a region composed of the maximum width axis of a rectangular leaf and two almost parallel leaf edges. The axis base of the axis of the oval leaf blade is at the midpoint of the former, and the axis of the Obovate leaf blade is the maximum width of the axis of the intersecting leaf at the midpoint of the former. At the same time, whether or not the leaves split, leaf color, young leaf color in addition to green, there are purple red, bright red and yellow. The old leaves have dark red in addition to green. Some old leaves become dark red or golden yellow, orange and other colors in autumn, as autumn leaves recorded in the specificity evaluation column. Green is divided into light green, dark green three levels [4]. Some young leaves are green, the leaves are respectively recorded by the surface and back of the hairy leaves, respectively, divided into dense, micro, only midvein, not four grades; The most important indexes for classification of ornamental begonia are leaf length, leaf width, middle width, broadest position and tip distance, so the measurement of leaf size mainly records these items. Leaf length refers to the length of leaf base to leaf tip, and leaf width refers to the distance between the two leaf edges at the broadest part of the leaf. The middle width of the leaf is the distance between the two leaf edges in the middle of the leaf, and the distance between the broadest part and the tip is to measure the length of the straight line from the leaf width to the tip, and the shape of the leaf tip is the area surrounding the edge of the leaf, which is slightly more than 25% at the upper end of the leaf. Apiculate, attenuate, mucronate, obtuse, and rounded [5]; leaf base shaped; leaf base refers to area surrounded by leaf margin slightly less than 25% of leaf base. Sharp, obtuse, narrowly cuneate, broadly cuneate, rounded, cordate, decurrent. The leaf margin is arc-shaped, with angle less than 90° as sharp tip and more than 90° as sharp point and more than 90° as obtuse; if the leaf margin is almost straight called wedge, the angle less than 90° is narrow cuneate and greater than 90° is broadly cuneate; the leaf edge is circular in arc shape at the base. The leaf margin of the ornamental begonia is mostly serrated, the whole leaf is very few, and the serrate is mostly single-serrated and the double-serrated is very few, so the records of the leaf margin are mainly recorded by the obtuse, sharp, neat and irregular of the serrated teeth. Petiole, mainly recorded petiole length, petiole coarseness, petiole color and coat, leaf blade texture subleathery and papery [6]. Nearly leathery leaf blade thick, hard, paper leaf thin, soft, leaf surface characteristics, mainly recorded smooth or not smooth, glossy or lustrous. Most of the leaves were spreading, some of them would appear leaf tip or leaf edge bending to the back. In the specific evaluation, inflorescence, ornamental malus inflorescence characters, mainly recorded the inflorescence type, the number of flowers per inflorescence, the number of leaves per inflorescence, and the number of leaves per inflorescence. Branches under inflorescences long, entire trees flowering and flowering. There are two types of inflorescences: umbels and umbels; the number of flowers per inflorescence, the number of leaves per inflorescence, the length of young branches under inflorescence, and the number of flowers per inflorescence, the number of leaves per inflorescence and the length of young branches in inflorescences are measured. The flower and fruit characters of flowering begonia are not only more stable than leaf characters, but also play an important role in classification, and they are also the main ornamental parts. The buds of begonia are always darker in color than the Corolla, and thus have higher ornamental value. Mainly record bud color and bud shape, bud color has purple, crimson, bright red, pink four kinds. Bud-shaped apical and round, Corolla, including Corolla diameter, color, there are no veins, flowers, and other recorded items. Corolla diameter: Measure the natural corolla diameter when the flowers are in full bloom. It is impossible to flatten the flowers artificially or measure the flowers that are not in full bloom [7], in cm. The flower color of the begonia was gradually dimmed from the first flower to the last flower. Therefore, the full flowering stage was taken as the standard in the record, and the flower color of the first and last flowering stage was recorded as a reference. If the flower color changes significantly during the flowering process, it should be recorded separately. Because the bud color of the begonia is darker than the petals, there will be dark veins appearing in the petals color, and whether or not the veins are recorded at the same time when the flower color is recorded; flower incense: recorded in the blooming stage, there are no two grades. Through the investigation and analysis of the varieties of Begonia, we can provide help to mark the varieties of different leaf colors, so as to realize the statistical work of difference.

2.2 Marking of Different Leaf Color Varieties of Begonia

Under the analysis of big data, the different leaf color varieties of ornamental begonia were labeled. In order to prepare for the statistical analysis of the difference between different leaf colors of ornamental begonia, isozyme and molecular marker methods were used to mark [8]. On the premise of defining the "species line" to which the variety belongs (or if it is the origin of the intraspecific or intergeneric hybrid, and the name of the hybrid or hybrid genus), three taxonomic units, namely, variety group, variety and grafted chimcra, are adopted, On the basis of the origin of natural taxo-nomic species (or hybrids and varieties), the varieties of ornamental begonia with different leaf colors were classified on the basis of source. The petals of most varieties of ornamental begonia are nearly rounded, ovoid or Obovate, apex obtuse, base with short claws. But the petals of 'lotus-like' begonia and 'double petal' Hubei begonia 'are ellipsoid, petal apex apical, petal-shaped like lotus flower; petals of' rolling calyx 'Liriodendron are not spreading, middle base has raised ridges, and petals above petals are tomentose; The inner buckle of the petals. Some double petals with large number of petals, double petal varieties due to spatial position of petal smaller, irregular shape or surface shrink phenomenon.

Different leaf colors of ornamental crabapple have the same or similar substrates, which catalyze the same reaction. Isozymes are the direct products of gene expression [9], in which the number of bands and mobility changes are largely determined by structural genes. Therefore, according to the phenotypes of isozymes, we can directly judge the different leaf color varieties of Begonia hypoglauca. The zymogram of iso-zymes in the progeny of the same vegetative line was always unchanged, and the zymogram characteristics of the same species or variety after asexual reproduction remained basically unchanged. In the same variety, most isozymes were relatively stable at different tree ages and at different stages of development, the basic zymogram of the original variety was still maintained in the tissue culture seedlings of the same variety, and some main enzyme bands of the same variety remained stable under different soil fertility conditions. Among them, molecular markers are a kind of genetic markers developed with the development of molecular cloning and recombinant DNA technology of ornamental begonia [10]. Molecular markers are expressed in the form of DNA directly in the tissues of plant, they can be detected in all developmental stages, not limited by season or environment, and the number is high, and the whole genome has polymorphism. The marker formula of analysis marker for different leaf color varieties of Begonia hypoglauca was as follows:

$$e = \frac{c(B_1, k)^{-1}}{v - rt_n} \tag{1}$$

In the formula, e represents the detected ornamental crabapple factor; t_n represents all third-party data; B_1 represents the plant tissue of crabapple; k represents the set of non-stop leaves of crabapple; This calculation is only for introducing coefficients, not for directional analysis. On this basis, a formal definition will be given. If and only if item r is to be marked item t_n, the form of Begonia mark can be recorded as $n(k) \Rightarrow x_i$.

According to the requirement of molecular marker [11], the marker function of different leaf color cultivars of Begonia crabapple was obtained by using $n(k) \Rightarrow x_i$ as the minimum support rule coefficient of marker without considering environmental limitation and quantity value.

$$M = \frac{B_n/f(t)}{K(cn)^2 \Rightarrow x_i} \tag{2}$$

In the formula, M represents the rule of molecular marking; B_n represents the parameter of marked crabapple; $f(t)$ represents the total number of marked crabapples in t time. This calculation does not do directional analysis.

By marking different leaf colors of ornamental begonia, it can provide a basis for statistical analysis of the differences among different leaf colors, so as to realize the difference statistics of different leaf colors.

2.3 Statistical Analysis on the Difference of Leaf Color of Ornamental Begonia (Tripterygium indica L.)

The statistical model design of the difference between different leaf colors of ornamental begonia was realized through the investigation and analysis of the variety resources and the marking of different leaf colors. Considering the difference of leaf color among begonia varieties [12], the difference of begonia varieties is calculated first, and the formula is as follows:

$$K_n = \sum_{v}^{N} d_q/F_c N_u \tag{3}$$

In the formula, K_n represents the quantity parameter of crabapple and F_c represents the quantity of different leaf colours. Formal definition of N, when d_q and only if the transaction item v are included, the results of different varieties of Begonia with different leaf colors are obtained. On this basis, the statistical model of the difference between different leaf colors of ornamental begonia was established, and the process map was shown as shown in the diagram (Fig. 1).

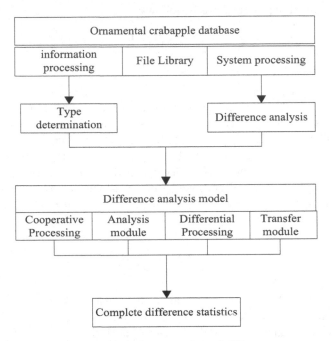

Fig. 1. Statistical process chart of differences

As shown in the chart, the statistical process map of the difference between different leaf colors is shown. According to the above-mentioned process, the difference statistics among different leaf color varieties are carried out, and on the basis of the results of the difference of different leaf colors, the results of the difference statistics between different leaf color varieties are obtained according to the above-mentioned process. To achieve the difference statistics among different leaf color varieties, the formula is as follows:

$$T_\eta = \sum_j^m c_j/m \times v_\sigma \times d \times g' \tag{4}$$

In the formula, T_η represents the number parameter of crabapple varieties, c_j represents the difference parameter in difference statistics, m represents the Initial Value of Different Leaf Colour Difference Data of Orange Begonia, v_σ represents the difference quantity of crabapple varieties, d represents the statistics of different leaf color differences. g' represents the introduced statistics. This calculation only introduces parameters, not directional analysis.

Through statistical calculation of difference, the statistical model design of the difference between different leaf colors of ornamental begonia was completed. In order to ensure the validity of the design, the following comparative experiments were carried out.

3 Results

The experimental materials were taken from a certain area, and more than 100 species of begonia were planted in the experimental area, and more than one hundred varieties of begonia were planted at home and abroad. The petal samples of Begonia begonia were collected at the bud stage, the full flowering stage and the last flowering stage respectively. According to the different growth position of the leaves, the young leaves at the top and the functional leaves at the middle part were collected respectively. The following is the design of color parameters of begonia varieties (Table 2):

Table 2. Design of color parameters of begonia varieties.

Color series and subseries	Cultivar number	L	a	b
Green	28	46.80 ± 3.52	−6.60 ± 3.81	28.92 ± 4.77
Dark green	15	46.20 ± 3.13 b	−7.03 ± 2.83 b	27.35 ± 2.31 b
Brownish green	3	42.72 ± 2.28 a 49.90 ± 2.10 a	−1.98 ± 1.98	22.13 ± 1.61
Bright green	7	32.50 ± 2.70 b	1.18 ± 1.98 a	9.46 ± 3.40 b
Reddish brown	20	38.20 ± 2.87 a	7.60 ± 2.42 b	21.80 ± 3.34 a

3.1 Processing Method

Analytic hierarchy process (AHP) is a multi-objective decision-making and evaluation method which combines qualitative analysis and quantitative analysis. The structural feature is that each element of the upper level is completely related to each factor of the next level, that is, each element of the upper level plays a role as the decision criterion of the next level. The whole operation process is completed by the analytic hierarchy process software Yaahp0.3.2 software package. The advantage of this software is: using the drawing method similar to Visio to complete the hierarchical structure model. The selection of fine ornamental begonia varieties is regarded as the target layer of difference statistics, that is, the difference analysis value obtained by comparison among the varieties, and the result as the evaluation layer of difference analysis.

3.2   Contrast Result

In the above environment, the experimental comparison is carried out, and the results are as follows (Fig. 2):

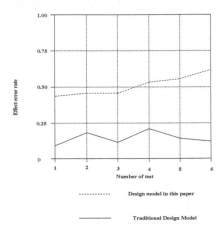

Fig. 2. Contrast chart of statistical accuracy of difference

Through the comparison chart, we can see that the precision of the difference statistical model design in this paper is high, and the error is small and the floating is low in the statistical time.

4   Conclusion

This paper puts forward the statistical model design of the difference between different leaf colors of ornamental begonia based on big data's analysis, and it is proved by experiments. The statistical model designed in this paper can improve the accuracy of difference statistics and help the further development of ornamental begonia. Therefore, it can be concluded that the statistical model designed in this paper is effective and can be applied to the statistical analysis of the difference between different leaf colors of ornamental begonia, and has a good prospect of application. However, the traditional statistical model is less accurate and more floating, so it is not very good for different leaf color varieties.

References

1. Li, H.: A Study on the Impact of Personalized Service on Customer Loyalty Based on O2 O Clothing Brand. Zhejiang University of Technology (2016)
2. Wang, R.M.: Patent Status Analysis and Development Strategy Research on Processing Technology of Traditional Chinese Medicine Pieces. Guangzhou University of Traditional Chinese Medicine (2017)

3. Liao, H.T.: Preliminary study on differential proteomics of nitrogen use in different maize inbred lines. Sichuan Agricultural University (2008)
4. Xie, Y.: Modern Agricultural Internet of Things Monitoring System Based on Cloud Computing. Southwest Jiaotong University (2015)
5. Wang, M.L., Yu, S.L., Chen, H.D., et al.: Based on large data analysis, the difference of adverse drug reactions between the Chinese Pharmacopoeia and other quality standards. Chin. J. New Drugs Clin. **12**, 752–756 (2017)
6. Jiang, W.L., Fan, J.J., Zhang, D.D., et al.: Colour characteristics of different leaf positions and exotic germplasm excavation of ornamental crabapple. J. Hortic. **44**(6), 1135–1144 (2017)
7. Zhang, J., Pu, J., Zhao, C., et al.: Dynamic analysis and primary selection of leaf color of offspring from three half-sib families of ornamental crabapple. J. Nanjing For. Univ. (Nat. Sci. Ed.) **42**(3), 37–44 (2018)
8. Zhang, R., Mao, M.M., Liu, Z.L., et al.: Pollen morphology of different cultivars of ornamental crabapple observed by scanning electron microscopy. Mol. Plant breed. **16**(16), 257–264 (2018)
9. Tian, Y., Shen, H.X., Zhang, J., et al.: Cloning of McANS gene from Malus ornamental crabapple and analysis of expression differences among different leaf color varieties. J. Hortic. **37**(6), 939–948 (2010)
10. Qin, X.X., Song, T.T., Zhang, J., et al.: Cloning and expression difference analysis of McF3'H among different cultivars of Begonia crabapple. J. Beijing Agric. Coll. **28**(2), 11–14 (2013)
11. Du, W.W., Duan, Q., Ma, L.L., et al.: Analysis of foliar variegation structure and genetic characteristics of seven Begonia species. Acta Botanica Boreali-Occidentalia Sinica **38**(11), 28–32 (2018)
12. Wang, Z., Wang, W.H., Zhang, J., et al.: Analysis of genetic diversity and genetic relationship of main ornamental crabapple cultivars. J. Fruit Tree **31**(6), 1005–1016 (2014)

Research on Radiation Damage Characteristics of Optical Fiber Materials Based on Data Mining and Machine Learning

Ang Li[✉] and Tian-hui Wang

Zhuhai College of Jilin University, Zhuhai, China
liangl22331@163.com

Abstract. In order to better analyze the damage characteristics of fiber materials under radiation environment, combined with data mining algorithm to calculate the degree of damage of material structure damage. Combine with machine learning method to analyze the calculation results, obtain the damage range of fiber material structure, standardize material damage characteristics and Grade, accurately determine the damage of material structure, and finally improve the radiation damage characteristics of fiber materials. Experiments show that the research on radiation damage characteristics of fiber materials based on data mining and machine learning is accurate and reasonable.

Keywords: Data mining · Machine learning · Fiber material · Radiation damage characteristics

1 Introduction

Research on the characteristics of radiation damage of materials and radiation protection have a wide range of applications. The effective analysis and control of radiation effects of radiation has been the focus of researchers [1]. In recent years, some scholars have studied the radiation damage characteristics of materials and achieved certain results. Literature [2] proposed the damage characteristics of two kinds of radiation sources on the irradiation of optical fiber materials. The irradiation damage characteristics of the three samples of single-mode fiber, erbium-doped fiber and erbium-doped fiber were studied by cobalt source and electron accelerator. The damage mechanism of two kinds of irradiation sources to optical fibers was compared and analyzed. It was found that the rare earth fibers used in the experiments had certain equivalent laws under the damage of two kinds of irradiation sources. The literature [3] proposed the effect of erbium-doped fiber radiation on the output characteristics of fiber-optic source. The gamma irradiation experiment was carried out on the erbium-doped fiber. According to the absorption coefficient and the emission coefficient test data of the erbium-doped fiber before and after irradiation, the absorption cross section and emission cross section of the erbium-doped fiber were calculated. Based on the power law model, the radiation model of the erbium-doped fiber absorption cross section and emission cross section is established. The radiation model of the absorption cross section and the emission cross section is substituted into the erbium-doped fiber

G. Gui and L. Yun (Eds.): ADHIP 2019, LNICST 301, pp. 410–418, 2019.
https://doi.org/10.1007/978-3-030-36402-1_44

source model, and the influence of the radiant effect of the erbium-doped fiber on the output spectrum and characteristic parameters of the erbium-doped fiber source is simulated. In order to better study the radiation damage characteristics of fiber materials. Therefore, combined with the mining algorithm to calculate the line energy transfer coefficient in the radiation ray, and based on the calculation results, the machine learning method is used to control the energy attenuation phenomenon in the fiber material. By analyzing the photoelectric absorption effect of the fiber material on the radiation ray, a large amount of photoelectrons are generated in the fiber material and accompanied by Auger electrons, thereby effectively preventing the damage of the material structure of the radiant fiber material, and completing the radiation damage characteristics of the fiber material.

2 Research Method of Radiation Damage Characteristics of Optical Fiber Materials

2.1 Radiation Damage Algorithm Based on Data Mining

The fiber structure information is refined to establish a material hierarchical structure decentralized database, the changes of the synthetic structure data under radiation are monitored and compared, the judgment matrix is formed, the damage characteristics are determined according to the structural safety judgment scale, and the judgment matrix is established as follows:

$$
\begin{array}{ccccccc}
G & G_1 & g_2 & \cdots & g_n & \cdots & g_m \\
G_1 & g_{11} & g_{12} & \cdots & g_{1n} & \cdots & g_{1m} \\
G_2 & g_{21} & g_{22} & \cdots & g_{2n} & \cdots & g_{2m} \\
\cdots & & & & & & \\
G_n & g_{n1} & g_{n2} & \cdots & g_{nn} & \cdots & g_{nm} \\
\cdots & & & & & & \\
G_m & g_{m1} & g_{m2} & \cdots & g_{mn} & \cdots & g_{mm}
\end{array}
\tag{1}
$$

Combining the above matrix to calculate the strain resistance of the material structure under radiation, the calculation method is as follows.

$$
\bar{G}_i = 2g_{ij}^b \frac{\Pi^c k_{ij}^a}{\sum\limits_{i=1}^{a} (\Pi^b k_{ij})^{\frac{1}{n}}}
\tag{2}
$$

Where i, j are the maximum and minimum parameters in the effective radiation tolerance range, and k is the radiation-dependent line energy transfer efficiency, a is the scale of the degree of radiation within the material, b represents the relative variability parameter of structural damage elements, by calculating the safety range of radiation damage of material structure, judging the degree of radiation damage, calculating the standard value of the radiation resistance capacity of the fiber material, combining the mining algorithm to evaluate the quality of the fiber material, and evaluating and constructing the change of suspected erosion elements in the radiation environment. The fiber erosion degree judgment matrix is as follows:

$$V = \begin{Bmatrix} v_{11} & v_{12} & \cdots & v_{1n} \\ v_{21} & v_{22} & \cdots & v_{2n} \\ \cdots & & & \\ v_{n1} & v_{n2} & \cdots & v_{nn} \end{Bmatrix} \tag{3}$$

The matrix is assigned, the assignment range is from 1 to 9, these values represent different meanings. The evaluation of the material quality index can be summarized as the eigenvector of the matrix and the calculation of the result. The component Q in the characteristic equation represents the weight of each quality index of the material. The specific steps for calculating the matrix characteristic equation are as follows. Calculate each row of security elements of matrix Q as follows:

$$Q = \prod_{i=1}^{j} \overline{G}_i V_{ij} (j = 1, 2, \ldots, n) \tag{4}$$

If m is the reference value of the calculation matrix, the calculation method of the radiation carrying load inside the fiber material structure is:

$$\overline{U} = m^2 \sqrt{Q_{ij}} (i = 1, 2, \ldots, n) \tag{5}$$

The linear energy normalization process for the numerical values calculated in the above steps can be used to calculate the line energy transfer coefficient as follows:

$$W_i = \frac{1}{n} \sum_{j=1}^{i} \overline{U} Q \frac{\delta_{max}}{m - 1} \tag{6}$$

The δ_{max} in the equation represents the characteristic equation root of material quality detection, n, m respectively represent the maximum and minimum values within the range of variation of the radiant ray eigenvectors. Calculate the quality assessment matrix B by combining the above formulas:

$$B = \frac{1}{2} \sqrt{(\overline{G}_i + \overline{U}_j)^{m-n} \delta_{max}} \tag{7}$$

In order to judge whether the material satisfies the average random consistency of radiation damage, the matrix is evaluated: When the matrix check value is less than or equal to 0.1, it is determined that the matrix B has consistency, otherwise the matrix needs to be readjusted. Establish a collection of material damage assessments $B = [b_1, b_2, \ldots, b_n]$, assess the degree and grade of damage to materials, The grades include {better, average, qualified, unqualified}. This level of detection set directly represents the radiation resistance of the material. The set of grades is assigned, and the set of factors affecting the radiation resistance of the factors affecting the evaluation factors is established. Finally, the data evaluation algorithm is used to multiply the set of quality assessments and the set of evaluation factors, and the final evaluation value is obtained. Effectively judge the degree of influence of material radiation combined with the final evaluation value [4].

2.2 Machine Learning-Based Material Radiation Influence Judgment Method

The radiation damage caused by the fiber material during the radiation process is mainly related to the action mechanism of the incident ray and the substance. Therefore, it is necessary to analyze the action mechanism of the ray and the substance in the process of studying the radiation damage effect [5]. In terms of radiation types, it can be mainly divided into ionizing radiation and non-ionizing radiation. The biological effects of radiation generated during radiation are related to the energy transfer between the radiating substances. Ionizing radiation refers to the direct or indirect ionization of substances, including particulate radiation and high-energy X-rays, gamma rays, etc. [6]. Non-ionizing radiation generally cannot cause ionization of matter molecules, but only causes vibration, rotation, etc. of molecules. These mainly include ultraviolet radiation and radiation with lower energy than ultraviolet light. The influence of non-ionizing radiation ionization on the ion structure of the fiber material is judged as shown in the figure below (Fig. 1).

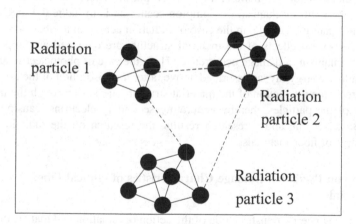

Fig. 1. Judgment of the influence of non-ionizing radiation ionization on the ion structure of fiber materials

As shown in the figure, the process of particle irradiation on fiber materials is an important part of studying the mechanism of radiation damage, Through the high-speed movement of protons, neutrons, mesons, electrons, etc. in the material, the changes of electrons, neutrons and some heavy nuclei are the key research objects in the research of radiation damage characteristics, just like electromagnetic radiation. In the process of fiber radiation, electrons, neutrons, and certain heavy nuclei transmit energy to other substances by losing their own kinetic energy. That is, the interaction with the substance realizes the energy transfer, which leads to the damage of the material structure in the process of particle motion and collision. The principle of determining the radiation influence degree is as follows (Fig. 2).

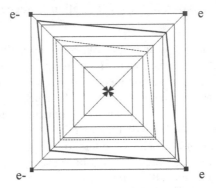

Fig. 2. Schematic diagram of the principle of radiation influence judgment

The study found that when the ray energy is higher than twice the minimum energy of forming electrons of 0.511 MeV, the electron pairing effect often occurs. For high-energy ray, the main mechanism of Compton scattering is to judge the mechanism of radiation and material damage, in the case of radiation acting on a substance, it is often the case that several effects of the material structure are damaged and appear in the form of a mechanism of damage occurrence [7]. In the case of photoelectric absorption as the main low-energy ray, as described above, after the absorption of the ray, the fiber material affects the interaction of the material structure particles through the transfer of the energy of the particles, thereby generating secondary electrons, causing material damage. Based on the above research results, the research on the radiation damage characteristics of fiber materials.

2.3   Study on Radiation Damage Characteristics of Optical Fiber Materials

According to the energy transfer mode of the action of radiation and matter, the process of action is divided into direct and indirect processes. Direct action means that ionizing radiation deposits energy directly on important biomolecules (or other components of the fiber material) and causes physical and chemical changes in these molecules, statistics on the probability of radiation and radiant energy deposition occurring on the same molecule [8]. Indirect action refers to the fact that ionizing radiation deposits energy on other molecules in the environment surrounding important biomolecules, causing physical and chemical changes of important biomolecules, using effects and radiant energy deposition to occur on different molecules. Under normal circumstances, direct and indirect effects always occur simultaneously, and their relative proportion depends on the water content in the living matter, it also depends on the form in which the molecules are "assembled" with each other and with other molecules in the structure of the fiber material. In order to ensure the accuracy of the study, the micro-focus beam performance parameters are statistically obtained, and the following table is obtained (Table 1).

Table 1. Study on performance parameters of microfocus beam.

Focused zone label	CZP_{23}	CZP_{32}	CZP_{45}
Center wavelength	2.1	2.6	3.0
Wavelength range	1.69–1.81	2.15–2.47	2.45–3.12
Radiation spacing	720–740	902–944	803–891
Outlet pinhole spacing	2.4	2.4	2.8
Material structure diameter	1512	1042	1064
Number of bands	432	431	616
Diffraction focal length	513	512	518

A special X-ray beam line dedicated to the study of radiation damage mechanism is established on the KEK2N synchrotron radiation device. The energy coverage is set in combination with the information in the table. From the soft ray to the monochromatic ray in the hard ray band, part of the radiation is carried out. Injury research [9]. At the same time, the radiation damage characteristics of fiber materials were studied by using Munakata and other devices, and the following research results were obtained (Fig. 3).

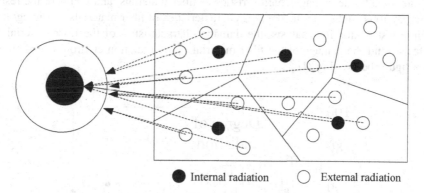

⬤ Internal radiation   ◯ External radiation

Fig. 3. Damage to the material by ray radiation

Studies have shown that synchrotron radiation can cause radiation damage to fiber materials to varying degrees, and the higher the absorption energy of the internal structure and elements of the material, the stronger the material damage effect, there is an enhancement effect on the radiation damage of fiber materials under different radiation environments [10]. In addition, the use of synchrotron radiation to different degrees of variation and damage to the radiation core, and the impact on the surface and structural deactivation damage of the fiber material is relatively large, resulting in different degrees of fiber material death, variation and radiation damage.

3   Analysis of Experimental Results

In order to verify the accuracy of the research results, a simulation experiment was carried out. Combined with the radiation damage algorithm of data mining, the radiation secretary of the fiber material was set, and the material damage value was calculated effectively. The specific information is as follows (Table 2):

Table 2. Experimental test data.

Experiment number	Radiation description	Damage degree
2	Radiation environment 400 rad	1412w
4	Radiation environment 420 rad	1124w
6	Radiation environment 450 rad	1349w
8	Radiation environment 520 rad	15674w
10	Radiation environment 540 rad	1430w

Combine the above table information for further data calculation, in order to accurately study the damage characteristics of fiber materials, and compare the results of the previous studies on the damage characteristics of fiber materials. By integrating multiple test results for analysis, the damage characteristics of the fiber material are displayed, and the damage of the fiber material under radiation environment is shown in the figure below (Fig. 4):

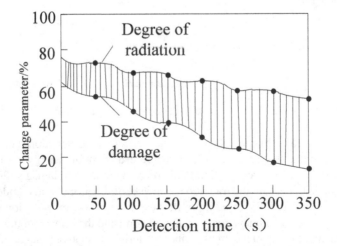

Fig. 4. Detection of damage of optical fiber material under radiation environment

According to the above test results, it can be found that the degree of radiation damage of the fiber material changes with the change of the degree of radiation in the case of changes in the degree of radiation, and the accuracy of the research results of the damage characteristics of the fiber material is repeatedly confirmed. In addition, it was found during use that the radiation damage of ordinary single-mode fibers is much smaller than that of doped fibers at the same radiation dose. Since the experimental results are not highly correlated with the previous research results and have no effect on the experimental results, they are not stated here.

4   Conclusions

According to the research of radiant radiation damage effect, using different radiation high brightness, energy continuously adjustable and other information for analysis and research, combined with data mining algorithm to calculate the radiation damage degree, according to the calculation results, the influence degree of the material radiation of the machine learning is judged, so as to realize the radiation damage effect on the fiber material.

Acknowledgments. Teaching Quality and Teaching Reform Project of Guangdong Undergraduate Colleges and Universities: Construction Project of Experiment Demonstration Center (2017002).

References

1. Shili, C., Haiyan, T., Xuliang, L., et al.: Urban functional area identification based on potential semantic information - GPS spatio-temporal data mining of floating cars in Guangzhou. J. Geogr. **71**(3), 471–483 (2016)
2. Shiwei, L., Bo, L., Haifeng, L., et al.: Research on radiation damage characteristics of optical fibers irradiated by two kinds of radiation sources. Opt. Commun. Technol. **09**, 64–66 (2017)
3. Yan, L., Keqin, L., Jing, J.: Influence of erbium-doped fiber's radiation effects on output characteristics of fiber source. Chin. J. Lasers **12**, 247–254 (2017)
4. Hongwei, Z., Huiyuan, S.: Application of data mining in document purchase decision of university library - taking Heilongjiang University of Traditional Chinese Medicine Library as an example. Chin. Med. Book J. Inf. **40**(2), 22–24 (2016)
5. Cheng, C., Ziyang, X., Jianhua, Y.: Preparation of PbSe quantum dot silicate glass fiber and its photoluminescence spectrum characteristics. Acta Photonica Sinica **46**(6), 61–67 (2017)
6. Wu Zhongli, W., Hongmei, T.L., et al.: Tm3+/Yb3+ Co - doped fluoride tellurite glass upconversion luminescence and optical temperature sensing. Acta Photonica Sinica **46**(9), 15–21 (2017)
7. Hu, Y., Wu, S., Zhang, S., et al.: Evolution of microstructure and mechanical properties of laser composite welding 7020 aluminum alloy based on 3D X - ray imaging. China Laser **1**, 78–86 (2016)

8. Mingqiang, S., Jiahe, W., Shengchao, Z., et al.: Application of PLC network control system in optical fiber material automation production line. Manufact. Autom. **39**(5), 19–21 (2017)
9. Raolan, Liu, Y., Xiao, H., et al.: Experimental study on the durability of optical fiber sensor packaging materials by the number of electrothermal cycles. Sensors Microsyst. **36**(7), 68–69 (2017)
10. Zhang, Z., Yu, A., Zhang, H., et al.: Application of organic anti-electromagnetic radiation materials in optimum design of Salisbury screen. J. Heilongjiang Inst. Technol. **30**(2), 42–45 (2016)

Analysis of Surface Compressive Strength of Optical Fiber Composites Under Low Velocity Impact Damage Based on Big Data

Ang Li[✉]

Basic Education School, Zhuhai College of Jilin University, Zhuhai, China
liangl22331@163.com

Abstract. The traditional method for analyzing the compressive strength of surface under low-speed impact damage of fiber-optic composites uses the aperture equivalent method to calculate the Compressive strength after impact (CAI) value with large error and insufficient accuracy. Aiming at the above problems, a method for calculating the CAI value of the fiber composite under low velocity impact damage by the damage accumulation method is proposed. Firstly, the materials and related equipment used in the experiment were selected, and then the initial damage state was determined by low-speed impact test. The failure state of the fiber composite under different compression loads was analyzed by compression test. Finally, the finite element model was established and the compressive strength was analyzed. The results show that compared with the open equivalent method, the calculation error of CAI value is reduced by 6.48%, the accuracy is improved, and the purpose of accurately analyzing the compressive strength is basically achieved.

Keywords: Optical fiber composites · Low speed impact · Impact damage · Compressive strength · Damage accumulation method · Finite element

1 Introduction

The history of human use of composite materials has been long, the adobe bricks that have been used since ancient times consist of straw or straw-reinforced clay. The reinforced concrete that has been used for more than 100 years is compounded by adding reinforcing steel to the concrete. In the middle of the 20th century, due to the needs of the aviation industry, glass fiber reinforced plastics have been developed, therefore, the name composite material appeared [1]. Composite materials are a large class of new materials. Its appearance has made the development of materials science rapid progress. Composite materials have high stiffness, high strength, light weight, and have anti-fatigue, high temperature, vibration reduction, many advantages such as designability, in recent decades, is widely used in aviation, aerospace, energy, construction, machinery, transportation, information, biological and other engineering fields and departments [2]. In contrast, fiber-optic composites refer to embedding optical fibers in composites. a new type of material that can be shared with them. With the addition of fiber, the strength of composites will not only decrease, instead, there is a certain degree of improvement. has been widely used in many fields, especially in

© ICST Institute for Computer Sciences, Social Informatics and Telecommunications Engineering 2019
Published by Springer Nature Switzerland AG 2019. All Rights Reserved
G. Gui and L. Yun (Eds.): ADHIP 2019, LNICST 301, pp. 419–428, 2019.
https://doi.org/10.1007/978-3-030-36402-1_45

aerospace and other military fields [3]. However, after the material is subjected to low speed impact, it is easy to generate a large number of matrix cracks and large-area delaminations inside. This hidden damage is very dangerous to the carrying structure [4]. It can seriously degrade the mechanical properties of laminated structures. Weaken the compressive strength of the structure, as a result, the carrying capacity is greatly reduced. potential threat to structural safety. Therefore, it is important to study the surface compressive strength (CAI) of optical fiber composites under low velocity impact damage using large data technology [5]. CAI is the maximum compressive stress that a surface is subjected to in a compression test until the surface of the specimen breaks (brittle material) or yields (non-brittle material). At present, there are mainly four methods for analyzing the compressive strength of optical fiber composites: softening inclusion method, sub-layer buckling method, opening equivalent method and damage accumulation method. The damage accumulation method is the most accurate method for calculating the CAI value. Based on the large data technology of this method, the surface compressive strength of fiber reinforced composite laminates after low velocity impact is calculated by establishing finite element model. This time through a specific experiment to analyze the compressive strength of optical fiber composites. First select the materials and related equipment used in the experiment, then, a low-speed impact was applied to the fiber composite laminate using an Instron 9250 HV drop hammer impact tester. then use the impact result (damage state) as the initial damage, finally, the compressive strength analysis of the optical fiber composite laminates with impact damage was performed by the damage accumulation method. To verify the accuracy of the CAI calculations by the damage accumulation method, a set of comparative experiments was performed together with the opening equivalent method. The results show: the damage accumulation method is used to calculate the surface compressive strength of the fiber composite material under low-speed impact damage. Compared with the opening equivalent method, the CAI calculation error is reduced by 6.48% increased accuracy. This proves that this method can analyze the compressive strength more effectively, helps improve the safety of fiber optic composites.

2 Evaluation Requirements and Research Status of Impact Resistance of Composite Materials Systems

With the structural design from static strength to structural integrity including static strength, stiffness, durability and damage tolerance, the concepts of material allowance and structural design allowance must be strictly distinguished. With the structural design from static strength to structural integrity including static strength, stiffness, durability and damage tolerance, the concepts of material allowance and structural design allowance must be strictly distinguished. Design allowables are: test results of specimens, components (including typical structural components), and the typical values of the materials allowed to represent the typical characteristics of the structure, according to the requirements of the specific project, and Design limit values determined based on design and use experience. It is pointed out that the allowable value of materials is a characterization of the mechanical properties of the material system, mainly used for material selection, acceptance and equivalence assessment. The design department shall, depending on the integrity requirements of the specific structure (usually including static strength, stiffness, durability, and damage tolerance), samples and components (including typical structural members) that have existing material allowable values and representative typical features of the structure. Based on the test results and design and experience, it is sometimes necessary to specify and verify the allowable values of the structural design based on the results of the assembly test to ensure that the structure designed according to the design allowable values meets its structural integrity requirements.

The impact resistance of the composite system was analyzed using the allowable values. Since the 1990s, a large number of studies have pointed out that the ability of composite systems to resist impact damage (damage impedance) and damage tolerance of composite systems are two different physical concepts, and damage resistance refers to the ability to resist impact events (Or the damage size caused by the impact force), and the damage tolerance is the effect of a certain damage state on the structural performance (or the intensity value corresponding to a given damage size). It is pointed out that a more complete understanding of the performance of the toughening system should be studied both the damage resistance and the damage tolerance. The above research results have been reflected in the latest US military manual, which clearly states that the damage characterization includes two elements, namely the impedance of the material to the damage caused by the impact (damage impedance), and the material or structure is safe after being damaged. Sexual ability (damage tolerance). But for a long time this concept has only stayed in the minds of a few researchers, and has not been accepted by the vast number of materials and engineering people. The author's experimental data also shows that the damage resistance of the composite depends not only on the toughness of the resin, but also on the elongation at break of the fiber and the interface between the resin and the fiber. The combination of the traditional brittle resin and different fibers may have different damage. Impedance composite system. The study of damage resistance in the United States began in the early 1990s. A large number of studies focused on the equivalence of low-speed drop hammer impact and quasi-static impact. The results show that the current low-speed drop hammer impact method can be simulated with quasi-static. The damage caused by the drop hammer impact and static indentation (QSI) methods with the same impact force is basically the same. At the same time, a large number of parameter impact studies were conducted. On this basis, ASTM released standard test methods for measuring damage resistance using quasi-static indentation (QSI) and drop impact test methods in 1998 and 2005, respectively.

3   Experimental Materials and Equipment

3.1   Experimental Materials

The optical fiber composite used for the test piece is CCF300/5228A, the fiber volume fraction in the material is approximately 60%. The laminate (test piece) made of fiber optic composite material has a thickness of 0.15 mm, a length of 825 mm and a width of 600 mm. The profile of the ribs is "H" type, the number of ribs is 4, the rib spacing is 150 mm. the ribs and the skin are formed by a co-curing process. Both ends of the test piece were glued to facilitate the compression test. The sequence of the test specimens is: [45/—45/0/—45/45/0/—45/45/90/45/—45/45/0] [6].

3.2 Experimental Equipment

The tests were conducted by the Instron 9250 HV drop hammer impact tester, the test process adopts the locking system. The secondary impact of the falling hammer is prevented from damaging the specimen. The impact energy is respectively 30 J and 50 J.

The impact test specimens were tested for post-impact compression strength on an INSTRON (3382) electronic drawing machine, continuous loading to specimen failure at a loading rate of 1.25 mm/min.

4 Low Speed Impact Test

According to the damage status of the material, impact is divided into high-speed impact and low-speed impact. When the impact causes penetrative damage to the material structure, that is high-speed impact; On the contrary, failure to cause penetration damage to the structure is a low velocity impact [7]. At low speeds, the experience time is very short, there will be no obvious damage to the laminate surface. therefore, it is not necessary to consider the correlation between creep effect and strain rate, however, matrix cracking and delamination damage occurred inside the laminate. However, matrix cracking and delamination damage occurred inside the laminate, the overall damage to the structure is potentially harmful [8].

Before the trial began, visually inspect all test pieces first, and sampling for non-destructive testing of ultrasound scans, make sure that there is no initial internal damage to the test piece. The test piece is placed on the support bracket during impact. In addition, it is also necessary to take another test piece for impact energy testing, determine the required impact energy. Due to the largest proportion of the skin between the ribs in the stiffened plate structure, according to the actual situation of the structure studied in the paper, a pit depth of about 1 mm will be generated at the impact position O as a criterion for selecting the impact energy, the impact is performed on the upper surface (skin surface). Through energy exploration tests, the final determination of impact energy is 50 J. then use 50 J energy to impact test the stiffened plate's impact position O, the impact pit depth and damage area were measured immediately after impact completion [9].

5 Compression Test After Impact

When performing compression tests, the fiber-optic composite laminate used shall retain the damage and deformation after the impact test is completed, instead of modeling on the basis of the assumption of the impact of human injury damage simulation [10].

Refer to ASTM D7137/D7137M-12 standard, compression test of specimens with low speed impact damage, the effect of impact damage at different locations on the load-carrying capacity of laminate specimens was investigated. The upper and lower ends of the test piece are fixed by single row bolts on both sides of the fixture. Before the test, a strain gauge is attached to the symmetry between the ribs of the test piece and the ribs. After the trial began, the compressive load is applied step by step with a load gradient of 5kN/s, after each load is loaded, the strain value corresponding to each strain measurement point is recorded by a static strain gauge, after the test, the load-strain curve is used to determine the structural instability load [6]. Record the phenomena that occurred during the test and the ultimate damage load and damage patterns.

6 Compression Strength Analysis

6.1 Establishing a Finite Element Analysis Model

In the low-speed impact test of optical fiber composites, the damage area mainly exists in the impacted area, the damage pattern is mainly matrix cracking, basic fiber shear and fiber breakage. According to experimental phenomena, observe the damage pattern of the material under different compression energy and measure the area of the corresponding damage area. According to the damage mode, select the above corresponding degradation mode. The stiffness of the damaged area is degraded, damage-free areas are assigned, this establishes a finite element analysis model of fiber optic composites.

The experimental finite element analysis model for the damage area of fiber composites under 50 kN compressive loads was measured, as shown in Fig. 1.

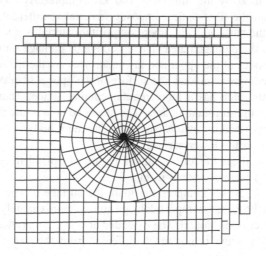

Fig. 1. Finite element analysis model of damage zone of optical fiber composite under 50 kN compressive load

When the compressive load is 50 kN, the test piece was subject to small cracks on the impact panel, there is a certain diverging phenomenon around the crack, however, the divergence area is not large. Basically confined to the affected area, the main type of damage is the cracking of the substrate, no fiber breakage occurred. A small amount of core material is accompanied by matrix cracking. there is no damage to the panel.

Finite element analysis model of damage zone of optical fiber composite under 100 kN compression load, as shown in Fig. 2.

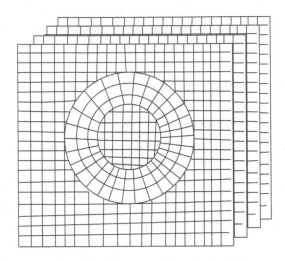

Fig. 2. Finite element analysis model of damage region of optical fiber composite under 100 kN compressive load

The damage caused by the impact of 100 kN compressive load and the 50 kN compressive load on the fiber optic composite material is different. Under the 0 kN compressive load, the surface of the fiber composite material is not broken, there is a slight depression in the damaged area. There is obvious damage on the lower surface. the main damage modes of the upper and lower surfaces are the matrix cracking mode. Under the 100 kN compression load, the surface of the optical fiber composite material is broken. The lesion area has a more regular circular shape. There is a significant damage extension in the surrounding area. The extended area is circular, the ring size is about 2 mm, mainly based on matrix cracking. The main body is cracking, there was no obvious damage on the lower surface.

Finite element analysis model of damage region of optical fiber composite under 150 kN compression load, as shown in Fig. 3.

For the effect of 150 kN compression load, the surface of the optical fiber composite is completely broken. the impact damage area is approximately circular, there are obvious damage extensions around. The extended area is circular, the ring size is about 2 mm, the extension range is not much different from the extension range of the

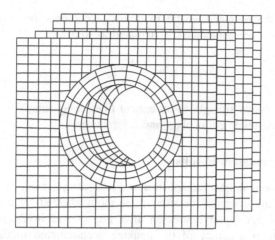

Fig. 3. Finite element analysis model of damage area of optical fiber composite under 150 kN compressive load

damage zone of the specimen under the 100 kN compression loa. The fibers in the impact zone are completely broken. The extended area is mostly matrix cracking damage, there is a small amount of fiber breakage.

6.2 Calculation of Compressive Elastic Modulus

Through the analysis of the compression performance of the finite element model, the stress caused by the displacement of the fiber-influenced area and the fiber-influenced area can be obtained separately, according to the number of implanted fibers. The calculation can obtain the average principal direction (X-axis direction) stress $\bar{\beta}_x$ generated when the entire intact specimen material is subjected to unit strain $\bar{\alpha}_x$. The material compressive elastic modulus T_c is:

$$T_c = \frac{\bar{\alpha}_x}{\bar{\beta}_x} \tag{1}$$

Substituting the calculation result of the finite element part, the elastic modulus of the test piece is shown in Table 1.

Table 1. Specimen elastic modulus.

Compression load (kN)	Compressible elastic simulation (GPa)	Relative change rate (%)
50	129.546	−0.064
100	150.458	−0.027
150	173.416	−0.154

According to the obtained elastic modulus of compression, calculate the compressive strength of fiber composites. Calculated as follows:

$$\wp = -\frac{P}{l \cdot h} T_c \tag{2}$$

$\wp$ is the compressive strength of an optical fiber composite; P is the compressive load; The width and thickness of the l and h laminates.

6.3 Strength Calculation Results

The structure of optical fiber composites is more complicated, the degree of fiber bending is large, the compressive strength is more affected by the impact energy, therefore, only the compressive strength after impact was investigated. In order to verify the calculation accuracy of the damage accumulation method, optical fiber composites were subjected to relevant experimental studies, the compressive strength test after low-speed impact was performed. The actual and experimental values are shown in Table 2.

Table 2. Damage cumulative method strength calculation results.

Compression load (kN)	Actual value (MPa)	Experimental value (MPa)	Error (%)	Average error (%)
50	78.5	78.5	0	0.25
100	60.8	60.0	0.25	
150	53.2	53.2	0	

To further verify the effectiveness of the damage accumulation method, the opening equivalent method was used to calculate the strength of the fiber composite material in the above test, the calculation results are shown in Table 3.

Table 3. Open equivalent strength calculation results.

Compression load (kN)	Actual value (MPa)	Experimental value (MPa)	Error (%)	Average error (%)
50	78.5	75.0	3.2	6.73%
100	60.8	52.3	8.4	
150	53.2	45.2	8.6	

Comparison between Tables 2 and 3 shows that, the average intensity of the former calculation is 0.25%, the latter's strength calculation error is 6.73%. Compared with the two methods, the cumulative damage method is less than 6.48% and the accuracy has been greatly improved. This proves the effectiveness of the method.

7 Conclusion

With the application of optical fiber composite materials, the low-speed impact problem has attracted more and more attention. The impact of fiber optic composites refers to the manufacture of fiber optic composite structures, during the use and maintenance process, the low speed impact of unexpected objects is inevitable. Causes structural damage and declining bearing capacity. causes visually undetectable internal damage to the material structure, there is no or only slight indentation on the surface of the composite structure, in addition, a large number of matrix cracks and large-area delaminations have been generated within the laminates. This hidden damage is very dangerous to the carrying structure. It can seriously degrade the mechanical properties of laminated structures. Strength can be weakened by 35% to 40%, as a result, the carrying capacity is greatly reduced, there is a potential threat to the overall destruction and failure of the structure. Therefore, it is of great significance to calculate the surface compressive strength (CAI value) of fiber composites under low-speed impact damage. Damage accumulation is the most common and most accurate method of calculation, this method mainly analyzes and calculates the composite strength by establishing a finite element model. Compared with the aperture equivalent method, the accuracy of calculation has been greatly improved, this is of great significance in determining the damage tolerance of the fiber optic composite structure and improving the reliability and optimal design of the composite material.

References

1. Vardhan, H., Bordoloi, S., Garg, A., et al.: Compressive strength analysis of soil reinforced with fiber extracted from water hyacinth. Eng. Comput. 34(2), 330–342 (2017)
2. Ingole, P.G., Choi, W.K., Lee, G.B., et al.: Thin-film-composite hollow-fiber membranes for water vapor separation. Desalination 403, 12–23 (2017)
3. Li, X., Wang, J., Yi, B., et al.: Cyclic behavior of damaged reinforced concrete columns repaired with high-performance fiber-reinforced cementitious composite. Eng. Struct. 136, 26–35 (2017)
4. Anilchandra, A., Bojja, R., Jagannathan, N., et al.: Prediction of mode II delamination propagation life under a standard spectrum loading in a carbon fiber composite. J. Compos. Mater. 51(20), 2827–2833 (2017)
5. Jing, W., Ping, C., Lu, C., et al.: Improvement of aramid fiber III reinforced bismaleimide composite interfacial adhesion by oxygen plasma treatment. Compos. Interfaces 25(2), 1–13 (2018)
6. Tian, K., Bo, W., Yan, Z., et al.: Proper-orthogonal-decomposition-based buckling analysis and optimization of hybrid fiber composite shells. AIAA J. 56(5), 1–8 (2018)
7. Shibuya, M., Yasukawa, M., Mishima, S., et al.: A thin-film composite-hollow fiber forward osmosis membrane with a polyketone hollow fiber membrane as a support. Desalination 402, 33–41 (2017)
8. Masoumi, V., Mohammadi, A., Khoshayand, M.R., et al.: Application of polyaniline–multiwalled carbon nanotubes composite fiber for determination of benzaldehyde in injectable pharmaceutical formulations by solid-phase microextraction GC–FID using experimental design. J. Anal. Chem. 72(3), 264–271 (2017)

9. Hui, L., Xue, P., Guan, Z., et al.: A new nonlinear vibration model of fiber-reinforced composite thin plate with amplitude-dependent property. Nonlinear Dyn. **94**(4), 2219–2241 (2018)
10. Lawan, I., Li, Q., Zhou, W., et al.: Modifications of hemp twine for use as a fiber in cement composite: effects of hybrid treatments. Cellulose **25**(6), 1–12 (2018)

Research on Data Mining Algorithm for Regional Photovoltaic Generation

Zhen Lei[1] and Yong-biao Yang[2(✉)]

[1] State Grid Jiangsu Electric Power Company, Nanjing, China
[2] Southeast University, Nanjing, China
danghongen2017@163.com

Abstract. Traditional data mining algorithms have problems such as poor applicability, high false positive rate or high false positive rate, resulting in low security and stability of the power system. For this reason, the regional photovoltaic power generation data mining algorithm is studied. Classification of data sources facilitates correlation calculations, and matrix relationships are used to calculate data associations. Combined with the data relevance, the association rules are output, and the output results inherit the clustering processing and time series distribution of the implicit data, thereby realizing the extraction of hidden data and completing the regional photovoltaic power generation data mining. The experimental results show that the regional PV power generation data mining algorithm has high stability and can effectively solve the system security problem.

Keywords: Raw input · Data acquisition · Data mining · Dynamic features

1 Introduction

The regional photovoltaic power generation array is the core component of the photovoltaic power generation system. The solar radiation to the ground energy is directly converted into electrical energy through the photovoltaic effect of the panel. Unlike other conventional energy sources such as thermal power, the output power of photovoltaic power generation systems is greatly affected by weather factors such as solar irradiance, temperature, humidity, wind speed and wind, and has obvious characteristics such as variability, intermittentness and uncertainty. The reliability of power system energy management requires that the generation, distribution and use of electric energy remain in a stable and balanced state for a long time. When large-scale photovoltaic power generation is connected to the large power grid for grid-connected power generation, photovoltaic power generation and grid-connected power generation will generate voltage balance between the two power generation system cabinets, which will have a huge impact on the safe and stable operation of the power system. If you want to make a large-scale photovoltaic power generation system smoothly connect to the large grid and generate electricity, the large power grid needs to provide a certain capacity of rotating standby to offset the fluctuation of photovoltaic power generation. It will cause a lot of waste of resources and reduce the economic benefits of photovoltaic power generation. However, due to energy shortages and environmental

G. Gui and L. Yun (Eds.): ADHIP 2019, LNICST 301, pp. 429–438, 2019.
https://doi.org/10.1007/978-3-030-36402-1_46

problems, it is necessary to develop and utilize solar energy as much as possible. In the face of the problem of grid-connected power generation of large-scale photovoltaic power generation systems, power grid companies are in a dilemma. Therefore, how to play the role of photovoltaic power generation as much as possible under the premise of meeting the safety, stability and economic operation of the power grid has become a problem to be solved in the field of photovoltaic power generation. One of the key technologies to solve this problem is to accurately predict the future PV power output to support the power system's power generation plan, power flow optimization, and adjustment of peak and frequency. Therefore, the topic of this paper has a very important role in the sustainable development and application of photovoltaic power generation [1].

2 Regional Photovoltaic Power Generation Data Mining Algorithm

2.1 Data Source Classification

Existing photovoltaic power generation forecasting methods are mainly divided into two broad categories: direct forecasting and indirect forecasting. The indirect prediction method is carried out in two steps. First, the solar irradiance is predicted by various weather factor prediction data at the solar power station, and then the irradiance is brought into the photoelectric conversion efficiency model to calculate the power generation. The direct prediction rule does not require measurement and prediction of solar irradiance, and is directly modeled based on meteorological information and historical power generation data. Predicting photovoltaic power Compared to indirect forecasting, direct prediction does not require irradiance monitoring and prediction. It is more versatile, less computationally intensive, and more predictive. Therefore, this paper uses the direct prediction method [2].

Based on the historical data of photovoltaic power generation for the past two years and the corresponding weather information, the combination of ambient temperature, humidity, wind speed and AQI is chosen instead of irradiance as the original input. Aiming at the problems of the original input variables and the compatibility, the regression-based forward selection method is used to reduce the original input variables by seasons, and the weather factors with moderate quantity and low correlation are selected as the input variables of the model. Then, for the problem of poor generalization ability of a single model, K-means clustering algorithm is used to cluster historical data, and the data is divided into similar weather types to complete the classification of data sources [3]. Its classification and practical application are as follows:

Table 1 is a classification and practical application. A categorical data source refers to a non-trivial process of extracting previously unknown, regular, and future-ready and understandable knowledge and information from a vast, fragmented, noisy, and fuzzy, random, historical data set. "Before unknown" refers to the fact that data mining information is not recognized by people before, that is, novel information, so the more innovative the information, the greater the value [4]. "Available in the future" means

Table 1. Classification and practical application

Type	Classification	Application example
Standalone photovoltaic Power generation system	Battery-free DC photovoltaic power generation system	DC photovoltaic water pump, charger, solar fan cap
	DC photovoltaic power generation system with battery	Solar flashlight, solar cell phone charger, solar lawn lamp
	AC and AC/DC hybrid photovoltaic power generation system	Microwave relay station and environmental monitoring station of AC solar household system Equipment Small ower stations in power-free areas
	Municipal electricity complementary photovoltaic power generation system	AC solar household system, small power plants in non-electric areas

that the extracted knowledge has potential use value, common-sense knowledge or facts, and unachievable knowledge are meaningless. "Can be understood" requires knowledge of the knowledge or discovered patterns that the user understands, and is better if it can be described in a natural language that is easy to understand. "Non-trivial" refers to the process of data mining is usually non-linear, difficult to be discovered, and can be summed up after continuous comparative analysis using dedicated massive data mining tools. A complete database knowledge discovery process first needs to analyze the requirements, clearly and clearly locate the business problems, and determine the purpose of knowledge discovery. Before starting a project, the final goal of knowledge discovery must be clarified through communication with target users and relevant industry experts [5].

2.2 Data Preprocessing

The main purpose of data preprocessing is to improve the quality of the data set and reduce the complexity of the data. In order to obtain similar meteorological conditions, the weather types are fuzzy identified and classified. Considering the limited conditions of the detection facilities of domestic PV power plants and the universality of the methods, the relevant weather type information predicted by the China Meteorological Forecasting Website is used as the identification factor of the weather type. Since these five factors have different dimensions and the magnitude difference is also large, the five factors can be fuzzly assigned. In this way, there is a weather type tag every day. In the photovoltaic power generation database, the weather type information can be fuzzy classified and marked above, and stored together with the power generation amount in the photovoltaic power generation database, which facilitates the subsequent data screening and processing [6].

After the previous data preprocessing and classification data sources, the sample information with similar weather types is obtained, but the number of samples obtained in this way is still relatively large and not accurate enough. The gray correlation theory can well select the sample weather forecast websites with high similarity and high correlation with the prediction ports from these samples to obtain the weather information of the predicted mouth. If the minimum temperature of the predicted port is 60 ° C, the maximum temperature is 25 °C, the relative humidity is 61%, the wind speed is 4, and the weather comprehensive information is cloudy, and the value is set to 3. Let the weather data comparison sequence be t, and obtain the following matrix formula;

$$(t_1, t_2, t_3 \ldots \ldots, t_n) = \begin{bmatrix} t_1(1) + t_3(3) + t_n \\ t_2(2) + t_4(4) + t_n \end{bmatrix} \tag{1}$$

In formula (1), t represents the meteorological data sample, and the correlation coefficient is calculated by the matrix formula, and the calculation result is as follows:

$$h(y) = \frac{\min\limits_{i}}{|h(k) - h_i|} \tag{2}$$

Equation (2) is the correlation coefficient result, where h represents the resolution coefficient, y represents the sequence vector, and k is the meteorological information. When the actual current is too large, the photovoltaic cell characteristic curve shifts to the second quadrant, and when the avalanche breakdown voltage is reached, the current is too fast, so this situation should be avoided. That is, when the photovoltaic cell flows excessively, it operates in the second quadrant, which is a drawback of the single-diode circuit, and the photovoltaic cell becomes a load-type power source. The current of the photovoltaic cell suddenly becomes very large in the case of avalanche breakdown. In practical applications, in order to avoid this, a parallel bypass diode is often required. That is, when a diode of a certain group of photovoltaic cells is connected in parallel, when the voltage across a photovoltaic cell becomes a negative value, the parallel diode is turned on, thereby preventing the photovoltaic module from becoming a load-bearing power source and absorbing the external energy, and avoiding the formation of hot spots [7].

3   Realizing Regional Photovoltaic Power Generation Data Mining Algorithm

3.1   Output of Association Rules

In terms of integrity and consistency analysis, traditional data mining algorithms provide support for scheduling methods such as peak and frequency adjustments, and then based on data preprocessing and classification data sources to clarify the range of association rules output. Regional photovoltaic power generation is mainly composed of *CM* junction, upper and lower electrode plates, surface passivation layer and reflective layer. It relies mainly on the photovoltaic effect to convert solar energy into electrical energy. The principle of power generation is as follows:

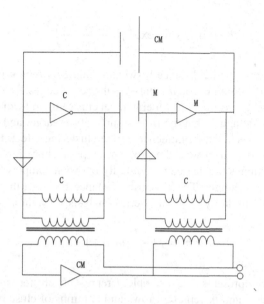

Fig. 1. Power generation principle

Figure 1 shows the principle of power generation. When sunlight is applied to the upper surface of the panel, the *CM* junction will absorb solar radiation energy to generate electron-hole pairs. Due to the influence of the internal electric field, electron-hole pairs will be separated, in which positively charged holes flow from the *M* region to the *C* region, and negatively charged electrons flow from the *C* region to the *M* region. By the flow of electron-holes, positive and negative charges are respectively concentrated near the boundary of the two electrodes, thereby generating a photo-generated electromotive force which is opposite to the electromotive force of the *CM* junction. When the *CM* junction is open, the junction current and the photo-generated current have the same size. Therefore, the two sides of the *CM* junction will produce a stable potential difference between the *C* region and the *M* region, which is the open circuit voltage of the photovoltaic cell. When we connect the *CM* junction to the circuit, under continuous illumination of the mouth, the *CM* junction is equivalent to the power supply [8], and the positive and negative charges continuously flow to form a current, which can convert the solar radiant energy into electrical energy. Expand the system space by limiting the output range of data association rules [9].

3.2   Implicit Data Extraction

A certain data set is satisfied for a given data set based on association rules. First, the data set is constructed into a cluster tree, and then decomposed according to the hierarchy of the cluster tree. The bottom-up and top-down constitute two decomposition sequences of hierarchical decomposition, and complete the function of data mining. The clustering formula is as follows;

$$b_e(l, s) = \left\{ w \cdot \exp\left(\beta \frac{-a(c_l, c_s)}{\varphi} \right) \right\} \tag{3}$$

In Eq. (3), b represents the distance between c_l and c_s, l represents the row of the matrix, s represents the column, and a represents the set of edges. The advantage of this formula is that it can be constructed by hierarchical clustering to form different levels of structure. The disadvantage is that the time complexity is large, and the choice of the decomposition point has a certain influence on the clustering effect. Furthermore, time series analysis is used to deal with the problem of poor clustering effect [10]. Time series analysis determines the degree of similarity between samples by calculating the distance between each sample. The closer the distance between the two samples, the higher the degree of similarity. The time series analysis formula is as follows:

$$b_e = f\left(\frac{-k}{\varphi} (b_l, b_s) \right) \tag{4}$$

In formula (4), b represents a data sample, f represents cluster value, k represents a cluster position, and b_l and b_s represent rows and columns of clusters. The sum of the squares of the total distances of all classes is as small as possible. The larger the value of k, the more classes the sample divides, and the f-value will monotonically decrease as the value of k increases [11]. When the value of k is small, an increase in the number of categories will cause the value of f to decrease rapidly. However, as the value of k increases to a certain value, the change in f value will gradually become flat until the value of k and the total number of samples. Time series analysis is fast and easy to implement. It is efficient when dealing with massive data, and has a certain degree of flexibility. The time complexity of the algorithm is close to linear.

The reason why the PV module array can output electric energy is to convert the energy radiated by the sunlight on the surface into DC electric energy through the photovoltaic effect, and then output the DC power to the battery or the inverter. Photovoltaic array is the most important component in photovoltaic power generation system. In the process of use, the power generation array should be connected in series and parallel according to the required voltage level and power level to meet the power generation needs. The time series analysis is used to decompose the data set and complete the data mining algorithm. In the process of data mining, the attributes of some data are related to time and will change with the passage of time. The time interval of these data can be constant or variable. Time series analysis is mainly to achieve the mining of patterns, similarity search and analysis of data trends [12]. The data mining algorithm flow is as follows (Fig. 2):

In the first step, after the requirements are clarified, the knowledge base data needs to be prepared. Through the integrity and consistency analysis, the data noise is removed and the missing attributes of the data are filled, and the invalid data is also deleted. In the second step, the preprocessor task is to record the data in the standard logger from the initial and final stages of port scanning of a source IP. When a certain log file is determined, the record type, destination IP address, and port are recorded and analyzed. The concept of port scanning is to complete the task of attempting a TCP

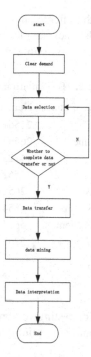

Fig. 2. Classification data source process

connection for more than P ports under the time limit of T (seconds), and it can be said that UDP packets are transmitted to more than P ports under the limitation of time T (seconds). The third step is to transform or unify the data into a form that is easy to mine. After completing the data preparation work, the next step is data mining. The fourth step is to analyze and process the data set according to the different needs of the customer and select the appropriate data mining method for the specific situation. In the fifth step, according to certain evaluation criteria, meaningful models and knowledge should be selected from the results of the mining, and visualization and knowledge expression techniques should be used to express knowledge that can be understood by users in natural language [13].

4   Experimental Results

In order to verify the effectiveness of the regional photovoltaic power generation data mining algorithm, the algorithm was tested. The simulated attack software used in the experiment, which can generate as many kinds of attack data, is an effective tool for testing. Network packets that are used to accurately and accurately record the actual attack process for each type of attack in the experiment. After encapsulation and automatic processing, an attack file is formed, thereby constructing a huge attack library to detect various attack recognition strategies. Simulate attack packets are sent with simulated attack software and saved to a log file. A total of about 2,000 attack packets were recorded to measure the effectiveness of system pre-detection. The system's pre-detection engine discards packets that are considered normal to reduce unnecessary abuse detection. The test environment is as follows:

Table 2. Test environment

Type of attack	Number
smurf	21561
neptune	26564
back	4123
Satan	4562
ipsweep	2651
portsweep	2654
warezclient	5654
teardrop	5265
Pod	322
land	235

Table 2 is a test environment for testing regional photovoltaic power generation data mining algorithms and traditional data mining algorithms. The test results are as follows:

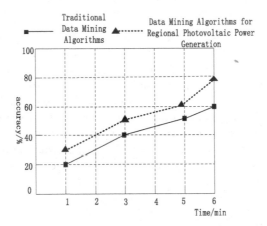

Fig. 3. Comparison of experimental results

Figure 3 is a comparison of experimental results, comparing traditional data mining algorithms with regional photovoltaic power generation data mining algorithms. It also compares the adaptive runtimes. As can be seen from Fig. 3, when the amount of data is small, the regional PV data mining algorithm does not show obvious advantages, and its running time is even slower than the traditional frequent item set mining algorithm. However, with the increase of data volume, the regional photovoltaic power generation data mining algorithm gradually shows its advantages, especially when the data volume is too large, the traditional frequent item set mining algorithm can not complete the calculation. However, regional photovoltaic power generation data mining algorithms make full use of their parallel advantages, and their speed is not affected by excessive data factors. In addition, after solving the problem of load imbalance, it can be seen that the running time of the regional photovoltaic power generation data mining algorithm is better than the common algorithm. It proves that the proposed regional photovoltaic power generation data mining algorithm has strong stability.

5 Conclusion

Traditional data mining algorithms have the following shortcomings: poor applicability, high false negative rate or false positive rate, too single detection, lack of extensive testing and analysis of rules, and excessive reliance on their own rule base. These deficiencies have not been able to cope with today's increasingly complex network environment. The regional photovoltaic power generation data mining algorithm can store all the relationships between the data items, and then split the entire database into smaller pieces of data for mining processing. The most powerful advantage of this algorithm is that it effectively reduces the number of scans and improves the efficiency, so this is often used for dynamic feature extraction data.

References

1. Wang, H., Li, F., Zhang, L., et al.: Research and application of big data mining technology in photovoltaic power prediction. Hebei Electr. Power Technol. **12**(2), 123–143 (2018)
2. Ge, J.: Research on large data mining algorithm for periodic performance of warships under load environment. Ship Sci. Technol. **23**(22), 121–123 (2017)
3. Xiaobo, Y.: Research on Data Mining Algorithms Based on Projection Pattern Support Set [J]. Computer Applications and Software **34**(7), 273–276 (2017)
4. Lv, Y., Huang, L.: Research and implementation of data mining algorithms based on Hadoop framework in Hongbo. Large data environment. Electron. Design Eng. **25**(7), 241–244 (2017)
5. Zheng, Z., Wu, W., Li, H.: Data mining algorithms based on CLUSTER optimization. J. Harbin Commercial Univ. (Nat. Sci. Ed.) **33**(6), 329–330 (2017)
6. Shibing, B.: Research on data mining algorithms based on neural network and particle swarm optimization. Laser J. **38**(3), 188–192 (2017)
7. Cheng, Z., Li, S., Han, L., et al.: Research on the prediction method of photovoltaic array power generation based on data mining. J. Solar Energy **38**(3), 726–733 (2017)
8. Yang, J., Lin, X., Yao, Q.: Study on wind power generation system based on hydraulic constant rense speed control. J. Xi'an Polytech. Univ. **2018**(05), 574–580 (2018)
9. Yongwen, Y., Fanyue, Q., Zaiqin, T., et al.: Data mining and analysis method for operation log of photovoltaic power plant. Sci. Technol. Econ. Guide **34**(2), 114–145 (2017)
10. Luo, R., Wang, Z., Wu, T., et al.: A pollution diagnosis method for photovoltaic modules based on large data mining of solar power regulation. CN107065829A [P] **33**(2), 134–135 (2017)

11. Ding, M., Li, C., Li, H., et al.: Fault detection method for photovoltaic inverters based on massive data mining. Electr. Autom. **33**(3), 154–165 (2018)
12. Gong, S., Pan, T., Wu, D., et al.: Research on the method of filling the missing photovoltaic data in microgrid based on MCMCMC. Renew. Energy **33**(3), 453–465 (2018)
13. Wang, H., Li, F., Zhang, L., et al.: Research and application of big data mining technology in photovoltaic power prediction. Hebei Electr. Power Technol. **12**(2), 345–367 (2018)

Distributed Learning Algorithm
for Distributed PV Large-Scale Access
to Power Grid Based on Machine Learning

Zhen Lei[1], Yong-biao Yang[2(✉)], and Xiao-hui Xu[3]

[1] State Grid Jiangsu Electric Power Company, Nanjing, China
[2] Southeast University, Nanjing, China
danghongen2017@163.com
[3] China Electric Power Research Institute, Nanjing, China

Abstract. Due to the long prediction time and the large range of data filtering, the traditional algorithm has low system operation efficiency. For this reason, distributed learning based on machine learning is widely used to predict the power grid output. First, establish a grid output prediction model to limit the system's line loss and transformer losses. Secondly, based on the distributed photovoltaic power generation output prediction model, the vector moment method and the information method are used to narrow the search space. Based on the data concentration and fitness function values, the calculation formula of voltage output prediction of distribution network nodes with distributed photovoltaics is derived to realize the power grid output prediction algorithm. Finally, it is proved by experiments that distributed PV large-scale access to power grid output prediction algorithm can effectively improve system operation efficiency.

Keywords: Operation efficiency · Photovoltaic capacity · Radial structure · Power system

1 Introduction

With the rapid development of the power industry, the access of distributed photovoltaics and charging piles for electric vehicles in distribution networks increases the complexity of the power usage mode. The core idea of grid output forecasting is to study the changing law of historical load data, as well as the impact of meteorological factors, economic factors and other related factors on the load. Describe the relationship between load and influencing factors by establishing a suitable mathematical model, and then make reasonable guesses about the load in the future period. According to the different time periods, the grid output prediction can be divided into four short-term, short-term, medium-term and long-term forecasts. The short-term grid output forecast period is generally one to several days, and the grid dispatcher specifies the regional power generation plan based on the results of the short-term forecast. If the forecast result is too high, the system operation efficiency will be too low, resulting in waste of resources. If the forecast result is low, there will be insufficient power supply to meet the social production needs and the people's power demand. Therefore, the importance

G. Gui and L. Yun (Eds.): ADHIP 2019, LNICST 301, pp. 439–447, 2019.
https://doi.org/10.1007/978-3-030-36402-1_47

of short-term load forecasting is self-evident. Therefore, finding the right method to reduce the prediction error is crucial. Literature [1] proposed an improved big bang algorithm for the grid-connection capacity of distributed pv, and solved the above model. Consider the impact on the power distribution system after the distributed photovoltaic (pv) grid, from the point of view of power distribution network planning, establishes a distributed photovoltaic (pv) grid acceptance ability as objective function, to run load voltage level, feeder rate, voltage total harmonic distortion rate and the short-circuit current level for the optimization model and application of the constraint of 33 nodes distribution network testing, comparing with other algorithm results this method has a certain error. In order to reduce the average prediction error of short-term load by 1%, a distributed PV large-scale power grid output prediction algorithm based on machine learning is proposed to ensure that the prediction result falls within the established range.

2 Distributed Photovoltaic Large-Scale Access Grid Output Prediction Algorithm

2.1 Power Grid Output Prediction Model

After distributed PV access to the distribution network, the impact on system network loss depends mainly on the location of access and the capacity of access. First, the impact of distributed PV access capacity on network loss. When the small-capacity photovoltaic is connected to the distribution network, the local compensation of the load absorption power can be realized, and the power flowing from the power supply node to the load node on the feeder line is reduced, thereby reducing the line loss and the transformer loss of the system. When the photovoltaic capacity is large, the uni-directional flow in the distribution network will have two-way flow and generate a new power distribution, which will increase the local network loss, but the total network loss of the system may be reduced. Second, the impact of distributed PV access locations on network loss. When the photovoltaic access is close to the head end of the line, a larger photovoltaic output can have a significant effect on the reduction of the network loss; As the photovoltaic position moves toward the end of the line, even if the access photovoltaic capacity is small, the network loss can be significantly reduced; Near the end of the line, the increase in PV capacity may increase the network loss, but still less than the network loss when there is no PV access [2].

Most of the distribution systems in urban and rural areas in China are mainly radial structures, and the power supply mode is simple. For medium voltage distribution networks in urban power distribution systems, radial operation is also performed under normal mode [3]. Therefore, this paper selects the radial distribution network as the research object, and the circuit diagram of the photovoltaic distribution network is as follows (Fig. 2):

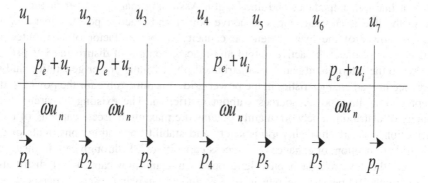

Fig. 1. Circuit diagram of photovoltaic distribution network

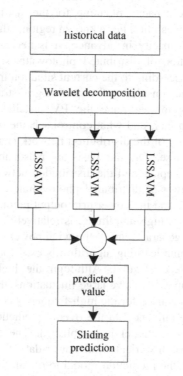

Fig. 2. Grid output prediction model

Since the wind power output has randomness, the fluctuation is large within a certain time range. If the machine learning algorithm is directly used, the prediction effect is not good. The low-frequency component obtained by using the wavelet to decompose the Fig. 1 is a circuit diagram of a photovoltaic distribution network. As can be seen from Fig. 1, the node voltage and line loss of the distribution network mainly depend on the load power, distributed PV output, distributed PV access position, line unit impedance and line length. Assuming that the power factor of each load in the line is constant, the load active power and reactive power depend on the apparent power of the load. When the capacity or power factor of distributed PV changes, it will affect the active output and reactive output of distributed PV [4].

Due to the intermittent nature of distributed photovoltaic power generation and the difference in load characteristics in the power grid, it is impossible for the power grid to accept photovoltaic power sources without restriction. The existing research on PV capacity of distribution network mainly obtains the maximum access capacity of PV in distribution network through various safety and stability operation constraints of grid after grid connection, or enhances the access capacity of PV through certain measures. However, the research on photovoltaic power transmission capacity of distribution network with PV penetration rate is scarce, and the existing research perspective is relatively simple. The impact of photovoltaic power on the distribution network and the support of photovoltaic energy to the distribution network cannot be fully reflected. Especially, the photovoltaic capacity planning for the distribution network is rarely involved on the basis of permeability. For a known regional distribution network, when planning the photovoltaic capacity in advance, it is necessary to conduct a macro assessment of the distribution of distributed photovoltaics from the perspective of power and energy balance according to the current situation in the region or the overall load curve in the future. And considering the specific grid structure and safe and stable operation restrictions, how to determine the PV installation location, installation method and installation capacity, and what control scheme is adopted to improve the PV maximum access capacity of the distribution network is a key consideration in the grid connection design phase. On the basis of reasonable penetration rate, the remaining distributed PV acceptance of the distribution network is announced in time. In order to improve the power of distributed photovoltaics, a power grid output prediction model is established, and the power grid output prediction model is as follows;

Wind power output has a high amplitude, is relatively stable, has a certain regularity, and can describe the general trend of the wind power output, and is dominant in each component. If a machine learning algorithm is used for the low frequency component, the prediction effect is good. Although the high-frequency components obtained by wavelet decomposition have large fluctuations, the amplitude is small. If a machine learning algorithm is used for the high-frequency components, even if a large prediction error occurs, the influence on the overall prediction effect is small. Therefore, a grid output prediction model is established. The model first uses wavelet decomposition to decompose historical wind power data, then puts the high and low frequency components into the prediction model to obtain the predicted values of the components, and finally adds all the component prediction values to obtain the final result [5].

When the distributed photovoltaic power generation system adopts the current-controlled inverter as the grid-connected interface, the output active power and the current amplitude are constant, and can be converted into multiple nodes for processing in the power flow calculation of the distribution network [6]. In order to output as much active power as possible, the distributed photovoltaic system can maintain a pure resistive power factor when it is integrated into the grid. In this control mode, distributed photovoltaics only output active power [7]. Its calculation formula is as follows:

$$h^e = \sqrt{n^2 \times (m-1)^2} \tag{1}$$

In the formula (1), h represents a node where the reactive power is 0, n represents the active power of the output, and m represents the active power. This formula is used to maintain a pure resistive power factor in a defined spatial range. From the simulation of the voltage influence of the distributed photovoltaic access distribution network, it can be known that the influence of the access location and capacity of the distributed photovoltaic on the voltage of the system node is very different. On the other hand, there are asymmetry in the distribution network, the transmission line is not cyclically transposed, and the three-phase load is asymmetrical [8]. If the access to the single-phase distributed PV is not restricted, the voltage and current three-phase unbalance of the distribution network may be aggravated. The model solves the problem of three-phase imbalance by reducing line loss and extending equipment life. The distributed photovoltaic power grid output prediction model is to access distributed photovoltaics as much as possible under the premise of satisfying the constraints of power balance [9], voltage deviation and three-phase unbalance, and reasonably configure the capacity of each node to access distributed photovoltaics [10]. So far, the construction of the distributed photovoltaic power output prediction model is completed.

2.2 Realize Power Grid Output Prediction Algorithm

After distributed PV access to the distribution network, the power supply network structure changes from a single power supply to multiple power supplies, and the magnitude and direction of the power flow may change, further affecting the voltage and loss of the distribution network. For the typical topology of the distributed photovoltaic access distribution network, the calculation formula for the voltage output prediction of the distribution network node with distributed photovoltaic is derived as follows;

$$|\langle f_e, t_u \rangle| = \max |\langle a_e, h_u \rangle| \tag{2}$$

In the formula (2), f represents a low frequency signal, t represents a signal to be decomposed, a represents a voltage consumption time, and h represents a position. When using the grid output prediction algorithm, each decomposition requires a large amount of inner product operations for each atom in the atom library and the signal to be decomposed. The vertical projection of the residual component of the signal on the selected atom has non-orthogonality, which makes the result of each decomposition not optimal, but a suboptimal solution. This will result in an increase in the number of iterations, an increase in the amount of calculations, and a lengthy calculation. In order to solve the above problems, based on the matching pursuit algorithm, this paper orthogonalizes the selected best matching atom and the selected best matching atom for each step decomposition. This allows for faster convergence on the basis of the same accuracy. In order to improve the convergence performance of the original algorithm, a speed expression for updating the system transmission data set is proposed. The formula is as follows:

$$a_i(y+1) = \Re(a_i \max(t)) + y_i \qquad (3)$$

In Eq. (3), a represents the convergence speed, y represents the spatial data set, and t represents the search space. The power grid output prediction algorithm has a vector moment method and an information method. Compared with the information method, the vector moment method can directly correspond to the fitness function of the optimization problem solution, which can effectively narrow the search space and avoid double counting. Therefore, a vector moment based concentration selection method is adopted in the improved grid output prediction algorithm. Suppose m antibodies form a non-spatial system set u. The specific flow of the concentration selection operation of the vector moment is as follows:

The first step is to initialize various parameters in the vector moment method, and the parameter data set is $t_1, t_2, t_3, \cdots, t_n$. In the second step, the data transmission speed in the solution space is initialized, and the initial position is set, and the initial position data set is $v_1, v_2, v_3, \cdots, v_n$. The third step is to determine whether the number of iterations satisfies the division criterion. If the number of iterations is $y_i \in 1$, the data is divided into two types. If the number of iterations is $y_i \notin 1$, then it is necessary to continue the iteration without satisfying the condition. In the fourth step, the data transmission speed is calculated according to the fitness function. The fitness function formula is as follows:

$$u_i = \Re(u_i \max(t)) \qquad (4)$$

In the formula (4), u represents the transmission speed, and t represents the data parameter. The fifth step is to evaluate the data results and update the speed and location of the data. The inertia weight and learning factor adopt a dynamic adjustment strategy. Record the optimal position of the data and the current optimal position of the data set. If the data set is divided, the worst position of the data and the current worst position of the population are recorded at the same time. In the sixth step, the concentration and fitness function values of each particle are calculated, and the individual extreme values of the particles and the extreme values of the population are updated according to the fitness function value. For the data set, the optimal extreme value of the data and the worst extreme value are updated at the same time. In the seventh step, the vector moment immune selection is performed according to the data transmission speed. The eighth step is to generate the next generation data set. In the ninth step, it is judged whether the convergence condition is satisfied, and if it is satisfied, the optimal solution is output, otherwise it returns to the third iteration to start the next iteration evolution.

In the iterative optimization process, the failed data set experienced is represented by the data itself or the data location with poor fitness in the population. For the speed and position update of the failure experience, it can be represented by formula (3), and the calculation formula is as follows:

$$j_i(y+1) = \Re(j_i) + k_i \tag{5}$$

In formula (4), j represents the data transmission position, y represents the transmission failure position, and k represents the worst position searched. Due to the large amount of data transmitted by the system, it is necessary to learn from successful experiences. For the failure experience, it only absorbs the effective information to guide the next iterative search and avoid returning to the failed position again. The final update position of the data set is still determined by Eq. (4).

Article method can reflect the intrinsic link between economy and safety when photovoltaics are connected to the distribution network. By calculating the current distributed PV permeability index group and photovoltaic utilization efficiency and utilization cost, it can effectively guide the orderly grid connection of distributed PV in the future, and provide an important reference for the pre-distribution planning of distributed PV in regional distribution network. For a specific distribution network, the geographical environment is basically determined by its photovoltaic output characteristics. Without considering other measures, its load characteristics have a greater impact on the PV capacity of the region. The correlation coefficient can reflect the correlation between the load characteristics and the photovoltaic output characteristics, and initially grasp the PV consumption capacity of the grid, and carry out reasonable photovoltaic grid layout to provide guidance for regional PV capacity planning. So far, the grid output prediction algorithm is implemented.

3 Experimental Results

In order to verify the effectiveness of the machine-based distributed PV large-scale access grid power prediction algorithm, the algorithm optimization, transmission speed and accuracy were tested. In the experiment, by comparing the response speeds of the two algorithms and analyzing the performance of the algorithm, the accuracy of the large-scale distributed PV output prediction algorithm based on machine learning is proved.

The machine learning-based distributed photovoltaic large-scale access grid output prediction algorithm is tested. The test results are as follows:

Figure 3 is a comparison of experimental results. From the above test data, it can be seen that it is more advantageous than literature [1] Method and literature [2] Method. From the results of the optimized scheduling in Fig. 3, the dispatching power at 100 min is 0, indicating that the grid-connected operation of the algorithm does not affect the voltage quality. Although the grid-connected operation of distributed photovoltaics can play a certain role in improving the network loss and voltage quality of the system, it is not superior from the economic perspective. This is mainly because the data transmission speed of the machine-based distributed photovoltaic large-scale access grid output prediction algorithm established in this paper is faster.

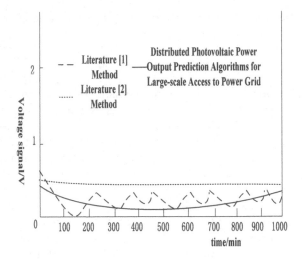

Fig. 3. Comparison of experimental results

4   Conclusion

Short-term grid forecasting is one of the indispensable tasks of the power dispatching department, and it is also a necessary process for the power dispatching department to realize modern management. Since the power generation plan and operation mode of the power grid are mainly determined by the load, high requirements are placed on the accuracy of load prediction. In this paper, based on machine learning, distributed PV large-scale access to power grid output prediction algorithm is established to establish a power grid output prediction model. Start with two aspects to improve the predictive effect of the model. The lack of objectivity for the model input selected by experience, and also affect the accuracy of prediction, the power grid output prediction algorithm is proposed, and the two algorithms are compared and analyzed through experimental simulation. The experimental results show that the input variables of the distributed PV large-scale access to the grid output prediction model will directly affect the prediction effect of the algorithm. In this paper, the grid output prediction algorithm can directly extract the features of numerical data. When selecting useful variables, the effects of redundant variables can be eliminated.

References

1. Liu, S., Luo, F., Wang, C., et al.: Calculation method of hosting capacity for distributed grid-connected photovoltaic based on improved big bang-big crunch algorithm. Proceedings of the CSU-EPSA **11**, 5–10 (2017)
2. Cheng, M., Dai, X., Wang, S., et al.: Study on voltage characteristics of distributed photovoltaic access to active distribution network. Northeast. Power Technol. **38**(5), 2118–2221 (2017)

3. Wang, H., Ge, L., Li, H., et al.: Summary of characteristics analysis and prediction methods of distributed photovoltaic power generation. Electr. Power Constr. **38**(7), 2321–2329 (2017)
4. Yang, F., Tian, C., Li, Z., et al.: Distributed photovoltaic spatial-temporal distribution prediction considering space capacity saturation. Power Grid Technol. **23**(12), 3917–3925 (2017)
5. Li, L., Wang, J., He, Y., et al.: Multi-point PV-DG day-ahead allocation plan based on K-means clustering particle swarm optimization. High Volt. Technol. **44**(4), 1263–1270 (2017)
6. Huang, W., Gao, Y., Zhang, Y., et al.: Limit capacity assessment of distributed photovoltaic access distribution network considering uncertainty. Power Syst. Prot. Control. **11**(14), 1453–1654 (2018)
7. Jin, Z., Xiang, T., Chen, H., et al.: Distributed photovoltaic access planning method considering power quality problems [J]. Power system protection and control **45**(9), 1231–1238 (2017)
8. Yang, C., Pan, Yu., Zeyang, W., et al.: Output optimization and capacity allocation method of distributed photovoltaic-energy storage system considering power loss. Renew. Energy **35**(2), 245–251 (2017)
9. He, X., Zhang, M., Zhu, Y., et al.: Application analysis of centralized and string inverter in photovoltaic power plant. J. Xi'an Polytech. Univ. **04**, 443–448 (2018)
10. Zhang, W., Qi, W., Xu, Q., et al.: Study on location and capacity of distributed photovoltaic access distribution network considering time series characteristics. J. Nanjing Norm. Univ. (Eng. Ed.) **17**(3), 1122–1128 (2017)

A Homomorphic Encryption Algorithm for Chaotic Image Coding Data in Cloud Computing

Bin-bin Jiang[(✉)]

School of Software, Nanyang Institute of Technology, Nanyang, China
gongzuo8788@163.com

Abstract. The traditional image data encryption methods tend to ignore the classification of encryption attack types, resulting in poor security and accuracy of encryption results. In order to better guarantee the performance of chaotic image coding, a homomorphic encryption algorithm for chaotic image coding data in cloud computing environment is proposed. First, the homomorphic encryption matrix of coded data is normalized, and the homomorphic encryption parameters are calculated according to the results of the specification. According to the encryption parameters, the image encoding instructions are set, the common encryption attack types are divided, the encryption instructions are selected according to the partition results, and the accurate encryption of chaotic image coding data is finally realized. Finally, the experimental results show that the homomorphic encryption algorithm of chaotic image coding data in cloud computing environment has higher security and accuracy than the traditional encryption algorithm. It is indicated that the proposed encryption algorithm has a certain feasibility.

Keywords: Cloud computing · Chaotic image · Coded data · Homomorphic encryption

1 Introduction

The characteristic of the image data information is that the information amount is large, the correlation is strong and the redundancy is large, and these characteristics determine that the encrypted digital image data information cannot be encrypted directly using the text encryption algorithm [1]. For this reason, a new field of password research is created, which is image encryption. The feature of the image data information causes the information security researchers to design a better image encryption algorithm to better protect the digital image data information. In the image data information, the operation of the spatial domain is a technique based on the direct operation of the pixels [2]. In cryptography, image encryption in spatial domain is the process of encrypting image pixel value directly. This method only allows the authorized party to retrieve the original information and read it. In the practical application of image encryption, symmetric key encryption system is more widely used than asymmetric key encryption system. With the development of chaos theory, chaos technology has also been applied to the field of digital image data encryption [3]. Compared with the traditional image

© ICST Institute for Computer Sciences, Social Informatics and Telecommunications Engineering 2019
Published by Springer Nature Switzerland AG 2019. All Rights Reserved
G. Gui and L. Yun (Eds.): ADHIP 2019, LNICST 301, pp. 448–457, 2019.
https://doi.org/10.1007/978-3-030-36402-1_48

encryption algorithm, the key space is generally small, the key space generated by the hybrid system is large, and the distribution of the key space is more random. In addition, chaotic system has three basic characteristics: high sensitivity of initial value and control parameters, pseudo-randomicity of motion trajectory and simple realization of software and hardware. Based on these three characteristics, chaos technology is applied to digital image data encryption, and a chaotic-based digital image data encryption method is proposed.

2   A Homomorphic Encryption Algorithm for Chaotic Image Coding Data in Cloud Computing

2.1   Coded Data Homomorphic Encryption Algorithm

Compared with text data, digital image data has the characteristics of large amount of data, strong correlation of adjacent pixel data and high redundancy of whole pixel data. These characteristics make the traditional cryptosystem based on text information no longer suitable for digital image data encryption system [4]. According to the different characteristics of the two stages of image acquisition and processing, there are two main branches in the research of image encryption system: One is the encryption and decryption processing system based on digital image data acquisition/display, which is called digital image data information encryption/decryption system; The second is an encryption and decryption system based on digital image data information stored and transmitted in digital signal form, called a digital image cryptographic system. The digital image encryption and decryption system based on chaotic system belongs to the digital image cryptosystem, which is referred to as chaotic digital image cryptosystem. Chaotic encryption is one of the best alternatives to ensure security [5]. Due to the extreme sensitivity of chaotic mapping to initial conditions, unpredictability and random behavior, an image encryption scheme based on chaotic mapping is proposed based on these properties.

Chaotic mapping image encryption is the combination of word key, number or expression to encrypt the original image data. Because of the basic role of chaotic image data in various applications, the security protection of chaotic image data information has become an important topic for most image and data processing researchers [6]. Chaotic image coded data homomorphism encryption algorithm is a mathematical function used in encryption and decryption process. By using different combinations of keywords, numbers or expressions to encrypt the original data, the key strength is improved. Therefore, it is necessary to set the key privacy strength attribute matrix first in the coding area, if the key confidentiality intensity attribute matrix is R_{ij}, and:

$$
R_{ij} - \begin{bmatrix}
1.104 & 0.942 & 1.241 & 1.547 & 1.648 \\
0.942 & 0.122 & 0.411 & 0.347 & 0.694 \\
1.012 & 1.042 & 0.924 & 1.044 & 1.651 \\
1.640 & 1.648 & 0.812 & 0.794 & 1.408 \\
0.841 & 1.105 & 1.351 & 1.054 & 1.918 \\
0.945 & 1.641 & 1.034 & 1.841 & 1.648
\end{bmatrix} \tag{1}
$$

If R_{ij} is data feature extraction symbol type attribute. In the process of data encryption and filtering, the data exchange and contrast algorithm is carried out.

Setting m_i to be a different data characteristic symbol type attribute, wherein the selection range is (x, y), and N is the corresponding bad data characteristic attribute discrimination parameter, and the D_{zir} is a thermal encryption information extraction range reference function, the image coding carrying symbol is s, and the mixed image data constraint range is (i, j), so as to complete the primary filtering processing calculation on the bad information vocabulary, and the algorithm is as follows:

$$
T_n = \log \frac{N}{Rm_i} [s(D_{zir}^2 + R_{ij}) - b] \tag{2}
$$

If T_n is the weight factor of data encryption feature lookup, fron is the primary agreement condition of information filtering [7].

In order to ensure the accuracy of information filtering, it is necessary to retrieve the threshold range of information filtering. In the course of secondary processing, the maximum detection threshold range should be selected first, and the information filtering should be processed twice within the effective detection range. The selected algorithms are as follows:

$$
\delta = \frac{1}{2} fron \sum_{j=1}^{i} T_n s(R_{ij} a_n - 1) f(x, y) \tag{3}
$$

In order to further encrypt the data, let $K(x_i, y_i)$ be the symbol attribute range of the data encoded by the information; e is the key word feature pre-processing screening parameter, the encryption parameters of chaotic image can be calculated effectively. The algorithm is as follows:

$$
v = \sum K(x_i, y_i) - \frac{1 + f(x, y)}{2\Delta\delta[\ln T_n - \ln R_{ij} - \delta] + \log(\ln e - 1)} \tag{4}
$$

Combined with the above algorithm, the security parameters of homomorphic encryption of chaotic image coded data can be accurately calculated, thus the massive intrusion data in cloud computing environment can be effectively prevented and filtered.

2.2   Chaotic Image Encoding Encryption Instruction Setting

The image encoding and encryption technology of hull usually adopts pixel replacement on image or video, which makes the data difficult to decipher. This technique ensures the security of image data to a certain extent, but also changes the relationship between adjacent pixel values, so that the subsequent compression operation to be less suitable [8]. Homomorphic data encryption technology is a new method to encrypt sensitive digital image data, which is important in human perception. It improves encryption efficiency, satisfies real-time requirements better, and keeps file format unchanged. According to the requirement of bandwidth during transmission, chaotic image is encoded by homomorphic encryption technology. The principle of chaotic image coding is shown in the following Fig. 1:

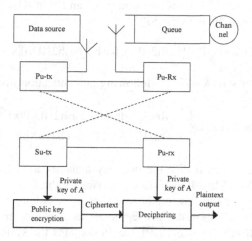

Fig. 1. Chaotic image coding principle

The chaotic image coding is optimized by homomorphic encryption algorithm. In the process of encryption and coding, the plaintext image is transcoded by encryption key, and the encrypted ciphertext image is obtained. Then the encrypted ciphertext image and encryption key are sent to the receiver [9]. The cipher text image encrypted by the receiving end uses the same key to decrypt, and the decrypted image is the plain text image, and the process completes the encrypted transmission of the digital image data information. Encryption on the spatial domain is the operation of each pixel value in plaintext image data, that is, the operation is done directly in pixels. Full and partial encryption can be performed on a spatial domain [10]. In complete encryption, consider the entire image value and encrypt each pixel. In the process of encryption, the main instructions of chaotic image encoding and encryption should be designed. Because the encryption password is relatively private, the imitating instruction proposed in this paper is used as a substitute. In order to describe the chaotic image symbols and their meanings, a password convention is carried out. The initial SP authentication convention instruction is constructed as follows:

(a) Suppose the server-side SP is identified as IDs, SP sending instructions to IDA:

$$SP \rightarrow IDA : \{(hash2(hash2(IDs)\|N)\}$$

(b) IDA authenticates SP with the following authentication instructions:

$$forIDA + \{Received(hash2(hash2(IDs)\|N)$$
$$= (hash2(hash2(IDs)\|x); x = x+1;\}$$

When the IDA again requests the SP to provide the transcoding encryption service, the saved image information list L can be used for verification, and the one-time public key is not needed to be constructed, and the IDA does not change the authentication method of the SP. The following is an example of an SP-to-IDA authentication:
(a) IDA sends instructions to the SP:

$$IDA \rightarrow SP : \{hash2(ID_i), hash2(hash2(ID_i)\|x)\}$$

(b) SP authenticates IDA with the following authentication instructions:

$$ForallH \in L \begin{cases} Receivedhash2(hash2(ID_i)\|x) \\ hash2(H\|N+1)N+1SaveNinL. \end{cases}$$

the encryption protocol can realize the two-way authentication between the terminal IDA and the server SP. When IDA visits the service for the first time, SP authenticates the IDA by verifying the one-time public key, that is, by judging whether the equation $e(P_i, P) = e(U_i, P)$ is valid or not. Only legitimate users registered in the TC can pass the authentication. If $e(P_i, P) = e(U_i, P)$, the Pi contains the system master key, as a result, the sender has registered. After IDA access, the x cannot be calculated even if the attacker intercepts, only the real SP owns the private key SP, through the calculate the random number x to provide the correct hash value $hash2(hash2(IDs), N)$. According to the security condition of hash function, it is difficult for the attacker to obtain the correct hash value under the condition of N unknown, thus realizing the validity of the current verification. In the post-IDA access, only legitimate terminals can authenticate IDA, through hash table lookup.

2.3   Realization of Homomorphic Encryption of Chaotic Image Coded Data

Because the digital image data information is different from the text data information, it has the characteristics of large amount of data, strong correlation of adjacent pixel data and high redundancy of the whole pixel data. For some reasons, traditional text data encryption algorithms such as RSA, DES can not be directly used in digital image data encryption. One of the reasons is that the size of the image is much larger than the text, so the traditional cryptosystem needs a lot of time to process the image data by direct public key cryptosystem. The public key cryptosystem is based on the mathematical one-way function. It uses two keys to separate the encryption and decryption functions, one key as the encryption key and one key as the decryption key. Through the conversion of encryption and decryption key, secure socket layer protocol for secure communication and digital signature can be realized by the same technology. Secure Sockets layer (SSL) is a secure data transmission technology developed by the company. It can prevent the communication between client and server applications from being eavesdropped by attackers, and can always authenticate the server and choose to authenticate the client. The advantage of the protocol is its independence from the application layer protocol. It ensures that the encryption algorithm is completed before the communication of the application layer protocol, the negotiation of the communication key and the authentication of the server. After that, the data transmitted by the application layer protocol will be encrypted. At the same time, because the transmitted message includes the integrity check of the message, the protocol provides a higher security channel is the confidentiality, integrity and reliability of the secure transaction protocol, complete the encoding and encryption of the image data. The detailed chaotic image coding data homomorphism encryption steps are shown in Fig. 2:

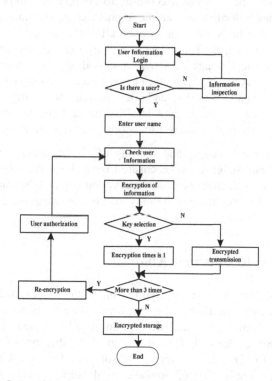

Fig. 2. Steps of homomorphic encryption of chaotic image coded data

In the process of homomorphic encryption of chaotic image coded data, the decrypted image with small distortion is acceptable. In addition, the security analysis of image encryption is a technique to decrypt all or part of the ciphertext without knowing the decryption key. Therefore, in the process of decryption, we need to rely on the information and control system, through encryption analysis to obtain the key or part of the key, decrypt the image or part of the decryption image. In the decryption process, the type of the image encryption attack is divided according to the difficulty degree of the attack, and the method comprises the following steps of:

(1) Ciphertext attack only: Also known as violent attacks, The cipher text image attacker can only master the cipher text data information, analyze the cipher text data by using the poor lifting method, and try to find out the key. This kind of attack is impossible to design and perfect the encryption system. Ability to prevent known ciphertext attacks is a minimum requirement for an encryption scheme

(2) Known plaintext attack: The encryption analyst has a string of clear text P and its corresponding ciphertext C, which will help the encryption analyst to determine the key or part of the key, thereby attacking the ciphertext image.

(3) Select clear text attack: The encryption analyst can choose to input the plaintext image data into a closed system containing encryption algorithm and encryption key. The closed system will output the corresponding ciphertext image data information, and after analysis, According to the relationship between the plaintext image data information and the ciphertext image data information, the encryption analyst finds out some or even all of the keys.

(4) Select a ciphertext attack: The encryption analyst can choose to input the information of ciphertext image data into a closed system containing encryption algorithm and encryption key, and the closed system will output the corresponding plaintext image data information, and after analysis, According to the relationship between the plaintext image data information and the ciphertext image data information, the encryption analyst finds out some or even all of the keys.

In order to ensure the security and stability of chaotic image data homomorphic encryption security and stability can be ensured by dividing the characteristics of the above attack types and selecting the coded encryption key and the transcode password in order to ensure the security and stability of chaotic image data homomorphism encryption.

3 Experimental Results and Analysis

The experiments of encryption and decryption of digital images of different sizes are carried out, and the time consuming of encryption and decryption process is recorded, and the statistics of encryption and decryption speed are analyzed. Experimental environment information for CPU Core dual-core 2.26 Ghz, memory 4 GB notebook computer, system for Debian7.5, simulation software for Matlab7.0. Because the quality of chaotic picture is relatively low and the definition is not enough, in order to get the characteristics of the image and encrypt it accurately, it is necessary to collect the bitmap and pixel of the image in the process of encrypting the transcode, and so on, in order to get the character of the image better and carry on the accurate transcoding encryption processing. The average encryption/decryption time of digital images with different pixel sizes is obtained, and the data is shown in the following Table 1.

Table 1. Parameters affecting chaotic Image encryption

Image size (pixels)	Bitmap (bit)	Average encryption time (s)
256 * 256 * 3	24	0.90
512 * 512 * 3	24	1.24
876 * 876 * 3	24	1.64
1024 * 1024 * 3	24	2.03
2063 * 2063 * 3	24	2.64

In the above parameter environment, the traditional encryption method and the homomorphic encryption method proposed in this paper are used to encrypt the image data respectively, and the accurate values of the authentication encryption method are

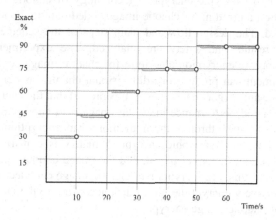

(a)Experimental group

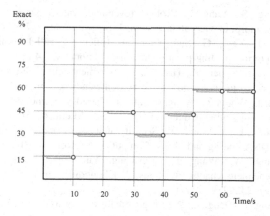

(b)Control group

Fig. 3. Comparison of experimental results

recorded and compared. In the process of detection, the higher the coding accuracy value is, the more accurate the image data is. The better the encryption, the better the security and stability. The test results are as shown in Fig. 3:

As shown in Fig. 3, the accuracy of traditional methods for encoding and encrypting chaotic images is relatively low. However, the encryption accuracy of the homomorphic addition algorithm for chaotic image coding data based on cloud computing environment is obviously better than that of traditional methods under the same experimental environment and parameters, which fully satisfies the research requirements.

4 Conclusion

In order to study the encryption technology of chaotic image data, a homomorphic encryption algorithm for chaotic image coded data in cloud computing environment is proposed. The design flow and main steps of the scheme are given, and the experimental results and safety are analyzed. The experimental results show that the homomorphic encryption algorithm for chaotic image coded data in cloud computing environment can produce one-dimensional chaotic sequences with better chaotic performance and larger chaotic range. It is proved that the encryption algorithm is effective and has good performance in digital image data encryption and various attacks.

In this paper, through the homomorphism encryption algorithm of encoded data, the encoded homomorphic encryption matrix is constructed, the common types of encryption attacks are analyzed, and the image coding instructions are segmented. On the basis of this, the encryption of chaotic image encoded data is realized. This method can effectively encrypt the image data according to the attack type, and provide a new idea for chaotic image encryption.

References

1. Xiang, S., Yang, L.: Robust reversible watermarking algorithm for images based on homomorphic encryption system. J. Softw. **29**(4), 957–972 (2018)
2. Shi, J., Yang, G., Sun, Y., et al.: Efficient parallel homomorphic encryption algorithm supporting floating point operations. Comput. Sci. **45**(5), 123–129 + 137 (2018)
3. Yang, X., Chen, Z., Han, T.: Improvement and application of homomorphic encryption algorithm in application scope and efficiency. Comput. Eng. Des. **38**(2), 318–322 (2017)
4. Qin, J., Wang, X., Wang, G.: Identity-based homomorphic encryption and its application in cloud computing. Comput. Program. Ski. Maint. **46**(6), 93–95 (2017)
5. Zhu, S., Li, J., Wang, W.: Security analysis of improved image encryption algorithm based on DNA coding and chaos. Comput. Appl. Res. **34**(10), 3090–3093 (2017)
6. Zhang, W., Wang, D., Meisheng, Yu.: Image encryption algorithm based on two independent chaotic functions. J. Chongqing Univ. Posts Telecommun. (Nat. Sci. Ed.) **29**(2), 232–239 (2017)
7. Xiong, J., Deng, Z.: An image stream encryption algorithm based on nonlinear chaos and data sharing. Electron. Technol. Softw. Eng. **53**(4), 194 (2017)

8. Niu, Y., Zhang, X.: Chaotic image encryption algorithm based on bit permutation and nucleic acid sequence library. Comput. Eng. Appl. **53**(17), 130–136 (2017)
9. Lei, J., Xiao, L.: Design of digital image chaotic encryption system based on SOC technology. Inn. Mong. Sci. Technol. Econ. **35**(19), 95–96 (2017)
10. Lin, Z., Hu, Q., Li, J., et al.: Image encryption algorithm based on hyperchaotic sequence and bit plane scrambling. J. Nanchang Univ. (Eng. Ed.) **39**(2), 169–174 (2017)

Quantitative Evaluation Model for Information Security Risk of Wireless Communication Networks Under Big Data

Bin-bin Jiang[✉]

School of Software, Nanyang Institute of Technology, Nanyang, China
gongzuo8788@163.com

Abstract. Quantitative evaluation of information security risk in wireless communication network can effectively guarantee the security of communication network. In order to solve the problem that the traditional network security evaluation method is not effective, a quantitative risk assessment model of wireless communication network information security under big data is constructed. Using the wireless composition and working principle, the risk assessment system of wireless communication is built, and the index weight is determined. On this basis, the network information function interface is deployed, and the initial probability is calculated, and the quantitative risk assessment model of wireless communication network information security under big data is constructed. The experimental results show that under the condition of increasing the frequency of network attack, the security potential value of the model is always at a higher level, which indicates that the model has better performance and is helpful to detect the security of the system. It is convenient to provide accurate safety protection measures in time to resist safety risks.

Keywords: Security risk assessment · Big data · Risk quantification · Information safety

1 Introduction

Because the communication mode and security level of different network systems are different, resulting in the unfavorable situation of network system isolation, the security level and protective measures of different elements in the same network system are not very clear, so it is difficult to ensure the accurate application of security measures to security vulnerabilities. Therefore, the construction of wireless communication network information security risk assessment model is an important basis for rational allocation of security protection resources. Through the information security risk assessment, we can clarify the information security requirements, help to formulate the optimal information security policy and select the corresponding risk control measures, so as to reduce the risk to an acceptable range. The quantitative measurement of information security risk is an objective and effective quantitative method, which has an intuitive understanding of the probability of risk occurrence and the possible loss after the risk occurs, and is more conducive to the organization of information security risk

© ICST Institute for Computer Sciences, Social Informatics and Telecommunications Engineering 2019
Published by Springer Nature Switzerland AG 2019. All Rights Reserved
G. Gui and L. Yun (Eds.): ADHIP 2019, LNICST 301, pp. 458–468, 2019.
https://doi.org/10.1007/978-3-030-36402-1_49

management and control. For the easy-to-issue information security incident, defensive measures can be taken early. Therefore, it is necessary to conduct research on quantitative measurement of information security risks, in order to manage and control information security risks with better cost-effectiveness [1].

Chen et al. proposed information security risk assessment based on BP neural network method. The process and method of information security risk assessment are introduced in detail. The non-linear BP neural network method is applied to the information security risk assessment model to overcome its subjectivity and artificial nature. It is an effective assessment method. The results are consistent with the theoretical analysis. The Reality of Successful Cases [2]. Li and Lian proposed network information security transmission simulation of large data mobile terminal. This paper designs a security mechanism for network reliability authentication and transmission encryption in the network transport layer to ensure the security of data transmission in the network [3]. However, the above methods have the problem of low evaluation results.

For this reason, the Quantitative Evaluation Model for Information Security Risk of Wireless Communication Networks Under Big Data method is proposed in this paper. The research results of this paper put forward new ideas for the information security risk quantification method, enriched the information security risk measurement method, and provided risk management theory and technical support. From the aspect of management, it promotes the optimal allocation of resources, rationally arranges the investment of information security funds, and carries out information security construction with better cost-effectiveness, reducing the losses caused by information security incidents; From the technical aspect, it provides a message. Security risk occurrence probability calculation model and an information security risk loss calculation idea; From the social aspect, through effective risk quantification, organizations and individuals have an intuitive understanding of information security risks, which is conducive to the protection and organization of personal information.

2 Establishment of Risk Assessment System for Wireless Communication

2.1 Determining the Weight of Assessment Indexes

According to the design principles of risk assessment index system and the security requirements of wireless communication at home and abroad, combined with the wireless composition and working principle, and comprehensively consider various factors affecting the security of wireless communication networks, this paper establishes a wireless communication security risk assessment index system. The evaluation system is mainly composed of five parts: communication transmission safety evaluation index; safety standard system evaluation index; networking safety technology evaluation index; formatted message evaluation index; each terminal safety evaluation index. The information transmitted by wireless communication has certain sensitivity and confidentiality. In order to ensure that information is not stolen by the enemy, the information is transmitted securely in the wireless network. Before the information is transmitted, various security measures must be adopted to encrypt the message.

Message encryption technology is the most commonly used method to protect data security during data transmission. It is also the most basic necessary technology. It is mainly based on a specific encryption method or encryption algorithm to convert the data to be encrypted into a garbled transmission. The data needs to be restored with the key when the message needs to be read. Transmission encryption is to perform pseudo-random code encryption on the transmitted signal before the terminal device is ready to transmit the data signal, and the frequency hopping pattern selection and the start of the message are shaken. The hopping spread pattern and the pseudo-random code are selected according to different communication networks. And the size of the encryption varies.

In this study, 10 network and wireless experts from different departments were invited to represent different perspectives on wireless security. Through the above simulation wireless throughput, effective throughput, packet loss rate and node transmission delay, etc. The analysis of the importance of the indicators of the evaluation indicators, according to the principle of fuzzy analytic analysis, the results of various indicators analysis [4]. As shown in Table 1:

Table 1. Weight analysis of wireless communication security evaluation index

Evaluation index of wireless communication security	Evaluation index of communication transmission security	Evaluation index of safety standard system	Evaluation index of network security technology	Format message evaluation index	Set up the safety evaluation index of each terminal
Credit/%	89	91	82	73	88
Effective throughput bit/s	354	521	501	497	483
Packet loss rate/%	1	2	2	1	2
Node transmission delay/s	0.020	0.045	0.024	0.084	0.064
Resource utilization rate/%	87.62	94.34	89.95	97.41	94.11

Through the evaluation of each demand risk value, the various elements of data link communication security and the quantitative weight of each factor can be analyzed, and the risk events with higher risk values can be analyzed to determine relevant perfect solutions, so that the existing risks can be effectively avoiding and reducing the occurrence of this risk, but also can effectively guarantee the security of data link communication [5].

2.2 Gray Assessment of Underlying Indicators

According to the weight analysis of the wireless communication security evaluation indicators shown in Table 1, the gray categories k $= \{1, 2, 3, 4, 5\}$ are classified into five categories according to the attack intensity, which are very low, low, medium, high, and very high. The various whitening weight functions are as follows:

First grey class: $k = 1$, very low, grey $\otimes_1 \in \{0, 1, 2\}$, the whitening weight function is f_1;

$$f_1(d_{ij}) = \{d_{ij}, x \in [0, 1]$$ (1)

Second grey class: $k = 2$, low, grey $\otimes_2 \in \{0, 2, 4\}$. The whitening weight function is f_2;

$$f_2(d_{ij}) = \{d_{ij}/2, x \in [0, 2]$$ (2)

Third grey class: $k = 3$, medium, grey $\otimes_3 \in \{0, 3, 6\}$. The whitening weight function is f_3;

$$f_3(d_{ij}) = \{d_{ij}/3, x \in [0, 3]$$ (3)

Fourth gray class: $k = 4$, high, grey $\otimes_4 \in \{0, 4, 8\}$. The whitening weight function is f_4;

$$f_4(d_{ij}) = \{d_{ij}/4, x \in [0, 4]$$ (4)

Fifth grey class: $k = 5$, very high, grey $\otimes_5 \in \{0, 5, \ldots\}$. The whitening weight function is f_5;

$$f_5(d_{ij}) = \{d_{ij}/5, x \in [0, \ldots 5]$$ (5)

Based on various whitening weight functions, the degree of quantitative evaluation of wireless communication network information security risk under big data is analyzed [6]. The methods used in each evaluation phase are described later in this chapter. Similarly, other evaluation indicators are calculated as follows:

It can be seen from the gray risk assessment results of the evaluation indicators in Fig. 1. The cybersecurity threat assessment has certain similarities with the threat assessment in the military field. In the military field, in order to assess the threat level of an air missile, in addition to considering the missile model (either tactical ballistic missiles, precision guided missiles, or ordinary cruise missiles, different types of missiles have different lethality), but also consider missiles. Information such as temporary space, route, distance, altitude, possible targets, and our defense measures [7].

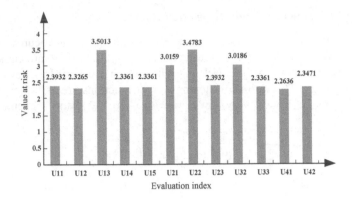

Fig. 1. Grey risk assessment results for assessment Indices

Similarly, in the cyberattack threat assessment process, the type of attack is first analyzed to determine its severity from the nature of the attack. In addition, factors such as the probability of success of the attack, the criticality of the attack against the asset, and the frequency of the attack should be considered to comprehensively assess the threat of the attack. The same type of attack may have different threat levels in different environments, which is related to factors such as network configuration and security policy [8]. This paper summarizes the factors affecting the threat of cyberattacks into six categories: attack destructiveness, environmental factors, probability of success, statistical factors, associated factors and attack effects.

3   Quantitative Risk Assessment of Information Security in Wireless Communication Network

3.1   Deployment of Network Information Functional Interface

The system function interface can be divided into two types: external interface and internal interface. The external interface is responsible for data interaction with the user through the front-end interface, including the user login interface, the management control interface, and the data entry interface. The management control interface further includes: first, a user management interface and an indicator management interface: implemented by a database communication interface; second, plug-in management interfaces: using class [9]. System, Reflection, Assembly, assembly loads an external DLL plug-in [10]. Users can input pre-assessment data through the data entry interface, and the administrator can extend the system through the control center. The internal interface is responsible for automatically processing the data according to the SEM model evaluation process, which is the data interaction interface of the internal modules of the program, as shown in Table 2;

Table 2. Deployment of network information function interface

Serial number	Interface name	Realization	Describe
1	Attack tree generation interface	Public *AttTree GenerateTree (VInfo *&vhead)	Taking the vulnerability information of wireless communication equipment as parameter, attack tree is generated and the root node pointer is returned
2	Theoretical security loss calculation interface	Public float Cal-I'ocLost *&treenode)	Taking the state node as a parameter, the theoretical security loss of the node is calculated and returned
3	Grey clustering interface	Public float Cal GreyCluster (String sql)	Calculate and return an array containing three grey clustering coefficients

Table 2 shows the deployment of the network information function interface, including the indicator system, user information, and plug-in information. It exists in the database before the system runs. It can only be modified by the control center, otherwise it remains unchanged; the dynamic table can be divided. For the pre-data table and the post-data table, the pre-data table includes network topology information, device vulnerability information, and network status specific values. The post-data table includes theoretical node loss, node clustering coefficient, actual node loss, and evaluation result. In the dynamic table, some data tables are manually entered by the user, and only occur before the evaluation calculation starts. Once it is determined that it cannot be changed; the data of the other part of the table is automatically changed according to the operation of the system evaluation work, and is not controlled by human factors.

3.2 Calculate Initial Probability

Monte Carlo simulation is used to calculate the maximum loss of information security risk. Here, geometric Brownian motion is chosen as a stochastic model to reflect the value change of information assets. First, the advantage of geometric Brownian motion to simulate the value of information assets is that the value of general Brownian motion may be negative, while the value of geometric Brownian motion can never be negative, satisfying the characteristic that the value of information assets is never negative; The geometric Brownian motion is consistent with the fluctuation of the information asset market; the geometric Brownian motion process and the real information asset value affected by the information security risk all show the same curved trajectory. Therefore, it can be expressed as:

$$\Delta S_{t+1} = S_t \left(\mu \Delta t + \rho \Im \sqrt{\Delta t} \right) \qquad (6)$$

In formula (6), Δt is the value of information assets at the moment of $t+1$; S_t is the value of information assets at the moment of t; μ is the average rate of return on information assets; ρ is the volatility of the rate of return on information assets. In this paper, $\Im$ is the ultimate source of information asset value risk, namely the occurrence of information security events. The occurrence of information security events directly leads to the change of the value of information assets, so the number of times of information security events also causes changes in the value of information assets. In the third chapter of this paper, it has been shown that the frequency of information security events follows Poisson distribution, so it can be assumed that random variables can be assumed. Obey Poisson distribution.

We set the holding period to one year, that is $\Delta t = 1$. We divide it into an average of 52 equal periods of time to simulate the value trend of information assets, S_t is the value of information assets at initial Tim, ΔS_{t+1} for the value of information assets at the moment of $t+1$, ΔS_{t+1} the amount of change in the value of information assets over a period of time. Then the average and standard deviation of the rate of return on information assets for each period of time is $\frac{\mu}{52}$ and $\frac{\rho}{52}$. The value of the information assets at the moment of $t+1$ is:

$$\Delta S_{t+1} = S_{t+i-1}\left(\frac{\rho}{52}\Delta t + \frac{\Im}{52}\right) \tag{7}$$

According to the probability calculation model of information security events established by formula (7), the mean value of occurrence frequency of information security events of different kinds of information security events is calculated respectively. Thus completed big data wireless communication network information security risk quantitative evaluation model design.

4 Experiment

In order to verify the validity of the quantitative risk assessment model for wireless communication network information security under big data, in the actual test, the model designed in this paper is set as the experimental group and the traditional evaluation model as the control group. The concrete steps are as follows.

4.1 Experimental Steps

The first step is to select 18 kinds of training samples with different characteristics, including 15 types of normal operation data and 3 types of attacked data, and calculate the expected values of each standard attribute of each training sample, namely, the group of feature information vectors of this kind of samples.

The second step is to input a certain amount of attack information randomly into the wireless sensor network and process the node running data once every 100 s to form the node operation information vector with standard attributes.

The third step is to pair the node's information vector with the elements in the feature vector group, and to express the set-pair relationship by the expression of the number of connections. The sensitivity of four Eigenvectors in the vector is calculated by analytic hierarchy process (AHP) according to the result of expert score. The calculation judgment matrix is;

Wormhole Judgment moment of attack:

$$
A_3 = \begin{bmatrix} 1, \dfrac{1}{2}, 1, \dfrac{1}{5} \\ .2, 1, 2, \dfrac{1}{2} \\ 1, \dfrac{1}{2}, 1, \dfrac{1}{5} \\ 5, 2, 5, 1 \end{bmatrix} \tag{8}
$$

The situation factor layer to the target layer weight is k = [0.2406, 0.2144, 0.1255, 0.4194]. The conformance test passed. According to formula (8), the degree of connection between the data and each element in the feature vector group is obtained, and the association degree array is formed.

4.2   Experimental Results

The security value of network information is obtained by counting the percentage of running states of all nodes in wireless communication network. The nodes matching one of the 15 types of normal operation data are considered as normal running nodes, and the nodes matching with one of the three types of abnormal operation data are considered as abnormal running nodes, and the nodes without classification or lack of data are classified as uncertain states. In this experiment, 11 groups of tests were carried out, and the attack intensity of the nodes in different test groups was different. In order to verify the effectiveness of this method, this experiment will choose the busy time of network use, that is, the time range is 6:00–24:00. Because most users are in the rest stage between 0:00–5:59, the frequency of network operation is low during this period, so it is not used as the detection period of this experiment. Where the formula for calculating the information security value and the percentage of nodes attacked in the network is:

$$
N_i = \frac{kf_n}{\Delta S_{t+1}} \tag{9}
$$

Through the previous analysis, when all the nodes are the information security values of wireless sensor networks, the information security values of sensor networks show a downward trend. Therefore, if this method is tested, if the same situation occurs, it indicates that the proposed method is effective and accurate. The relationship between the information security value of a wireless sensor network and the percentage of the node being attacked in the network is shown in Figs. 2 and 3:

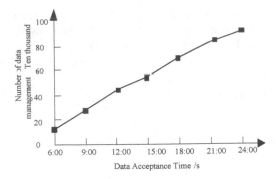

Fig. 2. Traditional forecasting model

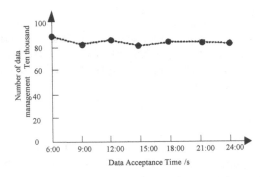

Fig. 3. Quantitative risk Assessment model of wireless communication network information security under large data

Through the analysis of experimental results, when the network tends to be absolutely safe, the wireless sensor network information security value is 35385 (prone to infinity). As the network attack frequency increases gradually, the sensor network information security value begins to decrease, when all nodes in the network are The wireless sensor network information security value is 2.61610 when attacked. As shown in Fig. 2, the abscissa is the frequency of the network attack (attack strength), and the ordinate is the security posture value calculated according to formula (7). According to the figure, the information security of the wireless sensor network decreases with the increase of attack intensity.

The margin of network information security is the amount by which the percentage of attacked nodes in the network increases by one percentage point, and the network information security value decreases. In order to verify the effectiveness of the model, the marginal rate of network information security of the model and the traditional model are compared, and the comparison results are shown in Table 3.

Table 3. Network information security marginal rate

Attack strength	Network information security edge rate /%		
	Running results of this model	Results of traditional model operation	Actual operation results
Very low	98.22	86.24	98.67
Low	85.56	76.03	85.23
Medium	76.83	52.88	76.15
High	63.45	32.86	63.40
Very high	52.05	20.53	51.98

It can be seen from Table 3 that with the increase of network attack intensity, the marginal value of information security of the two models gradually decreases, indicating that the two models are more sensitive to the changes of low-intensity attacks. The result of this model is higher than that of the traditional model, which is consistent with the actual operation. It shows that this model can correctly evaluate the security and risk of wireless communication network information.

5 Concluding Remarks

This paper analyzes the quantitative evaluation model of information security risk in wireless communication network under big data, and provides a model for calculating the probability of information security risk occurrence and a way of calculating information security risk loss. It is beneficial to protect the information security of organizations and individuals.

References

1. Liu, H.: Security evaluation and simulation of privacy information transmission based on big data analysis. Comput. Simul. **35**(2), 342–345 (2018)
2. Chen, X., Chen, H., Wang, C., et al.: Information security risk assessment based on BP neural network. Inf. Commun. **184**(4), 170–171 (2018)
3. Li, L., Lian, Y.: Network information security transmission simulation of large data mobile terminal. Comput. Simul. **35**(6), 194–198 (2018)
4. Chai, J., Wang, S., Liang, H., et al.: Quantitative method of information security risk assessment elements based on analytic hierarchy process. J. Chongqing Univ. **40**(4), 44–53 (2017)
5. Wang, H., Fan, K., Mo, W.: Information security risk assessment based on improved DS evidence theory and BN. Telev. Technol. **41**(6), 24–30 (2017)
6. Guan, T.: Design and implementation of information security risk assessment system for electric power industry. Netw. Secur. Technol. Appl. **11**, 122–124 (2017)
7. Tang, W., Wang, J., Yang, R., et al.: Quantitative risk assessment of large power grid operation based on support vector machine. J. Hefei Univ. Technol. (Nat. Sci. Ed.) **40**(4), 486–491 (2017)

8. Fu, C., Wang, X., Zhang, W., et al.: A component security attribute model driven information security risk assessment approach for train control center. Tiedao Xuebao/J. China Railw. Soc. **39**(8), 77–84 (2017)
9. Chai, T., Weng, J., Xiong, D.Q.: Development of a quantitative risk assessment model for ship collisions in fairways. Saf. Sci. **91**, 71–83 (2017)
10. Jing, X., Hu, H., Yang, H., et al.: A quantitative risk assessment model involving frequency and threat degree under line-of-business services for infrastructure of emerging sensor networks. Sensors **17**(3), 642 (2017)

Intelligent Recognition Method of Short Wave Communication Transmission Signal Based on the Blind Separation Algorithm

Yan-song Hu[(⊠)]

Liaoning Petrocchemical Vocational and Technology, Jinzhou, China
gfy087@126.com

Abstract. The traditional signal recognition method can not be quickly and efficiently identified by noise interference. In order to avoid the drawbacks of traditional methods, an intelligent identification method for short-wave communication transmission signals based on blind separation algorithm is proposed. According to the mathematical model, all the transmission signals in short-wave communication are modally decomposed, and the signal can be decomposed into functions of several different feature scales, and the time and frequency are extracted as the physical quantities of the signal characteristics. The blind separation algorithm is used for signal preprocessing. The short-time energy, short-term average amplitude and short-time zero-crossing rate are used as the starting point of the recognized speech signal. Under the fixed background noise, the normal signal and the noise signal are identified. It can be seen from the experimental results that the method has short recognition time and fast rate, which lays a foundation for short-wave communication transmission.

Keywords: Blind separation algorithm · Shortwave communication · Transmission signal · Intelligent identification

1 Introduction

The rapid development of communication technology, the specification of communication is also constantly improving, and short-wave is the earliest developed and utilized radio frequency band. Short-wave communication is one of the oldest modern communication means. When people continue to develop radio frequency bands such as ultrashort waves and microwaves in pursuit of communication capacity and various services, traditional long-wave and medium-wave communication can only be applied in special occasions because they lose their original advantages [1]. As a modern communication technology, short-wave communication, despite decades of development, still maintains its vitality with its flexibility, simple equipment and long communication distance. However, due to the large number of bad noises and many types of signals in short-wave communication, the work of the receivers is seriously affected [2].

The early signal identification method is a demodulator using a series of different modulation methods. After receiving the high frequency signal, the high frequency signal is converted into an intermediate frequency signal, and then input to each

G. Gui and L. Yun (Eds.): ADHIP 2019, LNICST 301, pp. 469–477, 2019.
https://doi.org/10.1007/978-3-030-36402-1_50

demodulator to obtain an observable or audible signal, and then the operator uses the earphone. Analytical recognition by oscilloscope or spectrum analyzer. The identification of manual participation requires an experienced operator. Generally, it can successfully identify the amplitude keying signal with longer duration and lower symbol rate, and can modulate the frequency-shifted keying signal with larger index, but cannot recognize the phase shift. Keying signal. This kind of manual participation identification method, the judgment result including the subjective factors of people, will vary from person to person, and the types that can be identified are also limited [3].

In order to achieve a satisfactory communication effect for short-wave communication, an intelligent identification method for short-wave communication transmission signals based on blind separation algorithm is proposed. The method has advantages in communication, biomedical signal processing, speech signal processing, array signal processing and general signal analysis. Wide application prospects [4]. It not only can effectively process signals, but also plays an active role in the development of neural network theory.

2 Research on Intelligent Recognition Method of Shortwave Communication Transmission Signal

Blind separation algorithm identification is based on the blind separation principle to identify each signal. In the recognition process, the combination of signal detection and estimation, feature selection, classification and recognition, etc., and the content itself constitute a huge theoretical system. The traditional recognition method has more constraints, so that the disturbance signal can be effectively recognized [5].

2.1 Mathematical Model

The research contents of blind separation can be divided into four parts: instantaneous linear mixing blind separation, convolutional aliasing blind separation, nonlinear aliasing blind separation and the application of blind separation. When the aliasing model is nonlinear, it is difficult to recover the source signal from the aliasing data unless there is further prior knowledge about the signal and the aliasing model [6].

Figure 1 is a schematic diagram of an instantaneous linear mixed-blind separation signal model.

In Fig. 1, the source signal $S = [s_1(t), s_2(t), \ldots, s_n(t)]^T$ is an unknown n-dimensional source signal vector, and A is an unknown mixing matrix, $m = [m_1(t), m_2(t), \ldots, m_n(t)]^T$ is an m-dimensional noise vector, $X = [x_1(t), x_2(t), \ldots, x_n(t)]^T$ is the m-dimensional observed signal vector of the sensor output, which has:

$$X = AS + m \tag{1}$$

The blind separation algorithm requires that only X be known to determine S or A. Independent component analysis is a kind of base station subsystem, and its basic meaning is to decompose the signal into several independent components [7]. In Fig. 1, the goal of independent component analysis is to find a separation matrix, and then

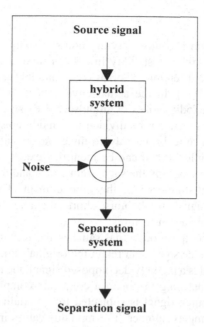

Fig. 1. Schematic diagram of instantaneous linear aliasing blind separation signal model

transform the matrix to obtain a new vector whose components are as independent as possible. The separated signal vector to be sought, that is, the estimated value of the source signal [8].

2.2   Mode Decomposition

Modal decomposition of all transmitted signals in short-wave communication can be used to decompose the signal into functions of several different feature scales. These functions satisfy the following conditions:

① The number of extreme points and zero crossings cannot exceed 1;
② At any point position, the average value of the data extremum is zero [9].
The established signal decomposition process is as follows:

(1)   The upper and lower envelopes can be obtained by fitting all the extreme points of the signal, obtain the difference between the fitted signal and the envelope mean value;
(2)   The difference obtained in step (1) is taken as a new fitting signal, and the above steps are repeated until the difference satisfies the eigenmode function condition, and the first decomposed modal component is consistent with the difference size.
(3)   Classify the modal components from the original signal, obtain a new fitting signal, repeat steps (1) and (2), and obtain modal components of different feature scales until the new fitting signal shows a monotonic trend [10, 11].

2.3   Feature Selection

Short-wave communication is a time-varying, non-stationary random process. Short-wave communication has relative stability in a short time, and its characteristics are considered to be constant. Therefore, short-wave communication transmission signals have short-term stability [12]. In the actual environment, in addition to broadband white noise, there are periodic noises or impulse noises such as machine roar, gun sound, etc., so the audio signal can be divided into mode noise, non-white noise and broadband white noise. The real-time waveforms of noise and normal signals can be seen to be significantly different and can be identified exactly. This indicates that the transmitted signal and noise occupy the same frequency band in the frequency domain, but there is a significant difference in the time domain. Therefore, the difference between the transmitted signal and the noise short-time autocorrelation function value can be used to extract the pattern features.

When the modal decomposition signal satisfies the routing information protocol standard, the acquired source signal can retain the original signal characteristics. Since the acquired source signal is a modally decomposed signal, the coefficient vector can be restored by orthogonal matching to obtain a conjugate complex number. Before the feature extraction, the source signal is subjected to a modulus conversion process to remove the conjugate complex number. The modulus values in the array are arranged from large to small and combined into a new source signal.

Using time and frequency as the physical quantities to characterize the signal, based on the new source signal, reveal the essential characteristics of the disturbance signal with fast frequency change, and construct the time domain and frequency domain bridge by blind separation to ensure that the signal characteristics can be in the region. show. The abnormal signal is introduced in the short-wave communication in time, and the normal signal and the abnormal signal can be distinguished in the aliasing phenomenon, and the blind disturbance signal pre-processing is performed on the normal disturbance signal that is not affected by the noise.

2.4   Blind Separation Signal Preprocessing

In the process of blind separation signal processing, in order to reduce the amount of calculation and improve the transmission efficiency, it is usually necessary to undergo preprocessing. Pre-processing generally includes centralization and whitening. Centralization is to make the mean value of the signal zero. Since the data obtained under normal conditions are related, it is usually required to perform preliminary whitening of the data because the whitening process can be removed. The correlation between the observed signals, thereby simplifying the extraction process of subsequent independent components.

Generally, the whitening of the data is better than the whitening of the data, and the algorithm has better convergence, less workload, and higher efficiency. The linear aliasing blind separation signal model generally adopts the method of independent component analysis. The main basis and premise of ICA is to assume that the source signal is independent. Therefore, it is naturally conceivable that the first step of the ICA algorithm is to establish an objective function to characterize the separation result. The degree of independence. After the objective function is determined, it can be optimized by various optimization algorithms to determine the separation matrix. The representative algorithms mainly include the maximum information method, the natural gradient method, the fast independent element analysis algorithm, the matrix eigenvalue decomposition method, etc. In the blind separation, the optimization operation is often used. As far as the optimization method is concerned, the algorithm and the natural gradient algorithm belong to the gradient descent (rise) optimization algorithm. The convergence speed is linear and the speed is slightly slower, but it belongs to the adaptive method and has Real-time online processing capability; independent component analysis algorithm is a fast and numerically stable method. It uses the quasi-Newton algorithm to achieve optimization and has super-linear convergence speed. Generally, the convergence speed is much faster than the gradient-decreasing optimization algorithm; Matrix Eigenvalue decomposition methods usually estimate separated Matrices by Eigen-decomposition or Generalized Eigen-decomposition of Matrices. This is an analytical method, which can directly find the formal solution. Since it has no iterative optimization process, it runs fastest.

2.5   Recognize the Starting Point of a Speech Signal

The basic short-time parameters of transmission signal are: short-time energy, short-time average amplitude and short-time zero-crossing rate.

$$E = \sum_{n=0}^{S=1} L_g^2(n)$$

$$F = \sum_{n=0}^{S=1} \left| L_g(n) \right| \tag{2}$$

$$Z = \frac{1}{2} \left\{ \sum_{n=1}^{S=1} \left| \text{sgn}\left[L_g(n) \right] - \text{sgn}\left[L_g(n-1) \right] \right| \right\} \tag{3}$$

In formulas (2) and (3): $L_g(n)$ is windowed transmission; S is window length; and E, F, Z represent short-term energy, short-term average amplitude and short-time zero-crossing rate, respectively.

The short-time parameter can be used to identify the starting point position of the short-wave communication transmission signal. Firstly, the probability density function in the case of a turbid transmission signal can be known through training. According to this, a threshold parameter can be determined. When the short-term parameter value of a frame input signal exceeds the threshold parameter, it can be confirmed that the frame signal is not silent, but May be voiced. According to the threshold parameter, it can be determined that the two points in the input signal are definitely between the two points, but the precise start and end points of the voice are also searched before and after the two points. To do this, set a low threshold parameter, which is forwarded by one of the points. This point can be determined when the short-term parameter value is reduced from large to small to the threshold parameter. Similar to this, by looking backwards from another point, you can determine the point, and it is still a voice segment between the two points.

Then, the search is performed with the short-term zero-crossing rate from the first point forward and the second point backward. According to the mean value of the short-time zero-crossing rate under the silent condition, a new parameter of short-time zero-crossing rate is set. If the short-time zero-crossing rate is always greater than 3 times of the new parameter when searching for the first point forward, these signal frames are considered to be It still belongs to the speech segment until the short-term zero-crossing rate suddenly drops to a new parameter below 3 short-time zero-crossing rate, at which point the exact starting point of the transmitted signal can be determined, and similar processing can be performed for the end point.

Recognizing the origin of speech is not only important for extracting data features, but also can separate speech more correctly. Because if the signal source has a silent part during the blind separation of the audio signal, the separated sound signal will have a silent part. The aliasing of other source signals is not conducive to the extraction of pure sound.

2.6   Transmission Signal Intelligent Identification

The purpose of transmitting signals in short-wave communication is to separate the transmitted signal from the received signal. Under fixed background noise, as long as the relative difference between the transmitted signal and the specific noise is extracted, the transmitted signal can be well recognized, but under varying background noise, it is necessary to find out between the transmitted signal and all other various noises. The difference in characteristics is not easy, because short-wave communication transmits signals and noise as a type of wave, and they have many commonalities. Especially in the case of low signal-to-noise ratio, the energy of most short-wave communication signals is very low relative to noise. Therefore, among the characteristics reflected by the analyzed signals, the characteristics of noise are the main components. In this case, it is particularly difficult to identify short-wave communication signals. Because it is a real-time short-wave communication signal identification method, the requirements for calculation amount are strict, and it is impossible to adopt an overly complex algorithm. According to this situation, the characteristics of noise can be classified according to the fact that some noise is in the time domain. The characteristics are obvious, and some noise features are more obvious in the frequency domain.

Under the optimal window, the blind separation algorithm can be used to cluster all the disturbance signals to the central position. Through signal conversion, all the transmission signals are collected together, which is convenient for users to obtain the demand signals. The specific implementation steps are as follows:

Assuming that the total number of extracted signals is m, and the amount of information contained in each signal is t, then the weight coefficient in the k th signal is x_k, and a coordinate point in the three-dimensional space is described according to the following formula. Disturbance signal recognition function under the influence of noise.

The disturbance signal identification function under the influence of noise is minimized to ensure that each signal has a fixed weight coefficient and fuzzy exponent in the process of clustering. The specific processing process of blind signal separation is as follows:

① Statistically disturb the number of signals, using blind separation processing, so that the signal blind separation index and weight coefficient reach the extreme value, and the processing threshold and the number of iterations reach the maximum value, and establish the signal initial matrix and the weight coefficient matrix;

② According to the weight coefficient matrix, the value of the objective function is set, and the number of times after the iterative processing is set is greater than the maximum value, then the selected objective function value will be smaller than the signal threshold, and the calculation can be stopped;

③ Error compensation for the center position of the blind separation space;

④ Using an iterative processing method to obtain a new blind separation center;

⑤ Update the signal attribute weight coefficient and return to step ②.

According to the above steps, the signal can be subjected to blind separation processing, and a blind separation algorithm is used to effectively identify the noise disturbance signal.

3 Check Analysis

In order to verify the rationality of the intelligent identification method of the short-wave communication transmission signal based on the blind separation algorithm, the following experiments are carried out.

3.1 Experimental Results and Analysis

3.1.1 Recognition Time

The identification time of the short-wave communication transmission signal is used as the standard of the transmission quality detection, and the recognition time is compared and analyzed by using the traditional identification technology and the identification technology based on the blind separation algorithm, and the result is shown in Fig. 2.

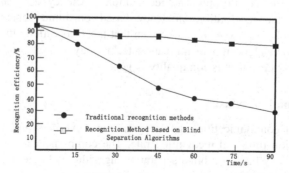

Fig. 2. Analysis of comparison of recognition time between two techniques

It can be seen from Fig. 2 that when the time is 15 s, the recognition efficiency by traditional technology is 80%, the recognition efficiency based on the blind separation algorithm identification technology is 90%; when the time is 45 s, the recognition efficiency by the traditional technology is 55%, based on blindness. The recognition efficiency of the separation algorithm identification technology is 88%; when the time is 75 s, the recognition efficiency by the traditional technology is 38%, and the recognition efficiency based on the blind separation algorithm identification technology is 82%. It can be seen that the recognition efficiency based on the blind separation algorithm identification technology is high, indicating that the communication signal transmission quality is good.

3.1.2. Recognition Rate

In the same way, the recognition time is compared and analyzed by using the traditional recognition technology and the identification technology based on the blind separation algorithm, and the result is shown in Fig. 3.

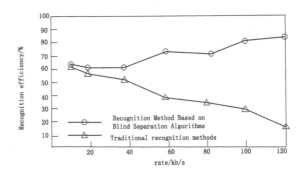

Fig. 3. Analysis of comparison results of recognition rate between two techniques

It can be seen from Fig. 3 that when the rate is 20 kb/s, the recognition efficiency is 55% by the conventional technique, the recognition efficiency based on the blind separation algorithm recognition technique is 65%, and when the rate is 60 kb/s, the recognition efficiency is determined by the conventional technique. For 38%, the recognition efficiency based on blind separation algorithm recognition technology is 75%; when the rate is 100 kb/s, the recognition efficiency is 32% by traditional technology, and the recognition efficiency based on blind separation algorithm recognition technology is 80%. It can be seen that the recognition efficiency based on the blind separation algorithm identification technology is high, indicating that the communication signal transmission quality is good.

3.2 Experimental Conclusions

The efficiency of communication signal recognition is verified and analyzed in two aspects: recognition time and recognition rate. The comparison results show that the recognition efficiency based on blind separation algorithm is higher, which shows that the communication signal transmission quality is better.

To sum up: the research on intelligent identification method of short-wave communication transmission signal based on blind separation algorithm is reasonable.

4 Conclusion

According to the actual environment of short-wave communication signal transmission, the short-wave communication signal recognition situation is analyzed. Therefore, researching signal recognition efficiency becomes a necessary condition for short-wave communication. Although this technology has higher recognition efficiency, it is still to be investigated for signal recognition in different environments. Therefore, in the future research work, the signal recognition in different environments is deeply studied.

References

1. Chunhai, H., Xin, S., Liu, B., et al.: Research on P300 recognition algorithm based on wavelet transform and blind source separation. J. Metrol. **38**(2), 12–15 (2017)
2. Tan, Y., Fan, H., Liu, M., et al.: Signal reconstruction of underwater wireless sensor networks based on blind source separation algorithm. Comput. Simul. **20**(2), 173–176 (2018)
3. Bo Tang, Yu., Zhang, H.Z.: Research on blind separation algorithms of MIMO radar signals based on alternating projection. J. Electron. **45**(9), 2092–2097 (2017)
4. Huang, Q., Hua, P., Li, T.P., et al.: Asymmetric PCMA blind separation algorithms based on soft information joint modification. J. Commun. **38**(4), 178–189 (2017)
5. Wang, C., Jia, R., Zeng, Y., et al.: Study on separation of overlapping electromagnetic signals based on blind source separation algorithm. Electro-optic Control **13**(2), 16–19 (2018)
6. Zhao, Z., Di, W.: Single channel BPSK signal blind separation algorithm using particle flow filtering. Data Acquis. Process. **33**(3), 25–31 (2018)
7. Jing, Y., Liu, C., Bi, F.: Blind source separation and identification of radiated noise of generating units based on signal analysis. Intern. Combust. Engine Eng. **38**(2), 141–145 (2017)
8. Guo, Y., Hua, P., Yong, Y., et al.: Blind separation algorithm for PCMA signals with different symbol rates based on DG-PSP. J. Commun. **38**(3), 92–100 (2017)
9. Ling, Q., Zhang, L., Yan, W.: Research on blind recognition algorithm of STBC-OFDM signal based on improved K-S detection. J. Commun. **38**(4), 46–54 (2017)
10. Xinyong, Yu., Guo, Y., Zhang, K., et al.: Multi-hop signal network sorting algorithm based on blind source separation. Sig. Process. **33**(8), 1082–1089 (2017)
11. Yang, G., Jing, J., Yang, M., et al.: Blind vibration source separation algorithm using aeroengine signal characteristics. J. Xi'an Jiaotong Univ. **51**(6), 20–27 (2017)
12. Wang, Yu., Li, X., Mao, Y., et al.: Radar signal research based on JADE blind source separation algorithm. Mod. Def. Technol. **45**(1), 18–19 (2017)

Research on Active Push Method
of Multi-source Patrol Information
in Large-Capacity Communication Network

Yan-song Hu$^{(\boxtimes)}$

Liaoning Petrochemical Vocational and Technology, Jinzhou, China
gfy087@126.com

Abstract. The traditional large-capacity communication network multi-source patrol information active push method has the defect of poor push effect. For this reason, the active push method of multi-source patrol information in large-capacity communication network is proposed. The differential filtering method is used to preprocess the collected multi-source patrol information, based on the processed multi-source patrol information obtained above. The multi-source patrol information is grouped and clustered to obtain a multi-source patrol information feature set, and the obtained multi-source patrol information feature set is collaboratively filtered to obtain a user-neighbor neighbor multi-source patrol information set. The active push algorithm is used to actively push the nearest neighbor multi-source patrol information, which realizes the active push of multi-source patrol information in the large-capacity communication network. Through experiments, the proposed multi-source patrol information active push method push response time of the large-capacity communication network is 4.1 S less than the traditional method. The proposed multi-source patrol information active push method for large-capacity communication network has better push effect.

Keywords: High capacity · Communications network · Multiple sources · Inspection information · Push

1 Introduction

Due to the openness of communication networks, the information resources of communication networks are also expanding, bringing more and more difficulties to people, and the result is that people are more and more difficult to obtain multiple inspection information in the communication network [1]. In response to this situation, the information initiative push method came into being and it has developed rapidly. The rapid development of the information push method brings new vitality to the active push of multi-source inspection information in large-capacity communication networks [2]. The multi-source patrol information active push method of the large-capacity communication network maximizes the user's multi-source patrol information of interest, saving the user's active search time and satisfying the user's needs.

G. Gui and L. Yun (Eds.): ADHIP 2019, LNICST 301, pp. 478–487, 2019.
https://doi.org/10.1007/978-3-030-36402-1_51

The traditional large-capacity communication network multi-source patrol information active push method has the defect of poor push effect, mainly because the push response time is too long, and the user's demand for multi-source patrol information cannot be satisfied. Therefore, a large-capacity communication network is proposed. Research on active push method of multi-source inspection information.

2 Design of Active Push Method for Multi-source Patrol Information in Large Capacity Communication Network

In the traditional method, the cluster analysis method is mainly used to analyze the characteristics of the user. Due to the insufficient degree of information analysis, the user cannot provide satisfactory multi-source inspection information [3]. In the proposed method, the main information is used to push the multi-source inspection information with accurate, high-quality and high satisfaction through the multi-level and all-round analysis. Push the multi-source inspection information of interest to the user according to the user's needs. Firstly, the collected multi-source patrol information is pre-processed, then clustered, and then collaborative filtering method based on clustering and service evaluation method based on user preference is taken into consideration, taking into account user needs and preferences. The user pushes multi-source inspection information of interest and demand. The multi-source patrol information active push method framework of the large-capacity communication network is shown in Fig. 1.

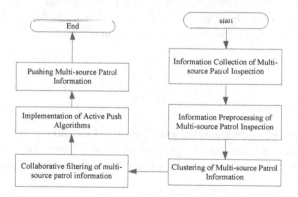

Fig. 1. Large-capacity communication network multi-source inspection information active push method framework diagram

As shown in Fig. 1, the active push method for multi-source patrol information in a large-capacity communication network is proposed to be implemented by multi-source patrol information pre-processing, clustering, collaborative filtering, and active derivation. The specific process is as follows.

2.1   Multi-source Inspection Information Preprocessing

Multi-source patrol information preprocessing plays an important role in the process of active push of multi-source patrol information. Multi-source patrol information pre-processing is mainly to remove the interference information in the collected multi-source patrol information, mainly Divided into two parts, namely interference information identification and interference information removal [4].

The multi-source patrol information pre-processing mainly deletes the information unrelated to the patrol information and processes the error information existing therein. Multi-source patrol information is mainly based on text content [5, 6]. Of course, there are also pictures, video, audio and other formats [7]. In general, the format is judged by the suffix of the information, and the multi-source patrol information can be prepro-cessed. The redundancy of the collected multi-source patrol information is significantly reduced, and the accuracy of the multi-source patrol information active push method is increased.

First, the collected multi-source inspection information format is unified, and the main unified process is:

$$A = \frac{1}{2}\left(\frac{1}{k \times X} + \frac{1}{k^2}\right) \tag{1}$$

Where A represents the multi-source inspection information with uniform format; X represents the collected multi-source inspection information; k represents the conversion factor.

The interference information present therein is then identified. Interference information identification mainly refers to the identification of irrelevant information and error information in a unified multi-source inspection information. The specific process is as follows:

$$D = \frac{1}{\alpha}\sum_{i=1}^{n}\frac{A}{\beta} \times \pi \tag{2}$$

Where in, D represents the identified interference information; α represents the identification parameter; β represents the proportion of interference information occupied; and n represents the number of multi-source inspection information in a uniform format.

Finally, based on the above-mentioned interference information recognition result, it is removed, and the differential interference method is mainly used to remove the identified interference information, and the removal formula is:

$$A' = A\left(1 - \frac{1}{\alpha}\right)\prod[1 - 2D + \zeta] \tag{3}$$

Where A' represents the multi-source patrol information after the interference information is removed; ζ represents the differential filtering parameter.

Through the above process, the multi-source patrol information of the collected communication network is preprocessed, and pure multi-source patrol information is obtained, which prepares for the active push of the multi-source patrol information of the communication network.

2.2   Multi-source Inspection Information Clustering

Based on the processed multi-source patrol information obtained above, the multi-source patrol information is grouped and clustered based on the user's demand characteristic attribute, and the following multi-source patrol information collaborative filtering is prepared [8, 9]. Multi-source patrol information clustering can greatly reduce the data sparsity problem in multi-source patrol information collaborative filtering, thereby improving the accuracy of multi-source patrol information active push. The multi-source inspection information clustering analysis process is shown in Fig. 2.

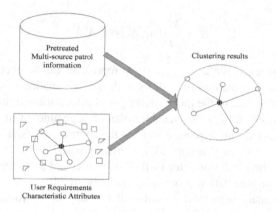

Fig. 2. Clustering design of multi-source detection information

Firstly, the demand characteristics of the user are obtained through the demand model. For the users who query the multi-source inspection information, the demand model can be divided into explicit demand and implicit demand. Use M to represent the user's total demand set, M_1 for the user's explicit demand set, and M_2 for the user's implicit demand set. Therefore, the user's total demand set is expressed as:

$$M = \{M_1, M_2\} \tag{4}$$

The user implicit demand set refers to the unconscious behavior record in the process of user search or query. It is important to analyze this part of the demand for the active push of multi-source inspection information. The analysis process of this part is mainly through the way of Web demand mining. The user's demand feature attribute is used to obtain the user's explicit requirement set, which refers to the user's conscious operation behavior during the search or query process, such as issuing the demand and other operational behaviors.

Web mining technology is one of the keys to realize the active push of multi-source inspection information in communication networks [10]. It is generally divided into three stages: preprocessing, pattern discovery, and pattern analysis. It is mainly divided into three categories, content mining, structure mining, and usage mining. The so-called Web demand mining method is essentially a process of extracting Web feature attributes centered on user needs. The specific user requirement feature attribute extraction process is:

$$M' = \prod_1^n \frac{2}{\beta} \times M^\chi \tag{5}$$

Where M' represents the extracted user demand feature attribute; β represents the extraction ratio; χ represents the extraction parameter.

The multi-source patrol information is grouped based on the obtained user demand characteristic attribute, and the process is:

$$A' = \frac{M'}{a} \left(A'_1, A'_2, \cdots, A'_m\right) \tag{6}$$

Where a represents the classification factor; m represents the number of categories.

The early clustering method only deals with the information of a single attribute type, and the attribute type of the multi-source patrol information of the communication network data is mixed and has the characteristics of large amount of information. The early clustering method cannot process it. With the continuous updating of technology, the spectral clustering method is applied. It is mainly based on the spectral theory and seeks the global optimal solution. This method does not need to set the initial clustering center. Accurate, the calculation process is relatively simple.

The clustering analysis method is used to cluster the above groups, and the feature set of the multi-source patrol information of each group is obtained as:

$$K = \sum_{i=1}^m \sqrt{(1+A')^2 + \eta} \tag{7}$$

Where K represents each set of multi-source inspection information feature sets; η represents calculation parameters:

It can be seen that the purpose of cluster analysis is to obtain feature sets of multi-source patrol information of the same category, which facilitates collaborative filtering of multi-source patrol information as described below.

2.3 Multi-source Inspection Information Collaborative Filtering

Based on the multi-source patrol information feature set obtained above, the multi-source patrol information is collaboratively filtered. In the obtained multi-source patrol information feature set, the relationship between user demand and information is a one-to-many relationship, and the multi-source patrol information contained therein has obvious similarity, and similar threshold information is found to find similar multi-source patrol information. The collection forms a collection of nearest neighbor multi-source inspection information, and provides multi-source inspection information for users to actively push.

Collaborative filtering refers to recommending information that is of interest to users according to certain preferences. The data is appropriately evaluated by a cooperative mechanism and recorded to achieve filtering purposes and to filter information. The collaborative filtering algorithm is mainly for users with search or query records. For new users, they do not have records of search or query. Therefore, when the collaborative filtering method is used to push multi-source inspection information, it is mainly through A multi-source patrol information set in the class feature set and its nearest neighbor to predict the multi-source patrol information of the user's interest or demand, and then actively push it according to the predicted result, the method solves the cooperation to some extent Cold start problem in the filtering algorithm. The process of collaborative filtering of multi-source inspection information is:

$$Q = \frac{K}{\varepsilon} \sum_{i=1}^{m} (1 + ang(K)) \tag{8}$$

Where in, Q represents a similar multi-source inspection information set; ε represents a set threshold; $ang()$ represents a similar information search formula;

The nearest neighbor multi-source inspection information set is expressed as:

$$K_o = \int_{1}^{m} \frac{Q}{\varepsilon^2} \times \pi \tag{9}$$

Where K_o represents the nearest neighbor multi-source inspection information set.

Through the above process, the user needs the nearest neighbor multi-source patrol information set to provide data support for the implementation of the following multi-source patrol information active push.

2.4   Implementation of Active Push of Multi-source Inspection Information

Based on the user-required nearest neighbor multi-source patrol information set obtained above, the active push algorithm is used to actively push the multi-source patrol information. The specific steps are shown in Table 1.

Table 1. Active push algorithm execution step table

Step	Concrete content
Step 1	Initialization, input user requirement nearest neighbor multi-source patrol information set
Step 2	Start matching, matching the nearest neighbor multi-source patrol information set according to the content of user search or query
Step 3	Judge whether to push multi-source patrol information to users, judge whether users are interested in information according to the content of users' search or query and whether they need it, and push information if they are interested. Continue to implement step 2 if you are not interested
Step 4	Pushing multi-source patrol information, first decoding the user's needs, then sorting the push multi-source patrol information according to the specific user's demand characteristics, and sorting according to the degree of demand
Step 5	Push sequence adjustment, according to the changes in user needs, constantly adjust its push multi-source patrol information

As shown in Table 1, the basic flow of the active push algorithm: firstly, according to the user search or query, it is determined whether multi-source patrol information push is required; secondly, the push content matching is performed according to the user's demand feature attribute, and the user's demand characteristic attribute and user are The nearest neighbor multi-source patrol information set is matched and sorted according to the degree of demand; finally, according to the change of the user demand, the order of the nearest neighbor multi-source patrol information collection is adjusted, and then actively pushed. The flow chart of the active push of multi-source patrol information in the large-capacity communication network is shown in Fig. 3.

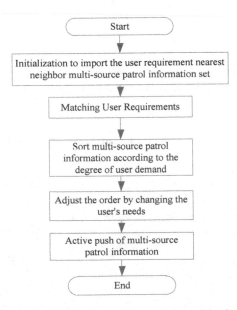

Fig. 3. Multi-source inspection information active push flow chart for large-capacity communication network

Through the above process, the active push of multi-source patrol information in the large-capacity communication network is realized, which provides power for the development of the large-capacity communication network.

3   Analysis of Push Effect of Active Push Method for Multi-source Inspection Information

The above-mentioned active push method of multi-source patrol information for large-capacity communication network has realized the active push of multi-source patrol information, which fully proves the feasibility of the proposed method, but the push effect needs further study. Therefore, the comparison experiment is used to analyze the push effect of the proposed multi-source patrol information active push method for large-capacity communication networks.

The experiment mainly uses the proposed multi-source patrol information active push method for large-capacity communication network and the traditional large-capacity communication network multi-source patrol information active push method to test the push response time. In order to facilitate the experiment, the proposed large capacity will be proposed. The active push method of the multi-source patrol information of the communication network is set as an experimental group, and the active push method of the multi-source patrol information of the traditional large-capacity communication network is set as the control group.

In order to obtain accurate experimental data, the experimental environment is set. Set the communication network mode to TCP mode, the threshold is 0.9, and the number of experiments is 100.

Experiments were carried out based on the set experimental environment parameters, and the response time of the multi-source inspection information active push method was tested. Because of the difference between the experimental group and the control group, it is not possible to conduct a direct comparative analysis. To this end, statistical software was used to record and compare experimental data. The push response time is shown in Table 2.

Table 2. Push response schedule

Number of experiments	Propose a method to push response time	Traditional methods push response time
10	1.6 s	6.4 s
20	1.8 s	4.4 s
30	1.2 s	4.4 s
40	2.6 s	6.4 s
50	0.8 s	6.4 s
60	1.8 s	4.6 s
70	2.0 s	7.2 s
80	1.5 s	5.6 s
90	2.2 s	4.6 s
100	2.8 s	4.0 s

The comparison of push response time is shown in Fig. 4.

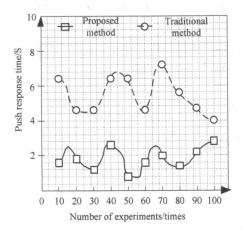

Fig. 4. Comparison of push response time

As shown in Fig. 4, the response time of the experimental group is significantly less than that of the control group. The minimum response time of the experimental group is 0.8 s, the average value is 1.8 s, and the minimum response time of the control group is 4.0 s. The average is 5.9 s. The average response time of the experimental group was 4.1 s less than the average of the response time of the control group. The proposed multi-source patrol information active push method for large-capacity communication network has better push effect.

Active push method of multi-source patrol information in large-capacity communication network is to improve the efficiency and quality of traditional network multi-source patrol information. Here we include the following points: the width of network multi-source patrol information is the key to affect the quality and efficiency of active push. With the rapid development of network technology, broadband technology has emerged, which greatly widens the width of network multi source patrol information, and thus improves the efficiency and quality of active push.

Because there are many interference signals in active push, the emergence of multi-source patrol information technology can improve the anti-interference ability of active push by restoring the signal and multi-channel technology. The diversification of multi-source patrol information in communication network is more common than that in traditional communication network, which transmits signals in words and languages, seriously affecting the quality of active push. Nowadays, the multi-source patrol information technology of communication network can carry out many new communication modes, such as video telephone, multi-person telephone, besides the communication modes of text and language. Therefore, diversified multi-source patrol information of communication network can improve the effect of active push.

4 Conclusion

The proposed multi-source patrol information active push method for large-capacity communication network realizes the active push of multi-source patrol information, which greatly reduces the push response time. However, due to the setting of the experimental process environment parameters, the influencing factors are ignored. The interference results in a certain error in the experimental results, but the overall trend is unchanged, so the impact on the experimental results is not large, but we still need to pay attention to the active push method for multi-source inspection information in large-capacity communication networks. Conduct further research and analysis.

References

1. Zhu, X., Yu, Z., Lin, Y., et al.: Research on multi-source geographic data push method based on model requirement template matching. Geogr. Geogr. Inf. Sci. **32**(1), 24–28 (2016)
2. Lu, J., Wang, C., Xiao, G., et al.: Research and application of cloud push platform for multi-source heterogeneous data. Comput. Sci. **43**(s1), 12–15 (2016)
3. Liu, J.: Huadian University Tong Qinjiashan 100,000 kW photovoltaic power station UAV automatic inspection and hot spot image automatic recognition. Solar Energy **56**(5), 45–48 (2017)
4. Liu, J.: Practice and understanding of the construction of integrated information system for oil field exploration and development. Contemp. Petrochem. **24**(10), 46–50 (2016)
5. Li, W., Wang, Y., Xu, B., et al.: The research on network management and online monitoring for communication network for smart distribution and consumption network. Autom. Instrum. **4**, 27–30 (2018)
6. Ding, W., Qiu, W., Chen, D., et al.: Application research of PTN technology in Shaoxing power telecommunication network. Zhejiang Electric Power **37**(5), 22–26 (2018)
7. Xie, Y., Wu, L., Zhang, S., et al.: Realization of security protection system for power communication network based on bigdata. Electron. Des. Eng. **25**(19), 131–135 (2017)
8. Cui, L., Geng, Z., Shu, Q., et al.: Key link identification in electric power communication network considering grid correlation degree. Electric Power Constr. **38**(5), 124–132 (2017)
9. Liu, Y.: Design and implementation of computer room patrol management system based on NFC technology. Financ. Technol. Time **10**, 48–51 (2017)
10. Liu, X.: Application of network communication technology in reality. Digit. Commun. World **169**(01), 206 (2019)

Research on Multi-master-slave Hybrid Coordinated Control Method in VANET Environment

Chao Song[(✉)]

Dalian University of Science and Technology, Dalian, China
lxyh201712@163.com

Abstract. To improve the quality and output efficiency of multi-master-slave hybrid operation, a coordinated control technology of multi-master-slave hybrid operation based on closed-loop error regulation in VANET environment is proposed. The constraint parameter model of multi-master-slave hybrid coordinated control is constructed, and the DC voltage stabilizing capacitance, DC voltage outer loop gain, interharmonic oscillation and electromagnetic loss are taken as the constraint parameters. An input-output closed-loop control system for multi-master-slave hybrid operation of power grid is constructed, and the internal loop feedback adjustment method is used to compensate the interharmonic output error. The steady state regulation method of open circuit voltage and short circuit current is used to realize the adaptive identification of control constraint parameters, and the coordinated control of multi-master-slave hybrid operation of power grid is realized. The simulation results show that this method can effectively realize the multi-master-slave coordinated control in VANET environment, increase the output efficiency of the power grid, and improve the output quality and gain of the power grid control.

Keywords: VANET environment · Power grid · Multi-master-slave mixing · Coordinated control

1 Introduction

With the development of large power grid distribution network technology, the scale of power grid in our country is increasing. Through the mixed operation of multi-master-slave power grid, all-weather, large area and fully covered power supply can be realized, and in the multi-master-slave hybrid operation of power grid [1]. The high voltage power supply and multi-terminal input and output control methods are used for power input and distribution, and the optimized multi-master-slave hybrid coordinated control method is used for the output power regulation and node distributed design of the power grid, so as to improve the output efficiency of the power grid. Reduce the power loss and promote the energy saving and efficiency of the multi-master-slave hybrid operation of the power grid. It is of great significance to study the coordinated control technology of multi-master-slave hybrid operation in order to improve the operation stability of power grid and the gain of DC voltage outer loop, and to reduce the power loss. The research of related control technology has attracted great attention [2].

© ICST Institute for Computer Sciences, Social Informatics and Telecommunications Engineering 2019
Published by Springer Nature Switzerland AG 2019. All Rights Reserved
G. Gui and L. Yun (Eds.): ADHIP 2019, LNICST 301, pp. 488–497, 2019.
https://doi.org/10.1007/978-3-030-36402-1_52

The research on energy saving, quality improvement and efficiency control technology of power grid distribution network is based on the optimal configuration and adaptive adjustment of power grid parameters. The multi-master-slave hybrid operation of power grid is affected by small disturbance and output steady-state error. As a result, the stability of the control is not high. The optimization of control technology was studied in the relevant literature. In reference [3], a multi-master-slave hybrid coordinated control method based on fuzzy PID control technology is proposed. The proportional resonance control technology is used to optimize and adjust the parameters of multi-master-slave hybrid operation to improve the output voltage gain and power gain, but the control algorithm can not effectively suppress the small disturbance interference, and the steady-state error of the control output is high. In reference [4], a coordinated control technology of multi-master-slave hybrid operation based on adaptive feedback regulation is proposed. The inertia link is used for analog output compensation control, and the differential evolution method is combined with the energy saving control of the power grid to improve the control stability. However, the computational overhead of this method is large and the real-time control is not good.

In order to solve the above problems, a coordinated control technology of multi-master-slave hybrid operation based on closed-loop error regulation in VANET environment is proposed in this paper. The constraint parameter model of multi-master-slave hybrid coordinated control is constructed, and the DC voltage stabilizing capacitance, DC voltage outer loop gain, interharmonic oscillation and electromagnetic loss are taken as the constraint parameters. An input-output closed-loop control system for multi-master-slave hybrid operation of power grid is constructed, and the internal loop feedback adjustment method is used to compensate the inter-harmonic output error. The steady state regulation method of open circuit voltage and short circuit current is used to realize the adaptive identification of the control constraint parameters and the control optimization is realized. Finally, the simulation experiment is carried out. The advantages of this method in improving the coordinated control performance of multi-master-slave hybrid operation are shown.

2 Multi-master-slave Hybrid Operation Modeling and Controlled Object Description of Power Grid

2.1 Analysis of Control and Confined Parameters for Multi-master and Master-Slave Hybrid Operation of Power Grid

In the multi-master-slave hybrid operation of the power grid, the DC/AC inverter model is mainly used to stabilize the voltage transmission and power output control, and the inner loop control model is used to construct the controlled object model of the multi-master-slave hybrid coordinated control of the power grid [5]. In order to realize the optimal control of multi-master-slave hybrid operation, the constrained parameter model of power grid control is analyzed. The output power coefficient of power grid in multi-master-slave hybrid operation is k_f, and the power modulation coefficient of voltage distribution in power grid is B_r. The magnetic density of the controller permanent magnet is as follows:

$$B_g = \frac{F_m}{A_g \Re} \tag{1}$$

Wherein, F_m is the three-phase current base on the grid side, A_g is the additional DC voltage stabilizing capacitance, $\Re$ is the DC voltage outer loop gain of the power grid, and when the power grid is in the steady state, the DC voltage stabilizing capacitance and the DC voltage outer loop gain of the power grid are taken as the DC voltage stabilizing capacitance and the DC voltage outer loop gain of the power grid. The interharmonic oscillations and electromagnetic losses are constraint parameters, and each constraint parameter can be estimated as follows:

$$F_m = \frac{B_r l_m}{\mu_0 \mu_{r1}} \tag{2}$$

$$A_g = l_s \frac{\beta \pi}{p} (r_r + l_g) \tag{3}$$

The DC voltage stabilizing capacitance and electromagnetic loss are added to the grid side, and the PI control method is used to describe the output electromagnetic gain in the d, q axis distributed at the distribution network nodes.

$$\Re = \frac{1}{\mu_0 l_s \beta \pi / p} \left(\frac{1}{\mu_{r1}} \int_{r_r - l_m}^{r_r} \frac{d_r}{r} + \int_{r_r}^{r_r + l_g} \frac{d_r}{r} + \frac{1}{\mu_{r2}} \int_{r_r + l_g}^{r_r + l_g + l_w} \frac{d_r}{r} \right) \tag{4}$$

The vacuum permeability $\mu_0 = 4\pi \times 10^{-7}$, μ_{r1} and μ_{r2} of the multi-master-slave hybrid operation of the power grid represent the transmission loss and output efficiency of the multi-master-slave hybrid operation of the power grid. When the power grid is in the steady-state operation state of the whole network, the steady-state error is introduced [6]. The distribution of control constraint parameters for multi-master-slave hybrid operation of power grid is obtained as follows:

$$I_x = (1 - k_2) L_{11} \tag{5}$$

$$L_{mx} = k^2 L_{11} \tag{6}$$

$$n_x = k \sqrt{\frac{L_{11}}{L_{22}}} \tag{7}$$

The power loss of the distribution network running at the resonance point is as follows:

$$B_g = \frac{B_r l_m}{(r_r + l_g) \ln(\frac{r_r + l_g + l_w}{r_r - l_m})} \tag{8}$$

Considering the influence of magnetic flux leakage coefficient k_1 and current loop k_β, energy saving compensation control is carried out by adaptive feedback adjustment. Through the above analysis, the constraint parameter model of coordinated control of multi-master-slave hybrid operation of power grid is constructed, which provides the model constraint conditions for the design of control algorithm [7].

2.2   Description of the Controlled Object

On the basis of the above control constraint parameter model, the DC/AC inverter model is used to construct the input and output network structure model of multi-master-slave hybrid operation, as shown in Fig. 1.

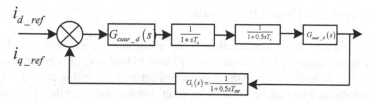

Fig. 1. Input and output structure block diagram of multi-master-slave hybrid operation in power grid

According to the input and output model given in Fig. 1, the controlled object model of multi-master-slave hybrid operation of power grid is constructed. T_s is used to represent the sampling time of current parameters in distribution network, and $\frac{1}{1+sT_s}$ is used to represent the control delay of multi-master-slave hybrid operation of power grid. i_{d_ref} represents the reference values of active current and reactive current in multi-master-slave hybrid operation of power grid, respectively. Ls represents the inductance on the grid side, $G_{cuur\_d}(s)$, $G_{cuur\_q}(s)$ indicate the current component of the inner loop operating grid on the d, Q axis, GS indicates the winding size, and R represents the current component of the inner ring operating on the d, q axis. i_{d_ref} is used to describe the power gain of d axis and q axis in multi-master-slave hybrid operation of power grid. Under the condition of small disturbance [8], the output torque and gain adjustment coefficient of the controller are expressed as follows:

$$T_{em} = \frac{\pi k_f k_c k_1 k_\beta B_r l_m l_s l_w (2r_r + 2l_g + l_w) J_{cu}}{\ln(\frac{r_r + l_g + l_w}{r_r - l_m})} \tag{9}$$

$$k_1 = 1 - \frac{1}{0.9[r_r/(\beta p(l_g + l_w))]^2 + 1} \tag{10}$$

Based on the analysis of the constraint parameters of the above large electrical equipment controller and the description of the controlled object, the modulation gain system function of the inner loop control of the multi-master-slave hybrid operation of the power grid is obtained as follows:

$$G_1(s) = \frac{1}{1 + 0.5sT_{SW}} \tag{11}$$

Wherein, s represents the reference voltage and I_{sd_ref} represents the current component on the outer loop of the distribution network, $T_{SW} = 1/f_{SW}$, the control object model of improving quality and increasing efficiency in multi-master-slave hybrid operation of power grid is constructed, and the control optimization by parameter adjustment and model identification is realized [9].

3   Control Algorithm Optimization

On the basis of the above construction of the constrained parameter model and the controlled object model of the multi-master-slave hybrid coordinated control of the power grid, the optimal design of the distribution network control is carried out. In this paper, a coordinated control technology of multi-master-slave hybrid operation based on closed-loop error regulation in VANET environment is proposed [10]. The equivalent circuit model of multi-master-slave hybrid operation of power network is constructed by using T-type equivalent circuit analysis method, as shown in Fig. 2.

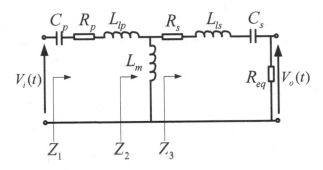

Fig. 2. Equivalent circuit model

According to the equivalent circuit model given in Fig. 2, an input-output closed-loop control system for multi-master-slave hybrid operation of power grid is constructed, and the output voltage $E = vl \times B$ of power grid is assumed. If the instantaneous current $v = r\omega_r$ and resistance are $r = r_r + l_g$, power factor $B = k_\beta k_1 B_g$, induction inductor $l = l_s k_f k_c A_w / A_c$, the energy function of multi-master-slave hybrid operation of power grid is as follows:

$$E = \frac{(r_r + l_g)k_\beta k_1 B_g \omega_r l_s k_f k_c A_w}{A_c} \tag{12}$$

The internal loop feedback adjustment method is used to compensate the inter-harmonic output error [11], and the parameter adjustment function is described as follows:

$$G_{cuur\_d}(s) = \frac{K_{P1}s + K_{11}}{sG_1(s)} \tag{13}$$

$$G_{cuur\_q}(s) = \frac{K_{P2}s + K_{12}}{sG_1(s)} \tag{14}$$

Wherein, K_{P1}, K_{11}, K_{P2}, K_{12} are used to describe the dq axis components of the output current adjusted by steady state in the process of multi-master-slave hybrid operation. Because the controller parameter K_{P1}, K_{11}, K_{P2}, K_{12} are unknown, according to the Lyapunov functional, the steady-state error convergence value of multi-master-slave hybrid operation of power grid satisfies $\begin{bmatrix} Y_{11} & Y_{12} \\ Y_{12}^T & Y_{22} \end{bmatrix} \geq 0, N = \begin{bmatrix} N_1 \\ N_2 \end{bmatrix}$, $M = \begin{bmatrix} M_1 \\ M_2 \end{bmatrix}$, under the constraint of model parameters. The fitness function of improving quality and increasing efficiency in multi-master-slave hybrid operation of power grid can be described as follows:

$$F_{inner\_dq} = \sum_{k=1}^{M} F|i_{dq}(k) - i_{dq\_cal}(k)| \tag{15}$$

Similarly, by using the steady state regulation of open circuit voltage and short circuit current [12], the fitness function of the outer loop controller with multi-master-slave hybrid operation can be described as follows:

$$F_{outer\_dq} = \sum_{k=1}^{M} F|i_d(k) - i_{d\_cal}(k)| \tag{16}$$

The i_{dq} represents the gain of the inertia phase, and finally the objective function of the coordinated control of the multi-master and slave hybrid operation of the power grid can be described as:

$$F = \sum_{k=1}^{M} |e(k)|G_{eq}(s) \tag{17}$$

Wherein, $G_{eq}(s)$ is the constraint function of three-phase control on the parallel side. Based on the above treatment, the steady-state regulation method of open-circuit voltage and short-circuit current is used to realize the adaptive identification of the control constraint parameters. The coordinated control of multi-master-slave hybrid operation of power network is realized.

4 Simulation Experiment and Performance Analysis

In order to test the application performance of the method to improve the quality and efficiency control in the multi-master and slave hybrid operation of the power grid, the simulation experiment is carried out, the experimental software platform is established on the MATLAB 7.0, the value of the permanent magnetic density of the distribution network transmission is between 1.2 and 2.3, the initial value of the electric loss is 1.24 Kw/h, The torque output of the multi-master-slave hybrid operation of the power grid is 10 N.m, the distance of the distribution network transmission coil is increased from 50 to 100 cm, the magnetic resonance resistance of the distribution network coil is SF, and the frequency of the voltage conversion is $R_{p1} = 45\ \Omega$, $f = 27.05$ MHz, $C_r = 14.6$ pF, $R_o = 30\ \Omega$ and the output of the optimized control variable is shown in Table 1.

Table 1. Optimal control variables for efficiency control of multi-master-slave hybrid operation system in power grid

Variable name	Lower limit	Superior limit	Optimization result
p	2	6	4
β	0.34	0.67	0.42
$l_m(m)$	0.045	0.065	0.053
$l_y(m)$	0.034	0.089	0.046
$l_w(m)$	0.043	0.065	0.087
$l_g(m)$	0.013	0.026	0.057
$r_r(m)$	0.021	0.134	0.323
λ	0.312	0.123	2.53
A_c	0.523	1	2.0

According to the above control parameter optimization design, the power grid multi-slave hybrid coordination control benefit analysis is carried out, the output power and the efficiency of the power grid are tested, and the results are as shown in Fig. 3.

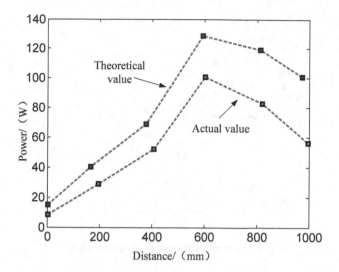

(a) Power test of multi-master-slave hybrid operation in power grid

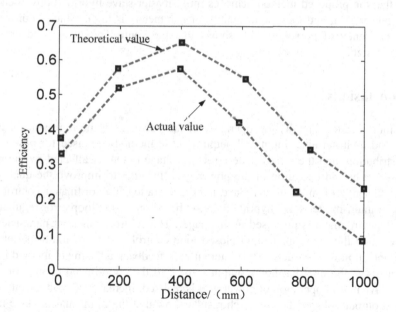

(b) Efficiency test of multi-master-slave hybrid operation in power grid

Fig. 3. Multi-master-slave hybrid operation of power grid

The analysis of Fig. 3 shows that the proposed method has good output power, high efficiency and good tracking and matching effect between the actual value and the theoretical value, which shows that the proposed method has a good performance of improving quality and increasing efficiency. By comparing different methods, the

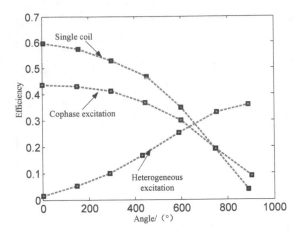

Fig. 4. Control performance comparison test

results of control performance comparison are shown in Fig. 4. Analysis of Fig. 4 shows that the proposed method achieves multi-master-slave hybrid coordinated control of power grid, and the output quality of parameters is high, which improves the output efficiency of power grid. It shows that the control quality of the proposed method is high.

5 Conclusions

In the multi-master-slave hybrid operation of the power grid, the high-voltage power supply and multi-terminal input and output control methods are used for power input and distribution, and the steady-state error of voltage output is affected by the multi-master-slave hybrid operation of the power grid. In order to improve the quality and output efficiency of multi-master-slave hybrid operation, a coordinated control technology of multi-master-slave hybrid operation based on closed-loop error regulation in VANET environment is proposed in this paper. The control constraint parameters are analyzed, and the input and output closed loop control system of multi-master-slave hybrid operation is constructed. The internal loop feedback adjustment method is used to compensate the inter-harmonic output error, and the coordinated control of multi-master-slave hybrid operation of power grid is realized. Increase DC voltage outer loop gain and output voltage. The research results show that the multi-master-slave hybrid coordinated control of power grid is carried out in this paper, and the output quality of parameters is high, which increases the output efficiency of power grid and improves the quality of power grid control, so it has good application value.

References

1. Seo, D.W., Lee, J.H., Lee, H.S.: Optimal coupling to achieve maximum output power in a WPT system. IEEE Trans. Power Electron. **31**(6), 3994–3998 (2016)
2. Liang, S., Hu, X., Zhang, D., et al.: Probabilistic models based evaluation method for capacity credit of photovoltaic generation. Autom. Electric Power Syst. **36**(13), 32–37 (2012)
3. Wang, Q., Dong, W., Yang, L.: A wind power/photovoltaic typical scenario set generation algorithm based on wasserstein distance metric and revised K-medoids cluster. Proc. CSEE **35**(11), 2654–2661 (2015)
4. Liu, J., Luo, X.: Short-term optimal environmental economic hydrothermal scheduling based on handling complicated constraints of multi-chain cascaded hydropower statio. Proc. CSEE **32**(14), 27–35 (2012)
5. Lin, D., Zang, M.: Research on impact fracture behavior of the laminated glass based on cohesive zone model. J. Mech. Eng. **53**(22), 176–181 (2017)
6. Chen, S., Zang, M., Xu, W.: A three-dimensional computational framework for impact fracture analysis of automotive laminated glass. Comput. Methods Appl. Mech. Eng. **294**, 72–99 (2015)
7. Mujumdar, A., Tamhane, B., Kurods, S.: Observer-based sliding mode control for a class of noncommensurate fractional-order systems. IEEE/ASME Trans. Mechatron. **20**(5), 2504–2512 (2015)
8. Aten, Q.T., Zirbel, S.A., Jensen, B.D., et al.: A numerical method for position analysis of compliant mechanisms with more degrees of freedom than inputs. J. Mech. Des. **133**(6), 491–502 (2010)
9. Zhong, F., Li, H., Zhong, S., et al.: An SOC estimation approach based on adaptive sliding mode observer and fractional order equivalent circuit model for lithium-ion batteries. Commun. Nonlinear Sci. Numer. Simul. **24**(3), 127–144 (2015)
10. Aguila Camacho, N., Duarte-Mermoud, M.A., Gallegos, J.A.: Lyapunov functions for fractional order systems. Commun. Nonlinear Sci. Numer. Simul. **19**(9), 2951–2957 (2014)
11. Li, Y.F., Fu, R.D., Jin, W., et al.: Image super-resolution using multi-channel convolution. J. Image Graph. **22**(12), 1690–1700 (2017)
12. Sun, X., Li, X.G., Li, J.F., et al.: Review on deep learning based image super-resolution restoration algorithms. Acta Automatica Sinica **43**(5), 697–709 (2017)

Design of Power Intelligent Control DCS Module Based on Improved PID

Chao Song[✉]

Dalian University of Science and Technology, Dalian, China
lxyh201712@163.com

Abstract. Distributed control system (DCS) is the core of power system control. A power intelligent control DCS module based on improved PID is studied to realize the output gain control of power electrical system and improve the control efficiency of power electrical system. Combined with integrated DSP information processing chip, a design of power intelligent control DCS module based on output power amplification and regulation is proposed. The overall model of DCS power control system is designed, and the DCS power control frequency doubling gain amplifier is constructed. The signal anti-interference design adopts cascade filter and output power amplification adjustment method to obtain the reset circuit of DCS controller. The output power amplification and adjustment algorithm are designed to equalize the gain distribution to improve the power control performance of DCS. The test results show that the output gain of intelligent power control is large, the adaptive performance is good, and the output stability is strong.

Keywords: Improved PID · Power intelligent control · DCS module · Amplification and regulation

1 Introduction

As one of the most important basic facilities, power system is related to the stability of people's life and the order of work and production. In the power system, the distribution of each power control node is scattered, so it is necessary to carry out effective decentralized control. How to use a reasonable control system to aggregate and dispatch the data information of each power node is the distributed control system (DCS) problems that need to be solved. With the development of integrated circuit and digital electronic technology, large-scale integrated chip is widely used in the design of power control system, and the accuracy of power control system is gradually improved. DCS is connected through PLC, executive components and data acquisition. It is of great significance to study the optimal design technology of power DSC control module based on PLC [1].

PLC programmable logic controller, which uses a class of programmable memory for its internal storage programs, performs logical operations, sequence control, timing, counting and arithmetic operations and other user-oriented instructions. The research on the optimization design of power intelligent control DCS module based on small Siemens PLC programmable logic controller has been paid more and more attention.

© ICST Institute for Computer Sciences, Social Informatics and Telecommunications Engineering 2019
Published by Springer Nature Switzerland AG 2019. All Rights Reserved
G. Gui and L. Yun (Eds.): ADHIP 2019, LNICST 301, pp. 498–506, 2019.
https://doi.org/10.1007/978-3-030-36402-1_53

the traditional controller design method mainly adopts PID control system and fuzzy neural network control system. Expert control system and other self-organizing learning and compound control schemes [2], in which the variable structure neural network control needs to monitor each separation unit in real time, and the synchronous tracking control performance is poor. In this paper, the improvement of control system design is carried out in the relevant literature, and a DCS power electromechanical control module design technology of small PLC based on adaptive fuzzy control technology is proposed in reference [3]. The global optimization method of deterministic bifurcation and boundary is used to improve the performance of power and electrical system, but the design scheme produces nonlinear distortion and the error compensation performance is not good. The linear combination control method in reference [4] changes the electromagnetic torque of the electric power generation system and obtains the learning input vector of the fuzzy PID neural network, but the operating environment of the model is harsh, which directly affects the economic benefit of the power generation system. A digital DCS power controller based on virtual impedance doubly-fed control is proposed in reference [5]. When the voltage rises sharply, the control performance decreases obviously and the energy constraint performance of power consumption is not good. In order to solve the above problems, combined with the integrated DSP information processing chip, this paper proposes a power intelligent control DCS module design based on output power amplification and regulation. Firstly, the overall design model and hardware design method of the system are described. The output power amplifier and regulation algorithm are designed for gain allocation equilibrium processing, which improves the power control performance of DCS. The integrated DSP information processing chip is used to realize the controller circuit design. Finally, the simulation experiment of the system is carried out, and the performance is verified.

The superior performance of the DCS controller designed in this paper is shown.

2 Overall Design Model and Hardware Design Method of DCS Power Control System

2.1 Description of PLC Programmable Logic Control Preparatory Knowledge and Construction of Its Overall Model

The power DSC controller adopts Siemens K9F1208UOB model PLC programmable logic control chip as NAND FLASH, its capacity is 64 MB, the working voltage is 2.7 V $\leq$ 3.6 V, and 3.3 V is used in this system. The performance of door small PLC programmable logic control is described as follows:

(1) PLC programmable logic control peripherals

In the hardware of PLC programmable logic control system, in addition to the main control component (MCU, DSP, EMPU, SOC), it also includes other hardware used to control storage, communication, debugging, display and other auxiliary performance, that is, PLC programmable logic control peripherals.

(2) PLC programmable logic control operating system

In order to make the PLC programmable logic control system develop more rapidly, it is necessary to have a software program which is responsible for managing memory allocation, interrupt processing, task scheduling and other functions, which is collectively called PLC programmable logic control operating system [6].

(3) PLC programmable logic control application software

PLC programmable logic control application software is aimed at a certain application area, based on a fixed program platform, to achieve the desired PLC programmable logic control software, because the user may have the goal of speed and accuracy. Therefore, some PLC programmable logic control programs need the support of PLC programmable logic control operating system.

The system design process includes the following aspects: (a) System requirement analysis: determining the design goal, planning and design specification commitment, and putting forward the acceptance standard of the design program. (b) Architecture design: design system to achieve functional and non-functional requirements, including hardware, software and system software, hardware selection and so on. (c) Hardware/software collaborative design: based on the architecture of the system software, hardware design in detail. (d) System integration: integrate the software, hardware and execution of the system into a development program to detect and improve the errors in the unit design process. (e) System test: debug the system program to check whether it meets the functional requirements [7].

According to the above analysis, the overall model of DCS power control system is designed. The data width of ISA bus is 16 bits and the working frequency is 8 MHz. Based on the low processing ability of 8086 and 80286, a bus standard with low performance of CPU is obtained [8]. The data line width of the K9F1208UOB of the power DSC controller is 8 bits, and the large storage performance of the NAND FLASH is encapsulated with the 48-foot TSOP. The system bus connection of the PLC programmable controller is shown in Fig. 1.

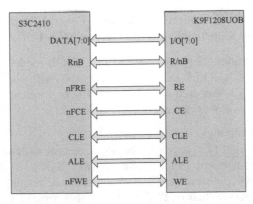

Fig. 1. System bus connection diagram of PLC programmable controller

2.2   Anti-interference FIR Filtering Controlled by Power DSC

The signal anti-interference design of power DSC controller adopts cascade filter, and the voltage stabilizing node of power DSC controller adopts triaxial acceleration sensor MMA7260Q. FIR band-pass filtering is based on PLC control chip. MMA7260Q-based PLC is a single-chip device that sensitively and accurately measures the fall, tilt, movement, placement, vibration and rocking of low gravity levels in three axis. Its package size is very small. Only small card space, battery power, to provide fast start and sleep mode. It can be widely used in falling detection, hard disk protection, electronic compass, seismic monitoring and other electronic products. In the design of DCS controller, PC automatically sets the number of signal output channels, signal center frequency [9], signal pulse width and output signal type (including CW, LFM, HFM, etc.) according to the received signal type information. The characteristics of the designed power DSC controller:

According to the above design index, the DCS power control frequency doubling gain amplifier is constructed, which is composed of processor, RF chip, external FLASH, USB bridge chip and other peripherals. Using small PLC programmable logic control software to improve DCS power control performance, the architecture of the whole small PLC programmable logic control system can be divided into four structures: PLC programmable logic control processor, Small PLC programmable logic control peripherals, small PLC programmable logic control operating system. The power DCS control signal output based on the improved PID is input to the main frequency amplifier through the tracker [10].

The improved PID is used to optimize the power control design. The induction potential energy T and high frequency noise components of the power DCS control system based on the improved PID are obtained:

$$T = \frac{1}{2}M_{RL}\dot{X}_{RL}^2 + \frac{1}{2}M_{RR}\dot{X}_{RR}^2 + \frac{1}{2}J_{RL}\,\dot{\theta}_{RL}^2$$
$$+ \frac{1}{2}J_{RR}\,\dot{\theta}_{RR}^2 + \frac{1}{2}M_p[(\dot{\theta}_pL\cos\theta_P + \dot{X}_{RM})^2 \tag{1}$$
$$+ (-\theta_pL\cos\theta_P)^2] + \frac{1}{2}J_{P\theta}\,\dot{\theta}_P^2 + \frac{1}{2}J_{P\delta}\,\dot{\delta}^2$$

$$V = M_pgL\cos_{\theta_p} \tag{2}$$

The transfer function of the control system is defined as:

$$\frac{Y(s)}{R(s)} = \frac{G_C(s)G_0(s)e^{-\tau s}}{1 + G_C(s)G_0(s)} \tag{3}$$

Wherein, $Y(s)$ is the output control parameter, $R(s)$ is the input control parameter, and $e^{-\tau s}$ is the fuzzy time delay characteristic parameter. Through the above analysis, the power DCS control system model based on improved PID is obtained. The step response curve method is used to suppress the time delay coupling of power electrical system, and the anti-interference FIR filter of power DSC control is realized [11].

3 Improved Design and Implementation of Power DCS Control Based on Output Power Amplification and Regulation

3.1 Output Power Amplification and Regulation Method

On the basis of the above model design and description, the output power amplification and regulation algorithm are used to realize the improvement of power DCS control coupling control based on improved PID [12]. According to the device manual and the actual requirements of the system, the reset circuit of DCS controller based on Siemens PLC chip is designed. The reset circuit of DCS controller is obtained by using the method of output power amplification and adjustment.

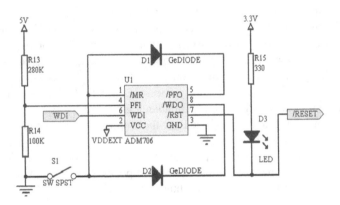

Fig. 2. Reset circuit of DCS controller

In Fig. 2, the PC0, PC1 controls the measurement range of the MMA7260 sensor, with a total of four 1.5G/2G/4G/6G ranges, corresponding to which the PC1, PC0 needs to enter a binary 0. 3. The PC2 of the amplitude modulation transmitter controls the dormancy mode of the MMA7260. When the PC2 input of the amplitude modu lation transmitter is low, the MMA7260 enters the sleep mode, at which time there is only 3 μ A current consumption. PC3 provides power support for MMA7260. Thus, the power gain allocation balance is realized, and the input tuning loop signal is represented as follows:

$$h_1 = \omega_0^2 M_{sr}^2 L_l^2 + R_s R_r L_l^2 + R_s R_o M_{rl}^2 \tag{4}$$

Wherein, $rect(t) = 1$, $|t| \leq 1/2$, current signal of the medium high frequency signal is easily affected by the high frequency signal. E_t is the working frequency of the static operating point of the intermediate frequency oscillator, ω_c is the carrier fre quency component, and the pre-whitening filter and cross-correlation receiver are used. After AC amplification, the gain distribution information of the amplitude modulation transmitter is obtained. the baseband signal of the amplitude modulation transmitter is filtered as follows:

$$w(t) = n(t) * h_w(t) \tag{5}$$

After frequency selection and filtering, the spectrum components falling in the passband of the system are equalized by gain allocation. At this time, the local oscillator oscillates and the output current amplitude is expressed as follows:

$$I_m = \frac{V_m}{Z} = \frac{V_S - V_{CE}}{Z} \tag{6}$$

When the phase margin of the closed-loop system is the maximum, the dynamic range of the analog preprocessing machine is −40 dB–+40 dB, and a large number of 80 dB is placed. The amplitude modulation transmitter adopts two-stage amplification to combat the interference of straight coupling noise, and adopts adaptive noise cancellation algorithm. Improve the anti-interference performance of the transmitter of power DSC controller.

3.2   Optimal Design and Implementation of Power DSC Controller

The power DSC controller system circuit is designed. The voltage signal output by D/A converter is between (0–4.095 V). Such a signal is not enough to provide enough transmission power to the acoustic array. VINB is connected to VREF and fixed to 2 V. So that the VINA range of the power DSC controller is 0–4 V. The level conversion circuit of power DSC controller is designed by ADG3301. ADG3301 is a single channel bidirectional level conversion chip produced by ADI. In this paper, the low frequency signal in high frequency signal can be detected by using phase detection method for reference. Sent to the low frequency circuit for amplification, the main point of the phase detection is to add the detected signal and the reference signal related to the detected to the input of the phase detection at the same time. The noise is effectively suppressed by using the characteristic that the output size is related to the phase difference between the two input signals, and the signal is extracted.

In this paper, the AC amplifier is designed by using double operational amplifier LM358, and a 16-order bandpass filter is composed of S3529 and S3528 stages. For the input signal S, the peak value is 2 V. The output voltage and output current collected by the data acquisition board are loaded into the MySQL database, and a lower sampling ratio is used to allow higher signal bandwidth, and a logic control circuit is designed. Finally, the optimal design of power intelligent control DCS module based on improved PID is realized. The core circuit of power DCS control based on PLC is shown in Fig. 3.

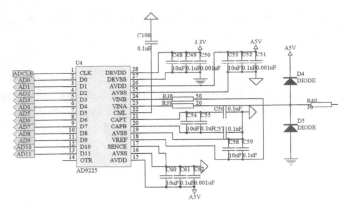

Fig. 3. Power DCS control based on PLC

4 Experimental Test and Result Analysis

In order to test the performance of the DCS power control module of the small PLC designed in this paper, the simulation experiment is carried out. The system simulation model is established based on the SIMULINK of MATLAB. The DCS power control system in the Machine library is selected as the controlled object, and the module resistance is $R_s = 0.7348 \, \Omega$, the load resistance $R_r = 0.7402 \, \Omega$, mutual inductance is $L_m = 0.1254$. In the power DCS control parameter setting based on improved PID, the stator resistance is $R_r = 0.7402 \, \Omega$, power intelligent control DCS module, the efficiency is 96%, the torque output is 10 Nm. The total loss is 56.7 W. after the power supply circuit is normal, the crystal oscillator circuit should be checked. If the crystal oscillator is normal, there should be a square wave output of 25 MHz at the third foot of the crystal oscillator. The power DCS control crystal oscillator input signal based on improved PID is obtained as shown in Fig. 4.

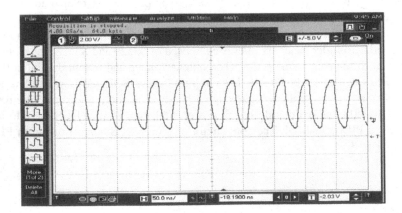

Fig. 4. Crystal oscillator input signal controlled by Power DCS based on improved PID

The sampling input signal is –4–0 V inusoidal signal, the voltage signal output by D/A converter is between (0–4.095 V), VINB is connected to VREF and fixed to 2 V, so that the VINA range of AM transmitter is 0–4 V. The level conversion circuit of amplitude modulation transmitter is designed by ADG3301. By using the control method designed in this paper, the output of power DCS control A/D sampling gain based on improved PID is obtained as shown in Fig. 5. It can be seen from the diagram that the traditional power DCS control model based on improved PID is used. The signal is composed of many narrow impulses, each pulse width is 2 V, the signal amplitude is less than 4 V, and there is a baseline drift of about 200 mV. Figure 5 shows the signal of the power control DCS baseline recovery after the output power amplification and adjustment control. It can be seen that the output base line of the power intelligent control DCS module is basically at zero level, which meets the compensation requirements, and after sudden loading, this paper has a shorter adjustment time, when the control process is stable, the rectifier coupling synchronous tracking control performance of the output voltage is better.

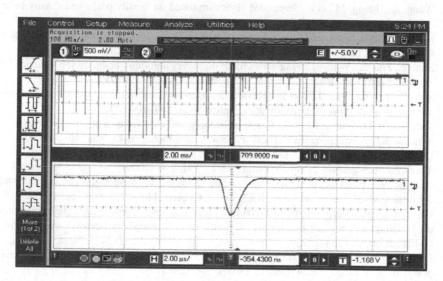

Fig. 5. Output gain control output of power intelligent control DCS module based on improved PID

5 Conclusions

In this paper, a power intelligent control DCS module based on improved PID is studied to realize the output gain control of power electrical system and improve the control efficiency of power electrical system. Combined with integrated DSP information processing chip, a design of power intelligent control DCS module based on output power amplification and regulation is proposed. The overall model of DCS power control system is designed, and the DCS power control frequency doubling gain amplifier is constructed. The signal anti-interference design adopts cascade filter and output power amplification adjustment method to obtain the reset circuit of DCS controller. The output power amplification and adjustment algorithm are designed to equalize the gain distribution to improve the power control performance of DCS. The test results show that the output gain of intelligent power control is large, the adaptive performance is good, and the output stability is strong. This method has good application value in power intelligent control.

References

1. Tu, B., Chuai, R., Xu, H.: Outlier detection based on K-mean distance outlier factor for gait signal. Inf. Control **48**(1), 16–21 (2019)
2. Wei, X.S., Luo, J.H., Wu, J.: Selective convolutional descriptor aggregation for fine-grained image retrieval. IEEE Trans. Image Process. **26**(6), 2868–2881 (2017)
3. Liu, Q., Guan, W., Li, S., Wang, F.: Indoor WiFi-PDR fusion location algorithm based on extended kalman filter. Comput. Eng. **45**(4), 66–71 (2019)
4. Wang, Z., Huang, M., et al.: Integrated algorithm based on density peaks and density-based clustering. J. Comput. Appl. **39**(2), 398–402 (2019)
5. He, H., Tan, Y.: Automatic pattern recognition of ECG signals using entropy-based adaptive dimensionality reduction and clustering. Appl. Soft Comput. **55**, 238–252 (2017)
6. Zhu, Y., Zhu, X., Wang, J.: Time series motif discovery algorithm based on subsequence full join and maximum clique. J. Comput. Appl. **39**(2), 414–420 (2019)
7. Sun, X., Li, X.G., Li, J.F., et al.: Review on deep learning based image super-resolution restoration algorithms. Acta Automatica Sinica **43**(5), 697–709 (2017)
8. Yan, S., Xu, D., Zhang, B., et al.: Graph embedding and extensions. a general framework for dimensionality reduction. IEEE Trans. Pattern Anal. Mach. Intell. **29**(1), 40–51 (2007)
9. Li, B., Wang, C., Huang, D.S.: Supervised feature extraction based on orthogonal discriminant projection. Neurocomputing **73**(1), 191–196 (2009)
10. Hou, C., Nie, F., Li, X., et al.: Joint embedding learning and sparse regression. a framework for unsupervised feature selection. IEEE Trans. Cybern. **44**(6), 793–804 (2014)
11. Liu, J., Luo, X.: Short-term optimal environmental economic hydrothermal scheduling based on handling complicated constraints of multi-chain cascaded hydropower station. Proc. CSEE **32**(14), 27–35 (2012)
12. Ding, Q., Lu, W., Xu, C., et al.: Passivity-based control of a three-phase shunt hybrid active power filter. J. Electr. Mach. Control **18**(05), 1–6 (2014)

Identification of Wireless User Perception Based on Unsupervised Machine Learning

Kaixuan Zhang, Guanghui Fan, Jun Zeng, and Guan Gui[✉]

College of Telecommunications and Information Engineering,
Nanjing University of Posts and Telecommunications, Nanjing 210003, China
guiguan@njupt.edu.cn

Abstract. Wireless user perception (WiUP) plays an important role in designing next-generation wireless communications systems. Users are very sensitive with the quality of WiUP. However, the bad quality of WiUP cannot be identified with traditional methods. In this paper, we propose an intelligent identification method using unsupervised machine learning. More precisely, we create an algorithm model based on historical data to realize feature extraction and clustering. The most similar cluster to those cells with bad WiUP is identified according to Euclidean distance. The experiment is conducted on the basis of a large amount of historical data. With several contrast experiments, Simulation results show that the method proposed achieves the accuracy of identification of bad WiUP over 93%. The study manifests that unsupervised machine learning is effective in identifying bad WiUP in wireless networks.

Keywords: Wireless user perception · Feature extraction · Clustering · Intelligent identification · Machine learning

1 Introduction

With the development of communication technologies [1–6] in last decades, users pay more attention to their service quality. It has always been an important means for operators to improve their competitiveness to improve the call quality by reducing the drop rate and increasing the coverage rate. Recently, bad wireless user perception (WiUP) appears in some cells, which cannot be identified effectively by key performance index (KPI) or key quality index (KQI). The research motivations come principally from user complaints.

The direct measurement of WiUP involves human participation and it requires a lot of time and effort. To improve quality of experience (QoE), a lot of methods were proposed theoretically [7, 8], which ignores the practical problems in real system [9, 10]. However, WiUP is highly reflected in the practical data. dimensionality reduction [11] is considered one of effective methods to realize the data visualization and lower computational complexity. For example, paper [12] uses principal component analysis (PCA) to achieve dimensional reduction of text features, but PCA based methods cannot explain the complex polynomial relationship between features. Supervised machine learning methods [13] have been used in the classification and identification, but unsupervised learning methods are very limited. Sometimes, it is hard to make the label

© ICST Institute for Computer Sciences, Social Informatics and Telecommunications Engineering 2019
Published by Springer Nature Switzerland AG 2019. All Rights Reserved
G. Gui and L. Yun (Eds.): ADHIP 2019, LNICST 301, pp. 507–515, 2019.
https://doi.org/10.1007/978-3-030-36402-1_54

in practical data. Under this context, unsupervised machine learning methods are better. Recently,

In this paper, we propose an effective WiUP identification method using unsupervised machine learning. Specifically, we create an algorithm model based on historical data to realize feature extraction and unsupervised clustering [19], and find out the most similar one to those with bad WiUP by Euclidean distance. During the process, dimensionality reduction should be paid more attention, we train an Auto-encoder neural network [20] for dimensionality reduction. Auto-encoder neural network for dimensionality reduction discards the disadvantage of linear algorithm and improves the identification accuracy by adjusting parameters. In this way, problems can be found and solutions can be formulated in advance. Computer simulations are provided to confirm the proposed method.

The rest of this paper is organized as follows. The system model is given in Sect. 2. Section 3 is the original data description. Section 4 gives these algorithms in this paper including dimensional reduction and clustering. The experimental results are presented in Sect. 5. Section 6 summarizes the full paper.

2 System Model

To realize intelligent identification of WiUP, the algorithm model is divided into three parts. Part I is data reading and preprocessing. Part II is dimensionality reduction and clustering. The last part is cluster identification. The whole system model can be depicted in Fig. 1.

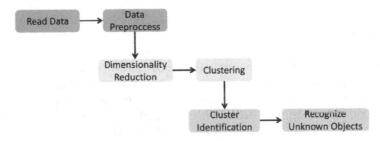

Fig. 1. The system model

3 Data Preprocessing

3.1 Data Description

The data sets are collected from wireless quality monitoring terminals. Table 1 gives the first 4 rows of a data set. Each row in this sheet contains 14 features which reflect the quality of WiUP in each hour. ECI is the ID of a cell. Each cell has 168 rows of data, the data in the whole week. In total, there are more than 10,000 cells. More than 80% of them is unknown historical data of cells and the rest is those identified as ones with bad WiUP. Even though a large number of historical data is available, not all of them is suitable for modeling. The data set need be evaluated in terms of missing value ratio and outlier ratio etc. Before the algorithm model is created, the data needs to be preprocessed, including normalization, correlation analysis [21] and vectorization.

Table 1. The head of the data sheet.

Cell name	ECI	Time	Page response success rate (%)	...	Initial cache delay (ms)
Cell1	126096558	2018-10-16-00	91.10	...	4688
Cell1	126096558	2018-10-16-01	76.32	...	11253
Cell1	126096558	2018-10-16-02	96.68	...	2563

For the sake of simple description, $F_i i = 1, 2, \cdots, 14$ is used to refer to the i-th feature. The map between F and features is listed in Table 2.

Table 2. The map between F and features.

F_i	Features name
F_1	Page response success rate (%)
F_2	Page response delay (ms)
F_3	Page display success rate (%)
F_4	Page display delay (ms)
F_5	Page download rate (kbps)
F_6	Video play success rate (%)
F_7	Video pause time per minute
F_8	Pause time ratio
F_9	Cache time delay (ms)
F_{10}	Stream media rate (kbps)
F_{11}	Instant communication response success rate (%)
F_{12}	Instant communication response delay (%)
F_{13}	Mobile game response success rate (%)
F_{14}	Mobile game response delay (ms)

3.2 Data Preprocessing

Normalization is to eliminate the dimensional influence among different features. And correlation analysis is to eliminate the redundancy among features with high correlation. On the other hand, we need to comprehensively consider the data of the whole day to evaluate the WiUP. Hence, we introduce vectorization to convert the data matrix to a vector.

According to the result of correlation analysis, F_1 is highly correlated to F_3. The high correlation also happens to F_7 and F_9. By this way, we delete F_3 and F_9 to eliminate the redundancy.

The vectorization plays an important role in the algorithm model. The process can be displayed as follows (Fig. 2).

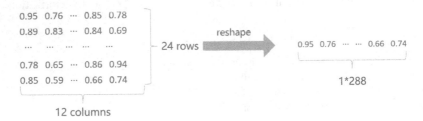

Fig. 2. The process of vectorization.

4   Proposed Methods

4.1   Dimensionality Reduction

Considering the invisibility and high computational complexity in the high dimensional space. Hence, it is necessary to encode the data from high dimensional into low dimensional. PCA is used widely due to its simplicity [22]. We propose a nonlinear generalization of PCA that is an adjustable, Auto-encoder neural network to realize dimensionality reduction. The encoder network transforms the high dimensional data into low dimensional code and the decoder network is responsible to recover the data. Figure 3 gives the structure of this neural network. In Fig. 3, the number in every layer means the number of neurons in this layer. The numbers of neurons and layers are adjustable for higher identification accuracy. w_i, b_i $(i = 1, \ldots, 8)$ represent the weights and deviations of the i-th layer respectively. Both the weights and deviations are updated by back propagation (BP) algorithm.

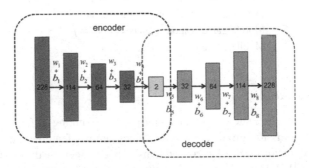

Fig. 3. The neural network for dimensionality reduction.

The neural network is trained with about 1000 pieces of history cells until that the value of the cost function is convergent or steady. The curve of the cost function value in the training process is shown in Fig. 4, and the cost function C is given as below

$$C = \frac{1}{2n}\sum_{i=1}^{n}\left\|y_i' - y_i^2\right\|$$ (1)

where n equals the number of objects. y_i' and y_i represent the value of output and input of i-th object respectively. $\left\|y_i' - y_i\right\|$ is denoted as the ℓ_2-norm of vector $y_i' - y_i$. ℓ_2-norm is defined as $\left\|v\right\|^2 = \sum_{i=1}^{n}\left|v_i\right|^2$. The change in a weight is given by

$$w_i' = w_i - \alpha\frac{\partial C}{\partial w_i}$$ (2)

where w_i' is the weight changed, α is a learning rate and the $\frac{\partial C}{\partial w_i}$ is the gradient of w_i computed by BP algorithm. In the same way, the change in a deviation is given by

$$b_i' = b_i - \alpha\frac{\partial C}{\partial b_i}$$ (3)

where b_i' is the deviation changed, the $\frac{\partial C}{\partial b_i}$ is the gradient of b_i computed by BP algorithm [23]. The model trained is saved to reduce the dimension of other objects, which saves the basic characteristic of the original data.

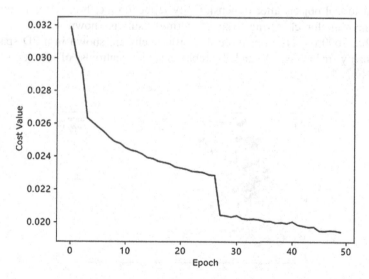

Fig. 4. The change curve of the cost function value in the training process.

In general, the performance of backpropagation deteriorates as the number of hidden layers gets larger. In this paper, we design a neural network with 7 hidden layers. Figure 4 shows the convergence of the neural network after 50 epochs training.

4.2   K-means Clustering

K-means clustering algorithm [24] is one of the most popular algorithms in unsupervised clustering. It owns simple principle and usually works with good results. Suppose that we are given a data set $X = \{x_1, \ldots, x_N\}, x_n \in R^d$. The M-clustering problem aims at partitioning this data set into M disjoint subsets (clusters) $C_1, \ldots, C_M$. The K-means clustering algorithm can be described as following steps:

Step 1: Label the number of clusters.
Step 2: Establish the centroid coordinate.
Step 3: Determine the distance of each object to the centroid.
Step 4: Group the objects based on minimum distance.

K-means clustering uses various distance function to measure the similarity among the objects. The distance function is measured by Euclidean distance [25]. The Euclidean distance between vector $X = (x_1, x_2, \cdots, x_n)$ and $Y = (y_1, y_2, \cdots, y_n)$ can be defined by

$$dist(X, Y) = \sqrt{\sum_{k=1}^{n} (x_k - y_k)^2} \tag{4}$$

The historical objects after dimensionality reduction are directly input into the k-means algorithm for clustering. The clustering result is shown in Fig. 5. We can observe that 7000 objects from more than 1000 cells are shown in a 2D space after dimensionality reduction. A and B represent the centroids of the two clusters respectively.

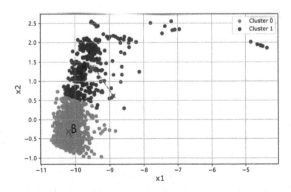

Fig. 5. The result of K-means clustering.

4.3   Identification of Target Cluster

Two centroids of clusters are found out by K-means but we cannot identify which cluster is the one with bad WiUP. In this paper, we divide those objects with bad WiUP into test-set and validation-set with ratio 7:3. To identify the target cluster, the validation-set is fed into the neural network for dimensionality reduction and then we compare the Euclidean distance to point A and point B. These objects are grouped into the closer cluster. After clustering, we view the cluster that contains more than 80% objects with bad WiUP as the target cluster. The flow chart is shown in Fig. 6.

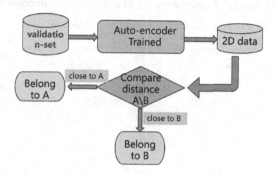

Fig. 6. Flow chart of algorithm for finding target cluster.

5   Experiment Results

5.1   Results Evaluation Method

As for the evaluation method of identification accuracy, we need to feed the test-set into the algorithm model shown in Fig. 6, and finally the proportion of objects correctly classified is output as the identification accuracy.

5.2   Results and Analysis

All 12 features are preserved. In other words, the input data is 228 dimensions. The only variate changed is the number of neurons in the code layer, which means the data is converted into different dimensions to compare the identification accuracy. The results are shown in Table 3. As we can see from the table, the best identification accuracy is achieved when the input is converted to two dimensions. On the other hand, correlation analysis is carried out on the original data to remove the features with high correlation to reduce the input redundancy. We also calculate the variance of all features and eliminate the features with small variance. Table 4 gives the comparison of results with different input dimensions.

Simulation results show that the highest identification accuracy can be achieved by eliminating the input dimensions and converting the data into two-dimension space.

Table 3. Identification accuracy of different dimensions in code layer.

Dimension of input	Dimension of code layer	Number of hidden layers	Recognition accuracy
336	2	7	86.50%
336	10	7	68.53%
336	50	7	61.60%
336	100	7	56.30%

Table 4. Identification accuracy of different input dimensions.

Dimension of input	Dimension of code layer	Number of hidden layers	Recognition accuracy
336	2	7	85.50%
264	2	7	68.85%
228	2	7	62.05%
96	2	7	93.70%

6 Conclusion

This paper has proposed an effective method to identify cells with bad WiUP. The whole algorithm model was created based on a large number of historical data with unsupervised machine learning. The model can be depicted by three parts including data preprocessing, dimensionality reduction and clustering. For higher identification accuracy, many parameters have been adjusted in this model and finally the identification accuracy can increase to 93.7%. The operators can formulate solutions to solve the bad WiUP according the precise identification. However, the identification accuracy need to be further improved. In the further research, the relationship between KQI and KPI should be analyzed in order to find out the basis reasons for bad WiUP.

References

1. Na, Z., Wang, Y., Li, X., Xia, J., Liu, X., Xiong, M.: Subcarrier allocation based Simultaneous Wireless Information and Power Transfer algorithm in 5G cooperative OFDM communication systems. Phys. Commun. **29**, 164–170 (2018)
2. Liu, X., Zhang, X., Jia, M., Fan, L., Lu, W., Zhai, X.: 5G-based green broadband communication system design with simultaneous wireless information and power transfer. Phys. Commun. **28**, 130–137 (2018)
3. Liu, M., Song, T., Gui, G.: Deep cognitive perspective: resource allocation for NOMA based heterogeneous IoT with imperfect SIC. IEEE Internet Things J. 1–11 (2018). https://doi.org/10.1109/jiot.2018.2876152
4. Liu, M., Yang, J., Song, T., Hu, J., Gui, G.: Deep learning-inspired message passing algorithm for efficient resource allocation in cognitive radio networks. IEEE Trans. Veh. Technol. **68**(1), 641–653 (2018)

5. Wu, J., Dong, M., Ota, K., Li, J., Guan, Z.: FCSS: fog computing based content-aware filtering for security services in information centric social networks. IEEE Trans. Emerg. Top. Comput. (2017). https://doi.org/10.1109/TETC.2017.2747158
6. Zhang, N., et al.: Software defined networking enabled wireless network virtualization: challenges and solutions. IEEE Netw. **31**(5), 42–49 (2017)
7. Cicalo, S., Sayadi, B., Faucheux, F., Tralli, V., Kerboeuf, S., Changuel, N.: Improving QoE and fairness in HTTP adaptive streaming over LTE network. IEEE Trans. Circuits Syst. Video Technol. **26**(12), 2284–2298 (2015)
8. Brito, I.V.S., Figueiredo, G.B.: Improving QoS and QoE through seamless handoff in software-defined IEEE 802.11 mesh networks. IEEE Commun. Lett. **21**(11), 2484–2487 (2017)
9. Kato, N., et al.: The deep learning vision for heterogeneous network traffic control: proposal, challenges, and future perspective. IEEE Wirel. Commun. **24**(3), 146–153 (2017)
10. Kato, N.: Challenges of content-centric mobile networks. IEEE Network **31**(1), 2 (2017)
11. Tan, S., Mayrovouniotis, M.L.: Reducing data dimensionality through optimizing neural network inputs. AIChE J. **41**(6), 1471–1480 (1995)
12. Abdulhussain, M.I., Gan, J.Q.: An experimental investigation on PCA based on cosine similarity and correlation for text feature dimensionality reduction. In: Computer Science and Electronic Engineering Conference (CCEC), pp. 1–4 (2015)
13. Li, X., et al.: Joint multilabel classification with community-aware label graph learning. IEEE Trans. Image Process. **25**(1), 484–493 (2016)
14. Fadlullah, Z.M., et al.: State-of-the-art deep learning: evolving machine intelligence toward tomorrow's intelligent network traffic control systems. IEEE Commun. Surv. Tutorials **19**(4), 2432–2455 (2017)
15. Wang, Y., Gui, G., Zhao, N., Yin, Y., Huang, H., Li, Y.: Deep learning for optical character recognition and its application to VAT invoice recognition (2018)
16. Huang, H., Gui, G., Sari, H., Adachi, F.: Deep learning for super-resolution DOA estimation in massive MIMO systems. In: 2018 IEEE 88th Vehicular Technology Conference (VTC Fall), Kansas, August 2018
17. Gao, X., Jin, S., Wen, C.K., Li, G.Y.: ComNet: combination of deep learning and expert knowledge in OFDM receivers. IEEE Commun. Lett. **22**(12), 2627–2630 (2018)
18. Wang, T., Wen, C., Wang, H., Gao, F., Jiang, T., Jin, S.: Deep learning for wireless physical layer: opportunities and challenges. China Commun. **14**(11), 92–111 (2017)
19. Lam, D., Wei, M., Wunsch, D.: Clustering data of mixed categorical and numerical type with unsupervised feature learning. IEEE Access **3**, 1605–1613 (2015)
20. Chen, K., Yang, S.: Effect of multi-hidden-layer structure on performance of BP neural network: probe. In: 2012 8th International Conference on Natural Computation, no. 2010, pp. 1–5 (2012)
21. Zhang, Z., Zhao, M., Chow, T.W.S.: Binary-and multi-class group sparse canonical correlation analysis for feature extraction and classification. IEEE Trans. Knowl. Data Eng. **25**(10), 2192–2205 (2013)
22. Agarwal, S., Ranjan, P., Ujlayan, A.: Comparative analysis of dimensionality reduction algorithms, case study: PCA. In: Proceedings of 2017 11th International Conference on Intelligent Systems and Control, ISCO 2017, pp. 255–259 (2017)
23. Liu, Y., Liu, S., Wang, Y., Lombardi, F., Han, J.: A stochastic computational multi-layer perceptron with backward propagation. IEEE Trans. Comput. **67**(9), 1273–1286 (2018)
24. Yang, F., Yang, L., Wang, D., Qi, P., Wang, H.: Method of modulation recognition based on combination algorithm of K-means clustering and grading training SVM. China Commun. **15**, 55–63 (2018)
25. Dokmanic, I., Parhizkar, R., Ranieri, J., Vetterli, M.: Euclidean distance matrices: essential theory, algorithms, and applications. IEEE Signal Process. Mag. **32**(6), 12–30 (2015)

Author Index

Printed in the United States
By Bookmasters